THE ILLUSTRATED
HISTORY OF THE CINEMA

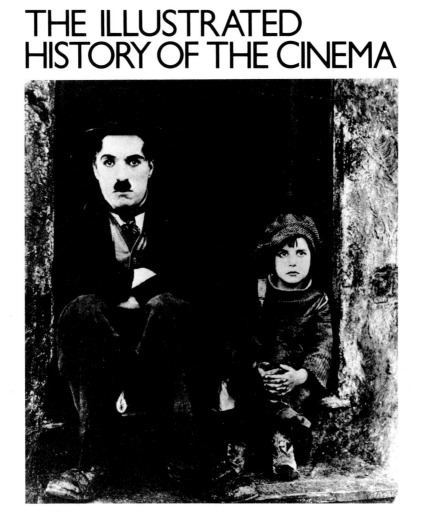

THE ILLUSTRATED
HISTORY OF THE CINEMA

Edited by Ann Lloyd
Consultant Editor: David Robinson

MACMILLAN PUBLISHING COMPANY
NEW YORK

Acknowledgements

The publishers would like to thank the following for their invaluable assistance: Gilbert Adair, Don Allen, Lindsay Anderson, Edgar Anstey, Barry Anthony, Susan d'Arcy, Roy Armes, David Atwell, Chris Auty, Martyn Auty, John Barnes, Peter Barnes, Brian Baxter, Robert Benayoun, Philip Bergson, Claude Beylie, Ian Birch, DeWitt Bodeen, John Brosnan, Geoff Brown, Kevin Brownlow, Freda Bruce Lockhart, Ken Cameron, Kingsley Canham, Andrew Casper, David Castell, John Caughie, Charlotte Chandler, Michel Ciment, Carlos Clarens, T.E.B. Clarke, Malcolm Coad, Jay Cocks, Brian Coe, Juliet Benita Colman, Richard Combs, Peter Cowie, Edgardo Cozarinsky, Dave Curtis, Robert Daudelin, Brenda Davies, Jan Dawson, Michael Dempsey, Arnold Desser, Deke Dusinberre, Steven Dwoskin, Richard Dyer, Mick Eaton, Barry Edson, Phil Edwards, Lotte H. Eisner, Derek Elley, John Ellis, Chester Erskine, Allen Eyles, Olivier Eyquem, Trader Faulkner, Raymond Fielding, Joel Finler, John Fleming, Margaret Ford, Leatrice Gilbert Fountain, Julian Fox, David Francis, Freddie Francis, Graham Fuller, Behroze Gandhy, Alain Garsault, Peter Gidal, Denis Gifford, John Gillett, Verina Glaessner, Joan Goodman, Hiroko Govaers, Jonathan Groucutt, John Halas, André Halimi, Ken G. Hall, Peter Hames, Paul Hammond, Bernard Happé, Phil Hardy, Ray Harryhausen, Molly Haskell, Stan Hayward, Anne Head, Gary Herman, Nina Hibbin, Sally Hibbin, Margaret Hinxman, Foster Hirsch, Herbert Holba, John Holmstrom, Peter Howden, Tom Hutchinson, Joris Ivens, Richard T. Jameson, Clyde Jeavons, Steve Jenkins, Albert Johnson, Allan Jones, Peter Jones, William Kenley, Michael Kerbel, George Kimball, Dennis Kimbley, Ian Knight, Gunter Knorr, John Kobal, Richard Koszarski, Zsolt Kézdi-Kovács, Jerome Kuehl, Karol Kulik, Mari Kuttna, Gavin Lambert, John Francis Lane, Gérard Legrand, Claire Leimbach, Antonín Liehm, Elizabeth Lodge, Jack Lodge, Bessie Love, Alan Lovell, Rachael Low, Colin McArthur, Donald McCaffrey, Malcolm McDowell, Sam McElfresh, Tom McGrath, Douglas McVay, Derek Malcolm, Pamela Mann, Roger Manvell, Dave Marsh, Rakesh Matthur, Samuel Marx, Scott Meek, Dan Millar, Tom Milne, Ivor Montagu, Doris Langley Moore, Sheridan Morley, George Morris, Mark Nash, Liam O'Leary, David Overbey, Christopher Palmer, Robert Parrish, Flavia Paulon, Chris Peachment, D.A. Pennebaker, Victor Perkins, Simon Perry, Julian Petley, Roy Pickard, Jim Pines, Dilys Powell, Michael Powell, Derek Prouse, Tim Pulleine, Michael Pye, Tony Rayns, Stanley Reed, Robert Reiner, Jeffrey Richards, David Robinson, Nick Roddick, David Roper, Cynthia Rose, Jonathan Rosenbaum, Richard Roud, Tom Ryall, Hans Saaltink, Barry Salt, David Samuelson, Victor Saville, Richard Schickel, Marie Seton, Colin Shindler, David Shipman, Brian Sibley, Charles Silver, Neil Sinyard, Monty Smith, Eugene Stavis, David Stratton, Philip Strick, Elizabeth Sussex, Martin Sutton, Bertrand Tavernier, John Russell Taylor, Paul Taylor, Richard Taylor, Bob Thomas, David Thomson, John Thomson, Mitch Tuchman, Richard Tucker, Adrian Turner, Alexander Walker, Marc Wanamaker, Tony Watts, Vicki Wegg-Prosser, Herman G. Weinberg, Sheila Whitaker, Alistair Whyte, Christopher Wicking, David Will, Richard Williams, Dana Wynter, Ken Wlaschin, Bob Woffinden, Steven Woolley, Basil Wright, Luce Vigo and Gene Youngblood.

Macmillan Publishing Company
A Division of Macmillan, Inc.
866 Third Avenue, New York, N.Y. 10022

Library of Congress Catalog Card Number: 86-18037

Printed in Italy

printing number
1 2 3 4 5 6 7 8 9 10

ISBN 0–02–919241–2

Library of Congress Cataloging in Publication Data

The Illustrated history of the cinema.
  Includes index.
  1. Moving-pictures—History I. Lloyd, Ann,
1945-   . II. Robinson, David, 1930-
PN1993.5.A1145   1987   791.43'09   86-18037
ISBN 0–02–919241–2

The Editors would like to acknowledge the valuable contributions to *The Illustrated History of the Cinema* of Dan Millar, Alastair Dougall and Arnold Desser.

Designer: Karen Bowen

Film dates
The dating of many films presents problems because production, completion and release may be separated by months or even years. We give here the date of the earliest known showing – whether private, trade or public – of the completed film.

Film titles
The original titles for English-speaking films have been preferred: e.g. *The Enforcer* (USA) and not *Murder, Inc.* (GB); *A Matter of Life and Death* (GB) and not *Stairway to Heaven* (USA). Foreign-language films are initially referred to by their original title, followed by a direct translation in brackets or, if one exists, the registered British/American title in italics.

Page 1: The Kid is one of Charlie Chaplin's best-loved masterpieces; it was, for its time, a courageous mix of near-tragedy and farce.

Pages 2 and 3: 'Watch the Skies' was the initial title of Spielberg's Close Encounters of the Third Kind (1977), the real stars of which were the immaculate special effects.

Contents

Introduction

Any history is recalcitrant; but the history of cinema is the hardest to contain of all the arts. It is so concentrated in time – the end of the first century is only just in sight – and so ranging geographically and stylistically. Imagine attempting a history of twentieth century literature which would take in writers from New York to Korea and West Africa, and genres from detective paper-back to political dissertation and poetical avant-garde. Yet that is what a history of movies must undertake.

Half a century ago, when Rotha and Bardeche and Brassillach attempted the first histories of the cinema, it was still reasonably possible for one person to maintain a fairly comprehensive grasp of world cinema (though time has shown that even then these authors remained ignorant, for instance, of the achievements of Japanese and Indian cinema). Today, with new centres of film production emerging annually in new territories of the world, it would be impossible. This is why we have attempted to compile a continuous and integrated history of the cinema from the contributions of a large number of specialist wrtiers: our HISTORY OF THE MOVIE, compiled in tandem with the more hetereogenous, partwork MOVIE, represents the combined efforts of over 200 historians whose individual contributions range from a paragraph or two to whole chapters.

A collaborative effort on this scale makes great demands on the executive editors, faced with the task of forming the work of so many authors into a continuous whole. At an early stage it was agreed that it was desirable to maintain the writers' idiosyncratic styles and personalities, even though they were not to be individually identified by name, rather than to impose a mechanical "house style". The effect, as the reader will quickly realise, is a continuous shifting of approach and viewpoint. One writer may find it more illuminating to come at his subject or era through studies of the individual artists; another through genres; another from an aesthetic angle; another from the point of view of a social or political historian. The editors quickly realised that, far from confusing the reader, such variation of attitude made for vitality: the effect is of a series of different voices, with different accents and tones, in turn taking up a single theme.

It is a long and complex story to summarize even in the 350,000 words of this book. The writers carry us from the optical toys and Victorian magic out of which the movies first evolved, to the technological complexities of *E.T.* or *Raiders of the Lost Ark*, from the one-minute films and gilt salon chairs of the first Lumière show of 1895 to the multi-billion-dollar business which is today's Hollywood. The story of the cinema takes in aesthetic discovery, industrial warfare, the needs and demands of a world-wide audience in a century of momentous historical events.

History is recalcitrant, maybe; but it seems to have its patterns and purposes. It is surely not without significance that the century which has seen the development of the most powerful weapons of destruction in the story of mankind has also witnessed the maturing of the most powerful and universal medium of communication that man has ever had in his hands since the start of history.

DAVID ROBINSON
January, 1986

Left: Ben Kingsley in the role of Ghandi *(1982), the film that for producer/director Richard Attenborough was some twenty years in the making. The result – one of the most garlanded films of all times, winning eight Oscars in addition to awards from all over the world.*

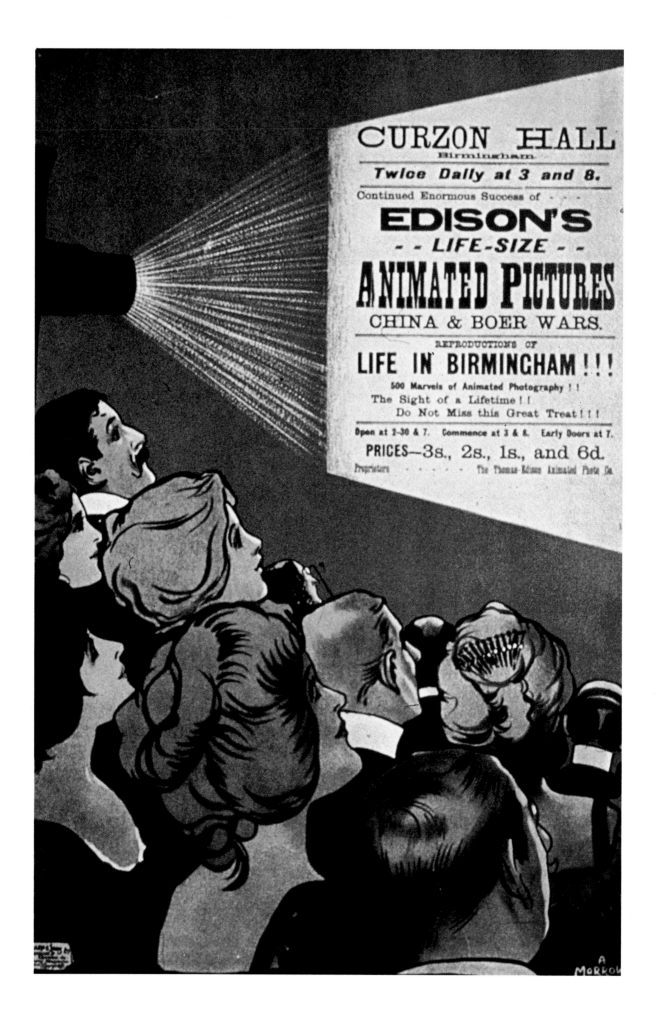

CHAPTER I
Birth of the Seventh Art

Motion pictures were not so much an invention as an evolution, the confluence and culmination of a number of separate lines of research that stretched back decades, and even centuries. Man seemed always to be groping towards the kind of optical entertainment of which the cinema was to be the apogee. Myths, folklore and fiction frequently explored the theme of magic glasses in which the world might be viewed in microcosm. Long before the cinema, audiences marvelled at the shadow show and the vague images of the first magic lanterns.

The second half of the eighteenth century, however, witnessed a quite new passion for optical entertainments which was to continue practically unabated until the advent of the cinematograph, and which may be associated with the growth of popular illustrated publications as printing became cheaper.

Shadows and Light

Throughout western Europe, shadow shows have always been known as *Ombres Chinoises* or 'Chinese Shadows'. Shadow shows were recorded in China at least by the eleventh century, and from the earliest times the repertory of the Chinese shadow theatre seems to have changed little. The figures – ingeniously articulated – were made of donkey skin, oiled to be translucent, then painted and cut out in exquisite filigree. As the operators made the two-dimensional figures move by a simple arrangement of rods and wires, coloured shadows were cast upon a screen of paper or silk.

It was in the 1770s, however, that the shadow show as sophisticated entertainment became a craze throughout the whole of western Europe. The path of the migration appears to have been from Italy through Germany (where no less a figure than the Romantic writer J.W. von Goethe set up his own shadow theatre) to France and eventually to England. The most significant contributor to this spread of interest was one Ambrogio (the name was modified in France and Britain to Ambroise) who launched his spectacle in Paris in 1772 before arriving in London in 1775, to take the town by storm. His performances in Panton Street were hailed by a critic of the time as 'absolutely the greatest Amusements that ever were exhibited in the metropolis', and Ambroise played to crowded and fashionable audiences who paid the then enormous admission price of five shillings. His best-liked and most spectacular sketch was a storm at sea, complete with

Left: an advertisement for Edison films shown in Birmingham c. 1900, with footage (that could have been authentic or faked) of the Boer War and Boxer Rebellion.

shipwreck, thunder and lightning, and his public performances ran in London for several successive seasons before eventually being taken over by the famous showman Philip Astley, who continued to include shadow entertainments in his Westminster Amphitheatre until 1790.

In the 1780s, an Edinburgh portrait painter, Robert Barker, had the idea of creating a huge continuous painting on the inner surface of a cylinder or rotunda. He was ready in 1788 to exhibit his great view of Edinburgh in a room in the Haymarket, London. It was a triumph with the London public. In 1791, Barker gave his invention a name, coining the word 'Panorama' from Greek words meaning 'a view all round' and in 1794 he opened a permanent brick Panorama building on the north side of Leicester Square. It was to remain a fashionable metropolitan entertainment for almost seventy years, finally closing its doors on December 12, 1863.

The arrangement of the Leicester Square building permitted the audience to see two separate paintings, the larger of which was 86m (283 feet) in circumference. Considering the enormous problems of painting and mounting a picture of such size, it is astonishing that the Panoramas were changed as often as once a year, though a big success, such as *The Coronation of George IV*, might pull such crowds that it could run for several years.

The high point of this era of the painting as show was the Diorama, launched in Paris in 1822 by Louis Jacques Mande Daguerre – whose work on photography, 17 years later, was to make another significant contribution to the evolution of the movies. The Diorama, which was re-created in London in 1823, consisted of huge paintings in which subtle effects of lighting and transformations were produced by the ingenious management of shutters and blinds controlling the light thrown from before and behind on the part-transparent image.

Of all optical entertainments, the magic lantern was the most venerable and the most durable. The magic lantern – whose basic form still survives in the modern slide projector – embodies the same essential principles as every moving-picture projector: a powerful light source, concentrated by a condenser and passed through a transparent image to project an enlarged impression of that image, in all its colour and detail, on a white screen.

The magic lantern was first described by the Jesuit scientist Athanasius Kircher in 1671; but it was certainly known before that. Throughout the late seventeenth and eighteenth centuries, everywhere in Europe and beyond, itinerant showmen travelled with their lanterns to delight, astound and terrify their simple audiences.

The magic lantern reached the height of sophistication in England in the late nineteenth century. English opticians developed magic lanterns, gleaming with the splendour of brass and polished mahogany, of such technical complexity that they required teams of people to operate them and libraries of manuals to explain their proper management.

From an early stage, showmen tried to give their audiences the extra thrill of movement on the screen. A slide pushed through the projector could give a persuasive impression of a procession of figures moving across the picture. Ingenious arrangements of levers and ratchets to manipulate or rotate circular glasses could produce mechanical movements in the pictures on the slides. Eyes could be made to roll, limbs to change position, fish to swim around a tank.

In the 1860s and 1870s, a more sophisticated means of producing the illusion of movement suggested itself. In the

Above: a Javanese shadow puppet worked by rods. Top: a Victorian artist's somewhat fanciful impression of a Chinese shadow show. Above right: the first illustration of the magic lantern, in Kircher's Ars Magna Lucis et Umbrae, *second edition, published in 1671. Right: a Zoetrope made in London by H. C. Clarke, c. 1860. Far right: the single moving image in the Zoetrope that the viewer saw by looking through the slots as the drum revolved.*

first third of the nineteenth century, physicists, including Michael Faraday and Peter Mark Roget, had been studying a phenomenon already observed since classical times, persistence of vision. The retina of the eye appears to retain an impression for a fraction of a second after the image producing that impression has been removed. One easy illustration of this is the effect produced if a point of light – a pocket torch, for instance – is rapidly revolved in the dark, when the eye receives the illusion of a continuous circle of light.

In 1833, quite independently of each other, two physicists – Joseph Plateau in Brussels and Simon Stampfer in Vienna – developed a toy to demonstrate this principle. Around the circumference of a disc were drawn a dozen little pictures representing successive phases of a continuing action. Slots were cut out between the pictures. When the disc was revolved rapidly, facing into a mirror, and the reflection was viewed through the slots as they passed before the eyes, the effect presented to the eyes was not a series of pictures but a single image in movement.

The device was quickly popularized as an instructive toy, the Phenakistiscope, and in time refined and varied. The Zoetrope, which came into vogue in the 1860s, replaced the system of disc and mirror by a hollow, open-topped drum, pierced with slots along its edge, around the inside of which were placed strips of paper printed with the appropriate series of phase drawings. In 1877, the Frenchman Emile Reynaud replaced the slots – the equivalent of the shutter in a modern movie projector – by a prismatic arrangement of mirrors. This he called the Praxinoscope.

In the 1850s and 1860s, the rotating disc of the Phenakistiscope had been adapted to the magic lantern resulting in flickering motion pictures being cast on to a screen. In 1892, Reynaud's Théâtre Optique adapted the principles of the Praxinoscope to project on to the screen what were virtually the first cartoon films.

The Living Image

One element was still missing. All these early moving-picture devices required the painstaking *drawing* of the images to be animated. But in 1839, with the perfection of Daguerre's Daguerreotype process in France and Henry Fox Talbot's Calotype (later Talbotype) in England, photography became a practical technique.

In the very early days of photography, Plateau suggested that the Daguerreotype and the Phenakistiscope could be combined; and in the 1860s and 1870s, there were a number of patents for the use of photographs in Zoetropes or similar devices. Henry R. Heyl's Phasmatrope, for instance, demonstrated in Philadelphia in 1870, gave movement to a series of photographs obtained by a painful process of positioning models for each successive phase of action. The problem that thwarted all these early attempts was how to take a series of photographs in a succession rapid enough to capture the individual phases of the action as they actually took place.

The problem was eventually to be solved by a number of scientists and photographers who initially had no particular interest in creating moving pictures, but simply sought means to analyse human and animal movement for the purposes of scientific study. Eadweard Muybridge (1830–1904), an English photographer who spent most of his active life in the United States, arrived in 1878 at a brilliant solution with a battery of cameras which were triggered – at first mechanically, eventually electrically – as a moving person or animal passed before them. Muybridge added to this considerable achievement when in 1879 he reconstructed the movements by projecting a disc of drawings, closely based on the photographic images, in series to create an animated picture on the screen. This development of the projecting Phenakistiscope was known as the Zoopraxiscope.

In Europe, Muybridge met Etienne Marey (1830–1904), a physiologist who had long experimented with graphic methods of recording animal and bird movement, and contemporaneously with Muybridge was applying photography to his work. Marey noted the example of the astronomer Jules Janssen, who in 1874 had succeeded in recording the passage of the planet Venus across the face of the sun by means of a 'photographic revolver'. Shaped like a gun, this ingenious camera used a single circular plate, which revolved each time the shutter was opened, to expose one small area of its sensitized surface.

Reynaud's Théâtre Optique (above) was a sophisticated form of his Praxinoscope (right). The latter used a central rotating mirrored polygon that integrated the phases of movement.

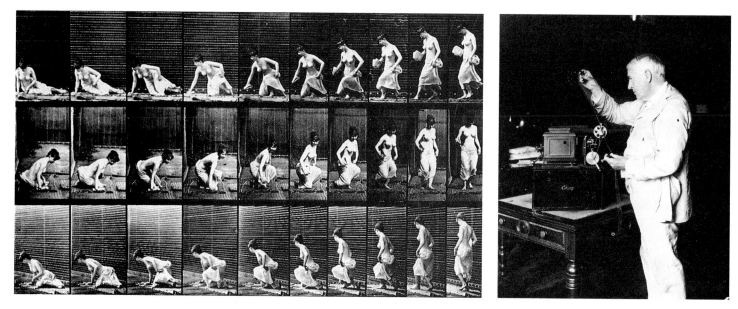

On much the same lines, Marey by 1882 had contrived a photographic gun *(fusil photographique)* which was capable of taking 12 individual photographs in one second. In 1885 in the USA, George Eastman perfected his paper roll film, which became very popular for still photography when he brought out the Kodak camera to use it in 1888. This development gave a new direction to Marey's experiments, and brought the motion-picture camera a considerable step nearer. Marey's Chronophotographe of 1888 used a continuous strip of paper film to record a sequence of individual photographs. When Eastman's celluloid roll film appeared in 1889, Marey promptly began to use that. In 1893, he suggested the construction of a projector to show the images he had recorded in a continuous sequence.

Edison and Company

The first public exploitation of cinematography took place in America. The great inventor and industrialist Thomas Alva Edison (1847–1931) became interested in the possibility of producing an optical equivalent to the sound recording and reproducing phonograph that he had invented in 1877. He was stimulated by the work of Muybridge and in February 1888 discussed with him the possibility of coupling the Zoopraxiscope projector with the phonograph. Developments are obscured by a cloud of misstatements thrown up by Edison and his Scottish collaborator William Kennedy Laurie Dickson (1860–1935) during subsequent legal proceedings. During 1888 and much of 1889, Dickson attempted to work out a camera design using an intermittently rotated sensitized cylinder on which a spiral arrangement of tiny pictures might be produced. Then Edison met Marey in Paris in August 1889 and saw his roll-film sequence camera. In November Edison described a design which used a long band of film passing from one reel to another, with toothed sprocket wheels engaging in rows of perforations on each side of the film and with an escapement mechanism, as in a watch or clock, to provide the necessary intermittent movement, so that the film stopped for exposure and moved on between exposures.

Dickson used Eastman's new celluloid roll film but also continued to work on the cylinder idea, which was brought to success in the autumn of 1890 but then abandoned. On August 24, 1891, Edison filed specifications for patents covering a Kinetograph camera and a Kinetoscope viewer, using perforated bands of film. A prototype of the Kinetoscope had been shown to the delegates of the National Federation Of Women's Clubs who visited the Edison laboratory at West Orange, New Jersey, on May 20, 1891; it was a small wooden box in which the picture was viewed through a hole in the top.

Dickson made such progress that in June 1892 Edison decided on the commercial introduction of the Kinetoscope. A new Kinetograph camera, with a vertical film feed instead of the previous horizontal running, was designed; it took a wider film strip, 35mm wide, perforated with four roughly rectangular perforations on each side of the 25mm by 19mm frame, approximately the same as is still in use. The Edison Kinetograph camera was the first to employ perforated celluloid film for accurate registration of the images and effective transport through the camera. It was driven by an electric motor, whereas most other early cameras were hand-cranked. The Kinetoscope viewer was an upright wooden box contaning a bank of spools over which 15m (nearly 50 feet) of film ran in an endless loop. The continuously moving film passed over an electric lamp and under a magnifying glass set in the top of the box. Between the lamp and the film passed a rotating disc shutter perforated with a narrow slit, which lit each frame so briefly that it 'froze' the movement of the film, presenting to the eye approximately forty images per second. The machine was set in motion by inserting a coin to activate the electric motor and gave a 'show' lasting about twenty seconds.

The new models were demonstrated in 1893 when full manufacture began, and the first Kinetoscope parlour was opened in New York City on April 14, 1894. This had ten machines, each showing a different subject, including a strong man, a wrestling match, a barber's shop, Highland dancing and a trapeze act. These had been filmed in a studio designed by Dickson, completed at the end of 1892 and known as the 'Black Maria' from its tarpaper exterior. It had a glass roof and could be rotated on a turntable to give the best light throughout the day.

The Kinetoscope was seen in Paris in August 1894 and in London in October 1894. By the end of the year, Kinetoscope parlours were open all over North America and Europe. Altogether over a thousand machines were sold before their popularity began to wane. Edison and Dickson thought of the peep-show form on the analogy of the phonograph parlours, which had earlier proved successful. The cinema still awaited its final stage, theatrical projection, which initially occurred not in the USA but in France.

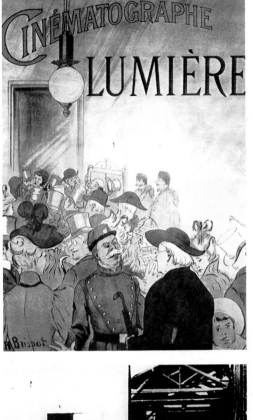

Far left: a woman sitting down, photographed synchronously (from right to left) from three points of view by Muybridge at the University of Pennsylvania c. 1887. Centre left: Thomas Edison with his 'Home Kinetoscope'. Left: Auguste and Louis Lumière. Right: a contemporary poster for their Cinématographe.

Pioneers of Projection

The two French brothers Auguste and Louis Lumière, (1862–1954 and 1864–1948), photographic-supplies manu-facturers of Lyons, were the first to achieve a satisfactory system for taking *and* projecting moving pictures made on a celluloid strip. They patented a combined hand-cranked camera and projector in France on February 13, 1895, which used a claw mechanism to pull on the film intermittently. They called it the Cinématographe, a name already used in 1892 and 1893 by Léon-Guillaume Bouly for a camera – but Bouly did not manage to project his pictures. The first public presentation of the Lumière Cinématographe was given at the Société d'Encouragement à l'Industrie Nationale on March 22, 1895. The film was *La Sortie des Usines* (1895, Leaving the Factory), a brief actuality of workers coming out of the Lumière factory that amazed the audience, who demanded a repetition. This first film was technically faultless and composed with the visual sense of an accomplished Victorian photographer. The Cinématographe was shown again at the Sorbonne on April 17, 1895. The next presentation on June 10, 1895 at Lyons, for the Congrès des Sociétés Françaises de Photographie, featured seven more subjects, including the first story film, *L'Arroseur Arrosé* (Watering the Gardener), about a joke played by a naughty boy with a hose-pipe.

Several more demonstrations followed, leading up to the first show for the general paying public in Paris on December 28, 1895. This took place at the Grand Café, 14 boulevard des Capucines, in a rented basement room containing about a hundred seats, with an entrance fee of one franc. The 30-minute show included 12 film subjects. The first day's takings were 33 francs, rising within three weeks to 2000 francs a day, the films were the Lumières' own home movies. They provided a faithful picture, sure to charm and flatter the public of the boulevards, of French middle-class life at the end of the nineteenth century – a time when few people could have foreseen the evens that were soon to destroy the illusion of unending security, prosperity and peace. Soon shows were taking place all over Europe and North America.

The Lumières were not long to retain their lead. In the USA Woodville Latham and his sons Otway and Gray became interested in the possibility of projecting a boxing film they had made at Edison's studio in 1894. In April 1895, Dickson left Edison and went to work with Latham on a projecting version of the Kinetoscope, using exactly the same principle of a moving film briefly illuminated frame by frame. The

Above: the Lumières' early films had a distinctive, 'documentary' flavour, striking in the way they portrayed people as they lived at that time.

Latham Eidoloscope was shown to the New York public in May 1895 and remained on show for a couple of years, but made little impression due to its poor picture quality.

The first projection of films in America based upon the intermittent projection of the film strip was the joint work of C. Francis Jenkins and Thomas Armat. They met in 1894, after Jenkins had patented a camera called the Phantascope,. They worked together on a Phantascope projector, using the 'beater' intermittent movement, invented by the Frenchman Georges Demenÿ in 1893, in which an eccentrically-mounted roller pulled on the film once per turn, and they exhibited the result at Atlanta, Georgia, in October 1895. Then they split up. Armat redesigned the machine and renamed it the Vitascope. Edison saw a demonstration in February 1896 and agreed with Armat for the supply of Vitascope projectors to be promoted under Edison's name. The first public show of the Vitascope was at Koster and Bial's Music Hall in New York on April 23, 1896. The 12 subjects, all Kinetoscope films, included two supplied by an Englishman, Robert W. Paul, and shot for him by Birt Acres. The Vitascope was a great success all over America but caused less excitement in Europe, which was already familiar with the Cinématographe and other forms of projection.

The first London show of the Cinématographe was at the Polytechnic, Regent Street, on February 20, 1896; but it was soon transferred to the Empire Theatre of Varieties in Leicester Square, where it ran continuously for over a year with great success, having opened on March 9, 1896. The programme consisted of ten films, billed by English titles as: 'Dinner Hour at the Factory Gate of M. Lumière at Lyons; Tea Time; The Blacksmith at Work; A Game at Ecarte; The Arrival of the Paris Express; Children at Play; A Practical Joke on the Gardener; Trewey's Serpentine Ribbon; Place des Cordeliers (Lyon); Bathing in the Mediterranean.'

However, the Cinématographe show was not the first to be given in England, where since the end of 1894 developments parallel to those in France had taken place.

Two men were involved, the London instrument-maker Robert W. Paul (1869–1943) and the photographer Birt Acres (1854–1918). After working well for a time, the partnership split up and a rancorous relationship developed, each man claiming that the other had made only minor contributions. Both afterwards presented their own views of what happened during the critical year, 1895, in which their brief association occurred.

By then, Paul was already making copies of the Kinetoscope machine, initially for a couple of Greek entrepreneurs, after having established that the design was not patented in England. But Edison's agents would supply films only to the purchasers of the original machines. Paul contacted Acres, who offered some ideas on how a camera might be made; by March 16, 1895 the camera was finished and Acres found and fitted a lens for it. The Paul-Acres camera was virtually identical in design to Marey's chronophotographic film camera of 1890, employing a sprung roller to pull the film, and it was used by Acres to take a dozen or so subjects, including the Oxford and Cambridge boat race in March and the Derby at Epsom in May. In May he also patented the Kinetic camera, using essentially the same design as the Paul-Acres camera. This unilateral action led to a breach between the two men, and Acres withdrew from their agreement in July. He needed to design a projector now that the outlet for his films, the Paul Kinetoscopes, was denied him. His first recorded presentation of projected films was to the Royal Photographic Society on January 14, 1896, using the Kinetic Lantern, soon renamed the Kineopticon. Though he showed films shot at 40 pictures per second to suit the Kinetoscope, he projected them at about fifteen pictures per second. His first public showing was on March 21, 1896, but a fire soon destroyed the show and Acres thereafter mainly confined himself to lecture and demonstration tours and to making more films.

By early 1896, Paul had developed a projector, the Theatrograph, whch he demonstrated at Finsbury Technical College on February 20, 1896, coinciding with the Lumière Cinématographe show. He improved this model, soon producing and selling over a hundred of these projectors. From March onward he presented shows at several music halls, including the Alhambra in Leicester Square. He also shot and commissioned new films, going on to become a leading producer, specializing in trick effects, many of which he pioneered. His manufacture and widespread sale of reliable equipment and his film-making earned him the deserved title of 'Father of the British Film Industry'.

The seaside town of Brighton seems a most unlikely place to figure in the early history of the British cinema, yet it was here that a number of pioneers were taking an active part in picture-making. This small but influential group comprised A. Esme Collings, G. Albert Smith, James Williamson and Alfred Darling. George Albert Smith did much to advance the technique of the film, and finally crowned his achievements by producing – in association with the American pioneer Charles Urban – the first commercially successful colour process, known as Kinemacolor.

The other European country where early motion picture development took place was Germany, where from 1879 a showman, Carl Skladanowsky, presented dissolving-view lantern shows, helped by his sons Emil and Max. It is claimed that Max built a sequence camera in 1892, using a continuously running film exposed through a very narrow slot in a rotating shutter, which gave very uneven picture spacing. To correct this, the negative film was cut up and reassembled to produce two positive strips with alternating frames, linked up into loops. These were shown on the Bioscop projector, patented in November 1895, which showed a frame from each of the films in turn, with a gradual transition between the images and no dark interval. On the day the patent was filed, Max and Emil gave their first public performance at the Berlin Wintergarten, presenting a 15-minute programme of eight films. They toured Europe in 1896, using a new Bioscop projector and a set of films made in an improved camera with an intermittent mechanism.

Also in 1896, Léon Gaumont's company persuaded Georges Demenÿ to redesign his 1893 camera so that it could use perforated film and be adaptable for projection. The resulting Chronophotographe used 60mm film, giving good picture detail. Another important early wide-film process was the American Biograph, originally developed to provide pictures for the Mutoscope, a flip-book peep-show machine, though in the event the projected version in 1896 antedated this other application, launched early in 1897 and often referred to as 'What the Butler Saw'. W.K.L. Dickson worked on the system with Herman Casler, using 68mm film, perforated between frames in the camera but unperforated in the projector, which tended to cause picture unsteadiness. The intermittent movement came from a pair of rollers, partially cut away. The Biograph remained popular into the 1900s.

Film Art, Film Language

The story is a good one, whether or not it is apocryphal: according to George Méliès (1861–1938), he approached Antoine Lumière (father of Auguste and Louis) after the first showing of the Cinématographe, to try to buy an apparatus to add to the attractions of his magic show at the Théâtre Robert-Houdin. The old gentleman refused:

'Young man, you should thank me. This invention is not for sale, but if it were it would ruin you. It can be exploited for a while as a scientific curiosity; beyond that it has no commercial future.'

George Méliès was largely responsible for the revolutionary discovery that films were not limited to photographing real life as and when it was found, but could be artistically composed for the purposes of entertainment. Méliès' discovery acquired added force from the fact that as a director he was an artist of a singular and charming fantasy. In 1884–85 he had visited London and, in the course of frequenting Maskelyne and Cooke's shows in Piccadilly, developed a passion for stage magic. In 1888 he was able to buy the most famous Parisian magic theatre, the Théâtre Robert-Houdin, where he specialized in elaborately staged and costumed spectacles. Undeterred by the Lumière rebuff, in 1896 Méliès bought a projector from Robert W. Paul in London, and with the help of a mechanic set about devising a camera to make his own films. At first he merely saw moving pictures as a supplementary attraction for his theatre; but film production was rapidly to usurp the magic theatre as his primary occupation.

The skills and versatility Méliès had learned in the theatre stood him in good stead as a film-maker. He acted as producer, director, scenarist, designer, sometimes cameraman and generally leading player. He also designed and built the world's first true film studio, an outsize glasshouse at Montreuil-sous-Bois, completed in 1897.

Between 1896 and 1913 he made more than five hundred films, ranging from action-packed one-minute trick films to twenty-minute stories and spectaculars. Applying all the practical ingenuity of a stage magician, he quickly found out the whole range of camera trickery: stop motion, superimposition, multiple exposure, even some devices that have still not been entirely explained. His quality, though, lies deeper than mere ingenuity. His trick films are distinguished by their pace, rhythm and invention.

Towards the end of 1896, Méliès made the first of the trick films that created his fame. This was *Escamotage d'une Dame chez Robert-Houdin* (The Vanishing Lady). In it a woman was changed into a skeleton and back again by stopping the camera and substituting one for the other. It remains questionable whether Méliès was the first to use double exposure and photography against a black background, since G.A. Smith was also using these techniques at the same time in England, though it is certain that the Frenchman did the most striking things with them. In late 1898 he made *Un Homme de Têtes* (*The Four Troublesome Heads*) in which the combination of the two devices allowed disconnected parts of the body to move round the set. After that date these methods, in combination with the 'stop-camera' effect, were his basis for large numbers of increasingly elaborate illusions.

Since trick films turned out to be merely a passing fashion in the long view of history, George Méliès' most important contribution is that he led the way to making longer films made up of many shots. The earliest example of this was *La Lune à un Mètre* (1898, *The Astronomer's Dream*), closely based on one of the miniature fantastic shows that he had previously staged in his theatre. As such it indicates how not

Left: George Méliès' glasshouse studio was equipped with blinds to control the amount of light, props rooms and a special stage with trap doors to allow for trick effects. Above: Méliès (left of centre) directing La Tour de Londres et les Derniers Moments d'Anne Boleyn (1905, The Tower of London). *He was reputed to be a difficult and demanding director, who disclosed little to his technicians and actors but expected rapid comprehension.*

only *his* films, but also those of other film-makers of the early years were frequently indebted to the stage for their subjects. *La Lune à un Mètre* was still not a very long film, being only three times the standard 65 feet (20m) i.e. 195 feet or 3 minutes' running time; but in 1899 Georges Méliès moved on to films that lasted about 10 minutes and were made up of many scenes. The most important of these was *L'Affaire Dreyfus* (1899, The Dreyfus Affair), which restaged the recent events surrounding the trial of Captain Dreyfus. Dreyfus, a Jew, had been convicted on trumped-up charges of treason in 1894, but at the instigation of the novelist Emile Zola was retried in 1899, finally being pardoned in 1906.

Some of Méliès films were inspired by the pantomimes and ballets of the London and Parisian theatres, or by the pioneer science fiction of Jules Verne. It was a film suggested by Verne's books, *Le Voyage dans la Lune 1902 (A Trip to the Moon)*, that definitively established Méliès on the international market. It had wit, brilliance and a mastery of scenic effect that were a revelation at the time, and still give the film an enduring charm.

Méliès' career achieved its peak around the time that he was elected president of the International Congress of Film Producers in 1909. After that his decline was rapid. His profits had been increasingly hit by widespread piracy of his films, notably in America. Audiences, moreover, were already beginning to tire of the artifice of his tiny stage; films had begun to use a wider world for their setting. The cinema was developing as a big business; and solitary creators such as Méliès were poorly armed for the battle with the new film empires. He made his last film in 1913.

Méliès' discovery of the magical possibilities of the cinema camera was part of the process of discovering the language of the new medium. Though for a long time film-makers would show a preference for shooting groups of people at full length, using the film frame as if it were a theatre proscenium, the highly sophisticated work of nineteenth-century still photographers suggested alternative possibilities. As early as 1895 the Lumière show, *Le Repas de Bébé* (The Baby's Meal) used a midshot of parents and child sitting at table. By 1900 George Albert Smith, in England, had made use of extreme close-up for comic effect in *Grandma's Reading Glass*. A Lumière cameraman, operating his camera in a gondola while moving down the Grand Canal in Venice, discovered the travelling shot. The backward or forward tracking movement was developed in the 1890s, when cameras were strapped to the front of moving locomotives to produce the 'phantom rides' beloved of audiences of that time.

Such manipulation of the content of individual shots provided the *vocabulary* of the film. The grammar followed. The earliest films were, quite literally, animated photographs, each one a single shot of a single scene or action. Their repertoire was analogous to that of picture postcards, stereoscope slides, lantern slides or pictorial jokes in illustrated magazines. Newspaper illustrations of current affairs also suggested the idea of 'reconstructing' for the camera impressions of topical events – there was no intent to deceive in such re-creations.

It was G.A. Smith (1864–1959) who invented the technique of breaking down a sequence into more than one shot or, to look at it another way, of making cuts within a scene, keeping continuity of action across them. He first did this in *Grandma's Reading Glass,* showing a little boy playing with the large magnifying glass which his grandmother (who is also present in the scene) uses to read with. As the child looks at a

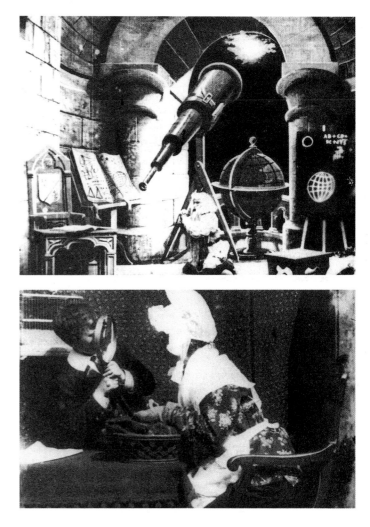

newspaper, a bird in a cage, his grandmother's eye and so on, there is a cut to a big close-up of each of the objects framed in a circular black vignette mask before the camera moves back to the more distant shot of the boy as he turns to look at something else.

The point-of-view shot immediately became popular in increasingly elaborate stories made in France and America about voyeuristic activities such as keyhole peeping, and by 1905 both it and the inserted close shot were standard elements of film technique.

At the same time the idea of action moving from one shot to another, with a direct cut between the shots, was being developed. The first films where this occurred were James Williamson's *Stop Thief!* (1901) and *Fire!* (1902). *Stop Thief!* was also the first chase film, but this genre was not properly established until 1903, which was the year things really started to move. Other English film-makers (the Mottershaws, the Haggars and Alf Collins) produced elaborate chase films – *A Daring Daylight Burglary, Desperate Poaching Affray* and *The Pickpocket* – which were all shown in the United States before Edison's director-cameraman, Edwin S. Porter, made *The Great Train Robbery* at the end of 1903. Besides the matter of taking the action out of one shot into another shot set in another location, *Desperate Poaching Affray* in particular showed the force that could be obtained by keeping the camera closer to the action than usual, and also by having the chase go out of the frame towards and past the camera in every shot. As a result this film still seems the fastest and most violent of those made in the early years.

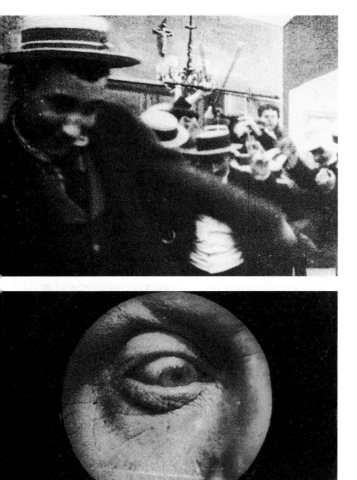

Far left and left: two consecutive stills from G.A. Smith's Grandma's Reading Glass, *demonstrating early use of the point-of-view shot. Above, far left: Méliès'* La Lune à un Mètre. *Above left: the courtroom brawl from* L'Affaire Dreyfus. *Above: Edwin S. Porter's* The Great Train Robbery, *which included variety of location, free movement from scene to scene and a degree of gripping action that was new in American cinema and was to affect subsequently how Westerns were made.*

The chase was one means used from 1903 onwards to extend the length of films – now one of the prime concerns of the film-makers in France, England and the United States, following on from the example of George Méliès. However, it was not Méliès but Charles Pathé (1863–1957) who put film-making on a truly industrial basis. Méliès insisted on personally participating in all the stages of the production of each of his films, whereas Charles Pathé merely organized the specialized services that backed up his ever-increasing number of production units. Within a few years after 1900 the Pathé company was the largest film producer in the world and continued to be so until World War I. In 1905–1906 the Pathé company produced 170 films with an average length of 300 feet (90m) and sold world-wide at least 300 copies of each – more than the entire American industry.

The films made by Pathé showed little in the way of innovation, being largely inspired by what was coming out of England and America; but they did have larger and more lavish sets, with better performers, and they were smoothly put together. Another advantage Pathé films had was that most of them could be obtained in coloured versions – hand-painted up to 1908, and in the more accurate and subtle stencil colouring from that date onwards.

At the beginning of the century American film production was confined to short knockabout sketches done in one or two shots, but by 1903 American film-makers were beginning to take up the European challenge. Edwin S. Porter (1869–1941), who made most of the Edison Company films from 1900 onwards, was the major single figure in the United States, but

his work was much more heavily dependent on that of his contemporaries than is usually realized, sometimes to the extent of direct imitation. For instance, his *Gay Shoe Clerk* (1903), which shows a shoe salesman taking the opportunity of a fitting to fondle the ankle of a young woman, with the crucial action revealed in an inserted close-up, is closely based on G.A. Smith's *As Seen Through a Telescope* (1901). In Smith's film the ankle-fondling is shown within a shot with circular masking, as representing what is seen from the point of view of an onlooker with a telescope, but Porter replaced this with the objective sort of close-up that Smith had also previously developed in a number of films such as *The Little Doctor* (1901), where he had cut to a closer shot when the little girl fed milk to the cat. The enormously popular boxed sets of lantern slides depicting the heroism of the fire services undoubtedly suggested to Porter the idea for his *Life of an American Fireman* (1903). He selected random scenes, already shot, of fires and firemen, added to them some new staged material that he shot himself, and even a close-up of a fire alarm and then assembled them together, in an entirely new order, to tell a continuous narrative about the rescue of a child from a burning house. Porter's most famous film *The Great Train Robbery* seems to have been based on an earlier stage melodrama rather than other films. Porter's principal technical contribution to film form was the use of panning shots to follow the action in fictional films.

The Great Train Robbery also makes use of such advanced editing devices as parallel and overlapping action. One scene, for instance, shows the bandits getting away after the crime;

Above: Sarah Bernhardt as Elizabeth I and Lou Tellegen as the Earl of Essex in Queen Elizabeth.

the next shows the rescue by his little daughter of the telegraph operator whom they have left bound and gagged; the next is a dance hall into which the exhausted but now freed operator suddenly bursts and tells of the robbery. The film – naive as it seems today – generated enormous excitement among the audiences of the time. Film-makers analysed and imitated Porter's techniques. *Rescued by Rover* (1905), an English film directed by Cecil Hepworth, shows how rapidly editing styles of great sophistication and fluidity had been assimilated by film-makers in the first decade of the century.

By 1905 a large enough number of films of substantial length had been produced to make it possible for film exhibition to move away from travelling fairground booths and items in vaudeville or variety shows into specialized theatres showing regularly changing programmes. The sudden expansion in numbers of these Nickelodeons in 1906 in the United States led to a world-wide film boom, and proper film industries appeared in Italy, Germany, Denmark and elsewhere to join those already existing in France, Great Britain and the United States. In the older film-making countries new production companies grew up to rival those already established.

For Art's Sake

The film had early discovered its natural role as an essentially popular entertainment; and it was in its most popular forms – Méliès' fantasies and fairy plays, the knockabout antics of the first comedians, the simple thrillers of the Porter school – that it discovered its role and style as art.

The early film-makers soon, however, enlarged their ambitions. They wanted respectability, recognition as artists and an audience other than the patrons of the music halls and fairgrounds. In 1906 Charles Pathé, always seeking new directions for expansion, formed the Société Cinématograph-

ique des Auteurs et Gens de Lettres (SCAGL) with a view to filming the classics of the modern theatrical and literary repertory. Two years later, also under the ultimate control of the omnipresent Pathé, the Société du Film d'Art was formed, to commission scenarios from the greatest living writers and to employ the greatest stars, including Sarah Bernhardt herself. Bernhardt did not appear in the heralded first production of the Film d'Art, *L'Assassinat du Duc de Guise* (1908, The Assassination of the Duke de Guise), which had a special musical accompaniment composed by Saint-Saëns; but she was to take the lead in several later films, including *La Dame aux Camélias* (1911, Camille) and *La Reine Elisabeth* (1912, Queen Elizabeth).

The film medium did not flatter the ageing and highly theatrical actress any more than it did such distinguished rivals as, for instance, Réjane in *Madame Sans-Gêne* (1911), based on the play by Victorien Sardou and Emile Moreau; but theatre enthusiasts must be grateful to the cinema for even such inadequate records of the stars of the nineteenth century.

Other companies were following the lead of the Société du Film d'Art in making their own *films d'art*, establishing a new and influential vogue. The productions of the *film d'art* today seem stuffy, stagy, overupholstered and declamatory. Nevertheless in their day their patently good connections did much to enhance the social respectability of the cinema.

The vogue of the *film d'art* left its legacies. In Italy its influence led to the development of a style of costume spectacle that earned the Italian cinema a brief period of international glory in the years preceding World War I. The taste for historical themes was evinced at least as early as 1905 with Filoteo Alberini's *La Presa di Roma* (The Fall of Rome). The *film d'art* and the discovery that films could be made in authentic classical locations produced a rich harvest after 1909, with the Cines, Itala Ambrosio and Aquila companies, among others, in fierce competition. The high point was Enrico Guazzoni's colossal *Quo Vadis?* (1912), whose unlimited extravagance, thousands of extras, conflagration of Rome and a menagerie of lions to devour the Christians ensured it a world-wide success. Its fame and the outbreak of World War I somewhat eclipsed a much more remarkable work, Giovanni Pastrone's *Cabiria* (1914), whose script was attributed (somewhat exaggeratedly, it seems) to the poet Gabriele D'Annunzio. The control of the narrative, the scale and splendour of the settings, which were brilliantly combined with actual locations, and the sophistication of acting, lighting and camerawork were never surpassed by the early Italian cinema.

It was the invasion of the *film d'art* that struck the first blow at the domination of the one-reel film in the exhibition systems of Britain and the United States. Producers and distributors insisted that the audience's powers of concentration could not extend beyond a single reel; and when, in 1911, D.W. Griffith decided that his *Enoch Arden* demanded to be made at the greater length of two reels, distributors – until shamed by the protests of audiences – insisted on releasing it in two separate parts.

At first the two-, three- and four-part films that began to arrive from the Continent with the *film d'art* vogue were indulgently accepted as foreign eccentricity. Then in 1912, Adolph Zukor (1873–1976), an exhibitor, had such success with Bernhardt's *Queen Elizabeth* that he was encouraged, despite the opposition of the Motion Picture Patents Company (which was trying to control all movie production), to launch his Famous Players company. Under the slogan 'Famous Players in Famous Plays', this was to produce 'feature' films, as the multi-reelers came to be known. The matter was clinched in 1913 by the overwhelming success in America of *Quo Vadis?* Launched in a legitimate theatre, the Astor, it defied the rooted beliefs of conservative producers and exhibitors. The public sat enthralled through the entire performance of nine reels, lasting more than two hours. The feature film, and the whole future of the American cinema, was established.

Right: lions seek Christians to devour in the arena in Quo Vadis? *Below right: one of* Cabiria's *lavish sets, the Temple of Moloch. Below:* Cabiria's *story of a gentleman's daughter who becomes a slave occurs against a backdrop of spectacular events, including Hannibal's crossing of the Alps.*

CHAPTER 2

The Early Days

The early years of the American film industry were far from peaceful. Competition for dominance in an increasingly profitable industry resulted in a 'patents war' that was at its most intense in the years between 1909 and 1915. An association of patent-holders, with Edison the most powerful, calling itself the Motion Picture Patents Company, endeavoured, though with gradually decreasing effectiveness, to monopolize motion-picture production and also, through a related company, distribution in the USA. This attempt was in violation of the spirit and ultimately the letter of the anti-trust laws, which forbade combinations of companies to interfere with the free market; the independent film-makers and distributors who eventually triumphed referred contemptuously to their would-be oppressors as 'the trust'. How had this situation arisen?

The Patents Company

For years Edison had been waging legal battles against the other main producers, claiming exclusive patents in cameras, projectors and even the sprocket-holes in the film invented and manufactured by George Eastman (this last large claim was upheld by a court in 1911 but reversed on appeal in 1912). By the end of 1907, most of the contending majors had agreed to become licensees of Edison, but Biograph, which used a camera invented by W.K.L. Dickson, Edison's former assistant, held out until the following year, being the last to join. The Motion Picture Patents Company was incorporated on September 9, 1908. Its members, besides Edison and Biograph, were Kalem, Vitagraph, Essanay, Lubin, Selig, George Kleine (distributor of Gaumont and other imported films), and the French-based companies Pathé and Méliès. Edison, Biograph, the inventor Thomas Armat (by this time associated with Biograph) and Vitagraph pooled 16 key patents – one for film, two for cameras and 13 for projectors. Edison's patents were regarded as basic and the other members agreed to pay him royalties. Only members could use the equipment licensed by the Patents Company, the idea was to freeze out the many small independent producers. Jeremiah J. Kennedy, the new president, enforced the trust's rules strictly. Producers had to pay a royalty of half a cent on each foot of film, and exhibitors were charged $2 a week, bringing in a total of $24,000 a week. A licensed studio could rent its films only to a licensed exhibitor. An exclusive contract was signed with Eastman, the main manufacturer of

Left: Mary Pickford as Mollie in William Beaudine's Sparrows *(1926), a Dickensian melodrama set in an orphanage in the Deep South.*

raw film stock in America. Kennedy kept close control on production and exhibition, prohibiting any publicity for actors, directors and writers in the film itself or in advertising. He also kept up the practice of the standard one-reel film and the consequent variety programme, lasting one to two hours.

To service distribution on behalf of the Patents Company members, the General Film Company was incorporated in 1910 to buy up the best-run and most prosperous film exchanges. By late 1911, it owned almost sixty of these and cancelled the licenses of those companies that refused to sell, denying them films to distribute.

Resistance had been growing since 1909, with Carl Laemmle always in the vanguard of the independents. But William Fox, who owned the principal film exchange in New York, now entered the struggle, not only refusing to sell but setting up his own production company and also suing the trust for conspiracy in restraint of trade. Fox's case went to hearing in January 1913. In 1915 the federal court ruled against the Patents Company, on the grounds that while an individual patent holder had a legitimate monopoly on his own invention, he could not combine his patent with that of others to create a monopoly. Already in decline because of its outdated policies, the company was pronounced legally dead in 1918, when its appeal was finally dismissed. By that time, nearly all of its members had ceased to produce films, with only Vitagraph surviving into the Twenties and passing its name on to Warners' Vitaphone sound films. The early history of American films is strewn with anecdotes about the often violent methods used in unsuccessful attempts to enforce the monopoly. The Patents War was also a factor in creating Hollywood, which provided a haven for the independents, far from the Patents Company members (who were mostly established on the East Coast or in Chicago) and conveniently near the Mexican border.

The Star System

Before the advent of the 'star' on the American screen, America was only one among many film-producing countries, and not the world power it would become. In the years prior to World War I, the French and then the Italian film-makers dominated the scene. The adoption and exploitation of the star system proved America's most important contribution to films and secured its prominence in the industry.

Although a star system was already flourishing on the European continent, this innovation met with surprisingly hard resistance from within the American film business. It was forced upon the industry in 1910 by a newcomer who saw star power as his means of surviving the warring world of movies by getting the public to prefer his product to the anonymous films being churned out by the big companies. The enterprising producer was an immigrant clothes salesman turned film distributor, Carl Laemmle (1867–1939); and his choice for securing his foothold was called the 'Biograph Girl'. She was one of the most popular faces on the screen, but the public knew nothing about her except what they saw. When Laemmle decided to employ her to star under her own name in films produced by his Independent Motion Picture Company (IMP), the pressure to publicize films' lead players by name was already strong, and it was only a matter of time before some other enterprising studio would have done the same. But to Carl Laemmle goes the honour of being the first American to do so, and Florence Lawrence (1886–1938), who flared for a brief time across the movie firmament, is forever-more enshrined in the history books as the first American film star to be billed under her own name.

Florence, who started her career in show business as 'Baby Flo, the Child Wonder Whistler', had been touring since she was four, and entered films like many out-of-work actors, eking out a living between stage roles. By 1909, when she joined Biograph to turn out nearly a hundred one-reelers in a year at a guaranteed weekly salary of $25, she had already been in films for three years. She was young and pretty, and she photographed well; the public began to look forward to her films. Members of the audience took to asking their local exhibitors if any of the Biograph films on the programme included 'that lovely young woman' whom they dubbed the 'Biograph Girl'. They also began to express interest in films with the 'Kalem Girl' (Gene Gauntier) or the 'Vitagraph Girl' (Florence Turner).

Whenever any of these early favourites appeared in a new film, attendances at the cinemas showing them went up. The exhibitors naturally asked the rental agents for more of the same, and these in turn relayed the message to the companies, where the early moguls suspected, quite rightly as it happened, that once actors found out how popular they were, they would ask to be paid more for their work. The rise of the stars was destined to transform the industry. But, refusing like so many King Canutes to heed the signs, the old guard stood on the shore of a new empire and most of them were swept away by the onrushing tide of enterprising newcomers to the film business who saw that victory lay in the stars.

In 1910, when Laemmle lured Lawrence away from Biograph, he set about publicizing his coup with means, both foul and funny, that introduced the other vital factor in America's dominance of the star system – publicity. First he put out a false press report that Florence Lawrence had been killed in a tram accident in St Louis. Then, blaming Biograph as the alleged instigator of this false rumour, he proclaimed in a newspaper advertisement that she was alive, well and working exclusively for his company, and he would prove it by sending her back to St Louis. The new IMP star's arrival in town provided the first demonstration of fan hysteria for any movie personality. Crowds, larger than those for President Taft's visit the previous week, met her at the station and along the way to the cinema showing her new film. The demure young girl, wearing a new frock and a pretty flower-covered picture hat, had the flowers torn from the hat, the hat from her head and the pins from her hair; by the time she arrived at the cinema, she was almost in a state of shock. The girl was terrified but her studio was delighted. The press, in St Louis and across the country, carried the news. The floodgates were open.

Now that it was recognized and accepted, star fever swept across America. It attracted to the studios in New York, Chicago and Los Angeles out-of-work actors, a schoolgirl from Brooklyn (Norma Talmadge), a sculptor's model (Francis X. Bushman – the screen's first 'great lover'), a US marshal (Tom Mix) and countless numbers of clerks and shopgirls, all eager for a chance of fame and fortune. Among these types more than any other lies the real key to the enormous popularity that the American film star had with the peoples of all nations – these early stars rose out of their own ranks.

Film stars became an authentic form of American royalty, with commensurate fortunes. The system was to provide legendary heroes – and it had its victims, one of the first of whom was to be poor Florence Lawrence. Unlike Mary Pickford (who later became known as 'America's sweetheart' and then 'the world's sweetheart') she does not appear to have been a very shrewd businesswoman. In 1911, possibly still traumatized by her experience of Carl Laemmle's business methods, she left him to join the Philadelphia-based Lubin Company, with a slight raise in salary. (Mary Pickford, who had become the new star of Biograph, now took Lawrence's place at IMP, who billed her as 'Little Mary', at $175 a week). A year later Florence Lawrence moved to the Victor Company, but soon she was to add another first to her achievements – she became the first movie star officially to retire from her hectic career in order to rest, contemplate and grow flowers. Then, in 1915, she became the first star to try for a comeback. But her time was over. More attempted comebacks followed and failed. By the mid-Thirties she was employed as an extra at Paramount and MGM and in 1938 she committed suicide.

What this goes to show is that the American public would not tolerate weakness and indecision in its idols. Mary Pickford (1893–1979) also moved from studio to studio, but in strength, with ever-increasing salaries and popularity, and with her spunky spirit unquenched. Whether playing adults or the child roles she is best remembered for, she was never the stereotyped heroine who meekly submitted to the problems her characters encountered – she bit and scratched or used her common sense.

After a successful return to the stage, where she had gained her first experience of acting, she came back to the movies for good, finding her popularity only increased by the horde of look-alikes that had sprung up and flourished in her absence. By 1912, when she signed with Adolph Zukor's Famous Players Company at $500 a week, she was undisputedly the cinema's biggest star. Later she received an offer from a studio to star in a 14-part serial at $4000 a week, but stayed with Famous Players at $2000 a week when provided with a guarantee of $104,000 for the year, rising in 1916 to a guaranteed minimum of $10,000 a week. By 1918 her only rival for popularity and salary was Charles Chaplin; and in a new deal with First National for $1,050,000 for three pictures, plus a $50,000 bonus to her mother and an additional contract to her brother Jack to make films, she became the highest-paid star. And her story was just beginning.

Meanwhile, new types of star gained public favour and these too received enormous fees in a mad competitive scramble for their services by rival companies that were springing up almost as fast as the stars they hired. Heroes, heroines, heart-throbs, fearless blondes and brunettes such as serial queens Pearl White (of *The Perils of Pauline*, 1914), Grace Cunard and Ruth Roland; animals (in 1911 Jean, a dog, became the first animal star) and clowns (Mack Sennett's Keystone films made their first appearance in 1912, and

Left: Francis X. Bushman in Graustark
*(1915). Above left: members of the Motion
Pictures Patents Company in 1908. Above:
Florence Lawrence in* A Girlish Impulse
*(1911). Below: 'America's Sweetheart' –
Mary Pickford.*

Chaplin joined Keystone in December 1913) – all these rose from obscurity to fame. They shared one vital quality – drive. Americans were doers.

During this period, Adolph Zukor bought a feature-length French film *La Reine Elisabeth* (1912, *Queen Elizabeth*), starring none other than France's legendary Sarah Bernhardt, an actress whose position in the theatre was that of a goddess. She was already an old woman and her film technique was non-existent, but her reputation was unassailable – if the most illustrious actress in theatrical history believed that movies were 'my once chance for immortality', then what American actor could presume to think otherwise? The film's success launched Zukor's Famous Players Film Company, and a stream of Broadway and opera stars began to appear in films.

But none of the famous stage names that made films – James O'Neill, Billie Burke, Geraldine Farrar, Lillian Russell and Enrico Caruso – was as lasting or as popular as the stars the public chose: Blanche Sweet, Douglas Fairbanks, Clara Kimball Young, Margaret Fischer, Mae Marsh, Henry B. Walthall, Wallace Reid, Gloria Swanson (who made her film debut in 1915), Lillian and Dorothy Gish. The greatest sensation of 1915 was also an unknown – Theda Bara, whose film *A Fool There Was* came out in January. Though Bara was borne up on a wave of publicity, her success was truly popular and enormous.

As stars' salaries kept rising upward, the rental fees of their films to the exhibitors rose too, and with them the standards of the movies being made. Mary Pickford would recall:

'As Mr Zukor, with much headshaking and ominous prophecy, went on acceding to my demands for higher pay, he raised the price of each film to the exhibitors, bringing the guarantee up from $35,000 to $65,000, then from $65,000 to $120,000, and finally, when he began paying me $10,000 a week, he boosted the fee to $165,000. This of course, had direct bearing on the type of picture we subsequently made.

We had educated both the exhibitors and the public away from the conception of a five-and-ten-cent movie, and sumptuous and spacious movie houses like the New York Strand soon sprang up to prove it'.

The producers, seeing their power shrink and fearing the imminent collapse of the whole structure, sought ways to clamp down on the stars' salaries, and bring them under their control. One way was the introduction of long-term contracts. Another was Samuel Goldwyn's idea of offering the public alternatives, as with the formation of his company to make films by famous authors. When a star's company went bankrupt, as happened to Clara Kimball Young's, the cause often lay not just in the product but in the producers' refusal to distribute the films in their cinemas.

It was as a reaction to such ominous schemes that the four most powerful names in the business, Mary Pickford, Douglas Fairbanks, Charles Chaplin and D.W. Griffith, joined together in 1919 to form their own company, United Artists. When the news leaked out prematurely, one observer is supposed to have commented: 'So the lunatics have taken charge of the asylum.' But in fact this move showed stars had reached a new peak. The world lay at their feet; and when Mary Pickford and Douglas Fairbanks were married on March 28, 1920, they were regarded as the uncrowned King and Queen of the Movies.

In the famous aphorism of Adolph Zukor, 'the public is never wrong'. But this stage of American predominance was not reached all at once. The Patents Company had made ineffectual efforts to slow down the introduction of the feature film, though some of its members were quick to leap on the band wagon, as when Kleine exhibited *Quo Vadis?* in New York. The independents Laemmle and Zukor had done much to establish the beginnings of the star system. Even in the field of comedy, where American success was finally sealed by the world-wide popularity of Charlie Chaplin, the

Right: Gloria Swanson (left) with Juanita Hansen in an early Mack Sennett comedy. Centre: Mae Marsh's blend of apparent frailty and inner strength made her a public favourite in the Twenties – particularly in the films of D.W. Griffith. Paddy-the-Next-Best-Thing (1923) was a rare British appearance. Far right: an early Fox publicity portrait of Theda Bara.

MAE MARSH – – – – in
Paddy-the-Next-Best-Thing.
by
GERTRUDE PAGE.

United States was at first surprisingly slow off the mark.

Comedy in France

Laughter is the surest of all best sellers. When things are bad, people want comedy to cheer them up; and when they are already happy, they want to seal their happiness with laughter. From the start film-makers recognized that they had in comedy a perennial money-spinner. From *L'Arroseur Arrosé* (1895, Watering the Gardener) onwards, comedy featured largely in the early film repertory.

These first films, barely one minute long, were confined to the sort of single-gag visual jokes that might have been inspired by cartoons in the comic papers – as, indeed, was *L'Arroseur Arrosé*. Even when films became longer and the action of comedies was extended and elaborated, what was funny was the happening, rather than the relationship to that happening of the people concerned. Of course it seemed funnier if the person who pulled the chair from under someone else was a cheeky-faced boy, and the victim was a stout and irascible old person who might wave his arms or stick and otherwise express anger in an extravagantly comical way. Yet, despite the hints offered by the appearance in films of music-hall comedians who occasionally recorded fragments of their acts for the camera, and the strong characterization in Méliès' comic films, it was not until the middle of the first decade of the century that the cinema screen saw the regular emergence of character clowns – comedians who produced laughter by their relationship to the world and events around them.

It was in France, which dominated the world cinema industry in the decade before World War I, that a genre of comedy was introduced where the humour depended on the personality of the comic actor. The first true movie clown was André Deed (1884–1938), born André Chapuis. Trained as a music-hall singer and acrobat, Deed entered films as a

supporting player for Georges Méliès. In 1905, Charles Pathé saw him on stage at the Châtelet Theatre in Paris and at once engaged him. After appearing in a chase film, *La Course à la Perruque* (1905, The Wig Chase), Deed went on to make a whole series of one-reel comedies, which within a few months established him as a favourite with audiences all over Europe.

Deed was the first of a generation of clowns who, though their proper names were unknown to the public at large, were lovingly styled by nicknames that were generally different in every country where their films were shown. In France, for instance, Deed was 'Boireau'. In Italy he was 'Beoncelli', in Spain, 'Sanchez', and so on. When in 1908 – perhaps nervous at the rise of a new rival, Max Linder, at Pathé – Deed accepted an offer to work for the Italia Film Company in Turin, his new Italian name was 'Cretinetti'. When the Cretinetti films were shown in France, he was renamed 'Gribouille'. The Spanish now named him 'Toribio', the Russians, 'Glupishkin', and the English, 'Foolshead'.

Perhaps this multiple nomenclature and change of nationality produced a kind of artistic schizophrenia, for Deed never established so clear-cut a personality as Linder and the later American clowns were to do. He was characterized by a glorious, irrepressible and incorrigible idiocy which, whether he was burning down his own house with a candle-lit Christmas tree or wrecking a cinema, generally resulted in apocalyptic destruction.

Deed was his own director and proved a good pupil of Méliès. He was the first director-comedian to exploit to the full the comic possibilities of accelerated action, stop motion and other comic trickery. His talent as a director was such that he continued to make films even when his own popularity as a star had waned, though his career did not survive the coming of sound. In his later days Deed is said to have worked as a night watchman at the Pathé studios, where once he had reigned.

Other Pathé stars were recruited from the variety theatres, including Dranem, whose fame as a comedian was already sufficiently large for his name not to be adapted, and Louis-Jacques Boucot (known as Boucot or 'Peinard Gavroche'), who was blessed with a funereal face, epileptic movements and a disconcerting manner of suddenly sticking out his tongue.

Pathé's greatest star – indeed, the greatest comic star of the years before World War I – was Max Linder. Born Gabriel-Maximilien Leuvielle in 1883 he began his career as a legitimate actor, but in 1905 began to eke out his small salary from the Théâtre de l'Ambigu by working days at the Pathé studios. He played bit parts and occasional leads until 1909, when the departure of Deed decided Pathé to star Max in a series of his own. Max was different from other comedians. While they strove for grotesque eccentricity, he affected the dress and style of a young, handsome boulevardier. The special flavour of his comedy lay in the contrast between his personal elegance and the ludicrous situations in which he found himself.

For all his elegance, Max's character in a way stood aside from the world he moved in. He wore that world's costume, but in his heart he didn't belong. His audiences must have felt that really he was one of them, and he helped them to feel this as best he could – hence the terrible jokes about fleas and smelly feet, seasickness and diarrhoea, which kept bursting in. He was mocking the bourgeois world (Jean Mitry emphasizes this in his monograph, *Max Linder*, published in 1966), and so now that that world has vanished, some of the

Above left: Fred Evans in Pimple's Wonderful Gramophone *(1913). Top left: Max Linder. Top right: Louis Feuillade. Above right: John Bunny hugely funny in the comedy Western* Her Hero *(1911).*

films starring two successive child comedians, first 'Bébé' Abeilard and then 'Bout-de-Zan' – a particularly unappealing child who was maliciously, and no doubt unjustly, reputed to be a dwarf of advanced years. The pranks which these mischievous juveniles played at the expense of guileless elders contributed notably to the more innocent merriment of the last days of the pre-war world.

The styles of French comedy were imitated everywhere, and French clowns were much in demand in Italy. Other countries attempted to follow the Latin style. In Germany the popular Jewish star of a crude slapstick series, 'Meyer', was later to achieve international fame as a director under his real name, Ernst Lubitsch. The Russians were inclined to import their comedy. A favourite comedian, generally characterized as a foppish suitor, 'Antosha' was a Pole, Antoni Fertner. The clown 'Giacomo' was Milanese, and 'Reynolds' was probably English.

Britain and the USA

Britain and America lagged behind continental Europe in the production and development of film comedy in these early years of the century – surprisingly, because both countries had rich theatrical traditions of vaudeville comedy. Some of the great comedians of the time permitted their variety acts to be filmed; but the only sustained English comedy series of the pre-war years were the films starring Fred Evans (1889–1915) as Pimple; he had a grotesque clown face and a very broad style in knockabout comedy, and tended to topicality in his choice of themes. Infrequent revivals of these films suggest that the titles were often the best part of them: *Pimple Up the Pole*, for instance, or *Pimple, the Bad Girl of the Family* (both 1915) – Evans had a particular taste for playing roles in drag. Rival series, such as Bamforth's films about Winky and Clarendon's comedies featuring the character Jack Spratt, were short-lived.

Few American comedies of note have survived from the first decade of the century; and it was not until around 1910 that the American companies began to experiment with character clowns in the European style. Vitagraph discovered American's first true comedy star, John Bunny (1863–1915). Bunny had been a successful stage actor and manager before, with rare foresight, he perceived the potential of moving pictures. At first he had some difficulty in persuading Vitagraph to accept his services; but in a matter of months he had established himself as a major box-office attraction. Bunny was stout and cheery, with a huge and irresistably comic face; he looked much older than his years – he was 46 when he made his first films for Vitagraph, and only 51 when he died in 1915. His usual partner was Flora Finch, generally playing the vinegary wife who frustrated his aspirations to amorous or other adventures.

Bunny's popularity launched American film comedy for the first time in the European market. The success of the John Bunny films produced new confidence among American makers of comic films. After 1910 comedy stars began to proliferate. Vitagraph enjoyed further success with the light domestic comedies of Mr and Mrs Sidney Drew as well as low-comedy one-reelers with Billy Quirk and an English comic from the Fred Karno music-hall troupe, Jimmy Aubrey. Essanay's long-running Snakeville Comedy series created characters who belonged to a comic-strip wild West, including Alkali Ike (played by Augustus Carney) and Mustang Pete (William Todd). Essanay, which was to score its greatest comic triumph a few years later, in 1915, when it captured

charm and point of the Max films has gone too. Max was a brilliant and prodigal inventor of comedy, with a gift for endless variations on a single, simple theme, such as taking a bath or putting on a pair of tight shoes. Gags that he devised still enrich every comedian's repertory. He also had a greater and more sophisticated appreciation than any among his contemporaries of the demands and the potential, for the comedian, of the cinema screen. Max's career ended in tragedy. Dogged by ill health, disheartened by his failure to establish himself in America, fearful of his declining popularity, he took his own life in October 1925.

At the Gaumont studios the guiding creative force (from 1907 onwards) was Louis Feuillade (1873–1925), who had not yet discovered his forte as a director of serial thrillers. Gaumont comedies were altogether more extravagant than those of Pathé, with prodigal use of trick camerawork and an unrestrained fantasy that anticipated both Mack Sennett and the surrealist film-makers of the Twenties.

Feuillade hit upon a particularly effective formula with

Charlie Chaplin from Mack Sennett's Keystone Company, also promoted a popular series starring Wallace Beery as Sweedie.

Comedies and their stars proved highly effective ammunition in the cut-throat industrial battles of the pre-war period. Character comedy had become a staple of the American silent cinema. It was to be carried to new heights of folk art, anarchism and inspired lunacy by Mack Sennett's Keystone studio.

The serial

The first true serial was the Selig company's *The Adventures of Kathlyn* (1913), starring Kathlyn Williams, billed as 'the girl without fear'. This ran through 13 instalments as the intrepid heroine faced a variety of bizarre and sinister dangers in India. In 1914 Pathé, the company that was to dominate the silent-serial market, produced its first venture in the type, *The Perils of Pauline*, starring Pearl White, still the best-remembered silent serial of them all. Pearl White's next vehicle was *The Exploits of Elaine* (1914), in which she was aided by Arnold Daly playing Craig Kennedy, the popular detective hero created by the novelist Arthur B. Reeve. Together they battled against a villain called The Clutching Hand – the first of many extravagantly-named menaces that were to thrill serial audiences. Pearl White repeated her role in two sequels *The New Exploits of Elaine* and *The Romance of Elaine* (both 1915), as well as starring in eight further serials in the next decade before retiring to France in 1924.

Meanwhile in Paris two popular writers, Pierre Souvestre and Marcel Allain, had published their phenomenally successful series of crime thrillers concerning the exploits of the master criminal, Fantômas.

There were 32 Fantômas stories, and for 6,000 fr. Gaumont bought the film rights. The studio's production-chief Louis Feuillade made the films in collaboration with the authors, who were often present during the shooting to lend a hand with the constant improvisation. However, Feuillade's *Fantômas* was not a genuine serial. It consisted of a series of self-contained films, released at intervals over a year (1913–14), and varying in length from three to five reels. But with it, the essential Feuillade style was born.

Vigorous and enjoyable as it is, *Fantômas* loses slightly today by being shown in one piece, that is, in a form for which it was never intended. Its repetitions become obtrusive and its climaxes misplaced. Also, René Navarre as the villain-hero lacks the panache of the central figures in *Les Vampires* (1915–16) and *Judex* (1916).

The immensely popular *Les Vampires* was a true serial, a continuous story released in ten episodes at irregular intervals during 1915–16. The Vampires are a band of criminals; they have a chief (the Great Vampire), but their inspiration is the ruthless, voluptuous Irma Vep (an anagram of Vampire), played with superb relish by the actress Musidora.

The locations are the great glory of *Les Vampires*. Forced on to the streets when wartime conditions made work in the studios difficult, Feuillade turned the bleak suburbs of Paris into his star. Grey, cobbled side roads, melancholy wasteland, gaunt factories, scattered bystanders, the occasional car gleaming with brass, all bathed in the light of a grey dawn or in a threatening twilight – this was the backcloth to Feuillade's drama of precarious good versus elemental (and exultant) evil.

The serial is magnificently acted. Feuillade had assembled his stock company mainly from people with little or no stage experience; he taught them the importance of *restraint* in film acting. Their naturalism amid all the wild developments of the plot lends the whole an uncanny conviction. Here and in the next serial, *Judex*, the hero's henchman was played by the great comic actor Marcel Lévesque. Tall, balding, sardonic, slow-moving, Lévesque made a valuable contribution to the serial, periodically bringing a disillusioned common sense to bear on the more bizarre aspects of the story.

Judex is almost as good as *Les Vampires*. Though less pleasurably shocking, because, the central figure of the Avenger (René Cresté) is on the side of good, it is as rich in poetry and as extravagant in invention. It also has the child Bout-de-Zan as The Liquorice Kid forming a marvellous partnership of unequals with Lévesque.

Feuillade felt he had to play it a little safer this time. The censor had held up *Les Vampires* for nearly ten weeks, until vamped into submission by Musidora in person, and the press had been shocked by the film's potential for corruption. They still found *Judex* beneath serious attention, but Feuillade worked for his audiences – and, without knowing it, for the future.

Below right: Feuillade's Fântomas. *Bottom right: René Cresté left) as* Judex. *Bottom left: Pearl White in* The Perils of Pauline. *Below:* The Adventures of Kathlyn, *with Kathlyn Williams.*

CHAPTER 3
The Rise of Hollywood

In 1883, a Kansas couple, Harvey and Daeida Wilcox, came to Los Angeles and opened a real-estate office. Three years later, they owned a 120-acre tract that was subdivided and advertised for sale under the name 'Hollywood'. In 1903 the residents voted for incorporation into the city of Los Angeles. The geographic area of Hollywood was determined to be from Normandie west to Fairfax Avenue and from the Santa Monica Mountains south to Fountain Avenue. This area, annexed to Los Angeles in 1910, was to become the focus of film production in the United States, and its name 'Hollywood' came to cover the film-making region, including the various outlying Los Angeles areas.

Los Angeles itself was far from an urban metropolis at the turn of the century. Most of its 100,000 residents were concentrated in the districts surrounding the downtown commercial hub. To the west lay great stretches of bean fields, orange groves and empty land all the way to the ocean. Entertainment was centred in the downtown area. The exhibitor Thomas Tally was among the first to show motion pictures in Los Angeles in 1896, and in 1902 he opened his Electric Theatre, installing 200 fixed seats and charging the high price of ten cents for admission. The films he showed there included those made in the East by the Thomas Edison Company, including *The Capture of the Biddle Brothers* and *New York in a Blizzard* (both 1902).

The first production pioneer was Colonel William Selig of the Chicago-based Selig Polyscope Company, who sent his director Francis Boggs to the East Coast early in 1907 to photograph coastal locations for *The Count of Monte Cristo* (1907). In 1908 Boggs rented a lot on Olive Street in downtown Los Angeles, and there made the first dramatic film shot completely in California, *The Heart of a Race Tout* (1909).

D.W. Griffith at Biograph
The American Mutoscope and Biograph Company sent its most prolific director, D.W. Griffith, to California for three seasons in 1910, 1911 and 1912. Griffith did not confine his activities to his studio in downtown Los Angeles. He travelled with his cameramen Arthur Marvin and Billy Bitzer, as well as his acting and production unit, to the actual places mentioned in the works he dramatized for the screen.

On 31 December 1913, D.W. Griffith announced his departure from the American Biograph Company with whom he had worked since 1908. In an advertisement in the *New*

Left: Charlie Chaplin directing The Gold Rush, *his first comedy feature for United Artists, the company he formed with Douglas Fairbanks, Mary Pickford and D.W. Griffith.*

York Dramatic Mirror, he summarized his achievements during the Biograph years, claiming that he had 'revolutionised motion picture drama' and 'founded the modern technique of the art'. To Griffith, on the strength of his own declarations, are normally credited the first uses of such devices as the close-up and the long-shot, the flashback (or, as he termed it, the 'switchback'), the fade-in and fade-out, the use of the iris lens to pick out details of action, the use of titles, the concept of editing for parallel action and 'dramatic continuity', the atmospheric use of lighting, and the encouragement of 'restraint in expression' in screen acting.

Some of these claims, particularly where restrained acting was concerned, were to find more substantial justification in the post-Biograph years. (By 1920, Griffith could reasonably be said to have pioneered the expressionist use of colour tinting, the concept of widescreen cinema, and the commissioning of original musical scores. By this time he had also sent a camera up in a balloon, and directed at least two of the greatest films the silent cinema would ever know). But there was no doubt that Griffith left both Biograph and film history the richer for a five-and-a-half-year output unequalled by any other film-maker in any other era.

Admittedly, evidence that has since emerged slightly diminishes Griffith's claims; Edwin S. Porter (for the Edison Company) and G.W. 'Billy' Bitzer (for Biograph) are no less amply revealed as authentic pioneers. Porter's *The Great Train Robbery* (1903) has long been established as a primitive example of parallel storytelling, and ends up (or starts, according to taste) with the medium close-up, in colour, of a bandit shooting at the camera and thus at the audience. But Porter's other Edison productions, from the turn of the century, are also full of dissolves, close-ups and camera movements. The effects are far from sophisticated – but they are there. Similarly, in such dramas as *Moonshiners* (1904) Bitzer pans fluently, if not particularly smoothly, around the countryside, while in *The Black Hand* (1906) he can be seen making use of titles, a two-shot, and a close-up. In both technique and subject (as with, for instance, *A Kentucky Feud*, 1905) he clearly marks out the territory that was subsequently to be claimed by Griffith. This indebtedness to the first film-makers is further reinforced by the irony that Griffith was directed by Porter in *Rescued From an Eagle's Nest*, when he was an aspiring actor and first worked at Biograph in 1907, and by Bitzer in *The Sculptor's Nightmare*, made in 1908, by which time he had officially joined the company. (Bitzer subsequently worked as Griffith's cinematographer for the next 16 years).

What D.W. Griffith brought to the movies when he started

directing at Biograph was a new vision of the dramatic possibilities of the medium rather than new techniques, which in many cases were already available, including cross-cutting between parallel actions. He introduced 'mixed' characters – the good-bad man (and good-bad girl) – which made possible extra twists and subtleties in the plots; and he used existing filmic devices for dramatically expressive purposes in new ways. A good example of this is seen in *The Country Doctor* (1909), which opens with a slow panning shot over the landscape in which the story is set, and which concludes after the tragic denouement with the same panning shot, but this time under darkened skies. Another example is his use of the car-mounted tracking shot, which also ante-dated his debut, to cover the interplay between the people in *two* vehicles, one carrying the hero and his fiancée, the other his jilted mistress, in *The Drive for a Life* (1909).

Griffith also led the way towards faster cutting, notably by developing cross-cutting between parallel actions into a major constructional device, applying it to the suspense of the last-minute rescue. Another device that he used more effectively than earlier film-makers was the insert shot, a close shot of some object other than an actor's face cut into a scene. Starting from more obvious examples such as the time-bomb ticking towards zero hour in *The Voice of the Violin* (1909), he moved on to reveal internal psychological states by repeated close-ups of hands and feet and symbolic insect activity in *The Avenging Conscience* (1914). It was the general dramatic power of his films that raised Griffith head and shoulders above his contemporaries. In other respects, however, some American film-makers were ahead of him. Vitagraph films, for example, showed greater naturalism of acting and staging, and were usually shot from closer in than Griffith's films. The further development of smoothness of continuity between shots by precise matching of action and the use of varied angles of shot within a scene (including reverse angles of actors facing each other) also took place elsewhere than at Biograph, mostly from 1912–13 onwards.

What Griffith brought significantly to the screen, then, was not a collection of technical tricks, but the skill to use them effectively to enhance his stories. It was a skill derived partly from the theatre – his first love – and partly from his family background, with its 'scholarly atmosphere'. But most cruci-ally, the skill grew inevitably from the experience of maintaining an output of around nine films a month through-out his stay with Biograph. Producing nearly five hundred films in five-and-a-half years, Griffith was given the unique opportunity – and had the responsive personality – to make every conceivable experiment in film-making at a time when the rules were few, the audience vast and enthusiastic, and the future unlimited.

Born on January 22, 1875 on a farm in Crestwood, Kentucky, Llewelyn Wark Griffith came of excellent South-ern stock. His father had been a colonel in the Confederate army, and his domestic life seems to have been ordered along firmly ethical and devout (but not ardently militaristic) lines. 'My parents always directed our studies and our thoughts towards the noble, the great in literature', he later said, and from the age of six he was determined to become 'a great literary man'.

Numerous early jobs included being a salesman for the *Encyclopaedia Britannica*, a hop-picker, a newspaper reporter, a drama critic in Louisville and an actor under the stage name of Lawrence Griffith in stock and touring companies. He wrote a play, *The Fool and the Girl*, which was produced in Washington and Baltimore in 1907 without much success. Taken by a friend to his first picture show, he found it 'silly, tiresome, inexcusable; any man who enjoys such a thing should be shot at sunrise'. But it led him to offer film stories to the Edison and Biograph studios in New York, and it was only a short step to finding employment as a bit-player for the cameras, along with his wife Linda Arvidson.

Mrs Griffith has described in her autobiography (*When the Movies Were Young*, published in 1925) how the Biograph Company, originally created to make the peepshow devices called Mutoscopes in rivalry to Edison's Kinetoscopes, were by 1908 desperately searching for good material. At the suggestion of Billy Bitzer's camera assistant, Arthur Marvin (who happened to be the general manager's brother), the studio offered a story by staff-writer Stanner Taylor (later to write many of Griffith's one-reelers) to the reluctant Lawrence Griffith – only when established did he become known as 'David' or 'D.W.' – on the assurance that he could have his acting job back if the project did not work out. Photographed by Marvin, *The Adventures of Dollie* (1908) starred Linda Arvidson and Arthur Johnson, a youth of no previous film experience whom Griffith picked from the street for his suitable appearance. It was shot in a week, premiered in New York on July 14, 1908 and judged successful enough

Far left: Griffith with his favourite cameraman Billy Bitzer. Centre: Lillian Gish in an early one-reeler, The Musketeers of Pig Alley. *Left:* Judith of Bethulia, *Griffith's first four-reeler (and his last film for Biograph) featured Lillian Gish, (left), with Blanche Sweet (right) in the title role.*

for Griffith to be granted a one-year contract which, with royalties, raised his salary from practically nothing to $500 a month. Apart from brief appearances when, in a crisis, there was nobody else to fill the walk-on roles, he never went back to acting.

The torrent of films that poured from Biograph for the next few years has remarkably survived intact. His one-reelers ventured into all conceivable territories long before they were defined (and later *confined*) as separate genres – in fact, the argument could be made that Griffith was the inventor of everything but fantasy cinema, which was pioneered by Georges Méliès and Thomas Edison, and the epic spectaculars, which he left to Italian film-makers until he could afford to outclass them.

His were among the first – if not *the* first – slapstick comedies (with *The Curtain Pole* in 1909 setting the scene for the Keystone antics of his Biograph colleague Mack Sennett), suspense thrillers, Westerns, gangster stories, social-realism dramas and romantic melodramas. He made costume films, adventure stories and war films, together with some adaptations, not always acknowledged, from such writers as Alfred Lord Tennyson, Leo Tolstoy, Guy de Maupassant, James Fenimore Cooper, and O. Henry. The variety of titles in any month picked at random from the Biograph list is astonishing: October 1908, for example, saw the release of *The Devil, The Zulu's Heart, Father Gets in the Game, The Barbarian Ingomar, The Vaquero's Vow, The Planter's Wife, Romance of a Jewess, The Call of the Wild* and *Concealing a Burglar.*

Today, just a handful of the Biograph works have a lasting reputation, though many more deserve attention. Among those most frequently reconsidered are *Pippa Passes*, which achieved the distinction of being the first film to be reviewed by the *New York Times* (on October 10, 1909); the Mary Pickford classic *The Lonely Villa* (1909), a suspense story of a family imprisoned in their own home by a marauder with a gun; *The Lonedale Operator* (1911), in which the camera was mounted on a locomotive to observe the struggle between the heroine (Blanche Sweet) and a railroad gang; and *Man's Genesis* (1912), a Stone Age parable in which an early screen dinosaur wobbled across the landscape.

If the one-reelers had anything in common (other than the 'AB' logo that featured in all the backgrounds to protect copyright), not surprisingly it was a sense of speed. They could be made on any inspiration, even the slender basis of a change in the weather; the unit would make up a story on the spot to unfold against the background of a recent snowfall, or to take advantage of a vista of autumn trees. And since there was not time to show insignificant detail, Griffith used titles more creatively than had previously been tried, in the place of cumbersome or irrelevant action, pushing his stories headlong from climax to climax. Marriages were made, broken and mended in ten minutes, wars fought and lost in the space of a single shot. His stories, springing from this frantic schedule, frequently based themselves on a race against time, and the need to show widely separate events interacting with each other led him to the logical solution of cross-cutting.

Despite the misgivings of the studio bosses, the obstinate vitality of Griffith's editing style never seemed to upset the one-reeler audiences:

'I borrowed the idea from Charles Dickens. Novelists think nothing of leaving one set of characters in the midst of affairs and going back to deal with earlier events in which another set of characters is involved. I found that the picture could carry, not merely two, but three or four simultaneous threads of action – all without confusing the spectator.'

As Griffith's experience grew, so did his ambition. His stories were increasingly complex, his cast ever larger, his budgets less convenient to Biograph. His later one-reelers, straying occasionally into two reels despite his producers' certainty that no audiences would tolerate such lengths, looked more and more like sketches and episodes from far grander projects. *The Battle* (1911) can now be seen as a rehearsal for *The Birth of a Nation* (1915), *The Musketeers of Pig Alley* (1912) for the modern story in *Intolerance* (1916), while *A Feud in the Kentucky Hills* (1912) anticipates both *The Massacre* (1913) and *The Battle of Elderbush Gulch* (1914), brilliant and spectacular films which in turn were preparing for the sophisticated performances and magnificent photography of the later epics.

The parting of the ways came with *Judith of Bethulia* (1913), which Griffith made as a four-reeler at such casual expense, and in the teeth of such opposition from Biograph, that there was no alternative but to fire him. When he left, he took his team with him – the teenagers who had matured to stardom in the same era that movie fandom had come into being as a direct response to the 'Biograph Girls', together with cameraman Bitzer, editor James Smith, and a score of designers and assistants.

The Griffith Features

Griffith's idea for a great film panorama of the American Civil War began to take shape one day in 1914 when his story editor, Frank Woods, brought him a copy of Thomas Dixon's novel *The Clansman*. Griffith had just begun working for Harry Aitken's Mutual; since his early features had cost on average around $10,000 apiece, it seemed reasonable that $40,000 would cover a film planned to be at least three times as long: $2,500 went to Dixon for the rights and Griffith, script in head and the rest of the money in hand, took off for the unknown.

After six weeks' rehearsal Griffith began filming, fittingly, on July 4. Soon sets, costumes and salaries had eaten up the $40,000. Aitken managed to raise $20,000 more, but that also disappeared with Griffith barely half way through shooting. He eventually turned to private investors and those who succumbed were later to be rewarded with their money back many times over. The Gish sisters gambled $300 and William Clune, a manager of the Los Angeles Auditorium, parted with $15,000. In the end the cost was around $110,000. Shooting had taken three months, editing and scoring a further three. What the film eventually grossed is unknown as accurate figures are only available for showings in the big cities. Some historians believe it finally made at least $50 million, but in any case it had far more admissions than any movie before or since.

Premiered at Clune's Auditorium on February 8, 1915 as *The Clansman*, the film opened in New York on March 3, with its title changed to *The Birth of a Nation*.

Provoking controversy even to this day, the film enjoys the uneasy honour of being both brilliantly innovative technically and also one of the most explicitly racist pictures ever made. It has been rightly venerated for its artistic achievements, and just as rightly condemned for its reactionary content.

The film deals with a prickly period in American history – the Civil War and the period of Reconstruction in the South, from which many Americans were still recovering when Griffith made the film. He himself was a Southerner, raised on the values and traditions of the Old South, though his depiction of that experience is laid out in epic proportions and succeeds in blurring sectional interests and antipathies. He does this by interweaving the lives of two families, the Stonemans and Camerons, respectively representing North and South, whose contrasting lives are eventually reconciled in the common interest of white supremacy or, as one of the film's intertitles puts it, 'in defence of their Aryan birthright'.

Such anti-black sentiments were not uncommon during the silent era, although most films tended to place emphasis on the traditional and relatively gentler image of devoted black servility, or use the black man for comic relief. Griffith's film follows the same pattern, but with greater force and with the emotive stress placed on the image of blacks as villains. These stereotypes play against the equally stereotyped whites in the film – men are aristocratic and paternalistic, women frail and vulnerable – but they do not express the interests of the blacks (played by whites in black-face) in the way that the white stereotypes express the interests of the whites.

The Birth of a Nation is one of few silent films to exploit the sexual stereotype of the black male in order to reinforce the doctrine of white supremacy. It achieves this through the use of the much-dreaded 'brute' figure – personified here by the renegade Gus, who not only betrays his former masters by joining the black revolt, but also commits the unspeakable crime of lusting after and causing the suicide of one of the Cameron daughters. This motif is duplicated in the character and actions of Silas Lynch, the mulatto leader of his people. The sexual racism that these characters exemplify plays a crucial part in the film's thematic development; and it comes to a head in the film's last-minute rescue finale which justifies the actions of the Ku Klux Klan, captioned by Griffith as 'the saviour of white civilization'.

Race feeling ran high wherever the film was shown, resulting in rioting in Boston and other cities. While the publicity this generated undoubtedly increased box-office receipts, Griffith himself was strongly attacked in the liberal and black press for his blatant racism and romanticizing of the murderous Ku Klux Klan (whose membership trebled within months of the film's release). Cinemas were picketed, and the newly-formed National Association for the Advancement of Coloured People (NAACP) managed to get the film banned in Kansas and a number of cities. To counteract the widespread turmoil over the 'White Supremacy' aspect of this film, Griffith went on to make his monumental epic *Intolerance* (1916). For this, his most ambitious film, he fashioned a filmic 'fugue' out of four separate stories taking place in four separate historical periods.

As a basis for his construction of *Intolerance*, Griffith started with a film with a contemporary setting which he had already completed, *The Mother and the Law* (eventually

Far left: Even at the time, The Birth of a Nation *was criticized for glorifying the racist Ku Klux Klan. Below: Griffith helped pioneer many techniques that were to form the basis of film narrative by emphasising the primacy of the imagination over the strict chronology of the events themselves. At the climax of* Intolerance, *he creates suspense by cutting between three centres of action – the site of an imminent execution on the gallows, a* group racing to the prison with the governor's pardon, and the condemned boy awaiting the pardon. Christ's Crucifixion (5) also appears briefly. Note how Griffith varies the angles of the train and car (1, 2, 3, 6) to increase the sense of movement, while he repeats the same angle of the gallows (8, 9, 14) to anchor the viewer. Tension is also built up by cuts to closer shots of the boy (8, 9, 10, 11).

Above: Richard Barthelmess and Lillian Gish in Way Down East, *Griffith's last major success.* *Right: in* Orphans of the Storm, *Dorothy and Lillian Gish played sisters who are separated by the horrors of the French Revolution and are only reunited in the final reel.*

released as a separate film in 1919). To this tale of a poor couple's struggle against social, economic and legal injustice he added three more stories: in ancient Babylon, a mountain girl rushes to warn her king, Belshazzar, of his betrayal by his judges and the onrush of Cyrus' Persian army; Christ struggles towards Calvary; and French mercenaries massacre a crowd on St Bartholomew's Day (while a Huguenot hero fights his way through a crowd to rescue his sweetheart). Finally, the four stories were linked thematically by a recurring refrain shot of Lillian Gish rocking a cradle, introduced and followed by intertitles adapted from lines by Walt Whitman: 'Out of the cradle endlessly rocking', 'Today as yesterday, endlessly rocking, ever bringing the same joys and sorrows'.

Perhaps the boldest of all Griffith's grand editing schemes was the combining of these interacting elements to make up *Intolerance*; but the scheme and idea failed with the general public almost as dramatically as *The Birth of a Nation* had succeeded. The grand design neither registered nor brought the sort of audience involvement and identification of its blockbuster predecessor. Yet *Intolerance* can still be regarded as a compendium of the possibilities of narrative editing.

Including the Reliance-Majestic productions, Griffith made 32 features after leaving Biograph. They were as disparate as his one-reelers had been, though only one or two achieved the undeniable, if controversial, classic status of *The Birth of a Nation*, and *Intolerance* – the delicate Limehouse fable *Broken Blossoms* (1919) and *Way Down East* (1920). This last was based on a hoary stage melodrama about a wronged woman (Lillian Gish) and her illegitimate baby. Griffith carried the drama to new heights, casting his heroine adrift on the ice floes for a last-minute rescue that helped to make the film his greatest box-office hit since *The Birth of a Nation* and·his last major commercial triumph: the film's success appeared to

justify his move back to New York, where he established his own studio at Mamaroneck, Long Island. Others were ambitious but sometimes only partly successful: *Orphans of the Storm* (1921), a panoramic tale of two sisters, one of them blind, involved in the French Revolution (the Gish sisters played these roles, with comedienne Dorothy as the blind girl); *America* (1924), the story of the War of Independence that did not match the power of *The Birth of a Nation* on the Civil War; and *Abraham Lincoln* (1930), a respectful sound-film version of the great president's life with a fine performance by Walter Huston. Time and modern criticism have reinstated such ventures as the compassionate *Isn't Life Wonderful?* (1924), shot on location in Germany, and *The Sorrows of Satan* (1926), a lavish version of Marie Corelli's antiquated novel, made under contract for Paramount with their excellent East Coast facilities, though a commercial failure. But the declining period at Mamaroneck and the subsequent Paramount connection also produced such oddities as *Sally of the Sawdust* and *That Royle Girl* (both 1925), both starring W.C. Fields as well as Griffith's favourite actress of the early Twenties, Carol Dempster. She was not without talent, but seemed to lack the wide appeal of earlier Griffith stars such as Blanche Sweet, Mae Marsh and the Gishes. Griffith, embroiled in financial difficulties, was unable to recapture the popular touch and gradually found himself without employment in Hollywood.

His final film, *The Struggle* (1931), a grim and obviously heartfelt warning of the perils of alcoholism, was a crushing commercial disaster. In the remaining 17 years of his life he made nothing further. He was shunned by the studios for whom he had almost single-handedly created the film industry, and forgotten by the public. When the D.W. Griffith Corporation went into bankruptcy and his films were auctioned, he bought the rights of 21 of them for only $500.

Thomas H. Ince

Thomas Harper Ince was born at Newport, Rhode Island, on November 16, 1882, the son of two stage performers, John and Emma Brennan Ince. In 1910 he entered films as an actor for Carl Laemmle's Independent Motion Picture Company and was the director of the Mary Pickford unit when Laemmle sent it to Cuba to make films out of the reach of the Patents Company.

In 1911 the New York Motion Picture Company (NYMPC) invited Ince to join their Bison Company studio in Edendale, California, where they made their own brand of Westerns. Towards the end of 1911 the NYMPC bosses Charles O. Baumann and Adam Kessel acquired rights from the Pacific Electric Company to use their coast-road property – 18,000 acres that lay four miles to the north of Santa Monica – for shooting films. The studio itself was situated on the slopes of the entrance of the Santa Ynez Canyon. Around the same time, the Miller Brothers 101 Ranch Real Wild West Show, a circus that made its own movies, arrived from its spread in Oklahoma to winter on the California coast, and Ince was authorized to engage their entire company to make 'real' Westerns. This consisted of '350 people, including riders, actors, cowboys and girls, Indians, horses, steers, mules, equipment and paraphernalia'. The whole studio – the Miller 101 Bison Ranch – became popularly known as 'Inceville'.

Thus equipped, the studio embarked on the prolific production of its famous Westerns. The first to feature the Inceville Indians was the two-reeler *War on the Plains* (1912), starring Ethel Grandin, a film praised for its 'Historical accuracy, correct costuming, perfect photography'. It was followed by *The Indian Massacre, Custer's Last Raid* (both 1912) and many more. For *Custer's Last Raid*, an expensive three-reeler starring Francis Ford as General Custer, Ince re-created the Battle of the Little Big Horn and arranged with the US government to use, in addition to his resident company of Sioux, over a hundred reservation Sioux as extras. Some of them had been there when the real Custer lost his life in 1876 – they were the boys who followed the warriors and looted the dead soldiers.

Ince was personally involved in the production and direction of all Bison's films from the autumn of 1911, when he first assumed responsibility for the brand, to the summer of 1912, when he divided the direction between himself and Francis Ford.

In 1912 NYMPC joined with Universal and a power struggle ensued within the company, the result of which was that NYMPC surrendered the 101 Bison brand-name to Universal's own Ince-inspired Westerns, while Kay Bee (the initials of Kessel and Baumann) became the new brand name for Ince's own product.

In 1914 Ince made *The Battle of Gettysburg*, employing eight hundred extras as soldiers in the first week of shooting, and using eight cameras (perched at different angles) simultaneously during each battle scene. One reviewer said that film presented 'war scenes on a larger scale than ever before attempted on the screen. . . . Thomas Ince may properly regard it as his masterpiece'.

Inceville continued to grow and by 1914 contained a Spanish mission, a Dutch village with a canal and windmill, an East Indian street, a Western town and a Sioux camp. There were about 520 inhabitants, all on the weekly payroll.

There was further expansion at the studio in 1914 and from then Ince's Kay Bee films were released by Henry E. Aitken's Mutual Masters Pictures. These included *The Bargain* (1914),

Above: Ince supervising the shooting of Civilization. *Eight years later he died on board William Randolph Hearst's yacht. Rumour had it that Hearst had shot him (mistaking him for Charles Chaplin who was having an affair with Hearst's mistress, actress Marion Davis.*

the film that established William S. Hart as a major Western Star. In 1915, in a further corporate shuffle, Aitken, now handling NYMPC's films, took Ince and Kay Bee into the new Triangle Film Corporation, along with D.W. Griffith's Reliance-Majestic and Mack Sennett's Keystone. Later that year the land-developer Harry Culver, who was working between Los Angeles and the Californian resort town of Venice, offered free land to anyone who would build a movie studio in the area he named Culver City. Ince intended to build a new plant for NYMPC and obtained from Culver a 16-acre parcel of the dusty, sun-baked land along the road which became Washington Boulevard.

Ince himself ceased directing around this time to concentrate on production (working with a team of eight directors) and the expansion of his company. But he retained creative control of his films, developing the shooting scripts (including dialogue and camera positions) and personally assembling each and every film. He was especially noted for his efficient and penetrating editing. In 1916 he produced his great epic *Civilization*, the story of war and peace in a mythical country, which was a contribution to President Woodrow Wilson's peace effort during World War I. In 1918 Ince fell out with Aitken, left Triangle and founded Ince Productions, building new studios at Culver City (a mile from the Triangle lot) and distributing his films through Paramount-Artcraft. The following year he began to release through Metro and formed Associated Producers, Inc. with Mack Sennett, Allan Dwan, Marshall Neilan, Maurice Tourneur and other producers and directors. This company merged with First National in 1922. Among the last significant films Ince produced were *Human Wreckage* (1923), a condemnation of drug abuse starring Bessie Love and Dorothy Davenport (the widow of the addicted star Wallace Reid), and *Anna Christie* (1923), with Blanche Sweet.

Mack Sennett's Comic World

An early protégé of Griffith at Biograph, as actor and then also as director, was a young Canadian of Irish origins, Michael Sinnott, who changed his name to Mack Sennett. Sennett directed comedies at Biograph in 1911–12 and then, financed by Adam Kessel and Charles O. Baumann's New York Motion Picture Company, set up a new company, Keystone, based at a studio in Edendale, Los Angeles, that had formerly been used by another Kessel and Baumann company, Bison. He took with him from Biograph his favourite comedienne Mabel Normand (with whom he had a stormy romance until her early death in 1930 at the age of 35), the plump actor Fred Mace and the actor-director Henry 'Pathé' Lehrman; and also discovered a stock company of new artists.

Sennett's Keystone developed a unique, surreal style of visual comedy. It enriched the folklore of America and the world with a universe of curious and colourful characters; and – quite incidentally to Sennett's aims, which were simply to make money out of comedy – advanced movie art, giving a new freedom to the camera which necessarily developed the same agility as the funny-men themselves.

Sennett recruited his artists from burlesque, circus, vaudeville, from building sites and even mental hospitals. At first he directed all the films himself, but as the Keystone output grew, to keep several units occupied at any one time, he recruited or created other directors, among them the comedians Mabel Normand, Fatty Arbuckle, Dell Henderson and Charles Parrott (alias Charlie Chase). The films were largely improvised; and a single prop (car, telephone, boat) or setting (a grocery store or a garage) was enough to inspire endless comic variations.

Keystone comedy drew its inspiration from comic strips, French slapstick cinema, vaudeville, pantomime; its techniques approached those of the old Italian *commedia dell'arte;* and yet it was different from all of these. The Keystone comedies remain a monument of twentieth-century popular art, transmuting the reality of the life and times of the first two decades of the century into a comedy that is basic and universal. The Sennett shorts were uncompromisingly anarchic, celebrating an orgiastic destruction of goods and possessions, cars, houses and crockery. Authority and dignity were regularly brought low – most notably by the Keystone Kops, a supremely incompetent law-enforcement troupe who were forever falling out of windows, tumbling down stairs or flying off their skidding patrol wagons. The inhabitants of Keystone's crazy world were larger and wilder and far more colourful than life. They might be fat or thin, giants or dwarfs, with oversize pants and undersized hats, entangled spectacles and uncontrollable moustaches. They were monstrous, wonderful caricatures of reality. After Normand and Mace, Sennett's long procession of stars was to include Ford Sterling, with his angry face and ludicrous goatee (generally the superintendent of the Kops); baby-faced Fatty Arbuckle; cross-eyed Ben Turpin, with his phenomenal Adam's apple; gangling Charlie Chase; walrus-moustached Billy Bevan; confused Chester Conklin and the gigantic Mack Swain. Two Keystone Kops, Eddie Sutherland and Edward Cline, became distinguished comedy directors, as did two Keystone gag men, Malcolm St Clair and Frank Capra. As well as Mabel Normand, the Sennett troupe of funny women included Polly Moran, Minta Durfee, Alice Davenport, Phyllis Allen, Louise Fazenda and Alice Howell. Of the greatest comedy artists who passed through the Keystone studios, Harold Lloyd failed to make his mark under Sennett; while Sennett's major discovery, Charlie Chaplin, left him after only one year and 35 one- or two-reel pictures. (Sennett, fearful of wage escalation, would never pay well enough to retain his most successful stars for long.)

In July 1915 Sennett was one of the Big Three – the others were D.W. Griffith and Thomas Ince – who were merged into the Triangle company. Triangle-Keystone, without forfeiting any of its allegiance to slapstick and to the public, was able to enlarge its ambitions. At first – in line with the aspirations of his sister companies for the prestige of famous names – Sennett engaged major stage comedy stars of the time, Raymond Hitchcock, Eddie Foy, Weber and Fields. The results were uneven, however, and Triangle-Keystone tended quite soon to revert to its own experienced screen stars.

Far left: Mack Sennett with Mabel Normand. The couple's stormy romance continued until Mabel's tragic death in 1930, aged only 35. Above left: Fatty Arbuckle and Normand find their home has been washed out to sea in Fatty and Mabel Adrift (1916). Left: the Keystone Kops get on the case. Above: Normand as the naive country girl in Mickey. Right: Marie Dressler and the Kops in the chase finale of Tillie's Punctured Romance.

At this time Sennett was able to extend his comedy production and embark on two and three-reelers. Production values were more elaborate; characterization was more developed. The old *commedia dell'arte* improvisation began to give way – with no appreciable loss of invention and freedom – to more careful scripting and pre-planning of production.

By 1917 however, the Triangle partnership was breaking up. In June of that year, Sennett succeeded in extricating himself from the contract, though the Keystone company remained part of the Triangle grouping. Without Sennett, its creator and guiding force, the unit finally foundered in 1919.

Though he had lost the company and the name, Sennett still retained his studio at Edendale, and continued in full production, releasing his films as 'Sennett Comedies' through Paramount. It was apparently at this period that the Sennett Bathing Beauties were first consciously promoted. Ornamental as their presence was in the films themselves, the object of the Bathing Beauties was rather to secure publicity for Sennett productions in magazines and newspapers. Sennett discovered early on that while picture editors were unenthusiastic about printing photographs of bewhiskered or cross-eyed comics, a photograph of a line of pretty girls in chic bathing dresses (and Sennett commissioned couturiers to design swim-suits that revealed more of the feminine shape than the usual patterns then in vogue) was irresistible.

In this period, too, Sennett's productions took new directions. Ben Turpin's grotesque style inspired him to a whole series of parodies of current Hollywood hits, with names like *The Shriek of Araby* (1923) and *Three Foolish Weeks* (1924). Love perhaps inspired Sennett to feature production. To placate Mabel, who had demanded more challenging parts, Sennett created the Mabel Normand Feature Film Company, and starred her in a full-length film, *Mickey* (1918). Hollywood was still sceptical about the idea of a feature-length comedy, despite Sennett's success in *Tillie's Punctured Romance* in 1914 and Sennett invested his own money in the project. He was wholly vindicated when the public took this modern Cinderella comedy to its hearts: the film is said to have grossed $16 million. Sennett was to star Mabel Normand,

whose later life was shadowed by drugs and scandals but whose charm was unimpaired, in the subsequent features, *Molly O* (1921) and *Suzanna* (1922).

In 1921 Sennett established Mack Sennett Inc., and released his films through First National. In 1923 he made further organizational changes, and from then until 1929 distributed his films through Pathé Exchange. The Pathé period was notable mainly for the series of films made with Harry Langdon, perhaps the oddest of the great comedy stars with his screen character of a middle-aged baby or a demented Pierrot Lunaire. Frank Capra, who directed or wrote Langdon's best features, notably *Long Pants* (1927), was later to claim that it was he, as a gag-man with Sennett, who first perceived Langdon's potential and modelled his screen character. Though it is true that Langdon's later efforts as his own director were less than successful, Capra's version, which has been accepted by history, disserves Langdon. For more than twenty years he had been a vaudeville star, with a very clearly defined comic character; and even before Capra, his whole essence was evident in a series of Sennett two-reelers directed by Harry Edwards.

Times were changing. Sennett responded uncertainly to the new audiences who felt that they were too sophisticated for the old styles of slapstick two-reelers. He knew that sound was not his element, though in 1928 he made his first sound feature, *The Lion's Roar,* and in 1930 experimented with colour.

Industrial reorganizations meant that Sennett films in 1929 were distributed by the ominously named Educational Film Company. In 1933 Sennett was obliged to close his studios. In 1935 the economic problems of Paramount had repercussions which resulted in the loss of Sennett's considerable personal fortune.

He moved back to Canada, where he worked for a while as an associate producer for Fox. Even by this time Sennett and the Keystone Kops had passed into Hollywood legend. But legend was of small benefit to Sennett. He died, still mourning his beloved Mabel, on November 5, 1960, in an old people's home in Hollywood.

Charlie Chaplin

Charles Chaplin, Hollywood's most universal figure, was born in south London in 1889. Soon his parents, both music-hall singers, separated and Mrs Chaplin was left to bring up Charles and his older half-brother Sydney alone. When she suffered a mental breakdown, the two boys spent long periods in orphanages. Chaplin claimed to have made his first stage appearance at five. At nine he joined a variety troupe and by 14 he was in regular work as a child actor.

In 1906, brother Sydney became a star comedian with the Karno comedy companies. Fred Karno, a former acrobat, had created what he accurately called his 'Fun Factory' in Camberwell Road, London. Here he rehearsed and equipped the several sketch companies which for many years proved the English music-hall's richest school of comedy. Sydney Chaplin persuaded Karno to engage his brother for a sketch called 'The Football Match'. Within a couple of years Charlie had become a leading comedian, and the star of companies that Karno sent on American tours during 1910–11 and 1912–13.

It was on the second of these tours that he was offered a year's contract with Mack Sennett's Keystone film company. Hesitantly, persuaded largely by the $150 a week that doubled his salary with Karno, he joined Sennett in California. Chaplin was at first uneasy in the new medium. He was disturbed by the chaos of the Sennett studios, and the Sennett slapstick comedians found his more refined style of comedy too slow. Little love was lost between Chaplin and his first director, Henry Lehrman, and he resented, equally, taking direction from his young, lovely and volatile co-star comedienne Mabel Normand.

His first film, *Making a Living* (1914), in which he was dressed as a dubious dandy, was indifferent, though well received by the trade press of the time. For his second film, a five-minute improvisation shot during the event which gave it its title, *Kid Auto Races at Venice* (1914), however, he adopted the costume that was to become world-famous. According to legend, it was made up from various items borrowed from other Sennett comedians: Fatty Arbuckle's huge trousers; Charles Avery's tiny jacket; a derby hat belonging to Arbuckle's father-in-law; Ford Sterling's boots, so oversize that they had to be worn on the wrong feet; and Mack Swain's moustache, sharply pruned.

Chaplin later wrote:

'I had no idea of the character. But the moment I was dressed, the clothes and the make-up made me feel the person he was. I began to know him, and by the time I walked on to the stage he was fully born.'

Over the next 22 years the character was to be refined and elaborated: the hero of *City Lights* (1931) or *Modern Times* (1936) is altogether more complex than the little tramp of the first frantic Sennett slapstick shorts as he scurries on one leg around corners, clutching his hat to his head while being chased by Keystone Kops or angry, bewhiskered giants. But the general lines of the character – the range of emotions from callousness to high sentiment, and of his actions from nobility to larceny, the supremely human resilience and fallibility of his nature – were fairly soon defined.

Chaplin spent 1914 at Keystone, serving a valuable apprenticeship to his art, and making 35 films. From the twelfth of these, *Caught in a Cabaret*, he began to take a hand in the direction, and from the twentieth, *Laughing Gas*, he was permanently established as his own director. Seen today, these films are fairly primitive. The stock jokes involve intoxication, illicit flirtations, mallets, dentists, jealous husbands, cops, dough, dynamite, lakes to be fallen into, cars to crash, benches and boxing rings from which to fall. Already, however, in *The New Janitor* for example, Chaplin was trying out subtler skills as a storyteller and actor.

These skills were to be developed further and faster at Essanay, the company Chaplin joined in January 1915 in the first of a series of much-publicized changes of employer that would dramatically increase his earnings. Chaplin was at first unhappy in Essanay's Chicago studio, though he knocked out a lively little comedy about the film business, aptly titled *His New Job* (1915). At the company's West Coast studio in Niles, California, Chaplin began to build a company around himself. His most important discovery was Edna Purviance, a beautiful stenographer with no screen experience. She was to remain his ideal leading lady for the next eight years. The warm and feminine quality of Edna's screen personality – in sharp contrast to the amusing madcap Mabel Normand – was probably partly responsible for the growing element of romantic yearning in Chaplin's work. This was most evident in two of Chaplin's earliest Essanay films, *The Tramp* and *The Bank* (both 1915). At the same time Chaplin was becoming more ambitious – he was taking more time over his films, and going on location. For *Shanghaied* (1915), he even blew up a small schooner to provide a dramatic climax. In his last film for Essanay, *Police* (1916), he first introduced touches of social irony that anticipated *The Kid* (1921) and *The Pilgrim* (1923).

With Chaplin's next move, his salary soared to $10,000 a week, with extra bonuses. He spent 16 months over the 12

two-reelers he made at his Lone Star studio for Mutual release. They were polished gag structures, mostly inspired by a location or a situation, as their titles – *The Floorwalker, The Fireman, Behind the Screen, The Rink* (all 1916) and *The Cure* (1917) – suggest. Some of them are feats of virtuosity: *One A.M.* (1916) is virtually a solo turn, with Charlie returning home inebriated to battle with a keyhole, a folding bed, a tigerskin rug and other domestic hazards; *The Pawn Shop* (1916) includes a long unbroken take of an autopsy on a customers's alarm clock. Other films, including *The Vagabond* (1916) and *The Immigrant* (1917), exploited Chaplin's developing gifts for drama and pathos.

A new distribution agreement with First National Distributors enabled Chaplin to fulfil his ambition of building his own studio, where he was to work for the next 24 years. His contract called for eight films to be made in eighteen months; instead, they took five years, and included at least three masterpieces. The first, *A Dog's Life* (1918), sharpened the henceforth ever-present element of social satire, drawing parallels between the existence of the Tramp and his faithful mongrel dog. Chaplin next boldly defied warnings that it was in the worst of taste, to make a comedy out of life at the front in World War I; the men who best knew that life took *Shoulder Arms* (1918) to their hearts, and today Chaplin's comic metamorphosis of the war may give a more vivid sense of those days than many more solemn dramatic treatments. *Sunnyside* (1919) is an uncharacteristic and only modestly successful pastoral comedy. *A Day's Pleasure* (1919) is a delightful slice of humble life, the misadventures of a little

Below left: Chaplin's film debut in Making a Living *was as a dubious swell who charms the ladies (Minta Durfee and Alice Davenport). Above left: Albert Austin looks on as Charlie examines an alarm clock in* The Pawn Shop. *Above: Tramp, girl and mother – Chaplin, Edna Purviance and Kitty Bradbury – arrive in America in* The Immigrant. *Purviance co-starred as a ministering angel or gamine in most of Chaplin's films between 1915 and 1923. Right: Charlie and* The Kid, *Jackie Coogan.*

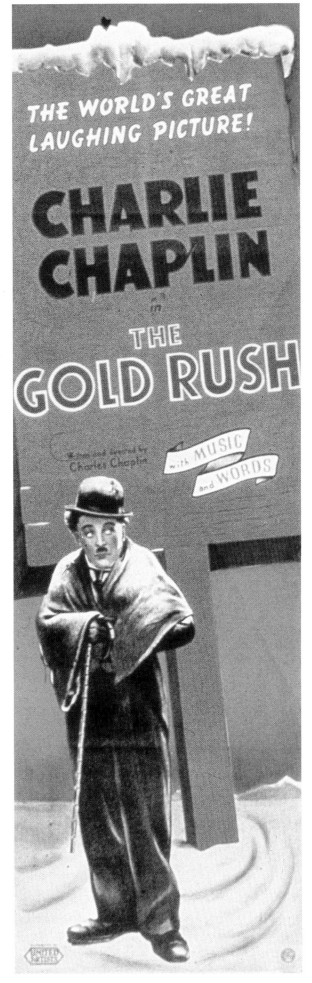

man taking his Ford and family on an outing; one of the children in the film was played by Jackie Coogan, whose uncanny acting ability partly inspired Chaplin's next film, *The Kid*. Here, a melodrama about an unmarried mother and her abandoned child provides the motive for a rich comedy about the Tramp's unwilling adoption of the foundling and the odd comic-pathetic bond that grows between them. After finishing the film, Chaplin decided to make a return visit to his homeland and to tour Europe. This was, perhaps, the peak of his career; few celebrities until this time had aroused the furore that attended every public appearance, or the adulation he received from the great men of the world.

The two films that he made on his return, *The Idle Class* (1921), a slapstick situation comedy with Chaplin in two roles, and *Pay Day* (1922), another slice-of-life comedy in which little Charlie is given a job, home and nagging wife, were only moderately successful; but with *The Pilgrim* his critical reputation soared again. This story of an escaped convict, who steals the clothes of a bathing priest and is mistaken for the new pastor of a little Midwest township, provided opportunities for nice irony at the expense of bigotry, hypocrisy and small-town manners.

Only when the First National contract was worked out was Chaplin free to make his first feature film for release by United Artists, the distribution organization he had formed in company with Douglas Fairbanks, Mary Pickford and D.W. Griffith four years before. *A Woman of Paris* (1923) was his first, long-contemplated attempt at serious drama. It was intended to launch the loyal Edna Purviance as a dramatic actress, and her elegant, restrained performance merited the chance, though her subsequent career was to be short-lived. Adolphe Menjou subtly partnered her and became a star. Chaplin himself appeared only in a walk-on part.

The film took the stuff of Victorian melodrama – the tragedy of a village girl turned courtesan and torn between an artist and a playboy – but applied to it an extremely sophisticated visual style, which was to influence the subsequent course of film comedy. To Chaplin's enduring chagrin, however, *A Woman of Paris,* despite its enthusiastic press, proved a commercial failure, but he was to recover his losses and his confidence with two of his best comedy features, *The Gold Rush* (1925) and *The Circus* (1928).

Chaplin has described how he 'strove, thought and brooded' for weeks, trying to get an idea. 'I kept saying to myself: "This next film must be an epic! The greatest!" The idea for *The Gold Rush* came to him one Sunday morning after breakfast with the Fairbankses at their home, Pickfair. Looking at steroscopic views of Alaska and the Klondike, he was particularly struck by:

'. . . a view of the Chilkoot Pass, with a long line of prospectors climbing up over its frozen mountains, with a caption printed on the back describing the trials and hardships endured in surmounting it. This was a wonderful theme, I thought, enough to stimulate my imagination. Immediately ideas and comedy business began to develop, and, although I had no story, the image of one began to grow.'

Further inspiration came from his reading a book on the Donner Party disaster, in which a group of 160 pioneers were snowbound in the Sierra Nevada, having missed the route to California. Only 18 survived out of the original 160, and hunger and cold drove them to cannibalism and to roasting

Left: The Gold Rush *was the first Chaplin comedy feature released by his United Artists company.*

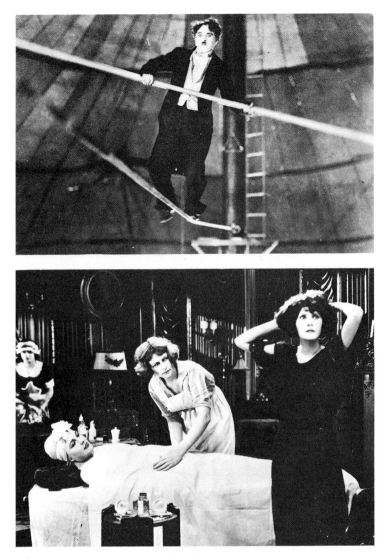

Below: Charlie makes dinner for his beloved Georgia and her friends, but they forget to come, in The Gold Rush. *Right: Chaplin walks a tightrope in* The Circus. *Below right: Edna Purviance, Nelly Bly Baker and Malvina Polo in* A Woman of Paris.

their moccasins for food. Chaplin was always fascinated by the macabre and this tragic affair was to inspire what is perhaps his most famous comic invention – the eating of the boot with all the airs of a gourmet, picking the nails as if they were the bones of some dainty game bird, and treating the laces as spaghetti.

After six months pondering over likely comedy sequences, Chaplin began shooting on February 8, 1924 without a script, relying on gag sequences and gag inspirations and the stimulus of set and location to suggest the narrative line. This was generally his method in silent days: he could afford the extravagance of time it involved, since he had at his disposal the facilities of a permanent studio and crew. Shooting was completed on May 21, 1925.

Parts of the film – notably the spectacular opening scene of the trail of prospectors – were shot on location in the high sierras of the California Rockies, at Mount Lincoln, where Chaplin had brought hundreds of down-and-outs who worked with enthusiasm, and provided their own costumes.

Chaplin sought a new leading lady to replace the loyal Edna Purviance, who had now grown too mature for youthful roles in his pictures. An early candidate was Lita Grey, who instead became, briefly and unhappily, Mrs Chaplin.

The eventual choice was Georgia Hale, a beautiful and spirited actress whom Josef von Sternberg had discovered as an extra and cast in his notable first film *The Salvation Hunters* (1925). Sternberg later, ungallantly, attributed her lively performance in *The Gold Rush* wholly to Chaplin's direction. Of the supporting players Mack Swain, as Big Jim, and Henry

Bergman, as the kindly prospector, were old Chaplin faithfuls. Tom Murray, who played Black Larsen, had been the Sheriff in Chaplin's *The Pilgrim*.

Even for those years the film was expensive; Chaplin reckoned the overall cost of production as $923,886. In 1942 he reissued the film, slightly cut and with a new synchronized musical score and narration spoken by himself. *The Circus* (1928) developed out of Chaplin's notion that he would like to create a gag which would put him in a perilous situation in some high place such as a high-wire. Although he may have been influenced in this idea by the success of Harold Lloyd's "thrill" comedies, it is tempting also to see in the concept a subconscious reflection of his current personal situation, and the threats to his private happiness and public reputation produced by a hopelessly unsuccessful marriage. His first idea was to set the story in a vaudeville theatre; but finally he settled on a circus for his comedy melodrama. A tent was erected on the studio lot, and Chaplin learnt to walk the high-wire with great expertise, and spent several days shooting in a cage with an unpredictable lion.

Few films have ever been so dogged by ill-luck: a large quantity of material was spoilt by laboratory errors; the tent was wrecked by gales, there was a costly fire in the studio, and Mrs Chaplin's divorce lawyers managed to close down the studios by seeking a distraint order on Chaplin's possessions. Perhaps for this reason Chaplin appears to have had little feeling for the film (he does not even mention it in his autobiography), although, neatly constructed and full of virtuoso gags, it has worn well.

CHAPTER 4
Cinema and the Great War

In the weeks immediately preceding the 1914–18 war and for the first few months of hostilities, the media in the embattled countries worked themselves into a chauvinistic frenzy. In the cinema this resulted in a rash of patriotic melodramas. With titles like *England Expects* (1914) and *Das Vaterland ruft* (1914, The Fatherland Calls), they bolstered recruitment by presenting issues in simple, emotive, jingoistic terms. The enemy were represented as unspeakable beasts who committed all sorts of dastardly crimes, most frequently rape and infanticide; the Allies were particularly successful in cultivating the image of The Savage Hun.

Typical of the genre on the English side is Hepworth's *The Outrage* (1915), in which a German man is killed in 1914 by the son of the girl he had raped in the Franco-Prussian War of 1870!

Occasionally subjects were treated with more credibility. The London Film Company's skilful American director, George Loane Tucker, made *OHMS* (1914), a realistic and unspectacular drama about German spies masquerading as city gentlemen to blow up an army train.

The pacifist and the shirker, the man reluctant to enlist, were favourite *bêtes noires*. In *England's Call* (1914) portraits of famous British heroes, such as Raleigh and Wellington, came to life to urge a slacker to do his bit. Pacifists were encouraged to set aside their scruples, in *An Englishman's Home* and *For the Empire* (both 1914).

Although such films, remarkably similar on both sides, helped for a while to spread the contagion of war-fever, the public began to tire of them as soon as some inkling of the true nature of the conflict began to filter back from Flanders. In France film production was to fall off considerably, but in Britain newsreel footage became popular, setting a trend that contributed to the start of a documentary tradition.

The early war newsreels were mostly non-action sequences; views of cities near the front, troops in training, or partly faked biographies of contemporary military leaders, such as *The Life of Lord Roberts VC* (1914). It became increasingly necessary, however, to satisfy the public's craving for details of what it was really like over there with footage of the actual fighting. Such material was not easy to get. Intrepid cameramen were not only exposed to the same dangers as the troops – they also faced the disapproval of the High Command, who were anxious to sanction only acceptable images of the fighting.

Left: Jim (John Gilbert) bids au revoir to his girl (Renée Adorée) in The Big Parade, *one of the first Hollywood films to describe an ordinary GI's war experiences.*

The German cameramen had an easier time, since they were granted passes allowing them access to the front. The first footage out of Germany caused so much excitement that the Allies were obliged to relax their conditions in order to keep up in the propaganda war. An official film about the Royal Flying Corps (RFC), *The Eyes of the Army* (1916), was such a success that it stimulated further documentary work.

The better-known British figures working in this field were Geoffrey Malins, who subsequently wrote a somewhat boastful book called *How I Filmed the War*, about his exploits as a war cinematographer, and J.B. McDowell, who was managing director of British and Colonial, a leading film company.

The string of battlefield newsreels made by Geoffrey Malins and J.B. McDowell had a tremendous impact on Home Front Britain. The best of Malins' and McDowell's work was edited together into four films, each focusing on one great battle: *The Battle of the Somme* (1916); *The Battle of St Quentin* (1916), an explicitly propagandistic effort which utilized evocative intertitles; *The Battle of Ancre* (1917), which contained sensational footage of the first tanks going on the attack; and *The Battle of Arras* (1917).

The Battle of the Somme (1916) was the first film to convey the reality of modern warfare, the grimness of life in the trenches and the pockmarked landscape. Its famous 'over the top' sequence, now thought to have been specially staged at a training camp behind the lines, is one of the best-known pieces of 'actuality' film to emerge from the war.

The USA
Both the early dramas and the later documentaries were distributed with an eye to propaganda in America. America began the war as a neutral and, with a large German immigrant population, its ultimate support of the Allies was by no means certain. The constant stream of pro-British films gradually helped to sway public opinion, however, and by the time *Britain Prepared* (1916), a newsreel featuring the Allied mobilization, was released it was received with great enthusiasm.

Yet America was not to enter the war until 1917, and before that much of its indigenous cinema reacted with a firmly pacifist and isolationist stance. Herbert Brenon's *War Bride* (1916) was an extraordinarily powerful piece of pacifist propaganda. Set in a mythical European country, not unlike Germany, it tells the story of a woman whose menfolk are killed in the war. She leads a campaign to unite women in promising to bear no more children until men give up fighting. When convinced that war will always exist, she commits suicide. Thomas H. Ince's *Civilization* of the same year resurrected Christ in the form of an anti-war campaigner.

Generally, though, the pacifists were swimming against an increasingly strong tide. In 1915 a German U-boat sank the civilian liner *Lusitania* and public opinion swung decisively away from neutrality. J. Stuart Blackton's *The Battle Cry of Peace* (1915) indicated the way the mood was going. Based on the writings of the munitions manufacturer Hiram Maxim (who vigorously denied any ulterior motive), *The Battle Cry of Peace* urged that America should be prepared for war. It showed what might happen if a foreign power – unnamed, of course, but remarkably like Germany – landed troops on the US mainland. With the active support of the former President Theodore Roosevelt, it went down well at the box-office.

The hawks found an ally, too, in Cecil B. DeMille, whose *The Little American* (1917) placed the symbolically-named Angela, played by America's sweetheart, Mary Pickford, at the mercy of the licentious Hun, a sight to send every self-respecting American male reaching for his gun. For some, the change in public attitude had come too quickly. Robert Goldstein was jailed for writing and producing his study of British atrocities in the American War of Independence, *The Spirit of '76* (1917). D.W. Griffith, following the failure of his peace-orientated *Intolerance* (1916), went on to make *Hearts of the World* (1918), a love story set in a beleaguered French village and starring the Gish sisters. Griffith made a much-publicized tour of the front to obtain actuality footage, but in the event used very little of it. Like many a producer after him, he realized that the grim conditions in the trenches were starkly short on those elements of adventure that made up the public view of heroism. 'Viewed as a drama,' he commented, 'the war is in some ways disappointing.'

Even Charlie Chaplin did his bit for morale with *Shoulder Arms* (1918). Humour had never been considered appropriate for war subjects, though the troops themselves, viewing tatty Hollywood prints at makeshift shelters behind the lines, understandably expressed a preference for comedy and escapism, and this began to spread to the Home Front towards the end of the war. A British film, *The Better 'Ole; or, The Romance of Old Bill* (1918), had featured an incarnation of Bruce Bairnsfather's popular cartoon character, Old Bill; but even so *Shoulder Arms* was breaking new ground. A warm human look at the absurdity of life in the trenches, it was a much-needed tonic.

The Post-War World

Almost as soon as the war itself came to a close, production of films concerning it slumped. There was a general feeling that

Right: The Germans were portrayed as 'brutish Huns' in British wartime propaganda like The Outrage. *Far right: Geoffrey Malins, official war cinematographer. Below right: a private dreams of doing deeds of heroism at the front in Chaplin's* Shoulder Arms. *Below: a sole survivor of the carnage in Pabst's* Westfront 1918.

Above right: Charles 'Buddy' Rogers, Richard Arlen and Gary Cooper in Wings. *Right: the ghosts of the dead make their own silent appeal for peace in* All Quiet on the Western Front.

the past was done, and a desire to look to the future. The war became a taboo subject. Such films as were made were usually bitterly vengeful, like *Behind the Door*, a 1919 drama in which a U-Boat commander is flayed alive by the survivor of one of the ships he has sunk. Abel Gance's masterly and impassioned plea for peace, *J'Accuse* (1918, I Accuse) was an honourable exception to the spirit of the times.

The post-war world was a very different one for the cinema. The British and French industries, both on the war's doorstep, suffered as a result of it and from the icy blast of financial depression that followed it. Hollywood, on the other hand, had blossomed, achieving a position of international domination it is reluctant to relinquish even today.

In America, the cinema's attitude to the war subtly mirrored the shifts in public attitudes towards militarism. Once the initial lull was over, the war crept back into fashion, most films attacking it for its destructive waste, yet carrying a certain tinge of nostalgia. In the vanguard of the new wave of World War I movies, Rex Ingram's *The Four Horsemen of the Apocalypse* (1921) perfectly illustrates this ambiguity. Although the film's stance is apparently pacifist, it paints so grim a portrait of the enemy, and so thrilling a picture of the battle scenes, that its tone is distinctly martial. The film also provided the first starring role for the most electric male lead

of the Twenties, Rudolph Valentino, whose reputation was made the moment he stepped onto the dance floor to tango with Beatrice Dominguez.

King Vidor's *The Big Parade* (1925) is the most powerful film about war from this period. Weak and sentimental its central love story might be, but the reconstruction of America's war experience, viewed through the eyes of its uncommitted hero, is vivid and harsh. Filmed with the aid of the US Army and employing dozens of veterans as extras and advisers, *The Big Parade* culminates in a full-scale reproduction of the attack on Belleau Wood in June 1918. Raoul Walsh's *What Price Glory?* (1926) was equally strong on action, but its anti-war stance was weakened by the obvious martial relish of its two central characters, played by Victor McLaglen and Edmund Lowe, buddies who spend their time fighting each other as much as the Germans. D.W. Griffith's *Isn't Life Wonderful?* (1924), a poignant study of the hardships in post-war Germany, was a refreshing contrast to the bombast of the battle pictures.

William Wellman's *Wings* (1927) was one of the first films to appreciate the value of the air war as spectacle. The air aces were the last of the individual warriors, engaged in exciting one-to-one conflicts, a long way removed from the anonymous, impersonal slaughter on the ground. While it was tasteless to present the war in the trenches as anything but ghastly, the aerial war offered scope for old-fashioned heroics. Although *Wings'* recreation of no-man's land is stark and grim, and its story a tragic one, it is the uplifting dogfight scenes that were clearly meant to steal the show. *Hell's Angels* (1930) boasted some classic aerial footage, later used in several smaller-budget films, while *The Dawn Patrol* of the same year (remade in 1938 with Errol Flynn and David Niven) attempted to deflate the romantic image of aerial war with its tale of the decimation of a Royal Flying Corps squadron by a more efficient enemy.

Anti-War Films

The Locarno Pact of 1925, effectively readmitting Germany to the community of nations, was followed by a period of reappraisal in the late Twenties. This was reflected by three of the greatest anti-war films ever made: Lewis Milestone's *All Quiet on the Western Front*, G.W. Pabst's *Westfront 1918* (both 1930) and Anthony Asquith's *Tell England* (1931). Milestone's film, remade as recently as 1980 but with less power and less passion, is perhaps the best-known and most admired of all films about World War I. Adapted from Erich Maria Remarque's novel, it tells of the gradual destruction of a group of young German recruits, mercilessly stripping the war of its glamour, and further enhancing its pacifist message by inviting audiences to sympathize with foreign (enemy) characters rather than American ones.

Pabst's *Westfront 1918* also follows the brutalization and elimination of a group of recruits, this time French, conveying the squalor and horror of life in the trenches with a grinding realism which some claim outstrips *All Quiet on the Western Front*. Marginally the weakest of the three, flawed by its nostalgic eulogy of the British class system, *Tell England* is nonetheless redeemed by its humanity. Its two young heroes are sent to Gallipoli, where the outdated concepts of honour and loyalty that compelled them to enlist are eroded until one is killed in a raid on the Turkish trenches. Peter Weir's Australian film *Gallipoli* (1981) has a curiously similar plot but a much greater eye for earthy realism and a very different national consciousness.

CHAPTER 5
Silent Cinema Around the World

Britain

The Blue Bird was the only film lasting longer than 15 minutes (a whole reel) made in Britain in 1910. There were many comic and dramatic 'subjects' turned out by the British producers but most were very short anecdotes rather than stories. The lively and inventive spirit which had given Britain a lead in film technique had petered out. Pioneers like G.A. Smith, James Williamson and R.W. Paul had given up making films. Production was led by the staid Cecil Hepworth, with his stock company and studio beside the Thames at Walton. Hepworth (1874–1953), the son of the well known lantern-show lecturer T.C. Hepworth, took an interest in photographic quality and beauty of setting that made his films visually outstanding, and his players were encouraged to act with unusual restraint. However, as films from abroad became longer and foreign stars came to be known by name it became clear that a more adventurous approach was needed. It was the arrival of a new producer, Will Barker (1867–1951), with his Bulldog brand, that signalled the revival. A rough diamond with big ideas and plenty of go, in 1910 he built the first Ealing studio, large for the time with two of its stages depending on sunlight and two on electricity. He created a sensation in 1911 with a shortened film version of Sir Herbert Beerbohm Tree's stage production of Shakespeare's *Henry VIII*, which lasted over half an hour. After this, other eminent actors decided to preserve potted versions of their own favourite roles on film. Sir Frank Benson, for example, was filmed playing Mark Antony in *Julius Caesar* and the title roles in *Macbeth* and *Richard III* (all 1911). Barker carried on with a couple of thumping melodramas, *East Lynne* and *The Road to Ruin* (both 1913), and broke new ground the same year with a film depicting scenes from the life of Queen Victoria called *Sixty Years a Queen*. Other companies made a conscious effort to get up to date – Cricks and Martin's futuristic airship story *The Pirates of 1920* (1911), although still just under a reel, was hailed as the first British 'feature film'. British multi-reel films became longer and more frequent.

Hepworth, realizing that the faces of his stock company were becoming familiar to the public, began to publicize them by name. As Chrissie White grew up to be a fair-haired blue-eyed English rose, she and Alma Taylor, darker and softer, played in many love stories with two new members of the company, the stage actors Henry Edwards and Stewart Rome. *Oliver Twist* (1912), a long film directed by Thomas Bentley, who was well known in the halls for his impersonations of characters from the novels of Charles Dickens, was the first of many literary adaptations in costume. Hepworth's *Hamlet*

(1913) showed the great actor Sir Johnston Forbes-Robertson, on the eve of retirement, as a very old Prince of Denmark in the Drury Lane production. These distinguished theatrical knights, ageing relics of the Victorian theatre, made little concession to the different medium and their larger-than-life style of classical acting contributed nothing to film technique, but they enhanced the prestige of the cinema. The beauty queen Ivy Close starred in films made by her husband, the Bond Street photographer Elwin Neame; self-consciously artistic, these also were part of a new tendency to take cinema seriously.

There were other newcomers before the war started in 1914. George Pearson (1875–1973), a former schoolmaster who had been making educational films for Pathé, ventured into feature production and soon became a leading director. Maurice Elvey (1887–1967) began 44 years of slick professional film-making in 1913. The Birmingham distributor G.B. Samuelson (1888–1947) established a studio at Worton Hall, Isleworth, and the director Percy Nash built one at Elstree, both near London. The London Film Company, a big public company with large capital resources, set new standards of business-like administration. Founded by Provincial Cinematograph Theatres, one of the biggest circuits, it turned an ice rink at Twickenham into a large studio and announced its intention of making films that reflected British life. Its top directors, writers and leading ladies, however, were all American, for the American presence in British production was already marked by this time.

The chief British studios were scattered around the smoke-free edges of London. The longer film, with its greater demands on the script, had already caused producers to turn to the stage for material, and the nearness of the London theatres reinforced this dependence by providing a convenient pool of acting talent. Immediately war broke out, there was an outburst of activity in the belief that American imports would fall. The numerous dramas from the London Film Company, many of them from plays, tended to be longer and more colourful than those from Hepworth. But Hepworth's major productions included two important adaptations from the plays of Arthur Wing Pinero, *Sweet Lavender* (1915) and *Trelawney of the Wells* (1916). Bentley continued to specialize in Dickens adaptations; and Barker made an historical drama about Edward IV's mistress *Jane Shore* (1915), which included spectacular crowd scenes.

Left: the young Alfred Hitchcock, aged 27, directing The Mountain Eagle *(1926), a film now lost. His future wife and long-time assistant, Alma Reville, stands behind him.*

The new Samuelson studio was enlarged in 1915, and Gaumont opened a studio at Shepherds Bush in west London, where Pearson filmed four adventures (1915–17) of his character Ultus the Avenger, created in answer to Léon Gaumont's request for a British equivalent of Louis Feuillade's Fantômas. Broadwest Film Company was founded during the war by Walter West. It specialized in racing dramas from the popular stories of Nat Gould, and daring society dramas and problem plays starring the beautifully-gowned Violet Hopson, formerly with Hepworth.

Unfortunately, in the light of all this home activity, American films, far from falling off during the war, now poured into Britain and vastly increased their share of the market. The multi-reel superpicture became common, with costly stars and settings, crowd scenes and elaborate costumes. The big American companies could in the first place spend more on their pictures because of their huge home market, and they were able with these attractive and well-advertised films to take over the British market as well.

The old 'open market' in films, involving sales of many copies of each film, was dead now, and the new expensive features were exploited by renters who bid for exclusive rights for particular areas. This 'exclusive' system gave renters great power over exhibitors, who found that they had to book large blocks of films in order to get the few they wanted. British producers with their few films, already suffering by comparison with their more lavish competitors, now found that there were fewer and fewer booking slots left for them, and their releases were often delayed for months.

British producers had sought import protection as early as 1915, and in 1917 had suggested a quota system to guarantee British films a proportion of screen time, but nothing had been done. In this unfavourable climate production tailed off. The London Film Company and Barker gave up and by 1923 most of the small pre-war companies had disappeared.

So, indeed, had two out of three much larger companies founded at the end of the war. The American firm Famous Players-Lasky had turned a barn-like former power station at Islington into a studio in 1919, bringing over technicians, stars and equipment from America. Using British actors, they claimed, like the London Film Company before them, that they wanted to make films with British themes but they gave up after four years. The big renting company Ideal, conscious of the importance of the story in these new longer films, took over the studio at Elstree and went into mass production of literary adaptations, mostly of English Victorian novels. Made on tight budgets, the films were poor and did not appeal to the more sophisticated post-war public. The theatre-owner Sir Oswald Stoll, also thinking of English writers as possible saviours of the British film, secured film rights to the works of many contemporary writers and went into even more massive production of the Eminent British Authors series in a former aircraft factory at Cricklewood in north London, with the directors Sinclair Hill and Elvey and many others. But as in the case of Ideal the films were churned out on the cheap and, despite three popular series of Sherlock Holmes films (1921–23), the critical tag, 'Stoll films are dull films', was only too true. Stoll lasted a little longer than Famous Players-Lasky and Ideal, but faded out in the mid-Twenties.

So bad was the slump in production by 1923 that producers got together to hold country-wide British National Film Weeks, in which their films were specially promoted with exhortations to the public to support them for patriotic reasons. Unfortunately no standard of selection seems to have been imposed and many of the films were far from good.

One of them, *Comin' Thro' the Rye* (1923), was Hepworth's favourite of all his films, yet it was one of his last, in production while his company, which he had unwisely tried to expand, was heading for the financial crash that ended his career. It was a sentimental tale of a broken engagement, with Alma Taylor as a gentle Victorian heroine, but it was sadly out of touch with the jazzy post-war era. Pearson on the other hand just managed to survive the Twenties, although he too was a Victorian at heart. He opened his own studio after the war and made a number of thoughtful and interesting films. But the real success of his company was fortuitous, and due to a series of comedies (1921–23) about a cockney flower girl, Squibs. Betty Balfour (b.1903), bubbly and gay as Squibs, became the one true British film star, ranking with the Hollywood stars as far as the British public was concerned. After she had left the company it floundered.

Output hit bottom in 1926, with only 37 new features, compared with 103 in 1919. Among them, however, were some excellent films of far higher quality than before, made by post-war newcomers to the industry.

Working in an old army hut at Elstree, Harry Bruce Woolfe, who had formed British Instructional Films in 1919, made an orginal contribution to cinema when he laboriously put together a compilation film with animated maps and diagrams, *The Battle of Jutland* (1921). Moving to a studio in

Surbiton, he then began a series of filmed reconstructions of famous wartime engagements, including *The Battles of the Coronel and Falkland Islands* (1927). This was made with Admiralty help, with naval vessels re-enacting their movements for the camera. Pioneering from the early Twenties onwards with *Secrets of Nature*, a brilliant series of films made by naturalists using stop-motion photography and microphotography, he led the way in the serious and factual film until the arrival of the documentarist John Grierson with *Drifters* in 1929. Harry Bruce Woolfe also turned to the production of features and gathered a band of young university graduates, one of whom, Anthony Asquith, the son of the former Prime Minister Herbert Asquith, dazzled the critics with a film about film-making, *Shooting Stars* (1927), which he wrote and co-directed. It was a melodrama, in which the starlet seeks to kill her husband so as to run off with a Chaplinesque lover, but contrives the latter's death instead. A display of technical virtuosity and wit, it showed the influence of German and Russian advances in film technique, and heralded the appearance of more intellectual films in Britain.

At this time, two young businessmen, Herbert Wilcox and Michael Balcon, entered production from renting. Both believed a share of the American market was necessary if films were to recoup the costs necessary to please British audiences used to Hollywood standards, and both tried hard to get their pictures released in the USA. The Irish-born Wilcox (1892–1977), producing and sometimes also directing, worked at first in hired studios and preferred stories with an obvious exploitation angle, often from stage successes and often in costume. He engaged American stars as part of his bid for American audiences including Mae Marsh in *Flames of Passion* (1922), directed by Graham Cutts, and Dorothy Gish in no less than five films, notably *Nell Gwyn* (1926). He hit the headlines when *Dawn* (1928) – in which Sybil Thorndike gave a memorable performance as Edith Cavell, the British nurse who had been shot as a spy by the Germans – was censored in case it offended Germany.

Top far left: Sir Johnston Forbe-Robertson as Hamlet. *Top left: in* Ultus and the Grey Lady *(1916),* Ultus the Avenger *(Aurele Sydney) is helped by Mary Ferris (Mary Dibley) to find the man who betrayed him and killed her father. Above: Ivy Ellison and Donald Calthorp in* Shooting Stars. *Above right: filming Stoll's* Sherlock Holmes *series at Cricklewood. Right: Alma Taylor and Shayle Gardner in* Comin' Thro' the Rye.

Michael Balcon (1896–1977), a young renter from the industrial Midlands, took over the Islington studio from Famous Players-Lasky with many of the staff, including a pudgy young assistant called Alfred Hitchcock. Hiring the American star Betty Compson at the unheard-of salary of £1000 a week, Balcon co-produced with Victor Saville the glamorous, tearful, rather daring and very successful *Woman to Woman* (1923), directed by Graham Cutts with Hitchcock as scriptwriter and art director. Balcon went on to make many of the best British films of the Twenties. A number of them starred the romantic dark-eyed matinée idol Ivor Novello (1893–1951), whose popularity with the British public rivalled that of Betty Balfour. In *The Rat* (1925), also directed by Cutts, the actor wrote himself a juicy part as a low-life Parisian apache, and the film was so successful that several sequels and remakes followed. Meanwhile Hitchcock rapidly showed himself to be an outstanding director: with the suspense and atmosphere of *The Lodger* (1926), in which Novello played the suspect for a series of Jack the Ripper murders, he hit the jackpot with both box-office and critics. It was the first

chance Hitchcock had had to pursue on screen his spare-time interest in murder, mayhem and the darker recesses of the human psyche. Hitchcock boldly shaped the story in largely atmospheric terms, building up the feeling of panic in the streets while the killer is on the loose, and the disturbed mental state of the unjustly-suspected hero, in a style more German than British or American. Hitchcock became at one stroke the leading director in British cinema eclipsing his one-time mentor Cutts.

Hitchcock does not seem to have felt then (or really ever) that he should confine himself exclusively to the thriller genre. Indeed, none of his other silent films is even remotely a thriller. In *Downhill* (1927) he continued the happy working relationship with Ivor Novello in a story, told with amazing flair and visual invention, of a public-school boy who goes picturesquely to the dogs after being expelled over a misunderstanding. *Easy Virtue* (1927) was based on one of Noel Coward's recent stage successes and *The Ring* (1927), was a love story with a boxing background. Hitchcock's last silent film, *The Manxman* (1929), was based on Hall Caine's best-

Top: Sybil Thorndike as Nurse Edith Cavell in Dawn. *Above: Ivor Novello in* The Lodger. *Right: man engaged to daughter but loves her mother – Jean Bradin, Eve Grey, with Olga Tschechowa (centre) as the mother, in* Moulin Rouge.

Above: Ivor Novello in Downhill *as a disgraced youth who marries a flighty actress (Isabel Jeans). Above left: Carl Brisson plays a boxer who stars at the fairground in* The Ring, *a love story about the rise of a prize-fighter and the effect this has on his marriage.*

selling novel about a love triangle on the Isle of Man, and is remarkable for the directness with which it expresses sensuality and desire.

Towards the end of the decade the Scottish solicitor John Maxwell, already the boss of a renting firm and a small circuit of cinemas, opened the huge new Elstree studio of British International Pictures. Hiring talent from all sides to fill it, including Hitchcock, he imitated Hollywood on a shoestring. Stars and technicians came from all over the world. Whereas Balcon had entered into Anglo-German production agreements so that Alfred Hitchcock made his first two films, *The Pleasure Garden* (1925) and *The Mountain Eagle* (1926), in Germany, Maxwell brought German directors and cameramen over to Elstree. A sombre film about the troubles in Ireland, *The Informer* (1929), was directed by Arthur Robison; *Moulin Rouge* (1928) and *Piccadilly* (1929), two would-be sophisticated films, were made by E.A. Dupont. Elstree was frequently described as the British Hollywood, and it was appropriate that here in 1929 Hitchcock made the film which signalled Britain's leap into the talkie era, *Blackmail*, his first

thriller since *The Lodger. Blackmail* was at first intended to be a completely silent film, so that it hardly mattered that a Czech actress played a suburban Londoner. But the producers decided that the last reel should use a new gimmick, sound; Hitchcock then persuaded them to turn *Blackmail* into a part talkie. Anny Ondra was dubbed – in a primitive but effective fashion – and Hitchcock had his biggest triumph since *The Lodger.*

When the Cinematograph Films Act of 1927, introducing a quota system at last, began operation on January 1, 1928, the initial reaction of the big American renters was to acquire for distribution the films of these few quality producers, in order to comply with their legal obligation. But the films were popular, and it soon became clear to the Americans that distribution on fair terms of pictures that would compete with their own was not good business. They looked around for cheap films that would pose no threat, and a whole industry was born. From now on, the production of 'quota quickies' was to account for at least half of British output, a situation that was to last for some years.

Above right: dinner is served – Marie Ault, Betty Compson and Clive Brook in Woman to Woman. *Hitchcock was the art director. Right:* The Rat *(Ivor Novello) and his girl (Mae Marsh) are separated in Graham Cutts' film of Novello's West-End hit.*

Scandinavia

Sweden pointed the way forward as early as 1907, when Charles Magnusson (1878–1948) was appointed production manager at AB Svenska Biografteatern – the company that still flourishes to this day as Svensk Filmindustri. Magnusson's gifts included a flair for cinematography – he had made his reputation with newsreels – and administrative efficiency that enabled him to stay at the top as the firm grew under him. He was also anxious to secure respectability for the new medium; he believed that the cinema could fulfil a reforming role and actually influence the way society acted and reacted. He felt more in tune with the Swedish countryside than the urban areas and he resolved to make more films on location, in natural surroundings.

Early in 1912, Magnusson gave contracts to Mauritz Stiller and Victor Sjöström. The three men became close friends and, through the next ten years or so, Sjöström and Stiller directed literally scores of films, an achievement that would establish the Golden Age of Swedish cinema, and that led eventually to both directors being recruited by Hollywood.

Mauritz Stiller (1883–1928) was born in Helsinki of a Russian Jewish family. At the age of 21, he emigrated to Sweden in order to escape military service (Finland was still at that time under Russian control) and, like Sjöström, was engaged in the theatre until the summons came from the astute Magnusson.

Victor Sjöström (1879–1960) was born in the heart of one of Sweden's most beautiful provinces, Värmland, near the Norwegian border. By his early thirties he had built up a modest reputation as a travelling actor in Finland and Sweden, eventually running his own repertory company in tandem with another actor. He was startled when Magnusson offered him 15,000 crowns (a tidy sum in those days) to join Svenska Bio.

The two men learned the craft of film-making together. They worked in a hot and glaring studio, built of glass, out on the island of Lidingö, to the east of Stockholm. Julius Jaenzon, one of the greatest photographers of the silent period, was already in residence and showed the new directors the ropes.

Sjöström and Stiller were both impressed and influenced by the neighbouring Danish cinema, which had set a fair course long before 1912. Nordisk Films Kompagni had been founded in November 1906 by Ole Olsen, once a penniless farmhand, later a fairground showman and subsequently a cinema owner. Under his leadership, the company became known throughout the world under its trademark – a polar bear atop the globe. All filming was done in the open air, with a hand-cranked camera and a few actors (paid only a meagre sum) posing in front of fragile sets painted to look like interiors. Olsen's early successes were two documentaries, *Bjørnen Løs* (1906, Hunting a Polar Bear) and *Løvejagten* (1908, *Lion Hunting*), the sales of which reached as high as 191 and 259 copies respectively, though Olsen's killing of two imported lions for the sake of realism incurred the wrath of the Minister of Justice, who promptly withdrew the showman's exhibitor's licence.

Lion Hunting marked a breakthrough on the international market for Nordisk, and between 1907 and 1910 more than 560 films were produced by Olsen's company. Celebrated stage actors were brought to the screen, among them Bodil Ipsen, Clara Pontoppidan, Olaf Fønns, Paul Reimert and the legendary Asta Nielsen.

Nordisk also housed some of the liveliest directors of the period, including August Blom, Carl Theodor Dreyer, Holger

Left: Nordisk, founded in 1906, is the world's oldest surviving film company. Below left: Renée Falconetti whose face, for director Carl Theodor Dreyer, was the window into – and the mirror of – the soul of Joan of Arc. *Above right: Asta Nielsen played an early prototype of the vamp in Urban Gad's* Afgrunden. *Above far right: Benjamin Christiansen's survey of* Witchcraft Through the Ages *was a mixture of horror and humour. Below far right: Karin Molander as a resourceful newspaper reporter in* Love and Journalism. *Below right:* Ingeborg Holm *concerned a poor widow who is forced to take her children to the poor house. It was a hard-hitting condemnation of the injustice of Sweden's Poor Laws.*

Madsen and George Schnéevoigt. Dreyer (1889–1968) began his career in the so-called 'Poets' Caravan' where Nordisk scriptwriters met and worked. He made his debut with *Praesidenten* (1919, The President), the story of a judge with a past, but also completed *Blade af Satans Bog* (1920, Pages From Satan's Book), an imitation of Griffith's *Intolerance* (1916) based on a Marie Corelli novel, before leaving Nordisk.

Prästänkan (1920, *The Parson's Widow*) was a Swedish film, but shot at Lillehammer in Norway in a preserved medieval village. Warm, serene and often very funny, the film is set in a country parsonage where a young man has just taken his place as the new incumbent. He has brought his fiancée with him, but local custom decrees that the new parson must marry the late parson's widow. The lady is very old and the young man will be her fourth husband. He agrees, and the fiancée is engaged as a maid. All this could have made a coarse rustic comedy, but with a flow of radiant images, Dreyer makes it into a tranquil celebration of old age and death. The lady knows very well what is going on, accepts its naturalness and, in her own time, gently dies.

Dreyer filmed *Die Gezeichneten* (1922, Love One Another), the story of a Russian village during the 1905 Revolution, at Lankwitz near Berlin. This little-known piece, once thought lost but rediscovered, is one of the director's most fascinating works. It is the account of a pogrom in which the crowd, unusually for Dreyer, is more important than any individual, and in which the scenes of swirling disturbance have a vivid reality.

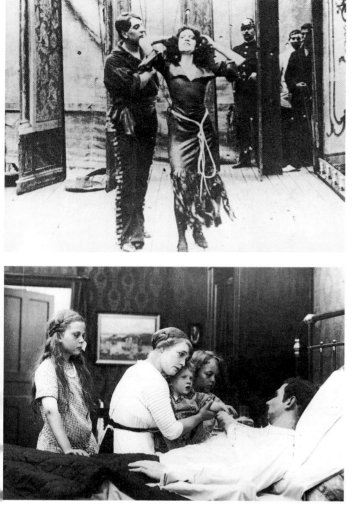

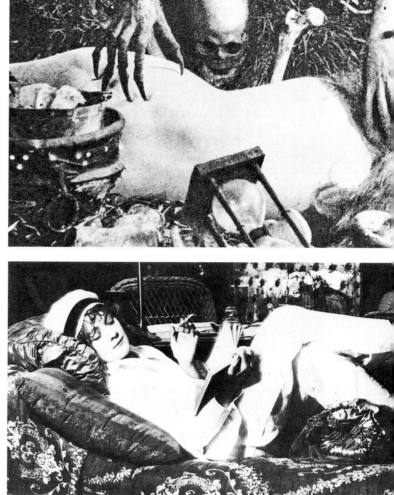

After *Der Van Engang* (1922, Once Upon a Time), a lost film said to be very slight, Dreyer returned to Germany for *Michael* (1924, *Heart's Desire*). The story of an elderly painter betrayed and cheated by his model whom he has adopted as his son – the homosexual overtones are unequivocal – *Michael* was enhanced by a lavish treatment from the producer Erich Pommer, the talents of two great cameramen, Karl Freund and Rudolph Maté, and a remarkable cast. The Danish and Hollywood actor and director Benjamin Christensen played the painter, the future character actor Walter Slezak played Michael, and the Austrian actress Nora Gregor – later to star in Jean Renoir's classic *La Règle du Jeu* (1939, *The Rules of the Game*) – was the princess who comes between them. The film was quintessential Dreyer: a steady, unhurried contemplation of a crisis in two lives and its resolution by death.

Back in Denmark, Dreyer made *Du Skal aere din Hustru* (1925, *Thou Shalt Honour Thy Wife*), a deliciously ironic account of a demanding husband's come-uppance at the hands of the old family nurse, and then, after making the minor *Glomdalsbruden* (1926, The Bride of Glomdal) in Norway, moved to France for his best-known film, *La Passion de Jeanne d'Arc* (1928, *The Passion of Joan of Arc*). Concentrating Joan's trial into one day and consisting largely of interrogations, this late silent film seems to cry out for sound and yet, miraculously, to transcend that necessity. The brilliance of the editing, Rudolph Maté's photography, the performance in her only film by the great French stage actress Renée Falconetti, the marvellously expressive faces, the

sublime and terrible ending – out of these Dreyer created a magnificent and unique study of the interior life of a human being.

Two other significant Danes of the pre-war period were Urban Gad (1879–1947), who helped to turn Asta Nielsen into a star with such films as *Afgrunden* (1910, The Abyss) and *Heisses Blut* (1911, Hot Blood); and the enigmatic Benjamin Christensen (1879–1959), who asserted himself as a master of the horror film before it became a genre, with *Det Hemmeligh-edsfulde X* (1913, The Mysterious X) and *Haevnens Nat* (1916, Night of Revenge). Christensen produced an extraordinary quasi-documentary in Sweden, *Häxan* (1922, *Witchcraft Through the Ages*), and after a spell in Germany he sailed for Hollywood, where a clutch of horror movies (the best being *Seven Footprints to Satan*, 1929) proclaimed him worthy of comparison with Louis Feuillade and Tod Browning.

Meanwhile, Sjöström and Stiller matched each other stride for stride, with Sjöström often acting in the films of his Finnish colleague. Of the 62 features they directed between 1912 and the end of 1916, virtually all have disappeared or been destroyed by fire. Sjöström's most important work, however, *Ingeborg Holm* (1913, *Give Us This Day*) has survived to attest to its director's attention to detail and fierce sense of social commitment.

Stiller's earliest masterpiece was *Kärlek och Journalistik* (1916, *Love and Journalism*), a sparkling comedy about a young female journalist who poses as a maid in the household of a top Antarctic explorer to obtain a scoop for her paper.

Sjöström embarked on a series of literary adaptations, each more striking than the last. His *Terje Vigen* (1917, *A Man There Was*) was based on the epic poem by Henrik Ibsen about a fisherman who pierces the English blockade of Norway during the Napoleonic Wars, is captured, and after a miserable life finally has the chance of avenging himself on his enemy; instead he relents and his hatred of humanity subsides. Sjöström also adapted several works of the Swedish novelist Selma Lagerlöf. Although Victor Sjöström and Mauritz Stiller each directed about five or six films a year between 1912 and 1916, their genius only began to blossom from about 1917 onwards. Their hectic pace slowed. They devoted more time to each production. The result was a steady stream of excellent, often brilliant, films that brought the Swedish cinema to the forefront – impressing even the Americans.

American producers have a long history of grabbing foreign talent. The undoubted gifts – and success – of *two* Swedish directors were indeed proof that Sweden knew a thing or two about film-making. In the early Twenties both were invited to Hollywood. But what the American moguls had failed to perceive was that Stiller and Sjöström – like many artists – drew direct inspiration from their country's emotions, experience and daily rhythm. In 1917, for example, Victor Sjöström took his tiny crew and his actors up to the mountains of Lappland to shoot *Berg-Ejvind och Hans Hustru* (1918, *The Outlaw and His Wife*), a dour story of a man, played by Sjöström himself, who steals a sheep to feed his starving family, is outlawed, and – in spite of the love of the loyal Halla (played by Sjöström's wife, Edith Erastoff) – comes to a miserable end in the mountains. But nature does at least grant the couple a brief summer to enjoy together.

Sjöström had grown up in the same province as the Nobel Prize-winning authoress Selma Lagerlöf, and brought to his adaptations of her work a lively sympathy and understanding. *Tösen Från Stormyrtorpet* (1917, *The Woman He Chose*) concerned a peasant girl saddled with an illegitimate child. *Ingmarssönerna* (1919, The Sons of Ingmar), released in two parts, was a morality tale about a stolid Swede who clambers towards heaven on a gigantic ladder in order to consult his ancestors about his difficulties on earth; and *Körkarlen* (1921, *The Phantom Carriage*) concerned the dangers of alcoholism.

Soon after making *Vem Dömer?* (1922, *Love's Crucible*) – a lavish, rather portentous evocation of Renaissance Italy – Sjöström was contacted by the Goldwyn Company, (which became part of MGM in 1924). So, on January 10, 1923, Victor Sjöström set sail for America, confident of the future and aware that, due to his having lived in the States for the first few years of his life (his father had settled there briefly), his fluency in English would enable him to cope with the rigours of filming in Hollywood.

Stiller, too, was destined to make the journey to Los Angeles, his achievements in the six years between 1918 and 1924 if anything having surpassed those of his great friend and rival. In *Erotikon* (1920, *Bonds That Chafe*), he established the pattern of sophisticated, upper-class comedy that would be elaborated upon in the years ahead by Lubitsch and DeMille. *Erotikon* remains an elegant pirouette of a film, sensational at the time because of its lack of inhibitions and its *risqué* innuendoes.

Like Sjöström, Mauritz Stiller turned to the stories of Selma Lagerlöf for some of his greatest works. *Herr Arnes Pengar* (1919, *Sir Arne's Treasure*) unfolds in sixteenth-century Sweden, with the discovery of a conspiracy among the Scottish mercenaries of King Johann III. Their rapacity leads to the death of the waif-like Elsalill (Mary Johnson), who has fallen in love with the mercenaries' leader; and the scene of her funeral cortège slowly wending over the ice at Marstrand constitutes one of the most enduring of all Swedish film images.

Another Lagerlöf novel, *Gunnar Hedes Saga* (1923, *Gunnar Hede's Saga*) breathes a strange power and fervency in its screen version by Stiller. Half-fantasy, half-documentary, the film demonstrates Stiller's ability to cope with both the epic genre and the fluctuations of memory – a fascination common to Lagerlöf, Sjöström and Stiller.

Gösta Berlings Saga (1924, *The Atonement of Gösta Berling*), based on one of Lagerlöf's greatest novels, was to be Stiller's last Swedish film, but the one destined to set a young Swedish actress, Greta Garbo, on the path to fame. The film survives as the swansong of Swedish silent cinema, rich in tableaux, yet laborious in pace.

Stiller was restless. He took Garbo and his cameraman, Julius Jaenzon, to Istanbul in the hope of shooting a film in Turkey for a German company. But the finance never materialized, and Stiller returned to Berlin, where he managed to strike a contract for Garbo to appear in G.W. Pabst's *Die freudlose Gasse* (1925, *The Joyless Street*). While in the German capital, he met Louis B. Mayer, who screened *The Atonement of Gösta Berling* and saw in Greta Garbo a potential star for MGM. Reluctantly, he took Stiller along on her coat-tails, although at this stage Garbo relied totally on her mentor for any decision concerning her career. And on July 5, 1925, they both arrived in New York, a little bewildered and somewhat neglected by the officials of MGM.

Left: Victor Sjöstrom (left) and Mauritz Stiller with Garbo in Hollywood. Below left: in The Wind, *Letty (Lillian Gish) buries the man she has killed. Right: Sir Archie (Richard Lund) woos Elsalill (Mary Johnson) in* Sir Arne's Treasure. *Far right: Greta Garbo as Elizabeth in* The Atonement of Gösta Berling, *the film that brought her to the attention of MGM's Louis B. Mayer. Below far right: Pola Negri as a servant and George Siegmann as a drunken officer in* Hotel Imperial. *Below right: Lon Chaney as the clown, with Norma Shearer and John Gilbert in* He Who Gets Slapped.

Although Victor Sjöström, with his command of the language and his sunnier nature, fared better than Stiller in the USA, the cruel fact is that neither of them really fulfilled Hollywood's high hopes.

For Stiller, the first year in America was hell. He suffered from rheumatism, was left without an assignment by MGM, and when at last he was allowed to direct Garbo in *The Temptress* (1926), he told Sjöström that:

'. . . they engage me because they think I have good ideas about how films should be made, and then I'm not allowed to do anything without the busybodies interfering everywhere.'

Sjöström's name was changed to Seastrom so that Americans might be spared the rotundities of Swedish pronunciation, and he completed nine features – including one with Garbo, *The Divine Woman* (1928) – during his six-year stay in Hollywood. From this point of view, he proved much more successful than Stiller, who worked on a mere five films, three of which were taken out of his hands and completed by journeyman directors.

Few of the American films of either man have survived. But *He Who Gets Slapped* (1924) is an astonishing achievement, in which Sjöström not only masters the more sophisticated technical apparatus available to him in Hollywood, but brings to this story of humiliation and revenge a blistering irony quite absent from his Swedish pictures.

Two films starring Lillian Gish assured the success of Sjöström's career in Hollywood. *The Scarlet Letter* (1926) was based on Nathaniel Hawthorne's classic novel, a stern tale of New England Puritan intolerance.

The Wind (1928) marks perhaps the peak of both Sjöström's and Gish's careers. Although inspired by a book by Dorothy Scarborough, set in a desolate stretch of Texas, the film exemplifies a particular theme of Sjöström's – that man drifts ultimately at the mercy of his environment and the elements. As Letty, the demure young woman forced to murder a mysterious assailant during a storm, Lillian Gish gives as convincing a portrayal of raw-nerved hysteria as she had done in *Broken Blossoms* (1919). Few scenes in silent cinema are so gripping as the climax of *The Wind*, with the gale whipping the sand inexorably away from the shallow grave where Letty has buried her victim.

In April 1930, Victor Sjöström returned permanently to Sweden, where he made the occasional picture but turned increasingly to acting, becoming a father-figure to many a new Swedish director. Among them was Ingmar Bergman, who paid homage to the master by starring him in both *Till Glädje* (1950, *To Joy*) and *Smultronstället* (1957, *Wild Strawberries*).

Of the various American productions on which Mauritz Stiller was unhappily involved, *Hotel Imperial* was accorded the best reception. Released in 1927, it was based on an espionage romance by the Hungarian writer Lájos Biró, and starred Pola Negri. Both reviews and box-office figures were excellent, and Stiller was whipped away from MGM by Paramount and paid $2500 a week. But poor health, combined with a refusal on Stiller's part to immerse himself in American life or society, contributed to the decline of his career. His final assignment, *The Street of Sin* (1928), was completed by Ludwig Berger, and Stiller, ailing and disillusioned, departed for Sweden. Less than a year later he collapsed and was rushed to hospital. Sjöström, home for a trip, managed to visit his bedside just before Stiller died aged only 45.

Germany

German exhibitors depended for a livelihood on a flow of films from Denmark prior to the outbreak of World War I and even beyond. Few local directors made any impact, although Richard Oswald, Max Mack and Max Reinhardt all came to the cinema around 1910. Significantly, when the Germans did make their first important film, revealing the themes that would obsess them in the years ahead, it was directed by a Dane, Stellan Rye. This was the first version of *Der Student von Prag* (1913, *The Student of Prague*), which was seen by Sjöström on its release and made a great impression on him. *The Student of Prague* reflected the bizarre, intense vision of the actor and co-writer Paul Wegener (1874–1948), who had acted under Reinhardt, and drew on the work of such writers as E.T.A. Hoffmann and Edgar Allan Poe and on the Faust legend, as well as Robert Louis Stevenson's novel *Dr Jekyll and Mr Hyde*, to paint the story of a man whose soul is divided fatally between two conflicting personalities.

Wegener acted in and co-directed *Der Golem* (1913, *The Golem*), which also displayed the penchant for the fantastic that was to distinguish German cinema in the Twenties. Seven years later he remade the picture, with greater resources and power.

At the height of World War I, General Ludendorff created a new office under the High Command to co-ordinate photography and film for the war effort. This initiative led to the gathering together of most of the main film companies under one organization: Ufa (Universum Film AG). In the wake of military defeat, the Reich abandoned its shares and control passed into the hands of the Deutsche Bank.

Siegfried Kracauer, in his seminal study of the German cinema *From Caligari to Hitler*, has emphasized the mood of intellectual excitement that swept through Germany after the Armistice, a mood described as *Aufbruch* (start, departure). The avant-garde, Expressionist painting and enthusiasm for the film as a medium were all as much to the fore in Germany as they were in the Soviet Union.

The omens were favourable. Ufa, with its immense financial resources, could offer film-makers every facility they could dream of, and during the last years of the war several directors had emerged, often working with one another,

stimulating each other and responding to the atmosphere of revolutionary optimism. Lupu Pick and Emil Jannings were prominent among players. Joe May, a specialist in thrillers, worked from screenplays written by a young Viennese, Fritz Lang. Arthur Robison and Ewald André Dupont had proved themselves skilled directors. And there was Lubitsch.

Ernst Lubitsch (1892–1947), like practically every bright young figure of the German film world at this time, had begun his career working for Max Reinhardt in the theatre. He had become an adroit and popular comedian, and by the end of the war was established as his own director. But his real surge to fame coincided with the expansion of Ufa. *Madame Dubarry* (1919, *Passion*) inaugurated Ufa's spectacular new showcase cinema in Berlin, the Ufa Palast am Zoo. One of Lubitsch's protégées was the fiery Polish actress Pola Negri, who had already smouldered in his 1918 version of *Carmen*, but who reached her apotheosis as a vamp in *Sumurun* (1920, *One Arabian Night*), Lubitsch's devastating parody of the Italian epic genre, with Negri as the vixen who dances her way to dusty death at the hands of a lecherous sheik. Lubitsch's gifts encompassed also the traditional German operetta, and he brought a delicate touch to the comedies *Die Austernprinzessin* (1919, The Oyster Princess) and *Kohlhiesels Töchter* (1920, Kohlhiesel's Daughters). Within a couple of years, Lubitsch was resident in the United States, transplanting his singular satirical talent to American soil and establishing himself with remarkable ease.

History has granted the glory to German directors for the films of the Twenties in Berlin; but Fritz Lang, Robert Wiene, F.W. Murnau and others would have been severely handicapped without the contributions of several distinguished screen-writers. Outstanding among these writers was Carl Mayer (1894–1944), an Austrian, who joined with the Czech poet Hans Janowitz in concocting the script for the most renowned of all German silent films, *Das Cabinet des Dr Caligari* (1919, *The Cabinet of Dr Caligari*). Directed by another Czech émigré, Robert Wiene, this nightmare of a movie, this living testament to the graphic powers of film expression, produced one of the cinema's immortal characters – Caligari (Werner Krauss), a maniac charlatan who exhibits his somnambulist giant Cesare (Conrad Veidt) at fairgrounds.

Far left: The Cabinet of Dr Caligari *opens with the arrival of a travelling fair in the town of Holstenwall. With it is the evil, shuffling Dr Caligari (Werner Krauss) and his somnambulist, Cesare (Conrad Veidt), slender, hollow-eyed and ashen-faced – one of the living dead. Left: Cesare, carrying off one of his victims over the roof tops whose harsh, jutting shapes reflect the maniacal vision of Caligari. Right: Siegfried (Paul Richter) is the heroic adventurer whose murder ends the first part of* Fritz Lang's Die Nibelungen, *based on a thirteenth-century German epic. The British director and film historian, Paul Rotha considered: 'For sheer pictorial beauty of structural architecture, Siegfried has never been equalled.'*

Walter Reimann, Hermann Warm and Walter Röhrig created the brilliant sets for *The Cabinet of Dr Caligari*, their twisting passages and triangular windows reflecting the vision of a madman. The characters shift in hideous harmony with the objects surrounding them, and in the dormant menace of Cesare lies the embryo of Nazism itself.

Mayer wrote *Hintertreppe* (1921, Backstairs) for Leopold Jessner and Paul Leni, and some key pictures for Murnau: *Schloss Vogelöd* (1921, Vogelöd Castle), a crime story; *Der letzte Mann* (1925, *The Last Laugh*); *Tartüff* (1925, *Tartuffe*); and Murnau's greatest film of his American period, *Sunrise* (1927). Mayer's genius comprised both subtle fantasy and social documentary – the documentary streak represented by his outline for Walter Ruttmann's *Berlin, die Symphonie einer Grosstadt* (1927, *The Symphony of a Great City*).

The winding path of fantasy and terror pursued by many of the German directors ended in a cul-de-sac. Films like Arthur Robison's *Schatten* (1923, *Warning Shadows*) and Paul Leni's *Das Wachsfigurenkabinett* (1924, *Waxworks*) have lost their hallucinatory quality with the years and linger as mere parodies of Expressionist art.

Fritz Lang (1890–1976) may be regarded as the most versatile of all German directors of the Twenties, able to turn his hand to everything from legend to fantasy, from thrillers to melodrama. In 1920, with the two-part commercial hit *Die Spinnen* (1919–20, *The Spiders*) behind him, he began writing screenplays with his future wife Thea von Harbou, and the following year earned his critical spurs with *Der Müde Tod* (1921, *Destiny*), an allegory about the struggle between Love and Death, notable for its awesome decors. Lang was attracted to figures of colossal dimensions, whether in the past or the present. His arch-criminal, Dr Mabuse, seemingly harbours a yearning to rule the world in *Dr Mabuse der Spieler* (1922, *Dr Mabuse, the Gambler*) and a similar villain predominates in *Spione* (1928, *Spies*). But these films were set in the present or immediate past. *Die Nibelungen* (1924) – made in two parts, *Siegfried* and *Kriemhilds Rache* (*Kriemhild's Revenge*) – plunged back into the Middle Ages, searching for a mythical, epic hero to inspire the Germans once more. The two films were shot in the months of 1923 that saw Germany reach its post-war nadir, with the currency plummeting in value,

members of the ultra-left manning the barricades in Hamburg, and Hitler leading an abortive *Putsch* in Munich. They were dominated by massive sets, enormous staircases, vast artificial forests – a feat of production design, curiously combining ancient and modern.

Yet Lang's insatiable imagination drew him to visions of the future too. The most spectacular of all his films remains *Metropolis* (1927), and if the early scenes appear lugubrious in pace, as groups of workers relieve each other with the metronomic shuffle of robots, this seems justified by the dynamic climax when the 'slaves' run riot, destroying the machines that oppress them and thereby flooding their own homes. Less trumpeted, yet more accurate in its prognosis of the future, was Lang's *Frau im Mond* (1929, *The Girl in the Moon*), a science-fiction story that anticipated the use of spacecraft in the Sixties and Seventies.

Around the middle of the decade, German artists came to contemplate their society with a numbed, somewhat cynical gaze, a feeling known as the *Neue Sachlichkeit* ('New Objectivity' or 'New Realism'). Resigned, disillusioned, appalled, these film-makers recorded the reality around them with a jaundiced eye. Walter Ruttman, in *Berlin: The Symphony of a Great City*, follows the life of the German capital from dawn to night; he shows a girl drowning herself, and observes the cold disdain mingled with curiosity in the faces of those watching from a nearby bridge. The inhabitants of Berlin respond to the promptings of the city with the blank indifference of automatons.

The director G.W. Pabst (1885–1967) also embraced the New Realism: 'What need is there for romantic treatment? Real life is too romantic, too ghastly.' *Die freudlose Gasse* (1925, *The Joyless Street*) brought its director to the forefront of German film-makers. Its sordid, lugubrious images of hunger and exploitation in post-war Vienna struck a far more exposed nerve among German audiences than the baroque and fantastic works of Fritz Lang.

Pabst could, however, rival both Lang and Murnau when flights of the imagination were required. In *Geheimnisse einer Seele* (1926, *Secrets of the Soul*) he related the case of an unfortunate doctor who descends into madness. As the doctor tells his psychiatrist about his recurring nightmares, his dreams mingle with everyday life to the point where the final, idyllic scene in the countryside carries a sense of entrapment rather than release.

Ilya Ehrenburg, the Soviet journalist based in Paris, wrote his novel *The Love of Jeanne Ney* as a condemnation of both communist extremism and bourgeois decadence. When Ufa assigned the property to Pabst, they insisted on his pruning the more controversial elements, but in *Die Liebe der Jeanne Ney* (1927, *The Love of Jeanne Ney*) Pabst managed to overcome these limitations with a brilliant visual sense. He and the cinematographer Fritz Arno Wagner used the camera as an additional character – an observer watching and creeping through one scene after another, expressing Pabst's love of the documentary approach. Jeanne Ney's turbulent love affair with the young Communist agent Andreas is undermined by the vicious adventurer Khalibiev during the civil war in the Crimea. The confusion of the war mirrors the turmoil of the lovers themselves.

Pabst's strength as a social analyst has been neglected. Even in an otherwise insignificant film like *Abwege* (1928, *Crisis*), he pins down the decadence of the post-war period in a microcosmic description of a nightclub to which a bored, wealthy woman (Brigitte Helm) repairs in an attempt to sublimate her disenchantment. Indeed, the nightclub

becomes for Pabst a recurring symbol of man's inability to escape his own narcissistic disillusionment: for example, the cabaret in *The Joyless Street* and the scenes of revelry in *Die Büchse der Pandora* (1929, *Pandora's Box*). In this film Pabst introduced the irridescent beauty of the American actress Louise Brooks to European audiences. She played the *femme fatale* Lulu, previously created by Asta Nielsen in Leopold Jessner's *Erdgeist* (1923, *Earth Spirit*), scripted by Mayer. In Frank Wedekind, from whose plays *Pandora's Box* was created, Pabst found a fellow spirit – a man who could penetrate deep into the corruption and deviousness of the monied classes while at the same time remaining objective in his appraisal of them.

Louise Brooks stayed on in Germany for Pabst's next film, *Das Tagebuch einer Verlorenen* (1929, *Diary of a Lost Girl*). With her demure features betrayed by her mocking, seductive eyes, Thymiane, the daughter of a chemist, quickly succumbs to the first lecherous advances made to her. She bears an illegitimate child and is promptly dispatched to a reformatory, ruled by a sadistic matron and her sinister male acolyte whose ingratiating smiles are as disturbing as any snarl. Thymiane and a friend escape during a commotion at the reformatory and are soon enrolled in a brothel. Here again, Pabst combines *joie de vivre* with acidulous observation, as he

Far left: Fritz Lang's Metropolis *is a giant high-tech city of the future. Left: servicing* Metropolis *is an army of ant-like slave workers labouring in the bowels of the earth. Below: George O'Brien as the peasant waits on the edge of a swamp for his mistress in* Sunrise. *Right: Louise Brooks as Lulu in* Pandora's Box. *Pursued by various men, she goes from riches to rags and ends up a prostitute who dies at the hands of Jack the Ripper. Below right: the tyrannical butcher, trampled underfoot by the angry, hungry poor in G.W. Pabst's* The Joyless Street.

would also do to such triumphant effect in *Die Dreigro-schenoper* (1931, *The Threepenny Opera*).

The film that bridged the past and the contemporary, taking pleasure in nostalgia while at the same time opting for a naturalism of tone, was E.A. Dupont's *Varieté* (1925, *Vaudeville*), based on a novel by Felix Holländer about a circus director (Emil Jannings) who abandons his wife for a luscious young trapeze artiste, only to be ousted by a handsome acrobat, whom he subsequently kills. Dupont (1891–1956), who in 1911 had flourished as one of the first film critics at work in Germany, here achieved the summit of his career; and Karl Freund, the cameraman, follows the curling flight of the trapeze with as much voluptuous delight as he follows the doomed man's sojourn in prison.

F.W. Murnau (1888–1931) survived the vicissitudes of the German cinema in the Twenties, and succeeded in his brief Hollywood heyday in establishing a name there also, above all for *Sunrise*, which won for its leading actress, Janet Gaynor, one of the first Academy Awards in 1928. Murnau had sought in his first major work, *Nosferatu, eine Symphonie des Grauens* (1922, *Nosferatu, the Vampire*), to tackle the extremes of fantasy with a realism that involved shooting in streets rather than in studios and testing the potential of deep-focus photography. The texture of *Nosferatu, the Vampire* (based on

Bram Stokers' *Dracula*) is boldly naturalistic. Superficially, Murnau's next masterpiece, *Der letzte Mann* (1925, *The Last Laugh*) could hardly be more different. *Nosferatu, the Vampire* is a perfect example of the dread-ridden German silent cinema – what the writer Lotte Eisner calls *The Haunted Screen* (the English title of her book on German silent cinema). *The Last Laugh* seems to belong to the opposite tradition, that of the minutely realistic study of everyday life based on the small-scale theatrical production, called the *Kammerspiel*, which Murnau's teacher, Reinhardt, had developed alongside his famous spectacles. Yet Murnau's story of a resplendently uniformed doorman's fall from glory is realized in images just as haunting and atmospheric as those in which he clothes his vampire tales. And Emil Jannings' performance in the principal role was also a potent factor in making the film the most universally noticed German feature of the year. It was, in fact, the immense American success of *The Last Laugh* which eventually brought both Jannings and Murnau to Hollywood.

All the resources of the Fox studios were placed at Murnau's disposal. He was able to bring over his favourite scriptwriter, Carl Mayer, to work with him on the adaptation of *The Journey to Tilsit*, Hermann Sundermann's novel about a peasant wooing. He worked completely without interference, building giant sets, shooting and reshooting until he had got just the effect he desired. The result – *Sunrise* – is really a completely German film made in America with American stars (Janet Gaynor and George O'Brien). Visually stunning and atmospherically sublime, it is constructed in a European style: the story itself remains slight, though Murnau's treatment develops it like a symphony, reaching a crescendo with the storm on the lake in which the reunited husband and wife are nearly separated for ever. *Sunrise* was greeted with critical acclaim, and went on to win all kinds of awards. But the great American public did not buy it, and this relative failure over-shadowed the progress of Murnau's two subsequent films for Fox.

The coming of sound did not help either, spreading uncertainty among the studios as to what they should do with the more expensive projects then in the works. Murnau's next film, a circus drama called *Four Devils* (1928), suffered from front-office interference. *Our Daily Bread* (1930) was begun with enormous ambition as a saga of the mid-Western grain lands, but got progressively cut down into a personal story of a city girl's problems with a hostile-seeming environment. Retitled *City Girl*, it was roughly re-edited with some talkie sequences (not by Murnau) to cash in on the new craze. Finally, though the silent version of the film contains some of the director's finest work, this was hardly noticed in the confusion of the talkies and his Hollywood career ended.

He did, however, manage to make one more film: the privately financed and evidently non-commerical *Tabu* (1930), begun in collaboration with the documentary film-maker Robert Flaherty and intended as a semi-documentary, was filmed entirely in South Sea locations with a non-professional cast of Polynesians. Lacking the documentarist's ideals, Murnau insisted on making it into a rhapsody on the theme of fated young love, as elaborately structured as any of his studio pictures. The result was a perfect swansong for the director – a hymn to natural beauty, of people and of landscape, and a triumph of aesthetic cinema. But it did not open until a few days after his death in a car accident in California, and what else he would have done – in America or Europe – remains open to intriguing speculation.

The USSR

When Lenin said 'Of all the arts the cinema is the most important', he fully intended that the cinema should provide the new revolutionary regime with its most effective weapon of agitation, propaganda and education. The cinema had certain attractions for the Bolsheviks. By the time they seized power in October 1917, the cinema was already the most popular form of entertainment in the towns and cities – the idea of the cinema therefore did not have to be 'sold' to the urban population. In the countryside it was still very much a novelty, with all the advantages which that implied, if only the industry could organize itself to provide the necessary equipment and the appropriate films. That was, however, to prove in the event a big 'if'.

The silent film was particularly attractive to the new Soviet authorities. The population, more than two-thirds illiterate, spoke a wide variety of languages. Written communication could therefore be effective only in the long run as the educational level improved, whereas the Bolsheviks were anxious to develop quickly the class consciousness of the masses. The silent film was an overwhelmingly *visual* medium – at its best, indeed, a *purely visual* medium – and was accessible to all sections of the people, while the moving image cut more deeply into the popular memory than did the poster, also widely used at that time.

Of course the silent film had its limitations: the dependence on relatively few intertitles to clarify the narrative meant that silent film plots had to remain fairly simple; but in this context such simplicity was to prove an enormous advantage. Films were first used on the agit-trains that toured the country for purposes of agitation and propaganda during the Civil War of 1918–21. These agitational shorts (*agitki*) were simple and direct. Their dynamism and economy of style were to exercise a great effect on subsequent Soviet film-making, as indeed were the people involved with them. Several of the foremost directors cut their cinematic teeth on the agit-trains. These trains distributed material from the centre to the provinces and gathered other material in the provinces to be taken back to the centre and used in future journeys. The film material gathered by them provided the content of the earliest Soviet newsreels and documentaries and also the themes for an important genre of fictional features about the Civil War.

Vital parts of the Soviet cinema network – in production, distribution and exhibition – remained in private hands until the industry was nationalized in 1919. But the problems were only just beginning: many of the private entrepreneurs fled the country, taking their equipment, their talent and their expertise with them. The ravages of war, civil war and general neglect had left studios (or 'film factories', as they were called) and cinemas in tatters, while a ban by the Western powers on the export of film stock to the Soviet Union meant that the authorities had virtually no new materials with which to make their own films.

Before the Revolution Russia had produced none of its own film materials; all stock and equipment had been imported. The Western blockade therefore dealt a particularly heavy blow to the nascent Soviet film industry. Desperation led Lenin to approve a deal with a certain Jacques Cibrario, who promptly disappeared with the money he had been given without providing the materials that had been paid for.

The disruption of war and civil war caused widespread starvation and epidemics. Hundreds of thousands died and millions more suffered. Fuel was scarce and power supplies erratic. The Russian winters increased the toll. Clearly the

Soviet cinema needed a massive injection of funds, but, equally clearly, the government had to concentrate its limited resources on the more immediate tasks of political survival. One positive step was taken: in 1919 the first State Film School was set up to train new cadres (groups of Party workers) of all sorts to people the cinema when times were better.

The advent of the New Economic Policy in 1921, with its limited return to private enterprise, provided temporary relief. The aim was to finance the restoration and development of the film industry from its own resources. Audiences were to be drawn to cinemas to see films that they were willing to pay to watch and the money that they paid was to be used to produce films that the authorities wanted them to view. Entertainment was to pay for propaganda.

Anatoli Lunacharsky who, as People's Commissar for Enlightenment, had overall responsibility for the cinema, was the architect of this policy of pragmatism. He preferred that audiences should come voluntarily to the cinema and that the propaganda should be concentrated in the newsreel. He himself was the author of several screenplays for 'psychological salon dramas', some of which provided a vehicle for his actress-wife Natalya Rozenel.

But Soviet audiences wanted to see foreign and, above all, Hollywood films. Charlie Chaplin, Buster Keaton, Harold Lloyd and, especially, Mary Pickford and Douglas Fairbanks were the staple diet of the Soviet cinemagoer during the Twenties. When Pickford and Fairbanks visited the Soviet Union in 1926, they were mobbed by fans; a feature film *Potselui Meri Pikford* (1927, *The Kiss of Mary Pickford*), from an idea by Lunacharsky himself, was made around their visit; and their comments on Sergei M. Eisenstein's *Bronenosets Potemkin* (1925, *Battleship Potemkin*) as 'the greatest film ever made' were used to relaunch the film after its disastrous first run.

By 1928 the Soviet authorities felt able to turn their attention to the political tasks of the Soviet cinema and it was in that year that the box-office receipts from Soviet films exceeded those from imported films for the first time. The new regime was now secure, even if Stalin's imagination did not always allow him to admit it, and the task of rapid industrialization that lay at the heart of the First Five Year Plan (1928–32) meant that the cinema could no longer be left to its own devices. The 'industrial revolution' was to be accompanied by a 'cultural revolution' in which the cinema's vital role was deemed to be the 'elevation of the cultural level of the masses'.

In March 1928 a Party Conference on Cinema outlined the task of the film industry and in 1929 a decree defined the responsibilities of the cadres of film workers. Despite reorganization of the industry in 1930, direct political control proved unexpectedly awkward to enforce. The attempt to impose it created its own troubles, and these were further complicated by the difficulties associated with the advent of sound and the refusal by many film-makers to recognize that sound was anything more than a passing novelty. Sound created problems in the West as well, but the by-now highly centralized organizational structure of the Soviet cinema turned those problems into nightmares.

Just as the political authorities had recognized the propaganda potential of the silent film, so a new generation of artists acclaimed the cinema as a new medium of artistic expression, as the new art form for the new epoch. Initially the political perspective merged with the artistic; but the political requirement of a medium of mass communication began to conflict with a need for artistic experiment, and the notion that here at last was an avant-garde which had the full support of the powers-that-be soon proved an illusion.

In addition to the functional attractions of the silent film, artists were drawn to the cinema as a relatively new medium untainted by a classical bourgeois tradition – unlike the theatre or literature, for instance – and with as yet untried but potentially limitless possibilities. For instance, the poet Vladimir Mayakovsky tried his hand at writing three film scenarios in 1918.

One of the leading exponents of the new art form was Lev Kuleshov (1899–1970), who has been described as the 'father of the Soviet cinema'. Like so many film directors Kuleshov came to the cinema after the Revolution and, like others too, he was astonishingly young – only 18 in October 1917. Since there was no film stock with which to make feature films, Kuleshov had to channel his energies into the establishment in 1921 of his own workshop at the new film school. Here Kuleshov and his students rehearsed films that would never be produced, the so-called 'films without film'. It was at this time that Kuleshov first developed the idea that the distinctive nature of cinema, its superiority to the theatre, lay in the principle of *montage* or editing. Experiments suggested to him that each film shot acquired meaning from its immediate context, from the shots that preceded and succeeded it on the screen and therefore in the perception of the audience. By altering the context, by placing the original shot in different sequences, the whole meaning could be transformed. This discovery, of crucial significance to the subsequent development of Soviet film theory, was to become known as the 'Kuleshov effect'.

Kuleshov acquired some experience of actual filming by travelling in the agit-trains and he used the material he collected for his agitational film *Na Krasnom Fronte* (1920, *On the Red Front*). His first fictional feature film was the remarkable satire *Neobychainye Priklyucheniya Mistera Vesta v Strane Bolshevikov* (1924, *The Extraordinary Adventures of Mr West in the Land of the Bolsheviks*), one of the most successful Soviet silent comedies. This was followed by the detective thriller *Luch Smerti* (1925, *The Death Ray*) and the more psychologically-orientated *Po Zakonu* (1926, *By the Law*), set in the Yukon during the Gold Rush. Kuleshov made three more silent films and in 1929 produced his major contribution to film theory. *Iskusstvo Kino* (The Art of the Cinema), a book still not translated in full into English.

Kuleshov's great importance goes beyond his own films, for he influenced almost every other Soviet film-maker, not only through his development of the idea of montage but also because of his attempts to encourage a new style of 'naturalistic' acting specific to cinema and in some ways resembling the stage and film director Vsevolod Meyerhold's experiments with bio-mechanics in training actors to use their bodies in the theatre.

Many of Kuleshov's ideas were taken up by a small group of very young film-makers in Petrograd (later Leningrad), led by Grigori Kozintsev, Leonid Trauberg and Sergei Yutkevich who called themselves FEKS or the Factory of the Eccentric Actor. Central to their ideas was the notion of 'impeded form': people and objects were to be portrayed in unfamiliar contexts, thus alienating the viewer in the sense, later used by the German playwright Bertolt Brecht, of forcing him to see things in a new light. Their most important films were: *Pokhozdeniya Oktyabriny* (1924, The Adventures of Oktyabrina), an anti-capitalist political allegory; *Mishka Protiv*

Top: the extraordinary dynamism and passion of Battleship Potemkin *has had a huge influence on film-makers. Above: the famous Odessa steps sequence – Tsarist militia fire on crowds cheering the mutinous sailors on the ship.*

Yudenicha (1925, Mishka versus Yudenich), a children's comedy which, in possible homage to Kuleshov, was subtitled 'The Unprecedented Adventures of Mishka the Paper-Boy Among the White Guards'; *Chertovo Koleso* (1926, *The Devil's Wheel*), a story of gangsters in Petrograd during the Civil War; *Shinel* (1926, *The Cloak*), based on Gogol's story about a poor clerk; *Bratishka* (1927, Little Brother), a comedy about a truck; *Soyuz Velikogo Dela* (1927,*The Club of the Big Deed – SVD*), concerning the Decembrist revolt in 1825 in St

Petersburg; and finally a film about the Paris Commune of 1871, *Novyi Vavilon* (1929, *New Babylon*), for which Shostakovich wrote a memorable score.

One of Kuleshov's leading actors, Vsevolod Pudovkin (1893–1953), became an important director and retained in his own films much of the balance between actor's characterization and director's editing that Kuleshov preached. Pudovkin's first feature film was *Mat* (1926, *Mother*), about a woman who is led by the example of her son into political activism; this was followed by *Konyets Sankt-Peterburga* (1927, *The End of St Petersburg*), concerning World War I and the Revolution, and *Potomok Chingis-Khana* (1928, *Storm Over Asia*), a tale of the Civil War in Mongolia. Pudovkin's films, like those of Kuleshov, were among the most popular Soviet films of the Twenties. These directors employed and built upon the techniques developed by Hollywood with which audiences were familiar: their films had a clear plot and an individual hero and villain so that audiences found them accessible and were able to identify with the message that the director and his team were trying to convey.

In fact the bulk of Soviet films of this period tried to adapt American techniques to Soviet themes — the *Miss Mend* serial (1926) is a good example — and it was these Soviet films that Soviet audiences went to see rather than the works later acclaimed as masterpieces. Two of the leading figures of this popular cinema were Fyodor Otsep (1895–1949), who directed *Zhivoi Trup* (1929, *The Living Corpse*), based on Leo Tolstoy's play, and Boris Barnet, (1902–65), who directed *Devushka s Korobkoi* (1927, *The Girl With the Hatbox*) and *Dom na Trubnoi* (1928, *The House on Trubnaya Square*), two satirical comedies. Both men were disciples of Kuleshov.

In the world-famous masterpieces, as Party activists were quick to point out, form often seemed to outweigh content, so that they were 'unintelligible to the millions'. The films of

Sergei M. Eisenstein (1898–1948) fell into this category, though the accusation of 'unintelligibility' reflected more on the accusers than the accused. Eisenstein was by no means alone among Soviet artists in thinking that a revolutionary *society* needed a revolutionary *culture* that would instil a revolutionary *consciousness* into the masses. This culture had to find new forms untainted by a bourgeois past and Eisenstein felt that the cinema was the ideal vehicle for this.

His silent films, beginning with *Stachka* (1925, *Strike*), were essentially experiments to find appropriate new forms.

Strike, instead of treating the story as subject, used images to convey the concept of 'collectivity', and the camera was allowed the greatest freedom. In the culminating sequence of the film, the slaughter of a bull is intercut to provide symbolic commentary on the slaughter of striking workers.

Eisenstein attributed the particular power of *Battleship Potemkin* to the original scenario written by Nina Agadzhanova-Shutko for the director's projected eight-episode *1905*, intended to celebrate the twentieth anniversary of the abortive 'dress-rehearsal' for the Russian Revolution. Shooting on the General Strike episode of *1905* began at the end of March in Leningrad. In August, the weather compelled Eisenstein's production unit to halt work and head south to Odessa to shoot the episode of the mutiny on the armoured cruiser *Potemkin*. Since Eisenstein's intention in shooting *1905* was 'to take the historical events just as they were and not to interfere . . . with the process as it was actually taking place', the *Potemkin* episode, absorbing the total atmosphere of the panorama of revolt, became synonymous of the whole. And so *1905* was abandoned and *Battleship Potemkin* became the work in hand. He wrote a new script (which adopted the classic five-act tragedy form) and integrated terse sub-titles to heighten the action. The climax of 'act four' was the famous seven-minute slaughter on the steps.

Traditional individual characterizations were abandoned as bourgeois relics in favour of symbolic ciphers representative of the mass and played by ordinary people who had had no training as actors. Eisenstein called this 'typage' and it was a highly stylized form of caricature. The characterization of the sailors and the middle-class people of Odessa in *Battleship Potemkin* is a good example. These figures were brought together by editing in a manner that challenged conventional narrative conceptions. In what Eisenstein described as 'intellectual montage', objects and characters were juxtaposed in a way that deliberately jarred on the audience: images commented on one another, forcing audiences out of complacent preconceptions and into a new consciousness of reality and meaning.

Eisenstein returned to Leningrad in 1926 to direct *Oktyabr* (1927, *October*) and the city where he had lived through the first eight months of the Revolution was put at his disposal. History seethes across the screen in *October* with the crowd as hero; except for Lenin, Trotsky and Kerensky, there are no individual characters in the original uncut version of the film. The powerfully reconstructed torrent of history is constantly interrupted by Eisenstein's addition of a multitude of impressions and ideas as he seeks to make his audience *think*. Suspending historical action, he weaves in a series of visual commentaries: for example, the crow pulling apart the statue of the tsar, which later jumps back together. Kerensky's rise to power as head of the provisional government in July 1917 is depicted with comic effect as explosive sub-titles indicating his ascending rank are intercut with shots of him climbing the stairs of the Winter Palace – at exactly the same pace.

An encyclopedia of imagery, *October* baffled the majority of spectators. Its release was delayed for five months when Eisenstein, who had been absorbed in his work, learned that Trotsky had fallen from power and that every shot indicating his presence in the film had to be cut.

Before starting *October*, Eisenstein had already begun its successor. *Staroye i Novoye* (1928, *The Old and the New*, sometimes known as *The General Line*), a picture of the changing Soviet village. Collectivization of farming having advanced while he was shooting *October*, he was compelled to write a new scenario. The peasant girl Marfa Lapkina, playing herself, became the first film heroine of the new Soviet society. Her evolution from oppressed farm worker to dynamic leader of her village is realized in a series of visually stunning experimental episodes. The two most famous show the awed peasants standing around a cream separator, and the astounding religious procession, where the silent images vividly suggest sound. Eisenstein, though blazing a trail in terms of artistic theory and practice, failed to appeal to the mass audience. The Party made clear its disappointment following the failure of *The Old and the New*, and Eisenstein temporarily fell from favour.

There were of course many other directors active in the Soviet cinema. One of the most famous was the Ukrainian Alexander Dovzhenko (1894–1956), maker of *Zemlya* (1930, *Earth*), whose films evoked a pastoral folkloristic idyll.

He began as scriptwriter and co-director on *Vasya Reformator* (1926, *Vasya the Reformer*), working with Danylo Demutsky, who was later to be his best cameraman. The following year came *Sumka Dipkurera* (1927, *The Diplomatic Pouch*), a spy thriller assigned to Dovzhenko's direction presumably on the strength of his experience as a fledgling diplomat abroad. But it was *Zvenigora* (1928) that really made his colleagues sit up and take notice. *Zvenigora* is founded on an elaborate pattern of legend, leaping from Viking times to a Paris theatre of the present. At its centre is a bandit and adventurer named Pavlo, who seeks the long-buried treasure of Zvenigora after responding to the tales of his grandfather. *Arsenal* (1929) was written by Dovzhenko in a fortnight, and he shot and edited it over a six-month period; he claimed:

'In making it, I set myself two tasks: to unmask reactionary Ukrainian nationalism and chauvinism, and to be the bard of the Ukrainian working class that had accomplished the social revolution.'

Like all Dovzhenko's films, it centres on death – death in the trenches, death at the barricades of a Kiev munitions factory.

Dovzhenko's next film, *Earth*, remains his most celebrated accomplishment. Youth and age join forces against the kulaks (rich peasants), the church and reactionary elements in society as crystallized in a small Ukrainian village where Vasili, a young idealist, brings the first tractor to the local farmers and tears down the fences dividing their land. The local kulaks resist the new move, fearing unity among the peasants, and one of them murders Vasili as he dances in exaltation through the village.

Earth was censured by several critics on its release for being too languorous in its conjunction of death and beauty. Harry Alan Potamkin, for example, found it *too* introspective, *too* reflective: 'The entire film has a poignancy too plaintive for its intention and sense of its theme.' Now, however, this moving poetic beauty sustains *Earth* whenever it is revived: the shots of apples and melons, ripe and sumptuous and sensual, and of the threshing machine attest to Dovzhenko's conviction that the world is more significant than the individuals who pass through it.

Dovzhenko's work did much to raise the reputation of film production to the Ukraine. There was also an active film industry in Georgia, which produced such works as *Krasniye Diavolyata* (1923, *Little Red Devils*), *Moya Babushka* (1929, *My Grandmother*) and, most notably, Mikhail Kalatozov's grim portrayal of the primitive customs and living conditions in the province of Svanetia *Sol Svanetii* (1930, *Salt for Svanetia*).

Other artists went further in their search for forms appropriate to the revolutionary Soviet cinema by denouncing fictional feature films altogether. 'The film drama is the opium of the people . . . Long live life as it is!' wrote Dziga Vertov (1896–1954). He was the leading exponent of the inherent superiority of the documentary and newsreel format, the founder and leading member of the Cine-Eye group. He had begun working with film on one of the agit-trains during the Civil War and, while editing the *Kinonedelya* (Cine-Week) newsreels in 1918–19, made three documentary films from the material that he had collected. He went on to produce the series of *Kino-Pravda* (Cine-Truth) newsreels in 1922–25, the most famous of which is the *Leninskaya Kino-Pravda* (1925, Leninist Cine-Truth) depicting the reaction to Lenin's death in 1924 and initiating themes later developed in his sound films *Tri Pesni o Lenine* (1934, *Three Songs of Lenin*) and *Kolybelnaya* (1937, Lullaby). But the most important of Vertov's silent documentaries were *Shagai, Soviet* (1926, Stride, Soviet), *Shestaya Chast Mira* (1926, *A Sixth of the Earth*), *Odinnadtsatyi* (1928, *The Eleventh Year*) and *Cheloviek s Kinoapparatom* (1929, *Man With a Movie Camera*), all depicting multifarious aspects of Soviet life with increasing virtuosity. In their manifestos the Cine-Eyes claimed to represent:

'. . . the art of organizing the necessary movements of objects in space and time into a rhythmic artistic whole, according to the characteristics of the whole and the internal rhythm of each object.'

They offered:

'Not a Pathé or a Gaumont newsreel (a newsreel of record), nor even a *Kino-Pravda* (a political newsreel), but a real Cine-Eye newsreel – a rapid survey of *visual* events interpreted by the film camera, pieces of *real* energy (as distinct from theatrical), brought by intervals to an accumulated whole by the great skill of montage.'

Through this montage the film-maker could organize 'life as it really is', improve upon it and 'see and show the world in the name of the world proletarian revolution'.

But by the end of the Twenties all this experimentation was giving way to the new orthodoxies of socialist realism. Soviet film directors initially wanted to use the new weapon of sound as an integral part of their concept of montage, with sound as counterpointing rather than merely illustrating the image; but the political situation had changed. Immersed in the world of collectivization and rapid industrialization, the Soviet cinema gradually adopted the tenets of socialist realism and attempted to 'describe not reality as it is but reality as it will be'. That became the clearly defined task of the Soviet cinema in the next decade.

France

At the time of the Armistice in 1918, the French national spirit was at a low ebb and French cinema was suffering one of its most severe creative crises. One man, Louis Delluc (1890–1924), did more to restore the quality of French film at this time than any other. He did so – much like François Truffaut and Jean-Luc Godard forty years later – by first writing the most trenchant criticism of his generation, and then putting his theories into practice on the screen.

As early as 1917, Delluc had been attacked for being too effusive in his praise of American movies. He admired the work of Thomas H. Ince and especially Charles Chaplin and D.W. Griffith. Delluc extolled the simplicity of Chaplin's art – a directness of appeal and imagery, the roots of which could be traced back to the conventions of medieval painting.

His view of French film was more disenchanted. He felt that Louis Feuillade, the master of the serial, had plunged into decline after 1914, and suggested that the French had no gift for the action cinema that was so brilliantly dominated by the Americans. Instead he thought they ought to return to the lack of self-consciousness and the lack of artifice practised by Lumière and his disciples, saying that it was through the straightforward depiction of reality, such as great events and natural phenomena, that 'the artisan finds the path to art'.

He and the directors whose work he did admire (Abel Gance, Germaine Dulac and Jean Epstein among them) looked eagerly at the Swedish films of Victor Sjöström and Mauritz Stiller with their use of natural locations and their unassuming decor. 'The French cinema must be *cinema*, the French cinema must be *French*!' was the exhortation that Delluc had printed on the masthead of his magazine *Cinéa*.

Delluc's best writings were quickly collected and issued in book form – *Cinéma et Cie*, *Photo-génie*, *Charlot* and *La Jungle du Cinéma*. He wrote eight screenplays, all but one of which he directed himself, between 1919 and 1923. His first script was for Germaine Dulac's *La Fête Espagnole* (1919, The Spanish Fête), a torrid story of the rivalry of two men for the same wayward woman. Ironically this wealthy temptress runs off with yet another admirer, while the two original adversaries proceed to dispose of each other in a duel.

Le Silence (1920, Silence), Delluc's first film as solo director, was described at the time as 'a monologue in images' concerning a man who is overwhelmed by remorse for having killed his wife. The film itself has vanished apart from a handful of tantalizing production stills.

His next film, *Fièvre* (1921, Fever), was, according to the cinema historian Georges Sadoul, the best directed by Delluc. The emphasis was on atmosphere rather than plot, and the photography established an impressionist mood with its welter of close-ups and revealing glimpses of dingy bars.

Although Delluc coined the word cinéaste, and now has the reputation of a somewhat fastidious aesthete, his own films sought a wide public. He acknowledged the commercial pressures and exigencies that marched side by side with the art of the film.

Eve Francis, his actress wife, starred in the majority of Delluc's films, and imposed herself on his best work, *La Femme de Nulle Part* (1922, Woman from Nowhere). This perfectly-wrought tale of persuasion and lost youth is striking for its use of natural landscape and for Delluc's startlingly sophisticated deployment of flashback. Inspired by Sjöström's *Karin Ingmarsdotter* (1920, God's Way), Delluc's final film was *L'Inondation* (1923, The Flood), in which a river floods the surrounding countryside. Delluc made his river the Rhône as it passes through the Vaucluse district, and his film excels in physical and bucolic detail.

On March 22, 1924, Delluc died, heavily in debt and overcome by the ravages of tuberculosis. He was only 33, and yet he had created a legendary name for himself. He should now be praised for his pioneer work in deep-focus cinematography, intercutting and the control of narrative structure in general. He also helped to introduce the idea of the cine club or 'film society' in France and arranged the first screening in Paris of *Das Cabinet des Dr Caligari* (1919, *The Cabinet of Dr Caligari*). The Prix Louis Delluc, awarded annually to the best French film, perpetuates his attainments. His ideas were carried on in the films of his (not very gifted) disciple Germaine Dulac and, to an extent, in the narrative-based work of Jean Epstein, Abel Gance and Marcel L'Herbier. Epstein, a theorist too, tried his hand at commercial features but was at his best in his dreamlike, Surrealist-influenced *La Chute de la Maison Usher* (1928, *The Fall of the House of Usher*), a version of Edgar Allan Poe's tale, and his sparse, eloquent documentaries of life in the fishing villages of Brittany, such as *Finis Terrae* (1929, The End of the Earth).

Abel Gance (1889–1981) was one of the few French film-makers Delluc consistently praised. Gance's *La Folie du Docteur Tube* (1915, The Madness of Dr Tube) has been called the first purely experimental film. Gance and Léonce-Henry Burel, the cameraman who worked with him throughout the silent period, used distorting mirrors to such remarkable effect that the bewildered Louis Nalpas (head of Le Film d'Art), considered that whatever the film was about it was not wartime entertainment, and refused to release it.

Discouraged, Gance bided his time and by turning out standard melodramas regained his producers' confidence. In 1917 he was given the chance to direct his first major film, *Mater Dolorosa* (Sorrowful Mother). Superficially a tearful bourgeois melodrama which would have been at home in any of the boulevard theatres of the day, the film easily transcends the genre. Richly mounted, and beautifully photographed by Burel, *Mater Dolorosa* is the work of a director totally involved with his material, caring enormously for his characters, and believing passionately in his medium.

Mater Dolorosa and its successor *La Dixième Symphonie* (1918, The Tenth Symphony) were critical and commercial successes. In the latter, Gance's old frend Séverin-Mars played opposite Emmy Lynn. His presence would be crucial in the two masterpieces that were to follow.

During the production of *La Dixième Symphonie* Gance was planning his great pacifist film *J'Accuse* (1918, I Accuse). He had been briefly mobilized into the cinematograph section of the army, but was soon discharged. When Charles Pathé – despite monetary difficulties at Le Film d'Art – gave him permission to go ahead with his project regardless of cost, Gance rejoined the cinematograph section to film at the front. With the making of *J'Accuse*, the two sides of Abel Gance were combined for the first time: the film-maker provided spectacular crowd scenes, telling close-ups and even a split-

Left: Alban (Philippe Hériat) is confronted by his fiancée (Ginette Maddie, standing) and his real love (Eve Francis) in L'Inondation. *Far left: a line drawing of Louis Delluc, whose writings on film were innovative and outspoken, and whose own films were both technically advanced and commercially successful. Below far left: distorting mirrors and trick photography were used to startling effect in* La Folie du Docteur Tube. *Below: the war dead in* J'Accuse.

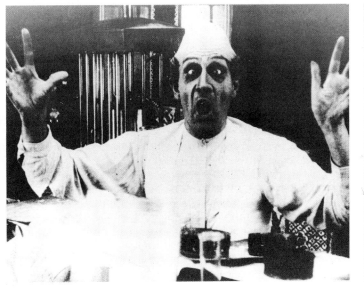

screen effect foreshadowing *Napoléon* (1927, *Napoleon*); the visionary writer, in collaboration with Blaise Cendrars (who had lost an arm in the war and had experienced all its horror), provided a script startling in its scope and intensity.

In *La Roue* (1923, The Wheel) a love story is the framework for much wider concerns. Sisif, an engine driver, and his son Elie both love Norma, a girl whom Sisif rescued from a train wreck when she was a child and brought up as his own daughter. Believing this, Norma marries another man, and the desperation of Sisif and Elie leads to tragedy. But the railway is the soul of the film. Gance constructed Sisif's house among the marshalling yards at Nice, and the smoke, dirt and din are an ever-present background. Much of the drama takes place on Sisif's engine, and Gance used rapid cutting as never before, creating a musical rhythm reinforced by a score from the composer Arthur Honegger. The film became a symbolist poem with the imagery of the wheel dominating. At the end, as Sisif quietly dies in a hut in the mountains, the villages below form a round dance – the final symbol – and it is clear that the wheel of the title is the wheel of Fate, that Sisif's suffering has from the beginning moved toward this ordained end.

On January 17, 1925, at the Billancourt studios in Paris, Abel Gance began filming *Napoleon*. He planned six long films covering the entire life of the Emperor. The first film, ending with Napoleon's invasion of Italy, was ready for release early in 1927. On April 7 came the triumphant first showing at the Paris Opéra, with two triple-screen sequences and a score by Arthur Honegger.

No film ever involved its audience more intensely. Others before Gance had set the camera free from constraint. Gance did more. He endowed the camera with a dynamic life of its own. For the pursuit across Corsica it was strapped to the back of a horse. Hand-held in the snowball battle at Brienne, it is a combatant, pelted but victorious. Swinging on a giant pendulum over the storm at sea and the storm in the Convention, it rocks in a dizzying frenzy. If the camera is a magical presence, the editing of the images which that camera caught is more astonishing still. Not only is there the intensely rapid cutting which Gance had introduced in *La Roue*; there are the three simultaneous images of the triptych (now reduced to one sequence, for in a time of despair Gance destroyed those of the storm in the Convention, and the Bal des Victimes, which had been added in 1928, leaving only that of the march into Italy); and there are multiple-image effects, employing in the fight in the dormitory up to nine divisions of the screen. Incredibly, all this was done by eye alone, laboriously matching and cutting without the aid of an editing machine.

The triptych of Italy works supremely well. Sometimes the action spreads unbroken across all three screens. Sometimes the central image is balanced by contrasting or complementary images on the outer screens. Often the left-hand screen carries a mirror image of the right. Gance said that the centre was prose, the wings poetry, the whole was cinema. And so it proves.

It would be wrong, however, to see *Napoleon* as entirely a display of new forms and new sensations. The quieter moments are as rewarding in their way: the gentle comedy of Napoleon's embarrassed courtship, the lovely invention (if invention it is) of the document-eaters who eat suspects' files and so save them from the guillotine, the trial of character in Italy between the new commander and the old generals, the sidelong view of the Revolution from Napoleon's obscure

Left: Albert Dieudonné magnificent in his embodiment of Napoleon. *Below: Jacques Feyder directs* The Kiss, *with Greta Garbo as a wife accused of killing her husband. Right:* Les Deux Timides, *a showcase of René Clair's technical skill. Below right: 'Once upon a time' a title reads; a man sharpens a razor and slits the eye of a young woman. So begins the Surrealist masterpiece* Un Chien Andalou.

window and, above all, everything that concerns the girl Violine, played by Annabella with such surpassing tenderness. These by themselves would have made Gance's film a masterwork.

At that high point, fate turned against Gance. With the coming of sound, no-one was interested in his achievements or his innovations. The film was shown in full in only eight European cities; in America, and in Europe too, after the first runs, shorter and increasingly travestied versions were the only ones available. Film historians came to speak of the piece as a monumental fiasco. What was on view bore them out. Of the five remaining parts, only the last, concerning Napoleon on St Helena, was ever made, and that by another hand. The respected Romanian director Lupu Pick filmed *Napoleon auf St Helena* (Napoleon in Saint Helena) in Germany, from Gance's script, in 1929. Gance's first sound film, *La Fin du Monde* (1930, The End of the World) was so savagely mutilated by the producers that he disowned it. He never again enjoyed full creative freedom.

Like many film-makers of his generation, Marcel L'Herbier (1890–1979) started off with avant-garde leanings. These were mainly evident in the decors and visual effects of early films such as *Rose France* (1919) and *Eldorado* (1921). *L'Inhumaine* (1924, *Futurism*) the less-than-convincing story of a *femme fatale* (Georgette Leblanc) and a scientist (Jacques Catelain), featured the eclectic designs of Alberto Cavalcanti, the art-deco architect Robert Mallet-Stevens and the painter

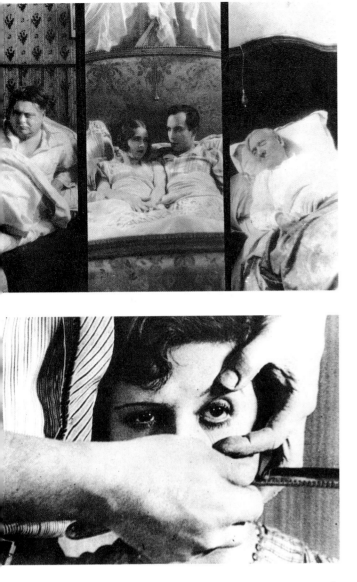

In 1922 Feyder made *Crainquebille* (*Ole Bill of Paris*), a daring and imaginative screen version of the introspective novel by Anatole France. Feyder subsequently appeared to become over-dependent on literary sources for his films. *Gribiche* (1925), *Carmen* (1926) and *Thérèse Raquin* (1928, *Thou Shalt Not*) were all anchored by the weight of their original novels in an aura of respectability and a kind of airless realism. *Gribiche* at least confirmed Feyder's marvellous flair for directing children, its story following the fortunes of a working-class boy 'adopted' by a rich woman and removed from the surroundings he knows and loves. This talent had first been revealed in *Visages d'Enfants* (1925, *Faces of Children*), shot, in a remote Swiss village during a three-month schedule in 1923, with considerable sensitivity and documentary awareness on the part of Feyder (and of his wife, the actress Françoise Rosay, who took over as director for two weeks in his absence).

In 1928, having completed the script of *Gardiens de Phare* (1929, *Lighthouse Keepers*), for the promising young director Jean Grémillon (1901–59), Feyder accepted the offer of a contract from MGM. It was the first such invitation extended to a French director since World War I, and Feyder travelled to Culver City, accompanied by his wife, with high hopes; but no major project evolved for several months. Finally came *The Kiss* (1929), featuring Greta Garbo as a murderess, in her last silent role. The two émigrés enjoyed working together, and Feyder also directed Garbo in both the German and the Swedish versions of *Anna Christie* (1930). Emil Jannings, F.W. Murnau and Ludwig Berger were also friends of the Feyders. But by 1932 the honeymoon was over. Feyder could no longer tolerate the attitude of the MGM management and returned to Paris early in 1933.

During the Twenties, other film-makers, or artists who had become interested in the cinema, became ambitious to escape traditional narrative modes altogether. One way of achieving this was through abstraction, and the French avant-garde during the decade threw up an important example, *Ballet Mécanique* (1924, *Mechanical Ballet*), a collaboration between the painter Fernand Léger and the American modernist artist Dudley Murphy. Its assembly of images seems wholly arbitrary – much of it abstract movement of gears, pendulums and the like – but the film culminates in long-shots of a working woman laboriously making her way up a flight of steps only to be repeatedly thrust back to climb and reclimb the same stairs. This sequence was credited with special social significance.

More numerous, more productive, and finally more influential were those film-makers more or less directly connected with Surrealism. At the time there were Surrealists, Dadaists, and people like Jean Cocteau who considered themselves violently opposed to Surrealism and everything it stood for. Films like *La Coquille et le Clergyman* (1927, *Seashell and the Clergyman*), directed by Germaine Dulac from a scenario by Antonin Artaud, the influential theorist of theatre, and Cocteau's cinematic debut *Le Sang d'un Poète* (1930, *The Blood of a Poet*) were regarded by their creators as anti-Surrealist. Today these works appear to resemble rather than differ radically from the 'true' Surrealism of Salvador Dalí and Luis Buñuel in *Un Chien Andalou* (1928) and the Dadaist knockabout comedy of such early René Clair films as *Paris Qui Dort* (1923, *The Crazy Ray*) and *Entr'acte* (1924).

Paris Qui Dort was the experimental first film of René Clair (1898–1981). It describes the delightful chaos that ensues when a maniac scientist sends the whole of Paris to sleep by

Fernand Léger – who designed the interior of the scientist's laboratory in 'Cubist' style. The film failed commercially, but L'Herbier had more success with *Feu Mathias Pascal* (1925, *The Late Mathias Pascal*), based on a Luigi Pirandello novel about a man wrongly believed to be dead. The work's Italian setting was attractively evoked in the sets of Cavalcanti and Lazare Meerson, and the film contained persuasive performances by the Russian actor Ivan Mozhukhin (known as Mosjoukine in France) as Mathias and Michel Simon in his first major role. Unfortunately the commercial failure of L'Herbier's ambitious Zola adaptation, *L'Argent* (1928, *Money*), which sacrificed social comment for elaborate camera acrobatics, ended his career as a director with serious, artistic pretensions. Henceforth he worked on commercial assignments and from the mid-Fifties in television. He is now best remembered for having founded France's most famous film school, the Institut des Hautes Etudes Cinematographiques (IDHEC), in 1943.

A more successful director, who nonetheless shared L'Herbier's literary predilections was Belgian-born Jacques Feyder (1885–1948). Early in 1916 he began directing for Gaumont churning out over a dozen films, mostly shorts, before being claimed for army service (mostly fulfilled with a theatrical troupe) from 1917 to 1919. In 1920 Feyder embarked on his first major movie, *L'Atlantide* (1921). Feyder insisted on going to the Sahara on location for this haunting fantasy, featuring the dancer Stacia Napierkowska.

Far left: riding through the Bois de Vincennes on his wedding day, Fadinard (Albert Préjean) is involved in an embarrassing incident when his horse nibbles The Italian Straw Hat *belonging to a young married woman who is in the bushes with her lover. Left: Catherine Hessling, Jean Renoir's first wife, dances in* Nana.

means of an infernal ray, and was only released in the wake of Clair's most celebrated silent film, *Entr'acte* (1924). A short of just 22 minutes, this film was prepared as an intermission entertainment for *Relâche*, a ballet by the multi-talented artist Francis Picabia. *Entr'acte* is not the satire that Clair perhaps intended it to be, for its notions and impulses are flung in all directions to create a torrent of images (including one worthy of Busby Berkeley, with the camera gazing up through a glass floor at the thighs of a ballet dancer). Several influential artists of the time participated in *Entr'acte*, among them Man Ray and Marcel Duchamp, as well as the composers Erik Satie and Georges Auric. Clair pressed on with his avant-gardiste efforts. But *Le Voyage Imaginaire* (1925, The Imaginary Voyage) was a flop. Intended as a tribute to Méliès, whose short films were then being dragged from obscurity, *Le Voyage Imaginaire* lacked zest and rhythm. *Un Chapeau de Paille d'Italie* (1927, The Italian Straw Hat) remains Clair's most successful film of the Twenties, although its source – a slice of vaudeville written by Eugène Labiche and Marc Michel – provided the director with a solid matrix from which he could build his effervescent gags.

In 1928, Clair continued to indulge his enthusiasm for the Parisian landscape with a short documentary on the Eiffel Tower, *La Tour* (The Tower). *Les Deux Timides* (1928, The Bashful Pair) was, like *The Italian Straw Hat*, based on a play by Labiche and Michel, but its parody of the police thriller did not quite come up to expectations. Still fighting against the introduction of sound ('It is the death of the film', he exclaimed to the American critic Harry Alan Potamkin during an interview on the set), Clair summoned up all his visual ingenuity to entertain the public, including the clever use of stills and frozen frames. As it turned out, the early sound years were to provide Clair with his period of greatest success.

Several of L'Herbier's, Epstein's, Feyder's and Clair's best films were made by a small Russian-émigré company, Albatros, run by the producer Alexander Kamenka. The original émigré group included the actor Mozhukhin, his co-star and (for a time) wife, Natalia Lissenko, the producer Josef Yermoliev, the directors Alexander Volkov, Victor Tourjansky and (briefly) Yakov Protazanov, and several more. This group began to break up soon after reaching Paris in 1920 and fell apart within a few years, though only Protazanov returned to the USSR. With Kamenka as producer and Volkov as director, Mozhukhin played the great English Shakespearian actor Edmund Kean in *Kean, ou Désordre et Génie* (1924, *Kean*), adapted from an Alexandre Dumas play. Mozhukhin also starred in, wrote and (with Volkov) co-

directed *Le Brasier Ardent* (1923, *Infatuation*), a detective fantasy. But the most original film by a Russian director was made independently under almost amateur conditions. This was Dmitri Kirsanov's *Ménilmontant* (1924), an atmospheric tale of two sisters who come to erotic grief in a Parisian suburb. It starred Kirsanov's then wife, Nadia Sibirskaia (born plain Jeanne Brunet in France), who was to grace several Renoir films in the Thirties, notably *Le Crime de Monsieur Lange* (1935, *The Crime of Monsieur Lange*).

In the Twenties, Jean Renoir (1894–1979) was in the process of discovering his characteristic style and themes. Early in his career, Renoir demonstrated that the vocation of cinematography lay in fantasy, even science fiction (*Charleston*, 1927), bending plots and characters to fit the conventions of fantasy. So the heroine of *La Fille de l'Eau* (1924, *The Whirlpool of Fate*), recklessly takes refuge in escapist daydreaming to console herself for the indignities of everyday life, as does the main character in *La Petite Marchande d'Allumettes* (1928, The Little Match Girl). In the same way *Nana* (1926) is firmly ensconced in a self-made woman's mythomania, while *Marquitta* (1927), a humble street-singer, imagines she is a grand-duchess. As for the madcap soldiers of *Tire au Flanc* (1928, Skiver), their substitute for the dull routine of the barracks is rowdyism, irreverence, wrangling, lechery and finally a wild bacchanalia.

Renoir claimed that he had only embarked on a career as a film-maker in order to make a star of his wife, Catherine Hessling, his father's former model. Ironically, it was only after he parted from her in 1930 and began to make sound films that he started to move to the forefront of French mainstream production.

French Documentaries

The Twenties and Thirties saw the creation of a small subgenre, the city symphony cycle. The ebb and flow of city life over a 24-hour time-span encouraged the editing of innumerable scenes into some kind of visual 'symphony'. Alberto Cavalcanti, a Brazilian working in Paris, produced the first major film in this field, *Rien que les Heures* (1926, Nothing But the Hours), which observed the passage of one day in Paris. There are many moments of commentary: a shot of a steak cuts into a slaughterhouse; at the very beginning of the film, a view of beautiful women descending a staircase – as if out of a Hollywood extravaganza – becomes a freeze-frame, and hands tear up the picture, tossing the pieces on to a real street. But Cavalcanti's film expresses a belief that the city has a life of its own and a history, in which individual thoughts and social movements are like passing phases. More cheerful still was Marcel Carné's first film *Nogent, Eldorado du Dimanche* (1929, Nogent, Sunday Eldorado), a movie essay on Parisians going to a weekend pleasure spot on the river.

Particularly memorable among the city films, however, is Jean Vigo's *A Propos de Nice* (1930, On the Subject of Nice), made by a young photographer who knew his life would be cut short by tuberculosis, and whose family history had been tragic. Vigo went to work in Nice for the sake of his health and was immediately struck by the extraordinary visual contrasts he saw there. The wealth, self-indulgence and excesses of egotism among the upper-class residents and visitors wintering in the pleasure city – or retiring to await death in supreme comfort – was in violent contrast with the poverty and deprivation of life in the slums. The spring ritual of the Battle of Flowers, in which youth celebrates and parades with huge, ugly caricature-effigies, is paralleled by the hideous splendour of the cemeteries for the rich, with their elaborate monuments to the undeserving dead. Using a semi-concealed camera to snatch revealing portraits of the decaying, aged citizens on the seafront, Vigo made a film of aesthetic protest that secured his lasting fame and established him as a professional film-maker. *A Propos de Nice* owed everything to the cine clubs that received it so enthusiastically. It crossed the borderline between the purely aesthetic documentaries of the Twenties and those of social comment characteristic of the years before World War II.

The Rest of the World

Austria, the gateway to Eastern Europe, first saw the Lumière Cinématographe on March 20, 1896, in Vienna, and around 1898 Karl Juhasz established a touring cinema. Five years later a permanent cinema opened in the Prater amusement park, and by 1910 the capital contained ten movie houses whose programmes consisted primarily of imported shorts. Count Alexander Kolowrat founded his Sascha-Filmfabrik studio in Pfraumberg in 1910, and in 1916 erected the first Austrian purpose-built studio in the Viennese suburb of Sievering.

With the coming of the Armistice, the Austrian cinema sprang forward. New studios were built, production companies mushroomed, and Kolowrat and his colleagues produced as many as a hundred films a year. The favourite genre was the epic; great overblown films emerged, such as *Sodom und Gomorrha* (1922, Sodom and Gomorrah) and *Die Sklavenkönigin* (1924, *The Moon of Israel*), adapted from a novel by H. Rider Haggard. But the stakes were too high – companies foundered, directors emigrated. Austria made a major contribution to the German silent cinema; talented émigrés included the actors Willi Forst and Walter Slezak, the writer Ladislaus Vajda and the director Robert Wiene – who returned after the triumph of *Das Cabinet des Dr Caligari* (1919, *The Cabinet of Dr Caligari*) to make the excellent *Orlacs Hände* (1925, *The Hands of Orlac*).

Neighbouring Hungary was dominated by Austro-Hungarian imperial traditions, and the cinema was soon popular throughout the country – there were 270 movie theatres in existence by 1912. In the same year, the first Hungarian studio was erected, a glass hall measuring 50 metres in length and 25 metres in width. The race to screen the first all-Hungarian film drama was won on September 14, 1912 by Ödön Uher's *Nóvérek* (Sisters), closely followed on October 14, 1912 by the more prestigious and artistic *Mae és Holnap* (Today and Tomorrow), directed by Mihály Kertész – who would later be known to Hollywood as Michael Curtiz.

The most prolific and significant of the talents to emerge in Hungary during the war period was Sándor Korda, who would become Sir Alexander Korda. In partnership with the producer Móricz Miklós Pásztory. Korda took over Corvin, a company to which he attracted several skilled writers to adapt major works of literature to the screen. Kertész, on the other hand, pressed forward with adventure and crime movies, scorning the literary genre. After completing 47 films in Hungary, he emigrated to Vienna in 1918. And as the 'White Terror' raged during the counter-revolutionary period following the brief months of Communist rule, Korda too left the country in 1919.

Poland did not enjoy a national identity, nor did it escape Russian domination, until 1918. But a favourite local comedian, Antoni Fertner, starred in *Antoś Pierwszy Raz w Warszawie* (Antoś' First Time in Warsaw) as early as 1908, and within a few years production companies were active, even if the first studio was not established until 1920. Therefore anti-Russian and anti-German films predominated, with the director Aleksander Hertz to the fore. During the Twenties, some ten to fifteen films were completed annually.

Czechoslovakia was among the first Eastern European countries to see the Lumière presentations, but local production was slow to develop. When it did, a strong folkloric tradition was immediately apparent, drawing on Bohemian and Slovak legends and ballads. Perhaps the most celebrated was *Jánošík* (1921), the story of an eighteenth-century highwayman, twice remade since. Gustav Machatý, later to achieve celebrity for Hedy Lamarr's nude scene in *Extase* (1933, *Ecstasy*), struck a fine note with *Kreutzerova Sonáta* (1926, The Kreutzer Sonata) and *Erotikon* (1928).

To the distant north, Finland was pursuing a more energetic course. In 1907, *Salaviinanpolttajat* (The Moonshiners) caused a stir as the first story film produced in Helsinki, and *Sylvi* (1913) aroused controversy with its fierce criticism of social conditions of the time. Erkki Karu was the oustanding talent, directing such comedies as *Kun Isällä on Hammassärky* (1923, When Father Has Toothache) and *Nummisuutarit* (1923, The Village Shoemakers); however most other Finnish films of the period remained plodding and ponderous.

The first Spanish film was made in Barcelona in 1900 by Fructuoso Gelabert, and showed a group of workers leaving their factory, in the style of the Lumière short *La Sortie des Usines* (1895, Leaving the Factory). Barcelona remained the centre of early Spanish cinema, and several documentaries devoted to bullfighting emerged, as well as a dramatic film on the subject, *Sangre y Arena* (1916, Blood and Sand), based on the novel by Vicente Blasco-Ibáñez. After World War I, and in a mood of national despondency brought on by the defeat in Morocco in 1921, the Spanish cinema succumbed to French and American imports, although Luis Buñuel established the first Spanish film society in Madrid in the early Twenties.

By 1897 Japanese audiences were aware of both the Vitascope and the inventions of the Lumière brothers. But Japan's own early silent cinema was dominated by the presence of the *benshi* – commentators who sat beside the screen narrating the story at each showing. This tradition stemmed from the Kabuki theatre, as did the female impersonator (*oyama*); and another stage inheritance that marked the movies was that of the *shimpa*, a romantic form of the Meiji era (1868–1912). In 1913 Shozo Makino, a producer-director, joined with the actor Matsunoke Onove to make the first of several versions of *Chushingura* (The Loyal 47 Ronin), and four years later animated cartoons began to emerge from the fledgling studios. In the early Twenties, three major directors made their debuts: Kenji Mizoguchi, Teinosuke Kinugasa and Yasujiro Ozu. Kinugasa's *Kurutta Ippeiji* (1926, *A Page of Madness*) and *Jujiro* (1928, *Crossroads*) were among two of the finest Japanese silent productions. But in 1923 an earthquake devastated most of the Tokyo studios and the industry had to start again.

In China on August 11, 1896, less than a year after the first Lumière screenings in Paris, Shanghai put on a performance of the new art, but Peking did not come into contact with the cinema until 1902. The first true Chinese film was, however, shot in Peking; *Dingjun shan* (1905, Dingjun Mountain), based on an opera story. A crucial landmark was the first feature film *Nanfu nanqi* (1912, A Nice Couple), directed by Zhang Shichuan and Zheng Zhengqiu, which satirized the feudal marriage practices still prevalent in China. The industry started to expand dramatically, and between 1915 and 1931, some three hundred features were produced in thirteen cities, notably Hongkong and Shanghai.

In India, at Watson's Hotel in Bombay in July 1896, the ubiquitous Lumière package was screened. Early in the new century, entrepreneurs like Jamjetji Framji Madan and Abdulally Esoofally used massive tents in which to show French and American shorts. Dadasaheb Phalke determined to rival these foreign film-makers, and travelled assiduously to gather knowledge and equipment. His first major film was *Raja Harischandra* (1913, King Harischandra) and was followed by around a hundred other productions during the next twenty years. Inventive, lively, extravagant, Phalke's talent coloured the early development of Indian cinema. Other interesting film pioneers included Dhiren Ganguly, Debaki Kumar Bose, Chandulal J. Shah and a German named Franz Osten who worked on several major German-Indian co-productions – for instance, as co-director of *Prem Sanyas* (1926, *Light of Asia*) and director of *Prapanch Pash* (1930, *A Throw of the Dice*). Ironically, the Indian industry, which is today the most prolific in the world, was as late as the mid-Twenties dominated by foreign product – and only about fiteen per cent of all films screened in India were domestically made.

Although the major flowering of South American cinema occurred after World War II, the continent boasts a complex and multi-faceted history of movies going right back to the first years of the century. Production in Brazil, for example, exceeded two hundred films a year in 1909 and 1910, while the Argentinian pioneer Max Glücksmann established a vast network of theatres in Uruguay and Chile as well as his own country. The first noteworthy Argentinian feature was *Nobleza Gaucho* (1915, Gaucho Nobility), directed by Eduardo Martínez de la Pera and Ernesto Gunche. A personality who would dominate the Thirties, José Agustin Ferreyra, made his mark in 1917 with *El Tango de la Muerte* (The Tango of Death).

Brazil remained the prime market for European films in the early part of the century, and not until the late Twenties did American cinema gain a dominant hold. Local film-makers concentrated on producing newsreels (immensely popular in Brazil) and fiction films influenced by local theatrical tradition. José Medina is regarded as the most vital pioneer of entertainment films in Brazil, and worked from studios in São Paulo.

Australia's first film, a horse-racing newsreel of the 1896 *Melbourne Cup*, was made by a Frenchman, Marius Sestier. Four years later, also in Melbourne, the Salvation Army made

Soldiers of the Cross (1900), at about 3000 feet (915m) probably the longest film anywhere in the world at the time. Even longer was *The Story of the Kelly Gang* (1906), possibly over 5000 feet (1520m). Other bushranger films followed the Ned Kelly epic, including *Robbery Under Arms* (1907), and the convict days up to 1850 were re-enacted in such films as *For the Term of His Natural Life* (1908).

The major film-maker of the silent era was Raymond Longford, an English seaman who had come ashore to act in, direct and produce movies – often in collaboration with Lottie Lyell, a talented screenwriter who was also one of Australia's first film stars. Longford's early films were all one- or two-reelers, and were each shot within a couple of days. Among them were *The Fatal Wedding* (1911), *The Tide of Death, Trooper Campbell, Taking His Chance* (all 1912), *The Silence of Dean Maitland* (1914), *A Maori Maid's Love, The Mutiny of the Bounty* (both 1916) and *The Woman Suffers* (1918). His crowning glory was *The Sentimental Bloke* (1918), adapted from a best-selling book of colloquial verse by C.J. Dennis and concerning the adventures of a man released from jail. Generally considered a classic of Australian silent cinema, the film had a successful run in London and English provincial theatres. Longford's last film of note was a version of the popular Australian rural comedy *On Our Selection* (1920). His films of the Twenties fell below the standard of his previous work, and he failed to make the transition to talkies. Lottie Lyell had meanwhile died prematurely in 1925. Tragically he met with financial trouble and finished his life working as a nightwatchman on a wharf in Sydney.

Other early film-makers included Franklyn Barrett and Beaumont Smith, known as 'One-take Beau' because he shot his low-budget productions so rapidly. World War I brought a rash of patriotic films; the best two were made by an American actor, Fred Niblo, better known a decade later for directing MGM's *Ben-Hur* (1925). The only notable documentarist was Captain Frank Hurley, who filmed Australian troops in action in France. He had previously been with Sir Ernest Shackleton's disastrous South Pole expedition of 1912, and his *In the Grip of the Polar Ice* (1917) was a great success, as was his New Guinea documentary feature, *Pearls and Savages* (1921). However, two dramatic features made in New Guinea for Stoll of London did not match the brilliance of his documentaries.

In 1927 Australasian Films imported American actors and technicians in an attempt to establish an Australian 'Hollywood' in Sydney. Their remake of *For the Term of His Natural Life* (1927) succeeded; but the Fiji-made *The Adorable Outcast* (1928) was a dismal flop, and the experiment ended.

Two indigenous Australian film-makers emerged towards the end of the silent era, Charles Chauvel and Ken G. Hall; but they had to await the coming of sound before making their mark on the Australian and international scene.

Top right: abnormality is conjured up in several hallucinatory sequences seen through the eyes of lunatic asylum inmates in Kinugasa's A Page of Madness. *Bottom right: Raymond Longford's 1916 film of the famous mutiny. Top far right: a scene from* Light of Asia, *a German–Indian co-production, with Himansu Rai and Sita Devi (seated left and right respectively) on a resplendent elephant. Far right centre: a shoot-out in the 1906 Australian film,* The Story of the Kelly Gang. *Far right bottom: Frank Hurley went deep into the head-hunting region of New Guinea, parts of which had never before been seen by Europeans, and returned with* Pearls and Savages, *an outstanding documentary feature.*

CHAPTER 6

The Twenties and the End of the Silents

The war had crippled the European picture business, but the same period witnessed the emergence of an American film industry. Hollywood was about to become the cultural centre of the world's popular imagination, the factory that merged the two American ideals of making real money and chasing fantastic happiness without a tremor of inconsistency. Between 1912 and 1919, important changes occurred in America. The Motion Picture Patents Company failed in its attempt to dominate the mass of small companies engaged in picture production, film exchanges and exhibition. Those companies and individuals most resistant to the Patents Company monopoly were among those who moved westwards and began to organize an industry to their own liking. Incidentally, they discovered cheap real estate, lower labour costs, lax local laws, a convenient variety of locations and 300 days' sunshine a year. D W. Griffith, following the lead of films imported from Europe, demonstrated that audiences could and would remain concentrated on a 'photoplay' lasting more than 30 minutes. This level of audience involvement was greatly encouraged by the promotion of 'star' careers and by the building of movie theatres, more comfortable than the converted shops, arcade parlours and tent shows that had been common places of exhibition before 1914.

There were landmarks in time and place. In 1911, the Nestor company opened a studio in Hollywood itself. Two years later, Cecil B. DeMille found a barn near Hollywood and Vine, and shot *The Squaw Man* (1913) there. In 1915, Carl Laemmle built Universal in the San Fernando Valley and Mack Sennett worked out of the Keystone studio in Edendale. In 1918 Samuel Goldwyn moved from New Jersey to Culver City, taking over studios built by Thomas H. Ince. Most pictures were still under an hour, and land remained a bargain. Chaplin put up his own studio on North La Brea in 1918 for $35,000.

The turning point was 1919–20. Loew's, Inc. was set up in 1919, a chain of exhibition outlets enriched by a $9 million bank loan and urged forward by Marcus Loew's decision to buy the Metro company, which he acquired in 1920. It was in 1919 that Louis B. Mayer moved his new production company to Los Angeles, having set it up with the profits earned in distribution in New England. A few years later, Metro, the Goldwyn Company (without Goldwyn himself) and Mayer merged and the pattern of the industry was set: a West Coast production factory, led by Mayer and Irving Thalberg (who

Left: Rudolph Valentino – here with Vilma Banky in his last film, The Son of the Sheik *– was the decade's supreme male romantic idol at the time of his sudden death in 1926.*

had been hired by Carl Laemmle in 1919, when he was only 20); and a New York base of film distribution, theatre-owning and fund-raising, controlled by Loew and later Nicholas Schenck. Paramount went the same way. With Jesse Lasky, and then B.P. Schulberg, running production in Los Angeles, Adolph Zukor ruled from New York, raising another huge bank loan in 1919 to buy and build more theatres.

It was in the early Twenties that most of the great movie palaces were conceived and constructed. Their extravagance and decoration reflect the helpless profitability of the business. They also manifest the vulgar but heartfelt belief of the new moguls that their profession was using science, art and 'spirituality' to address the peoples of the world. Money-making might not have been as unrestrained but for the weird accompaniment of high-mindedness.

The artists tried to unite in 1919: prompted by the advice of Oscar Price of the US Treasury Department, who had been with them on a tour to sell war bonds. Chaplin, D. W. Griffith, Douglas Fairbanks and Mary Pickford formed United Artists as a way of ensuring that stars and film-makers kept as much of the total film rental as possible. Their company would have an honourable career, but those first artists were not its most active supporters. Griffith was a pioneer but a Victorian, and his post-war films suffered from his failure to grasp new attitudes or stories. Chaplin was a lone wolf and a slow worker. Doug was something of a playboy, 'Little Mary' had the best business head of them all. But not even her marriage to Fairbanks, and the royal life-style they created at Pickfair, their Beverley Hills home, could enable United Artists to rival the other studios.

The Twenties

By 1927, 'Hollywood' meant the greater Los Angeles area, a board game in which several powerhouses competed with one another and excluded newcomers; MGM, Paramount, Universal, Fox, Warners and a retinue of smaller studios including Columbia – mostly in what was known as 'Poverty Row', which was the Gower Street district. The majors were alike in that they generally had factories in and around Los Angeles, East Coast financing and distribution, large holdings in theatres and a head of production who gave out long-term contracts, watched over every film on the lot and ensured that the factory machine stayed active. A film director was still a professional assigned to a picture, not a lordly visionary: John Ford, King Vidor, Raoul Walsh, Frank Capra, Frank Borzage, Allan Dwan – a generation of great talents who did as they were told, or who cultivated that reputation. Irving Thalberg had consolidated the role of the producer, someone who made

Top: Cecil B. DeMille (left) and Company on location for The Squaw Man. *Centre: Louis B. Mayer, Western director Reginald Barker and Irving Thalberg. Above: Carl Laemmle, paternalistic boss of Universal, with Mona Ray and Virginia Gray on the set of* Uncle Tom's Cabin *(1928).*

sure a picture kept on schedule and under budget, who ran a project from script concept to final cut. No incident had so demonstrated the significance of the producer as when Thalberg dismissed Erich von Stroheim from *Greed* (1924) and then turned the monstrous masterpiece over to a series of editors with instructions to gut it for showing. Thalberg also intervened on *Ben-Hur* (1925), making key personnel changes and bringing it back from foreign location.

The audience for pictures was huge; the annual box-office take just before sound in America was over $500 million (when 25 cents bought admission to most films), and more films were being made than at any other time. The profits were immense and income tax was still low. Los Angeles filled out with prosperity. More mansions went up, in styles as diverse as those on the back lot. Between them there appeared the less opulent but still spacious houses of supporting actors, technicians, agents, publicity people, lawyers, doctors and every kind of soothsayer. The new money bought cars, pools, clothes, divorces and a variety of new sensations. There were shops and hotels catering to all tastes. As Alla Nazimova's acting career slumped, she sold her property and it was turned into a hotel, the Garden of Allah.

Musso & Frank's Grill, the first 'in' restaurant, opened on Hollywood Boulevard in 1919, and the original Brown Derby, a huge hat-shaped building, appeared on Wilshire in 1926. The 'Hollywoodland' sign went up, the ad for a housing development scheme, and a few years later a forlorn starlet threw herself to her death from on top of the H. Grauman's Chinese Theatre and the Pantages sought to prove that Los Angeles had the gaudiest theatres. Sea-shore homes were built off the Pacific Coast Highway and in Malibu. Bel-Air, a private housing estate, bloomed and a few magnificent dwellings were perched up in the hills. Gaiety and conspicuous self-indulgence reigned, and Hollywood won its reputation for decadent money-mindedness and ostentatious extravagance.

The mood of the pictures had changed; skirts, spirits and profits went up together after World War I. In 1919, for instance, Griffith was still locked into the pious moralizing of *True Heart Susie* and the pained virtue of Lillian Gish. But DeMille made a new kind of film – like *Male and Female* (1919) – racy, daring and frivolous, and centred on the pent-up bee-stung mouth of Gloria Swanson, who made her name playing working girls and flappers. Clara Bow's knowing sex appeal made Theda Bara look like a female impersonator. There were new stars – Rudolph Valentino, John Gilbert, Greta Garbo, Pola Negri, Ronald Colman, Marion Davies – who had an erotic vitality (cheerful or brooding) that was soon to be recognized as the energy of the Jazz Age. Buster Keaton and Lon Chaney were extreme examples of silent male appeal – frozen beauty and seething beastliness.

The audience enjoyed this new excitement and the speed of pictures, but some were suspicious and fearful of the movies' influence. Then, in the early Twenties, a series of real-life scandals confused the standards of Hollywood private life and the rules of motion pictures. On Labor Day, September 5, 1921 – not in Los Angeles, but in San Franciso – Fatty Arbuckle threw a party that ended in the death of bit-part actress Virginia Rappe. Fatty was charged with manslaughter and eventually acquitted. But the legend of notoriety stuck – from the earliest days, audiences were eager to believe the worst of stars. A few months later, the director William Desmond Taylor was found shot to death. Investigations dragged Mabel Normand and Mary Miles Minter into a circle

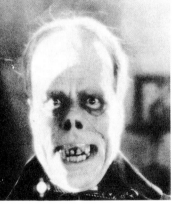

Among the new stars to bring a breath of fresh air to movies in the Twenties were Lon Chaney (above), in The Phantom of the Opera; *Clara Bow, in* Dancing Mothers *(1926); Buster Keaton (top right), in* Sherlock, Jr, *with Kathryn*

McGuire; Gloria Swanson (above), with Thomas Meighan in Male and Female; *Pola Negri (left); and the 'love team' of Greta Garbo and John Gilbert (above left), providing fire and smoke in* Flesh and the Devil *(1926).*

of orgies and drug-taking. Within another year, the actor Wallace Reid was dead from the effects of drugs.

The industry was afraid for its reputation, and alarmed that the various educational and religious guardians of moral America might intimidate the audience. In 1922, the leaders of the picture business founded the Motion Picture Producers and Distributors of America (MPPDA), and they appointed Will H. Hays to be its president. Hays spoke for Hollywood, and he helped to create the impression that the place was sober and responsible. He organized Central Casting as the agency for extras in 1926, and he eased the way for what passed for unions in the very conservative industry. He introduced a Production Code in 1930, the first step towards systematic self-censorship in pictures. The industry formed its own Academy (of Motion Picture Arts and Sciences) in 1927, and designed annual prizes – Oscars – to show how well-behaved and diligent it really was.

Pictures got organized; the kingdom acquired bureaucracy. But the studio system could hardly count the money it made. Europe was ransacked of talent: Ernst Lubitsch, F.W. Murnau, Michael Curtiz and Victor Sjötröm as well as stars like Greta Garbo. Only Rex Ingram and Louise Brooks went from America to Europe, and they both paid for their originality. By 1927, Los Angeles was a big city. The Picture business had a structure that is still visible, and it was on the point of going over to sound – the step that reduced audiences, mortgaged the industry to Eastern banks and allowed the chance that movies might be as demanding as plays or books. The kingdom still has power and glamour, no matter that Hollywood has sold out to many fresher sensations – pop music, TV, real estate, health foods and child prostitution. But in the Twenties, a few immigrants who had suffered under the old tyrannies of Europe discovered, with unashamed glee, that they could be emperors in Los Angeles.

The First Westerns

The Western is one of the finest creations of American culture, and the cowboy one of the great macho heroes of the world. Historically, the supreme era of the cowboy was short. It lasted from the end of the American Civil War in 1865 to the 1880s, a period when the cry was for beef to feed the hungry, growing nation. These were the days of the epic cattle drives up the famous trails like the Goodnight and the Chisholm, the days of the cattle empires, of the wide-open cow towns like Abilene and Dodge City, of range wars and murderous rivalries – the raw material of cowboy legend. But disastrous weather, bad management and the collapse of the beef market put an end to the boom; the arrival of homesteaders and the spread of barbed wire terminated the open range. Cowboys continued to exist and to ply their trade; but the old expansive, free-wheeling life had ended. Many cowboys moved on and the destination of some of them was Hollywood. By the Twenties, it was estimated that 500 a year came to Hollywood from ranches in Arizona and Colorado that were going broke.

The earliest Westerns therefore not only reconstructed the story and the life-style of the Old West – they overlapped with it and actually continued it. Real-life western characters appeared in films about their exploits: outlaws such as Al Jennings and Emmett Dalton and lawmen such as Bill Tilghman, last of the great western marshals. Tilghman made a number of films, actually interrupting the shooting of one of them to round up some bank robbers, thus mingling fantasy and reality with a vengeance. For the epic film *North of 36* (1924), the director Irvin Willat staged the first longhorn cattle drive for nearly thirty-five years, exactly reproducing the conditions of the drives in the 1870s.

But for all the documentary-style realism of some of these Western reconstructions, the mass audience went to Westerns primarily for dashing heroes and plenty of action, preferably in impressive locations. So the films that the real-life cowboys helped to make in Hollywood gave worldwide currency to a romantic archetype which had been established even before the film industry came into being. The cowboy was seen as the embodiment of the virtues of the American frontier. These had been described by the historian Frederick Jackson Turner in 1893:

'That coarseness and strength combined with acuteness and inquisitiveness; that practical, inventive turn of mind, quick to find expedients; that masterful grasp of material things, lacking in the artistic but powerful to effect great ends; that restless, nervous energy; that dominant individualism working for good and for evil, and withal that buoyancy and exuberance which comes with freedom'.

These characteristics were blended with the essential elements of the chivalric gentleman of the Old World – courtesy, bravery and nobility – to create an ideal Westerner. This image was perfected by three men, all Easterners, all friends, all intoxicated by the heroic vision of the West and all destined to influence the Hollywood version of it. Owen Wister, a Philadelphian, made the cowboy the hero of his novel *The Virginian*, published in 1902. It was the first serious Western novel and gave the cowboy pride of place over the previously preferred heroes, the dime-novel favourites – the outlaw, the lawman, the pioneer, the trapper and the scout. Frederic Remington, a New Yorker, in his paintings of cattle drives and round-ups, gunfights and hold-ups, recorded a West made up of swirls of action and colour, with manly cowboys at its centre. Theodore Roosevelt, aristocractic President, explorer and big-game hunter, preached in his life and in his books a militant Anglo-Saxonism of which the cowboy was the proud exemplar. The first epic Western film, *The Covered Wagon* (1923), was to be dedicated to his memory. The impact of the cowboy can be gauged from the fact that the terms 'Western film' and 'cowboy film' became interchangeable, although many Western films actually featured no cowboys as such.

Although the cowboy was being ennobled for the first time, the process was built on the tradition of the dime novels. From the 1860s onwards, as the West seized the imagination of America, a flood of cheap novels, written according to a few formulas, had poured from the presses, dramatizing and romanticizing the adventures of real and fictional Western heroes. Dime novels became one of the primary sources of film content, reinforced by stage melodramas with Western settings and the Wild West shows which popularized what became the great set-pieces of Western films – the stagecoach chase, the wagon-train attack and the cavalry charge.

One figure tapped all these sources of inspiration – Colonel William F. Cody, 'Buffalo Bill' himself. A real-life scout and buffalo hunter, he was taken up by the leading dime novelist, Ned Buntline, who started a long series of novels describing his fictional adventures. Cody took to the stage in 1872 in a rather bad melodrama called *The Scouts of the Plains* and, discovering that he lacked aptitude as an actor, launched his celebrated Wild West show in 1883. Towards the end of his life, he brought the wheel full circle by producing and starring in a film of his Western exploits, made in 1913 and known by various titles, including *The Adventures of Buffalo Bill*. His career is the perfect demonstration of how historical reality shaded into cinematic fiction.

It was inevitable that films would follow the lead of the stage and the printed page, and Westerns became a staple of the new entertainment medium early on. The first recorded Western is a one-minute vignette entitled *Cripple Creek Bar Room*, produced in 1898. The first Western story film, *The Great Train Robbery*, followed in 1903. Directed by Edwin S. Porter, it was actually filmed in New Jersey but told a classic story of robbery, chase and retribution. It had enormous success at the box-office and was extensively imitated. One thing it did not have was a hero. But in the cast was an actor called Gilbert M. Anderson (1882–1971), who was soon ready to remedy this defect. Overcoming an initial tendency to fall off his horse, he saw the potential in the cowboy hero, launched a new company (Essanay) and took a film unit off first to Colorado and then to California, where he began producing one- and two-reel Westerns, many of them featuring Anderson himself as a sentimental tough guy called Broncho Billy Anderson, who appeared in hundreds of Broncho Billy films between 1908 and 1916, thus became the first Western hero. Business problems kept him off the screen for over a year and when he returned he found that new idols had risen and his career faded.

Lone Stars

The artistic possibilities in the Western became clear in the work of two of the cinema's great innovators – D.W. Griffith and Thomas H. Ince. Griffith in his years at Biograph brought his increasingly sophisticated technique and powerful visual sense to Westerns, imbuing such projects as *The Last Drop of Water* (1911), *The Massacre* (1913) and *The Battle at Elderbush Gulch* (1914) with truly epic qualities. Thomas H. Ince, the first producer to insist on fully detailed and comprehensive scripts for the guidance of the production team as well as the actors, and an organizational genius when it came to staging large-scale action, hired the Miller Brothers 101 Ranch Real Wild West Show, to provide him with a ready-made stock company of cowboys and Indians, longhorn cattle, stage-coaches and wagons. He turned out Westerns from his Inceville studios, one of the most successful of which was *Custer's Last Raid* (1912), directed by and starring Francis Ford (though Ince officially took the directorial credit). This film so impressed Carl Laemmle that he lured Ford away from Ince and set him to work at Universal, which was to become one of the major producers of Westerns. Francis Ford was eventually to be eclipsed as a director by his younger brother John Ford and as an actor by Harry Carey and then Hoot Gibson, who both starred in many popular Westerns for Universal, some of them directed by the up-and-coming John (then known as Jack) Ford.

Ince, however, found a more-than-adequate replacement for Francis Ford in William S. Hart (1870–1946), who entered films in 1914 at the age of 44. Previously a stage actor, who had appeared not only in Shakespeare and *Ben-Hur* but also in such popular Western stage melodramas as *The Squaw Man* and *The Virginian*. Hart was an incurable romantic. He had been raised in the West, loved it and wanted to depict it realistically on the screen. First with Ince and later with Paramount, he succeeded in his aim, giving his films a gritty surface realism of austere, dusty townships and authentic cowboy costume and accoutrements. But with this went another side of his romanticism, plots that were sentimental, melodramatic and heavily moralistic. In his films he played a succession of ramrod-straight, grim-visaged badmen with names like Black Deering, Blaze Tracey and Draw Egan, who were underneath it all chivalric and sentimental and whose moral regeneration was a central theme of the stories. In *Hell's*

Hinges (1916), he actually burns down a sinful town, in a sequence eerily prefiguring Clint Eastwood's *High Plains Drifter* (1973). Hart's horse Fritz became the first of a long line of star movie horses who became as well-known as their riders. But Hart's popularity waned and the piety, sentiment-ality and comparatively slow pace of his films came to seem increasingly old-fashioned with the rise of a very different sort of star – Tom Mix. Hart refused to change his style and after a final film, *Tumbleweeds* (1925), he retired. *Tumbleweeds* represents the triumphant summation of Hart's vision of the West and takes place symbolically against the background of the end of the open range and the arrival of the homesteaders. It also contains a stunningly executed and majestically shot set-piece, the Cherokee Strip land rush, which ranks with the best of its kind in the genre.

Where Hart had prided himself on the authenticity of his films, those of Tom Mix (1880–1940) were pure fantasy. He had first entered films in mid-1909 as a stockman and supporting player in a rodeo picture, *Ranch Life in the Great Southwest* (1910), and from then until 1917 he worked for the Selig company turning out something like a hundred West-erns, one- and two-reelers, which he often wrote and directed as well as starring in. But in 1917 he moved to Fox and his career took off. The inspiration of his films was the circus and the Wild West show, where Hart's had been Victorian melodrama and photographic realism. Tom Mix's cowboy hero, flamboyantly costumed, involved himself in fast-moving, far-fetched stories, strong on stunts, action and comedy. Fleet of foot, keen of eye and effortlessly gallant, Tom Mix became the Doug Fairbanks of the sagebrush. He set the style and pattern for the Westerns of a host of rivals and imitators. Indeed from his own supporting casts emerged Buck Jones and George O'Brien, who were both promoted as clean-cut Western stars by Fox in the Twenties.

Far left: the redoubtable William S. Hart as The Gun Fighter *(1917). Left: Tom Mix, the nattily dressed* Son of the Golden West *(1928). Above: shot in Thomas Edison's Black Maria Studio in New Jersey,* Cripple Creek Barroom *was the first Western saloon interior ever filmed.*

Above: The Covered Wagon *was shot in conditions almost as arduous as those suffered by the authentic original pioneers.*

Cowboy Epics

Westerns received a tremendous boost in 1923 when Paramount released the first indisputable Western epic, *The Covered Wagon*. Based on Emerson Hough's novel, it began as a conventional programmer about a wagon boss falsely accused of a crime by his rival for the heroine's affections, but expanded to become the saga of wagons westward on the Oregon Trail in 1848. It exists now only in an incomplete print. Nevertheless it can be said that despite such assets as the grandeur of Karl Brown's photography, the documentary look imparted by eight weeks' location shooting to such large-scale action sequences as the wagon train's departure, the river crossing and a buffalo hunt, and the rich character comedy of Ernest Torrence and Tully Marshall as two old frontiersmen, it is a flawed film. The director, James Cruze, whatever his strengths, was weak on action highlights and suspense, and the Indian attack on the wagon train and its rescue are clumsily handled.

But the film was a great box-office success, and it emboldened Fox to turn its new Western *The Iron Horse* (1924) into an epic. So the familiar story of a young man seeking the murderer of his father burgeoned into a full-scale reconstruction of the building of the transcontinental railroad. In John Ford, Fox had a director who could combine visual sweep and exciting action sequences, rich comedy interludes and acutely-observed details of everyday life to counterpoint the epic theme. In George O'Brien, Ford found a wholly convincing Western star, virile, natural and likeable. The result was one of the great achievements of the silent cinema. Other epics followed, such as Irvin Willat's *North of 36* and James Cruze's *The Pony Express* (1925). But none of them achieved the success of *The Covered Wagon* and *The Iron Horse,* and it became clear that large-scale evocations of nationalistic sentiment were not entirely to the public's taste.

Interestingly, after his magisterial land-rush epic *Three Bad Men* (1926), John Ford was not to make another Western until *Stagecoach* (1939).

Programme Westerns, however, flourished and production of them trebled in the year following *The Covered Wagon*. Films on the streamlined, action-packed Tom Mix model were what was required, and in his wake a posse of immortals galloped across the screen. These were the men in white hats riding white horses, the idols of the Saturday matinées.

MGM launched a group of historical Westerns starring the stalwart Colonel Tim McCoy, a former Indian agent who had handled the Indians used in the making of *The Covered Wagon*. At First National, Ken Maynard starred in rousing Western adventures, whose spectacular set-piece highlights were to be re-used constantly as stock footage throughout the Thirties. At FBO, Fred Thomson, a former Presbyterian minister and Boy Scout leader, now forgotten but idolized in his day, rode and fought his way into the hearts of a legion of young admirers. From Paramount between 1921 and 1928 (and thereafter in the sound era) came an impressive series of adaptations of the novels of Zane Grey, arguably the most popular of Western writers. With classic plots and evocative titles like *The Thundering Herd, The Vanishing American* and *Wild Horse Mesa* (all 1925), they generally starred steely-eyed Jack Holt or rugged Richard Dix.

By 1926, however, a glut of cheap Westerns took the edge off public demand and the coming of sound apparently signalled their doom. Short on that essential commodity, dialogue, they were dubbed old-fashioned and over-romantic. The vogue was for bang-up-to-date films that could exploit the new medium, and Westerns were eclipsed by gangster films with their screeching cars and machine-gun battles and by musicals – 'all-talking, all-singing, all-dancing'. Production of Westerns was cut by as much as 75 per cent and in 1929 *Photoplay* magazine declared: 'Western novel and motion picture heroes have slunk away into the brush, never to return.'

Heroes from the Past

In the early nineteenth century, the spread of industrialization led to the growth of a vast and teeming urban proletariat. Mass media entertainment developed to provide colourful escapism for the toiling millions. An unending flow of cheap books and magazines, mass-produced prints of popular paintings and action-packed stage melodramas catered for this need. Prominent among the perennial subjects for these media were swashbucklers, historical epics and horror fantasies. When the cinema arose to provide a new source of entertainment for this same audience, it inevitably turned to these tried-and-true staples of popular literature; but it sought to do them bigger and better than before.

The cinema swashbuckler is very largely the work of one man – Douglas Fairbanks Sr. He did not direct his films but he masterminded their creation, writing the screen stories, selecting the cast, supervising the production details and collaborating on stunt design. The great tales of costume adventure – 'Zorro', the 'Three Musketeers', 'Robin Hood' – were refashioned to fit them to the Fairbanks formula. The ingredients – character archetypes, elaborate sets, acrobatic content – were definitively set by Fairbanks' films of the Twenties, beginning with *The Mark of Zorro* in 1920 and ending with *The Iron Mask,* directed by Allan Dwan, nine years later. Each new film dazzled the audiences and evoked fresh praise from the critics. The *New York Times* declared of

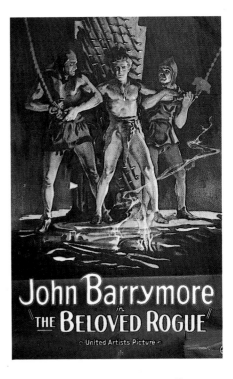

Right: a knife-edged moment for The Son of the Sheik. *Valentino played both father and son. Below: Ronald Colman and Vilma Banky in* The Night of Love. *Below right:* The Black Pirate *(Douglas Fairbanks) defeats the enemy in true swashbuckling fashion.*

Above: even torture cannot quell the spirit of the vagabond poet François Villon (John Barrymore).

Robin Hood (made in 1922, released 1923):

'He has made a picture which for magnificence of setting, richness of pageantry, beauty and elegance of photography, and impressiveness of action has probably never been equalled before.'

Only a year later, it was declaring *The Thief of Bagdad* (1924), 'a feat of motion picture art that has never been equalled'. Before Fairbanks, there had been adaptations of the old heroic stories – but adaptations that were still literal and literary in conception. After Fairbanks, the swashbuckler took off as a cinematic genre, in which physical movement and visual style predominated. But his sheer verve and vitality were to remain unsurpassed.

Although no other silent star sought to make a career out of swashbuckling, many silent idols donned cape and sword for forays into a field already being described as Fairbanksian. Among the best examples were two films starring John Barrymore and directed by Alan Crosland, *Don Juan* (1926) and *The Beloved Rogue* (1927). Both films combined acrobatic action, passionate lovemaking, sly humour and some stunning art direction. Ben Carrés sixteenth-century Rome in *Don Juan* was the height of Romantic stylization and William Cameron Menzies created an unforgettable quasi-Expressionist medieval Paris for *The Beloved Rogue*. John Barrymore, at the peak of his powers, made Don Juan and the poet-thief Francois Villon, the beloved rogue, both irresistibly attractive adventurers.

John Gilbert cut a dash in the title role of King Vidor's *Bardelys the Magnificent* (1926), only a fragment of which survives. But stills and reviews indicate lavish sets, fine photography and well-handled acrobatic action in this Rafael Sabatini tale of intrigue and romance in seventeenth-century France.

The screen's Latin lovers were also anxious to demonstrate swashbuckling skill. Rudolph Valentino took the title role in Sidney Olcott's *Monsieur Beaucaire* (1924), which one critic described as 'a masterpiece of the united arts of the scene

builder, the decorator, the costumier and the cameraman'. As the French duke posing as a barber in eighteenth-century Bath, Valentino fenced gracefully, wooed ardently and at one point disguised himself as a woman. *The Eagle* (1925), Clarence Brown's elegant comedy of manners in the Lubitsch style, masquerading as costume romance, cast Valentino as a dashing Cossack guards officer resisting the amorous advances of Catherine the Great and ridding his local district of a tyrant. But George Fitzmaurice's engaging oriental extravaganza *The Son of the Sheik* (1926) allowed him to take time off from ravishing the dancing girl Yasmin (Vilma Banky) in his desert encampment to fight off hundreds of opponents, swing from chandeliers and give whirlwind horseback chase to the villain, Ghabah the Moor (Montague Love).

Ramon Novarro got his first big break as the ruthless, dandified Rupert of Hentzau in Rex Ingram's *The Prisoner of Zenda* (1922), a film which displayed the pictorial genius, attention to detail and unmatched feeling for composition that distinguished Ingram's best work. Ingram surpassed this achievement and attained a painterly pictorialism of the highest order in *Scaramouche* (1923), in which Novarro played the title role. Rod La Rocque played the novelist A. Conan Doyle's gallant and vainglorious Brigadier Gerard in Donald Crisp's stylish and light-hearted *The Fighting Eagle* (1927). Ronald Colman, who – rather improbably in the light of his subsequent career – was being built up as a new Valentino by Samuel Goldwyn, was teamed with Valentino's erstwhile co-star Vilma Banky in a series of costume romances which mingled swashbuckling and passion. He was a medieval Spanish gypsy avenging the rape of his betrothed in *The Night of Love,* a dissolute crown prince and his circus-clown double in *The Magic Flame* (both 1927) and a Flemish freedom-fighter resisting the Spanish occupation of the Netherlands in the seventeenth century in *Two Lovers* (1928).

Although Fairbanks' *The Black Pirate* (1927) created the ultimate in witty and stylized pirate pictures, several large-scale piratical sagas vied with it for popular favour, notably

Frank Lloyd's *The Sea Hawk* (1924), one of the silent screen's largest money-makers, David Smith's *Captain Blood* (1924) with J. Warren Kerrigan and a climactic battle which one critic described as 'the biggest and rowdiest thing yet seen on the silent screen', and Lloyd's *The Eagle of the Sea* (1926) with Ricardo Cortez as the pirate Jean Lafitte involved in a plot to rescue Napoleon from St Helena. So pervasive was the lure of the swashbuckler that such unlikely candidates for fencing honours as Richard Barthelmess, in *The Fighting Blade* (1923), and Tom Mix, in *Dick Turpin* (1925), tried their hands at it – but without presenting a real threat to Fairbanks. The coming of sound led to the abandonment of swashbucklers in favour of more up-to-date genres. Fairbanks symbolically died on screen for the first time in *The Iron Mask*. The revival of the genre awaited the arrival of Errol Flynn.

Historical Epics

Where Victorian stage melodrama had been the initial inspiration of the swashbucklers, it was Victorian spectacular theatre and spectacle painting that inspired the historical epics. The nineteenth-century vogue for epic canvases with vast settings, massive crowds and apocalyptic action (the fall of Babylon, the destruction of Nineveh, the Last Judgment), typified by the paintings of John Martin, had a marked influence on stage productions. A passion for size and spectacle was matched by a passion for historical accuracy and archaeological exactitude, stimulated by the discovery of the lost cities of Pompeii, Nineveh and Troy, and popularized in the idealized Roman and Greek reconstructions of painters like Sir Lawrence Alma-Tadema. Historical dramas, particularly Shakespeare's were now staged to conform to the demand for spectacle and historical accuracy. Interestingly *The Times* described Sir Herbert Beerbohm Tree's production of *Henry VIII* as 'kinematographic' and indeed a film version (1911), now lost, was made of the production.

As with swashbucklers, the stage-to-screen transition was almost a matter of natural progression. Both D.W. Griffith and Cecil B. DeMille (1881–1959), the principal creators of the silent-screen epic, were deeply rooted in the Victorian theatrical tradition and strongly influenced by its trends to spectacle and to accuracy in their film work. Griffith, for instance, included on his title cards historical verification of scenes and of artefacts used, while DeMille employed teams of historical researchers to assemble material for reconstructing the past.

Despite their theatrical roots, what Griffith and DeMille produced on the screen was essentially and distinctively cinematic. DeMille perfected the blend of sex and moralism that was to make him the master of the biblical epic. Several of his films had spectacular flashbacks to the past in them, *Manslaughter* (1922), for instance, counterpointed the drama of its modern tale of the irresponsibility and sensation-seeking of the idle rich with a re-creation of the decadence of Ancient Rome. *The Ten Commandments* (1923) went even further. The first half re-created on a massive scale the exodus from Egypt, the worship of the Golden Calf and the granting of the commandments to Moses. The second half told the modern story of a crooked builder who constructs a defective cathedral, a story designed to illustrate the continuing importance of the commandments. *Photoplay* called the resulting film 'The greatest theatrical spectacle in history'.

Even when DeMille devoted the whole of a film to the Bible, as he did with *The King of Kings* (1927), telling the familiar New Testament stories of Christ with great flair and

compositional skill, he managed to open on a note of unforgettable decadence, at the villa of Mary Magdalene, lovingly depicted as overflowing with half-naked slaves, dancing girls, ostrich-feather fans, swans and pet leopards. Mary herself sweeps out, on her way to see Christ, with the immortal line: 'Harness my zebras – gift of the Numidian king'.

Other directors followed in DeMille's footsteps, Michael Curtiz, who had established a reputation as a director of European spectacles was imported to direct *Noah's Ark* (1928), with parallel modern and biblical stories; Raoul Walsh directed *The Wanderer* (1926), the story of the Prodigal Son; and, after considerable production difficulties and changes of director and cast, Fred Niblo finished MGM's first version of *Ben-Hur*, complete with climactic chariot race.

Horror

Elements of both the historical epic and the swashbuckler found their way into three of the silent screen's great horror fantasies, all done on a large scale with elaborate period reconstructions and spectacular action sequences. *The Hunch-back of Notre Dame* (1923) and *The Phantom of the Opera* (1925), set in medieval and nineteenth-century Paris respectively, showcased the amazing talents of Lon Chaney (1883–1930). Chaney not only created makeup of unequalled grotesquerie, but he also carried the art of mime to new tragic heights. He was not available for *The Man Who Laughs* (1928),

a story strongly paralleling *The Hunchback of Notre Dame* in its elaboration of the 'Beauty and the Beast' theme. Conrad Veidt stepped in as Gwynplaine, whose face had been surgically altered to make it fixed in a permanent smile. With its background of torture chamber, gibbet, fairground and corrupt royal court, its erotic subplot and its mixture of pathos and terror, it was turned by the director Paul Leni into as striking a piece of imaginative fantasy as ever came out of Hollywood. Sadly, the film's impact was diminished by the arrival of the talkies and it failed at the box-office.

Chaney was unable to accept the part of Gwynplaine because he had signed for MGM and there, with the talented but decidedly quirky director Tod Browning, he had appeared in a group of bizarre, obsessive and unusual horror films, often centring on physical deformity – *The Unknown, London After Midnight* (both 1927), *West of Zanzibar* (1928). One of them, however, *The Unholy Three* (1925), with its larcenous trio of transvestite ventriloquist, murderous midget and circus strong man, emerged as a classic of black comedy. It was this film that was chosen for a remake (1930) as Chaney's talkie debut, directed this time by Jack Conway. Chaney died just after its completion.

The silent screen produced two other classics of the macabre. Rex Ingram's *The Magician* (1926), superbly photographed on atmospheric French locations, centred on the activities of a sinister, caped, black-magic practitioner (Paul Wegener), a character based on the contemporary diabolist Aleister Crowley. It featured a drug-induced vision of Hell, an orgy of fauns and satyrs, powerful, erotic, inspired by the engravings of Gustave Doré. The climax of the film came in a storm-wracked tower where the magician and his dwarf assistant sought to drain the heroine (Alice Terry) of her blood. John S. Robertson's *Dr Jekyll and Mr Hyde* (1920), which fleshed out Robert Louis Stevenson's short novel with elements from Oscar Wilde's novel *The Picture of Dorian Gray* and set the action in a highly stylized Victorian London, provided a marvellous opportunity for John Barrymore. With the noble profile as yet unimpaired by drink and self-indulgence, he was perfectly cast as the saintly Dr Jekyll but he transformed himself into the evil Hyde with gleeful bravura, emerging, hunchbacked and beetle-browed, to commit mayhem.

An important sub-genre of late silent horror films was the 'old dark house' variety. The best of them allowed continental directors to revel in fluid camera movements, chiaroscuro lighting and the paraphernalia of sliding panels, clutching hands and vanishing corpses to create elegant exercises in terror, such as Roland West's *The Bat,* (1926), Paul Leni's *The Cat and the Canary* (1927), and Benjamin Christensen's *The Haunted House* (1928) and *Seven Footprints to Satan* (1929). Based as they were on hit Broadway plays, most of them were immediately remade as soon as sound was established, but the genre reached its triumphant summation in James Whale's appropriately named *The Old Dark House* (1932).

Left: pious moralizing (and outrageous scenes of debauchery – seen here in Manslaughter*) were typical of Cecil B. DeMille's films. Above: Lon Chaney proving himself the master of disguise in* The Hunchback of Notre Dame. *Above far right: Conrad Veidt as the disfigured Gwynplaine in* The Man Who Laughs. *Far right: John Barrymore, suitably demoniacal as* Dr Jekyll and Mr Hyde. *Right: an heiress (Laura La Plante) menaced in* The Cat and the Canary, *a classic old-dark-house mystery.*

Comedy

The full flowering of silent-screen comedy came in the mid-Twenties, partly as a result of previous vigorous activity. Before 1920, humour had generally been confined to one- and two-reelers, with the feature-length film, Mack Sennett's *Tillie's Punctured Romance* (1914), as a singular and most successful exception. Full-length features were usually made only by the most successful comedians – those who had achieved popular acclaim and big box-office receipts for their shorts. Until the Twenties, short-story-like films were favoured even by Charles Chaplin and Harold Lloyd, who were reluctant to commit themselves to longer works.

The USA was blessed in the 1910s by the migration of British music-hall comedians, including Charles Chaplin and Stan Laurel, who had served their apprenticeship with Fred Karno's music-hall troupes. Others would follow, lured by the American comedy explosion. Such skilled stage comics as Billie Ritchie and Lupino Laine took leading roles in short films for Hollywood companies. Most of these actors were drawn to America by the higher pay and the many companies that offered them a chance to ply their trade. Walter Forde, considered the leading British comedian of the early Twenties, was one of the few to return to his homeland to gain more success as both a star and director.

The Kid (1921), Chaplins first feature as director and star, proved to be a milestone. Ironically, Chaplin had been so successful with his two- and three-reel shorts that he feared he would not be able to handle a longer film of five or six reels, and felt he might have to retire from the screen. But, by an intuitive sense that some critics would call genius, Chaplin was able to blend the necessary ingredients of emotional appeal and of lively slapstick in the comic style of Mack Sennett.

Unlike Chaplin, whose universal stories seemed to exist in a world untouched by time, most other makers of comedy films in the Twenties were content to follow along the lines of the earlier, off-the-cuff improvised plots or else the popular humorous stories of books and magazines, faddish inventions of the age. Sennett, rather than seeing the advantage of combining elements to give variety and dimension to his features, rigidly produced two types of film – one that followed the slapstick tradition of the 1910s, such as *A Small Town Idol* (1921), and another in the genteel tradition of polite situation comedy, such as *Molly O* (1921), starring Mabel Normand. Since Mabel Normand was one of the best American comediennes, this standard formula might have worked if she had not become involved in a scandal when an English film director, William Desmond Taylor, was mysteriously murdered. Sennett was forced to withdraw *Molly O* from circulation because of public indignation, and Mabel Normand's career was destroyed.

The genteel-humour tradition was more fully exploited by such American light comedians as Johnny Hines, Douglas Maclean, Charles Ray and Wallace Reid, with typical magazine short-story material. Johnny Hines, having graduated from two-reel comedies in the late 1910s in which he played 'the average American boy next door', went on to features with such titles as *Burn 'Em Up Barnes* (1921), *Luck* (1923), *The Early Bird* (1924) and *The Live Wire* (1925), which focused on the struggles of a young man trying to make good, in the manner of the nineteenth-century novelist Horatio Alger's success stories. Maclean, Ray and Reid achieved acclaim in the early Twenties using this same type of material. Representative of the light-comedy actresses of the day was

Colleen Moore, who became one of the highest-paid women of the silent screen in the late Twenties. She starred in such features as *Ella Cinders* (1926), a mild comedy based on a famous comic strip of the day.

But there were some attempts to break the mould of popular fiction in the Twenties. In England, for example, the music-hall comedian George Robey, after appearing in a series of shorts based on the short stories of W.W. Jacobs, was given the role of Sancho Panza in *Don Quixote* (1923), based on Miguel de Cervantes' classic novel, with Jerrold Robertshaw in the title role. Ten years later, in a talkie version directed by G.W. Pabst, Robey played the same role to the Don Quixote of Fyodor Chaliapin, the famous Russian opera singer, and the result was a considerable improvement on the earlier film. In the USA, the Fox Film Corporation released an updated rendering of the famous Mark Twain novel of 1889, *A Connecticut Yankee at King Arthur's Court*, made in 1921 and starring Harry Myers, later best known for his role as the drunken millionaire in Charles Chaplin's *City Lights* (1931). The famous comedian's brother, Syd Chaplin, appeared in a successful screen adaptation of Brandon Thomas' highly popular late-nineteenth- century farce *Charley's Aunt* in 1925. A year earlier the pixie-like comedienne Betty Bronson was featured as the boy-hero in a Famous Players-Lasky adaptation of the playwright J.M. Barrie's *Peter Pan*, directed by Herbert Brenon.

Trying to improve the image of movies by adapting literary 'classics' and often employing famous stage actors and actresses, Famous Players-Lasky produced in 1925 a film of Ferenc Molnár's sophisticated stage comedy *The Swan*, starring Adolphe Menjou. In fact, quite a few sophisticated films were made in the mid-period of the decade. Ernst Lubitsch transposed Oscar Wilde's famous 1892 play *Lady Windermere's Fan* to the screen in 1925. James Cruze, best known for his Western *The Covered Wagon*, directed *Beggar on Horseback* (1925), based on a contemporary play, the most satirical of the George S. Kaufman and Marc Connelly collaborations. A delightful, satirical farce from France, *Un Chapeau de Paille d'Italie* (1927, *The Italian Straw Hat*), did not seem to suffer in the transmigration from stage to silent screen. But most of these translations from the more verbal media (novel and play) suffered oversimplification as adaptors tried to appeal to a mass audience. The use of intertitles also presented problems. Lubitsch, obviously trying to avoid a flood of titles for his Oscar Wilde adaptation, even omitted the famous playwright's forte, the epigrams. Not until the screen found its voice did such literary works as Shakespeare's *The Taming of the Shrew* achieve the full dimension of which the medium is capable; the 1929 version, directed by Sam Taylor (who was one of Harold Lloyd's directors), starred Mary Pickford and Douglas Fairbanks.

While literary works tended to please the critics, the general public flocked to the films of the famous four of the decade, Charles Chaplin, Harold Lloyd, Buster Keaton and Harry Langdon. In that magical year of 1925 when the comedy feature came to full fruition, Chaplin released *The Gold Rush* and Lloyd offered *The Freshman*, both of which achieved depth of comic character, a rarity in the full-length humorous films of the period. Chaplin, Lloyd and also Keaton kept the total production of each film under their supervision, usually serving (uncredited in the case of Lloyd) as story editor or author, director or co-director as well as star.

Harold Lloyd (1893–1971), based many of his feature films on a modern psychological version of the Horatio Alger success story. He employed a clutch of gag writers and avoided directly adapting the popular literature of the time, as was the practice of such genteel comedians as Douglas MacLean and Charles Ray. He cleverly blended their humour with the slapstick tradition to achieve character dimension. His first five-reeler, *Grandma's Boy* (1922), told the story of a shy young man who is psychologically weak in asserting his rights when a macho rival in love constantly embarrasses him in front of the girl, the object of both their affections. His grandmother gives him a magic amulet that she claims will cure his meekness. Believing her little ruse, he becomes a dashing young man who turns into the town hero. *Grandma's Boy* proved to be a box-office smash hit, and the comedian became a rival of Chaplin for the audiences of the time. His college-life picture *The Freshman* was also a success in which elaborate character development was combined with many brilliantly-conceived, action-filled comedy sequences. Lloyd became closeley identified with 'thrill-comedy' typified by his clock-hanging, human-fly antics in *Safety Last* (1923). In *The Freshman* he is a naive youth going about winning acceptance at college in quite the wrong way. He triumphs in the end, but his road there is hard, and his humiliations on the way are lacerating. *The Kid Brother* (1927) is a more mature version of *Grandma's Boy*, with Lloyd eventually winning the respect of his tough father and brothers. The climax is a fight that is genuinely thrilling and full of inspired gags. His final silent movie was *Speedy* (Lloyd's own juvenile nickname), a model comedy made in 1928. Here, a dreamy baseball fan (Lloyd) not only meets the great Babe Ruth but single-handedly (save for an intelligent dog – Lloyd's dogs and cats are worth a study in themselves) routs the crooks who are trying to eliminate the last surviving horse-drawn trolley-car in New York. Swift, economical, beautifully timed and attractively shot on location in New York (a new departure for Lloyd), *Speedy* falls little short of the great comedies of Keaton and Chaplin. But before Lloyd could progress any further sound arrived, changing the whole basis of comedy and undermining him.

Buster Keaton (1895–1966), developed an understated portrait of the small man struggling in a big world that seemed full of obstacles poised to crush him, both physically and spiritually. Often in some difficult situation he appeared lost (or actually was) and stood in a characteristic pose like a poker-faced Indian surveying the horizon, one hand shielding his eyes from the sun. Keaton displayed an obsession with gadgets – many of his two-reelers and his features focused on machines. In *Our Hospitality* (1923) and *The General* (1926) the locomotive practically became a co-actor. *The Navigator* (1924) had an ocean liner that could have stolen scenes from Keaton if he had not been so closely enmeshed in it. But the actor had more than this type of material going for him. Like Lloyd he was a master at developing one long series of gags from a basic situation. Controlling the total production of his films until the late Twenties, Buster Keaton enjoyed a popularity second only to Harold Lloyd's. But after this period never again would his films reflect the sheer un-cluttered exuberance of his comic timing and his magical visual sense.

The hallmark of a Keaton comedy is the energy of its central character, all the animation that others display on their faces being expressed by Buster in a headlong ballet of acrobatics which he performed himself, in long-shot and without cuts. There is no trickery about the log-bouncing scene in *The General*, or Buster's high dive from the top of the ship in *The*

Above: Harold Lloyd in true Boy's Own style, heading Back to the Woods *(1919). Top: One of Lloyd's most famous scenes, hanging on for dear life in* Safety Last.

JOSEPH M. SCHENCK presents

BUSTER KEATON in "The General"

UNITED ARTISTS PICTURE

Navigator, or the vaulting ease with which he skims down the riverboat decks in *Steamboat Bill, Jr* (1928) and all the way up again a moment later. In *Spite Marriage,* a single shot follows his desperate battle with the villain from one end of the luxury yacht to the other where, flung into the ocean, he is carried by the current back to the lifeboat trailing at the stern and hauls himself up over the side to resume the struggle. During his career, as he often reported in later years, he broke every bone in his body. In *The Paleface* (1921) he dropped 85 feet from a suspension bridge into a net; he was nearly drowned under a waterfall in *Our Hospitality*; and during the train sequence in *Sherlock, Jr* (1924) he actually broke his neck yet continued stunting and filming despite months of blinding headaches. Nevertheless, it is not as a stuntman but as a unique tragi-comic personality that he survives as the most fascinating of the silent comedians. As if pursuing a redefinition of his private experience, his films illustrate the purgatorial struggles of an inconsequential reject, habitually

Left: a moustachioed Buster Keaton doing his homework as an amateur detective in Sherlock, Jr. *Right: a cyclone blows the front of a house onto* Steamboat Bill, Jr — *fortunately a window is open. In performing this stunt Keaton allowed himself only two inches to spare on either side.*

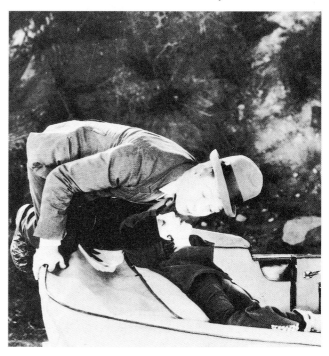

Top: comedy or no, every shot of The General *looks as authentic as a Civil War photograph by Matthew Brady. Johnny Gray (Keaton), a railway engineer, is a lone, brave, foolish figure who is besotted with two loves – The General (his locomotive), and Annabelle Lee (his girl). Above left: during a chase in* The

General, Johnny sees a log blocking the line ahead. Miraculously, he manages to struggle to the front of the train with another huge log and, just at the vital moment, throws it on to the threatening obstacle, bounces it clear of the track and saves The General from destruction.

bullied by a scornful father or disdainfully ignored by an unappreciative girl, who by sheer persistence and ingenuous courage (physical danger never seems to occur to him as a possibility) battles his way to social acceptability. In his tenacious war against the forces of evil, his endurance in restoring the rightness of things, and his enigmatic face that gives nothing away – no promises, no denials – he is one of the screen's great martyrs. Yet at the same time, he has an uncanny gift for adapting technology to provide unexpected comforts; he uses a swordfish for protection, a boiler for a bedroom and a lobster-pot for an egg-holder in *The Navigator,* lazy tongs for a traffic indicator and a telephone for controlling a horse in *Cops* (1922), and can whip up a brisk asbestos suit in order to survive burning at the stake in *The Paleface.* As if in reward for his ingenuity, and for his obvious innocence, Providence is on his side, carrying him placidly off in an airborne canoe at the end of *The Balloonatic* (1923), or dropping the two-ton façade of a building over his body – he

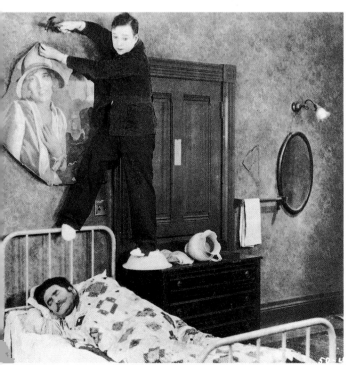

Above left: Harry Langdon (here in Long Pants*), the least assertive of the great silent clowns, was described as being 'bland as milk'. Above: Harry Logan (Langdon) puts up a poster of his beloved Betty Burton (Joan Crawford) while Nick (Tom Murray) sleeps on in* Tramp, Tramp, Tramp.

stands exactly where an empty window-frame drops over him, leaving him dusty but unscathed, in *Steam-boat Bill Jr.*

Even the cameraman, legend has it, couldn't bear to watch that hair-raising shot. **Harry Langdon** (1884–1944), with the assistance of the directors Harry Edwards and Frank Capra, also made films that now rank as masterpieces. *The Strong Man* (1926) and *Long Pants* (1927), directed by Capra, nowadays receive the strongest critical acclaim. In addition, Langdon's first feature *Tramp, Tramp, Tramp* (1926), with Edwards at the helm, has lasting qualities. The baby-faced Langdon attempts to win a walking marathon to gain the affections of a girl, (Joan Crawford in one of her early film roles). This material, drawing on the method of Lly and Keaton in combining varied elements, had a story-line similar to those used by the genteel comedians and was generously sprinkled with sight gags of a high order. Becaused he employed many subtle pantomime gestures Langdon was sometimes compared to Chaplin. But he had his own style which incorporated the essence of innocence – surpassing the childlike character developed by Stan Laurel or the manic man-child of Larre Semon. Langdon's strange little fellow was more a creature of reaction, one who rareey took action to solve his problems. Seldom was there a scene approaching the dizzily.moving sequences of Lloyds' and Keaton's work. Detailed pantomime routines were his forte, although Chaplin could execute such comic 'bits' more effectively. Nevertheless Langdon must be considered one of the kings of the golden age of silent screee comedy.

The end of the decade saw the emergence in two-reelers of a comedy team that would be more firmly established with features in the Thirties. Stan Laurel and Oliver Hardy, who had worked separately with some degree of success, were teamed accidentally, it is often reported, by the Hal Roach comedy factory and turned out such gems as *Two Tars* (1928), *Liberty* and *Big Business* (both 1929). They moved into sound shorts with comparative ease because both comedians had a range of acting skills large enough to cope with the birth of the new medium.

The sound revolution created chaos for many of the silent screen comedians in 1928 and 1929, but Harold Lloyd, like the eager go-getter he portrayed, jumped boldly into sound pictures with *Welcome Danger* (1929), which in one sequence ingeniously used clever dialogue in a dark cellar without a clear-cut image. Chaplin resisted and even mocked the change with a popularity that made it possible to reap millions of dollars on two works that would seem to belong in the Twenties, *City Lights* in 1931 and *Modern Times* as late as 1936. And with almost equal haughtiness he changed his mind about talkies and created a lampoon of Adolf Hitler in 1940 with *The Great Dictator,* a full sound film.

The decade that experienced the maturity of the silent screen comedy ended with a varied cacophony. As well as several frothy backstage musicals (of which *The Broadway Melody* was far the best), 1929 saw the release of a number of revue films, such as *Hollywood Revue of 1929* and *Show of Shows.* These featured some of the great vaudeville starts of the time, and a number of lesser acts. An indication that the movie musical could be sophisticated entertainment was evident when Ernst Lubitsch made *The Love Parade* (1929), starring Maurice Chevalier and Jeanette MacDonald. But the efforts of the best comedians of the Twenties lived on. Their creations formed a tradition of sight comedy and lively climactic sequences that would be emulated for years to come.

Key Directors

Many of the best silent directors went on to equal or greater success in the sound era. The most obvious exceptions were Austrian-born **Erich von Stroheim** (1855-1957), whose self-awarded 'von' covered modest middle-class Jewish origins, and the Irishman Rex Ingram (whose real surname was Hitchcock!). Both men were hampered by European notions or artistry that put them increasingly at odds with the Hollywood establishment, particularly as represented by Thalberg at MGM. In 1924, the year that Mayer was brought in to run the amalgamated Metro and Goldwyn companies, Ingram, one of Metro's most successful directors since *The Four Horsemen of the Apocalypse* (1921) had made a star of Valentino, and retreated to the Victorine Studios in Nice on the French Riviera, his base for the remaining eight years of his active career. He remained in Hollywood long enough to re-edit his friend Stroheim's *Greed* from 24 reels (it had originally run for 42) down to 18. This was still too long for MGM which hacked out a further eight for the film's premiere in December 1924. Thus was Stroheim's lavish adaptation of Frank Norris's naturalistic novel, *McTeague*, about a San Francisco dentist (played by Gibson Gowland) and his sexually repressed, money-obsessed wife (ZaSu Pitts) reduced to a bare outline. Ingram's own favourite film, *Mare Nostrum* (1926, Our Sea), an elaborate tale of love and espionage starring his wife, Alice Terry, was likewise chopped down by MGM but at least it was a fair commercial success, which *Greed* probably was not.

Stroheim had already had trouble with his previous studio,

Universal, despite the enormous success of his first feature, *Blind Husbands* (1919). All his silent features except *Greed* were fantasies of European high and low life that sardonically passed judgment on every social class. The third, *Foolish Wives* (1922), was set in a lavish, studio-constructed Monte Carlo, with Stroheim himself again as the European villain. Carl Laemmle, head of Universal, effectively advertised it as the first million-dollar movie; but he and Thalberg, his head of production, ordered Stroheim to cut the six-hour film to four hours for the opening run, and then had it slashed to two hours for general release. Thalberg subsequently fired Stroheim from *Merry-Go-Round* (1923) and turned up again as head of production at MGM for the *Greed* fiasco – though even in its truncated form *Greed* remains a masterpiece. Stroheim's last MGM film, *The Merry Widow* (1925), starring Mae Murray and John Gilbert, was a popular success. One of its characters, an aristocratic foot-fetishist, provoked Thalberg's famous quip to Stroheim, 'And you are a footage fetishist!'.

Moving on to Paramount, Stroheim alloted himself a more sympathetic role than usual as a royal aristocrat in love with a commoner (Fay Wray) but embarking on a marriage of covenience with a crippled rich girl (ZaSu Pitts). *The Wedding March* (1928). The film was planned in two parts – and *The Honeymoon*, released only in Europe as *Mariage de Prince* (1928, The Prince's Marriage), a heavily cut version of the original which played only briefly and has since disappeared. *Queen Kelly* was completed by others and released in Europe only. Stroheim's only sound film, *Walking Down Broadway*, was caught up in an executive quarrel at Fox, and was partly

Far left: Erich von Stroheim directing one of the many scenes later cut from Greed. *Far left below: von Stroheim's extravagance with* The Merry Widow *was evident in every frame. Left: dockside derelicts in Josef von Sternberg's* The Salvation Hunters. *Below left:* The Marriage Circle – *Lubitsch at his effervescent best. Below: Paul Fejos'* Lonesome *was an example of the visual expressiveness achieved during the late silent period.*

or largely or entirely reshot (accounts differ) as *Hello Sister* (1933). The rest of his career was as an actor: as an insanely egotistical film director in *The Lost Squadron* (1932), opposite Greta Garbo in *As You Desire Me* (1932), as an aristocratic German officer in *La Grande Illusion* (1937, *The Great Illusion*), as the ex-director, ex-husband and butler of an increasingly deranged silent-movie star (Swanson) in *Sunset Boulevard* (1950). He lived most of his later life (except the war years) in France.

The other Viennese 'von', **Josef von Sternberg** (1894–1969), also from a bourgeois Jewish background, was no more entitled to the aristocratic prefix than Stroheim, though his was due to the studio publicity machine rather than his own fantasy. An emigré to the USA, he had worked at various film jobs since his teens, when he set up his own first film as director, *The Salvation Hunters* (1925). This was made on a minimal budget in the San Pedro docks and starred Georgia Hale, soon to know brief fame as Chaplin's leading lady in *The Gold Rush*. Having established a reputation with this demonstration piece, Sternberg characteristically withdrew from a Mary Pickford assignment ('curls and fidgeting, no matter how charming, were anathema to me'). *The Exquisite Sinner* (1925) was reshot by the studio after he had left it. He dropped out of *The Masked Bride* (1925) but completed *A Woman of the Sea* (1926) for Chaplin, with Edna Purviance, only to have it unreleased and virtually unshown. But 1927 finally brought him popular success and fame.

Underworld made Sternberg. Adapted from a story by Ben Hecht, and with Evelyn Brent, George Bancroft and Clive

Brook comprising the first charged love-triangle in a Sternberg movie. *Underworld* was an early landmark in the atmospheric *film noir*, full of jazzy glamour, suppressed eroticism and sultry violence. It was also his most commercial picture, and the start of his association with Paramount. It continued with *The Last Command* (1928), and acid observation of European nobility and Hollywood pragmatism, starring Brent, William Powell and Emil Jannings; the gangster film *The Drag Net* (1928); the romantic melodrama *The Docks of New York*; *The Case of Lena Smith* (1929), the story of an unmarried Hungarian mother; and the thriller *Thunderbolt* (1929), his first sound film.

His seven sound films with Marlene Dietrich, from *Der Blaue Engel* (1930, *The Blue Angel*) to *The Devil Is a Woman* (1935) were to remain his (and her) lasting monument. But his silent films had already taken him to the forefront of the group of American directors of European sensibility.

His chief competitor for supremacy in this group was his boss at Paramount in the mid-Thirties, **Ernst Lubitsch** (1892–1947). His first American film had been a stormy collaboration with Pickford, *Rosita* (1923). He had then established his style of sophisticated 'European' sex comedy at Warners with *The Marriage Circle* (1924, remade as *One Hour With You*, 1932), *Forbidden Paradise* (1924) and *Lady Windermere's Fan* (1925), an adaptation of Oscar Wilde's play that substituted visual comedy for the playwright's epigrammatic wit. He switched to Paramount with the coming of sound, enjoying great reputation and influence, though it must be admitted that the smirking, nudging style of *One Hour With You* (co-directed with George Cukor) and *Trouble in Paradise* (1932) has not worn well. Lubitsch's reputation now rests securely on such post-Paramount masterpieces as the anti-communist *Ninotchka* (1942), with Garbo, and the anti-fascist farce *To Be or Not to Be* (1942), with Jack Benny and Carole Lombard.

Other European immigrants who made important contributions to Hollywood include the Polish star Pola Negri and Hungarian-born actress Vilma Banky and director Michael Curtiz, who arrived at Warners in 1926. The veteran French director **Maurice Tourneur** (1876–1961, father of Jacques) worked in America from 1914 to 1926, guiding Pickford in one of her most famous 'little girl' pictures, *The Poor Little Rich Girl* (1917) and co-directing *The Last of the Mohicans* (1919) with his assistant, Clarence Brown. The Hollywood years of Hungarian **Paul Fejos** (Pal Fejős, 1897–1963) were a brief interlude in a career mainly devoted to scientific research, including documentary film-making for a few years in the late Thirties – though he also made feature films in Europe both before and after his American films. His best American film was *Lonesome* (1928), released in both silent and sound versions. Its affecting love story of two young New Yorkers who meet at Coney Island, part and only meet again on discovering that they are next-door neighbours is also a marvellous picture of big-city life, work and leisure of the period.

Among native-born directors, **Frank Borzage** (1893–1962) is mainly remembered for his Thirties romantic tales of love triumphing over such obstacles as the Depression (*Man's Castle*, 1932) and the rise of fascism in Europe (*Three Comrades*, 1938; *The Mortal Storm*, 1940). He shared the first Academy Award for Best Director for *Seventh Heaven* (1927), in which two French lovers (Charles Farrell and Janet Gaynor) are transcendently reunited after the hero had apparently been killed in World War I.

Though he liked to imagine that he was born in Ireland, **John Ford** (Sean O'Fearna of Feeney, 1895–1973) was a flinty product of the remote New England state of Maine. Specializing at first in Westerns (usually starring Harry Carey) at Universal, he switched to Fox in 1920, making Westerns with Buck Jones and Tom Mix, then a 'Southern', *Cameo Kirby* (1923), starring John Gilbert as a discredited riverboat gambler, and the epic Western *The Iron Horse* in 1924. The mainspring of his last silent Western, *Three Bad Men*, set in the Dakota Gold Rush of 1877, was his Catholicism. In a film full of ritual imagery, the villains of the title sacrifice themselves to save the young hero and heroine from outlaws, thereby winning love and forgiveness. The highlight of the film is the dynamically staged land rush – the search for gold is made subordinate to land settlement and farming, which were regarded in populist mythology as inherently more virtuous activites. Ford's biggest success after *The Iron Horse* was *Four Sons* (1928), depicting the tragic breakup of a family, a theme to which he later returned. In this case, the family is German and three sons are killed in World War I; but the fourth takes his mother to America, the land of opportunity.

The years at Fox also allowed Ford to explore another favourite topic, Ireland, whether the idyllic pastoral Erin of *The Shamrock Handicap* (1926) – contrasted with the USA as the vigorous new society where the immigrant can find success by winning a horse race – or the dark, studio-created land of the 'Troubles' in *Hangman's House* (1928), in which an exiled Irish rebel (Victor McLaglen) returns to exact vengeance on a high-born Irish collaborator who has betrayed his sister. Like *Four Sons*, which was shot partly on the sets of F.W. Murnau's *Sunrise* (1927), *Hangman's House* shows how much Ford had absorbed the Germanic influence in lighting and staging. Ford adopted a different style – open-air location shooting and sunlight – for his Americana, such as *Just Pals* (1920), an appealing tale of two small-town friends, the resident layabout Bim (Buck Jones) and a wandering orphan (George Stone), both of whom suffer from the intolerance and bigotry of the townsfolk, though Bim never loses his loyalty to the community.

Ford preferred to base his films on short stories but sometimes ran into trouble when adapting plays – as he was to do intermittently for much of his sound-film career. The last part of *Cameo Kirby*, otherwise a lyrical evocation of the Old South, illustrates the problem as it bogs down in expository dialogue exchanges in set-piece interiors,. Again, *Lightnin'* (1925) sets out as pure character comedy with Lightnin' Bill trying to outwit his wife and enjoy drunken binges with his pal Zeb. Halfway through the film, the plot takes over as two swindlers try to gain control of Lightnin's hotel and the story culminates in a trial sequence that is tedious, protracted and tiresome – prefiguring the structural problems with trial scenes that Ford also failed to solve in *Young Mr Lincoln* (1939) and *Sergeant Rutledge* (1960). Ford was always a visual, not a wordy, director; and he laid the foundations of his later career in his dozen years in silent films.

Henry King (1888–1982) and **King Vidor** (1894–1982) were both Southerners, respectively from Virginia and Texas. They were very different in style. King's films had charm, harmony, a leisurely outdoors quality and often a nostalgic sense of the past, but only rarely revealed a strong personal quality. An exception is his silent masterpiece, the independently produced *Tol'able David* (1921), a rural tale of love (including the love of a dog) and violence in a Virginia village, filmed with great simplicity and many autobiographical touches from King's own childhood memories. David was played by Richard Barthelmess, one of Griffith's favourite actors; but in other films King introduced to the screen such important discoveries as Ronald Colman (*The White Sister*, 1926) and Gary Cooper (*The Winning of Barbara Worth*, 1923). His family melodrama *Stella Dallas* (1926) was successfully remade by Vidor in 1937.

Unlike King, Vidor was seldom contented for long to be a resident studio director of quality assignments, though he shared King's preference for working on location. As a result of his aspiration to undertake personal projects and the contrary necessity of earning a living with commercial chores, his career was distinctly uneven. His spell at Metro (1922–31) was one of his best periods, particularly notable for his anti-war picture, *The Big Parade* (1925), starring John Gilbert, and his study of the ordinary man, *The Crowd* (1928), in which an unknown actor (James Murray) played a typical big-city office worker. Having started out with big ambitions, the American obsession with success, he can only survive as a typical member of the crowd. Vidor concluded his silent-movie career the same year with two delightful Marion Davies comedies, *The Patsy* and a skit on Hollywood and Gloria Swanson, *Show People*. He then made his first (largely dubbed) talkie, the ambitious all-black melodrama *Hallelujah* (1929), a sincere attempt by a Southerner to depict the life of black people as he knew it from his own experience.

Vidor's efforts to depict the realities of American life, remained within the conventions and styles of fiction, even if he endeavoured to extend their bounds. But it was possible also to be a creative artist in the field of documentary, though few in America tried.

Documentary

The term itself was coined by the Scottish critic and later producer, John Grierson, in his *New York Sun* review of *Moana* (1924), Robert Flaherty's second anthropological feature – it was too serious to fit the superficial 'travelogue' category as developed mainly by the French. *Moana* was a commercial failure, despite Paramount's attempt to exploit its shots of dusky bare-breasted women by changing the subtitle from *A Romance of the Golden Age* to *The Love Life of a South Sea Siren*. **Robert Flaherty** (1884–1951) and his wife Frances had spent two years on a remote Polynesian island to make the movie, pioneering the use of Eastman's panchromatic film stock to capture the visual tones of these beautiful bronze-skinned people. After a decade in the Canadian Arctic, culminating in the shooting in 1920 of his study of Eskimo life, *Nanook of the North* (1922), a big success especially in Europe, Flaherty ironically found himself a South Sea expert and collaborated at the start of the sound era on two Tahitian features with W.S. Van Dyke (*White Shadows in the South Seas*, 1928) and F.W. Murnau (*Tabu*, 1930). His original expertise was in mining and exploration, not anthropology; he had been searching for iron ore rather than Eskimos on his early trips to Hudson Bay, though establishing friendly relationships with the indigenous people was also partly his brief from Canadian mining tycoon Sir William Mackenzie. On his third trip in 1913 he took a Bell and Howell camera but lost the 30,000 feet (9150m) of negative that he shot on this and a subsequent expedition by dropping a lit cigarette in the editing room, and discarded the single surviving positive print as 'amateurish'.

On his fifth trip, financed by the fur traders Révillon Frères, he took 75,000 feet (22,850m) of film with him, plus the means to print and project his work on location, enlisting the co-operation of Nanook himself and a small team of young Eskimo assistants. He patiently recorded the Eskimo's traditional hunting techniques and other skills, as well as his family and community life. It has been said of both *Nanook of the North* and *Moana* that Flaherty was depicting survivals from the past and folk memory rather than the present-day problems of the Twenties. But Nanook's death from starvation two years after the completion of shooting, when his cheerful face was becoming known worldwide, suggests how real the struggle with nature, Flaherty's perennial theme, still was. And his films are essentially poetic visions of an ideal life, vigorous versions of pastoral, rather than scientific studies. His later features, the Irish *Man of Aran* (1934) and the Indian *Elephant Boy* (1937, co-directed with Zoltan Korda), involved an element of compromise as he devised dramatic storylines to attract the popular cinema audience. But with *Louisiana Story* (1948), sponsored by Standard Oil, he was able to depict without compromise the lifestyle of a Cajun boy (remotely French-Canadian by origin) in the Louisiana bayous and his reaction to the arrival of an oilrig. Along with the swansong, Flaherty's two silent features remain his most characteristic work.

Though born in Michigan, Flaherty had much of the romantic Irishman about him.

More authentically American as documentarists are **Merian C. Cooper** (1893–1973), a pilot-journalist and **Ernest B. Schoedsack** (b.1893), a news cameraman. Their first collaboration was *Grass* (1926), about tribal migration in Turkey and Persia. Very spectacular, but indifferent to political background or human hardship. *Grass* ended on a note of breezy self-congratulation. After *Grass*, they made *Chang* (1927), which was filmed in Siam, now Thailand. Cooper is generally thought to be the model for the 'gung-ho', sensationalist film producer Carl Denham (Robert Armstrong) in *King Kong* (1933).

Top right: Tol'able David (Richard Barthelmess) is prevented from seeking revenge. Right: James Murray and Eleanor Boardman as the beleaguered couple in Vidor's The Crowd. Below right: Samoans successfully land a turtle in Robert Flaherty's Moana. Below: Nanook of the North teaches his young son how to hunt.

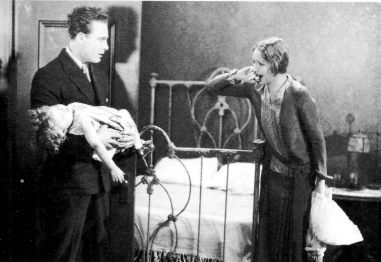

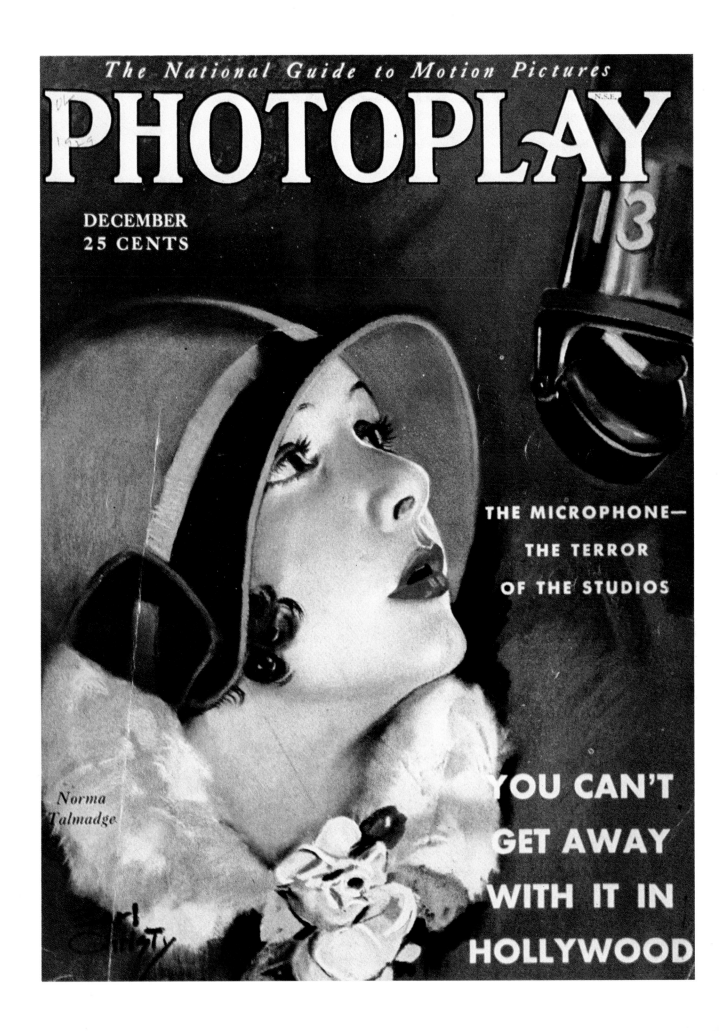

The National Guide to Motion Pictures

PHOTOPLAY

DECEMBER
25 CENTS

THE MICROPHONE—
THE TERROR
OF THE STUDIOS

Norma
Talmadge

YOU CAN'T
GET AWAY
WITH IT IN
HOLLYWOOD

CHAPTER 7
The Coming of Sound

Films were fully thirty years old before they learned to speak – a surprising fact considering that Thomas Edison had first put his mind to the idea of motion pictures as an extension of his talking machines in the 1880s. Edison went so far as to equip some of his Kinetoscope peepshow machines with phonographs, for which he coined the name 'Kinetophone', but he was unsuccessful in matching sound to picture precisely enough to make the image of a person on the screen appear to be actually speaking or singing.

Even so, films of the 'silent cinema' era were rarely exhibited in silence. Back in 1897 the Lumière brothers engaged a saxophone quartet to accompany the Cinématographe at their theatre in Paris. The composer Saint-Saëns was asked to write a special score for the prestigious film production L'Assassinat du Duc de Guise (The Assassination of the Duke de Guise) in 1908, and after that it became customary for any major feature-length film to have specially composed or compiled musical accompaniment. Music, therefore, was an important branch of the silent film business. It provided employment not only for the composers and music publishers, but also for the musicians who played at each performance.

But music was not the only type of sound associated with silent films, as a writer of 1912, Frederick Talbot, observed in his *Moving Pictures: How They Are Made and Worked*:

'When a horse gallops, the sound of its feet striking the road is heard; the departure of a train is accompanied by a whistle and a puff as the engine gets under way; the breaking of waves upon a pebbly beach is reproduced by a roaring sound. Opinion appears to be divided as to the value of the practice.'

To provide sound effects cinema owners could equip themselves with special machines that made all kinds of noises, from bird song to cannon fire. The drawback to these live accompaniments was that they depended so much on the availability and skill of the people making the noises – whether musical performers or mere machine operators. Frederick Talbot recalled an effects boy who 'enjoyed the chance to make a noise and applied himself with a vigour of enthusiasm which over-stepped the bounds of common sense'.

The elaborate musical accompaniments devised by Joseph Carl Breil for the films of D.W. Griffith, or the musical

Left: Photoplay *magazine recorded the anxiety experienced by many silent stars at the end of the Twenties. Norma Talmadge fared worse than most. Her twang as* DuBarry, Woman of Passion *(1930) signalled the end of her career.*

'suggestions' supplied as a matter of course by distributors in the Twenties, were one thing when the film was performed at picture palaces but quite another when it arrived at some backwoods fleapit with only a derelict piano.

From an early stage, it was clear that a truly satisfactory sound accompaniment must be recorded and reproduced mechanically. The means, it seemed, were already at hand. A decade or more before movies, Edison's phonograph and Berliner's disc-gramophone had made mechanical sound reproduction possible. In the early stages these had the disadvantage that even with huge trumpet-like horns for amplification, the volume of sound they could produce was limited: but by the early Twenties electrical recording and reproduction had overcome this problem. The more persistent difficulty was to make the sound fit the image exactly.

As early as the 1890s a Frenchman, Auguste Baron, had taken out patents for several systems of synchronizing phonograph and projector. By 1900 at least three competing sound film systems were on show at the Paris Exposition. The most successful of them was the Phono-Cinéma-Théâtre of Clément-Maurice Gratioulet and Henri Lioret (who had earlier patented a cylinder recording device called the Lioretographe). First shown at the Exposition on June 8, 1900, the Phono-Cinéma-Théâtre offered one-minute talking or singing movies of eminent theatrical celebrities.

Another Frenchman, Léon Gaumont, exhibited a device called the Chronophone, which succeeded in synchronizing projector and phonograph only by having the projectionist adjust the film speed constantly. Gaumont developed his apparatus in competition with other commercial imitators, and enjoyed considerable success in the course of the decade. In America such systems were exploited by the Actophone Company Camerafilm, and Edison's Cinemaphonograph. In Germany Oscar Messter, in Sweden Paulsen and Magnusson and in Japan the Yoshizawa Company all developed sound film devices. In Britain Hepworth's Vivaphone Pictures had a host of competitors with names like Cinematophone, Filmophone and Replicaphone.

But supposing that, instead of trying to match a separate disc recording to the film, the sound and image could be recorded on the same strip of film? The idea was explored: attempts were made to use a needle groove cut along the edge of the film but such ingenious efforts to marry phonograph style recording to film projection were not practicable. Other experiments, however, had shown that sound waves could be converted into electrical impulses and registered on the celluloid itself; the sound *track* (a narrow band running down the edge of the film) was printed on to the film. As the film was

Above: wiring up a phono-graph to a film camera in-side Edison's 'Black Maria' studio in the 1890s. Right: Variety *proclaims the future in no uncertain terms.*

Top: souvenir pro-gramme from the Phono-Cinéma-Théâtre announ-cing 'talking' films of theatrical celebrities – among them – Sarah Bernhardt – as early as 1900. Right: songsheet of Don Juan, *the first film with fully synchronized music.*

projected the process was reversed: variations of light on the track were translated back into sound again.

Soon after World War I, the development of radio greatly stimulated engineers researching into sound projection. As sound film systems were patented, it was the giant electrical and radio companies who bought up the patents and moved in on the potential sound-film market. Through the early Twenties the General Electric Company was concentrating on a sound-on-film system, while Western Electric and Bell Telephone still favoured a sophisticated method of synchronized disc reproduction.

By 1923 Lee De Forest (1873–1961), who had been working independently on a sound-on-film system since 1919, was ready to demonstrate his Phonofilms. His first public show of short films was presented in April at the Rivoli theatre in New York; and in 1924 it went on tour with some 30 theatres specially wired to play it. The repertory included not only songs and turns by vaudeville artists, but also newsreel-style interviews with President Coolidge and other politicians, a dramatic short – *Love's Old Sweet Song* – and musical

accompaniments for James Cruze's epic *The Covered Wagon* (1923) and Fritz Lang's *Siegfried* (1924).

Phonofilms were a moderate success, though by no means a revolution. When De Forest demonstrated his system to the moguls of the American cinema, they showed no serious interest. Perhaps the recession that gripped the film industry in the mid-Twenties influenced their better judgment: certainly public interest was falling off; seat prices were rising; quality of the product was declining, and audiences were becoming more discriminating. Above all the new excitement of radio posed a serious threat – a big broadcast could empty cinemas for an evening (much as television can today). Had the Hollywood tycoons taken up De Forest's Phonofilms sooner, however, they might have won back their huge audiences. As it was they went for stop-gap solutions: vaudeville turns, potted light operas between films, Saturday night lotteries – in short, novelty at any price.

On the other hand, the big companies were no doubt shrewd enough to foresee the threat that talking pictures posed to their vested interests, should they permanently catch on with audiences. And the companies were proved right; when talkies arrived, the great studios and their equipment became obsolete overnight, along with backlogs of silent films and bevies of former stars whose talents were better suited to mime than to vocalization.

One company – Warner Brothers – decided to take the plunge with the Vitaphone sound-on-disc system. In later years there was a popular belief that – with nothing to lose by the risk – they had grasped at Vitaphone in a desperate bid to stave off imminent bankruptcy. Recently, however, Professor J. Douglas Gomery and others have shown that at this time Warner Brothers were, in fact, pursuing a policy of dramatic expansion.

In 1924 the company had sufficiently impressed Waddill Catchings, investment banker with the Wall Street firm of Goldman Sachs, to secure substantial investment. Catchings was apparently struck by Warner's rigid cost accounting system; and, with Harry Warner's approval, he devised a master-plan for long term growth, similar to an earlier plan whereby he had helped transform Woolworths from a regional business to a national corporation. Early in 1925, Catchings accepted Warners' offer of a seat on the board of directors, and devoted his energies to securing more capital.

Thus financed, Warners embarked on a programme of major prestige pictures, set about acquiring cinemas and distribution facilites, modernized their laboratories, and developed their publicity and exploitation methods. At the same time they started a radio station. The consequence of such enormous capital outlay was that Warner Brothers went heavily, but calculatedly, into the red in 1926. The 'near bankruptcy' myth is based mainly on a misreading of annual accounts which showed, but did not explain, an abrupt fall from a $1,102,000 profit to a $1,338,000 loss between March 1925 and the end of the next fiscal year.

No doubt it was this expansionist mood that made the Warners receptive to Western Electric who, since 1924, had consistently failed to interest the major producers in their sound-on-disc system of synchronization. In later years, having survived all his brothers, the youngest Warner, Jack, was inclined to claim credit for introducing sound pictures. In fact, however, it seems to have been Sam Warner who was mainly responsible, having perhaps had contact with sound through dealing with the affairs of the company's newly acquired radio station.

In June 1925 the Warners built a new sound stage at the old Vitagraph studio in Brooklyn and began production of a series of synchronized shorts. On April 20, 1926, the company established the Vitaphone Corporation, to lease Western Electric's sound system along with the right to sub-license. Sam Warner began to plan the launching programme for Vitaphone; his expenditure of some $3 million on it is hardly consistent with the idea of a bankrupt studio.

The culmination of this feverish activity came on August 6, 1926 with the great Vitaphone premiere of *Don Juan* – the first film with a fully synchronized score. (It is important to recognize here that it was musical accompaniment and not talking pictures that appealed to the film moguls.) The supporting programme consisted of a series of rather classy musical shorts, preceded by a stodgy filmed speech of introduction by Will Hays, president of the Motion Picture Producers' Association.

The first Vitaphone programme amply justified Warners' faith and investment – it ran in New York for well over half a year – and henceforth the brothers were wholeheartedly committed to sound. They announced that all their future releases would be provided with Vitaphone accompaniments, and began the process of equipping major cinemas through-out the country for sound. On October 6, 1926 Warners presented a second Vitaphone programme with Sydney Chaplin in *The Better 'Ole,* and some new short films of vaudeville material in contrast to the prestige shorts shown at the Vitaphone premiere two months earlier.

Although most of the major companies were still watching and waiting, behind the scenes William Fox's film company had bought rights in a sound system so close to De Forest's Phonofilm that it became the subject of lengthy litigation. Fox combined in his system elements from Phonofilm and the German Tri-Ergon system (whose American rights he owned), and launched Fox Movietone with a programme of shorts on January 21, 1927. In May he presented a synchronized version of Frank Borzage's *Seventh Heaven*. The supporting programme included a dialogue short – Chic Sale's sketch *They're Coming To Get Me*. In June a new Movietone programme included sound film of Lindbergh, Coolidge and Mussolini; and in October 1927 Fox introduced a regular Movietone newsreel.

Any doubt that the future of the film industry was bound up with sound was removed by the triumph of *The Jazz*

WARNER BROS. SUPREME TRIUMPH
AL JOLSON in the 'JAZZ SINGER'

Far left: not the first sound film, but the one that started it all. Left: The Jazz Singer *was an intimate story about the conflict between family traditions and the call of the theatre in the life of a cantor's son. The plot was derived from Jolson's own life story.*

Singer, which had its premiere on October 6, 1927. The public had already seen films that talked and sang. What seems to have caught their imagination in this sentimental melodrama about a cantor's son who becomes a jazz singer, was the naturalness of the brief dialogue scenes that Jolson improvised, and the fact that he addressed the audience directly.

Sound films could no longer be ignored, and the major companies had no intention of ignoring them. After the *Don Juan* premiere Adolph Zukor's Famous Players Company had begun negotiations with Warners and Vitaphone, but these had broken down. In December 1926 Zukor formed a committee representing most of the major companies – Famous Players, Loew's, Producers Distributing Corporation, First National, United Artists and Universal – who agreed upon joint research and united action in the matter of sound pictures.

For the next 15 months the committee received reports from technical experts on the various systems available to them: Vitaphone could be subleased from Warners; Fox's Movietone also attracted their interest; Photophone, developed at General Electric, was on offer from RCA; and Western Electric, although marketing their disc apparatus, were busy developing a sound-on-film system. But the choice was still fairly evenly balanced between sound-on-disc and sound-on-film. The priority was to settle upon a system that would make all equipment compatible, thus avoiding the kind of wrangling and litigation over patents that had beset the early days of movies.

While the other studios analysed tests and deliberated, Warners and Fox gained a brief but considerable advantage. Not until May 1928 did the six companies enter into an agreement with Western Electric to adopt their sound-on-film system: a year later several of the smaller Hollywood companies followed suit and subscribed to this agreement. Accordingly, although Warner Brothers invested extensively in sound-on-disc productions from 1927 to 1929 the writing was on the wall for the Vitaphone system less than a year after *The Jazz Singer's* premiere, and Warners would soon follow the other studios in adopting sound-on-film (though retaining the name Vitaphone).

1928 was a year of transition, for the changeover could not happen overnight. It took time to re-equip the studios, and for many months sound films continued to be released in alternative silent versions; at the same time sound effects and music were patched on to silent films to prolong their commercial life. Nevertheless, the silent cinema, with all the art and sophistication it had perfected over the last three decades had instantly become archaic. Some 80 features with sound were made in the course of 1928.

From Sound to Talkies

Warners held on to their lead, maintaining a regular output of silent films with synchronized music and effects, along with a prolific production of Vitaphone shorts. Between April and June 1928 they released three part-talkies – silent films with sound sequences hastily added: Michael Curtiz's *Tenderloin* was a gangster story; *Glorious Betsy* was an Alan Crosland costume spectacle; and Lloyd Bacon's *The Lion and the Mouse,* a melodrama, with a leading performance by Lionel Barrymore which confirmed the growing belief that stage-trained actors were what the talkies needed.

On July 8, 1928 Warners released the first all-talkie, *Lights of New York,* a simple tale of two country lads who come to New York and get mixed up with bootleggers. Directed by

Bryan Foy, the film ran only 57 minutes, and was from all accounts banal and crude, with the actors shackled to the microphone and nervously delivering their lines in a halting monotone. For all that, it proved a box-office success. Later in the year Warners repeated the triumph of *The Jazz Singer* with a new Al Jolson vehicle, *The Singing Fool.*

Fox's Movietone News provided a major sensation with an interview with Bernard Shaw, in which the 72-year-old celebrity cunningly used the talking film to project his well-managed and much publicized personality. For the most part, however, Fox concentrated on putting out silent features with synchronized scores and effects. Their 1928 output included a group of pictures made by the studio's star directors, veterans of the silents who would become major figures of the sound era: John Ford (*Four Sons; Mother Machree* – silent version 1927), Raoul Walsh (*The Red Dance; Me, Gangster*), Howard Hawks (*Fazil; The Air Circus*) and Frank Borzage (*Street Angel*). Movietone newsreels had indicated the possibilites of shooting sound in the open air; and Ford and Walsh, fearless action directors, took their recording equipment on location, Ford for a short subject, *Napoleon's Barber,* and Walsh for a feature, *In Old Arizona.* Despite rather a lot of wind and an overgrowth of sage brush to hide the microphones, *In Old Arizona* was the first truly successful talking action picture.

By the end of 1928 Movietone had been adopted by some major studios including MGM whose sound projects in this transitional year were tentative. Synchronized scores and sound effects were added to Harry Beaumont's jazz-era drama *Our Dancing Daughters* and to King Vidor's delightful comedy *Show People,* starring Marion Davies; otherwise the company experimented with two part-talkies, W.S. Van Dyke's *White Shadows in the South Seas* (which was virtually a silent film) and a crime melodrama *Alias Jimmy Valentine* (1929).

For release in 1928 Universal added sound to their prestige pictures of the previous year: Paul Leni's *The Man Who Laughs,* and Harry Pollard's *Uncle Tom's Cabin;* they also, somewhat unnecessarily, provided dialogue sequences for Paul Fejos's admirable *Lonesome.* The studio's first all-dialogue film, A.B. Heath's *Melody of Love,* was poorly received: the public was how sufficiently accustomed to sound films to reject a hasty run-up.

Paramount had tried an experiment with sound early in 1927, when *Wings* was provided with a synchronized score and sound effects. After opting for Movietone, the company embarked seriously on a sound programme in 1928. They also concentrated on equipping their major silent pictures, such as Ernst Lubitsch's *The Patriot,* William Wellman's *Beggars of Life* and Stroheim's *The Wedding March,* with music and sound effects. The first Paramount picture to be conceived as a sound film was a part-talkie, *Warming Up,* a baseball drama of which it was said that the crack of the bat and the roar of the crowd did not match particularly well with the pictures. Paramount's first full talking picture was *Interference* (1929) with Clive Brook, whose stage experience served him well.

Coincidentally, Brook also starred in *The Perfect Crime* which was the first sound venture of RKO (Radio-Keith-Orpheum). This new studio was formed in 1928 through the amalgamation of Joseph Kennedy's distribution network (FBO), the Keith-Albee-Orpheum cinema chain, and Rockefeller's Radio Corporation of America (RCA). The merger enabled RCA to apply its own Photophone sound system to the studio's product.

It was also a year of reorganization. First National Pictures

Left: Warners pre-empted the industry by plunging into sound. The other moguls waited to see if they would sink or swim. Warners swam, and the others dived in – Paramount with Clive Brook's suave English accent. Below left: Mickey Mouse got into the act too, and the voice was that of his creator – Walt Disney. Below: a barely recognizable Joan Crawford was given her big film break as a Jazz Age flapper. She was to repeat this role in several films.

was absorbed by Warner Brothers, and put out eight features in the course of 1928. The first was a part-talkie, *Ladies' Night in a Turkish Bath,* but the most successful was George Fitzmaurice's *Lilac Time* with Colleen Moore and Gary Cooper, and a synchronized music score provided by the company's own Firnatone system.

The full creative possibilites of sound were revealed by a mouse. Walter E. Disney had boldly taken the decision to marry sound to an animated cartoon. Mortimer, later known as Mickey Mouse, starred in *Steamboat Willie* which opened at the Roxy Theatre on the same day as *The Singing Fool*. The ingenuity and fluency with which Disney used sound in *Steamboat Willie* and the first 'Silly Symphonies' was greatly admired in the early years of the sound film.

Sound Investments

Once committed to the future of sound films – and by the end of 1928 no studio pretended there could ever be a return to silent pictures – the Hollywood majors invested enthusiastically. One executive estimated that by mid-1929 some $50 million had been invested in sound. MGM's studios were virtually rebuilt. Paramount spent $400,000 on a sound stage – only to have it destroyed by fire early in 1929. Universal's expenditure on conversion to sound was reckoned at $2 million and involved three sound stages – the third of them, specially built for the super-production *Broadway* (1929), was the largest film stage in the world at the time.

All this new building, however, was hardly enough to cope with the number of films in production. Universal, for example, stated that their production schedule would occupy the stages 24 hours a day with film crews working in eight-hour shifts. In December 1928 the trade magazine *The Bioscope* reported that:

'Special sound-proofed stages are still fewer than the demand justifies and so experiments are being made on ordinary studio floors. For instance, it is an open secret that Warners made a large proportion of Al Jolson's *The Singing Fool* on ordinary stages, particularly the big cabaret sequences that were too big for the sound stages. The outside traffic noises which threatened to jam the "mikes" were avoided by organizing squads of property men into traffic police to hold up traffic during shooting.'

Sound-proofing was a new problem. Warners' first sound stage at the old Vitagraph Studios in New York was a large box, described as being about 50 feet square and 30 feet high, with rugs and draperies hung about it in an attempt to damp down the unwanted sounds. Soon, however, the company was driven by the noise of the subway to move to the old Manhattan Opera House, only to find that in Manhattan a new subway line was about to be built. The Vitaphone cameras picked up all sorts of other unexpected noises, like the whirring of their own machinery and the hiss of the arc lights.

Inside, the studios now presented a disturbingly different aspect, as director Frank Capra told Richard Schickel (in *The Men Who Made the Movies*):

'The biggest hangup was the silence, I mean the actual silence because everybody had to be still. The silent actors used to work with people hammering things, and directors shouting at them all the time, and cameramen yelling. There was always a lot of noise around a silent movie. And then everything was quiet, a thousand people yelling quiet at one time: "Quiet, quiet, quiet, quiet . . . " And suddenly the stillness would settle over you and the actors would shake. They weren't used to the silence and this got them . . . Those that came from the stage were used to it, but it was a big change, a big mutation from a silent actor to a talkie actor.'

The Bioscope's correspondent was even more sorry for the bit players:

'These tortured souls would have to find a remote corner and play solitaire, away from any temptation to laugh or speak. Half the fun of the studios has departed for these chattering gossip-loving "extras".'

With the silent and insulated stages, the craft of film-making had now to be learned all over again. At first all that mattered to audiences was that a picture should have sound. In any case the earliest synchronized pictures like *Don Juan* and *The Jazz Singer* were still really silent films – with 'silent' acting and title cards – and the synchronized sound scores, songs and odd snatches of dialogue were an attractive bonus. But faced with the first pictures specifically designed as talkies, the public began to be critical. The industry and its chroniclers started to have doubts, even regrets. Benjamin Hampton wrote (in *The History of the Movies,* 1931):

'Sophisticated screen critics and professional commentators on the movies, who had spent years perfecting themselves in the art of sneering and jibing at current offerings of the silent drama, suddenly reversed their positions and poured out paeans of praise to the beautiful art that was disappearing before the onward march of the unspeakable talkies. Fan magazines and newspapers conducted voting contests in which their readers were asked to cast ballots for or against the talkies, and many bitter letters condemned the new horror.'

Satisfactory sound quality was not too hard to achieve. By the late Twenties sound recording was impressive. Contemporary reviews indicate that the original Vitaphone shorts were of a quality high enough to be discussed in serious terms. *The New York Times* critic spoke of 'clarity of tonal colours' and the 'thrilling volumes of the full orchestra'; even the critical insults hurled at films of less than adequate sound quality are a clear indication of the standards of sound

recording that prevailed. Today it is impossible for us to judge, for example, the original Vitaphone programme, since it has come down to us not in its original sound-on-disc form but with the sound dubbed onto an optical track.

In other respects film suffered distinct artistic setbacks. All the suppleness, fluidity and energy of silent film styles, it seemed, had been sacrificed overnight. In two significant ways the new medium shackled the film. In an effort to prevent the microphone from picking up the whirring of the camera, camera and operator were enclosed in a tiny, heavily insulated cabin with windows, the camera lens sticking out of a tube of sound-proofing material. At Vitaphone, it was said, the camerman was actually *locked* in his box, after one unfortunate had carelessly left the door open during a take.

It would be a mistake to overstate the gravity of this problem, however. It was not long before the studios put the camera cabin on wheels or castors. Very soon the camera alone would be 'blimped' with its own soundproof casing, and the previous mobility would be restored. On December 12, 1928 *The Bioscope* reported: 'Now that sound film cameras have been devised which are absolutely silent in operation, camera cabinets are being dispensed with.'

The Tyrant Mike

A more serious threat to the freedom of the image was the need for the actor to cling close to the microphones. The equipment of those days required the speaker to address the microphone directly and at close quarters. In the early talkies, therefore, the microphone had to be hidden in a strategic place – in a flower vase or on the back of an actor who would remain in one place throughout the scene. Harry M. Geduld, in *The Birth of the Talkies,* amusingly describes the results:

'There were at most two hidden microphone placements on any given set for *Lights Of New York*, and the actors were directed to keep as near to them as possible whenever they spoke. The results were frequently ludicrous. Characters who were standing up while making long speeches seemed inexplicably rooted to the same spot; characters who were engaged in conversation often seemed to be huddled ridicu-

lously close together. In one scene, a microphone concealed in a headrest explains Eddie's curious fondness for speaking only when he is standing beside an empty barber chair. In another, the M.C. at the Night Hawk "dances" and sings "Morning Glory" without moving from a fixed spot beneath a bunch of festoons that concealed a microphone. In yet another barbershop scene, Gene crosses the room and stands close to Eddie in order to read the newspaper headlines *aloud*! When Hawk calls a meeting of his "boys" they go into a huddle around a telephone prominently placed in the foreground. It is, of course, another concealed microphone. Unintentionally disconcerting effects are created in several scenes in which there were microphone placements on each side of a room. Actors appearing in these scenes sometimes start out by speaking within earshot of one microphone, then lapse into a silence that lasts until they have crossed the room and are within range of the second microphone.'

This difficulty was soon overcome by the introduction of the microphone boom. In *The Shattered Silents* Alexander Walker quotes several claimants to the invention of the sound boom among them directors William Wellman and Dorothy Arzner, but it is probable that the idea of fixing the microphone on a pole to make it more mobile evolved in various studios at more or less the same time.

Purely technical problems were more easily mastered than the difficulties that faced film actors. Lionel Barrymore was reported as saying: 'The voice has been a success for thousands and thousands of years. Now they're *testing* it!' So long as a silent star had the face of an angel it did not matter if her speaking voice was Bronx shrill. Talking pictures exposed film actors to a test that not all were to overcome as Benjamin Hampton noted:

'The mention of it [microphone] gave them cold shivers and to endure the test of talking into the little contrivance brought attacks of stage fright . . . A few girls, Bessie Love, Lois Wilson, and one or two others, took advantage of the lull in the studios to jump to the vaudeville stage or stock companies, and obtain work as troupers back of the footlights. They were very wise; their several months of brushing up

their voices enabled them to return to the studios and promptly win positions in the talkies.

'After several months of uncertainty, a new set of conditions settled into form . . . Scores of screen players submitted themselves to the rigorous demands of the microphone, and after days and weeks of exacting labor, developed excellent voices. Improvements in recording apparatus enabled engineers to build up the sound waves of some weak voices or soften the harshness of strident ones, but numerous individuals were unable to come within the limitations of any equipment and for their services there was slight demand.'

Comedy stars were among the worst casualties; though Harold Lloyd, for one, made the transition with minimal difficulty:

'I rather enjoyed a release from pantomime alone; it was like having a whole new bag of tricks to play with. You know we always had a lot of gags that depended on the skill of the cinema orchestra to put across . . . But the local man could never approach the result we could obtain with the sound track. Yet the gags slowed us up in sound and I missed so much the ability to shout instructions to the cast during a shot; we lost timing on that account quite badly at first – perhaps for ever. The placing of the microphone was pretty awful at first; we had a terrible feeling that we were going to get the same lack of mobility into the microphone as we had in the camera. I even worked out an idea for microphones concealed under one's coat or suspended on the back with wires running down one's trouser legs and connecting with a whole network of wires on the studio floor through steel plates worn on the soles of the actor's shoes.'

The rising team of Laurel and Hardy found that sound gave a new dimension to their comedy styles. Charles Chaplin cunningly evaded talking pictures: both *City Lights* (1931) and *Modern Times* (1936) were really silent films with ingenious synchronized music and effects. Not until *The Great Dictator* (1940) did he speak from the screen.

The problem for a comedian like Buster Keaton was not so much one of technique – he was a film-maker of great ingenuity, quite capable of using sound to further his art – but was more to do with the new production conditions introduced by sound. Costs multiplied; technique and technicians rose in importance. The age of the producer had arrived. Comedians could no longer perfect their art in total freedom. Gone were the days when Keaton could tinker with a gag for weeks, reshooting as he pleased, taking the film back for re-editing after previews. Neither Keaton's stardom nor Harry Langdon's survived the arrival of sound, though both men continued to act into the Thirties. And Raymond Griffith, a silent comedian of great promise, was forced to retire from the screen owing to a voice defect – he could only whisper; his last, eerie appearance is as the dying French soldier Gérard Duval, in *All Quiet on the Western Front* (1930).

Hollywood turned to the legitimate theatre for support: stage people, stage plays, stage experience were seen as the answer to all the problems that talking pictures presented. Among the Broadway actors brought West in the early sound era were Bette Davis, Ann Harding, Ruth Chatterton, Fredric March, Edward G. Robinson, Katharine Hepburn, and the song-and-dance man James Cagney. Along with the actors came voice and elocution coaches. Some of them were celebrated old stage players like Constance Collier and Mrs Patrick Campbell; having assisted, respectively, Colleen Moore and Norma Shearer with their voice problems, they carved out small Hollywood careers for themselves as

Far left: 'To kill the camera noise', wrote director Frank Capra, 'our moving cameras were mummified and entombed in thick padded booths . . . Of course the cameraman was stuffed into his booth with his camera and couldn't hear a blessed thing . . .' Centre: a front view of the camera booth, lens and cameraman peering through their plate-glass window. Everyone but Bessie Love looks anxious. Left: a voice coach spreads panic among the acting fraternity and no doubt makes a killing out of others' insecurities.

supporting players. A few of the stage directors who were rushed out West – among them Rouben Mamoulian – took readily to the new medium. Another great Hollywood director of the future, George Cukor, originally came from Broadway as a dialogue director (one of the first films on which he worked was *All Quiet on the Western Front*). In *The Men Who Made the Movies* he describes those early days:

'I came out when everything seemed very strange. Everybody had been thrown for a loop – the actors weren't trained, the places were not equipped and the sound technicians, as I remember, had been radio operators on boats. So it was rather clumsy.'

The spoken word had come to stay, but Hollywood rapidly learned that drawing-room comedies in three acts could not be simply transferred from the stage – at least if the audience was to remain interested. Warners learned the hard way, casting the great Austrian actor Alexander Moissi as Edmund Kean in a film of his great stage triumph *The Royal Box* (1929). The film was not a success and was to be his only appearance on the screen in America.

One of the most successful adaptations from Broadway was to have a revolutionary effect on comedy styles: a former vaudeville team, the Marx Brothers, had a stage hit with a show called *The Cocoanuts* in 1925. Its success led them in 1928 to devise a new show, *Animal Crackers*, and to film *The Cocoanuts* (1929) in New York's Astoria Studios. A year later they were back in the same studios shooting *Animal Crackers* (1930). A new era of comedy had dawned.

New and Revived Genres

The arrival of sound coincided with a golden era for stage musicals, and it was inevitable that Hollywood should buy them up, along with the rest of what Broadway had to offer. Joan Crawford had already starred in a silent *Rose-Marie* (1928). Now John Boles sang in *The Desert Song* (1929), Helen Morgan re-created her original role in *Show Boat* (1929) and Lawrence Tibbett starred in *The Rogue Song* (1930). Jeanette MacDonald, another introduction from the musical stage, made her film debut with Ernst Lubitsch's *The Love Parade* (1929) and in 1930 sang in five films, *Let's Go Native, The Lottery Bride, Monte Carlo, Oh, for a Man!* and *The Vagabond King*. An earlier stage success, *Gold Diggers of Broadway,* was filmed with sound in 1929 and provided a durable format for Warner musicals throughout the Thirties and early Forties.

Hollywood rapidly began to develop its own musical forms. The revue-style film was a product of these early years. The numbers could be filmed individually on small stages while proper sound facilities were being prepared. Moreover the revue served to test the vocal abilities of the stars: MGM's *Hollywood Revue of 1929* revealed the talkie talents of Laurel and Hardy, Joan Crawford, Bessie Love and Marie Dressler; the outstanding success of *Paramount on Parade* (1930) – assembled by Ernst Lubitsch – was Maurice Chevalier. In Warners' *Show of Shows* (1929), canine star Rin-Tin-Tin personally introduced each act. Fox made *Movietone Follies of 1929*, and Universal's *King of Jazz* (1930) featured Paul Whiteman's band with Bing Crosby and the Rhythm Boys as one of the supporting acts. A film of more lasting influence, as the prototype of all Hollywood backstage musicals, was Harry Beaumont's *The Broadway Melody* (1929). Unique among the musical productions of these years, however, was King Vidor's all-black music drama *Hallelujah* (1929). It was remarkable for its use of black folk music and the accuracy of its cotton-country settings.

The great Western migration also included musicians: but while Tin Pan Alley song writers were hurried to Hollywood, the transition to sound had a dire effect upon professional musicians elsewhere. Not only accompanists in cinemas, but all the instrumentalists and orchestras who had been employed in the days of silent film-making to inspire actors with mood music became obsolete. Tens of thousands of professional performers now found themselves unemployed. The effects were to be felt in the music business for many years afterwards.

Other Hollywood genres acquired new life. Gangsters had begun to capture the public imagination in silent pictures, but now the audience could actually hear the squeal of the cars, the rattle of the guns and the catchy underworld slang. Mervyn LeRoy's *Little Caesar* (1930), which established Edward G. Robinson as a star, remains one of the most brilliant and memorable films of the period. The Western enjoyed a surprising revival – the great open spaces, too, had their characteristic and haunting sounds. Westerns of 1928–31 included: *The Trail of '98* (1928), *The Wagon Master* (1929), *The Big Trail* (1930), and *Cimarron,* (1931), a prototype of the family saga. The war film had a renewed success with the addition of sound. *Hell's Angels* (1930) spectacularly recreated early aerial warfare; Lewis Milestone's *All Quiet on the Western Front,* a moving reflection upon the waste of war, was instantly established as a classic of literary adaptation.

It was not altogether surprising that the directors who seemed most rapidly to master the new medium were the émigrés who, as non-native speakers, had perhaps a special sensitivity to words and mime. Lewis Milestone was himself of Russian origin. F.W. Murnau, one of the many Germans working in Hollywood first used sound in *Four Devils* (1928). The Armenian Rouben Mamoulian manipulated sound and images to complement each other in *Applause* (1929) and *City Streets* (1931). The Austrian-born Josef von Sternberg, who had begun his career in Hollywood in the silent days, returned from his German triumph with *Der Blaue Engel* (1930, *The Blue Angel*) to direct Marlene Dietrich in the exquisitely romantic *Morocco* (1930). Ernst Lubitsch, another German, began a brilliant new career as a creator of film operetta with *The Love Parade* (1929) which united the newly-discovered film talents of Maurice Chevalier and Jeanette MacDonald.

Sound films, then, had survived their early novelty value and were becoming acclaimed in their own right. The great D.W. Griffith had been one of the few directors of the silent era to welcome sound: 'Just think', he said, 'You can get all the movement, the swing, the rhythm, and the drive of the best of the old silent pictures . . . added to this you have the human voice.'

Britain

In the transitional year of 1929 Hollywood was supplying talkies faster than British exhibitors could refit themselves for sound, and as late as 1930 some 47 silent films were still being distributed to those smaller cinemas as yet unequipped for sound.

When Alfred Hitchcock's *Blackmail*, the first British talkie, was released in June 1929 some 400 cinemas were already wired for sound. This figure grew to 1000 by the end of the year, and the majority of British cinemas had been converted by the end of 1931.

The changeover to sound caused some painful adjustments; many small independent cinemas disappeared in favour of

Left: a Revue film was half-way towards a musical and the best way of advertising a studio's talent; some sang, others told jokes, but everyone talked. Far left: the Marx Brothers were among the first comedians to realize the new potential for talking film comedy. Groucho's verbal repartee combined with the knock-about clowning of Chico and Harpo (who continued to play dumb throughout his career). Below far left: words take second place to images and movement in Rouben Mamoulian's Applause. Mamoulian used sound with exceptional ease and freedom and refused to let his camera be immobilized by the requirements of the microphones. Below: Hollywood animals also had to face the dreaded microphone – Rin Tin Tin has his very own voice test.

Above: Hitchcock listens in as Blackmail, the first British talkie, is filmed. Right: Bessie Love, Anita Page and Charles King in The Broadway Melody.

Above and right: a solution to the new problem of making films marketable in foreign countries was to make the same film in several languages simultaneously. Far right: Gainsborough's Balcon.

more modern circuit houses. Not only was the new equipment expensive but at first it was not clear whether disc or sound-on-film would prove the best system.

Even though Hollywood sorted itself out as to which sound systems it was going to use, the British film industry in 1930 found itself using a multiplicity of sound-film processes. At first many films planned or already made as silents were hastily fitted with synchronized soundtracks. Strange hybrids boasting music, sound effects or dialogue sequences (or all three) appeared during the transition. By the end of 1930 all the main British studios had converted to true sound production.

From 1926 to 1929 De Forest Phonofilms, running a small UK subsidiary based at Wembley, London, had been busy turning out many short, novelty sound films. In April 1929 their UK patents and Wembley studio were acquired by British Talking Pictures, who changed their name to Associated Sound Film Industries.

ASFI's first feature with sound was rather a half-baked attempt. Made with a mixed German and English cast from a script by Edgar Wallace, The Crimson Circle (1929) was actually a German film (Der Rote Kreis) to which were added several English dialogue sequences recorded on British Talking Pictures discs. It was an unsatisfactory way of making a film available in a foreign language. Far more promising was the system of foreign versions, although once producers had discovered the sales potential of multi-language versions the practice escalated into a factory-style production-line, until it was superseded by the technique of dubbing.

John Maxwell's company hit the jackpot with Blackmail, and quickly converted British International Pictures into a sound film studio, BIP turned out a multitude of the usual music and comedy shorts; they revamped their recent silent films and full talkie production was under way in the second half of 1929. First on to the screen was an adaptation of Thomas Hardy's Under the Greenwood Tree, directed by Harry Lachman, soon followed by another period drama The American Prisoner. Both films used sound with imagination. The studio followed its tri-lingual Atlantic with another shipboard drama The Hate Ship, this one shot in English and

French versions only. Finally, at the end of this busy year, Maxwell's company produced an adaptation of Sean O'Casey's Juno and the Paycock (1930), in which Hitchcock failed to repeat his brilliant cinematic use of sound in Blackmail.

Another of the older companies, Gaumont-British had been working for some time on a sound system called British-Acoustic. It was first used in a full talking version of High Treason (1929), a futuristic play that had been a recent hit in London's West End, and concerned the struggle of women to prevent financiers from engineering a world war in 1940.

Herbert Wilcox (1892–1977) was eager to use sound, and, while his Imperial studio at Elstree was being built and fitted with a Western Electric recording system, he made Black Waters (1929) on a hired back-lot in Hollywood. But Wilcox's first British talkie was Wolves (1929), a thriller for which he brought Dorothy Gish from Hollywood and cast Charles Laughton in a supporting role. Wilcox's British and Dominions Company then released Rookery Nook (1930), the first of a long and popular series of stage farces – known as the Aldwych farces – transferred to film with the collaboration of the Aldwych Theatre team, writer Ben Travers and comedians Tom Walls and Ralph Lynn.

From his backgound in theatre, **Basil Dean** (1888–1978) looked upon the dialogue film as a chance for Britain to contribute something unique and distinguished to the cinema. His chance came with a play by John Galsworthy called Escape (1930) in which Gerald du Maurier had starred on the London stage. Both writer and actor were friends of Dean and a film version was rapidly put together and shot at Beaconsfield. By the end of 1931 Dean had his own studios at Ealing, the first in Europe to be custom-built for sound.

In November 1929 Victor Saville's remake of Woman to Woman, a romance set in wartime France, was released by Gainsborough and three months later the World War I classic Journey's End was premiered in London. Both films were made in America; and the writer of Journey's End, R.C. Sherriff, and its young director, James Whale, were to stay on in Hollywood.

Michael Balcon (1896–1977) of Gainsborough Pictures, one of the most intelligent producers, was one of the slowest to change to sound. His crime film *The Return of the Rat*, directed by Graham Cutts and starring Ivor Novello, appeared in April 1929 as a silent but took off very successfully when re-released with a British Acoustic soundtrack in October of the same year.

Balcon's approach to sound films differed little from that of his fellow-producers: the inevitable series of musical shorts – the variety programmes of their day – *Sugar and Spice* and *Gainsborough Gems* preceded the company's first full talkie *Symphony in Two Flats* (1930).

British Lion and British Instructional Films had been early converts to sound but neither prospered. British Lion had been formed in 1927 because the writer Edgar Wallace, many of whose stories had already successfully transferred to the stage, now had his eye on the cinema.

In December Wallace himself started directing British Lion's first true sound film *The Squeaker* (1930), made on the RCA Photophone system at Beaconsfield. Unfortunately the

Below: the films of George Formby capitalized on the British love for the underdog fighting against the odds. Below left: A Cottage on Dartmoor with Hans Schlettow and Uno Henning. Bottom left: Anna Neagle's cleavage as Nell Gwyn (1926) caused the American censors to blush.

Above: Will Hay as an irascible and incompetent school teacher.

Below: Hulbert and Courtneidge were a popular musical comedy team.

Below: Victor Saville gave style and glamour to the British musical.

Below: Jessie Matthews was Britain's top musical star of the Thirties.

company was too small to take the heavy losses their silent films incurred, and in 1932 Wallace died of pneumonia in Hollywood, after which British Lion went into quota production for a time, later to resurface in a variety of indifferent guises throughout the history of British cinema.

British Instructional Films, on the other had, had bought rights in the German Tobis-Klangfilm sound system and built a specially equipped sound studio at Welwyn in 1929. The first feature made by BIF with sound was Anthony Asquith's *A Cottage on Dartmoor* (1929), originally released silent but later put out with music and one dialogue scene recorded on discs. By August 1930 the Welwyn studio had a brand new sound stage ready for the filming of their prestige movie about the Gallipoli landing, *Tell England,* again directed by Anthony Asquith but not released until 1931.

After a series of experiments during the summer of 1929, Julius Hagen initiated full sound production at his Twickenham studios with a melodrama, *At The Villa Rose* (1930), filmed in English and French. With one sound stage and a Visatone van for location shooting. Hagen's team made multilanguage films with cut-price efficiency (one language unit working by day and another by night) and succeeded in producing films of great variety, each taking only two or three weeks to complete.

The next task facing British producers was to create talkie stars and establish a national style for their films that would have an international appeal, especially in America. Basil Dean found that regional music hall comedians Gracie Fields and, later, George Formby, although highly paid, were in fact the bread-and-butter which made his serious and often stage-based films possible.

Herbert Wilcox, always seeking a formula, also relied on home-grown comedy, including the Aldwych farces, but found star material first in the musical comedy idol Jack Buchanan and later in Anna Neagle, whom he promoted with devotion and finally launched as a box-office attraction in America as *Victoria the Great* (1937).

Michael Balcon, who after 1931 managed the combined production of Gainsborough and Gaumont-British, was responsible for many well-remembered films, including

Hitchcock's finest British thrillers, the early work of Robert Stevenson – *Falling For You* (1933), *Tudor Rose* (1936) and *King Solomon's Mines* (1937) – and the thrillers and comedies directed by former comedian Walter Forde, such as *The Ghost Train* (1931), *Jack's the Boy* (1932) and *Rome Express* (1932).

Also working with Balcon was the supremely professional **Victor Saville** (1897–1979), who both produced and directed some of the most successful films of the decade, including musicals such as *The Good Companions* (1933), *Evergreen* (1934), *First a Girl* (1935), and *It's Love Again* (1936),starring the London girl Jessie Matthews, a talented singer and dancer with an adoring following in her own country.

The output from BIP was enormous and varied, over 160 features between *Blackmail* (1929) and the end of 1936, embracing films by Hitchcock and including costume muscials, heavy drama, the early films of comedian Will Hay, and the work of many foreign visitors.

Germany

The Jazz Singer and the early talkies arrived in Europe in 1928. This new challenge from across the Atlantic affected the highly developed film industries of Germany and France in remarkably different ways. The French film studios were totally unprepared for the introduction of sound, and the lucrative domestic market was consequently invaded by the better-organized American and German film companies. Yet in Germany too – although filmgoers had seen talking picutres as early as 1922 – the Americans were allowed to take the lead in exploiting sound, as a result of under-investment, lack of interest, and wasted opportunities on the part of German business.

The legal battles fought over the rights to sound film systems were not resoled until 1930 when a conference in Paris passed a worldwide patents agreement. This resolution went some way towards vindicating the work of a number of European sound-film pioneers whose claim to a place in cinema history might otherwise have been over-shadowed by their American counterparts.

In 1918, three Germans, Hans Vogt, Joseph Massolle and Joseph Engl, patented a sound-film system they called

Tri-Ergon ('the work of three people'). Theirs was a sound-on-film system (see Chapter 1) and was extremely advanced for its time. On September 17, 1922, Vogt, Massolle and Engl mounted the first public show of their invention at the Alhambra Cinema in Berlin. The audience saw – and heard – a two-hour film progamme of musical numbers and recitations.

By all accounts the Tri-Ergon system scored an immediate hit with the public who were thrilled at the perfect synchronization of lip movements and sound. Under normal circumstances Tri-Ergon would have been ripe for commercial exploitation, but its inventors were to receive much the same kind of negative reaction from sponsors as the American De Forest had encountered for his Phonofilms. Furthermore, Germany had scarcely recovered from the devastation of World War I, and the economy was at its most inflationary.

For a crucial couple of years the ownersip of Tri-Ergon sound-film patents passed from one company to another, with none of them succeeding in capitalizing on the system. Late in 1924 a contract was signed linking Tri-Ergon with Ufa (Universum Film Aktiengesellschaft), Germany's biggest film-making company, for the purpose of atempting a sound feature film. The result was *Das Mädchen mit den Schwefelhölzen* (1924, also known as *Armes kleines Mädchen*) which was based on Hans Christian Andersen's tale 'The Little Match Girl'. A studio with the necessary technical equipment was constructed and the film was shot at a breathtaking pace. Its premiere on December 20, 1925, however, was bedevilled with breakdowns and technical mishaps. As a result Ufa turned down the offer of world rights to the Tri-Ergon system.

Three months later, on a visit to Europe, the movie mogul William Fox purchased the American rights. The following year the first of Fox's Movietone Newsreels, showing Lindbergh's triumphal crossing of the Atlantic, was watched in Germany by enthusiastic filmgoers and red-faced Ufa executives who had finally realized their mistake in not taking up the option on the Tri-Ergon system.

As far as sound-film production was concerned, little progress was made in the three years following the failure of *Das Mädchen mit den Schwefelhölzern*, but the merger of the Tobis and Klangfilm companies in March 1929 signalled a combined attack on the European film markets.

Early in 1929 the Deutsches Lichtspiel Company gave a sneak preview in Berlin. Two popular stars of the silent screen – Harry Liedtke and Marlene Dietrich – were billed to appear in *Ich küsse ihre Hand, Madame* (1929 *I Kiss Your Hand, Madam*). The film was screened and, to everyone's surprise, Liedtke *sang* the title song to the film. Actually the voice was that of the famous tenor Richard Tauber, but the effect on the screen was totally believable: Liedtke had opened his mouth and sung; the German sound film had arrived.

By the end of the Twenties, then, German film producers were convinced of the future of sound films. As in America, it had taken some time to persuade them. But having decided in favour of the optical sound solution, the German pioneers represented a genuine challenge to the American Vitaphone system. It is not surprising that when *The Singing Fool* was shown in Germany in the late Twenties, projection room doors were firmly locked to prevent industrial espionage. From this point on the production of German sound flms began in earnest: Walter Ruttmann's *Melodie der Welt* (1929), a kind of travelogue with story sequences made by Tobis Studios for the Hamburg–American steamship line, is generally taken to be the first German sound feature.

During the transitional period of 1928–9, German producers tried to recapture the markets lost to the Americans at the time of the release of *The Singing Fool* (1928). Typical of their efforts was *Das Land ohne Frauen* (1929, The Land Without Women), which was begun as a silent film but had music and some dialogue added before its release on September 20, 1929. This film was a spectacular production featuring love stories and stirring action, directed by the Italian Carmine Gallone, with Conrad Veidt in the leading role,. Veidt had been a top box-office star in Germany since *Das Cabinet des Dr Caligari* (1919, *The Cabinet of Dr Caligari*), and his debut in talking pictures certanly did not disappoint audiences who had come to love his hypersensitive, full-blown acting style. As he ranged from outburst of insanity, through quiet sobbing to hysterical laughter, audiences rose to their feet and applauded. A few critics were slightly more reserved, suggesting that the addition of sound to certain sequences in an otherwise silent film disrupted the style and continuity of the movie.

By another quirk of history the honour of making the first 100 per cent talking film went not to Ufa, Germany's biggest production outfit, but to Afa Film with a production called *Dich hab'Ich geliebt* (1929, I Loved You). The explanation for Ufa's delay in getting into sound production lies in the disputes over sound-film patents.

In Berlin, Ufa completed the building of four sound studios in the Babelsberg suburb, and were then fully geared up for sound production. The new head of production at Ufa was Erich Pommer, who had spent three years in Hollywood and was now assigned the task of promoting Germany's sound films both at home and abroad. Ufa's first full sound film was a prestige picture called *Melodie des Herzens* (1929, *Melody of the Heart*), premiered on December 13, 1929. To maximize its distribution, the film was shot simultaneously in German, English, French and Hungarian, and was thus an early example of the foreign-version, or 'multi-language', film.

As well as mounting an unprecedented export drive for their first sound feature, Ufa were keen to saturate the home market. Special spreads appeared in film magazines: the script of *Melodie des Herzens* was published in book form (another promotional novelty permitted by the introduction of dialogue in films). The stars of the film, Willy Fritsch and Dita Parlo, made public appearances to sign autographs and promote records of the film's hit songs. Ufa's massive advertising campaign hammered home the message 'The Victory of German Sound Films'.

A new transatlantic war had replaced the one fought over sound patents: the objective of American and German film producers was to sell their product to as many different countries (or 'territories', to use the film trade term) as possible. Foreign version films were expedient for this purpose though rarely successful in themselves. All too often the process of making them resembled a factory production line; untried directors were often assigned to them, and even where respected and experienced directors made foreign versions they rarely turned in very good work.

With the arrival of the talkies, production in Germany increased rapidly. From 14 sound films made in 1929 the number climbed to 127 the following year and to 200 by 1931. During this production boom, melodramas and light-hearted operettas seemed to represent the most popular box-office fare. Fairytale escapism was predictably successful at the height of the economic depression when cinema-goers were badly in need of distraction.

Typical of the German musical genre was *Liebeswalzer* (1930, *Love Waltzes*), directed by Wilhelm Thiele, featuring the partnership of Lilian Harvey and Willy Fritsch, already a popular duo in silent films, who went on to become cult figures and wealthy stars. The story concerned a princess in a fictitious, small country who is supposed to marry a monarch, and instead falls in love with the son of an American automobile millionaire. Thiele's other famous musical-comedy of the same year was *Die Drei von der Tankstelle* (1930, *Three Men and Lilian*). Both films were made in several different language versions and were as successful abroad as they were in Germany. The following year Erik Charell made *Der Kongress Tanzt* (1931, *Congress Dances*), again in English and French, as well as in German, with the versatile Lilian Harvey appearing in all three versions. It became one of the best-known German films of the period and an effective challenge to the Hollywood musical revue film.

While film production increased, many cinemas in Germany were still waiting to be equipped for sound films. In the severe economic climate of the early Thirties independent exhibitors were naturally cautious about installing sound equipment. As late as the end of 1932, one in three German cinemas had no sound facilities. This delay meant that some genuinely silent films had a longer run for their money than might have been expected. But there was no question that sound was what the public wanted. Any lingering doubt on this matter was dispelled by the enormous success of *The Blue Angel*. Directed by Josef von Sternberg – who had already made a talkie in America – and starring Emil Jannings and Marlene Dietrich, the film was undoubtedly the hit of the year. It was made simultaneously in English and has since gone on to become one of the all-time classic movies.

Perhaps more typical of the German filmgoers' taste, however, was an all-talking, all-singing film called *Die Privatsekretärin* (1931, *The Private Secretary*) starring Renate Müller as a clever country girl who comes to Berlin and gets a job as a secretary. On its appearance in America the *New York Times* critic commented, 'Miss Müller sings, dances and chatters her way through one and a quarter hours of gay music and comic situations. The theme song, "Today I fell so happy", sums up the mood.' As the Depression continued, the demand for light-hearted fairytale films increased. Titles like *Es wird schon wieder besser* (Things Are Sure to Get Better Again) and *Einmal möcht' ich keine Sorgen haben* (For once I'd Like to Have No Worries) or, more deceptively, *Man braucht kein Geld* (You Don't Need Any Money), all appeared in 1931–2.

More serious material established Robert Siodmak's reputation as a director and would launch him on a highly successful Hollywood career later in the Thirties. From his debut on the naturalistic film *Menschen Am Sonntag* (1929, *People on Sunday*) Siodmak had distinguished himself as a serious-minded and skilful director. His early work was in the harshly 'realistic' style known as *Neue Sachlichkeit* ('new objectivity'). His first sound film, *Abschied* (1930, *Farewell*), was set in Berlin's slums and recalled the urban 'street' films of Gerhard Lamprecht in the mid-Twenties. However worthy his films were, austerity was bad news at the box-office, and Ufa hastily tacked on a happy ending to try and salvage their investment. *Abschied* was not, however, without influence. Its treatment of social issues was reflected in films like Piel Jutzi's *Berlin Alexanderplatz*, Lupu Pick's *Gassenhauer* (Street Ballad) and Georg Klaren's *Kinder von Gericht* (Children Before the Courts) all made in 1931.

Undoubtedly the most significant social comment film of this period is *Kuhle Wampe oder Wem Gehört die Welt?* (1932, *Whither Germany?*), famous not so much for what it said about the conditions of the German working class, but for how it put its message across. The film was the result of collaboration between the writer and dramatist Bertolt Brecht and the director Slatan Dudow and was sponsored by the communist party who approved its radical style; even the Nazis could not overlook it.

Another director noted for his outspoken views, at least at the beginning of the decade, was George Wilhelm Pabst. His pacifist masterpiece *Westfront 1918* (1930) ranks alongside Milestone's anti-war classic, *All Quiet on the Western Front*, which was released in the same year. If his use of sound was not original in itself, it certainly enhanced the atmosphere of the film. Sound was to play a much more important role in Pabst's next feature *Die Dreigroschenoper* (1931, The Threepenny Opera), where Kurt Weill's music was intended to carry a dramatic and political charge. The film, however, was subjected to a protracted court case after Brecht had seen and declared his objections to it. Pabst's other commercial success of the year was *Kameradschaft* (1931, Comradeship), the story of a pit disaster in Alsace-Lorraine where, in defiance of national frontiers, German miners came to the rescue of their French comrades.

By the time Fritz Lang's *M* was released in May 1931 sound films in themselves no longer surprised audiences. Lang's use of sound in *M* was nevertheless quite original; the voice of the mother calling her daughter over a shot of the child's empty chair, the tune whistled by the murderer which eventually gives him away, and the atmospheric roaring of the crowd conveying all the threat of the lynch mob. It is still surprising, however, that Lang uses very little direct sound—noise recorded on set at the time of filming – to heighten his effects, whereas Robert Siodmak's murder-hunt thriller *Voruntersuchung* (1931, Preliminary Investigation) clearly demonstrates how effective the dramatic use of direct sound could be.

The attack on militarism implicit in Richard Oswald's *Dreyfus* (1931) is one of the earliest indications of the way films reflected the political events of the day. The direction the German cinema was taking at the beginning of the Thirties was made more politically explicit in the pre-Nazi films of Gustav Ucicky whose *Das Flötenkonzert von Sanssouci* (*The Flute Concert at Sanssouci*, 1930*)* was a portrait of Frederick the Great of Prussia. Ucicky's *Yorok* (1931) was a more aggressively militaristic account of a Prussian general who rebels against his king (not Frederick) to represent the true Prussian spirit. The shape of things to come could be discerned at least two years before the Nazis took over.

France

In sharp contrast to the preparations made in Germany, the French film industry was caught napping when the talkies arrived. The great Danish director Carl Dreyer was brought to Paris in 1928 to direct *La Passion de Jeanne d'Arc* (*The Passion of Joan of Arc)*, a film he intended as a talking picture, only to discover that the studios were not equipped for sound, and so the film was shot silent. The same lack of sound facilities forced enterprising French producers to make the earliest French talkies in London; among these were *Les Trois Masques* (1929, The Three Masks) and two films starring Léon Mathot.

There was a vociferous demand for French-speaking films; when *Lights of New York* was shown in Paris late in 1928 the

Left: in this scene from Fritz Lang's M, the child-murderer's voice is heard off screen saying 'What a nice ball you have. What's your name?' and the implied threat is felt all the more for his not being seen. Far left: Emil Jannings' schoolmaster is obsessed, seduced and destroyed by a night club singer in The Blue Angel. Below left: G.W. Pabst directs a scene from The Threepenny Opera. Below: René Clair's Sous les Toits de Paris made exceptional use of songs, musical score, atmospheric sound and dialogue. His charming Thirties studies of Paris life were created entirely within the studio.

sound was drowned by angry cries of 'In French!' Part of the problem was that the manufacturing end of the French film business was entirely foreign-owned. The German or American companies who controlled the means of production were therefore largely free to decide where and when to install sound-reproducing equipment in cinemas.

Of all the American studios Paramount went in deepest; not content to make foreign versions in Hollywood, with expatriate actors and directors, they financed and built an entire multi-studio complex at Joinville, outside Paris, reported by one historian to look more like Hollywood than the real thing. Production chief Robert T. Kane was put in charge of this 'Hollywood-sur-Seine' which consisted of nine sound stages, laboratories and luxury accommodation for the stars. With the French film industry at a low ebb, Paris appeared ripe for colonization by the commercially stronger Americans and Germans; and at the same time as Paramount moved in, the German Tobis-Klangfilm set up a Paris office and shortly afterwards built a studio at Epinay. It was here that René Clair made his first sound film Sous les Toits de Paris (1930, Under the Roofs of Paris), as a German production, but in time these foreign-owned studios would pass into French hands.

The Germans were perhaps more sensitive than the Americans to the taste and needs of the European film market. Tobis pursued a policy of making specifically French films in Paris; everything, except the capital and share of the profits, was French, and in this way Sous les Toits de Paris could legitimately be welcomed, by critic Georges Sadoul, as the first flowering of the new spring of French cinema. Clair's next three films were made for Tobis at Epinay, but remained resolutely French. By 1934, however, Clair had run into problems with Tobis, now under the eye of Dr Goebbels, and was forced to take his film Le Dernier Milliardaire (The Last Millionaire) to another studio.

Gradually the French film industry caught up with its foreign competitors. A leading financier named Bernard Natan bought a sizeable share-holding in the pioneer firm of Pathé and set up a sound-film production programme. A parallel development from the equally famous Gaumont company resulted in there being two sound-film combines in operation by 1930. Suddenly the indigenous French cinema had a new lease of life; in 1930 the output of talking pictures was double the previous year, and rose to 130 by 1931 and over 150 in 1932.

But business did not go well for Paramount; hand-me-down Hollywood simply was not popular with French audiences. The Joinville studios were run down, staff were dismissed and contracts were liquidated. But the studios did continue to function for dubbing purposes, and a number of French actors and actresses found work speaking their lines over the lip movements of famous Hollywood stars.

In order to prevent American-dubbed films swamping the market, the French government limited the number of foreign films – English, Italian, German as well as American – that could be shown in France. At last the French seemed to be gaining a measure of control over their industry, and, with Paramount pulling out of Joinville, they now had major production facilites to hand. Pathé-Natan took over Joinville.

After a late start in the sound film stakes, one of the richest periods of world cinema was about to begin: Vigo, Renoir, Carné, Feyder and Duvivier would soon be dazzling filmgoers in France and abroad with their talents.

CHAPTER 8

Hollywood in the Thirties

From the Thirties to the Fifties, American production was dominated by a handful of Hollywood film companies: Paramount, MGM, Warner Brothers, 20th Century-Fox and RKO Radio. Often referred to as the Big Five or the 'majors', they were not just production companies and international distributors of motion pictures but also owned massive cinema circuits, thus controlling the entire movie business from film-making through to exhibition.

In the second division of the studio league were two studios, Universal and Columbia, and a releasing company, United Artists. These companies differed from the majors in that they owned few or no cinemas. In addition, United Artists was not a studio but a distribution company formed in 1919 by Mary Pickford, Douglas Fairbanks, Charlie Chaplin and D.W. Griffith in order to gain greater control over the marketing of their films.

Finally there was a group of minor studios, known collectively as 'Poverty Row', that specialized in B pictures. Of these only Republic and Monogram (later to become Allied Artists) lasted for any length of time or made much impression on film history.

The financing of motion pictures was based in New York. Wall Street had consolidated its hold on the big film companies during the financial crises of the late Twenties and early Thirties when the cost of equipping for sound and rapid acquisitions of theatres stretched the resources of most companies to snapping point.

But it was on the West Coast that the flamboyant and legendary moguls who had built their dream factories in Hollywood created, through their individual enterprises, a superstructure that became known as the studio system. This system was an attempt to make films in the most efficient and orderly way possible. Studios not only had directors, actors, supporting players and writers on contract but also cameramen, art directors, special effects men, editors and composers.

At RKO David O. Selznick (1902–1965) was appointed head of production in October 1931 and promised a completely free hand to carry out the studio's merger with Pathé. But interference from one of RKO's backers soon caused Selznick to leave and join MGM. Even there, under the benevolent eye of his father-in-law, Louis B. Mayer, Selznick felt curbed and in 1935 he left to form an independent company. Later at RKO another production chief, Dore Schary, responsible for

Left: 'He gave her class, she gave him sex-appeal' – so Katharine Hepburn (RKO's other major star) is reported to have described the magic of Fred Astaire and Ginger Rogers, seen here in one of their best musicals, Swing Time.

encouraging new talent like directors Robert Wise and Edward Dymtryk, was harried out of office by the studio's last owner, the eccentric millionaire Howard Hughes.

Universal's problems in the early Thirties stemmed largely from boss Carl Laemmle's practice of nepotism. As Universal's founder he gave his son the post of head of production for a twenty-first birthday present. Laemmle's faith in youth could be forgiven, for back in 1920 he had appointed the 20-year-old Irving Thalberg to run the studio but Thalberg had taken his estimable talent off to MGM and left Universal to the Laemmles. Although Carl Laemmle Jr initiated a memorable horror-film cycle with *Dracula* and *Frankenstein* (both 1931) the company's overall output was not strong enough to withstand the ill winds of the Depression and both father and son were eventually forced out of office. At this time it was proved, in the words of a popular rhyme, that 'Carl Laemmle had such a large family', for over 70 relatives and dependents had found their way onto the studio payroll. Universal went through the next decade excessively dependent on the few major stars – Deanna Durbin, Abbot and Costello – it was lucky enough to discover.

More than anyone, Irving Thalberg at MGM refined the system of delegated responsibility that became a management blueprint for other stuidos. Louis B. Mayer handled the temperamental actors, looked for new talent, welcomed important guests, made big speeches; Thalberg, who abhorred publicity and declined any form of screen credit, chose the pictures and got them made.

After Thalberg's early death in 1936, Mayer reigned supreme over the studio until 1948, and encouraged a committee system of decision-making, rather than allowing a single production chief to dominate the studio. MGM was extremely well-funded and certainly the richest studio for talent: it had a regular staff of some 20 directors, 75 writers and 250 players on the payroll, and an annual profit that went from $4 million (in a bad year!) to $10 million in a good year.

Warner Brothers' Darryl F. Zanuck (1902–1979) had been a screenwriter before his promotion to production chief. It was Zanuck who launched the gangster and musical cycles that carried Warners to success past the initial boost provided by Vitaphone talkies. Zanuck and Jack Warner understood each other, but Harry's meanness eventually led to Zanuck's resignation and Hal B. Wallis took over. Wallis kept Warners in the money with his shrewd choice of supervisors, directors and writers.

After Zanuck's departure, Jack Warner's workhorse regime provoked some famous quarrels. Stars like Bette Davis and James Cagney protested at the films they were forced to

Above: the trademarks of Hollywood's foremost studios. A company's product could also be recognized by its distinctive visual style and subject-matter.

make. Miss Davis hoped to go to Britain to make better films but was defeated in the courts. Cagney managed to make two independent films but both Davis and Cagney returned to Warner Brothers with the satisfaction of being offered better parts.

Darryl Zanuck's status after he left Warners was sufficient for the money-man Joe Schenck to finance a wholly new company, 20th Century Productions. In the first place they simply produced films, releasing them through United Artists but in 1935 when they merged with the ailing Fox Films Corporation, the new 20th Century-Fox company made its own movies in its own studio and took care of its own releasing.

At Paramount creativity was given a freer hand. Indeed the company went so far as to appoint a major established artist, the producer-director Ernst Lubitsch, to run the studio. Unfortunately this was not a happy move and he soon returned to directing. In the late Thirties certain directors, like William Wellman and Mark Sandrich, were permitted to produce their own films.

How well the studio system worked for RKO depended largely on who was running the 'shop'. When George Schaefer was appointed head of production, he brought in Orson Welles with his Mercury Players and gave him

unprecedented freedom. The result was *Citizen Kane* (1940). Schaefer's policy failed, however, to produce profits. His successor, Charles Koerner, was the production chief who put an end to Welles' activities at the studio.

Columbia studios were run by the notoriously foul-mouthed Harry Cohn (1891–1958). In the Thirties his hottest property was the director, Frank Capra, whose *Lost Horizon* (1937) was one of a string of films that conferred profits and prestige upon the studio, and enabled it to attract other major film directors like John Ford, Howard Hawks and George Stevens. In the Thirties the studio had no big stars: Cohn had to borrow Clark Gable from MGM and Claudette Colbert from Paramount for Capra's *It Happened One Night* (1934), and Edward G. Robinson from Warners for Ford's *The Whole Town's Talking* (1935). Fortunately Columbia developed some stars of its own, notably Rita Hayworth and Jack Lemmon, in the Forties and Fifties. Whatever Harry Cohn's faults he had picture-making in his blood; it was his penny-pinching brother Jack who brought about Capra's exit from Columbia when he refused to allow the director to make *The Life of Chopin* in colour.

Down on 'Poverty Row' two studios stood out from the rest: Monogram made itself known for series films like the Charlie Chan mysteries (from an original story bought from 20th Century-Fox) and the Bowery Boys (the Dead End Kids, taken over from Warners). Republic, on the other hand, had flirtations with the big time thanks to a contract they held with John Wayne. Having loaned him out for *Stagecoach*

(1939), which made him a major star. Republic toplined him in *The Dark Command* (1940), even though they had to borrow a director (Raoul Walsh from Warners) and co-star (Walter Pidgeon from MGM) to ensure first-feature quality.

Republic's powerful boss Herbert J. Yates (1880–1966) also had Western stars Gene Autry and Roy Rogers on contract, but it was Wayne's films which made the really big money until Yates backed out of a deal to let Wayne make his cherished project *The Alamo* in 1951 and lost the star's services for good. Yates further handicapped Republic by insisting that Vera Ralston, later to become Mrs Herbert J. Yates, starred in the company's pictures even though her box-office appeal was dubious.

The studio system was never so rigid as to justify the 'factory production line' label sometimes attributed to it, but it is important to recognize a consistency in the product of each studio.

While it is true that Warners specialized in topical, tightly edited, realistic pictures in the early Thirties, that MGM made classy comedies and musicals, that Paramount encouraged a Continental sophistication (in their Thirties films) and that Universal went from horror movies in the Thirties to Technicolored adventure films in the Forties, every studio also made films that ran counter to its prevailing image.

When a studio is said to have possessed a certain visual style, this often refers to the 'look' of a film as determined by the laboratory processing favoured by each individual studio. An experienced film editor might tell at a glance which studio had made the film according to the graininess of the black and white or the tones of the colour.

An easier although less reliable guide to the studio origins of a particular film lay in the recurrence of particular stars in one studio's movies: Tyrone Power, for example, was identified with 20th Century-Fox, Alan Ladd with Paramount, Gable with MGM, and so on down the list of supporting players and technicians.

The studio system encouraged high standards of technical excellence. Most independently made films of the Thirties and Forties looked tatty by comparison, lacking the strong casts and lavish settings that the big studios could always provide. Goldwyn and Selznick certainly spent money on a scale equivalent to that of the majors, if not in excess of it, but other independents were usually either short of cash or keen to spend as little money as possible to get adequate results.

The studio system offered 'the safety of a prison', said Bette Davis. But good films were made, nonetheless, and every company permitted the occasional experiment. Paramount, Columbia and Republic, for example, all indulged the offbeat notions of the writer-director Ben Hecht. Orson Welles, however fiercely single-minded, was more productive while the big studios were flourishing than he has been at any time since.

Escapist Entertainment

At the beginning of the Thirties the Hollywood tycoons did not have to look too hard for a formula to match the mood of their audience. Faith in American capitalism had been badly dented by the Wall Street Crash: millions of citizens were victims of the Depression and of the accompanying unemployment. It was the era of 'Buddy can you spare a dime?' What people needed was a means of escaping, if only temporarily, from the harsh realities of life.

Every kind of film gained a new dimension with the introduction of sound; but one genre, the musical film,

Above and top: examples of Berkeley's spectacular routines, from Gold Diggers of 1935 *(1935) and* Dames *(1934).*

appeared to evolve specifically for the purpose of escapism – and that was what Hollywood was in business to provide.

This magical world of the musical was opened up by some of Hollywood's finest directors. Thanks to Mamoulian and Lubitsch, the camera was liberated from its early sound-proof boxes. Lubitsch's *Monte Carlo* (1930) had Jeanette MacDonald in a moving railway train singing 'Beyond the Blue Horizon' while what seemed to be all the peasantry of Europe waved back at her as she passed; for the opening sequence of Mamoulian's *Love Me Tonight* (1932) the camera swooped and swerved over early morning Paris.

To the freedom regained by the cameras and the microphones could now be re-united something at which Hollywood had always excelled – spectacle. The man responsible for the biggest production numbers in the history of the musical was Busby Berkeley (1895–1976). In his peacock displays of female pulchritude nothing was too lavish or extravagant.

From his early films like *42nd Street* and *Footlight Parade* (both 1933) through to the surrealistic *The Gang's All Here* (1943), his choreographic style accurately reflected the shifting moods of the movie-going public.

Perhaps the most significant Berkeley musical of the era was *Gold Diggers of 1933* which was the story of a backstage show foreclosed by the bank. In the space of one number

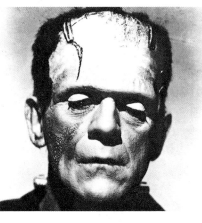

Above: the Thirties' supreme musical team. Above right: Bela Lugosi as Dracula. *Right: Boris Karloff in* Frankenstein. *Far right: enter* King Kong.

entitled 'Remember My Forgotten Man' Berkeley has his singers and dancers describe the progress of young American men from the trenches of World War I to the dole queues of the early Thirties.

At RKO the musical was not so much an ensemble spectacle as a vehicle for the brilliant duo of Fred Astaire and Ginger Rogers. The titles of their films formed a sort of litany of escapism: *Flying down to Rio* (1933), *The Gay Divorcee* (1934), *Top Hat* (1935), *Shall We Dance?* (1937), and *Carefree* (1938). The perfection of their dancing, the pellucid black and white photography, the excellence of the music and dialogue made every one of their films a masterpiece.

There were other avenues of escape available to moviegoers. One of these was the cathartic process of enjoying a good fright. In the silent days horror films had enjoyed something of a vogue, but the addition of sound increased their impact immensely — owls hooted, stairs creaked and heroines screamed.

Universal earned its reputation as Hollywood's home of horror with three films it made at the beginning of the Thirties. Tod Browning's *Dracula*, released on St Valentine's Day 1931, with Bela Lugosi repeating the role of the bloodsucking Transylvanian Count he had created on Broadway in 1927, soon emerged as the studio's leading contender for money-maker of the year. Then came *Frankenstein*, which was originally scheduled to be directed by Robert Florey, but was finally made by James Whale. It starred Boris Karloff after Lugosi had refused to appear in a non-speaking role as the Monster. Released in November 1931, the film grossed twice as much at the box-office as *Dracula*. Lugosi and Florey emerged with their consolation prize for missing out on *Frankenstein* when they made *Murders in the Rue Morgue* (1932). It was another major success for Universal though less profitable.

Like Robert Wiene's *Das Cabinet des Dr Caligari* (1919,

The Cabinet of Dr Caligari), all three films featured white-robed maidens assailed by mad geniuses and monsters (even if *Dracula* combined the two latter roles into one). And all three had the same atmosphere of dark, fairy-tale magic, a quality which was later so effectively tapped by other film-makers — Cocteau, for example in his superlative version of *La Belle et la Bête* (1945, *Beauty and the Beast*). Although James Whale (1889–1957) made only four horror films, they remain Universal's unmatched masterpieces. *Frankenstein* (1931), the first and best known, is also, for all its sombre visual beauty and archetypal quality, the least successful. Whale was most at home with comedy of manners in which he could express his yearning for gracious living and at the same time puncture it with malicious wit. It is possible that Whale, an English working-class boy who made good, was compensating for his dubious upper-crust position in society. In his horror films the results are irresistible: the waspishly effeminate Horace Fenn (Ernest Thesiger) in *The Old Dark House* (1932), serenely observing the social niceties in a household that includes a mute, drunken giant of a butler, a killer with a knife, and a pyromaniac; the unseen hero (Claude Rains) of *The Invisible Man* (1933), gloating over his new-found power but lamenting that an invisible man must be hungry, naked and spotlessly clean; the frizz-wigged, adder-tongued woman (Elsa Lanchester) created for the Monster (Karloff) in *Bride of Frankenstein* (1935), glancing at her intended mate and hissing with dismay. Without ever jeopardizing the grave beauty he found in horror, Whale was able to laugh long before the audience began.

From this great wave of horror films, MGM's *Freaks*, directed by Tod Browning in 1932, earned the distinction of being one of the most censored films in the history of the cinema, on account of its portrayal of malformed human exhibits in a travelling circus show. Highly unusual for its time, *Freaks* suggests a community that, though physically

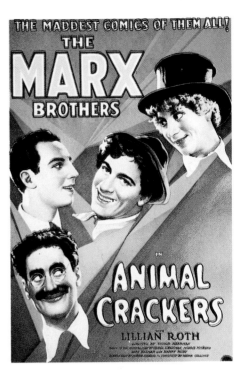

Left: 'I used to be Snow White, but I drifted' – Mae West's breezy, bawdy repartee and hourglass curves won her a huge following, though her film career was frequently hampered by Hays Office censorship. Above centre W.C. Fields with director

A. Edward Sutherland, with whom he worked on several occasions. Above: Animal Crackers, based on a Broadway hit, let the Brothers unleash their mayhem in high society.

abnormal, constitutes a challenge to the 'civilized' normal world of the early Thirties. If any one horror movie undermined that world, however, it was Ernest B. Schoedsack and Merian C. Cooper's *King Kong* (1933). In a thrilling narrative composed of potent images of destruction, the theme of nature reclaiming 'civilization' emerges as a powerful reaction to the bankruptcy of twentieth-century life. The film enlists our sympathy for the ape by underscoring the corruption of modern urban man – the hunters, reporters, photographers and the showmen are all targets of abuse.

Laughter, on the other hand, was an equally potent antidote to the Depression blues, and the Thirties was one of the richest decades for film comedies. Laurel and Hardy, originally teamed together in the silent era, had no hesitation in adapting to sound films. Their voices were perfect, especially the veneer of refinement which Hardy built up from the underlying softness of a Southern accent. Few other screen comedians made such subtle and brilliant use of sound. From 50-odd two-reel shorts, they extended their art into features such as *Fra Diavolo* (1933), *Bonnie Scotland* (1935), *Our Relations* (1936), *Way Out West* (1937), *Swiss Miss* (1938) and *A Chump at Oxford* (1940); of these their comic dance routine from *Way Out West* has become a classic scene as has their rendering of the song 'The Trail of the Lonesome Pine'.

Their formula was simple. Setting out to be helpful or to do a good job they managed with the best will in the world to reduce all around them to chaos and confusion. They performed each piece of mayhem with a slapstick style that often achieved a dreamlike quality. Such scenes removed the audience so far from the harsh realities of life that they felt able to participate in the orgies of destruction.

The same was also true of W.C. Fields (1879–1946), another comedian who found fulfilment in the sound film. It was not until the coming of sound, when his nasal, gin-soaked voice

was finally heard, that Fields' persona flowered like some gorgeous tropical, flesh-eating plant. His sound films can be divided into two kinds: 'wormy' and 'demonic'. In his 'wormy' films, like *It's a Gift* (1934) and *The Man on the Flying Trapeze* (1935), he is the hen-pecked husband who never raises rebellion to more than a constant mutter. They contain classic moments but they lack the invigorating destructive energy of his 'demonic' films in which he plays the bombastic huckster, ham and fraud. These include *The Old Fashioned Way* (1934), *You Can't Cheat an Honest Man* (1939) – Fields' favourite title, for like every successful con man, he believed there are no honest men – and *Never Give a Sucker an Even Break* (1941). The two modes, 'wormy' and 'demonic', co-exist in the masterly *The Bank Dick* (1940). The film is every middle-class male's Walter Mitty fantasy: any lazy, incompetent bank employee with an obnoxious wife and children can be a hero, financial genius, great writer, Hollywood director, *bon vivant* and general all-round good fellow. All you need is a little luck.

The teaming of Fields and Mae West, in *My Little Chickadee* (1940), did not work. Their egos and slow, drawling styles were too similar. But those who wish to take Fields neat – as undiluted as he took his own gin – must go to the shorts he made for Mack Sennett: *The Pharmacist*, *The Barber Shop* and, best of all, *The Fatal Glass of Beer* (all 1933).

At their best the Marx Brothers' films carried the same anarchic charge as those of Fields. After a long career in vaudeville, the brothers had a New York success in 1924 with *I'll Say She Is*, a show they devised themselves. Two even bigger Broadway hits followed: *The Cocoanuts* in 1925 and *Animal Crackers* in 1928. Both were later filmed in New York – 1929 and 1930 respectively – almost exactly as they were presented on the stage.

After filming *Animal Crackers*, the Marx Brothers left for California, where they remained. Their first three Hollywood pictures were produced for Paramount by Herman J. Mankiewicz, the future writer of *Citizen Kane* (1940) and one of Hollywood's great nonconformists. (Assigned to write a Rin-Tin-Tin picture he had the courageous police dog carry the baby *into* a burning building instead of out of it. He was never assigned to a Rin-Tin-Tin film again.) The Marx Brothers' pictures of this period – *Monkey Business* (1931), *Horse Feathers* (1932), and *Duck Soup* (1933) – all bear the imprint of their iconoclastic producer. The next two films, *A Night at the Opera* (1935) and *A Day at the Races* (1937), were produced by Irving Thalberg at MGM. Groucho credited Thalberg with saving their careers after *Duck Soup* had done poorly at the box office. Thalberg felt that the Marx Brothers were appealing only to a minority, and that they were missing especially the female audience that so often decided which film the family attended. He found the Marx Brothers characters of the Paramount films 'unsympathetic' because they were not helping anyone. To remedy this, he reinforced the plots so that they could stand alone as romantic comedies, recast the Marx Brothers as helpful avuncular types rather than totally uninhibited anarchists, and added the kind of lavish production numbers that a major studio like MGM could afford. He also allowed the Marx Brothers to try out material for their next picture in front of audiences on a road tour; this was especially helpful, as the Marx Brothers had always depended heavily on the reaction of live audiences to their ad libs. Thalberg in this way returned to the original successful formula of George S. Kaufman who, with Morrie Ryskind, had conceived and written *The Cocoanuts* and *Animal Crackers*; and at Groucho's behest, Kaufman and Ryskind were imported from the East Coast to write *A Night at the Opera*.

Thalberg's premature death during the filming of *A Day at the Races* marked a crucial point in the Marx Brothers' career as a team. No longer did they have their champion at the biggest studio in Hollywood. After the RKO version of a Broadway hit, *Room Service* (1938), their next three pictures, *At the Circus* (1939), *Go West* (1940), and *The Big Store* (1941), were made for MGM on a production-line basis, and by 1942 they were ready to retire as a team, each brother going his own way professionally, though they reunited a couple of times in the late Forties.

From the Thirties onwards, Charles Chaplin greatly slowed his output, taking not less than five years on each film. By the time he embarked on *City Lights* (1931), sound pictures had arrived, and Chaplin had witnessed the downfall of other great silent comedians. He decided not to risk the voiceless character he had created on his vast international market by trying dialogue. *City Lights* is a silent movie with musical accompaniment. It is based on a series of comic variations built around an ironic melodrama about a blind girl and the sad little Tramp whose efforts give back the sight that enables her to see his pathetic reality. In *Modern Times* (1936), which marked the last appearance of the Tramp, he risked a few moments of comic gibberish, though elsewhere retained his old mimetic comic style. With this film Chaplin first attracted the hostile and persistent line of criticism that charged the comedian with exceeding his 'proper' brief, and setting himself up as a philosopher. It was a criticism that inevitably attached no less to *The Great Dictator* (1940), a comic satire on totalitarianism. For all the anger underlying the laughter, Chaplin later said that had he known the truth about Hitler's concentration camps he would not have had the temerity to make the film.

Realism

The other side of the coin from escapism was a new gritty realism in films of the Thirties. The collapse of traditional American values, that began with the introduction of Prohibition in 1919 and culminated in the Wall Street Crash of 1929, provided Hollywood with 'realistic' material that ranged from the sensational, newspaper-headline stuff of the gangster movies to the more earnest, socially aware films reflecting the spirit of Franklin D. Roosevelt's New Deal.

It would indeed have been extraordinary if Hollywood had not sought to exploit the breakdown of law and order as potential film themes. Among the gangster films William Wellman's *The Public Enemy* (1931) starring James Cagney aroused official opinion against the genre on account of its unprecedented violence. Howard Hawks' *Scarface* (1931) pushed official antagonism further and had the effect of sharpening Hollywood censorship, owing to the close parallels the film made with the real-life story of Al Capone. Never had murder been shown so casually and light heartedly as in the machine-gunning of the restaurant; never had massacre been so nonchalantly filmed as in the famous St Valentine's Day Massacre sequence; never before had Hollywood got close to depicting incest as in the relations between Scarface (brilliantly played by Paul Muni) and his sister. But the gangster always got his comeuppance. Justice was meted out and injustice was rooted out; such was the moral code of the

Warners 'social-conscience' movies, as well as of *Scarface*, an independent Howard Hughes production. Hollywood made a few bold, if compromised, attempts to deal with the rigours of the Depression. Warner Brothers took the lead in this sensitive field and the work of two directors, Mervyn LeRoy (b.1900) and William Wellman (1896–1975), gave the studio a reputation for honest, no-punches-pulled film making. Films like *I Am a Fugitive From a Chain Gang* (1932), *Heroes for Sale* (1933) and *Wild Boys of the Road* (1933) attributed the plight of their 'heroes' to the Depression. Mervyn LeRoy, who had made *Little Caesar* in 1930, starring Edward G. Robinson as Rico, consolidated his reputation for tough, uncompromising films with *I Am a Fugitive From a Chain Gang*. Once again Paul Muni gave a wonderful performance, this time as a man unjustly accused, condemned, tortured and finally turned into a hunted escapee.

LeRoy delved further behind the headlines in *Five Star Final* (1931), exposing the gutter press, and in *Hard to Handle* (1932), a satire on the money-grubbing race of con men. It was LeRoy, too, who in 1937 made an anti-lynching film, *They Won't Forget*, which on balance improved upon Fritz Lang's *Fury* of the previous year, if only because it avoided Lang's implicit excuse that lynchers are 'only human'. In *They Won't Forget* LeRoy makes no such excuses; he excludes forgiveness. Claude Rains plays the shifty local governor who gets his way by dubious and questionable means. LeRoy employs some

stunningly effective high-angle shots (of an interrogation; of a girl's body crumpled at the bottom of a lift shaft), and builds to a sickening climax when the hanging of the innocent school-master is conveyed by the startling image of a high-speed train snatching a mailbag off its post.

LeRoy's *I Am a Fugitive From a Chain Gang* and Wellman's *Heroes for Sale* both portray war veterans returning to encounter unemployment and falling 'innocently' into crime. *Chain Gang* amounts to an indictment not only of the penal system but of the society that forces its hero (Paul Muni) outside the law. *Heroes for Sale* is less clear about its targets. Richard Barthelmess plays Tom Holmes, a victim of the post-war years who is at root an (American) individualist, frustrated by the contemporary hard times. A muddled, desperate film that is by turns anti-capitalist and anti-communist, *Heroes for Sale* nevertheless provides some memorable images of the dole queue and the breadline.

Wellman's next film *Wild Boys of the Road* is reputed to have been inspired by screenings of Nikolai Ekks' *Putyevka v Zhizn* (1931, *The Road to Life*), a Russian film about roving gangs of youths rendered homeless by the Civil War. *Wild Boys* takes up the same theme, billing it as 'the story of half a million young Americans, neglected, maltreated and marching to hell' pitting innocent children against seasoned hobos and freight car guards, as the unemployed ride the trains in search of work. When the boys make their home in 'Sewer

Far left: the last of Chaplin's Little Tramp – from Modern Times. *Far left, above: Margaret Dumont almost qualified as an honorary Marx Brother, playing 'straight lady' in seven of their films; here she is wooed by Groucho in* Animal Crackers. *Above left: Tom Powers (James Cagney) sees his partner Matt (Edward Woods) shot down in* The Public Enemy. *Above: Rico (Edward G. Robinson) tries to shoot his way out in* Little Caesar. *Left: Paul Muni (second from left) as gang boss Tony Camonte with George Raft (right) in* Scarface.

City' they are raided by police and fight back with stones, an anti-authoritarian gesture that made the film trade jittery. Again, despite the genuine concern with injustice, the film stops short of attacking the social ills or of suggesting solutions to them.

In a parallel development the documentary movement began to make its presence felt on film-goers. The work of the American 'father' of documentary, Robert Flaherty, and the influence of John Grierson's British documentary group had not gone unnoticed in the United States. Various young film-makers became interested in this new approach to cinema in terms of realism and public education.

One of these directors was Pare Lorentz (b.1905), a former film critic, who made *The Plow That Broke the Plains* (1936), an imaginative documentary on the dust-bowl. The same subject was given a fictional treatment a few years later by John Ford in *The Grapes of Wrath* (1940) – a dramatization of John Steinbeck's novel about one family's heroic attempts to escape the misery of agricultural poverty.

Lorentz returned to the dust-bowl phenomenon – and the specific problems of the Mississippi basin – in his next film *The River* (1937). Both *The Plow* and *The River* had declamatory narrations, and powerful musical scores by the distinguished composer Virgil Thomson. These films attracted the attention of President Roosevelt, who set up a government film agency whose purpose was to assist the production of this kind of film.

Lorentz planned two more films: one, on unemployment, never came to fruition; the other, *The Fight for Life* (1940), about Chicago's maternity services, was impressive enough to be banned in Chicago and highly praised elsewhere.

Some of the ideas about the portrayal of reality and the 'truthfulness' of the documentary image surfaced in the *March of Time* series in the mid to late Thirties. An offshoot of the magazines *Time* and *Life*, this dramatized account of world events set out to be provocative. Departing from the principle of documentary film, the series mixed actualities with reconstructed scenes using actors and look-alikes.

Certainly the series created an easier climate of opinion for genuine documentaries like *The City* (1939), a critique of slum conditions directed by Ralph Steiner and Willard van Dyke. In the same period, Frontier Films made *China Strikes Back*, (1937), which dared to suggest that Mao Tse-tung, and not Chiang Kai Shek, might prove to be the country's saviour.

Below: The Plow That Broke the Plains *spoke of hope of future prosperity for dust-bowl farmers.*

Gangster Films

The gangster film proper, after its early wave of 1930–2, soon fell into formulaic repetitions or self-parody, as in *Lady Killer* (1933), in which James Cagney played an amateur criminal who becomes a movie actor of tough-guy roles. Similarly, in *The Little Giant* (1933), Edward G. Robinson played a superannuated bootlegger who tries to move into the smart set and is quickly cheated with dud bonds by 'respectable' people. Robinson's reluctance to be identified with gangster roles – he was a cultured man who collected Impressionist paintings – was dramatized with almost schizophrenic vividness in *The Whole Town's Talking*, where he was the innocent double of a gangster as well as the bad guy himself, killing off his evil alter ego by briefly assuming his identity.

Both Cagney and Robinson figured prominently, however, in the second wave of gangster movies from 1935 onwards, in which the hero, instead of being a gangster was a law-enforcer – though not infrequently an undercover one, who could behave like a hoodlum for much of the film. Several factors contributed to this development. Increased censorship was imposed when the Hays Code, formulated in 1930 for the Motion Picture Producers and Distributors of America (MPPDA, later MPAA), began to be strictly enforced under the administration of Joseph Breen. Simultaneously, Catholic pressure led to the formation of the Legion of Decency, which initiated an influential ratings system. Meanwhile, the FBI, which had failed to make much impression on organized crime under Prohibition or after it, was galvanized into new initiatives, under its publicity-conscious director J. Edgar Hoover, when Congress extended its mandate to a whole new list of federal crimes, in the wake of the Lindbergh kidnapping. Hoover's agents gunned down a clutch of small-town bank-robbers in 1934–5, notably John Dillinger (though in that case the famous shooting outside the Biograph cinema in Chicago on July 22, 1934 quite possibly nailed the wrong man). Appropriately, then, William Keighley's *G-Men* (1935) inaugurated the new policy at Warner Brothers, with Cagney as the ambiguous undercover government agent or 'G-Man' (a nickname attributed to George 'Machine Gun' Kelly, later commemorated in Roger Corman's 1958 biopic). Robinson followed with an undercover (though not specifically FBI) role in Keighley's *Bullets or Ballots* (1936), pitted against malevolent gang-boss Humphrey Bogart.

Bogart also figured prominently in another strand of mid-Thirties gangster movies, a somewhat sterile one – adapted Broadway plays. He was in the film version of Robert E. Sherwood's *The Petrified Forest* (1936) as Duke Mantee, a gangster on the run, who eventually shoots a talkative writer (Leslie Howard). Bogart left Maxwell Anderson's verse-play *Winterset* (1936) to Burgess Meredith and Eduardo Ciannelli, but was on-set again for a somewhat studio-bound version of Sidney Kingsley's *Dead End* (1937, dir. William Wyler), now chiefly remembered for inaugurating the Dead End Kids (Leo Gorcey *et al*), who went through several name changes, finally becoming the Bowery Boys.

Their best subsequent effort was Michael Curtiz's *Angels With Dirty Faces* (1938), which also took over the theme of the social origins of crime from *Dead End*. Bogart's crooked lawyer is again irredeemably evil, but tough-guy Rocky (Cagney) has his better side and kills two treacherous associates to save his boyhood pal, now the parish priest (Pat O'Brien). More significantly, he is persuaded to pretend to be yellow when facing the electric chair, proving to the hero-worshipping local lads that crime does not pay. However, the

theory that poverty produces crime was somewhat undercut by having both good guy and bad guy come from identical backgrounds. When this pattern re-emerged in post-war films (such as *Cry of the City*, 1948), it had lost its sociological element altogether and become a device of psychological, almost metaphysical, doubling and contrast.

Also inevitably influenced by social themes were the perennially popular prison films – if slums were the high schools of crime, prisons were seen as its universities. Yet reform was possible, even if instigated from within, as in Keighley's *Each Dawn I Die* (1939), by a crusading journalist (Cagney), framed for manslaughter by a crooked DA, and a 'good' gangster (George Raft). Even the Dead End Kids did a spell in the reformatory in *Crime School* (1938), under the benevolent supervision of a liberal Commissioner of Correction (Bogart).

Bogart reverted to type in Raoul Walsh's *The Roaring Twenties* (1939), which not only summed up much of what the gangster movie had become during the decade but also helped to popularise the retrospective, even nostalgic, mode that has since so largely characterized the genre. If Bogart's bootlegger, George, is again psychopathically evil, Cagney's cabdriver, Eddie, becomes a big-time hood almost by accident, rises with the boom, and declines in the Depression, is driven by unrequited love for a singer (Priscilla Lane) to sample the booze he had previously shunned, and finally redeems himself by sacrificing his life to save an old buddy, now married to the girl. This fairy-tale of old Manhattan, originally written by New York crime reporter (later producer)

Mark Hellinger, is interspersed with elaborately symbolic quasi-documentary montages, probably directed by the young Don Siegel, that established each section of scenes' economic and social context.

This was Cagney's farewell to gangster roles for a decade; but Bogart continued with *Brother Orchid* (1940, opposite Edward G. Robinson), and *The Big Shot* (1942). The turning point of his career came with *High Sierra* (1941), produced by Hellinger and directed by Walsh. This time, Bogart's Roy 'Mad Dog' Earle (vaguely based on Dillinger) is poised between unrequited love and a sympathetic moll (Ida Lupino). But he is an ageing loner rather than a ex-big shot, and his inevitable death occurs in the rural isolation of the mountains, far from the big city. The film was tinged throughout with nostalgia.

The classic gangster movie was soon to give way to the private-eye genre and the dark perversities of the *film noir* The next brief flurry of activity involved using the names, if not the true stories, of real gangsters, as in *Roger Touhy, Gangster* (1944) and *Dillinger* (1945), a practice previously forbidden by the Production Code; but the fashion for biopics did not come to fruition until the late Fifties.

Formulas

Hollywood spent the first decade of sound films looking for trade marks – for a way to slap a corporate identity on movies that would attact consumer loyalty. MGM wanted the aura of Ford for cars or Kellogg for cereals. But studio trade marks of this kind did not work. Furthermore the names of individual stars were too risky, since they might unaccountably wax or wane according to audience taste. What the studios most wanted were packages – simple ways to put together stars, stories, characters, again and again, so that the public was seldom surprised, rarely disappointed.

The means they found were the star teams, the so-called love teams, and the series. Star teams could be heavily promoted and their films re-released at will. Series could be extended indefinitely. Instead of the Hollywood nightmare of story starvation – the producer B.P. Schulberg of Paramount reckoned Hollywood had to invent 400 new stories a year to fill the gap between movies made and novels and stage plays to adapt – there was a chance of smooth, cheap assembly-line production. Above all, there was a way to build audience loyalty. Seen from the front office, the exotic adventures of Charlie Chan and the Thin Man, the domestic ructions of the Hardy Family and the moral dilemmas of Dr Kildare, the love-making of Clark Gable and Jean Harlow, Errol Flynn and Olivia de Havilland, Jeanette MacDonald and Nelson Eddy were all devices to rationalize the one uncontrolled force in the movies – the audience.

Each MacDonald and Eddy picture was a soft and glossy operetta; each partnering of Ruby Keeler and Dick Powell saw an undercover rich man hoofing his way to the love of a showgirl; Judy Garland and Mickey Rooney, whether in the movies about Andy Hardy or the MGM musicals after *Babes in Arms* (1939), exuded vibrant naivety. The names made the product predictable. They were brand names. Sometimes, as with Garland and Rooney, star teams and series formulas can be seen to overlap. It is hard to distinguish between the standard appeal of the stories and the standard appeal of the star personalities. William Powell and Myrna Loy in the Thin Man movies could be either a love team of particular charm and skill, all the more remarkable for representing a married couple, or else the skilled functionaries of a carefully contrived series package.

Love teams were not unbreakable, nor were they constant. Producers would sometimes underestimate the power of a particular combination of personalities. Nelson Eddy and Jeanette MacDonald had breathed some sharp life into the revival of (sugary) operetta which Louis. B. Mayer had decreed for his studio. Together they made *Naughty Marietta* (1935) work commercially where the cynicism of Lubitsch's *The Merry Widow* (1934) with MacDonald and Chevalier had proved unpopular. In the next two years Eddy and MacDonald were reunited for *Rose Marie* (1936) and the astonishingly lush *Maytime* (1937). When MGM decided to gamble on their separate drawing-power, however, it became clear that Eddy and MacDonald clicked at the box-office only as a team. Eddy and MacDonald is a trade mark, as exact about the product it represents as, say, Rolls (and) Royce. The same is true of Janet Gaynor and Charles Farrell the bright teaming of an unlikely couple who could radiate on screen a haze of virtuous passion in pictures like *Sunny Side Up* (1929).

Dick Powell and Ruby Keeler also acted out the same screen relationship in movie after movie. Their partnership began in *42nd Street* (1933), the Darryl Zanuck-inspired production that revived the Warners musical. Keeler had made only one

Right: Dick Powell and Ruby Keeler take a stroll down Flirtation Walk *(1934), one of the pair's several wholesome musicals. Far right: Myrna Loy and William Powell were brought together for the first time by producer David O. Selznick for* Manhattan Melodrama *(1934). Below far right: Clark Gable as the boss of a rubber plantation is strangely attracted to low-down Jean Harlow in* Red Dust. *Centre right: Gable's other notable partner of the period was Joan Crawford, here as a show-biz hopeful in* Dancing Lady *(1933). Below right: the king and queen of film operetta – Nelson Eddy and Jeanette MacDonald. Below: the Michael Curtiz swashbuckler* Captain Blood, *about a doctor forced to turn pirate inaugurated the romantic team of Errol Flynn and Olivia De Havilland.*

film before, a guest appearance in *Show Girl in Hollywood* (1930); she was best known as Mrs Al Jolson.

Nevertheless Powell and Keeler emerged, charming and lovable, from the self-conscious spectacle around them. As Powell's radio career took off, so his billing improved, until he and Keeler had to have their names on separate lines. By the time of *Colleen* (1936) the team had run its course. Powell was by then the established star, and Keeler, after a handful of solo appearances, left Warners when her husband fell out with the studio hierarchy. She made only one further screen appearance following her divorce from Jolson.

Clark Gable's two great partnerships of the Thirties, with Jean Harlow and Joan Crawford, show just how varied the actual movies of the strongest love teams could be. Gable and Crawford turned out melodramas like *Dance, Fools, Dance* (1931) and musicals like *Dancing Lady* (1933) and even production-line screwball comedies. After the success of Gable with the brilliant Claudette Colbert in *It Happened One Night* (1934), Gable and Crawford made *Love on the Run* (1936), in which they went through the motions of the earlier movie's main plot points, but on European locations. Each star in a love team had a general appeal; each movie was a separate product; the effect of the love team was to bolster the pulling power of the words on the cinema billboard and to improve the standing of the valuable star.

The extraordinary screen warmth between Gable and Harlow was helped by timing: *Red Dust* (1932) emerged before the Hays Code could bridle their passions. They had

previously starred in *The Secret Six* (1931), an outstanding gangster movie in which they supported Wallace Beery, and went on to make various assorted dramas of tropical passion on land and sea, usually the Orient; they even made a soap opera set in a publisher's office called *Wife vs Secretary* (1936) in which Gable virtually ignores Harlow's attractions, and the usual brute virility is buried under a conventional, even stuffy character. In the bedroom scene Harlow's most physical act is to remove Gable's shoes.

The vast majority of series hinged on two devices: they took exotic matters, usually crime, and presented them through familiar characters; or else they took domestic drama and by presenting it either as farce or melodrama, made it seem exotic.

The most remarkable example of the dramatization of domestic lives was the saga of the Hardy Family, first seen in *A Family Affair* (1937) and substantially recast for the first of the 14 movies in the series proper.

Andy Hardy's adventures in middle-class, small-town America were the pet project of Louis B. Mayer, who carefully vetted the films, the best of which teamed Mickey Rooney as Andy with Judy Garland. The MGM script department worked out Judge Hardy's salary precisely and tailored everything in the movies to fit the family budget. Warm and loving, with a father who was always right, the Hardys were supposed to epitomize the standards, if not the circumstances, of the ideal American family. In fact, the plotlines are remarkably exotic. Father is a judge who may

Above: Judy Garland and Mickey Rooney fall in love over ice-cream sodas in Love Finds Andy Hardy.

inherit, briefly, a huge fortune, or be summoned to Washington to head a committee. Andy Hardy, the all-American boy, spends an entire movie trying to gate-crash Manhattan's social elite. Since realities like debt are carefully excluded as plot devices, all that remains is the extraordinary.

The exotic was tamed and domesticated by conventions in the crime series. Scripts were literally interchangeable. Fox had both Charlie Chan, aphoristic Chinese gentleman, and Mr Moto, quiet Japanese jujitsu champion. When Warner Oland, the best of the Chans, died during production of one episode, both script and footage were converted into a Mr Moto adventure *Mr Moto's Gamble* (1938), in which Chan's Number One Son makes a rather uncomfortable appearance apparently as Moto's side-kick. Rules of narrative were, it seems, rigid and general. Everybody knew a Thin Man mystery ended with characters assembled to be told what had happened.

Medical matters always involved a problem-solving older doctor, a kind of shaman who could cure all ills, resolve all conflict. The Dr Kildare movies dealt with subject matter that ranged from plagues to the more controversial territory of socialized medicine, but always within a format of 'problem-solving' and therefore comforting, narratives.

Crime is as sanitized as medicine in the series. Heroes always win; equivocal characters like The Saint acquire virtue; Boston Blackie, Lone Wolf and The Falcon beat their adversaries every time. In the end plot values gave way to mayhem, which was easier to invent, and the Ellery Queen series in particular simply piled fist-fight on fist-fight in place of elegant deduction.

One of Hollywood's longest-running and most popular series reached its peak in the Thirties – the Tarzan films, based on Edgar Rice Burroughs' stories and novels about a British aristocrat orphaned in the African jungle and brought up by apes. The first Tarzan movie, starring Elmo Lincoln, had reached the screen in 1918, but the King of the Jungle did not become a major box-office attraction until the late Twenties when, thanks to the coming of sound, audiences were permitted to experience the thrill of roaring lions, chattering monkeys, trumpeting elephants and Tarzan's own cry.

In 1932, former Olympic swimming champion, Johnny Weissmuller became the first talking Tarzan in MGM's *Tarzan the Ape Man*, directed by W.S. Van Dyke. In addition to the movie's excellent jungle footage, its enduring merits derive from the charm of the script (by Cyril Hume and Ivor Novello) and the playing of Weissmuller and co-star Maureen O'Sullivan. The film's success resulted in a series of Tarzan adventures; Weissmuller remained virtually unchallenged in the lead role until 1948. Following his departure to less taxing work, largely in television, Lex Barker, Gordon Scott, Daniel Miller, Jock Mahoney, Mike Henry and Ron Ely all assayed the character of Tarzan with varying degrees of success in low budget films and TV series. In 1983 British director Hugh Hudson bravely attempted to rekindle audience respect for the King of the Apes with his spectacular *Greystoke – The Legend of Tarzan, Lord of the Apes*.

In the Thirties, another ex-Olympic swimming champion gained world-wide stardom as a fantasy hero, Buster Crabbe, who achieved popularity playing Tarzan, Billy the Kid, Thunda and, especially, Flash Gordon. Universal's serial *Flash Gordon* (1936) was the most expensive ever made and the first with a science-fiction theme. Its success resulted in several sequels and set the style for Republic's and Columbia's many sci-fi serials of the Thirties, Forties and Fifties.

Family Films

In the mid Thirties Hollywood was only dimly aware that World War II was just around the corner, and that an even greater menace called television was to threaten its existence after the war. Consequently the phenomenon of family cinema-going was, perhaps for the last time, a factor to be reckoned with in the film industry. Louis B. Mayer, a 'family man' even among movie moguls, once asked rhetorically:

Above: Tarzan the Ape Man *sensitively combined exoticism and eroticism. Above right: in this 1938 Charlie Chan mystery, Sidney Toler succeeded Warner Oland as the famous Chinese detective and inventor of proverbs. Far right: Hollywood's hottest property in the mid to late Thirties was Shirley Temple. During the filming of* Captain January *she was troubled by the loss of her baby teeth. Right: serial saviours of the Universe Dale Arden (Jean Rogers) and Flash Gordon (Buster Crabbe).*

'What will people say about Louis B. Mayer if he puts his name on a picture he's ashamed to let his family see?'

As TV companies were to discover later, family viewing was big business; what's more it meant that film producers could comfortably keep on the right side of the rigorous requirements of the Production Code and the strident demands of the Catholic Legion of Decency.

One obvious approach to dealing with the Catholic lobby was to have a priest for a hero. In a most improbable piece of casting, Spencer Tracy played a priest in *San Francisco* (1936) – up to this point he had been playing convicts, gangsters and con men. It was a powerful performance that earned Tracy his first Oscar nomination and set the pattern for his playing of the saintly Father Flanagan in *Boys Town* (1938). *San Francisco*, quite apart from Tracy, had everything: Clark Gable at his rugged best as a gambling, brawling saloon-keeper, whose final reformation in no way affects one's enjoyment of his wicked career; Jeanette MacDonald's silvery voice putting over a memorable theme song; and the climactic earthquake, a triumph of the art of special effects.

Boys' Town was a sentimental but effective account of how a dedicated priest who believes that there is no such thing as a 'bad' boy runs a home for juvenile delinquents. The chief delinquent was played by the mercurial Mickey Rooney – then 16 but short in stature and ideally suited to go on playing juvenile roles well into his adolescence. Rooney was one of many highly talented American screen children whose films provided much of the popular fare for family audiences. Child stars were nothing new of course, and had always been an essential ingredient of 'family pictures'. Rooney and Jackie Cooper were the outstanding boy stars of the Thirties, with Jackie Searl often in close support as the sneak or sissy who was a necessary foil.

Among the little girls Shirley Temple (b.1928) reigned supreme. A fully-fledged star at five, she had a range of talents that has tended to be obscured by the saccharine image created for her by largely cynical critics. Her foil, as a mischievous and sometimes unpleasant child, was Jane Withers, but Bonita Granville was an even more remarkable performer of nasty little girls as her portrayal of the malevolent talebearer in *These Three* (1936) attested.

In the late Thirties MGM brought forward two young girls, both exceptionally talented musically. Judy Garland (1922–1969) was the less successful at first, despite the hit she made in *The Wizard of Oz* (1939), but Deanna Durbin (b.1921), dropped by MGM and taken up by Universal, became a box-office phenomenon – especially in Britain – from her very first film, *Three Smart Girls* (1937).

Deanna had a light, remarkably controlled soprano voice and a repertoire of popular classics. In *One Hundred Men and a Girl* (1937) she helped make so-called serious music more popular. But her singing would not have done the trick had she not had an exceptionally likeable personality. What really sold her to the public was the wholesome charm which made her every parent's favourite dream daughter.

As might be expected *Three Smart Girls* spawned a sequel – *Three Smart Girls Grow Up* (1939).

The Three Smart Girls films were directed by Henry Koster and featured Deanna as the youngest of three sisters. In the first she reconciles her estranged parents and in the second she helps to marry off her older sisters. Plot, however, is less important to these movies than the freshness and vitality of the girls, the support of a strong cast and the judicious blend of popular and classical songs.

A rather similar and appropriately titled 'family' series was launched in *Four Daughters* (1938). Featuring the attractive Lane sisters (Lola, Rosemary and Priscilla) and Gale Page as the daughters of a musician, the film was also notable for the debut of John Garfield, who made a big impression as a poor boy with a chip on his shoulder. This and two of the sequels, *Daughters Courageous* (1939) and *Four Wives* (1939), were made by Michael Curtiz. Both these sequels shared the virtues

Above: the Lane sisters and Gale Page as musician Claude Rains' Four Daughters, *an archetypal Hollywood 'family' film.*

Top: Paul Muni (right) in the title role of The Life of Emile Zola *centring on the year 1898, when the famous author came to the aid of Captain Alfred Dreyfus, a Jewish officer in the French army wrongly accused of treason. Above: Henry Fonda as the future President in* Young Mr Lincoln, *which showed him fighting injustice as a humble country lawyer.*

of the original film but the next, William Keighley's *Four Mothers* (1941), was not able to sustain the momentum. What all the films had in common was a thorough-going endorsement of the notion of family; the fact too, that stories were located in small-town, middle-American contributed to the image of a homogenized society based on traditional family values.

Literary classics were another cornerstone of family entertainment in the Thirties and provided a further extension of the daughters, wives and families themes already noted. The works of authors like Charles Dickens, Louis May Alcott and Frances Hodgson Burnett suggest sentimentality, but in the hands of sensitive directors like George Cukor and John Cromwell the authors were well served; as Cukor himself said, 'If you really respect a work, you must respect the weaknesses, the vagaries, as well as the strength'.

Neither he nor Cromwell believed in tidying up a story to fit modern concepts and their versions are consequently as timeless as the originals. Cukor has said that he had thought of *Little Women* as a story little girls read:

'When I came to read it I was startled. It's not sentimental or saccharine, but very strong-minded, full of character, and a wonderful picture of New England family life. It's full of that admirable New England sternness, about sacrifice and austerity.'

Cukors' film of *Little Women* (1933) was equally vigorous, thanks largely to Katharine Hepburn's wonderfully fresh and tender portrayal of Jo. The director went on to film *David Copperfield* (1935), in collaboration with David O. Selznick. It was the same producer who set John Cromwell to work on *Little Lord Fauntleroy* (1936) and *The Prisoner of Zenda* (1937). From its reputation as a legendary tear-jerker *Little Lord Fauntleroy* emerged, under Cromwell's careful guidance, as a sharply observed and humorous story whose hero, played by Freddie Bartholomew, was a natural, likeable child. Cromwell's version of *The Prisoner of Zenda* is one of the great swashbucklers of all time and it provided Douglas Fairbanks Jr with a fine romantic part.

Costume drama that revolved around a family situation continued to be reliable family-audience fare. Katharine Hepburn, following her success in *Little Women*, was also featured in two adaptations from stories by J.M. Barrie, produced by Pandro S. Berman for RKO. She was radiant as the wild and wilful Babbie in *The Little Minister* (1934) and, in a very different mood, gave a restrained and elegant account of the ageing spinster in *Quality Street* (1937, dir. George Stevens). Stevens directed her in another of her best characterizations – that of the funny but pathetic small-town snob in Booth Tarkington's *Alice Adams* (1935).

It was Selznick again who produced one of the best Mark Twain adaptations: *The Adventures of Tom Sawyer* (1938), directed by Norman Taurog (who had made a version of *Huckleberry Finn* with Jackie Coogan back in 1931). This version, the second in Hollywood during the decade, starred Tommy Kelly and Jackie Moran and had a strong cast of character players including Victor Jory as Injun Joe. The film owed much to the art direction of William Cameron Menzies and reflected once again Selznick's tireless quest for the perfect team in each production. Indeed it is a notable fact – borne out by MGM's *A Tale of Two Cities* (1935) in which Ronald Colman gave the definitive performance of Sydney Carton – that wherever several versions exist of the same classic novel it is almost always the Selznick version that is best remembered.

Literary adaptations were safe bets: they had already succeeded in another medium and they were respectable. This meant that the whole family could enjoy them and the self-appointed guardians of America's morals would approve of them. In a similar vein the stories of the lives of famous men and women provided good doses of moral uplift. The success of these 'biopics' in the Thirties may be compared with the historical biographies so popular on television today. *The Story of Louis Pasteur* (1935), *The Life of Emile Zola* (1937) and *Juarez* (1939) were all directed by William Dieterle. The careers of famous statesmen were also reckoned to be acceptable subjects for audiences of all ages and in *Disraeli* (1939), starring George Arliss, and *Clive of India* (1935), starring Ronald Colman, the vital ingredient of adventure was never overlooked. Towards the end of the decade Hollywood got around to dramatizing the lives of American statesmen. Henry Fonda, for example, played Lincoln in Ford's *Young Mr Lincoln* (1939) and Raymond Massey took over the role in Cromwell's follow-up *Abe Lincoln in Illinois* (1940).

In the final analysis Hollywood's formula for building the

loyalty of family audiences was to base its films on happy families, famous lives or famous books, often scaled down to the comfortable, familiar environment of the all-purpose small town. It was as though Alexander Graham Bell (played by Don Ameche in the 1939 film), Tom Sawyer and the Hardy family all grew up and lived in the same town: a place that was as familiar an image of America as the idyllic village was of England, and a place where the Hollywood moguls may have imagined their audiences to live.

Down to Earth

The arrival of talkies in America at the same time as the Depression introduced a new kind of star to the movies: screen heroes and heroines who talked the same language as the moviegoers. These were characters with whom the audience could readily identify: men who were street-wise and girls who played the game of life according to their own rules.

Perhaps more than any other performer, Will Rogers personified the man who expressed the home truths that every American wanted to utter but could not articulate. Rogers was born in Oklahoma in 1879. He had a varied career as a cowboy, merchant seaman, variety artist in Wild West shows and as a raconteur in Flo Ziegfeld's Broadway spectaculars.

Rogers was first signed by Sam Goldwyn to appear in silent movies as a cowboy trickster. The essence of Rogers, however, was his homespun, insular philosophizing about ordinary folk having a tough time but coming through it all with a laugh. Only in his talkies could this aspect be exploited, and so it was after he signed for Fox that he became a big success in films like *A Connecticut Yankee* (1931, dir. David Butler), *Ambassador Bill* (1932, dir. Sam Taylor), *State Fair* (1933, dir. Henry King) and *Judge Priest* (1934, dir. John Ford).

His role as the people's spokesman, in films like *Down to Earth* (1932) where he offers advice on how to cope with the Depression, was considered influential in getting Franklin D. Roosevelt elected the following year. And certainly he was never more popular than in FDR's campaign year of 1932, when Rogers found himself ninth in the Hollywood popularity polls. His last film was *Steamboat Round the Bend* (1935)

again for Ford. Later that same year he died in an air crash. His life story was made into a film, *The Will Rogers Story* (1952), in which Will Rogers Jr portrayed his father.

In the Thirties, a new kind of film hero emerged and caught the imagination of the public. Loosely based on the archetypal Will Rogers character, these were men who spoke only when they had something vital to say; men who lived by standards that were rooted in the pioneer existence of the birth of an independent United States. They were, above all, men of personal pride. In Westerns they were typically played by Gary Cooper, Henry Fonda and Joel McCrea.

But the grass-roots hero also found his way into more sophisticated films. Gary Cooper played the title role in Capra's *Mr Deeds Goes to Town* (1936) – a provincial man who inherits a fortune and wants to spend it helping poor people in the Depression. In Capra's subsequent 'Everyman' film, *Mr Smith Goes to Washington* (1939), James Stewart played the hick from a small town who is taken for a ride by big city smart guys. In the jungle of big business and politics Mr Deeds and Mr Smith fought for their basic beliefs in the American way of life and for their right to denounce a corrupt and corruptible Establishment.

The city was the true jungle. And the early Thirties gangster movies were not the only films to portray the tough nature of street life. In *No Greater Glory* (1934), set in pre-war Hungary, Frank Borzage showed the city ghettoes as places where boys grew up either honest or corrupt and had to fight for moral supremacy. Children are also the victims of urban deprivation in Wyler's *Dead End* (1937), and the same gang of boys, the Dead End Kids, were to continue struggling against their environment well into the Forties as the Little Tough Guys, the East Side Kids and later as the Bowery Boys.

More than any other group in society it was the women in films who bore the brunt of the Depression. They fought their way up from the bottom, often made profitable marriages, but were nearly always thwarted in their ambitions. As Marjorie Rosen writes in *Popcorn Venus* 'Women were the sacrificial lambs of the Depression'. They were required to run the gamut of moral, and sometimes physical, suffering and thereby made the working girls in the audience feel better.

Pictures that featured working women arrived on the scene at the same time as talkies. In her book *From Reverence to*

Left: Ford's film gave Will Rogers one of his best vehicles. Above: Wyler's Dead End *dealt with the trials and tribulations of growing up in the slums.*

Rape, Molly Haskell describes how the Depression created 'a demand for a more down-to-earth heroine'. And you could hardly get more down-to-earth than *Five or Ten Cent Annie* (1928) or *The Girl From Woolworths* (1929).

These magazine-inspired movies soon developed into a wholesale genre that was particularly lucrative for RKO and MGM. The 'confessional' films, as these melodramas came to be known, not only gave flesh to the fantasies of ordinary working girls but also administered a dose of the puritanical medicine that society seems to prescribe during periods of economic hardship.

A film called *Common Clay* (1930), in which Constance Bennett and Lew Ayres battled in the courts for custody of their illegitimate child, set the tone for subsequent Constance Bennett tear-jerkers whose titles included: *Sin Takes a Holiday* (1930), *Born to Love*, *The Common Law*, *The Easiest Way* (all 1931) and *Rockabye* (1932).

At Paramount the soon-to-be-famous director George Cukor was cutting his teeth on similar 'women's pictures'. In *Tarnished Lady* (1931) Tallulah Bankhead plays a spoiled socialite who marries for money, falls in love with her husband (Clive Brook), deserts him to find self-realization in motherhood and a nine-to-five job, but finally returns to his side after he has been wiped out by the disastrous Crash of 1929.

Bankhead followed this with *Faithless* (1932) at MGM in which, according to *Picturegoer*, she ran 'the gamut of sex and degradation'. MGM's other 'suffering' ladies of the period included Joan Crawford in *Possessed* (1931) opposite Clark Gable, and Helen Twelvetrees in a string of pictures with indicative titles like *Unashamed*, *Compromised* (both 1932) and *Disgraced* (1933).

In the eyes of the movie moguls, and indeed the public, Joan Crawford, Norma Shearer, Helen Twelvetrees and Constance Bennett personified the kind of woman who had come up the hard way and achieved an elegant style, but who lived to regret her denial of her humble background. This made the girls behind the counter at the 'five-and-dime' store feel they'd made a better choice after all in marrying the boy next door.

Later in the decade a tougher breed of women made their presence felt: Sylvia Sidney, Bette Davis, Ann Sheridan and Alice Faye. But they were inherently the same sort of women. In *Dead End* Sylvia Sidney struggles to bring up her young brother in New York's grim East Side ghetto. In *Marked Woman* (1937) Bette Davis as a nightclub hostess suffered a hideous penalty for testifying against an underworld boss. Joan Blondell wise-cracked her way through several 'gold-digger' parts like *Millie* (1931) in which she supported Helen Twelvetrees. And it was Blondell, in *Gold Diggers of 1933*, who sang the poignant number 'Remember My Forgotten Man' – an epitaph for all the menfolk who survived World War I and came home to a USA teetering on the brink of the Depression.

Unemployment scarred American badly. In 1930 it was estimated that ten million American women went out to work. Two years later a fifth of them were jobless. The early Thirties were tough on the masses. Hollywood's primary response was to venture into new forms of realism. But of equal importance was the blending of Victorian sentiment and backwoods 'pioneer' spirit with contemporary setting and stories. The Will Rogers corny comedies and the working-girl weepies were as much a feature of moviegoing on the bleakest evenings of the Depression as any gangster film. Soon, however, Roosevelt's New Deal was the national talking point and the movies, especially those of Capra and Vidor, swiftly reflected the public's new mood of optimism, engendered by the President's economic measures.

Above: Hugh Herbert mistreats his mistress, Tallulah Bankhead, in Faithless. *Above right: wounded soldier Paul Cavanagh meets selfless nurse Constance Bennett in* Born to Love. *Far right: Helen Twelvetrees in* Millie, *in which she is 'betrayed' by no less than five men. Right: Charles Delaney makes a play for Alice Faye in* The Girl From Woolworths.

Swashbucklers and Epics

With the advent of sound several of the staple genres of the silent screen went into eclipse, notably Westerns, swashbucklers and historical epics. But when, in 1934, Hollywood strictly enforced the Hays Code, which had been drawn up in 1927 and rewritten in 1930, the film companies returned to such 'safe' subjects. These were films which were generally set in distant eras, far-off countries, and societies whose moral codes stressed romance, patriotism, gallantry and clean-cut action rather than sex, violence and sensationalism.

The most purely escapist films were the swashbucklers, which had owed so much to the talent of Douglas Fairbanks Sr. The archetypal characters of dashing hero, double-dyed villain and damsel in distress, the elaborate sets, the acrobatic set pieces and the stylized plots were established by Douglas Fairbanks in an unforgettable series of films that began with *The Mark of Zorro* (1920) and ended with *The Iron Mask* (1929) almost a decade later. The new cycle of swashbucklers adhered to this pattern, but added sound and colour.

Errol Flynn, cast by Warner Brothers at short notice in *Captain Blood*, proved the ideal successor to Douglas Fairbanks Sr. The combination of lithe, animal grace, clear-eyed youthfulness, pure English-speaking voice and athletic prowess was irresistible. Warners assembled a memorable supporting cast headed by Olivia de Havilland, as a radiantly lovely heroine, and Basil Rathbone, sneering, arrogant, virile and flamboyant, as a definitive villain. Fred Cavens provided the thrilling sword-play, Anton Grot designed the stylized, semi-Expressionist sets, Erich Wolfgang Korngold wrote the symphonic score, the whole wealth of skills being blended together by director Michael Curtiz into the classic pirate adventure.

With occasional changes of personnel, the same talented team went on to create two more swashbucklers which set the standard that all rivals and successors would have to aim for. *The Adventures of Robin Hood* (1938), shot in lustrous Technicolor, still ravishes the senses and stirs the blood. The action highlights of the film are the outlaws' attack on a gold shipment in Sherwood Forest and the climactic sword fight between Flynn and Rathbone.

The Sea Hawk (1940) starred Flynn as a privateer, modelled on Sir Francis Drake. It was a film of sumptuous visual style, spell-binding skill, breath-taking action and full-hearted commitment. Two stirring sea-battles between actual-size ships were staged in the new Warners studio tank and a furious final duel between Flynn and the villain Henry Daniell was fought, with the protagonists dwarfed by huge flickering shadows on the walls.

The Warners style was closely copied by 20th Century-Fox when they produced two swashbucklers with their leading male star, Tyrone Power. Rouben Mamoulian's elegant *The Mark of Zorro* (1940) utilized Fred Cavens' sword-play and a score that echoed Korngold's style. Several Warners supporting players embellished a dream-like sequence of horseback chases, sword-fights and sardonic encounters. Henry King's *The Black Swan* (1942) was Fox's answer to *Captain Blood*, complete with flame-haired Maureen O'Hara and villainy from George Sanders.

Douglas Fairbanks Jr took up his father's mantle to star in John Cromwell's *The Prisoner of Zenda* (1937). Ronald Colman, Madeleine Carroll, Raymond Massey and Fairbanks Jr could not have been bettered as the protagonists in this timeless Ruritanian romance, and the film climaxed with one of the best and wittiest of screen duels, choreographed by Ralph Faulkner (who, along with Cavens, had a virtual monopoly of fight arranging in the Thirties). Fairbanks Jr followed this in 1941 with a lively double role in Gregory Ratoff's *The Corsican Brothers*.

Left: the classic duel in the bowels of Nottingham castle between the villainous Guy of Gisborne (Basil Rathbone) and Robin (Errol Flynn) in The Adventures of Robin Hood. *Above: Tyrone Power (right) as the dashing Zorro duels with Rathbone in Mamoulian's remake of Douglas Fairbanks' 1920 swashbuckler.*

Where the keynotes of the swashbuckler were grace, speed and humour, those of the historical epic were size, scale and seriousness. The latter was also frequently used to point up a moral, religious or even political message. The great showman Cecil B. DeMille was the acknowledged master of the historical epic.

Although he prided himself on imparting moral uplift, DeMille's promotion of Christian values was virtually lost beneath glittering spectacle and slyly titillating scenes of eroticism and sadism. *The Sign of the Cross* (1932), *Cleopatra* (1934) and *The Crusades* (1935) remain his finest achievements. They celebrate on the one hand an almost pagan sensuality, with shimmering photography and languorous camera movements weaving scenes of luxurious seduction. In *Cleopatra*, amid clouds of incense, showers of rose petals, fluttering doves and strutting peacocks, scantily-clad slaves attended Claudette Colbert as she wallowed naked in a bath of asses' milk. On the other hand the films appeal to a primitive blood-lust, featuring cruel games in the Roman arenas and the torture or slaughter of captive Christians. Bloody battles are frequent set pieces – monstrous siege-engines roll inexorably forward over human bodies, torrents of flame pour from city walls onto the soldiers beneath and battalions of knights wade through corpses with swords whirling around their heads.

In the late Thirties, however, DeMille turned his eye on American history and dramatized the expansion of the United States in *The Plainsman* (1936), *The Buccaneer* (1938) and *Union Pacific* (1939) which, although replete with battles, charges and train wrecks, lacked both the erotic and sadistic edge of his earlier films. In the same vein, the decade ended with David. O. Selznick's *Gone With the Wind* (1939), the single most famous film of the era and the one which celebrated the rebirth of the nation after the trauma of civil war.

Hollywood boasted two other profitable lines in epics. The box-office success of Henry Hathaway's *The Lives of a Bengal Lancer* (1935), in which Gary Cooper put down a native uprising on the North West Frontier of India, began a vogue for imperial epics to which almost every studio contributed.

Warner Brothers countered with *The Charge of the Light Brigade* (1936). The film offered a tiger hunt, a wild horse drive and had Errol Flynn leading the climactic charge which was unforgettably staged by second-unit director B. Reeves Eason. Fox presented *Wee Willie Winkie* (1937) in which Shirley Temple brought peace to the Indian North-West Frontier under the direction of John Ford. At the same time Universal produced *The Sun Never Sets* (1939) and RKO made *Gunga Din* (1939), adapted from Rudyard Kipling's famous poem.

Even Republic Pictures, home of Gene Autry and Captain Marvel, contributed *Storm Over Bengal* (1938). These Indian adventures, whose location work was usually done at Lone Pine, California, contained generous action sequences and constituted another exotic form of escapism. But their insistence on a racial hierarchy headed by the white man, their implicit (and sometimes explicit) justification of the British Imperial presence in India and Africa tended to reinforce the political *status quo*.

Disaster epics were equally successful action pictures. They might be classified as films that sought to live up to Sam Goldwyn's celebrated injunction to a scriptwriter, 'I want you to begin with an earthquake and work up to a climax'. Invariably they brought together a group of characters with individual and collective problems and caused these pro-

Above: in defiance of history, Captain Vickers (Errol Flynn) leads his Bengal Lancers 'into the valley of death' in The Charge of the Light Brigade.

blems to be resolved in one way or another by a spectacular final holocaust.

The Hollywood special effects departments had a field day, creating ever more grandoise disasters. They succeeded in destroying New York by tidal wave (*Deluge*, 1933), San Franciso by earthquake (*San Francisco*, 1936), Chicago by fire (*In Old Chicago*, 1938), the South Sea island of Manikura by hurricane (*The Hurricane*, 1937), a Chinese province by locust plague (*The Good Earth*, 1937) and the Indian city of Ranchipur by damburst (*The Rains Came*, 1939).

The epic form also appealed to other countries, particularly those with totalitarian regimes, which used the cinema to rewrite and restage dramatic episodes from their countries' past, imbuing them with nationalistic and militaristic messages.

Although the totalitarian countries carried on the production of epic films into the war, the USA's entry into World War II signalled the demise in Hollywood of these kinds of historical action films. Swashbuckling movies set on the Spanish Main, imperial epics located on India's North-West Frontier and historical epics set in Ancient Rome, all seemed suddenly irrelevant. War films and Westerns enjoyed an instant revival – the former for obvious reasons, the latter because they laid stress on America's national consciousness, ideals and traditions. The historical epic, the swashbuckler, the imperial drama and the disaster film were out for the duration of the war.

Westerns

In the Western actions usually spoke louder than 'words', but when the sound revolution occurred the craze was for films with plenty of dialogue – comedies and musicals. So in the early days of talkies the immediate outlook for the Western was bleak. To make matters worse the sound engineers claimed that recording outdoors would be difficult, if not impossible.

In the ensuing uncertainty, the big Western stars of the silent cinema – Tom Mix, Ken Maynard, Tim McCoy – were dropped by their studios. Only Universal persevered, pumping out more of its Hoot Gibson Westerns and later snapping up Maynard and McCoy. But it was the director Raoul Walsh and the crew of *In Old Arizona* (1929) who quashed any reservations about applying sound to outdoor subjects.

The film was a modest Cisco Kid drama based on a story by O. Henry with a typical twist in which the Kid neatly revenges himself on a double-crossing señorita and outwits the law at the same time. The incidental sounds were laid on somewhat heavily, but audiences were thrilled at the clear recording of lips being smacked after a character had swallowed a drink, of eggs and bacon frying, and of horses' hoofs fading away as riders departed. There was also a zestful performance by Warner Baxter as the laughing bandit who serenaded his faithless señorita with the song 'My Tonia'. Baxter won the Academy Award in 1929 for Best Actor and *In Old Arizona* was the smash hit that restored Westerns to favour.

The same year saw Victor Fleming's painstaking screen version of the thrice-filmed story *The Virginian* (1929) in which Gary Cooper made a suitably laconic hero forced to hang the friend who has turned cattle-rustler.

The Western was so strong a box-office prospect that by 1930 it was seen as a suitable candidate for wide-screen experimentation. MGM made *Billy the Kid* (1930) which was shot in the 70mm Realife process; Fox released its epic *The Big Trail* (1930) which ran 158 minutes in its Fox Grandeur version and 125 minutes in the standard 35mm version (both were shot simultaneously). Warners contributed *The Lash* (1930), a romantic adventure set in the California of the 1850s with Richard Barthelmess as a Spanish nobleman who turns bandit in order to overthrow a crooked American land commissioner. This movie was released in yet another wide-screen process: 65mm Vitascope.

Despite the resurgence of interest in Westerns, these three films flopped at the box-office owing to resistance on the part of exhibitors to the cost of installing wide-screen systems in their cinemas. Experimentation with 65mm and 70mm film gauges had raised the production cost enormously, and because of their failure the Western was once again brought into disrepute as far as the big producers were concerned.

The only Western ever to win the Academy Award for the year's Best Picture was *Cimarron* (1931). But this was more than a Western: based on one of Edna Ferber's vast, sprawling, generation-spanning sagas, it was an epic about the development of Oklahoma. It began with a spectacular reconstruction of the Cherokee Strip land-rush and continued through to the oil boom of the twentieth century. The success of *Cimarron* spawned such imitations as *The Conquerors* (1932) with the same star, Richard Dix, and *Secrets* (1933), with Mary Pickford and Leslie Howard. The latter film was the only main feature Western among the sixty or so released in 1933.

Before the genre went into the wilderness of the B movie there was one notable, medium-scale Western, *Law and Order*

(dir. Edward Cahn, 1932) which drew heavily on the story of Wyatt Earp bringing law to Tombstone and of the gunfight at the OK Corral. Walter Huston brought his usual authority to the central role and the script was written in part by his son John Huston.

After this production, however, it was left to the B picture units and the Poverty Row studios to keep the Western alive, though usually in the series format. In 1935, however, minor Westerns doubled in number in response to public demand, and two important developments in the genre occurred. First there was the arrival of Gene Autry (b. 1907) a former radio singer, who made his debut as a singing cowboy in the serial *The Phantom Empire* and the feature *Tumbling Tumbleweeds* (both 1935). Songs and comedy became major ingredients in Autry's work and his bland easy-going personality set the tone for the relaxed quality of his films which non-metropolitan audiences found especially to their liking. His stories were set in a fantasy land where contemporary and period details merged – aircraft, for example, could co-exist comfortably with old-fashioned stagecoaches.

The second key development was the Hopalong Cassidy series starring William Boyd (1898–1972) as the blond knight of the range. Boyd was an accomplished performer who could handle action as ably as he could deliver lines; responding to a query about his guns in *Bar 20 Rides Again* (1935), he says, 'I just wear them to keep my legs warm'. The Hopalong Cassidy series was a success and encouraged Paramount, who had distributed it, to venture into big Westerns again.

So in 1936 King Vidor made *The Texas Rangers* with Fred MacMurray as the former stagecoach robber who joins the lawmen and brings an old partner (played by Lloyd Nolan) to justice. More significant, however, was Cecil B. DeMille's *The Plainsman* (1936) a lavish pot-pourri that starred Gary Cooper as Wild Bill Hickok, Jean Arthur as Calamity Jane, James Ellison as Buffalo Bill, John Miljan as Custer and Frank McGlynn Sr as Abraham Lincoln. Its robust action scenes, filmed by the second-unit director Arthur Rosson, blended awkwardly with studio close-ups of the stars firing at back-projections of marauding Indians – but at least DeMille insisted on a factual conclusion with Hickok being shot in the back and dying. Paramount followed this slice of comic-strip history with Frank Lloyd's static *Wells Fargo* (1937), starring Joel McCrea, and James Hogan's livelier *The Texans* (1938), with Randolph Scott, Joan Bennett and Walter Brennan.

Surprisingly, although three-strip Technicolor was being used by Paramount and other studios on outdoor subjects it was not used in Westerns until *Jesse James* (1939), although a number of Warners' outdoor films – *God's Country and the Woman* (1936), *Gold Is Where You Find It* and *Heart of the North* (both 1938) – were almost Westerns. Then two films, Fox's *Jesse James* and Paramount's DeMille extravaganza *Union Pacific* (1939) triggered a great Western boom; the trade paper *Variety* noted the trend early in 1939.

Variety's explanation for the revival of the genre was the cyclical nature of the business and the copy-cat techniques of the studios; all of them were making Westerns for fear of being left out of a forthcoming box-office bonanza. But other factors may have come into play. *Variety*'s report of a 'surge of Americanism' in film subject-matter was only to be expected as the European situation worsened. Key foreign markets were threatened or already lost, and films with strong domestic appeal made sense at the box-office.

Furthermore, cinema attendance figures in the United States had become static despite the rise in population and the

Top: the late Thirties Western boom persuaded gangster film paradigms Cagney (centre) and Bogart (right) to don Stetsons in The Oklahoma Kid. *Above right:* The Westerner *began a brief vogue of big-budget Westerns. Above: James Stewart as the peace-loving tenderfoot Destry, who cleans up a frontier town in* Destry Rides Again *with the help of tough saloon-girl Frenchie (Marlene Dietrich).*

studios were consequently making changes in film content in the hope of building new audiences.

One picture has come to stand out from all the rest in the bumper crop of 1939: *Stagecoach*. It was John Ford's first Western since *Three Bad Men* (1926) but was not an outstanding success commercially.

But the praise heaped on the film and the evident skill of Ford's direction did have a strong influence on other film-makers: it made the Western a respectable subject for quality films. If the year had not been dominated by *Gone With the Wind*, the film would have won more Oscars than the two it did.

In a dramatic sense *Stagecoach* was not essentially a Western – its carefully assorted band of passengers could have been assembled in any setting and exposed to an equivalent danger to show their reaction under stress. And almost all the scenes involving the leading players were filmed in the studio. But besides John Ford's inimitable use of Monument Valley and his striking chase sequence across salt flats, there was his masterful treatment of the traditional gunfight on main street. Moreover the dynamic performance of John Wayne, in such moments as the halting of the runaway stage or when he dives to the ground to fire on his opponents in the climactic shoot-out, assured the actor of the front-rank stardom that had eluded him since *The Big Trail*.

Both *Jesse James* and *Dodge City* (1939) eclipsed *Stagecoach* in box-office terms; they had top stars and were in Technicolor. *The Oklahoma Kid* (1939) was another success. James Cagney wore a ten-gallon hat and brought his city-slicker mannerisms to the role of the Robin Hood of Oklahoma, and Humphrey Bogart, dressed in black from tip to toe, played the dastardly villain, but the movie was tongue-in-cheek and deserved its success. *Jesse James* was a romanticized depiction of the celebrated outlaw's life with sympathetic portrayals

from both Tyrone Power as Jesse and Henry Fonda as his brother Frank; the two of them take up robbery only after the railroad's representative (played by Brian Donlevy) has burnt down the family farm and killed their mother. Jesse's actual death (he was shot in the back) was retained but the newspaper editor, acting as chorus or commentator, gave the film an upbeat ending eulogizing Jesse.

The cue had been given for the Old West's other badmen to be covered in Hollywood whitewash. MGM remade *Billy the Kid* (1941) with Robert Taylor; Gene Tierney appeared as the notorious *Belle Starr* (1941) and Universal told of *When the Daltons Rode* (1940).

DeMille's *Union Pacific* was the epic story of the construction of the first transcontinental railway. The main plot featured Joel McCrea as the overseer fighting saboteurs (led by Brian Donlevy, the period's most hard-working screen villain) while avenging the death of a friend at the same time. The narrative was stronger than that of *The Plainsman* and DeMille gained some inspiration from John Ford's *The Iron Horse* (1924) which had had the same historical background.

Even Republic, the leading source of B Westerns, with its singing cowboys Gene Autry and Roy Rogers, decided the time was right to move upmarket. Borrowing a star, Richard Dix, a director, George Nichols Jr, and a supporting actress, Joan Fontaine, they made *Man of Conquest* (1939), the story of the pioneer Sam Houston, that culminated in a rousing reconstruction of the battle of San Jacinto. So contagious was the fever for big Westerns that even the 'quality film' specialist Sam Goldwyn succumbed and hired William Wyler to make *The Westerner* (1940), Goldwyn's second (and last) horse opera.

At the turn of the decade the Western was in such strong shape that it even encouraged the satirical treatment of George Marshall's *Destry Rides Again* (1939), a light-hearted re-working of a Max Brand story that had been filmed straight in 1927 as Tom Mix's first sound film. James Stewart played the apparently naive and helpless Destry who helps clean up a town while Marlene Dietrich was the saloon singer who fell for his good looks and innocent charm.

The astonishing recovery of the genre put it back on its feet apparently for good, but the excitement and vitality of the Westerns of the 1939–41 period was only short-lived.

Walt Disney

Walt Disney (1901–1966) was born in Chicago, attended classes at Kansas City Art Institute, and served in the Ambulance Corps in World War I. After the War he worked for a commercial art studio, where he first met Ub Iwerks who was later to be his most important collaborator. In 1920 he began to make animated advertising films for the Kansas City Film Advertising Company, and began to produce his own 'Laugh-O-Grams'. His 'Laugh-O-Gram' company went into liquidation, however, and in 1923 he went to Hollywood with his brother Roy (1894–1971) and established his own studio. From 1923 to 1926 he made the *Alice in Cartoonland* series, combining live and animated action, for the distributor M.J. Winkler. After 1925 he was joined by Ub Iwerks, who worked with him on developing the *Oswald the Lucky Rabbit* (1927–28) and *Mickey Mouse* series (1928–53).

In 1928 Disney formed Walt Disney Productions and broke into sound with *Steamboat Willie* (1928). This and *Skeleton Dance* (1929), which inaugurated his Silly Symphonies, gave him an ascendancy over every other American animation firm which was never seriously to be challenged. In 1932 he first used colour in *Flowers and Trees*; and in 1937, with *The Old Mill*, revealed the full potential of the three-dimensional effects he could give his animation pictures with his Multiplane process – involving the accurate focusing of animated images arranged in a sequence of planes.

Throughout the Thirties Disney was producing an average of 18 cartoon shorts a year, and developing his world-famous repertory company of Mickey and Minnie Mouse, Donald Duck, Pluto, Goofy and their supporting players. In 1937 he released his first feature-length cartoon *Snow White and the Seven Dwarfs*. It was followed by *Pinocchio* and *Fantasia* (both 1940), *Dumbo* (1941) and *Bambi* (1942).

Technicolor

The full emergence of Technicolor as the pre-eminent name in colour film-making dates from 1932 with the development of the three-strip process. Where previously only two primary colours – red and green – had been possible, the third, blue, was now introduced. As a result 'natural' colours were possible for the first time.

Despite the increase in expense – filming in Technicolor added about fifty per cent to the negative cost – Hollywood was eager to experiment with the new medium. With varying degrees of success, every kind of film – costume pictures, musicals, Westerns, even screwball comedy – was seen by audiences for the first time 'In Glorious Technicolor'.

Disney paved the way with the animated film *Flowers and Trees* (1932). Then in 1935 Rouben Mamoulian, another film-maker always eager to try something new, completed the feature which is acknowledged as the first modern colour film – *Becky Sharp*. Virtually the whole of *Becky Sharp* is confined to studio interiors, allowing Mamoulian and designer Robert Edmund Jones exceptional control over colour and mood. However, Mamoulian's anti-realistic, symbolic approach was misunderstood or was not entirely successful; *Becky Sharp* had little immediate influence on future colour productions.

The effectiveness of Technicolor in capturing the colours and textures of natural settings was first exploited in Paramount's *The Trail of the Lonesome Pine* (1936). Critics were quick to praise the film's colour landscape photography.

The Trail of the Lonesome Pine was followed in 1936 by a diverse group of colour films which have been largely forgotten. These include the first three-strip Technicolor musical, *The Dancing Pirate*, produced by Pioneer Pictures/RKO (of which no prints appear to survive); *Ramona* from 20th Century-Fox, *The Garden of Allah* produced by

Disney's innovative early films included Steamboat Willie *(top) and* Skeleton Dance *(above), which combined superb animation with exciting experiments in sound;* Flowers and Trees *(above right)*

was the first film in three-strip Technicolor. Other notable early Technicolor films were Becky Sharp *(above right) and* The Adventures of Robin Hood *(right), the definitive swashbuckler.*

David O. Selznick, and Warner Brothers' *God's Country and the Woman*. Thus each of the major studios (apart from MGM) had made an attempt to jump onto the colour bandwagon. However, *Ramona*, *The Garden of Allah* and *God's Country and the Woman* were all adapted from weak stories and failed at the box-office; *The Garden of Allah*, in particular, was a financial disaster having cost over $2 million. Selznick was quick to redeem his reputation with *A Star Is Born* and *Nothing Sacred* (both 1937, and both directed by William Wellman). *A Star is Born* was nominated for seven Oscars and won two – for best original story (Wellman) and a special award for colour cinematography (W. Howard Greene). In both films colour was used in a restrained and realistic way in keeping with their stories about contemporary life in America, providing a unique picture of what the world of the Thirties looked like in colour.

For most film companies 1937 was a boom year; the recession which followed in 1938 hit the industry hard. Despite this, the number of Technicolor films grew steadily throughout the late Thirties and early Forties. Perhaps the novelty value of colour was regarded as a means of fighting the slump – certainly the three aspiring majors, Fox, Paramount and Warners, saw colour as a means of competing in prestige with the top company MGM, where the attitude was, 'If our films make money in black and white, what do we need colour for?'

Warners' first big prestige colour film was *The Adventures of Robin Hood* (1938) which cost over $1.5 million. The striking colour photography – with much of the picture filmed on location – was achieved by Sol Polito, Tony Gaudio and W. Howard Greene. The film strikes an ideal balance between intimate moments, spectacle and action sequences, and between a toned-down, restrained use of colour and the brighter, more lavish scenes featuring the costumes of Milo Anderson.

Despite all this, the reaction of film audiences at the time was disappointing; the picture hardly managed to recoup its substantial cost. A new incentive for filming in colour – with a new emphasis on musical fantasy – was supplied by the smash success of Disney's *Snow White and the Seven Dwarfs* (1937). In addition, Selznick finally embarked on filming *Gone With the Wind* (released in 1939).

From the beginning of his work on the project, Selznick had been firmly committed to colour. He was particularly insistent that the film should not be confined to the kind of neutral and pastel shades favoured by the colour consultants assigned to the project by the Technicolor company. He commented:

'This picture in particular gives us the opportunity occasionally to throw a violent dab of colour at the audience to sharply make a dramatic point.'

The film's director, Victor Fleming, accomplished the remarkable feat of making the other most famous movie of 1939 – *The Wizard of Oz*, MGM's most expensive film up to that date. In view of its substantial cost the film was not a commercial success on its initial release, reinforcing MGM's prejudice against the added cost of Technicolor.

In marked contrast to MGM's reluctance, the producer Darryl Zanuck had, towards the end of 1938, embarked on a series of Technicolor pictures at 20th Century-Fox which continued into the Forties and averaged five or six films per year. This represented the first substantial and lasting commitment to colour by any of the major studios and established the pattern of colour-filming for the Forties. Although he concentrated on musicals and Westerns, Zanuck nevertheless provided the opportunity for a number of important directors to express their individual styles in colour for the first time, including John Ford (*Drums Along the Mohawk*, 1939) Fritz Lang (*The Return of Frank James,* 1940), Ernst Lubitsch (*Heaven Can Wait*, 1943) and Busby Berkeley (*The Gang's All Here*, 1943).

The preference for escapist entertainment during the war meant that colour films were predominantly musicals or other lightweight fare. Many of the leading directors of the Forties avoided colour entirely, including Capra, Cukor, Huston and Wyler, while Hawks, Sturges, Welles and Wilder directed only one minor colour film apiece. Even Ford, Lang, and cameraman James Wong Howe, all of whom had done some distinguished colour work during the late Thirties, returned to black and white.

The first substantial move into colour did not take place until the early and middle Fifties to counteract the effects of TV on movie audiences. There remained a widespread prejudice against colour for certain types of film – particularly gangster pictures and psychological dramas. Both from an artistic point of view and also from 'realistic' considerations – owing perhaps to the fact that documentaries were filmed in black and white – colour was frequently disparaged by critics. A typical comment was made by leading film critic James Agee:

'Colour is very nice for costume pieces and musical comedies, and has a great aesthetic future in films, but it still gets fatally in the way of any serious imitation of reality.'

The contradictions inherent in this statement would not be realized for several years.

Right: Marlene Dietrich with a colour test card for The Garden of Allah. *However even Technicolor failed to rescue this romantic hokum (about a socialite's love for a monk) at the box-office. Far right: at the start colour was primarily used for adventure or fantasy films such as* The Wizard of Oz.

Left: the troubled romance between Rhett Butler (Clark Gable) and the wilful Scarlett O'Hara (Vivien Leigh) in Gone With the Wind *begins with a flirtation at a charity ball in aid of the doomed Confederate war effort.*

Gone With the Wind

In May 1936 David O. Selznick's East Coast story editor, Katherine Brown, sent her boss a pre-publication copy and a synopsis of *Gone With the Wind* with an enthusiastic recommendation that he purchase the rights. Selznick, however, was more than reluctant, and understandably so. A month before its publication no-one could have foreseen that Margaret Mitchell's novel would fast become a publishing phenomenon and a national craze.

Although several studios were interested initially, the insistence of Mitchell's agents that the bids stay extremely high discouraged even the wealthy MGM studio. However, when Jock Hay Whitney, Chairman of the Board of Selznick International, wired Selznick that no matter what the decision in Hollywood, he himself intended to purchase the rights for the company. Selznick relented and paid the then-unequalled price of $50,000 for the book – a sum which was to be one of the lesser expenses in the production of the film.

Once he had acquired the rights, Selznick characteristically threw himself into the project and pursued it with obsessional energy for the next three years. Even after the premiere in Atlanta, Georgia on December 15, 1939, Selznick continued to fire off his famous memos to everyone involved in the sale and distribution of the film.

The playwright and film scenarist Sidney Howard was the first writer Selznick engaged to work on the script of *Gone With the Wind*. George Cukor was hired to direct and Selznick sent both men to Atlanta to discuss the film with Margaret Mitchell, for Selznick was adamant that his *Gone With the Wind* should be faithful in spirit and in letter to hers.

Even before a first script was finished, William Cameron Menzies was engaged to design the production, beginning with those sets they knew they would need no matter what the final form of the scenario. When a completed script was ready, Menzies was to sketch the entire film shot by shot, including camera set-ups, lighting and colour motifs. Lee Garmes was hired as director of photography. The film was, at this point, budgeted around $1.5 million, which remained the highest figure spoken of at Selznick International until the autumn of 1938 when MGM became involved (as a result of Selznick's desire to borrow Clark Gable for the male lead) the budget rose to $2.25 millions.

For over a year after he purchased the rights, Selznick went ahead assembling a script and getting a production design completed, but was stalled in almost every other aspect of the project. In May 1938, because of his company's financial difficulties, he was tempted to accept Louis B. Mayer's offer to buy the project outright (with a substantial profit for Selznick International) and to hire Selznick himself to produce the film at MGM. His mistrust of his father-in-law (Mayer) and his fear of losing his independence led him to refuse the offer, despite the fact that MGM had greater production facilities and a more prestigious roster of stars for the cast. Above all, they had Clark Gable, who was the public's overwhelming choice for the role of Rhett Butler.

Surprisingly, Clark Gable was not Selznick's first choice. He wanted Gary Cooper, then under contract to Samuel Goldwyn, partially because it would have allowed him to release *Gone With the Wind* through United Artists. Goldwyn did not so much refuse Selznick's request for the loan of Cooper as ignore it. Selznick then considered other actors, including Warners' Errol Flynn. Warner Brothers, after initial indifference, agreed to loan Flynn if Selznick would cast Bette Davis as Scarlett. In her autobiography, Davis claimed that she was attracted to the part of Scarlett but that the thought of Flynn as Rhett Butler appalled her. Controversy still surrounds the differences of opinion between Selznick and Warners, but Davis found compensation in a similar role in *Jezebel* (1938), elements of which film were so close to the story of *Gone With the Wind* that Selznick bombarded Warner Brothers with bitter memos accusing them of profiting from his production and insisting that certain sequences be cut from their film.

Finally, however, giving in to public pressure, he made a deal with MGM for Gable's services, the terms of which were to continue to rankle with him for the rest of his career. In exchange for Gable and $1.25 million, MGM was to have the distribution rights and 50 per cent of the profits (which, 25 years after initial release, totalled $41 million).

Although the great hunt for a Scarlett has become a major part of the *Gone With the Wind* story, none of the casting was automatic or easy. Leslie Howard now seems the obvious choice for Ashley Wilkes and was one of the first actors considered, but Howard was reluctant to play 'yet another weak and ineffectual character' and had to be promised a producers' function on Selznick's upcoming production *Intermezzo* before he would sign. Other actors considered were Ray Milland, Melvyn Douglas (who almost got the part after a splendid test) and even Humphrey Bogart.

A great many actresses were also considered and tested for Melanie Hamilton, and at one point Joan Fontaine peevishly refused with the remark, 'If you want someone to play

Melanie, I suggest you call my sister'. Cukor did and found Olivia de Havilland exactly what he wanted, but she was under contract to Warner Brothers who, after the Davis debacle and the *Jezebel* trouble, wanted nothing more to do with *Gone With the Wind*. De Havilland persisted, however, and Warners gave in when Selznick offered to loan them James Stewart, whose services he had for a single film. Even the smaller roles of Dr Mead, Ellen O'Hara, Belle Watling and Careen O'Hara were first intended for Lionel Barrymore, Lillian Gish, Tallulah Bankhead (who had, amazingly, been an early contender for the role of Scarlett) and Judy Garland.

Still it was the casting of Scarlett that provided the biggest problem and which garnered the most publicity. For the $50,000 Selznick admitted spending on the search for the perfect Scarlett, he had the entire nation talking about *Gone With the Wind*. But the talent hunt cannot be entirely and easily dismissed as merely the greatest publicity stunt ever pulled off in Hollywood. From reading his countless memos on the subject, it is clear that Selznick was sincere in wanting to find an actress who would please as many readers of the novel as possible.

While Gable was Rhett in the public imagination, no current female star held an equal place as Scarlett. Thousands of unknown girls from all over the USA, but primarily, for obvious reasons, from the South, were interviewed and many were tested. Every major star in Hollywood was considered and a number of them submitted to the indignity of a screen test.

Katharine Hepburn wanted the part badly but refused to test and was rejected, as were all who did test, including Susan Hayward, Lana Turner and Lucille Ball. Seriously considered were Joan Bennett, Miriam Hopkins, Joan Crawford, Margaret Sullavan, Jean Arthur, Ann Sheridan and Carole Lombard. Selznick had just about decided to give the role to Paulette Goddard (if she could produce proof she had actually married Charles Chaplin, and thus avoid any scandal), when Selznick's agent brother Myron introduced him to Vivien Leigh.

Selznick was later to claim that he had never seen her before, although he mentions her by name after seeing *A Yank at Oxford* (1938) while looking for an actress to cast in *Young at Heart* (1938). Nonetheless he liked what he saw, tested her immediately, and when it was clear that she was as good as she looked, could handle a Southern accent, and that her eyes would match the colour of Scarlett's in the novel, she was signed to a seven-year contract.

While the search for the perfect cast went on, so did that for a perfect script. In 1937, Selznick had given Sidney Howard a copy of the novel with his own notations and kept in close communication with the writer and with Cukor who was advising him. Selznick admired the script, but it would have taken over five hours of screen time to film. Howard, however, considered that he had done what he had contracted to do and refused to stay in Hollywood, to write another version.

Rejecting the idea that *Gone With the Wind* become two films, Selznick began himself to compress the script. He then hired playwright Oliver Garrett to revise Howard's work. Dissatisfied with that, Selznick soon found himself with three scripts. Summarizing the situation in his memos, he noted: '. . . the Sidney Howard script, the so-called Howard–Garrett script, and the script that we are shooting . . . We have everything that we need in the book and in the Howard and Howard–Garrett scripts. The job that remains to be done is to telescope the three in the shortest possible form.

Along the way, Scott Fitzgerald, Charles MacArthur, Edwin Justus Mayer, Ben Hecht, John Van Druten and others were hired to rewrite single scenes, supply lines of dialogue, or to search through the original novel for alternative dialogue. But Selznick recognized Howard's contribution by giving him sole screen credit for the screenplay.

The directional credits are just as muddled. George Cukor was involved deeply in pre-production and directed three weeks of the actual shooting at which time he was discharged. Several reasons for his replacement have been suggested, and probably all played their part. Gable objected that Cukor, even then known as a 'woman's director', paid far more attention to Leigh and de Havilland than to himself. Selznick maintained that Cukor had a firm grasp on the intimate aspects of the story but none on the more epic sequences. The producer also complained in memos that Cukor was changing lines of dialogue from the 'finished script' – this from a man whose daily revisions often arrived *during* the shooting of a scene.

Cukor left *Gone With the Wind* to do *The Women* (1939), although he continued to advise and direct both Leigh and de Havilland on the interpretation of their roles in secret throughout the making of *Gone With the Wind*.

Cukor was replaced by Victor Fleming, who was Gable's choice from a list of directors submitted to him by Selznick. Fleming's stated intention of making *Gone With the Wind* 'a flamboyant melodrama' seemed to fit Selznick's own ambitions for the film. The shooting went fairly smoothly for some weeks. They had started filming on January 26, 1939, though the key scene of Atlanta burning had been shot on December 10, 1938, the night of the instant casting of Vivien Leigh. By July 1 all the film was in the can and Selznick began to immerse himself in the task of promoting and planning distribution. During the shooting the strains of working at high pitch on a complicated and costly production began to tell. At one point, for example, Leigh (who never cared for Fleming) balked at doing a scene. Fleming rolled the script in his hand into a tube shape, threw it at Leigh and told her graphically what she could do with it. He then stalked off.

Production stopped for two days until Fleming could be placated and enticed back to work. Selznick began to worry about Fleming's health and ability to continue, and asked Sam Wood to prepare himself to take over. Fleming did eventually collapse. Wood directed during the two weeks that Fleming was absent and continued to shoot upon his return. And so the cast often found themselves being directed by Fleming in the mornings and by Wood in the afternoons. Selznick estimated later that about 33 minutes of Wood's work remained in the final film. At the same time, no matter who was directing the major sequences, there were never less than three second units shooting 'atmosphere' and action sequences elsewhere on the sets or on the various locations.

In a letter to Frank Capra, then president of the Screen Directors' Guild, Selznick explained that he had given full credit for directing the film to Victor Fleming (both Cukor and Wood had refused to take screen credit) in spite of the fact that, as he put it, 'I alone had the reins of the picture in my hands'. He went on to suggest that if the full truth were known, either William Cameron Menzies or he – Selznick – deserved directional credit far more than any director who had worked on the film.

The hundreds of memos, letters and notes that Selznick sent to everyone involved in *Gone With the Wind* suggest that

**In new screen splendor...
The most magnificent picture ever!**

DAVID O. SELZNICK'S PRODUCTION OF MARGARET MITCHELL'S

"GONE WITH THE WIND"

STARRING

**CLARK GABLE
VIVIEN LEIGH
LESLIE HOWARD OLIVIA de HAVILLAND**

A SELZNICK INTERNATIONAL PICTURE · DIRECTED BY VICTOR FLEMING · SCREEN PLAY BY SIDNEY HOWARD · METRO-GOLDWYN-MAYER INC. · Music by MAX STEINER

Left: a monument to the studio system, Gone With the Wind *was planned from over 3000 full-colour sketches by art director William Cameron Menzies, involved a cast of 2400 extras and was completed in just under a year — a schedule that would astonish today's producers of multi-million-dollar projects. The film itself lived up to producer D.O. Selznick's ambitions and the public's eager expectations. Below: in the search for a Scarlett to play opposite Gable's Rhett Butler, 1400 actresses were interviewed and 90 screen tested. Eventually Selznick's brother, the powerful agent Myron, found the ideal lady, Vivien Leigh, who was visiting the USA with her future husband Laurence Olivier. Bottom: Gable arrives in style at the* Gone With the Wind *premiere in Atlanta, Georgia with his wife, Carole Lombard.*

he was right. He insisted that Walter Plunkett redesign Gable's costumes and produce no less than 27 copies of Scarlett's calico dress in order that the same costume could be seen in various stages of deterioration during the film. He further instructed his camerman (and though Ernest Haller received sole credit after the early departure of Lee Garmes, there were many who worked on the picture) to follow his specifications of lighting and filters. Even though the Technicolor company provided advisors, Selznick required that they follow his and Menzies' notions of what was possible in colour. He even ordered the makeup and costume department to rebuild Vivien Leigh's bosom. In short, there was no detail, however small, which he did not have a hand in shaping, making *Gone With the Wind* the prime example of a producer's film, perhaps even a case for arguing Selznick as *auteur* — a term usually reserved to describe the artistic creation and control of a director.

Key Directors

During the Thirties **John Ford** (1895–1973) gradually emerged as Hollywood's leading director, establishing his 'art-movie' reputation decisively with his gloomy IRA melodrama *The Informer* (1935), which won the first of his four Oscars – the others were for *The Grapes of Wrath* (1940), *How Green Was My Valley* (1941) and *The Quiet Man* (1952). All were based on modestly respectable novels – two Irish, one Welsh and one Californian – and none was a Western, though they dealt with the theme of external forces disrupting a family, group or community, which also formed the subject matter of many of his Westerns. Apart from the silents and *Stagecoach* (1939), his major Westerns belong to the period from 1946 (*My Darling Clementine*) to 1964 (*Cheyenne Autumn*) and even that has gaps (*Rio Grande*, 1950 – *The Searchers*, 1956 – *The Horse Soldiers*, 1959). In the Thirties he went in more for 'Southerns' like the Will Rogers trilogy – *Doctor Bull* (1933), *Judge Priest* (1934) and *Steamboat Round the Bend* (1935) – or, by extension, *The Grapes of Wrath* and certainly *Tobacco Road* (1941) – not the most obvious material for an Irish-American from the north-east of New England. But he was then still optimistic about the essential unity of the United States, which seemed increasingly problematic among the loners and outsiders of the later films, whose fate was exile in place or time or race or indeed death.

Howard Hawks (1896–1977) did not achieve the same degree of recognition (he won no Oscars then or ever), though much of his work has proved just as long-lasting in its appeal.

Broadly his work fell into two types, action and crazy comedy, which themselves often crossed over. A recurrent theme was the all-male group that accepts women only on masculine terms and indeed rejects men who fail to live up to its standards of professional excellence. The obverse of this is the comic humiliation of the hero, sometimes by a domineering woman (*Bringing Up Baby*, 1938, *Ball of Fire*, 1941; *I Was a Male War Bride*, 1949), though it may be the woman who suffers if she is playing a masculine role (the ex-wife reporter, Rosalind Russell, in *His Girl Friday*, 1940). The possibilities of deviant sexuality within these themes are always restrained by a kind of ritual decorum rigorously adhered to through the wildest adventures and mishaps. In addition, there is generally an unspoken mutual respect between Hawks' men and women that undercuts their apparent antagonism or indifference. In *The Big Sleep* (1946), some time after a fascinatingly inconclusive discussion of sexual techniques, Vivian (Lauren Bacall) even says to Philip Marlow (Humphrey Bogart), 'I guess I'm in love with you'; to which, after some plot-forwarding chat, he replies, 'I guess I'm in love with *you*'. But then Marlowe is a loner, more like a hero of Hawksian *comedy* in that he needs a woman to make a team. In the other special case *Gentlemen Prefer Blondes* (1953), the female heroes (Marilyn Monroe and Jane Russell) need each other in their hunt for men and, of course, in performing their musical numbers.

With Griffith and Stroheim out of the running and Chaplin in splendid isolation, the principal survivors from the silent era, apart from Ford and Hawks, were Cecil B. DeMille, Michael Curtiz, King Vidor, Josef von Sternberg, William Wellman, William Wyler (from routine Westerns), Frank Capra (from Harry Langdon and Sennett comedies), Leo McCarey (from Roach comedies), Clarence Brown, Frank Borzage, Ernst Lubitsch, Lewis Milestone, Mervyn LeRoy (who started by playing juveniles), Victor Fleming, Allan Dwan, Raoul Walsh, Tod Browning (Lon Chaney's favourite

Above: the evicted Joad family search in vain for a new life in California in Ford's The Grapes of Wrath. *Top: Humphrey Bogart and Lauren Bacall in Hawks' version of Hemingway's novel* To Have and Have Not.

director), Henry King, Gregory La Cava, W.S. Van Dyke and Sidney Franklin.

Casualties included Herbert Brenon, who went back to England in 1933 and retired in 1940, and another Irish-born director, Rex Ingram, whose only sound film was *Baroud* (1932). Buster Keaton lost control of his productions and, despite considerable popular success in the early Thirties, declined into mediocrity and alcoholism.

King Vidor (1894–1982) had success with large-scale Westerns – *Billy the Kid* (1930), with Johnny Mack Brown, *The Texas Ranger* (1936), with Fred MacMurray, as well as the later *Duel in the Sun* (1946), produced by David O. Selznick as a vehicle for Jennifer Jones – but his heart was in social pictures like *Our Daily Bread* (1934), about a cooperative farm, and *The Citadel* (1938), a plea for socialized medicine, made in Britain. He also excelled in superior tearjerkers like *The Champ* (1931), with Wallace Beery as the boxer and Jackie

Above: Claude Rains, Paul Henreid, Humphrey Bogart and Ingrid Bergman in Curtiz's Casablanca. *Top: Hepburn, Grant and 'Baby', the leopard that brings them together, in Hawks' classic comedy of errors.*

Above: Curtiz's Mildred Pierce *provided an Oscar-winning role for Joan Crawford. Top: Carole Lombard, Walter Connolly and Fredric March in Wellman's satire on the yellow press* Nothing Sacred, *produced by David O. Selznick.*

Cooper as his boy supporter, and *Stella Dallas* (1937), in which Barbara Stanwyck suffered as a self-sacrificing mother.

Michael Curtiz (1888–1962) was the top action and horror director at the Warner's factory, averaging four and a half features a year in the Thirties. He made a star of Errol Flynn in *Captain Blood* (1935), *The Charge of the Light Brigade* (1936), *The Adventures of Robin Hood* (1938), *The Private Lives of Elizabeth and Essex* (1939), *The Sea Hawk* (1940) and several Westerns. He also guided Spencer Tracy and Bette Davis in *20,000 Years in Sing Sing* (1932), Boris Karloff in *The Walking Dead* (1936), James Cagney in *Angels With Dirty Faces* (1938), with Humphrey Bogart, and *Yankee Doodle Dandy* (1942), Bogart again, with Ingrid Bergman, in *Casablanca* (1942), Edward G. Robinson in *Kid Galahad* (1937) and Joan Crawford in *Mildred Pierce* (1945). From the late Forties his career declined; he left Warners in 1954 but continued to work until his death in 1962.

William Wellman (1896–1975) turned out 17 films in his three year with Warners, the best-remembered being *The Public Enemy* (1931) and *Wild Boys of the Road* (1933). His Western *Robin Hood of El Dorado* (1936) anticipated his better-known *The Ox-Bow Incident* (1943) in its criticism of American attitudes. He made *A Star Is Born* and *Nothing Sacred* (both 1937) in colour for David O. Selznick, winning his only Oscar for the original story of *A Star Is Born; Nothing Sacred* was written by the prolific ex-Chicago journalist Ben Hecht. Wellman then won a producer-director contract at Paramount where he successfully filmed three Robert Carson scripts, *Men With Wings* (1938), about aerial warfare, *Beau Geste* (1939), The French Foreign Legion tale, and *The Light That Failed* (1939), from a Rudyard Kipling story, with Ronald Colman as the painter going blind and Ida Lupino as his cockney model. During the war he shifted from snappy, cynical satires centring round hard-boiled dames such as

Ginger Rogers in *Roxie Hart* (1942) and Barbara Stanwyck in *Lady of Burlesque* (1943) to the almost documentary immediacy of his celebrated war film *The Story of GI Joe* (1945).

William Wyler (1902–1981) gained his reputation as Sam Goldwyn's house director with *These Three* (1936), from Lillian Hellman's play *The Children's Hour* depicting teachers smeared by a child's accusations, *Dodsworth* (1936), from Sinclair Lewis' novel, *Dead End* (1937), *Jezebel* (1938), *Wuthering Heights* (1939), *The Little Foxes* (1941), *Mrs Miniver* (1942), with Greer Garson and Walter Pidgeon, and several more, culminating in *The Best Years of Our Lives* (1946). He was a perfectionist on-set, frequently clashing with Bette Davis and other stars, but collaborating closely with deep-focus cinematographer Gregg Toland. His brand of realism was championed by the French critic André Bazin; but his ponderous and literary style made him decreasingly fashionable by the Sixties, despite (or because of) his third Oscar for *Ben-Hur* (1959), though with the Barbra Streisand musical *Funny Girl* (1968) his direction was less anachronistic.

Lewis Milestone (1895–1980) never surpassed *All Quiet on the Western Front* (1930) but diversified with the newspaper comedy *The Front Page* (1931), the oddball musical *Hallelujah I'm a Bum* (1933), the Chinese adventure *The General Died at Dawn* (1936), and an adaptation of John Steinbeck's *Of Mice and Men* (1939), with Lon Chaney Jr as the half-witted giant murderer and Burgess Meredith as the friend who has to kill

him. Milestone's returns to the war film included *The North Star* (1943), written by Lillian Hellman and subsequently branded as communist propaganda, and *A Walk in the Sun* (1945). His last film was the underrated remake of *Mutiny on the Bounty* (1962), with Marlon Brando and Trevor Howard.

Tol'able David (1921) by **Henry King** was 'Too good, dear boy. Too good. Too good', according to D.W. Griffith, and arguably King (1888–1982) never equalled it. His better films of the Thirties included *Lightnin'* (1930) and *State Fair* (1933), both with Will Rogers, *In Old Chicago* and *Alexander's Ragtime Band* (both 1938), with Tyrone Power, Don Ameche and Alice Faye, and *Jesse James* (1939). His later reputation was sustained by *Twelve O'Clock High* (1949) and *The Gunfighter* (1950), both with Gregory Peck; and towards the end of his career he turned to classic American novels with *The Sun Also Rises* (1957) and *Tender Is the Night* (1962).

Newcomers of the sound era included George Cukor, Rouben Mamoulian and the veteran German Fritz Lang, who, though offered work by the Nazis had elected to leave for the US in 1933. His first American film was *Fury* (1936), which examined his favourite theme of the evils of revenge. After *You Only Live Once*, a moving study of a small-time crook framed for murder with Henry Fonda and Sylvia Sidney, he teamed Sidney with George Raft in the less successful crime comedy *You and Me* (1938). He then immersed himself in Americana, making the Westerns *The Return of Frank James*

Above: Laurence Olivier as Heathcliff, Merle Oberon as Cathy in Wyler's film version of Wuthering Heights. *Above right: William Wyler and Bette Davis confer during the making of* The Little Foxes. *Right: Greta Garbo as the consumptive heroine, Robert Taylor as her young admirer, in the final moments of Cukor's* Camille.

(1940), with Fonda and Gene Tierney, and *Western Union* (1941), with Randolph Scott. Lang did his bit for the allied war effort with *Man Hunt* (1941), which pitted Hitler's near-assassin (Walter Pidgeon) against a smoothly villainous Nazi (George Sanders), and *Hangmen Also Die!* (1943), which followed up the assassination of Hitler's representative, Heydrich, in Czechoslovakia, and was notable for the only American screen credit of German playwright Bertolt Brecht.

George Cukor (1899–1983) made his solo debut with *Tarnished Lady* (1931), starring Tallulah Bankhead as a mercenary wife to Clive Brook, and soon followed it with the gold-digger story *Girls About Town*. Teaming up with producer David O. Selznick, he hit his stride with *What Price Hollywood?* (1932), *A Bill of Divorcement* (1932), Katharine Hepburn's debut, and the witty comedy *Dinner at Eight* (1933), with Marie Dressler, John Barrymore, Lionel Barrymore, Wallace Beery and Jean Harlow. His version of *Little Women* (1933), with Hepburn again, launched him on a programme of literary adaptations – *David Copperfield* (1935), *Romeo and Juliet* (1936) with Norma Shearer, Leslie Howard and John Barrymore, and *Camille* (1936), with Garbo and Robert Taylor. After these period pieces, his modern subjects included two adaptations from Philip Barry plays, *Holiday* (1938) and *The Philadelphia Story* (1940), both with Hepburn and Cary Grant. By Hollywood logic, Cukor's homosexuality made him a 'woman's director' so he was fired from the epic

Gone With the Wind (1939) by his old employer Selznick but ideally suited to the all-female cast of *The Women* (1939). His subsequent collaborations with Hepburn and Spencer Tracy (1943–52) and the writers Ruth Gordon and Garson Kanin (1947–54) were among the highlights of his career.

Rouben Mamoulian (b. 1898) was primarily a theatre director who made 14 of his 16 films between 1929 and 1942. An innovator in the use of sound, visual effects and colour, he made his debut with the backstage tragedy *Applause* (1929), invented the interior monologue in *City Streets* (1931) – though Eisenstein had the same idea for his unmade version of *An American Tragedy* – experimented with the tight close-ups and colour filters to effect the protagonist's transformation in *Dr Jekyll and Mr Hyde* (1932). *Love Me Tonight* (1932) was among the most inventive of early musicals, symphonically combining sounds, music and words. *Becky Sharp* (1935) used the newly available three-colour Technicolor with restraint, adding colour as the film progressed, whereas the bull-fighting story *Blood and Sand* (1941) was anti-realist in its derivation from the great Spanish painters El Greco and Velázquez. His last film, *Silk Stockings* (1957), was a musical remake in colour and wide-screen of *Ninotchka* (1939), with the essential romantic development expressed in the dancing of Fred Astaire and Cyd Charisse. It reveals Mamoulian still at the height of his powers, making one regret that his regular career scarcely outlasted the Thirties.

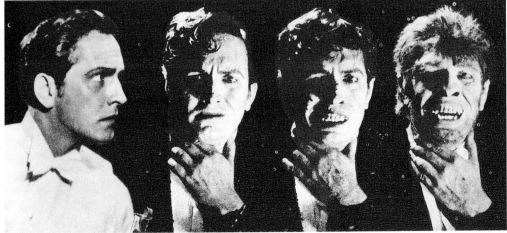

Above far left: Gary Cooper and Madeleine Carroll in Milestone's The General Died at Dawn, *a thriller with an exotic, Eastern setting. Above: Sylvia Sidney and Henry Fonda as a poor, young couple on the wrong side of the law in Lang's* You Only Live Once. *Left: Dr Jekyll (Fredric March) slowly turns into the horrific Mr Hyde in Mamoulian's 1932 film – all done with hand-made colour filters.*

Nr. 2302

Für den Inhalt verantwortlich Hermann Weist, Berlin-Mariendorf
Verlag "Neue Film Kurier" Verlagsgesellschaft m.b.H., Berlin W 9
Köthener Straße 37 Kupfertiefdruck August Scherl GmbH., Berlin SW 68

CHAPTER 9
The Thirties in Europe

The Realist Influence

John Grierson (1898–1972) coined the word 'documentary' in 1926 to describe Robert Flaherty's *Moana*, but many films made long before this date could well have been called documentaries.

What was so different and new about the British movement Grierson founded in 1929 was fundamentally the nature of its sponsorship and the publicity line Grierson adopted in order to attract that sponsorship. The money for *Drifters* (1929) – and for setting up a new film unit – came from a government department, the Empire Marketing Board, so the operation had to seem prestigious. Grierson, through his writing, quickly created such an image for it. His propaganda – rather than the films – enabled his unit to survive the EMB's dissolution in 1933, when it was taken over by the General Post Office and began fully to flower.

Grierson's young recruits, Basil Wright, John Taylor, Arthur Elton, Edgar Anstey, Stuart Legg and Harry Watt, had unprecedented opportunities for all kinds of experiment, even personal expression – a rare situation at any time. Even so, their creative freedom had definite political limits. Despite the movement's left-wing sympathies Grierson's sponsors were always either government departments or private industry, and the British establishment, than as now, does not pay for working-class propaganda. The message had to be indirect. Consequently, most of the documentaries reflected another strong British tradition, that of compromise.

The working man tended to be idealized in the films of the documentary movement, which for the most part had little to do with the desperate plight of large numbers of working-class people during the Depression years of the Thirties. Even at the time it was made, the famous *Drifters* was attacked for failing to include any mention of the price the fishermen got (and paid) for their large haul. But some of the later films were bolder. It took genius to see that the gas industry could be persuaded to pay for such indictments of living conditions as *Housing Problems* (1935) and *Enough to Eat?* (1936).

Housing Problems, officially directed by Elton and Anstey, owes its success to interviews with slum tenants in their homes. Grierson's sister, Ruby, credited as assistant on *Housing Problems,* is remembered for her ability to win people's confidence, and there seems little doubt that the sincerity of the interviews is due to her and to John Taylor, who was cameraman.

Left: the might of Nazism, soon to be unleashed on an unsuspecting Europe, as depicted in Leni Riefenstahl's propaganda documentary Triumph of the Will.

In this context also, the work of **Paul Rotha** (1907–1984), a maverick independent whose early association with the Grierson unit was brief, must be mentioned. His grim shots of industrial England in *The Face of Britain* (1935), the tragic picture of unemployed miners in the Rhondda valley in *Today We Live* (produced by Rotha with Ruby Grierson and Ralph Bond as directors in 1937) showed a profound social concern that pointed the way to Rotha's later and better known *World of Plenty* (1943), *Land of Promise* (1945) and *The World is Rich* (1947).

Grierson began to lose interest in the aesthetic side of filmmaking during the Thirties; his reputation still rests on the experimental work that he made possible (both in Britain and in Canada) and on the talent he had the inspiration to employ; in Britain, in addition to the American documentarist Robert Flaherty, the list of names includes Richard Massingham and Lotte Reiniger, Norman McLaren and Len Lye. However the single individual crucial to the consolidation of Grierson's original ambitions for his unit was **Alberto Cavalcanti**.

Cavalcanti (1897–1982) was a professional film director who had worked with the industry and the *avant-garde* in France. He joined Grierson in 1934. The unit had just acquired its own sound recording equipment and Cavalcanti was vitally interested in experimenting with sound. Under his leadership, the whole unit involved itself in a crazy parody of middle-class suburbia called *Pett and Pott*, for which they recorded the sound first and added the picture afterwards.

Cavalcanti proceeded to salvage a good deal of material that had been shot without sound. The outstanding case of this was *Coal Face* (1935), which consisted of coal mining shots that had been lying around for several years, padded out with additional material shot by almost everyone in the unit. All this Cavalcanti edited together with an inspired soundtrack based on a poem by W.H. Auden and with music by Benjamin Britten, both unknown names at the time. Auden was a personal friend of Basil Wright whose contribution to the success of a collaboration that continued into *Night Mail* (1936) is as incalculable as that of Cavalcanti himself.

Before *Night Mail*, Wright had completed his beautiful *Song of Ceylon* (1934). This film too depended very much on its sound track, on which Wright worked with the composer Walter Leigh.

Of all the films of the Thirties, *Night Mail* was probably most responsible for putting the British documentary on the map. It made first-class entertainment out of the overnight journey of the mail train from London to Glasgow.

Night Mail is also perhaps the most authentic example of creative teamwork, as opposed to being the inspiration of any

single *auteur*. Certainly Basil Wright, Harry Watt, Cavalcanti and Grierson himself all made valid contributions, and it seems fitting that this is the film by which the movement as a whole is most often remembered.

Almost immediately after *Night Mail* the movement split up. In June 1937 Grierson resigned from the GPO film unit in order to set up Film Centre, which had some kind of formal link with Shell. At the same time his interest in developing non-theatrical distribution became apparent. GPO films were already being taken to schools and educational institutions throughout the country by travelling projection units, but up to this point the main idea had been to get them shown in the cinemas. Grierson proposed stepping right out of the entertainment business, and redirecting documentary to the fields of education or propaganda. He then took up an even greater challenge than that of setting up the British documentary movement by founding the National Film Board of Canada.

Basil Wright, Arthur Elton, Stuart Legg and John Taylor were among those who followed the new pattern set by Grierson. From then on, they had little time for developing their personal style, and in the main became producers dedicated to the idea of extending the field of documentary.

Meanwhile Harry Watt, Humphrey Jennings and Pat Jackson – who later directed the distinguished feature documentary *Western Approaches* (1944) – remained with Cavalcanti at the GPO. Watt (b.1906) made the excellent dramatized documentary about ship-to-shore radio, *North Sea* (1938), Jennings (1907–1950) made *Spare Time* (1939), a film about the leisure activities of ordinary people, while Anstey (b.1907) became British Director of Productions of the *March of Time* series. The group Grierson left behind him lifted British documentary to its second peak of achievement during World War II. Later the movement foundered owing to lack of leadership and an inflated sense of its own importance, left over from the golden years when a handful of films miraculously succeeded in living up to the expectations aroused for them by Grierson's persuasive prose.

Towards the end of the decade there were signs that the documentary idea was having some influence on feature films in Britain, notably in King Vidor's *The Citadel* (1938), Carol Reed's *The Stars Look Down* (1939) and Pen Tennyson's *The Proud Valley* (1939), all fictional films set against the harsh world of mining communities.

Soviet Socialist Realism

The 1930s were contradictory years for Soviet cinema. On the

one hand, repressive official measures put a virtual end to the high-spirited experiments and originality of the revolutionary cinema of the silent Twenties and led to a number of heavy-handed, conformist productions. On the other, several directors, with new facilities at their disposal, were able to operate within the imposed limits to create some remarkable films.

In line with the first Five Year Plan (1928), the film industry was harnessed to the country's over-riding task of reconstruction after the devastation of revolution, civil war and the wars of intervention. 'Socialist realism' was the order of the day for all the arts: film, as the most popular and influential of them, was given prime importance. 'Socialist realism', as interpreted by the film bureaucracy, meant a concentration on optimistic stories about individual achievements during the revolution and its aftermath, or about inspiring personal examples of the work of reconstruction.

The 'reality' of socialism could, of course, have been encapsulated in a variety of styles' 'Socialist realism', however, was posed as the opposite of 'formalism' – a term used as a blanket condemnation of any deviation from 'naturalism' or straightforward narrative style. This stemmed, in part, from a paternalistic underestimation of what the 'masses' would

understand or accept – in some ways a political counterpart of the commercial pressures under which the Hollywood studios operated.

The main victims of crude anti-formalism, especially under the film administration structure of 1934–8, were the greats of the silent era – Eisenstein, Pudovkin and Dovzhenko. Eisenstein was not allowed to complete his film about agricultural policy, *Bezhin lug* (1935, *Bezhin Meadow*). (A might-have-been compilation of surviving sequences and stills was put together by Yutkevich and Kleimann in 1967.) The progress of Pudovkin's *Prostoi sluchai* (1932, *A Simple Case*) and his *Dezertir* (1933, *The Deserter*), was fraught with difficulties.

Dovzhenko suffered cuts and hindrances over *Ivan* (1932) and *Aerograd* (1935), although both proved to be powerful, poetic films. The Georgian director Kalatozov, whose much-neglected masterpiece *Sol Svanetii* (1930, *Salt for Svanetia*,) had been sharply criticised, ran into difficutlies with *Gvozd v sapoge* (1932, *The Nail in the Shoe*) which was banned after completion.

After the failure of his experimental *Entuziazm* (1931, *Symphony of the Donbas*), Vertov had to face many battles before completing his lyrical *Tri Pesni o Leninye* (1934, *Three Songs of Lenin*) based on revolutionary folk-lore from Soviet Central Asia.

Directors embarking on complex political themes, like Yutkevich and Ermler with *Vstrechni* (1932 *Counterplan*) were particularly vulnerable to official interference.

Many of the film-makers, however, seized on another aspect of 'socialist realism' – the depiction of individual characters rather than generalized heroes – and made films of considerable charm and panache in whch vivid characterizations provided the main dynamic. Films ranging from Ekk's *Putyovka v zhizn* (1931, *Road to Life*), the first fully-fledged Soviet talkie, about a settlement for young delinquents orphaned by the revolution, to Raizman's *Poslednaya noch* (1937, *The Last Night*) about a sailor on the night before the revolution, were rich in character observation.

So were *Deputat Baltiki* (1936, *Baltic Deputy*) with the great Cherkasov as a lonely, ageing professor who finds friendship among the Baltic fleet sailors, and *Chlen pravitelstva* (1939, *Member of the Government*) with Vera Maretskaya as a peasant elected to the Supreme Soviet. Both were directed by Zarkhi and Heifitz. Dzigan's film about events in the Baltic, *My iz Kronstadt* (1936, *We from Kronstadt*) was more hidebound and didactic.

Chapayev (1934), made by the Vassiliev brothers – an affectionate and gently humorous study of a highly individualistic partisan fighter, with the official political 'line' unobtrusively introduced through an idealized secondary character – was held up as a model of socialist realism. It was tremendously popular in its time and remains a favourite with modern audiences.

One of the most original film-makers of the period was Medvedkin, who in 1931 worked on the celebrated film train that took cinema and film-making out to remote areas. Among his quirky, satirical pastoral comedies was the delightful *Schast* (1934, *Happiness*).

Considering all the difficulties and restrictions, there was a fair range of genres. Arnhem was the leading exponent of a trend for romances; Alexandrov directed mainly escapist musicals featuring the popular actress Orlova (whom he later married), while Pyriev made naive and folksy excursions into the realms of musical socialist realism. *Byeleyet parus odinoky*

(1937, *Lone White Sail*), directed by Legoshin, was an outstanding film for children.

In 1938, a change of the film administrative structure led to new film-making initiatives in which Stalin often took direct control. It was Stalin who suggested the subject for Dovzhenko's *Schors* (1938), which was to be the 'Ukrainian Chapayev'. Although Dovzhenko had to pay the price of intensive interference by Stalin and Beria, it turned out to be his finest and most visually exciting film. Stalin's initiation of a trend for massive, epic historicals, enabled Eisenstein to re-emerge with his superb *Alexander Nevsky* (1938). With its magnificent camerawork by Tisse, its evocative score by Prokofiev and its dazzling battle-on-the-ice climax, it made a striking contrast to the worthy stolidity of Petrov's two-part epic *Pyotr I* (1938, *Peter the Great*).

Stalin also encouraged a series of hagiographic films about Lenin, including Yutkevich's *Cheloveks ruzhyom* (1938, *Man with a Gun*) and Mikhail Romm's *Lenin v Oktyabre* (1937, *Lenin in October*) and *Lenin v 1918* (1939, *Lenin in 1918*), with imposing Lenin look-alike performances by Maxim Strauch (*Man with a Gun*) and Boris Shulkin. By the end of the decade the figure of Stalin was appearing in films in semi-godlike form, often in a gleaming white uniform – an indication of his increasingly oppressive influence on the film industry.

In 1937, Donskoi started work on his celebrated trilogy based on the autobiography of Maxim Gorky. The films, *Detstvo Gorkovo* (1938, *The Childhood of Gorky*), *V lyudyaki* (1939, *My Apprenticeship*) and *Moi universiteti* (1940, *My Universities*), teem with life and character, and feature and unforgettable performance by Varvara Massalitinova as the robust and earthy grandmother. The trilogy, with its vivid recreation of the hardships and humour of a bygone age, is among the greatest achievements of Soviet cinema in its most difficult and complex decade.

Newsreels

By the Thirties newsreel audiences seldom questioned the truthfulness of the images presented to them on the screen. Viewers outside Germany and Italy were thus not aware that all film coming from these countries had been shot by accredited members of the *Reichsfilmkammer*, nor that the vast amount of footage of goose-stepping Italian troops had been shot by LUCE cameramen. No-one, except a tiny minority of left-wing film-makers, expected the newsreels to provide anything but additional entertainment alongside the weekly feature film. All the major American, British and French newsreel outfits (Fox Movietone, Hearst Metrotone, Pathé, Paramount, Gaumont British, Pathé Frères and Gaumont) did, in fact, swap footage with Ufa and LUCE film crews.

Politicians were among the first to exploit the value of sound news, making themselves available for carefully vetted 'interviews' which usually gave the politician a golden opportunity to state a policy without any fear of it being criticized. When Germany walked out of the League of Nations in 1933, Goebbels did not even condescend to speak into Movietone's microphone – he merely sat at a desk while his interviewer stated Germany's reasons for quitting the League. Equally, when an interviewee chose to say something out of line with government policy, the American parent companies could be relied upon to suppress the offending passages at the request of the relevant European ambassador. A 'quiet word', for example, ensured that no film of the Duke of Windsor's wedding appeared on British screens.

Throughout the Thirties American and non-fascist European newsreels were anxious not to 'rock the boat'. Strikes and demonstrations by the millions of unemployed were largely ignored. Official censure, local government banning or private lawsuits would ensue whenever anything politically or morally controversial was shown. None of this excuses, however, the newsreel companies' failure to report what was happening to the Jews in Nazi Germany.

Newsreels were happiest covering 'action'; and when Mussolini invaded Abyssinia they adopted an almost festive air. The mood changed to one of more responsible journalism as civil war wrough havoc in Spain, although the 'Reds' came in for more biased criticism than the Nationalist forces. Actuality footage of disasters was still what the average newsreel cameraman craved and occasionally got: moments like the assassination of King Alexander I of Yugoslavia in 1934, the explosion of the zeppelin *Hindenburg* in May 1937 and the bombing of the US gunboat *Panay* by Japanese aircraft in December 1937.

The regular output of American and British newsreels in the Thirties was criticized by many (including Dr Goebbels) for being trivial, ephemeral and often frivolous in content and commentary. The American *March of Time* series always aimed to take a provocative stance in its treatment of current events. At first each monthly edition considered two or three hard new topics in depth; later, each was devoted to a single subject. Unfortunately it did little to influence the fare of contemporary newsreels and was, of course, subject to censorship. But the *March of Time* was able to avoid Nazi controls on location shooting by shamelessly reconstructing or faking the events under discussion.

Inside Nazi Germany (1939), the most famous of *March of Time*'s reports of this period, contained vivid shots of people in prison and of Jewish scientists being shut out from their laboratories, with no indication on the commentary that these 'authentic' scenes had been filmed in American studios.

On both sides of the impending struggle, film could be used as open propaganda and as a subtle means of influencing public opinion. But the problem was also one for the moviegoer – of how to know when a film was telling the truth.

Italy and Germany

In the aftermath of World War I, Western governments sought to contain the two opposing forces of National Socialism (or fascism) and International Socialism (or communism). The democracies of Britain, the USA, France and the Scandinavian countries survived, to a greater or lesser extent, through to the outbreak of World War II. Elsewhere in Europe the forces of fascism triumphed: in Italy Benito Mussolini had assumed totalitarian control with the aid of the Fascist Grand Council and was to survive as 'Il Duce' until the tide of World War II turned against him; in Germany Adolf Hitler's Nazi Party came to power in 1933 and the following year Hitler was proclaimed 'Fuhrer of the German Reich'.

The instability of the pre-fascist period and the growth of totalitarian rule is reflected in the inter-war cinema of Italy and Germany.

After a 'Golden Age' of epic splendour, the Italian cinema of the Twenties represented something of a decline. Starved of foreign capital and of indigenous talent many film-makers, actors and technicians had emigrated to the USA, France and Germany. When Mussolini came to power, however, he took a keen personal interest in the cinema, as befitted his nationalistic vanity. In 1926 he approved a ten per cent quota

Above left: a scene from March of Time*'s famous exposé* Inside Nazi Germany. *Above: Mindful of the importance of film as propaganda, Mussolini inspects the building of the Cinecittà studios in 1937.*

(later increased to 25 per cent) of Italian films in all cinemas. He also implemented a recommendation to turn the privately owned L'Unione Cinematrografia Educativa (LUCE) into a state-controlled institution under his direct supervision. LUCE was instructed to make and distribute films:

'... of an essentially scientific, historical and patriotic nature ... to correct public taste which has been corrupted by films whose moral and aesthetic qualities have all too often left much to be desired.'

LUCE quickly became a vehicle for state propaganda, disseminating official news via its newsreel, *Luce Gazette*. It also put out idealized documentaries such as *Il Duce* (a three-part saga of Mussolini and his blackshirts) and *La Strada degli Eroi* (1936, *Path of the Heroes*), an account of the Italian invasion of Abyssinia in 1935–6.

Screening of LUCE titles was compulsory in Italian cinemas and the exhibition of these films abroad was assisted by massive state subsidies.

State control of the feature film industry was not so easy to impose. In 1929 Mussolini banned the screening of foreign-language films and entrusted Stefano Pittaluga, a veteran from the early days of Italian cinema, with the task of converting the native film industry to sound. Initially his efforts were concentrated on dubbing the persistently popular French and American films, but he gradually gained a monopoly of the Italian-speaking film production. When Pittaluga died, the writer and art critic Emilio Cecchi took over the re-equipped Cines studios and pursued a policy of collaboration with the cinemas of sympathetic nations. Walter Ruttmann was hired from Germany in 1933 to film a Pirandello novella *Acciaio* (1933, *Steel*) – the first example of cross-fertilization between the Italian and German fascist cinemas.

The Cines studios proved incapable of leading a forceful revival of Italian film production, and during one of its periods of bankruptcy Mussolini set up a General Office for the Discipline and Guidance of Film Production. In this way he was able to intervene more directly, controlling films at the script and exhibition stages, while not subjecting film-makers to the kind of rigorous regime imposed by Goebbels in Germany.

Military success in Africa encouraged Mussolini to invest further in a cinema that should be worthy of his country's imperial past and present. In 1935 he approved the founding of the Centro Sperimentale di Cinematografia to train film technicians. In the same year building began on what was to become the great studio of Cineccità. By the time this monument to Mussolini's cinema was completed in April 1937, the Italian feature film industry had been put back on its feet.

The Italian silent cinema had been famous for its historical epics and had re-created virtually every story from the classical past; from Spartacus to Nero, from the Fall of Troy to Julius Caesar, from Oedipus Rex to Attila the Hun. The cinema of the Fascist era could not manage an output of epics comparable to that of the great age of Italian cinema, but Carmine Gallone's *Scipione l'Africano* (1937, *Scipio Africanus*) was a lavish re-creation of the Roman general's victorious campaigns in North Africa, intended to justify Mussolini's African campaigns. Other directors turned to the epic in order to escape contemporary reality and avoid entanglement with the controversial present. Many films, such as the 1937 version of *Gli Ultimi Giorni di Pompeii* (*The Last Days of Pompeii*), were remakes of silent successes. The historian Richard Griffith has written that 'they reflected nothing but the frozen values of a paralyzed society. Even the Fascists were bored by them'.

Underlying the blandness of most of the films of this period was the 'realist' style that recurs throughout the history of the Italian cinema. The work of **Alessandro Blasetti** (b.1900) is typical here. In his first film *Sole* (1929, Sun) he tackled the government's land reclamation policies with a realism that recalled the 'verismo' ('truthlikeness') style of Italian films prior to World War I. The heroes of the film are the peasant workers in the Pontine marshes, captured and framed on film as in a still life. Blasetti is better remembered, however, for his 1933 epic *1860* which deals with an episode in Garibaldi's campaign for the liberation of Sicily – a most inappropriate subject for a fascist regime to endorse! In his 1935 film *Vecchia Guardia* (*The Old Guard*) Blasetti paid tribute to the Fascists who had marched on Rome in 1922, but his subsequent films were less overtly propagandist and his historical fantasy *La Corona di Ferro* (1941, The Iron Crown) looks, with hindsight, a worthy predecessor to the Italian costume epics of the Sixties.

Blasetti had an inspired vision of creating a recognizably Italian cinema; his own career went some way towards realizing that ambition.

By contrast the other outstanding Italian director of the Thirties, **Mario Camerini** (b.1895), retreated to comedy instead of to history as a means of avoiding official censorship. He achieved international success in 1932 with his comedy *Gli Uomini, Che Mascalzoni* (*What Rascals Men Are!*) which starred Vittorio De Sica in the first of his many roles as a weak but charming lover. Like any other contemporary director, however, Camerini was obliged to make a piece of fascist propaganda and his *Il Grande Appello* (1936, The Great Roll-Call) was one of a spate of 'Africa' films which followed in the wake of Mussolini's conquest of Abyssinia.

Camerini's light comedies were often an inspiration to many lesser Italian directors who otherwise churned out a depressingly large number of anodyne 'telefoni bianchi' films, which took their nickname from the white telephones over which so many of the heroines languished. That these films were so distant from the realities of life under Il Duce was a constant source of embarrassment to all subsequent schools of Italian film-making. They also reveal the way in which the fascist ideology can be embodied in escapist entertainment.

Recent analyses of the films of the Third Reich have revealed a similar process at work in the German cinema of the Thirties, instead of the traditional view of a marked distinction between overt propaganda and mere escapist cinema.

In Germany the forceful realism of *Neue Sachlichkeit* ('new objectivity'), the strong avant-garde movement in the arts, and the implicit threat posed by Expressionist art and cinema, all conspired to make the Nazi ideologists anxious to control film. In retaliating they not only commissioned their own Party films but also mounted a campaign of attack on subversive trends within German cinema, staging 'spontaneous' demonstrations against several films of the early Thirties that exhibited some socio-political awareness.

Pabst's World War I pacifist epic *Westfront 1918* (1930) was a victim of these attacks. Banned seven months after its premiere, it was severely cut and rescreened in late 1931 before being completely banned in the spring of 1933. A similar fate befell the same director's *Kameradschaft* (1931, Comradeship) which was an appeal to international solidarity among working men.

The psychological themes that characterized the German Expressionist films persisted into the early sound period. Leontine Sagan's *Mädchen in Uniform* (1931, *Girls in Uniform*) is, in fact, more striking as a study in female psychology than as a plea for a human system of education. The survival of the same undercurrent of psychological anxiety that made the German films of the Twenties so disturbing is evident in the films of Fritz Lang – especially *Das Testament von Dr Mabuse* (1932, *The Testament of Dr Mabuse*), in which the manic Doctor attempts to take over the world from his base in a lunatic asylum.

By 1936 systematic purges of the German film industry – prohibition of Jews, abolition of film criticism and the operation of a ruthless censorship – ensured that a large proportion of the native German film talent had emigrated, most of it to the USA. Hollywood had benefitted from the influx of talent represented by directors and actors like Fritz Lang, William Dieterle, Robert Siodmak, Edgar G. Ulmer, Marlene Dietrich, Conrad Veidt, Billy Wilder, Peter Lorre and Fred Zinnemann.

The combined effect of Goebbels' control of the bureaucracy of film-making (under the aegis of the *Reichsfilmkammer* or Chamber of Film) and Alfred Hugenberg's financial control of Ufa (the country's major production company) was to bring about the gradual nationalization of the German film industry.

By 1933 *Reichsfilmkammer* members were the only people allowed to make films. They enjoyed exclusive filming rights in Germany free from foreign competition. As it grew in strength the *Reichsfilmkammer* introduced a series of prizes and approved a system of grading films as culturally and politically valuable. By 1935 they took control of all exports of German films and newsreels: all cinematic images of Germany seen abroad now stemmed from the *Reichsfilmkammer*.

Top left: Mädchen in Uniform *was an unusual film in the context of mainstream German cinema of the early Thirties. An account of the oppressive discipline in a girls boarding school, it was one of the first films to deal sensitively with the attraction between young girls. Top right: the actor-director Luis Trenker played the hero of* Der Rebell, *billed as 'a film of freedom from the mountains'. Above: members of the Hitler Youth in* Hitlerjunge Quex, *which helped woo the German working-classes away from communism and towards National Socialism and its promise of a bright future.*

Ufa had been responsible for financing the peculiarly German genre of 'mountain films', such as Arnold Fanck's *Die Weisse Hölle von Piz Palü* (1929, *The White Hell of Pitz Palu*) and Luis Trenker's *Der Rebell* (1932, The Rebel). The appeal of these films resided in the monumental grandeur of the glaciers and rocks and the selfless idealism of the Aryan heroes. From these films it was only a short step to overtly Nazi films like *Hitlerjunge Quex* (1933, Hitler Youth Quex).

Tobis, Ufa's only real rival in film production, conformed equally to the edicts issued by the *Reichsfilmkammer*. Both companies issued regular newsreels – *Deutsche Tonwoche* (Tobis) and *Deutsche Wochenshau* (Ufa) – which were blatantly used by Goebbels as mouthpieces for National Socialist policies and activities.

Outstanding among Third Reich films were the documentaries of **Leni Riefenstahl** (b.1902), which stand analysis both as propaganda and as art. In 1934 she won Hitler's approval with the Nuremberg Rally film *Triumph des Willens* (*Triumph of the Will*). *Olympia* (1938, *Berlin Olympiad*), her

lyrical epic of the 1936 Olympic Games, was made under the scrutiny, if not direct supervision, of Dr Goebbels, Hitler's propaganda minister.

The overtly propagandist feature films of the Nazi period followed certain themes and archetypes. They encouraged the cult of the leader and the Fatherland; they celebrated discipline and comradeship; they advocated euthanasia and anti-Semitism and they promoted an image of 'Perfidious Albion' as a means of attacking British imperialism. At the same time it was always Goebbels' intention that propaganda should work, to use his own words:

'. . . invisibly to penetrate the whole of life without the public having any knowledge at all of the propagandist initiative.'

Both Stalin's Russia and Hitler's Germany promoted historical epics to glorify the submission of a people to their national destiny and to hold up for admiration the all-powerful, all-knowing, all-seeing leader. In Russia the two-part film *Pyotr Pervyi* (1937/8, *Peter the Great*) and in Germany the Fridericus

Left: the concept of the beauty, grace and strength of the ideal Aryan form was extolled by Leni Riefenstahl through her images of athletes in Olympia, *a documentary of the 1936 Olympic Games. Below left: Riefenstahl with Adolf Hitler at the Nuremberg Rally of 1934. Below: the ominous pomp of the Nazis at Nuremberg, as captured by the documentary* Triumph of the Will.

series of films about the Prussian king Frederick the Great preached just that message. Eisenstein's Soviet epic *Aleksandr Nevskii* (1938, *Alexander Nevsky*) was a nationalistic, anti-German drama about the thirteenth-century Russian prince who defeated an invasion by the Teutonic knights.

In Germany the foremost historical epic was *Condottieri* (1937, *Knights of the Black Eagle*) filmed by a German company on location in Italy and directed by Luis Trenker. As a piece of pure film-making the movie is outstanding for its majestic use of Italian settings and buildings, a soaring symphonic score and graphically-staged battles and sieges.

France

The structure of the film industry in France changed markedly with the arrival of sound in 1930. The extra costs of talkie production eliminated many of the smaller film companies, though others continued to proliferate throughout the decade, albeit undercapitalized and short-lived; in 1936 alone, for example, 175 new film companies were founded.

Financial considerations also led to the creation of two massive and vertically-integrated companies (embracing production, distribution and exhibition) formed out of the pioneering companies of Charles Pathé and Léon Gaumont. Both the resulting companies, however, withdrew from film production in the mid-Thirties, partly as a result of the illegal financial manipulations of Bernard Natan who had taken over the Pathé company in 1929.

From an output of some fifty feature films in 1929, French film production doubled by 1930 and more than tripled by 1932. But the native film industry never supplied any more than 25 per cent of the movies distributed annually in France. Moreover these were years of chaos and disorder in the industry: technical crews struggled with the limitations of unwieldy new sound-recording equipment; cinema owners required considerable capital to convert their buildings to sound; and producers contrived to add sound to projects conceived originally as silent films. For a while the cumbersome business of multi-language shooting occupied the studios until dubbing and subtitling enabled French films to be distributed abroad with ease.

Certainly in the confusion of the early years of the decade, much of the specifically French quality of the national film production was lost. France had a slow start in talkies since patent rights to the most successful sound systems were owned by American and German companies. The early Thirties had also seen the establishment of large-scale multi-language production in Paris, by the American Paramount company and the German Tobis company, operating from studios at Joinville and Epinay respectively.

The upheavals of sound were followed, from the middle of the decade onwards, by further crises which reflected the contradictions of contemporary French society as much as the inherent problems of the film industry itself.

In this climate a sense of national identity was difficult to achieve and sustain even after the era of multi-language production had come to an end. Germany, in particular, was a major foreign influence. On the one hand co-productions with Ufa at the Neubabelsberg studios in Berlin continued to provide work for French directors, writers and actors throughout the decade. On the other hand, the advent of Hitler to power in 1933 caused a mass emigration to Paris of German producers, directors and technicians. Figures as important as Erich Pommer, Fritz Lang, Billy Wilder, Robert Siodmak, G.W. Pabst and Eugen Schüfftan worked, some of

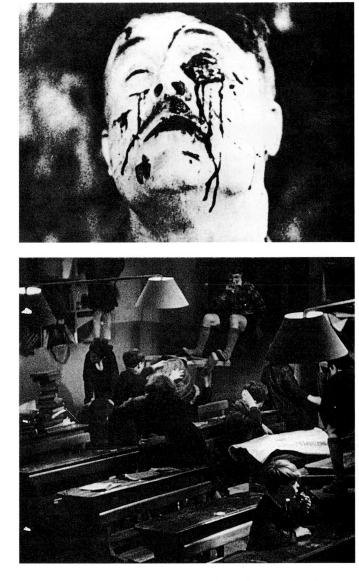

them for several years, in the French film industry. It has been estimated that up to a third of French cinema in the Thirties was strongly shaped and influenced by emigrés like, for example, the Austrian Max Ophuls who spent eight years of the decade in France. Ophuls achieved some impressive melodramas that portrayed the misfortunes of beautiful women: *Divine* (1935), *La Tendre Enemie* (1935, Tender Enemy), *Yoshiwara* (1937) and *Sans Lendemain* (1939, No Tomorrow).

The demands of sound-film production resulted in the loss of many of the characteristic features of earlier French cinema, in particular the visual experiment associated with the various avant-garde movements of the Twenties.

The interaction of film with Surrealism in France had reached a climax by 1930 with the premiere of Luis Buñuel's *L'Age d'Or* (*The Golden Age*), a masterly indictment of society which provoked riots when first shown in Paris. In the same year Buñuel's sponsor, the Vicomte de Noailles, financed Jean Cocteau's *Le Sang d'un Poète* (1930 *The Blood of a Poet*), but with the increased costs of sound-film production this kind of private patronage of independent film-making came to an end. *Le Sang d'un Poète* was Cocteau's first venture into film and though attacked and derided by the Surrealists on its first appearance, the film now stands as a major achievement and a statement of the personal vision that would be fully orchestrated in *Orphée* (1950, *Orpheus*) some twenty years later.

Sound meant that other key figures of French silent cinema,

Below far left: the beginnings of anarchy in the classroom from Vigo's disturbing comedy, Zero de Conduite, *which was largely inspired by his unhappy years in provincial boarding-schools. The content and satirical force of the film strongly influenced Lindsay Anderson when, in 1967, he came to du ect the British public-school satire* If .... *Far left: Gaston Modot falls a prey to 'L'amour fou' in Buñuel's* L'Age d'Or, *which was acknowledged as the first authentic*

Surrealist sound film. Left: a typically satiric image of the leisured classes from Vigo's avant-garde documentary, A Propos de Nice. *Below: ex-jailbirds Emile (Henri Marchand) and Louis (Raymond Cordy) renew their friendship in Clair's* A Nous la Liberté. *Below left: the artist's sculpture comes mysteriously to life in Cocteau's oblique reworking of the Pygmalion myth,* Le Sang d'un Poète, *initially disparaged as parlour surrealism.*

such as Abel Gance, Marcel L'Herbier and Jean Epstein were reduced to merely commercial film-making. Gance, for example, alternated remakes of some of his earlier successes – he made a sound version of his famous *Napoléon* (1927) in 1935 – with routine assignments which offered only rare opportunities to show his full talents. L'Herbier made a couple of lively thrillers, adapted from the novels of Gaston Leroux – *Le Mystère de la Chambre Jaune* (1930, The Mystery of the Yellow Room) and *Le Parfum de la Dame en Noir* (1931, The Perfume of the Lady in Black). Otherwise his output was restricted to dull historical spectacles, while Epstein's work of the Thirties was equally compromised by unsuitable scripts and financial restraints.

One thread of continuity is provided by the career of **René Clair**, the master of silent cinema whose writings of the late Twenties opposed the notion of sound (and particularly talking) films but who was one of the first in France to exploit the new form with wit and inventiveness.

The five Clair comedies released in the early Thirties create a distinctive universe where the entanglements of his characters are presented with good-humoured sympathy, and where good eventually triumphs over evil. His first sound film, the internationally successful *Sous les Toits de Paris* (1930, *Under the Roofs of Paris*) with its treatment of characters living on the fringes of society, is an early precursor of what was later to be called 'poetic realism'. Generally, however, Clair's comedies are much lighter and

involve a great use of the interplay of dream and reality.

Clair is at his weakest when attempting abstract statements about society, as at the end of *A Nous la Liberté* (1931, Freedom Is Ours), or politics, which form the background of *Le Dernier Milliardaire* (1934, *The Last Millionaire*). But despite the reticence and restraint which characterizes all his work, Clair's films of the early Thirties remain genuinely moving and affectionate works.

He left for England in 1935 and was absent from France for 12 years except for a brief period during 1939 when he began, but failed to complete, *Air Pur* (Pure Air).

Another great loss to the French film industry was that of **Jean Vigo**, who died in 1934 at the age of 29. Vigo was one of France's most talented and promising young film-makers, whose entire output amounted to two documentaries and two longer fictional works.

After a penetrating study of Nice, *A Propos de Nice* (1930), which blends documentary and surrealist elements, and a short film about a champion swimmer, *Taris* (1931), Vigo made the two films on which his reputation principally rests. Both were dogged by misfortune. The 47-minute *Zéro de Conduite* (1933, *Nought for Behaviour*), a surreal study of life in a boarding-school, was banned by the French censor until 1945, and the feature-length *L'Atalante* (1934, The Atalanta) was re-edited and redubbed by its producers while Vigo himself lay dying.

Through both films runs a unique vein of poetry. The

world of childhood has seldom been so accurately captured as in *Zéro de Conduite* and the combination in *L'Atalante* of realistically detailed barge life with larger-than-life elements (such as the figure of the mate, brilliantly played by Michel Simon) is a successful fusion of fantasy and reality.

The oustanding film-maker throughout the decade, however, was **Jean Renoir** (1894–1979) – the son of the painter Auguste Renoir. Like Clair, he had made a number of films during the silent period, but the Thirties, when he made some fifteen films, were the richest years of his career. His work is enormously varied and combines elements drawn from his father's Impressionist style and from the naturalism of the nineteenth-century novel or theatre.

Renoir's work during the early years of the decade is marked by his collaborations with the actor Michel Simon.

Bottom: Renoir (left of camera) directing Toni *on location in the South of France. Below: Jenny Hélia and Charles Blavette in* Toni, *based on a real-life crime of passion. Below right:* Un Carnet de Bal *related a woman's nostalgic search for the beaux of her youth. Bottom right: this poster evokes the 'slice of life' atmosphere of Pagnol's trilogy.*

The first film they made together was a farce called *On Purge Bébé* (1931, Purging Baby). Next they did two splendidly amoral tales designed to exploit the actor's remarkable talents: Simon excels as Legrand in *La Chienne* (1931, The Bitch), a timid cashier turned painter who murders his faithless mistress and allows her lover to be executed for the crime. He is equally impressive as Boudu, the tramp in *Boudu Sauvé des Eaux* (1932, *Boudu Saved From Drowning*) who rewards his rescuer by seducing both his wife and his mistress. The anarchism celebrated in the figure of the tramp links the Renoir film with Vigo's *L'Atalante* and to some extent with the mood at the end of Clair's *A Nous la Liberté*. It is a measure of Renoir's versatility that he could subsequently follow adaptations of Simenon – *La Nuit du Carrefour* (1932, Night at the Crossroads) – and Flaubert's *Madame Bovary* (1934) with *Toni* (1934), a sober study of migrant workers shot on location and in a style that anticipates some aspects of post-war Italian neo-realism.

Many of Renoir's greatest films like *Une Partie de Campagne* (1936, A Day in the Country), *La Bête Humaine* (1938, *Judas was a Woman*) and *La Règle du Jeu* (1939, *The Rules of the Game*) were made from his own scripts. *Le Crime de Monsieur*

THE THIRTIES IN EUROPE 147

Lange (1935, *The Crime of Monsier Lange*), however, announces a new orientation for his work since it was made in collaboration with the poet and scriptwriter **Jacques Prévert** (1900–1977).

The two of them captured the essential socialist optimism of the Popular Front period and subsequently Renoir found himself caught up in political activity to the extent of making *La Vie Est à Nous* (1936, *People of France*), an explicit propaganda piece for the Communist Party.

The following year he made *La Grande Illusion* (1937, *The Great Illusion*), a passionate anti-war statement and a triumph of human observation, controlled rhetoric and total professionalism. At the end of the decade Renoir completed his masterpiece *La Règle du Jeu*, a perceptive dissection of a divided society which amounts to his personal statement on the eve of world war. When the film was first shown, in July 1939, it caused a riot and attempts were made to burn down the cinema. The film ran for a mere three weeks. In October the French government, no doubt bewildered by the film's blend of drama, comedy and farce, banned it, claiming it was morally unacceptable. The ban was lifted some months later but re-enforced when the Germans occupied Paris.

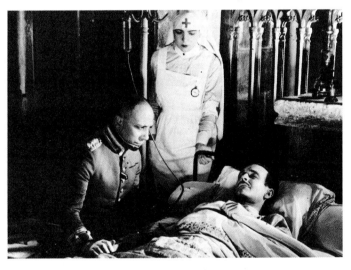

Top: Rauffenstein, the prison commandant (Erich von Stroheim), visits the bedside of Boeldieu (Pierre Fresnay) in La Grande Illusion. *Above: mayhem among the servants of the chateau in* La Règle du Jeu.

In the theoretical debate about sound, and particularly talking pictures, two highly successful French dramatists declared themselves opposed to the traditional view of the primacy of the image. **Sacha Guitry** and **Marcel Pagnol** both initially turned to the cinema simply as a means of recording their own work written for the theatre. Both of them had plays adapted for the cinema by other directors in 1931 and then began to direct their own work for the screen a few years later. The results were paradoxical. Their best films, far from being stage-bound, show a freedom shared only by Renoir among their contemporaries.

Guitry (1885–1957) was a prolific dramatist who wrote some hundred and thirty plays; most of his Thirties films are simple adaptations, but in his original work written for the screen he shows a freedom of construction, a light and playful style of performance and an inventive approach to the relationship of image and sound which would later be acknowledged as an influence by post-war directors like Alain Resnais. Among Guitry's notable films are: *Le Roman d'un Tricheur* (1936 Story of a Cheat), *Les Perles de la Couronne* (1937, Pearls of the Crown), *Remontons les Champs-Elysées* (1938, Let's Go Up the Champs-Elysées) and *Ils Etaient Neuf Célibataires* (1939, They Were Nine Bachelors).

The work of Pagnol (1895–1974), too, has its surprises. His first contact with the cinema was through his own adaptations of his famous Marseilles trilogy – *Marius* (1931), *Fanny* (1932), and *César* (1936, directed by Pagnol himself). He later made his own film adaptation of his play *Topaze* in 1936, which has subsequently been much filmed.

The success of these works in the tradition of filmed theatre allowed Pagnol to build his own studio and exercise total control over production, even to the extent of remaking films that displeased him, either through defects of sound, as in *Merlusse* (1935) or of interpretation, as in *Cigalon* (1935).

Most of Pagnol's best films of the Thirties, however, were adapted not from his own plays, but from novels and stories by the popular author Jean Giono. *Angèle* (1934) and *Regain* (1937, *Harvest*) with Fernandel, and *La Femme du Boulanger* (1938, *The Baker's Wife*) with the great Raimu, were filmed away from the studios on location in Provence so as to make the most of the landscape. The construction and the direction of these films is characterized by a freedom that still appears extremely modern.

The gifted **Jean Grémillon** (1901–1959) had greater difficulty establishing himself in feature film production. His first sound film, *La Petite Lise* (1930, Little Lise), was a box-office failure and from then on he was condemned to make films that were guaranteed commercial projects or, subsequently, to seek work abroad in Spain and Germany.

Working at the Ufa studios in Berlin, Grémillon made two films from scripts by Charles Spaak. Both *Gueule d'Amour* (1937, Mouth of Love) starring Jean Gabin and *L'Etrange Monsieur Victor* (1937, The Strange Mr Victor) with Raimu had considerable merits.

In 1939, Grémillon was given the opportunity to direct the ideal couple of the period – Jean Gabin and Michéle Morgan – in Jacques Prévert's scenario *Remorques* (*Stormy Waters*), the plan to make the film was disrupted by the outbreak of World War II, though the film was completed in 1940.

Key Directors

Jacques Feyder (1888–1948), the Belgian-born director, returned from Hollywood to make three films that re-established his European reputation built up during the silent

Above: love briefly transforms despair into irrational hope for the protagonists of Quai des Brumes.

era. These were *Le Grand Jeu* (1933, *The Great Game*), *Pension Mimosas* (1934) and *La Kermesse Héroïque* (1935, *Carnival in Flanders*) and the team of technicians Feyder assembled to make them included the designer Lazare Meerson, the photographer Harry Stradling and a young assistant, Marcel Carné.

All three films starred Feyder's wife, Françoise Rosay, and were scripted by **Charles Spaak** (1903–1975), another Belgian who had earlier worked with Feyder on *Les Nouveaux Messieurs* (1928, The New Gentlemen). The writer's contribution, not only to the surface brilliance of the dialogue but also to the structural organization of the plot, was vital. It was to be the first of several writer-director collaborations that characterized the French cinema of the period.

Spaak himself went on to work with another veteran of silent cinema, **Julien Duvivier** (1896–1967). They made two films starring Jean Gabin: both *La Bandera* (1935) and *La Belle Equipe* (1936, The Fine Team) captured the confused aspirations of the period when the left-wing Popular Front government came to power in France.

Duvivier's other major script collaborator was the more superficial but nonetheless brilliantly witty writer Henri Jeanson. Together they worked on the gangster film *Pépé-le-Moko* (1936), a striking example of the romantic pessimism of the time, starring Jean Gabin and the nostalgic *Un Carnet de Bal* (1937, *Christine*) in which a woman seeks out all the men whose names appear on an old dance card to discover what fate had befallen them.

The talent of **Marcel Carné** (b.1909) is defined by a single period and style. Carné was the protégé of Feyder and had proved himself a brilliant organizer of artistic collaborators

like the designer Alexandre Trauner and the composer Maurice Jaubert. Before he was 30, Carné had completed five star-studded features, four of them from scripts by Jacques Prévert.

After his debut with *Jenny* (1936), he made the striking comedy *Drôle de Drame* (1937, *Bizarre, Bizarre*), a comparatively rare example of Prévert's purely comic gifts. Carné and Prévert's two master-pieces *Quai de Brumes* (1938, *Quay of Shadows*) and *Le Jour se Lève* (1939, Daybreak) are both fatalistic pieces in which Jean Gabin loses all chance of happiness with the woman he loves after a confrontation with two personifications of evil, respectively portrayed by Michel Simon and Jules Berry. The combination of Prévert's anarchic poetry and Carné's technical prowess creates an unforgettable mixture that is echoed in the Carné-Jeanson collaboration *Hôtel du Nord* (1938, Northern Hotel).

The achievements of Clair and Vigo in the early Thirties and, later in the decade of Feyder, Duviver, Renoir and Carné, together with their writers Spaak, Jeanson and Prévert, combined to make this a seminal period in the development of French cinema. Its influence extends not only to post-war France but also to Italian neo-realism.

Britain

By the time sound films arrived, the British film industry was used to growing up in the shadow of the American cinema. But the particular struggles over what is known in the film business as exploitation (the hiring out or releasing of films by distributors, and the promotion and showing of films by exhibitors) demonstrate the depth of Hollywood's involvement in Britain.

It was against this background of competition – some would say colonization – from America, that the British cinema of the Thirties evolved its characteristic mixture of parochial comedies, occasional prestige pictures of international appeal, and harshly 'realistic' documentaries. Whatever kind of films they were, they constituted a challenge to Hollywood by the very fact of being British-made. The problem was to get them on to the screens in the home country so that they would have a chance to earn revenue.

Even prior to the talkies British producers were less and less successful in securing a share of screen time in Britain, because the Hollywood companies exerted a large measure of control over UK distribution.

The same companies strengthened their hand by block booking (packaging less popular films with the most prestigious) and blind booking (scheduling groups of films far in advance, often fixing playdates for films that were still uncompleted).

So serious was the threat to the home industry that the Government stepped in with the Cinematograph Films Act of 1927, designed to afford some protection to British producers. Initially and superficially the law did help. It ensured the distribution and exhibition of a rising proportion, or *quota*, of British feature films and thus provided a stimulus to production.

But the drawbacks to the Act soon became apparent. Throughout the next decade the malpractices of block/blind booking proved impossible to prosecute or eradicate. Moreover British producers realized that a protected market was oblivious to quality. The law required merely that the quota be met: distributors had to supply their customers, the cinema owners, with a proportion of British-made product; the exhibitors were obliged to screen it. Quantity and not quality was the order of the day.

In many cases the distributors were branches of major Hollywood studios whose pictures they were in business to promote. Handling British quota films was simply a routine that had to be gone through: the films were treated as second-class product.

The market required cheap pictures, and, as early as the spring of 1929, the term 'quota quickies' was current to describe shortish features made as quickly and as cheaply as possible to satisfy the legal requirements for distributors and exhibitors.

Suddenly there was too much British product, of the worst kind. The quota became overfulfilled as producers rushed to supply the industry with any old film, however feeble, that could be registered as British and then used as programming fodder. It was rumoured among the film trade in London that by showing bad British films the Americans were conspiring to ruin the reputation of British production. The same paranoid attitude attended even the most successful British films whose producers saw inferior American movies earning more money at the box-office simply because the Americans could afford to spend more on publicity.

The attitudes of the major American film companies towards the native British industry ranged from tentatively co-operative to outright exploitative. Until the late Thirties MGM, and to a lesser extent Universal, were notorious for programming poor-quality quota films to their UK distribution schedules. RKO, on the other hand, made a reciprocal deal with Basil Dean, head of ATP at the Ealing studios: Dean would then supply them with quota films and in return they were to promote his pictures in the USA. The second half of the deal was never fulfilled. Fox, and later Columbia, made arrangements with various small-time British producers to make cheap quota films for UK distribution.

Americans had made pictures in Britain before. One of the earliest examples was part of D.W. Griffith's *Hearts of the World* (1918) in 1917. But having a measure of control over the British distribution network, it now seemed logical to the Americans that they should produce in England films for the English market. No-one really believed the Hollywood majors, however, when they announced that American films made in England would compete with home-grown product back in the USA.

Most of the Hollywood companies had UK subsidiaries and produced their films on a one-off basis, sometimes in collaboration with British film companies, often in rented studios. The only genuine attempt to establish an American production company in Britain in the early Thirties was that of Warner Brothers – First National who bought the Teddington studio that today houses Thames Television. From 1931 it was run like a miniature Hollywood factory, competently turning out a stream of very similar films under a strong editorial directive from California, with a nucleus of American technical staff and a thrifty use and re-use of both players and sets.

Several categories of producer began to emerge. The serious ones, like Basil Dean, Michael Balcon and Herbert Wilcox, wanted to make films of good quality and they knew they would have to sell their films abroad, especially in the USA. The chief proponent of this view was Alexander Korda, who arrived in England to make quota films for Paramount towards the end of 1931, but made a strong case for quality

British cinema with *The Private Life of Henry VIII* (1933).

Companies of more limited ambition, like Warner Brothers – First National and John Maxwell's British International Pictures, aimed first at the home market, and made a modest but assured profit from a steady turnover of romantic comedies and English whodunnits. Other producers, who might be called 'quota kings', went after small profits on a large output of ruthlessly cheap pictures.

Cheaper budget productions from the smaller firms tended to prefer show business stories: popular variety turns were cobbled together into rudimentary story films. But High Society, as represented on the London stage was equally popular fare for audiences in the Thirties. It was against this detachment from reality that the new British documentary movement was reacting with ever increasing strength.

The Quota Act had done little more than give protection to cheap British films. But American domination of the British film industry remained as powerful as ever and manifested itself in a variety of ways. American companies, for example, were able to pay higher salaries, owing to their greater box-office revenues, and so many English actors, writers and directors drifted off to America. The size of the British colony in Hollywood reflected this trend.

The migration of talent was not entirely one way. A number of second-rate American actors and technicians were borrowed soon after the Quota Act, but several competent professionals also came to Britain on a more permanent basis.

Rather different in its contribution was the immigration from Europe of refugees, exiles or birds of passage – technicians, actors and directors – who brought an unfamiliar sophistication to the industry. The little group of first class cameramen, like Georges Périnal, and art directors, like Vincent Korda and Alfred Junge, helped to add a new visual gloss to the appearance of British films.

Actors like Conrad Veidt, Elisabeth Bergner and singer Richard Tauber grafted their exotic talents onto the homely British film. Already established foreign producers and

Above: shooting the banquet scene in The Private Life of Henry VIII, *with Laughton at the table.*

directors, among them Erich Pommer, Lothar Mendes, Kurt Bernhardt, Karl Grune worked for a while in England before moving on. Others, like the three Korda brothers (producer-director Alexander, art director Vincent, and director Zoltan), stayed and set up shop in Britain.

By the mid-Thirties it was clear that the quota had failed to create a flourishing industry after all. Those producers who believed that the production of quality films was only viable if they had an American market had found that the vital cinema circuits were controlled by American production interests, and so were implacably barred to those people trying to distribute British films in the USA. Producer and director Victor Saville claimed that even in Britain the financial terms of distribution were less favourable to British producers than to Americans.

In the second half of the decade, the slump hit the British film industry. Gaumont-British had decided to cease production at Shepherd's Bush by the end of 1936. Around the same time Korda was running into financial trouble after building the large studios at Denham. Financial backers in the City of London were beginning to realize that they had been lending short-term capital without adequate security and at least one producer, Julius Hagen of Twickenham was declared bankrupt. All the Quota Act had done was to encourage an unhealthy expansion of cheap production. The Act was due for renewal in 1938 anyway, but a government committee under Lord Moyne met several times during 1937 to reconsider the Quota and other means of dealing with the American influence. In this crucial period of uncertainty, investment in production fell away and the big American companies began to take over studios that had been expanded during the boom period. Britain was by this time a fully geared-up movie colony ripe for big-budget American productions.

Hitchcock in England In 1934, Alfred Hitchcock (1899–1980) began the great series of six suspense thrillers, made in four years and concluding with *The Lady Vanishes* (1938), which carried his reputation round the world and finally took him to Hollywood in 1939. The first of them, *The Man Who Knew Too Much*, established his penchant for the brilliantly conceived effect as the basis of film-making. A family staying in St Moritz witness the murder of a secret agent who, before he dies, tells them of a plan to assassinate a foreign diplomat in London. Realizing this, the enemy spies kidnap the couple's daughter to ensure their silence. The couple have to thwart the villains' plans without police help.

Whereas in *The Lodger* (1926) and *Blackmail* (1929) the tricks had tended to stand out from the overall texture, *The Man Who Knew Too Much* was virtually a succession of memorable scenes and incidents which kept the audience totally at the director's mercy. This became Hitchcock's hallmark during the Thirties and remained an important part of his style.

Not everyone approved – Graham Greene, then influential film critic of the *Spectator*, wrote of *The Secret Agent* (1936):

'His films consist of a series of small "amusing" melodramatic situations: the murderer's button dropped on the baccarat board; the strangled organist's hands prolonging the notes in the empty church; the fugitives hiding in the bell-tower when the bell begins to swing. Very perfunctorily he builds up to these tricky situations (paying no attention on the way to inconsistencies, loose ends, psychological absurdities) and then drops them: they mean nothing: they lead to nothing.'

It is curious that Greene, of all people should have been quite so unsympathetic to what Hitchcock was doing in these films, since it was so close to those stories of his own that he labelled 'entertainments'. Hitchcock was always first and foremost a popular entertainer, with no overt pretensions, leaving others to find deeper meanings in his work. His way of involving his audience was to deploy his unique technical skills and extraordinary inventive faculties in the elaboration of telling incident through specific effect. There are many single shots in the British thrillers which everyone who has seen them remembers. There is, for instance, the famous shot near the end of *Young and Innocent* (1937) in which the camera travels slowly across a crowded ball-room during a *thé dansant*, moving closer and closer to the black-face band, then concentrating on the drummer and finally pausing in an arresting close-up of his eye twitching – the crucial identifying mark of the murderer.

But memorable though such isolated moments are, and though Hitchcock enjoyed devising them and making them work, the dramatic effects in his films are usually more far-reaching. There are whole sequences that use or exploit well-known conventions of suspense. Take, for example, the idea of there being 'safety in numbers'. In *The Thirty-Nine Steps* (1935), the hero, Hannay, hotly pursued by foreign agents, stumbles into a political meeting. Realizing that his only hope of escape is to get up and speak, he delivers an absurd, off-the-cuff speech and makes himself so conspicuous that the villains are unable to do anything to him for fear of giving themselves away. Hitchcock liked this idea so well that he later used variations of it in the two American films which had similar chase formulas to *The Thirty-Nine Steps*, *Saboteur* (1942) and *North by Northwest* (1959).

Yet crowds and public places are not always havens from danger – they can also conceal it. The climactic scene of *The Man Who Knew Too Much* occurs at the Royal Albert Hall during the performance of a cantata; the sound of the assassin's bullet is planned to coincide with the clash of cymbals at the end of the piece. In *The Thirty-Nine Steps*, Mr Memory is murdered on stage in full view of the music-hall audience. In *Sabotage* (1936), a bomb unknowingly carried by a boy explodes on a crowded London bus. An elderly Englishwoman disappears on a European train in *The Lady Vanishes*, and the British contingent only gradually organizes to rescue her from her fascist captors. It was not on this warning note but after a stagey version of Daphne du Maurier's famous novel, *Jamaica Inn* (1939), that Hitchcock went to settle in the USA.

Alexander Korda Born Sándor Kellner on September 16, 1893, near Túrkeve, Hungary, Korda worked as a journalist and editor of a film magazine before directing his first film in 1914. Two younger brothers, Zoltán and Vincent, later worked with him as director and art director respectively.

Korda's turbulent 25 years in Britain tend to overshadow his previous 17 years as a director first in Hungary and subsequently in Vienna, Berlin, Hollywood and Paris. Although he and Michael Curtiz dominated the early Hungarian film industry between 1917 and 1919, Korda was scarcely known outside his own country during that period.

When the communist regime of Béla Kun fell in 1919, Korda fled the country. He emigrated with his actress wife, Maria Corda, to Vienna where he directed four films. The first, an adaptation of Mark Twain's novel *The Prince and the Pauper*, was successfully released in America. The praise for its evocative recreation of British pageantry convinced Korda that foreign directors could effectively handle national

subjects outside their own experience. In Berlin, from 1922–26, with films like *Das Unbekannte Morgen* (1923, *The Unknown Tomorrow*) he accommodated his own preference for light romantic subjects, adopting the Expressionist preoccupations with destiny and mysticism then fashionable in German cinema. Determined to make films that would attract Hollywood, Korda directed the lavish and sophisticated *Eine Dubarry von Heute* (*A Modern Dubarry*) in 1926. It earned him a contract with First National in Hollywood which he took up early in 1927.

During his four years in Hollywood (1927–30), however, Korda was typecast as a director of female stars or of films with Hungarian settings. The only notable film he made there, *The Private Life of Helen of Troy* (1927), was an impressively photographed version of the Greek legend, reshaped into a marital comedy, with the characters given contemporary speech and attitudes. This humanizing approach to history though anticipated by Lubitsch's German costume pictures, became the model for Korda's later films.

Korda returned to Europe in 1930. At Paramount's French subsidiary at Joinville he made *Marius* (1931), the first of the trilogy of film adaptations from Marcel Pagnol's plays about Marseilles life.

Above: nymphs and satyrs sport together in Korda's The Private Life of Helen of Troy, *his only successful Hollywood film. Top left: Dream Factory on the High Street – Twickenham studios in the early Thirties. Top: Madeleine Carroll and John Gielgud in* The Secret Agent.

In the autumn of 1931 Alexander Korda came to Britain to direct 'quota' pictures for Paramount's British subsidiary, but within a few months he had decided to form his own company, London Film Productions. The company's sixth production, *The Private Life of Henry VIII* (1933), achieved Korda's goal of successful competition in world markets. It captured the American box-office and earned ten times its cost in its first world run. Historical costume films were considered passé at the time, but Korda 'humanized' a well-known historical subject, turning it into a sex romp which owed much to the vitality of Charles Laughton's performance.

For the next seven years, Korda sought to build on this film's success, first with other 'private life' films (*The Rise of Catherine the Great* and *The Private Life of Don Juan* in 1934, both box-office failures) and then with a series of over 30 prestige films for which Korda mixed and matched the nationalities and talents he had collected to achieve an international production. Although none of the subsequent films equalled *Henry*'s profitability (as they all cost much more to make, they could hardly be expected to recoup proportionally as much), even a selective list shows how much the British film industry owed to this emigré Hungarian: *The Scarlet Pimpernel* (1934), *Things to Come* and *Rembrandt* (both 1936), *Fire Over England* and *Knight Without Armour* (both 1937), *The Drum* (1938), *The Four Feathers* (1939) and *The Thief of Bagdad* (1940).

All these films exhibited the Korda stamp in varying degrees, according to the amount of control he exerted as head of production. This stamp is best defined by a brief analysis of his strengths and weaknesses as a film director. Although associated with all the 100 films which London Films produced between 1932 and 1956, he directed only 8 of them. The subjects he chose tended to fall into two categories: the satirical, high-society comedies: *Wedding Rehearsal* (1933), *The Girl from Maxim's* (1933) and *An Ideal Husband* (1947); and the 'private life' films – *The Private Life of Henry VIII, The Private Life of Don Juan, Rembrandt* and *Lady Hamilton* (1941).

The most outstanding quality common to all these films is their visual polish, which owes much to French cameraman Georges Périnal and to Korda's brother Vincent, London Films' head of art direction. These two men created impressive films that rivalled anything produced in Hollywood, both in grandeur of scope and sumptuousness of detail. Established actors and actresses were chosen for the lead parts, while Korda cast the supporting roles from his stable of young contract starlets. The films he directed and those he produced mostly share a nostalgic view of Britain and proudly champion her past glories.

However his main talents were entrepreneurial rather than directorial. As a film impresario, he combined a fertile imagination with a journalist's understanding of publicity and promotion. His special gift was his ability to manipulate finance and financiers, and it was this which was to be most exercised during the late Thirties.

The business of making internationally marketable films was an expensive one, and London Films required immense financial investment. This came from two sources: the American United Artists Company (in which Korda became a full partner in 1935) and the City of London's Prudential Assurance Company. The United Artists tie-up was a mixed blessing as UA owned no cinema chains itself and could not guarantee American distribution for Korda's films. Heavy

Right: Ann Boleyn (Merle Oberon), unjustly accused of infidelity by Henry, lays her head on the block in The Private Life of Henry VIII. *Far right:* Rembrandt *gave Laughton one of his finest screen roles. He responded with a restrained, warm-hearted performance. Below right and below:* The Drum *and* The Four Feathers *were action-packed films that recalled the heyday of the British Empire. Both were directed by Alexander Korda's brother, Zoltan.*

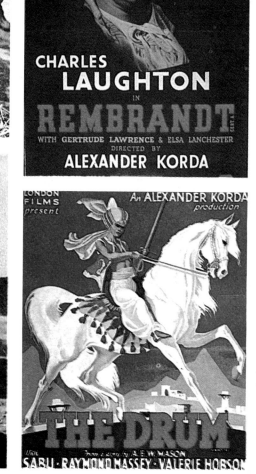

investment by the Prudential became Korda's mainstay in the Thirties and led to the building of Denham studios. Opened in 1936, Denham was the most up-to-date studio in Europe, yet it was too large for a single producer and, by the time it was fully operational, the investment boom in the film industry, caused by the success of *Henry VIII*, had given way to a slump. Korda gradually lost control of Denham to the financiers (eventually to J. Arthur Rank). He was finally forced to become a tenant producer in the studio he had built just a few years before.

Having gone to Hollywood in 1940 to supervise the completion of *The Thief of Bagdad*, Korda stayed there to direct *Lady Hamilton* in which Nelson's efforts against the French became an open metaphor for Britain's current war with Germany. This film earned him a subpoena from isolationist American senators who charged him with making the American branch of his company a centre for pro-British propaganda. Although criticized by many in Britain for having 'deserted' to Hollywood, Korda did in fact make several trans-atlantic crossings during the war and it now seems clear that he was acting as a courier for Winston Churchill. In 1942 he was knighted by King George VI, the first film personality to be so honoured.

In the summer of 1943, Sir Alexander Korda returned to London and spent two frustrating years trying to set up the merged MGM–British/London Film Productions company from which he then resigned in late 1945 having completed only one film. *Perfect Strangers* (1945). Throughout 1946 he was busy resurrecting London Films as a separate company. Korda, tired of directing, was now the executive producer – an administrator and businessman. After 1947, his name ceased to appear on the film credits, and as the name disappeared, so did the old Korda style. His major triumph during his last years was in drawing a large number of independent British film-makers to his company and allowing them freedom to work without interference. Directors like Michael Powell and Emeric Pressburger, Carol Reed, David Lean, Anthony Asquith, Frank Launder and Sidney Gilliat and Laurence Olivier made some of their best films while working under the aegis of Korda's umbrella organization.

To obtain adequate distribution for these films, Korda gained control of British Lion in 1946, and rebuilt and refitted Shepperton Studios which became London Film's production base. During the 1948 financial crisis in the film industry, Korda's British Lion secured the first government loan to the film business through the newly created National Film

Right: Laurence Olivier defeating the Spanish Armada in Fire Over England, *directed by Hollywood director William K. Howard and filmed by ace American cameraman James Wong Howe. Below: another American, the art director William Cameron Menzies was recruited by Korda for the futuristic, spectacular* Things to Come.

Above: The American title and poster for Lady Hamilton *tended to draw attention to the film's romantic or erotic content. However it provoked far more controversy in the USA for its thinly veiled anti-fascist message – delivered by Nelson (Laurence Olivier) in the form of an impassioned speech against the ambitions of Napoleon Bonaparte – which warned particularly against the dangers of attempting to appease the forces of tyranny.*

Finance Corporation. By 1954 the NFFC loan, amounting to £3 million, had still not been repaid, and with the appointment of an official receiver for British Lion, the second Korda film empire collapsed. Even after this debacle, Korda was able to form new financial alliances which enabled him to continue producing films until his death in 1956.

Korda was almost as famous for the films he did not make as for the ones he did – indeed, he received the honour of having an entire television documentary devoted to footage from a film, *I Claudius* (directed by Josef von Sternberg), which was abandoned after a month's shooting. He was more successful as a producer than as a director and his reputation for extravagance now seems deserved. Yet he demonstrated to the world 'that in spectacle and lavishness of production the British industry could legitimately hope to match the best that America could produce'.

The Late Thirties

After a decade of the quota regulations, the potential had gone out of British production companies. On the other hand the cinema business was booming. Throughout the Thirties audiences grew and grew. Funds poured into the exhibition side of the business which remained profitable even during the Depression. Gaumont – British and Associated British Cinemas both became highly profitable circuits and were organized as large vertical combines, with their own production, renting and exhibition branches.

Gaumont–British Picture Corporation, run by the Ostrer family, was made up of three companies: the Gaumont and Gainsborough studios in London, a nation-wide film distribution network and the Gaumont–British cinema circuit. By 1929 the company controlled 287 cinemas throughout Britain. Their chief competitor was ABC, headed by the tough, aggressive John Maxwell, who later tried to wrest control of Gaumont–British from the Ostrer family. At the beginning of the Thirties ABC owned 88 cinemas, the prolific British International Pictures studio at Elstree and the distribution firm Wardour Films. During the winter of 1933–34, the company was reorganized as the Associated British Picture Corporation and by 1938 it had increased its number of cinemas to 325.

Another major film exhibitor was the energetic and likeable Oscar Deutsch, whose chain of Odeon cinemas was built up over the decade, his first cinema having been built at Perry Bar, Birmingham in 1930. A new approach to urban planning in the Thirties created large suburbs which contained ideal sites for the new Odeons. These cinemas were broadly uniform in their functional art-deco appearance and created a modern brand image for the circuit.

In 1937 Odeon merged with County Cinemas to form a circuit of 250 cinemas and had first call on all United Artists and Korda films. At this point Odeon became the third circuit in size and worth £6 million as a company. Towards the end of 1939, the Odeon board was enlarged to include two members of the new General Cinema Finance Corporation; one of them was the future mogul J. Arthur Rank.

A Methodist millionaire with flour-milling and other business interests, Rank had entered films in the early Thirties to improve the production of religious films. In 1936 his company moved into feature production and studio ownership. His arrival on the board of Odeon was his first step into exhibition – a business he all but monopolized.

While film exhibition was flourishing, production was depressed. A government committee under the then Lord Moyne studied the problem and tried to accommodate the opposing interests of the big combines (Gaumont–British and ABC) and the independent producers like Basil Dean. The problem continued to be the quality of British films and the difficulty of selling them in America. The new Quota Act was finally passed in 1938. The committee who had framed the legislation had attempted to ensure higher quality in British films by insisting that a film should meet certain minimum costs in order to be eligible for distribution as a quota film.

As might have been hoped, the introduction of the minimum-cost clause killed off the cheap 'quota quickie'. It also put a premium on expensive films and led to the production of some high-quality pictures. But film production as a whole did not revive. In the first year of the new quota regulations, no feature films emerged from eight of the British studios. The labour union claimed that unemployment among technicians stood at 80 per cent. Fewer 'quota quickies' meant, moreover, that film production continued to decline numerically.

Worse still for those who had hoped for a truly national picture-making industry, statistics revealed that all but 25 per cent of films made in 1938 were American productions of one kind or another. The dilemma central to the British film industry remained unsolved: quality films were expensive and to cover their costs they had to be exported to the USA. Once again the effort to achieve this had put the industry in the hands of the American major companies.

In order to forestall the British government's moves against them, the American majors had begun serious production in Britain on a large scale. Twentieth Century-Fox made a horse-racing drama, *Wings of the Morning* (1937), that had the distinction of being the first British film in Technicolor. The film starred Henry Fonda and the popular French star Annabella and was produced by Robert T. Kane, who had been Paramount's chief in Paris at the start of the Thirties. Kane retained Annabella for his next English production, *Under the Red Robe* (1937). This historical romance was another prestige picture, with Conrad Veidt starring opposite Annabella. The film brought together the great talents of cameramen Georges Périnal and James Wong Howe, under the direction of the Swedish director Victor Sjöström.

Columbia embarked on production at Korda's Denham studio, making several good thrillers, among them *Q-Planes* and *The Spy in Black* (both 1939), which promoted the beautiful Valerie Hobson into a star, after she had been neglected for several years by British producers.

MGM made perhaps the biggest impact of all. The plans they announced when Michael Balcon joined them as head of production early in 1937 included *A Yank at Oxford* and one film he was to make in Hollywood. But Balcon and MGM were to part company within 18 months of agreeing a long-term producer's contract.

A Yank at Oxford (1938) was a massive undertaking that involved a mixed American/British cast. A vast and varied collection of writers that included John Monk Saunders, Sidney Gilliat, Hugh Walpole, Ben Travers, Herman J. Mankiewicz and F. Scott Fitzgerald had a shot at the script. Jack Conway was the director and the film sold well on both sides of the Atlantic.

Balcon's old friend Victor Saville took a different approach to MGM. As an independent producer he had prudently acquired the film rights to A.J. Cronin's recent best-selling novel *The Citadel* a book that MGM wished Balcon to produce. Saville was not inhibited by the MGM regime and he

Below left: Annabella and Henry Fonda in the charming racing romance Wings of the Morning. *Left: Robert Donat in the leading role of the shy schoolmaster in* Goodbye, Mr Chips, *for which he won the 1939 Best Actor Oscar, narrowly beating Clark Gable, who had been nominated for another MGM film –* Gone With the Wind. *Below: filming* A Yank at Oxford *with (left to right) American director Jack Conway, British producer Michael Balcon and Hollywood star Robert Taylor.*

soon found himself producing both *The Citadel* and *Goodbye Mr Chips* (1939). Once again the directors, King Vidor and Sam Wood, were American but the main star of both was the British actor Robert Donat. These two films were highly successful and earned Saville his passport to Hollywood, where he was to remain during the war.

During the late Thirties other top British film-makers like Hitchcock, Wilcox and Korda found their way to Hollywood. Balcon, however, turned his back on the American market and was to spend the rest of his career in the British cinema. He stepped into Basil Dean's shoes at Ealing Studios where Dean had come under increasing criticism from the board. Balcon assembled many of his former Gaumont team and continued the Ealing tradition of providing vehicles for music-hall comics, but in certain other films he introduced a more realistic treatment of ordinary people and themes. *There*

Ain't No Justice (1939), an unassuming film starring Jimmy Hanley as a young boxer, was scarcely noticed as a forerunner of what later became known as the Ealing style.

By the end of the decade, British film technicians and directors who had proved themselves in the tough training school of 'quota quickies' and documentary film production, were ready to undertake the difficult task of filming the war. On its own the 1938 Quota Act is unlikely to have fostered a prosperous national industry. Early in 1939, an important daily newspaper carried the headline 'Films Act Has Failed'. The following day its correspondence columns had a letter from Basil Dean saying bitterly, 'I told you so'. Whether the making of quality American films would have expanded in the Forties is hard to say; with the outbreak of war the American majors withdrew from Britain and the character of the native industry was to change beyond recognition.

CHAPTER 10
The World at War

When Archduke Ferdinand was assassinated at Sarajevo in June 1914, precipitating World War I, the movie industry was still in its infancy. Many pioneers were just getting into their stride, exploring the power of the medium and its potential hold over audiences. When Hitler invaded Poland in September 1939, precipitating World War II, a huge, profitable, world-wide industry had long been established with massive resources of equipment, manpower and 'star power'.

Britain

Britain's television service, only three years old and serving a tiny minority, was promptly shut down at the start of the war. Film-studio space was requisitioned for storing ammunition, greatcoats and all the paraphernalia of war. But the industry continued. Indeed, the experience of working with limited resources under pressure concentrated the minds of many film-makers. And the involvement of the entire country in the war effort – all classes, both sexes – made many old cinema genres and attitudes inadequate. No longer could studios rely upon laboured farces or thrillers featuring stereotypes of the elegant rich or the rude poor.

The transformation, however, did not occur overnight. Alexander Korda's *The Lion Has Wings* (dir. Michael Powell, Brian Desmond Hurst, Adrian Brunel), a hopeful salute to the fighting power of the RAF, was rushed into release in the autumn of 1939. The film was a mixture of newsreel footage, and mocked-up battles but was over-burdened by a quaintly genteel, fictional sub-plot.

Yet slowly the industry buckled to. The Ministry of Information, after many changes of personnel and unfortunate gestures like the slogan '*Your* Courage, *Your* Cheerfulness, *Your* Resolution, will Bring *Us* Victory' (hardly the best way to bind a nation together), established a solid system of film distribution, sending out to cinemas short films on war topics every week. In addition, travelling projectionists showed films in those parts of the country where there were no proper cinemas.

Style and subject in these shorts varied tremendously. Most artistically polished were the poetic essays of Humphrey Jennings, who found in the war an ideal way of expressing his strong feelings for Britain's cultural heritage. Richard Massingham found a similar niche providing crisp, comic illustrations of wartime regulations, such as bathing in only five inches of water.

Left: an Air Raid Precautions (ARP) Rescue Squad search a bombed building for survivors – from Fox Newsfilm footage, taken during World War II.

At the other end of the scale there were filmed lectures given by Ministry men seated behind desks and blinking nervously. These films were so embarrassing that cinema managers occasionally showed them with the curtains tactfully drawn. But it is clear that some of this huge output had considerable effect abroad – particularly in America, uninvolved in the fighting until Japan attacked Pearl Harbor in December 1941.

Jennings' and Harry Watt's *London Can Take It* (devised for showing in Allied countries in 1940) filled out its blitz images with a commentary by the American journalist Quentin Reynolds, full of praise for London's 'unconquerable spirit and courage'. Later, there was much direct film cooperation between the Allies, as each arm of the services prepared photographed accounts of their operations. In the war's last stages Carol Reed and the American Garson Kanin came together to produce *The True Glory* (1945), a film charting Europe's liberation.

But the greatest changes in British cinema occurred in feature films. Previously the feature industry had been inhibited by American competition, and the presence of so many foreign moguls and visiting directors hardly promoted indigenous product. But with the war, the visitors returned home and rising talent, previously confined to scriptwriting or editing, eagerly moved into the director's chair – David Lean, Charles Frend, Frank Launder, Sidney Gilliat were among them.

Initially the cinema continued to reflect the rigidly stratified class system enshrined in British films of the Thirties, remaining resolutely middle class in tone and values. The epitome of the romanticized, class-bound and hopelessly out-of-touch war film was Ealing's *Ships With Wings* (dir. Sergei Nolbandov, 1941). Michael Balcon, the head of Ealing studios, resolved henceforth to produce essentially realistic stories of Britain at war. He turned, therefore, to the only group in Britain familiar with the evocation of real-life – the documentarists. This group of talented film-makers, nurtured by John Grierson in the Thirties, was committed to the concept of realism in setting, mood, and content and to the dramatizing of the everyday experience of ordinary people. Several members, notably Harry Watt and Alberto Cavalcanti, went to work for Ealing studios, and the documentary influence permeated feature-film production.

The image of a nation divided by class barriers was replaced by the concept of 'The People's War', the idea of ordinary people pulling together to defeat a common foe. Ealing's war films exemplified this new image: *The Foreman Went to France* (dir. Charles Frend, 1942) told how a determined foreman (Clifford Evans) retrieves a vital piece of machinery from France, aided by two soldiers (a Cockney and a Scot) and an American secretary: *San Demetrio, London* (dir. Charles Frend, 1943) recounted the true story of the salvaging of a merchant-navy tanker by part of its crew, a cross-section of various types of men. A similar cross-section made up an army patrol pinned down in a desert oasis in *Nine Men* (dir. Harry Watt, 1943); *The Bells Go Down* (dir. Basil Dearden, 1943) dramatized the work of the Auxiliary Fire Service in London, stressing the comradeship and dedication of the team. Significantly, none of these films had an officer hero. Indeed the personality and attitudes of the old-style officer and gentleman were comprehensively demolished in Michael Powell and Emeric Pressburger's *The Life and Death of Colonel Blimp* (1943). The title figure (played by Roger Livesey), an officer, gentleman and sportsman of the old Imperial school who would rather lose the war than resort to using the methods of the Germans, is shown as a touching but wholly anachronistic figure. Comradeship and cooperation, dedication to duty and self-sacrifice, a self-deprecating good humour and unselfconscious modesty characterized the films of the fighting services. The war produced a masterpiece for each service. For the navy, there was *In Which We Serve* (1942), written, produced, co-directed (with David Lean) and scored by Noel Coward, who also played the lead role. It was based on the true story of HMS *Kelly*, which had been commanded by Coward's friend Lord Louis Mountbatten and had been sunk off Crete. The film focuses on three characters: the captain, a petty officer and an ordinary seaman. Their differences of status, background and situation are submerged by their common loyalty to their ship. The army film – Carol Reed's *The Way Ahead* (1944), scripted by Peter Ustinov and Eric Ambler – was a semi-documentary account of how a group of conscripts from all walks of life are brought together and welded into a disciplined fighting army unit. And Anthony Asquith's *The Way to the Stars* (1945), scripted by Terence Rattigan, recalled life on a single RAF station between 1940 and 1944 with its joys and losses, its tragedies and its camaraderie. The film also took in the arrival and integration of the Americans into the war in Europe.

The contribution of women to the war effort was vital, and the cinema paid tribute to them, reflecting the dramatic change in their social roles and expectations. Leslie Howard's *The Gentle Sex* (1943) was a female version of *The Way Ahead*, a realistic account of the training of a group of women from all classes and backgrounds in the Auxiliary Territorial Service (ATS). Frank Launder and Sidney Gilliat's moving and memorable *Millions Like Us* (1943) dramatized the experiences of a group of girls drafted to work in an aircraft factory.

These were films with sympathetic and realistic characters and situations to which ordinary people could relate.

In retrospect, the most redundant propaganda features

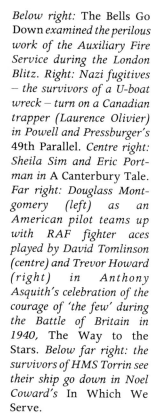

Below right: The Bells Go Down *examined the perilous work of the Auxiliary Fire Service during the London Blitz. Right: Nazi fugitives – the survivors of a U-boat wreck – turn on a Canadian trapper (Laurence Olivier) in Powell and Pressburger's* 49th Parallel. *Centre right: Sheila Sim and Eric Portman in* A Canterbury Tale. *Far right: Douglass Montgomery (left) as an American pilot teams up with RAF fighter aces played by David Tomlinson (centre) and Trevor Howard (right) in Anthony Asquith's celebration of the courage of 'the few' during the Battle of Britain in 1940,* The Way to the Stars. *Below far right: the survivors of HMS Torrin see their ship go down in Noel Coward's* In Which We Serve.

were those warning against the danger from fifth columnists — simply because there were no fifth columnists in Britain. But warnings against complacency were never wasted and the cycle produced at least two memorable films. Thorold Dickinson's *Next of Kin* (1942) was a chilling illustration of the slogan 'Careless Talk Costs Lives', demonstrating the way in which a chain of fifth columnists and Nazi spies assemble the information enabling them to destroy a British landing on the French coast. Alberto Cavalcanti's *Went the Day Well?* (1942) was an equally compelling account of a group of Nazi paratroopers taking over an English village (with the aid of the local squire) until defeated by the gallant villagers.

Why Britain Fought   Films about *why* Britain was fighting were rarer than films about *how* she was fighting, perhaps because of the difficulty of rendering ideological and philosophical concepts as acceptable entertainment. Perhaps the best programmatic account was provided by Michael Powell's *49th Parallel* (1941). Financed by the Ministry of Information and filmed partly in Canada with an all-star cast, it told the gripping story of the stranded crew-members of a Nazi submarine travelling across Canada towards neutral USA and encountering *en route* various representatives of democracy. An uncommitted French-Canadian trapper (Laurence Olivier) turns against them when they maltreat the 'racially inferior' Eskimos. A democratic Christian community of Hutterite exiles demonstrate the workability of a system of equality and

cooperation. A donnish aesthete (Leslie Howard) beats one of the Germans to a pulp when they burn his books and pictures. Finally a Canadian soldier (Raymond Massey) takes on and defeats the fanatical commander of the fugitives (Eric Portman).

Michael Powell (with Emeric Pressburger) also directed *A Canterbury Tale* (1944), a complex, absorbing fable which mystified contemporary critics. It evoked the England of Chaucer and Shakespeare, the Kent countryside, half-timbered cottages and quiet churchyards. The spirit of this England was embodied by Thomas Culpeper (Eric Portman), gentleman farmer and amateur historian, who seeks to communicate its values to a group of latter-day Canterbury pilgrims, all unseeing and unfeeling products of a modern, materialist world. It represented a sense of the living past, the beauty of the English countryside and the enduring relationship of man and the soil. Less mystical, but no less engaging, was Bernard Miles' *Tawny Pipit* (1944), in which a hierarchical rural society, led by the squire and the vicar, bands together to preserve the nesting place of the rare British bird, the tawny pipit.

Anthony Asquith's *The Demi-Paradise* (1943) artfully demonstrated how the preconceived notions about Britain held by an earnest Russian engineer (Laurence Olivier) are dispelled by his actual encounters with the living power of tradition and indicates what several other films divined as the British secret weapon – their sense of humour. The England that these films summoned up was essentially a mythic one – pre-industrial, timeless and hierarchical. It was the dream of a different sort of England that was to lead to the Labour victory of 1945, the logical culmination of those other films which had stressed the lowering of class barriers, the solidarity of ordinary people and the ideals of freedom and justice for the oppressed.

British films found an audience and a popularity they had never enjoyed before. As the war went on escapist entertainment increased in volume and popularity. Traditional tosh was given a topical inflection in *Dangerous Moonlight* (1941), where a Polish concert pianist joined the RAF and played Richard Addinsell's popular 'Warsaw Concerto'. Gainsborough studios produced period melodramas like *The Man in Grey* (1943), with ladies and gentlemen behaving amorally, dressed in wigs, masks and riding boots. On a far higher artistic level Laurence Olivier's *Henry V* (1944), dedicated to the commandos, used Shakespeare's heroic poetry as a clarion call to the nation. And no world war, however devastating, could halt Gabriel Pascal's determination to film Shaw's *Caesar and Cleopatra* (1945), which began shooting at Denham six days after D-Day, despite the threat of flying bombs and the difficulties of securing nubile young ladies and white peacocks to flit by in the backgrounds.

Germany

While British cinema stumbled uncertainly into war production, Germany began with its propaganda machine in top working condition. Ever since Hitler secured control in 1933, his propaganda minister Josef Goebbels had organized the industry to fit Nazi requirements. Jews were banned immediately; a film censor office was established in 1934; film criticism (and all arts criticism) was abolished in 1936; thereafter newspapers could print only facts, not opinions. The independent studios, including the mighty Ufa, were absorbed by the government during 1937. By 1939 many of Germany's best film talents had emigrated; those that re-

Right: the pseudo-documentary Der Ewige Jude *was among the most virulent anti-Semitic propaganda shown in wartime Germany.* Below right: Ohm Krüger *charged the British with brutality in the course of their imperialist adventures in Africa. Far right: the epic* Kadetten *extolled the bravery of young men dying for the Fatherland. Opposite page, right: Nikolai Cherkasov as the aging Tsar in Eisenstein's* Ivan the Terrible. *Above left: the closing moments of Visconti's debut film* Ossessione: *Giovanna (Clara Calamai) dies in the arms of her lover Gino (Massimo Girotti). Below left: Pina (Anna Magnani) falls foul of German troops in* Rome, Open City.

mained were regarded as part of the country's fighting forces.

Goebbels sensed how powerful a weapon film could be, but he had known for a long time that audiences resented hard-core propaganda in fictional, dramatic formats. Instead propaganda was channelled into newsreels, compiled or doctored from material shot at the fighting fronts and decked out with animated maps full of pulsating arrows that indicated German advances.

The newsreels were eventually lengthened to as much as forty minutes, and there are reports that cinema doors were carefully secured so that there was no possibility of escape. Special productions were concocted to lower the morale of countries about to be occupied; *Feuertaufe* (1940, Baptism of Fire), a film that gloried the Luftwaffe's conquest of Poland, was shown at the German Embassy in Oslo four days before the invasion of Norway in April 1940. The most notorious production of all, however was *Der Ewige Jude* (1940, The Eternal Jew), an illustrated lecture by Dr Fritz Hippler designed to fan the flames of anti-Semitism.

Once the newsreels were over, audiences could settle down to suffer bombastic epics glorifying various sections of the armed forces, or Veit Harlan's viciously anti-Semitic *Jud Süss* (1940, Jew Süss) – a key exhibit in the post-war trials. Other films attempted to influence German youth, including *Kadetten* (1941, Cadets) which told the story of young Prussians fighting in 1760 during the Seven Years' War. History, in fact, proved a boon for German film-makers who wanted to please their Nazi overlords without being rabidly propagandistic. German history was, after all, well-stocked with belligerently nationalistic heroes. Films about Frederick the Great of Prussia had long formed a separate genre and the actor Otto Gebühr did little else but play him.

Colonial activities in Africa and the Boer War proved a

fruitful source of anti-British propaganda. *Ohm Krüger* (1941, Uncle Kruger), though one of the more impressive productions, offered a wickedly coarse caricature of Queen Victoria and credited the British with inventing concentration camps. Other films slanted the same way included *Titanic* (1943), where the ship hit the iceberg as a result of the sins of Jewish–English plutocracy, and two films by Goebbels' brother-in-law Max Kimmich, portraying British brutalities in Ireland: *Der Fuchs von Glenarvon* (1940, The Fox of Glenarvon) and *Mein Leben für Irland* (1941, My Life for Ireland).

Many other films were simply escapist entertainment with the odd twinge of propaganda. Goebbels spent much money developing Agfacolor so that German audiences would not lose out on colour films while the rest of the world was enjoying the early Technicolor movies. In celebration of Ufa's twenty-fifth anniversary, Goebbels planned the highly elaborate fantasy film *Münchhausen* (1943), studied Disney's feature cartoons and Korda's *The Thief of Bagdad* (1940), and produced something almost comparable. But his monumental undertaking was *Kolberg*, begun in 1943 and completed towards the end of 1944. Geared to the declining course of the war, the film shrewdly portrayed the citizens of Kolberg, beseiged during the Napoleonic wars and heroically holding out against amazing odds. By the time the film was ready for release in early 1945, it had no value as propaganda for Germany was close to defeat.

Italy

Italy, Germany's ally in Europe, went about its film-making as it went about its fighting, with little of the manic fervour displayed by Goebbels. Most of the country's fascist tub-thumping had been performed in the late Thirties, when

mammoth spectacles like *Scipione l'Africano* (1937, Scipio Africanus) were mounted to reflect Italy's new image as an imperial, conquering power. Mussolini had ensured that the film industry was well equipped for the task. The vast Cinecittà film studios were built outside Rome and a film school (the Centro Sperimentale di Cinematografia) was established. Mussolini's own son Vittorio pursued an active interest in the medium, securing his name on film credits and on the mast-head of a cinema magazine.

Many directors in the war avoided overt propaganda by retreating to unassuming romantic comedies and tales of provincial life. Some talents did manage to cut through the dross. Alessandro Blasetti's *Quattro Passi fra le Nuvole* (1942, *Four Steps in the Clouds*) focused sharply on the torments of daily life and had a script co-written by Cesare Zavattini, who was later associated with the director Vittorio De Sica and the neo-realist movement. In the same year, Luchino Visconti's *Ossessione* (1942, Obsession), a story of adultery and murder, exploded onto the screen with a kind of brute force unseen before in the Italian cinema and proved to be a precursor of neo-realism.

Equally distinctive, though now largely forgotten, were the films of Francesco De Robertis. He was head of the Naval Ministry's film department and made features such as *Uomini sul Fondo* (1941, *SOS Submarine*), imbued with the spirit, and often the footage, of documentary, with non-professional players and location shooting. *La Nave Bianca* (1941, The White Ship), for instance, began as a straight documentary about the brave work of a hospital ship. When the authorities wanted to boost the Italian entries at the 1941 Venice Film Festival, De Robertis obligingly built in a love story. Despite such compromises, his films had great impact, and his assistant, Roberto Rossellini (effectively the director of *La*

Nave Bianca), followed this style in his own wartime films, *Un Pilota Ritorna* (1942, A Pilot Returns) and *L'Uomo della Croce* (1943, The Man of the Cross).

When Italy surrendered to the Allies and declared war on Germany, it only produced more turmoil with facilities, equipment and talent scattered throughout the country. De Robertis went north, obstinately loyal to Mussolini who was now installed as puppet-head of the short-lived Salò Republic. Rossellini went south and helped establish the cinema branch of the Committee of National Liberation. A few weeks before the Allies entered Rome in June 1944, his film *Roma, Città Aperta* (1945, *Rome, Open City*) went into production. It was a harsh, moving tale of a Resistance leader's betrayal. But the Italian cinema had already encountered its own kind of liberation.

The USSR

The Soviet Union's path through the war was just as chequered as Italy's. After several years of mounting tension on its western borders with the dismembered parts of the old Austro–Hungarian Empire, Stalin concluded the Non-Aggression Pact with Hitler in 1939. Feature films described the occupation of Poland, the invasion of Finland: items with anti-German leanings such as *Professor Mamlock* (1938) and *Aleksandr Nevskii* (1938, *Alexander Nevsky*) swiftly returned to the vaults. But they soon emerged after June 22, 1941, when Germany's shock invasion brought the pact to an end. Film studios were now uprooted from Moscow to safer surroundings. Various Soviet policies were modified and the customary anti-religious bias was abandoned. Suddenly the much-despised Tsarist generals received homage from the cinema for their part in the Napoleonic wars and other conflicts. There were also new forms of presenting films in the

Soviet Union during the war. From August 1941 so-called 'Fighting Film Albums' appeared in cinemas every month: these were a mixture of short films that included miniature dramas, satiric japes and war-effort propaganda. Cameramen at the front maintained a constant stream of filmed dispatches which were edited into powerful documentaries. Alexander Dovzhenko supervised and wrote a moving commentary for *Bitva za Nashu Sovetskuyu Ukrainu* (1943, *The Fight for Our Soviet Ukraine*) that reflected his feelings for his homeland.

Soviet features tended to follow the usual propaganda pattern, spotlighting German atrocities or the heroic activities of the partisans. But as in other countries pure entertainment was never neglected; indeed its quantity increased as the war continued. One of the most popular films of 1944 was a musical entitled *V Shest Chasov Vechera Posle Voiny* (*At 6 pm After the War*).

The celebrated Soviet director Sergei Eisenstein spent most of the war engaged on *Ivan Grozny* (*Ivan the Terrible*) in Mosfilm's wartime headquarters at Alma-Ata in Kazakhstan. By the end of December 1944, the first part of the projected trilogy was ready for release. The film was a ferocious and monumental excursion into Russia's past, with Tsar Ivan bludgeoning his way from childhood to coronation and conquest. As a cinematic history lesson, the film was complex and unsettling for audiences.

France

On June 22, 1940, Marshal Pétain, the French Chief of State, signed an armistice with Germany. Under its terms Paris became part of an occupied zone, and was to remain so for just over four years. In June 1944 the Allies landed on the French coast; by August Paris was liberated.

However deep a resentment and humiliation the French people may have felt at their subjugation to Nazism, the French cinema flourished as never before. Something above three hundred and fifty features were made in these fifty months of occupation, including such landmarks of French film as *Le Corbeau* (1943, *The Raven*) and *Les Anges du Péché* (1943, *Angels of Sin*).

Yet there is remarkably little record of overt and willing collaboration by French film-makers with the Nazi Party and its ideologies. Indeed, a number of those artists who remained active – among them the directors Jacques Becker, Jean Grémillon, Jean Painlevé and the actor Pierre Blanchar – were responsible for the formation of the clandestine 'Committee of Liberation of the French Cinema'.

This is not to say that Goebbels did not exert comprehensive control over the French film industry. For years before the war, German films had been successfully infiltrating the French market. With the Occupation – and to an extent through the expropriation of Jewish interests – the Germans acquired complete economic control of about a third of the industry: production, press, distribution and theatres. French film was subjected to a dual censorship by the German Propaganda Ministry, and by the German-backed Vichy government whose powers in this respect nominally covered only the so-called 'free' zone of France.

Two factors contributed to the freedom allowed to French film-makers. One was the failure of German-made pictures to attract the French public. At the start of the Occupation there was a determined effort to put German films onto French screens, but audiences tacitly boycotted them. As a result, receipts for French films rose considerably, thereby enhancing the financial prosperity of the home industry. Moreover,

the Germans looked to French production to replace the films they were no longer buying from Hollywood, and so left film-makers a free hand in the field of what were regarded as purely entertainment pictures.

The only direct injection of German money into French production was through the German-owned Continental company which produced thirty of the more expensive pictures of the period. Continental concentrated particularly on 'American-style' subjects, such as Henri Decoin's light comedy *Premier Rendez-vous* (1941, First Meeting) and detective thrillers. Henri-Georges Clouzot, who had made a number of German versions of French films in Berlin in the early Thirties, scripted two of the most important of these thrillers: Georges Lacombe's *Le Dernier des Six* (1941, Last of the Six) and Decoin's *Les Inconnus Dans la Maison* (1942, *Strangers in the House*), adapted from a pre-war Georges Simenon novel but turned into an attack on non-Aryans, useful as propaganda for the Vichy government.

Clouzot went on to make his debut as a director with a thriller, *L'Assassin Habite au 21* (1942, The Killer Lives at No. 21), which remains one of his best works. His next film, *Le Corbeau*, based on a real-life story concerning the circulation of poison-pen letters in a French village, became the centre of a bitter controversy when the Nazis used it as anti-French propaganda in Occupied Europe.

Jacques Becker, who also began his directing career during the Occupation, was a pupil of Jean Renoir and worked in a

Below: in Le Corbeau, *Pierre Fresnay played a doctor victimized by a writer of poison-pen letters.*

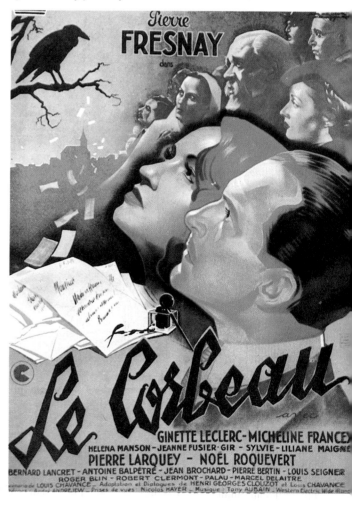

realist style that combined elements from French pre-war cinema and from the American detective genre. His first film was *Le Dernier Atout* (1942, The Trump Card), a brilliant and commercially successful detective thriller. With *Goupi Mains Rouges* (1943, *It Happened at the Inn*), Becker went beyond his detective-story plot to create a rich portrayal of French rural life. *Falbalas* (1945, *Paris Frills*), completed around the time of the Liberation, was the first of the Parisian subjects on which his later fame was to rest. Set in a top fashion house, the film is a wonderfully detailed description of the French bourgeoisie under the Occupation.

Jean Grémillon made two of the few strictly realist works of the period. *Lumière d'Eté* (1943, Summer Light) contrasted the life of construction workers on a dam with the decadence of their employers (evidently intended to symbolize the way of life under the Vichy administration). *Le Ciel Est à Vous* (1944, The Sky Is Yours), based on the real-life story of two ordinary Frenchmen who achieved a world flying record, was seen as a symbol of French aspirations towards liberation.

Robert Bresson commenced a career of unparalleled, uncompromising creative independence with *Les Anges du Péché*, bringing cinema audiences their first encounter with his metaphysical and spiritual concerns and his severe, demanding style. It was followed by a no less austere modernization of Diderot in *Les Dames du Bois de Boulogne* (1945, Ladies of the Bois de Boulogne), scripted by Jean Cocteau.

The most characteristic films from the Occupation period,

Below: Maria Cesarès in Les Dames du Bois de Boulogne.
Bottom: Les Visiteurs du Soir.

however, are a handful of glittering flights into fantastic worlds or romantic periods – areas where neither Goebbels' nor Vichy's film censors could follow. The veteran Marcel L'Herbier made *La Nuit Fantastique* (1942, *Fantastic Night*), Jean Delannoy followed *Pontcarral, Colonel d'Empire* (1942, Pontcarral, Colonel of the Empire) – a historical drama that had clear contemporary references – with *L'Eternel Retour* (1943, *Love Eternal*), a modern version of the legend of Tristan and Iseult. Both the latter and *Le Baron Fantôme* (1943, The Phantom Baron), a charming trifle directed by Serge de Poligny, were scripted by Cocteau. Claude Autant-Lara concentrated upon the decorative past in *Lettres d'Amour* (1942, Love Letters), *Le Mariage de Chiffon* (1943, The Chiffon Marriage) and *Douce* (1943). The prolific Abel Gance dedicated *La Vénus Aveugle* (1941, Blind Venus) to Marshal Pétain, and followed it with another work of characteristic romanticism, *Le Capitaine Fracasse* (1942, Captain Fracasse).

Two films above all stand as monuments of the French cinema under Nazi Occupation. Marcel Carné moved into a new phase of his career with *Les Visiteurs du Soir* (1942, *The Devil's Own Envoy*). Visually superb, this evocation of a medieval world, in which the Devil visits a castle at night but is unable to conquer true love, seemed to audiences a symbol of Hitler's final inability to crush the nation's spirit. *Les Enfants du Paradis* (1945, *Children of Paradise*) remains Carné's masterpiece and the most memorable work of the time. This fable of Love and Death, Good and Evil, is set in the Paris of the 1840s. With its pictorial splendour and the complexity of its intertwining of life and theatre, the film has lost none of its attraction for succeeding generations.

Left: Madeleine Sologne and Jean Marais in L'Eternal Retour. *Below: Barrault and Arletty in* Les Enfants du Paradis.

CHAPTER II
The Show Goes On

World War II – which for Europe lasted from September 1939 to May 1945, for the USA from December 1941 to August 1945 – galvanized Hollywood to satisfy a boom in the home market that fully compensated for the widespread loss of European audiences. Cinemagoers were not only eager to see war and war-related films; they desperately wanted escapist entertainment, in particular comedies, musicals and Westerns. In addition, the general mood of anxiety and fear generated by the war created a new Hollywood genre, comprising complex, disturbing private-eye movies and crime films, later termed *film noir*.

The style of *film noir* was characterized by dramatic use of light and shade, unusual camera angles, complex cutting, and disjointed time scales, whereby a story would be told by means of flashbacks, dream sequences or from different points of view. Though some of these devices had been employed before – notably in the German Expressionist films of the Twenties – the director Orson Welles helped popularize their use in the Forties, combining them with deep-focus photography and overlapping sound in his highly influential debut film *Citizen Kane* (1940).

Other artistic conquests of the period included the development of a sophisticated style of film musical exemplified by MGM's *Meet Me in St Louis* (1944) and *On the Town* (1949). The economies forced on Hollywood in the late Forties resulted in a realist tendency parallel to, and perhaps influenced by, developments in Europe. Hollywood film-makers began to take their cameras out of the studios and into the streets.

Musicals
When the Fred Astaire-Ginger Rogers team broke up in 1939 after *The Story of Vernon and Irene Castle*, it was the end of an era. Gone were the suave elegance and deco chic of the Thirties and gone was the musical based on the romantic tussles of a dancing team – for although people kept looking for a new partner for Fred Astaire, he never found one for more than two films together.

Obviously tastes were making that noticeable, if not exactly definable, shift which seems to occur every decade or so. Musicals, apparently, were particularly vulnerable to this change. In a spirit of try-anything-once, film-makers hit on two new gimmicks – youth and the popular classics. Of course, if the two could be combined in one package that would be even better. As luck would have it, just such a

Left: Lucille Ball tames her 'panthers' in the 'Bring on the Beautiful Girls' sequence of MGM's star-studded musical revue, Ziegfeld Follies.

combination was waiting in the wings – Deanna Durbin (b.1921). She was pretty, wholesome and hardly more than a child, but with a true adult coloratura soprano.

Durbin had made her first appearance in an MGM short, *Every Sunday* (1936) with another singing hopeful, Judy Garland. She was then snapped up by Joe Pasternak at Universal and put into a cheery comedy with music – *Three Smart Girls* (1937) – a low-budget film which made millions and saved the company from bankruptcy.

The high-school musical which provided a favourite location for 'jazzing the classics' flourished both at MGM, in the early days of Mickey Rooney and Judy Garland – *Babes in Arms* (1939) and its successors – and, in much humbler circumstances, at Universal. There Donald O'Connor and Peggy Ryan, who were hep, and Gloria Jean, who was not, appeared variously combined in any number of B films about co-eds, young army recruits and the like; all three were in *When Johnny Comes Marching Home*, *Mr Big* (both 1943) and *Follow the Boys* (1944).

Even MGM, which tended to be a law unto itself, had – as well as its fading singing duo, Jeanette MacDonald and Nelson Eddy, and its teenage threats, Garland and Rooney – its own big dancing star, Eleanor Powell (1912–82). She was an extraordinary, stainless-steel-clad lady who was no great shakes as an actress but, once she started on her machine-gun taps, was so magnetic that she could manage single-handed to hold the audiences' attention through such otherwise tiresome and patchy vehicles as *Broadway Melody of 1936* (1935), *Broadway Melody of 1938* (1937) and *Rosalie* (1937). In *Broadway Melody of 1940* (1940), for about the only time in her career, she was given a partner of equal standing, Fred Astaire, and some of their splendid routines, set to Cole Porter's music (particularly a long version of 'Begin the Beguine'), represent a degree of sheer style and technique rarely matched in the Hollywood musical. This proved to be the high point of her career: within three years she was reduced to playing second fiddle to Red Skelton, the company's new comic sensation; she retired gracefully.

At Paramount, Bing Crosby was the reigning king of musicals, Bob Hope was the leading comedy star and sang a little, and four principal girls divided most of the plum feminine roles at the studio between them. Paulette Goddard got the fiery dramatic parts, Dorothy Lamour was exotic in a sarong, Veronica Lake was the resident siren and Betty Hutton was the hard-sell musical comedienne. Their areas were clearly defined and no-one stepped on anyone else's toes: they could all, from time to time, let their hair down (or put it up, according to the fashion of the moment) to play in comedy or even musical roles – though only Betty Hutton specialized in the genre with occasional assistance from former band singer Dorothy Lamour.

Many aspirants to screen stardom during the Thirties and Forties originally sang with bands – including Bing Crosby (1901–1947). Paramount had snapped him up in 1932, after he had become an instant sensation with his own radio show, and kept him for 24 years (although he was occasionally loaned out to other companies). With his lazy charm and seemingly effortless crooning, he was the constant factor in Paramount musicals. He was never teamed with any particular leading lady for long, apart from the series of seven 'Road' films, starting with *Road to Singapore* (1940), in which he and Bob Hope vied for the affections of Dorothy Lamour. Otherwise, Mary Martin was nearest to a romantic partner in *Rhythm on the River* (1940) and *The Birth of the Blues* (1941) when Paramount were trying to transform her from a Broadway to a Hollywood star – without success.

Curiously enough, Crosby was only once teamed with Paramount's female musical star, Betty Hutton (or perhaps one should say twice, since in *Here Comes the Waves* (1944) she played twins – one was quiet and refined and the other her usual raucous self). Perhaps Paramount feared that Crosby's relaxed, easy style would not blend with the Hutton oversell; they teamed her instead with Eddie Bracken in *The Fleet's In* (1942), *Star Spangled Rhythm*, and *The Miracle of Morgan's Creek* (both 1943) or with Sonny Tufts in *Cross My Heart* (1945) since they offered no competition and did not have to be protected from her onslaughts.

The great government drive towards Pan-American friendship and the Good Neighbor policy encouraged producers to look for a suitably Pan-American star to decorate films with titles like *Down Argentine Way* (1940), *That Night in Rio* and *Weekend in Havana* (both 1941). They found Carmen Miranda (who was in fact born in Portugal but nobody quibbled) – the Brazilian Bombshell. Miranda (1909–1955) belonged to another class of Forties star, the speciality star. As far as anyone could tell, all she was ever able to do was her characteristic hip-wagging, finger-twisting, pseudo-Latin number (usually written for her by old Hollywood stalwarts like Harry Warren) and wear her notorious tutti-frutti hats.

Carmen Miranda was the most famous – or notorious – speciality star, but not the biggest. For that honour it was a close competition between skating Sonja Henie and swimming Esther Williams. Sonja Henie prettily skated her way to music through nearly a dozen films at 20th Century-Fox from *One in a Million* (1936) to *The Countess of Monte Cristo* (1948) and retired from the screen to make a fortune promoting ice shows. Esther Williams, MGM's home-grown mermaid, began in *Bathing Beauty* (1944) and was a regular in ever more exotic and elaborate watergoing romances until *Jupiter's Darling* (1955); she also retired with a fortune. Where Carmen Miranda was an incidental attraction, never called upon to provide more than semi-comic relief, Williams and Henie were undoubtedly stars, with whole big-budget films built around them. But then it was the era, above all, of the star musical.

Warners no longer had any tame musical stars, but then Warners did not make many musicals in the Forties. They produced only a handful of dramas with music which were quite frequently based on the life of a popular composer like George M. Cohan (*Yankee Doodle Dandy*, 1942), George Gershwin (*Rhapsody in Blue*, 1945) or Cole Porter (*Night and Day*, 1946). This continued until 1948 when they discovered

yet another band singer, called Doris Day, and made her into a star with her first movie – *Romance on the High Seas*.

Columbia had Rita Hayworth and, since she was about all they had, they had to make her go a long way. Unfortunately she could not sing – or nobody could spare the time to coach her. But she could dance and, in between weightier assignments, she proved, in *You'll Never Get Rich* (1941) and *You Were Never Lovelier* (1942), to be one of the best partners Fred Astaire ever had and worked surprisingly well with Gene Kelly in *Cover Girl* (1944).

The best that RKO could come up with as a musical substitute for Astaire and Rogers was Anna Neagle, who was in Hollywood under contract at the beginning of the war in Europe and made such innocuous, undistinguished musicals as *Irene* (1940), *No, No, Nanette* and *Sunny* (both 1941).

Of the major independents, David Selznick had bigger things to do than bother his head with such frivolity, but Samuel Goldwyn discovered a musical comic in 1943 and unleashed Danny Kaye on the waiting world in *Up in Arms* (1944) and a succession of other semi-musical vehicles.

But the big studio for musical stars and star musicals during the Forties was 20th Century-Fox. They had something for just about every taste. At the beginning of the decade there was still Shirley Temple, Sonja Henie skating and soon after Carmen Miranda doing whatever she always did. Then when the studio went in for band singers the whole band would come along; two lively musicals featuring Glenn Miller and his orchestra – *Sun Valley Serenade* (1941) and *Orchestra Wives* (1942) – were made at that studio.

There were also the serious musical stars. Chief among them were Betty Grable and Alice Faye – both were blondes, both were Forces' sweethearts, but they were otherwise very different in style. Betty Grable had worked her way up from the chorus and did a bit of everything sufficiently, if nothing very well. She had bounce and good humour and rather short, pudgy legs which were regarded as the epitome of feminine allure. It was, perhaps, her very ordinariness that made her the great wartime pinup – soldiers felt that, given the right breaks, the girl-next-door back home could probably do just as well, and they enjoyed Grable for being a trier. Alice Faye had been a band singer and, with her quivering bee-stung lips and throaty mezzo, was perfect for being soulful and singing melancholy torch songs like 'You'll Never Know' and 'No Love, No Nothing'.

Like goddesses of dissimilar races, they were usually kept apart, each in her own particular sphere, but it was a fair guess that one or other of them would be in any major 20th Century-Fox musical. The men who played opposite them – Don Ameche, John Payne, even Dan Dailey – were merely moral support for the duration of the film. The films which surrounded them were brash and vulgar, conceived in the glaring tints of saturated Technicolor, and made no grand claim to be works of art. They were, one might say, primitive Hollywood at its best, and as such they retain their vitality even today when many more pretentious offerings have long since faded.

Art, of course, is something else again. But for that one has to look elsewhere: to that special area of MGM where Arthur Freed and his team were up to something new and exciting and completely different.

Right: Carmen Miranda in Busby Berkeley's The Gang's All Here *(1943). Far right: Forces' favourites Alice Faye and Betty Grable played sisters in* Tin Pan Alley *(1940).*

Right: two of the Forties' most popular young musical talents were Deanna Durbin and Judy Garland, here in an MGM test short Every Sunday. *Far right: Esther Williams indulges in a spot of underwater ballet in* Neptune's Daughter. *Below far right: the 'Road' team of Bing Crosby, Dorothy Lamour, and Bob Hope – here in* Road to Zanzibar *– was a superb combination of the musical, the glamorous and the humorous. Below right: Hollywood's favourite ice-skater, Sonja Henie, in her last Fox musical, made in 1943. Below: following the break up of the Astaire–Rogers partnership, Fred was partnered by tap-dancing queen Eleanor Powell in* Broadway Melody of 1940. *Their dancing to Porter's 'Begin the Beguine' was one of its many highlights.*

Key Directors

The early years of the Forties saw the emergence of one of America's most innovative film-makers, **Orson Welles**, (b.1915), who had soared to prominence as an actor/producer for stage and radio; his 1938 radio production of H.G. Wells' *War of the Worlds* had been so vivid that many listeners had genuinely believed that Martians were invading Earth. In 1939, RKO studios, badly in need of a major success, decided to offer Welles a Hollywood contract. Given virtually *carte blanche* by George J. Schaefer, president of RKO, Welles, after a couple of false starts, created the innovative and controversial masterpiece, *Citizen Kane*. Although hard hit by a systematic press campaign organized by newspaper magnate William Randolph Hearst (upon whom the film's protagonist was largely based), the film received many enthusiastic critical reviews. However its unremarkable performance at the box-office prompted RKO to curb Welles' creative freedom. The studio cut his next film, *The Magnificent Ambersons* (1942), a stylish, evocative adaptation of Booth Tarkington's novel of life in a small American town in the nineteenth century, by a third, and relieved him of all control over another, *Journey Into Fear* (1942, dir. Norman Forster).

Branded an expensive eccentric by Hollywood, Welles fell back on his acting skills, playing Mr Rochester in *Jane Eyre* (dir. Robert Stevenson, 1943) and starring opposite Claudette Colbert in *Tomorrow Is Forever* (dir. Irving Pichel, 1946). He got a rare chance to direct with *The Stranger* (1946), in which he also starred as an escaped Nazi war criminal, and the following year he directed his wife, Rita Hayworth (they married in 1943, she sued for divorce four years later) in the classic melodrama *The Lady From Shanghai* for Columbia. He then embarked upon a low-budget version of *Macbeth* (1948) for Republic, his last film within the old studio system. Between 1949 and 1952 he struggled to complete a film version of *Othello*. Among the many roles he took to finance the project was that of black-marketeer Harry Lime in Carol Reed's *The Third Man* (1949), perhaps the most memorable of his many cameo roles.

After completing a disappointing mystery thriller, *Mr Arkadin* (1954), Welles was given a belated chance by Universal studios to re-establish himself in Hollywood as a director with *Touch of Evil* (1958), a thriller of nightmare seediness about a corrupt policeman, Quinlan (Welles), who frames those who his 'instinct' tells him are guilty. Though hailed as a masterpiece in Europe, the film fared poorly in the USA, killing Welles' chances of a Hollywood comeback.

Thanks to Spanish and Swiss finance, he was able to complete *Campanadas a Medianoche* (1966, *Chimes at Midnight* (1966, *Falstaff*) a brilliant asemblage of scenes from various Shakespeare plays that might be alternatively titled 'The Tragedy of Sir John Falstaff'. Without any violence to Shakespeare's own, essentially comic, vision of Falstaff, Welles extracts a character that is heroic in his humour and generosity and finally tragic in his incomprehension of the ingratitude of the great and powerful.

Following a short feature made for French television, *Histoire Immortelle* (1968, *Immortal Story*), about a rich, impotent, man who invites a young mariner to sleep with his beautiful wife (Jeanne Moreau), Welles created one of his most engaging, enigmatic works in collaboration with François Reichenbach, *Vérités et Mensonges* (1973, *F for Fake*), This concerned the exploits of the notorious art forger Elmyr de Hory and the faker of Howard Hughes' 'autobiography', Clifford Irving, as well as some of Welles' own artistic japes –

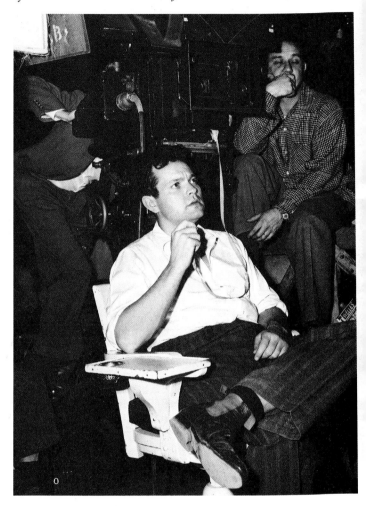

such as his *War of the Worlds* broadcast.

Welles continues to relish his film persona of magician and charlatan, aimiably deceiving his willing audience with wonderful sleight of hand. Yet his place in movie history is nearer, in reality, to one of his tragic characterizations. Potentially one of the most gifted figures of world cinema, his output has sadly been small.

A major director in the silent period, **Raoul Walsh** (1887–1980) had had little control over his projects in the Thirties, but found congenial conditions at Warners (1939–51), directing Cagney at his most manic in *The Roaring Twenties* (1939) and *White Heat* (1949), with *The Strawberry Blonde* (1941) as a quieter interlude; guiding Bogart in his transition from deep-dyed villain (*The Roaring Twenties*) to more sympathetic roles in *They Drive by Night* (1940), with George Raft, and *High Sierra* (1941), co-starring Ida Lupino; and taking over as Errol Flynn's regular director in seven vehicles from the Custer epic *They Died With Their Boots On* to the contemporary war movie *Objective, Burma!* (1945), little liked in Britain for minimizing the British role in that theatre of war. *Salty O'Rourke* (1945) was memorable for the mel-

ancholy beauty of Gail Russell as teacher trying to redeem a gambler, dully played by Alan Ladd; and *Pursued*, with Robert Mitchum and Teresa Wright, is often described as the first psychological (indeed Freudian) Western.

John Huston (b.1906), son of the actor Walter Huston, had established a reputation as a scriptwriter at Warners before writing and directing his first film, *The Maltese Falcon* (1941), the third and best version of Dashiell Hammett's hard-boiled thriller, with Humphrey Bogart as the private-eye Sam Spade, Mary Astor as the treacherous Brigid O'Shaughnessy and a supporting cast of villains including Sydney Greenstreet, Peter Lorre and Elisha Cook Jr. After a Bette Davis vehicle, *In This Our Life* (1942), he reassembled most of the *Maltese Falcon* team for an inconsequential spy comedy-thriller, *Across the Pacific* (1942). He then joined the army and made several controversial war documentaries of great quality. *The Treasure of the Sierra Madre* (1948) reunited him with Bogart in the Mexican tale of three men lured to disaster by gold – Walter Huston and Tim Holt co-starred. In the gangster melodrama *Key Largo* (1948), Bogart now played the good guy (loved by Lauren Bacall) and Edward G. Robinson was the

gangster trying to re-enter the USA by way of the Florida Keys. *We Were Strangers* (1949) was a gloomy tale of Cuban revolutionaries, starring John Garfield and Jennifer Jones. *The Asphalt Jungle* (1950) was among the first and best of the heist movies, detailing a large-scale robbery, and the excellent cast included Sam Jaffe as the mastermind, Sterling Hayden as a 'hooligan' with longings to return to his pastoral horse-breeding roots in Kentucky, Jean Hagen as his put-upon girlfriend, Louis Calhern as a double-crossing lawyer and Marilyn Monroe as his child-like mistress. Moving to MGM, Huston attempted to put Stephen Crane's great Civil War novel on film in *The Red Badge of Courage* (1951) with Audie Murphy, the most-decorated American serviceman of World War II, as the novice soldier. The project caused a permanent rift between Louis B. Mayer and his new production chief, Dore Schary, as detailed in Lillian Ross's entertaining blow-by-blow account of the film's making, *Picture*. *The African Queen* (1951), co-scripted by James Agee, and with excellent star roles for Bogart (who won an Oscar) and Katharine Hepburn as ill-matched lovers taking on the German navy in World War I Africa, restored Huston's commercial reputation. In 1952 he went to live in Ireland with his fourth wife and thereafter worked mostly away from Hollywood but still essentially within the American film industry, for the most part (later he moved to Mexico). He also resumed his acting career, after an interval of thirty years, but in this as in the films he directed, the occasional remarkable artistic successes were outnumbered by the disasters (though there is not 100 per cent agreement among critics on which is which). Among the best of his subsequent films as a director were *The Misfits* (1961), scripted by Arthur Miller, in which Clark Gable played his last role, as a disillusioned, latter-day cowboy, who becomes involved with a sensitive divorcée (Marilyn Monroe); *Fat City* (1972) a subuded, low-life story about an ageing, alcoholic boxer (Stacy Keach) making a hopeless attempt at a comeback; *Wise Blood* (1979), a disturbing, black-comic study of religious obsession in America's bible belt, featuring a compelling performance by Brad Dourif; and *Under the Volcano* (1984), a brave attempt to bring to the screen Malcolm Lowry's 'unfilmable' novel about an eccentric British diplomat (Albert Finney) dying of despair and alcohol in Mexico.

Jules Dassin (b. 1911), after such whimsies as *The Canterville Ghost* (1943) and the witty *Two Smart People* (1946), found his direction with *Brute Force, The Naked City* and *Thieves' Highway* (1949), the last of which starred Richard Conte as a truck driver fighting off the mobsters and Valentina Cortese as the reformed girlfriend of the chief hoodlum (Lee J. Cobb). His last 'Hollywood' film for many years was made in London: *Night and the City* (1950) starred Richard Widmark as a would-be wrestling promoter on the run from gangland reprisal – British players Googie Withers and Francis L. Sullivan also made the most of their roles as nightclub owners. After a gap, Dassin concluded this successful run with an ambitious French heist movie, *Du Rififi Chez les Hommes* (1955, *Rififi*). He then began to indulge a taste for European culture and arty movies, usually starring his wife, Melina Mercouri, later to become minister for the arts in the Greek government. His one popular success was a rather curious dramatization of this relationship, *Pote Tin Kyriaki* (1959, *Never on Sunday*), with Mercouri as a waterfront prostitute

Above: Harry Dean Stanton and Brad Dourif in Wise Blood, *John Huston's black-comic vision of religious fanaticism set in America's 'Bible Belt'.*

and himself as an American intellectual – he had started his career as an actor in the New York Yiddish Theater. A return to the heist (rechristened 'caper') movie, the joky *Topkapi* (1964), was also widely shown; but most of his other films have fallen into the gap between genuine art movies and popular entertainment, disappearing rapidly from sight and seldom surfacing even on TV.

Though an American citizen from his teens, **Jacques Tourneur** (1904–1977) made his early films in France, delaying his American debut until 1939. He directed three of the best psychological horror-films produced by the Val Lewton unit at RKO, *Cat People, I Walked With a Zombie* (1943), a voodoo movie set in the West Indies, and *The Leopard Man*, based on a novel by Cornell Woolrich.

The other Lewton movies were directed by alumni editors of Orson Welles' earliest productions, Mark Robson (four) and Robert Wise (two). Wise (b.1914) went on to make the notable boxing picture, *The Set-Up* (1949), with Robert Ryan, and eventually such overblown musicals as *West Side Story* (1961) and *The Sound of Music* (1965). Robson (1918–1978) directed the Kirk Douglas boxing picture *Champion, Home of the Brave* (both 1949) and Bogart's last film, *The Harder They Fall* (1956), another boxing picture, from a Schulberg novel. Tourneur never made the big-time like his colleagues, though his work is more highly rated by *auteur* critics. *Out of the Past* (1947) is among the most complex and fascinating of *film noirs*, with Jane Greer as a *femme fatale* ensnaring private-eye Robert Mitchum and gangster Kirk Douglas, with fatal results. *Stars in My Crown* (1950), with Joel McCrea as a gun-toting preacher in the lawless West, was among Tourneur's own favourites; and the English-made *Night of the Demon* (1957), based on an M.R. James story, has a cult following. Robson's later films were mostly straightforward commercial propositions, the best of which – *Von Ryan's Express* (1965), *Valley of the Dolls* (1967) and *Earthquake* (1974) – were solid, if somewhat simple-minded, entertainment, aimed fairly and squarely at mass audiences.

Vincente Minnelli (b.1910), a native Chicagoan despite his exotic name, became best known as a director of musicals, including *Meet Me in St Louis, Yolanda and the Thief, An American in Paris, The Band Wagon, Gigi* and *On a Clear Day You Can See Forever*. However, from the outset of his career he occasionally diversified into other genres, in particular family (or group) melodrama (*Undercurrent*, 1946) and domestic comedy (*Father of the Bride*, 1950). Certain themes are common to most of his films: a concern with illusion and reality, sexual role playing and social convention. He was married to Judy Garland from 1945 to 1951; Liza Minnelli (b.1946) is their daughter.

Finally, Charles Chaplin completed only one more film in the Forties after *The Great Dictator*. A feeling for the dark and macabre had never been far absent from his films, and it surfaced most strongly in *Monsieur Verdoux* (1947), the story of a French Bluebeard, wife-killer between the wars, with Martha Raye, Isobel Elsom and Marilyn Nash. The philosophic contrast that Verdoux draws between his own kind of murder and the kind that is licensed by war was not popular in the Cold War years and the character was made a weapon of that persecution which led to Chaplin's permanent exile from America in 1952, after nearly forty years' residence.

European Emigrés

The rise of Nazism and the ravages of war in Europe resulted in a number of the continent's leading film-makers seeking refuge in Hollywood – Fritz Lang, Max Ophuls, Douglas Sirk, Robert Siodmak, Otto Preminger and Billy Wilder from Germany or Austria, and Jean Renoir, René Clair and Julien Duvivier from France. Other notable foreign additions to Hollywood were Alfred Hitchcock and Robert Stevenson from England. Alexander Korda directed a single film in the US, *Lady Hamilton* (1941) before returning to England; his art director brother, Zoltan, however, remained in the USA until the end of the Forties. His former assistant, the director André de Toth, married Veronica Lake in 1944 (they divorced in 1952) and worked in Hollywood until the late Fifties.

By the time **Max Ophuls** (1902–1957) came to the USA in 1941, he had directed films in Germany, France, Italy and Holland. When he was finally hired in 1946 by Howard Hughes for *Vendetta* (1950), he was fired after only a few days' shooting. He completed an amusing swashbuckler, *The Exile* (1947), written by and starring Douglas Fairbanks Jr, and went on to make a touching re-creation of Vienna in *Letter From an Unknown Woman* (1948), based on Stefan Zweig's novella, with Joan Fontaine as the girl who sacrifices all for love and Louis Jourdan as the philandering concert pianist who fails to recognize her lifelong devotion, though he fathers her child in a brief affair. A happy partnership with English voluntary exile James Mason produced two American melodramas; *Caught* (1948), with Mason as a kindly doctor, Barbara Bel Geddes as a poor but ambitious girl and Robert Ryan as the sadistic millionaire who marries her; and *The Reckless Moment* (1949) with Mason as an Irish blackmailer who falls in love with the woman (Joan Bennett) he is persecuting. Ophuls then returned to France to make two of his finest films, *La Ronde* (1950) and *Lola Montès* (1955) before his premature death.

Like Ophuls, **Robert Siodmak** (1900–1973) was Jewish and had been based in France from 1933; but unlike him, Siodmak was continuously employed in Hollywood from 1941 to 1951, at first on such trifles of Universal's expressionistic fantasy as *Son of Dracula* (1943) and the exotic Maria Montez vehicle *Cobra Woman* (1944). In 1944 he found his own line in *film noir* thrillers with *Phantom Lady*, in which a girl (Ella Raines) searches New York for the elusive woman who can prove her boss innocent of murder, assisted by the real culprit (Franchot Tone); *Christmas Holiday*, in which a bride (Deanna Durbin) discovers that her effete husband (Gene Kelly) is a murderer; and *The Suspect*, in which Charles Laughton is a Crippen-like wife-killer. *The Strange Affair of Uncle Harry* (1945) was followed by Siodmak's best-known American film, *The Spiral Staircase* (1945), in which a dumb girl (Dorothy McGuire) is menaced by a fastidious slayer of handicapped women. *The Dark Mirror* (1946), with Olivia de Havilland, was on the popular Forties theme of twins, one virtuous and the other wicked, which Siodmak had earlier handled in *Cobra Woman*. Siodmak ended his Hollywood career (he returned to Europe in the early Fifties), with some first-rate thrillers – *The Killers* (1946), which brought Burt Lancaster instant stardom, *Cry of the City* (1948), and *Criss Cross* (1949).

The British directors who made most impact in Forties Hollywood, **Alfred Hitchcock** and **Robert Stevenson**, were brought to the USA by producer David O. Selznick. Stevenson (b.1905) made *Jane Eyre* and a much later series of films for Disney, including *Mary Poppins* (1964). Hitchcock, who already had a strong British track record, culminating in *The Lady Vanishes* (1938), re-created rural English settings in *Rebecca* (1940), with Joan Fontaine and Laurence Olivier, and

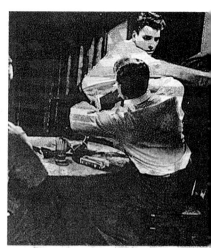

Above: Chaplin's version of the Bluebeard story was one of his most personal and bitter works. It coincided with the political witch hunt against him, and was attacked for its 'un-American' bleak irony. Above right: Swede (Burt Lancaster) and Colfax (Albert Dekker) fall out over Ava Gardner in The Killers. *Right:* Lola Montès, *a visually stunning glimpse of the courtesan's life is widely acknowledged as Ophuls' masterpiece.*

Above: time runs out for Jeff (Robert Mitchum), trapped by his ex-girlfriend (Jane Greer) and her gangster lover (Kirk Douglas) in Out of the Past.

Left: the Tucker family contemplate their devastated home in Renoir's The Southerner. *Below: Mrs Danvers (Judith Anderson), the sinister housekeeper of Manderley, startles the second Mrs de Winter (Joan Fontaine) in Hitchcock's* Rebecca. *Bottom: Alicia (Ingrid Bergman) realizes that she is being poisoned by her Nazi husband's mother in* Notorious.

Suspicion (1941), with Fontaine and Cary Grant. Both were romantic melodramas of tremulous wives and possibly murderous husbands, with Fontaine, eye-avoiding mistress of masochism, at her most vulnerably crushable. *Foreign Correspondent* (1940) and *Saboteur* (1942) were headline stuff for the war effort, but *Shadow of a Doubt* (1943) was Hitchcock's first real attempt to portray small-town America – he shot the exteriors on location in California several years before this became fashionable, and employed the playwright Thornton Wilder to supply authentic American dialogue.

Back with Selznick, Hitchcock affirmed his persisting interest in the psychological with *Spellbound*, set in a mental institution, with Ingrid Bergman as a doctor and Gregory Peck as an amnesiac impostor suspected of murder and racked by guilt feelings from childhood. *Notorious* (1946) starred Bergman again as a loose-living lady, persuaded by an American agent (Cary Grant) to infiltrate a Nazi group in Rio de Janeiro by marrying one of its leaders (Claude Rains). Selznick himself scripted *The Paradine Case* (1947) from a dusty courtroom novel by Robert Hichens; Alida Valli was a fascinating murderess in the dock and Charles Laughton presided as a hanging judge in Hitchcock's first colour film. In *Rope* (1948), based on the Leopold-Loeb murder case, he experimented with ten-minute takes and with intimations of homosexuality, daring at the time; James Stewart played the professor whose students translate his Nietzchean (and implicitly Nazi) theories into unmotivated murder. Hitchcock returned to England for *Under Capricorn* (1949), set in studio-based nineteenth-century Australia with Ingrid Bergman as a guilt-ridden Anglo-Irish aristocrat married to a surly ex-convict (Joseph Cotten), and being slowly poisoned by her maid (Margaret Leighton). The mainly British cast of *Stage Fright* (1949) was given star appeal by importing Jane Wyman as a drama student out to prove the innocence of her lover (Richard Todd) and the guilt of the murder victim's actress wife (Marlene Dietrich). The film's main technical innovation was the 'lying flashback'. After this somewhat uncertain period Hitchcock returned to peak form with *Strangers on a Train* (1951) and remained consistently successful for the next dozen years.

The French directors **René Clair** and **Julien Duvivier** did not become 'American' film-makers as Hitchcock did. They sat out the war and took what opportunities they could. Clair's best American films, *I Married a Witch* and *It Happened Tomorrow* (1944), were fantasies in the vein of his early silents: 'these . . . films saved me from American realism for which I did not feel gifted, because I wasn't American . . .' Duvivier remade *Un Carnet de Bal* (1937, *Christine*) as *Lydia* (1941) for Alexander Korda, with Merle Oberon as the woman seeking out the dancing partners of her youth. The all-star, episodic *Tales of Manhattan* (1942) was followed by the similar *Flesh and Fantasy* (1943) – Charles Boyer, Edward G. Robinson and Thomas Mitchell appeared in both. *The Impostor* (1944) was one of Jean Gabin's two relatively undistinguished American appearances.

Jean Renoir stayed longer and was more productive than his compatriots. He retained a permanent base in California after returning to France in 1951, though his career as a Hollywood film-maker lasted only seven years and was regarded by him as a mainly unsuccessful interlude. He tried to make 'American' films, like *Swamp Water* (1941), set in Georgia and filmed partly on location with Walter Brennan as a fugitive and Anne Baxter as his loyal daughter, and *The Southerner* (1945), a *Grapes of Wrath*-like tale set in Texas, with script advice from William Faulkner. He even attempted a sort of *film noir* in *The Woman on the Beach*, a melodrama with Charles Beckford as a blinded painter, Joan Bennett as his *femme fatale* wife and Robert Ryan as a shell-shocked army veteran. His 'French' films were *This Land Is Mine* (1943), a resistance drama with Charles Laughton as a self-sacrificing schoolteacher, and *Diary of a Chambermaid* (1946), based on Octave Mirbeau's risqué minor classic, with Paulette Goddard and Burgess Meredith, who also co-wrote with Renoir and co-produced. Having found no secure place in the Hollywood system, he made *The River* (1951) as an independent production in India, before returning to work in Europe.

Animation

The Disney Features For animation, that strangely peripheral art which existed within the comparatively new medium of cinema, the Forties represented a decade of real expansion and self-discovery. In its infancy, animation had been little more than short silent cartoons accompanied by lively musical motifs knocked out on the cinema piano. Walt Disney, however, had turned this small-scale art into a viable industrial wing of movie entertainment and by 1940 he dominated the scene in Hollywood.

The success of his first feature-length picture – *Snow White and the Seven Dwarfs* (1937) – and his prolific output of cartoons meant that other potential animators, lacking the resources and business acumen which lay behind Walt Disney Enterprises, barely survived the high costs of production and could ill afford the specialized kind of marketing that animated films required if they were to be widely distributed.

Nevertheless, in spite of these problems, animators found new forms of expression through the demands of wartime propaganda. The post-war period saw the development of allied forms of animation, especially puppetry, and the many kinds of abstract, mobile designs pioneered by Norman McLaren in Canada.

The early Forties, however, belonged to Disney. For him it was a period of continued achievement in the particular style he had made his own. Moving on from the simple black-and-white, semi-silhouette stylization that had characterized the

early cartoons, such as *Felix the Cat* and Disney's own *Steamboat Willie* (1928) or *Skeleton Dance* (1929), Disney's artists had been encouraged towards a degree of pictorial naturalism which was often at odds with the fantasy of his subjects. While Pluto, Goofy, Donald Duck and Mickey Mouse were all splendid creatures born of the comic imagination. Disney's more naturalistic humans – from Snow White onwards – were conceived with a kind of childishly sentimental artistry. Their movements were given a spurious activity derived from the technique known as rotoscope, whereby the human figure was recorded in movement with a live-action camera and the resultant images were then traced in the form of graphics and used as models for the animation process.

Disney gradually abandoned the production of shorts in favour of features. The sheer dramatic force of his early feature films was often admirable and was so strong, indeed, that *Snow White and the Seven Dwarfs* was restricted by the censorship authorities in Britain because it was felt the scenes with the witch would be frightening to children.

Pinocchio (1940) also had sequences that were reckoned to alarm the young. Costing $2.5 million, the film is a masterpiece of animation, containing stunning set-pieces such as the opening multi-plane camera shot of Gepetto's village by starlight, the underwater sequences and the climactic whale chase, all of which proved that Disney's work could no longer be adequately described by the word 'cartoon'. *Pinocchio's* pictorial richness, imaginative camera angles and fast-moving storyline were enhanced by such superb characterizations as Stromboli, the volcanic puppet-master, and the foxy Dickensian villian J. Worthington Foulfellow. The film also had an exceptional musical score, highlighted by the Oscar-winning song, 'When You Wish Upon a Star', sung by Jiminy Cricket,

Bottom far left: Pinocchio desperately tries to escape the whale's enfolding jaws. Below far left: Walt Disney in the late Thirties, when he and his studio laid down many of the basic principles of animation. Below left: his first feature, Snow White and the Seven Dwarfs. *Below: the 'Dance of the Hours' sequence from* Fantasia.

© 1985 Walt Disney Productions

© 1985 Walt Disney Productions

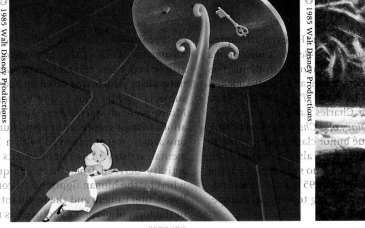

Right: Alice tries to reach the key to the door of Wonderland in Alice in Wonderland. *Far right:* Bambi *with his mother, just before she is killed by hunters leaving him alone to fend for himself in the forest.*

whose moralistic role as Pinocchio's 'official conscience' helps the film to avoid undue sentimentality. The song, with its promise of dreams coming true, became the touchstone of Disney's screen philosophy.

The year 1940 also saw the premiere of *Fantasia*, a film made possible by the skills developed while working on *Snow White and the Seven Dwarfs* and *Pinocchio*, but which came to a public quite unprepared for anything more than another fairy-tale. *Fantasia* grew out of Disney's search for a starring vehicle for Mickey Mouse. Paul Dukas' 'The Sorcerer's Apprentice' was chosen as a musical pantomime for Mickey, and in 1938, Disney invited conductor Leopold Stokowski to record the music. This collaboration developed into the notion of 'The Concert Feature', as *Fantasia* was first called, for which Disney's artists would animate an entire programme of classical music. The musicologist Deems Taylor was enlisted as an advisor and remained to provide the film's linking narration. Perhaps the selection of compositions was too diverse, perhaps the differing approaches of the various sequence directors is too perceptible – whatever the reason, the film is a patchwork of the brilliant and the banal.

Fantasia remains a brave experiment, and a clear development of the use of music in the early Silly Symphonies, but Disney's uneasiness in the 'highbrow' atmosphere of the concert hall is reflected in the completed film.

Fantasia was initially a financial failure, at a time when Disney could least afford one. The war in Europe was curtailing overseas markets and had already affected the earning potential of *Pinocchio*. In addition, Disney's other major project, *Bambi* (1942, in production since 1937), was costing vast sums of money.

Disney made economies and quickly put two less ambitious films into production. The first of these, *The Reluctant Dragon* (1941), combined live-action footage (featuring Robert Benchley on a tour of the studio) with three short cartoons. The second was the fully animated *Dumbo* (1941). Running for just 64 minutes, the film tells a simple story dramatically and with great poignancy – and at a cost of only $700,000. The only extraneous sequence is that in which Dumbo has alcoholic hallucinations of pink elephants, and that is pardonable because of its sheer inventiveness.

There are many appealing qualities about *Dumbo*: the circus-poster colourings, the ingenious score of funny songs and wistful ballads and the animation set-pieces, such as the raising of the big top by night in torrential rain.

Released a year later, *Bambi* was a very different movie, being as naturalistic as *Dumbo* was stylized. *Dumbo* has the frenzied pace of the circus-ring, but *Bambi* has a hauntingly lyrical rhythm; and, whereas Dumbo's triumph over adversity is lightly handled, the same moral in *Bambi* is heavily underlined.

Although the animals in *Bambi* were modelled on life studies, they were sufficiently 'Disneyfied' to make them appear uncomfortable residents in the film's beautiful forest settings. The stock cartoon gags used from time to time are intrusive and the animal's childish voices only proved how right the studio had been to keep Dumbo dumb.

There are, nevertheless, moments of animation in *Bambi* which remain unsurpassed; in particular, the battle of the stags (impressively shot in dramatic browns and purples), and the terrifyingly vivid forest-fire sequence. However, American audiences of 1942, now fighting the war they had once hoped would pass them by, found little in the sequestered glades of Bambi's forest with which to identify.

The studio became a factory employing a large staff of highly talented designers and technicians to whom Disney permitted little artistic freedom. Among the major artists who worked for him were several who were later to become celebrated animators in their own right. It came as a grave shock to Disney when, during the summer of 1941, recurrent labour disputes came to a head and closed the studio down for nine weeks. The staff grievances not only involved wages and hours of work but also the lack of recognition given to the senior artists. Disney was sent on a goodwill tour of South America while the strike was settled.

The studio survived the war years by making propaganda and training films for the government, and executed, among many other subjects, the mobile maps illustrating the progress of war with huge probing arrows for the *Why We Fight* series. Disney's standards of professionalism often led him to subsidize the official budgets. The most significant of these movies was *Victory Through Air Power* (1943), which had animated sequences of great potency, as when the American Eagle battles with a grotesque Japanese octopus to free the world from its tentacled grasp.

The material gathered on Disney's South American tour was made into two features: *Saludos Amigos* (1943) and *The Three Caballeros* (1945). The first of these films, running for just 43 minutes, scarcely merits feature status, although it contains some remarkable sequences, particularly the concluding 'Acquarela do Brazil' ('Watercolour of Brazil'), in which an animated paint brush creates a lush jungle background against which a Brazilian parrot, José Carioca, teaches Donald Duck how to dance the samba. This episode heralded even wilder flights of surreal fancy in *The Three Caballeros* which combined real and animated characters. It was this technique which was later to be used in several other features, including *Song of the South* (1946), based on Joel Chandler Harris's Uncle Remus stories about Brer Rabbit, *Mary Poppins* (1964) and *Pete's Dragon* (1978).

The compilation format used in the South American movies

was employed to construct a number of so-called features which contained anything from two to ten short subjects. These films, sometimes linked with live action, are a random rag-bag, in which even the best sequences are hardly masterpieces. Among the highlights are 'Peter and the Wolf' and 'The Whale Who Wanted to Sing at the Met' from *Make Mine Music* (1946); 'Mickey and the Beanstalk' from *Fun and Fancy Free* (1947) and 'Johnny Appleseed' and 'Little Toot', from *Melody Time* (1948).

This inconsistent, unsatisfying period concluded with the patchy Washington Irving adaptation *Ichabod and Mr Toad* (1949). *Cinderella* (1950) marked the beginning of a new era. This was the first animated feature since *Bambi*, and tried hard to re-create the brilliance of the studio's earlier films without quite capturing their graphic quality of line. *Cinderella* is a graceful film, but its heroine lacks the sympathetic qualities of Snow White, and much of the film's success is due to the mouse characters, Jac and Gus, and their running battle with Lucifer the cat.

Alice in Wonderland followed in 1951, and, despite the critics' unanimous disapproval, is still the screen's most satisfying interpretation of Lewis Carroll's book. True, the crazy characters are constantly upstaging one another, and the pace is a shade too frenetic, but the comic invention never flags and there is much fine animation, especially in the 'March of Cards' sequence and the Daliesque nightmare of the finale.

Increasingly in this period we find Disney making concessions to meet what he supposed were the narrow expectations and limitations of his audiences. In *Alice in Wonderland*, he failed to grasp the implicit seriousness of Lewis Carroll's humour and abandoned most of the disturbing elements in the story. Similarly in *Peter Pan* (1953) Disney shows no understanding of the story's sinister and emotional depths or the tragedy that is implicit in Peter's perennial youth. Disney's Peter has charm and bravado but lacks the self-sacrificing heroism of the original, while the whimpering buffoonery of the film's Captain Hook has nothing of the genuine malevolence of J.M. Barrie's black-hearted Old Etonian.

The increased production of live-action movies and the studio's diversification into television and the amusement-park business (Disneyland opened in 1955) contributed to a slowing up of Disney's output of animated films. His next feature, *Lady and the Tramp* (1955), was the first to use CinemaScope; Disney filled the wider screen with a picturesque conception of America at the turn of the century, with its opulent 'gingerbread' architecture and its seedy tenements. The canine characterizations are believable and endearing and the film has much adult appeal, not least because of Peggy Lee's bluesy songs and her sophisticated vocal performance as Peg, the 'Dietrich' of the dog pound.

Sleeping Beauty in 1959 marked the end of another era at the Disney studios, being the last feature to have its characters inked onto the cels by hand – a costly process replaced, in *101 Dalmatians* (1961), by the freer, but less stylish, method of using Xeroxed drawings.

Sleeping Beauty cost an astronomical $6 million and was a financial disaster. It was poorly received by the critics, perhaps because the storyline seemed too close to *Snow White and the Seven Dwarfs*. But its neglect is undeserved; the wicked fairy Maleficent is the embodiment of evil, the ornate settings are full of gothic horror and the final battle between the Prince and the dragon is a *tour de force*.

The transition from traditional fables and established classics to contemporary stories like *101 Dalmatians* (also the first feature in which songs were of minimal importance) was the most suprising development in the studio's history. However the studio failed to follow up the success of this film with its next movie, *The Sword and the Stone* (1963), having to wait until *The Jungle Book* (1967) for its next triumph, which Disney, who died on December 15, 1966, was never to witness.

Released 30 years after the premiere of *Snow White and the Seven Dwarfs*, *The Jungle Book* was the last animated film to be personally produced by Disney. He gave the stories by Rudyard Kipling a decidedly up-beat treatment, and his cast of finely delineated characters jive and swing through rich jungle landscapes. Much of the film's strength was derived from the use of the voice-actor's personalities as character models – particularly George Sanders' sneering Shere Khan, the tiger.

This proved so successful that it became adopted as a standard feature of the studio's post-Disney productions, *The Aristocats* (1970) and *Robin Hood* (1973), presumably in the hope of strengthening stories which show a singular lack of imagination and originality. *Robin Hood* also has the dubious distinction of being technically the worst animated film the studio has ever made, with much of its animation plundered wholesale from earlier films.

Not until *The Rescuers* (1977), did the Disney studio produce a movie which re-established its supremacy of line. Possessing a plot which balances drama with humour and sentiment it is a film that is worthy of the name of the dream-merchant who 40 years before had laboured at building a folly that became a gateway to a realm of enchantment for millions of cinemagoers.

Cartoon Shorts

The general popularity of short cartoons supporting the normal live-action feature films led the larger film corporations to found their own animation units. At Warner Brothers, for example, violence of action prevailed to the point of burlesque. In the Forties many new cartoon series rivalled the popularity of Disney films – with work at once cruder and more anarchically vital than anything his studio could devise.

Walter Lantz became celebrated for his Woody Woodpecker character and Paul Terry for Terrytoons. Tex Avery and Chuck Jones developed the characters of Bugs Bunny for Warners and stayed at that studio from 1938 to 1952, working in the wooden animation building known as Termite Terrace. Chuck Jones worked on many established cartoon characters including Bugs Bunny, Daffy Duck, Porky Pig, Sylvester and Tweety Pie. He even directed a propaganda film, *Hell Bent for Election* (1944), on behalf of Franklin D. Roosevelt's last election campaign. Jones also developed the fearful rivalries of Wile E. Coyote and Mimi the Road Runner: the road runner is the State bird of Arizona and Mimi emerged as an extraordinary, ostrich-like bird, totally indestructible, with the capacity to tear along highways in the desert at supersonic speeds – leaving a plume of smoke behind.

Friz Freleng revelled in the ceaseless pursuit of the diminutive bird Tweety Pie by the scraggy scavenger-cat Sylvester, who always gets the worst of Tweety Pie's distructive stratagems. At MGM, William Hanna, Joseph Barbera and Fred Quimby created the savagely fought cat-and-mouse wars of Tom and Jerry.

These films normally consisted of six minutes of mayhem in the form of cumulative gags lasting about one minute each, in which the pursuer aims to 'get' the pursued, only in turn to be foiled by the superior wits of his intended victim.

The characters, drawn with little or no solid moulding to suggest bodily vulnerability, are subjected to every form of catastrophic destruction. They are crushed by massive, falling weights, pressed into the ground in incredible shapes or flattened against walls in hard-line, geometric patterns. For such highly schematic figures, no physical destruction is possible. The crudity of the gags flowed with insatiable, mischievous ingenuity from their tireless creators. The big factor in such animation was continuous movement; as Chuck Jones has put it: 'Movement is how animation *acts*. What makes a cartoon character significant is not how it looks, it's how it moves.'

The particular pictorial style of cartooning represented by Disney and his rivals did not go unchallenged in the USA. European animators of the Twenties and Thirties, such as Oskar Fischinger, Hans Richter, Viking Eggeling, Anthony Gross and Len Lye, had shown that animation could make effective use of many forms of art, however stylized and abstract. Indeed, the more stylized they were, the more the drawn characters appeared to belong naturally and organically to the art world of animation. The labour dispute at Walt Disney's studios in 1941 had had some effect. Gradually the artists who had led the protests left to work on their own. New styles of animation were already being evolved during the war years. John Hubley, Bill Hurtz and Bob Cannon all worked in the Air Force Motion Picture Unit during the war, experimenting with new ideas. Stephen Bosustow worked for Hughes Aircraft and made films on industrial safety, as well as a propaganda film, *Flat-Hatting* (1945), for the US navy.

UPA In the late Forties, a group of American animators, determined to counteract the influence of Disney, joined up with the Disney break-away Stephen Bosustow to form UPA (United Productions of America). Artists followed their own inclinations in the more abstract or stylized art forms, some of them basing their designs on Matisse's linear, graphic style. The UPA style, insofar as one style existed, was spare and economical; the artists employed the vaguest suggestion of background, furniture or properties necessary for the action. As in the classical Chinese theatre, if a door or table were needed for momentary use, it would be sketched in for the duration of the action, disappearing the moment it was no longer needed. Otherwise, backgrounds were quite blank.

The UPA group stayed together for only a few years, but the collective experience of working together was a strong influence on each member's later, independent work. UPA was, indeed, an off-Hollywood springboard for these valiant independents. The more celebrated UPA films – Bob Cannon's *Gerald McBoing Boing* (1950) and *Madelene* (1952), John Hubley and Pete Burness's Mister Magoo films, Hubley's *Rooty-Toot-Toot* (1952) were all products of the Fifties, but their origins lay in the collaborative work of UPA in the late Forties. UPA was fortunate in securing distribution for their films through Columbia and thus the initial Mr Magoo films – *Ragtime Bear* and *Fuddy Duddy Buddy* (both 1949) – were released along with films like *Jolson Sings Again* (1949).

The broad distinction between the Disney style and the UPA school of animation has been analysed by John Smith, an

Below: some of the most popular cartoon characters that came to fame in Forties shorts, including MGM's Tom and Jerry (far left), Paramount's Popeye, Olive Oyl and Bluto (below left) and Warners' Bugs Bunny and Daffy Duck (below).

Above: an animator's cell from a UPA Mr Magoo cartoons. This good-natured character with his chronic myopia was one of the studio's most popular creations. Right: the Jack-in-the-box and the dancing doll, animated toy figures from Paul Grimault's innovative short Le Petit Soldat.

animator of Halas and Batchelor's studio in Britain, in the following terms:

'In Disney's cartoon films, the rich, even sugary colouring and bulbous forms are matched by movements that resemble a bladder of water … The sentimentality of mood is matched with cute, coy, easy movement … excessive distortion and squashing. UPA artists favour simplicity of form and movement, the essence without the frills. Acid colours and sharp forms are matched by movement the way cane or wire would move – springy, whippy, staccato. The wit and cynicism of these cartoons is acted out in slapstick of a high but blasé kind.'

Canada   In 1941, John Grierson, who headed the newly-founded National Film Board of Canada, invited the Scottish artist and film-maker Norman McLaren to join his staff. 'I can only afford one artist,' said Grierson characteristically. McLaren's technique was derived from his experiments in drawing, scratching and painting directly onto celluloid. The majority of McLaren's films were, therefore, made without the use of the camera; his technical triumph was to synchronize the scratch marks on the celluloid with the beat of the music so that his lines moved precisely according to the rhythm of the soundtrack. Through films like *Stars and Stripes* (1939), *Hen Hop* (1942), *Fiddle-De-Dee* (1947) and *Begone Dull Care* (1949), McLaren developed many forms of experimental animation, drawing on his distinctive wit and ingenuity.

McLaren was not the only animator to create a highly personal style for the National Film Board of Canada. George Dunning, who became most famous for his Beatles film *Yellow Submarine* (1968), began his career in the Forties along with Jean-Paul Ladouceur, René Jodoin and Grant Munro, all of whom collaborated on films such as *C'Est l'Aviron* (1944, It's the Oar) and *Là-Haut sur les Montagnes* (1945, Up There in the Mountains) adapted from a French folksong.

Alexandre Alexeieff of France and his American wife Claire Parker devised the infinitely laborious 'pin screen' technique whereby lateral lighting was cast over an area covered by closely set pins which could be raised and lowered to create an irregular surface with highlights and shadows. Very few films were made by this process, the most famous being *Une Nuit sur le Mont Chauve* (1933, Night on a Bare Mountain). But *En Passant* (1943), Alexeieff and Parker's contribution to the National Film Board of Canada's Chants Populaires series, was a remarkable achievement.

Western Europe   In Britain in 1940, a new animation unit was established by Hungarian artist, John Halas, who worked with his wife Joy Batchelor. During the war years, Halas and Batchelor began in the field of specialized technical instruction and propaganda; but their style of design, however simplified for speed of turnover, was in marked contrast to the styles of artwork traditionally associated with the cartoon film.

Halas and Batchelor brought panache to such seemingly pedestrian subjects as cultivation of allotments in wartime and the virtues of saving and recycling waste. The climax of *Dustbin Parade* (1943), for example, was choreographed like a ballet with music by Matyas Seiber, who became one of the more distinguished composers for animated films.

The Home Office sponsored Halas and Batchelor to make *Water for Fire-Fighting* (1948). The twin techniques of graphic and model animation were used to give these films maximum clarity. Britain's post-war socialist government then commis-sioned the series of films about a character named Charley. These cartoons aimed to explain key points in the government's reformist legislation, such as the new Education Act, in terms of Charley's initial opposition and eventual conversion to the policies of the day. As a relief from five years of making propaganda films Halas and Batchelor, working with the artist Peter Foldes, made a symbolistic film about freedom of the spirit. *Magic Canvas* (1951), for which Seiber composed one of his finest scores.

In France, new forms of dramatic imagery were being explored. Paul Grimault and his associate Andre Sarrut made *Le Petit Soldat* (1947), a grim fairy-tale played out by animated toy figures. Grimault then embarked on the feature-length *La Bergère et le Ramoneur* (1952, The Shepherdess and the Chimney Sweep). Other experimental artists who flourished in the post-war years were Omer Boucquey and the Hungarian-born Jean Image.

Eastern Europe   Zagreb in Yugoslavia and Prague in Czechoslovakia were the centres of the animation industry for which Eastern Europe became famous. The Zagreb school of Dušan Vukotić, Nikola Kostelac and Vatroslav Mimica belongs essentially to the Fifties and Sixties, but the groundwork for their careers was laid in the Forties. The Zagreb artists pursued the linear, schematic stylization – started by Anthony Gross in the Thirties and developed by UPA in the Forties – to its logical conclusion. Never have so few lines been needed to achieve such richness in character and action.

In Prague, one of the greatest of all talents in international animation was Jiří Trnka, a pre-war puppeteer who began working in films after the war. One of Trnka's earliest films was done in harsh black-and-white line drawings: *Pérák a SS* (1946, The Springer and the SS) told the story of a chimney-sweep who turns violent in his resistance to the Nazis. Trnka went on to make films with puppets using the stop-frame principle common to all animated films to effect movement in his puppet characters. His talent for endowing his vast range of puppet characters with uncanny life began in the Forties with such films as the spoof Western *Arie prérie* (1949, The Song of the Prairie) and his traditional Czech subject *Špaliček* (1947, The Czech Year). Other notable graphic animators whose careers began at the same time as Trnka's, were Jiří Brdečka, Zdenek Miler and Eduard Hofman. At the end of the Forties another Czech, Karel Zeman, created a new form of puppetry using animated figures made of glass in films like *Inspirace* (1949, Inspiration).

In both Europe and North America animation underwent widespread diversification during the Forties. The most advanced forms of design moved in the direction of a simplicity of line that recalled the experiments of early animators like Emile Cohl in France and Winsor McCay in the USA, re-establishing the essentials of the art. The finest animators of the Forties believed that animation should remain a highly stylized graphic form that delighted in its own wit of subject and artifice of line. They were also concerned to reduce the complexity of the image so that the labour costs which had made Disney's overheads so enormous could be substantially reduced. Indeed a new era had begun for animation. By the Fifties, it had become an internationally established part of creative cinema, matching every mood from comic caricature to political satire, from folklore to serious drama, from fantasy to the outer limits of mobile abstract art. In subsequent decades animation was to become the most technologically advanced form of film-making in existence.

CHAPTER 12

The Post-War Years

There never was a year like 1946 for Hollywood. Servicemen waiting for demobilization were trapped in camps across America, eager for films to pass the time. When they finally got home, they were courting and going out to the movies. American cinemas sold more than 4000 million tickets – producing a box-office take of nearly $17000 million. The latter figure was not matched again until 1974, though by that time this represented only a quarter of the number of tickets. After the wonderful year of 1946, only inflation made Hollywood's take look good.

Trouble in Paradise

In the four years following the end of the war, however, Hollywood went from boom to nervous disarray, its structure radically altered by law, its morale shattered by paranoia, its audience thinned away. Those captive servicemen went home, married, built a suburban lifestyle away from the down-town cinemas. They wanted entertainment in the home and when they could get it they wanted television.

Lifestyles that had been denied by the Depression and the war were now embraced with wild relief. The women who had worked in the munitions factories went home, settled down, had babies and stopped going to the movies.

Between 1946 and 1948, even before television was nationwide, movie admissions dropped by 15.7 per cent. In the inner councils of the industry, moguls and bankers alike saw estimates that the fall-off would exceed 25 per cent. They did not publish the figures, but they took action. In 1946 MGM had already decreed a slimming of its product. It was to be a little less long, a little less lavish. Anticipating keener competition for dwindling audiences, 20th Century-Fox concentrated its resources on fewer but bigger inducements to draw audiences back to the cinemas. Columbia and Universal, on the other hand, tried to make their product more glamorous.

Fewer admissions were bad enough. Worse, for the majors, was the continuing interest of the US Department of Justice in the financing of Hollywood and in particular the cosy cartel operated by the big studios.

From the early Thirties, the Department of Justice had been trying to break the stranglehold of the majors over independent cinemas. Its aim was to force the film production and distribution companies to sell off their highly lucrative cinema divisions. Since most of the majors made almost all their money in film exhibition, rather than in distribution or

Left: Lamberto Maggiorani and Enzo Staiola in Vittorio De Sica's neo-realist classic, Bicycle Thieves.

When, in 1946, the world opened up again, only the USA had generous supplies of film stock – the raw materials with which to carry on the trade of film-making and win markets. Alongside the 20 films made in the Soviet Union in 1946 and the mere 54 that Italy completed at the height of the neo-realist movement, Hollywood's total of 432 was staggering. Furthermore, the American film industry had a backlog of movies from the war years still unreleased in many foreign territories. Even though the US Department of Commerce announced 'only the movies which put America's best foot forward will be sent abroad', the stage was set for American domination of the world film trade.

There was a catch in this apparently open-ended market. American films covered the screens of Europe but the revenue was going back across the Atlantic. In 1946, the French authorities conceded that three-quarters of the nation's screen production. Hollywood resisted as long as it could.

Cases were brought before the courts in 1938 and 1940 but the war delayed their impact. In 1946, the Department of Justice began to strip away the major privileges (and major profits) of the big-league motion-picture companies. The change was even more radical than most observers admit. Along with new tax laws (the biggest external influence on movies) the anti-trust decisions of the late Forties changed the basis of movie financing, and so of movie-making.

By 1946 the pattern of the business was changing; the small-town cinema owner was no longer confronted with a salesman who would make him take everything a studio might produce, on pain of getting nothing at all. He did not have to accept prices before seeing movies and he could bid competitively. It would be naive to suggest that this made for open competition in the movie business, but it did mean movies were not automatically guaranteed success. They had to convince cinema owners first.

Independent producers now had a better chance of selling their movies. The new tax laws made it wise for stars and star directors to form themselves into independent corporations. If each movie project were a corporation in its own right, sold, when completed, to a distributor for a profit then the profit would attract only 25 per cent capital-gains tax. The majors had to compete for these independent productions and for stars who also wanted their independence.

The majors were made to sell their cinema chains by a series of legal settlements reached between 1949 and 1959. These sales took away the largest element in profit and cash-flow from the studios. Banks were short of lending money in the immediate post-war period and were thus inclined to examine individual movie projects as well as corporate credits. In this way the idea of the 'bankable' star emerged. The strict hierarchy of first-run and second-run cinemas was shaken and this too altered the financial base of movie-making.

World War II had effectively closed most of America's traditional markets for film, except Britain. Attempts were made to open up larger business in South America notably with Carmen Miranda in musicals like *Down Argentine Way* (1940), *That Night in Rio* and *Weekend in Havana* (both 1941). Such moves did not, however, compensate for the loss of European markets. One of the problems with South America was the difficulty of shipping films there during wartime.

MGM had calculated rightly that the domestic US market was at saturation point in 1946. Abroad, American movies never had such a success as they did in the late Forties. But this did not bring as much money as expected back to the studios.

When, in 1946, the world opened up again, only the USA had generous supplies of film stock – the raw materials with which to carry on the trade of film-making and win new markets. Alongside the 20 films made in the Soviet Union in 1948 and the mere 54 that Italy completed at the height of the neo-realist movement, Hollywood's total of 432 was staggering. Furthermore, the American film industry had a backlog of movies from the war years still unreleased in many foreign territories. Even though the US Department of Commerce announced 'only the movies which put America's best foot forward will be sent abroad', the stage was set for American domination of the world film trade.

There was a catch in this apparently open-ended market. American films covered the screens of Europe but the revenue was going back across the Atlantic. In 1946, the French authorities conceded that three-quarters of the nation's screen time should be filled by Hollywood product, but in 1948 they insisted that only $3.6 million out of an annual $14 million take could be sent back to the USA. For their part, the British allowed $17 million to leave the country each year but about twice as much remained blocked by foreign-exchange regulations. Hollywood needed the cash but could not touch it. In time these blocked funds would form the basis of 'runaway' productions – American movies made outside America. Until this money could be made into new movies, Hollywood had a wild but profitless success on its hands.

Back in California the system was breaking up. United Artists tore itself apart – Pickford and Chaplin bad-mouthing each other across the nation, threatening to sell their shares and suing their absentee partner David O. Selznick. When a masterpiece of a film like *Red River* (1948) went $1 million over budget, United Artists could not support it. The production passed to an independent company. Such visible troubles did not help confidence. As a result of their experiences after 1948, at least half-a-dozen banks left the movie industry alone.

Labour trouble was the next problem to hit Hollywood. Post-war prices demanded new wage scales. Clean-ups in the

Above: violence erupts during a strike by workers at the Warner Brothers studio in 1946. Above right: A year later HUAC called its first witnesses. Disney claimed that communist propaganda was drawn in cartoon studios. Right: Garry Cooper on communism to HUAC – 'From what I hear I don't like it because it isn't on the level.' Centre: Robert Montgomery – 'I gave up my job to fight a totalitarianism called fascism. I am ready to do it again to fight the totalitarianism called communism'. Far right: the Hollywood Ten and their laywers. Far right above: Bogart and Bacall lead a protest march against the investigations.

craft unions in the early Forties had made the usual studio policy of buying off the union leaders impracticable. Those leaders were fierce and liberal, yet at the same time they included men like Ronald Reagan.

All this change and trouble and decline made for bad nerves, especially where Wall Street bankers or government support were involved. It was this nervousness that produced the sordid business of blacklists and blackmail. The political paranoia in Hollywood in the late Forties was fed by the uncertainties that abounded in the industry.

Hollywood had been blooded politically in the Thirties, with the vicious resistance to the author and screenwriter Upton Sinclair who ran for Governor of California. Prominent figures within the industry had taken part in a campaign of blatantly reactionary propaganda. Its political mood was always conciliatory to those in power, eager to avoid trouble, dissension or scandal. The flimsy wartime alliance between the USA and the USSR was terminated with the end of the war. The Left was characterized as both enemy abroad and

enemy within. It was not surprising that when the House Un-American Activities Committee, bearing the banner of the right wing, came out to investigate, Hollywood caved in. HUAC, as it was generally known, calculated quite shrewdly that Hollywood names would make headlines, and resistance would be soft. They were right.

HUAC Formed in 1937 as a committee of the House Of Representatives, the lower house of Congress, HUAC was officially re-established in 1945. It exploited public ignorance and hysteria about a 'communist-inspired conspiracy'. Officially, its members had the power only to suggest alterations to any law. In fact they had the power to destroy people's lives, using innuendo, hearsay and malice, under the aegis of a right-wing press.

Public interest in 'the communist threat' had subsided during World War II, but the beginnings of the Cold War made possible new opportunities to highlight and justify the hearings of HUAC. Two of the most active members, John Rankin, who was blatantly anti-Semitic, and the chairman, J. Parnell Thomas, who was rabidly anti-New Deal, had long memories. They recalled the 'intellectuals' of the Thirties; the writers, teachers and lawyers who had been attracted to leftist activity.

As many of these writers and lawyers were now working in the film industry, Hollywood was an obvious target. Early investigations in 1940 had been 'promising'. In 1947, HUAC opened its attack and subpoenaed 19 'unfriendly' witnesses – writers, directors, producers and actors. The hearings opened privately in the spring of 1947 with the appearance of helpful witnesses, like Ginger Rogers' mother, Lela, who revealed her daughter's stubborn refusal to speak the line 'Share and share alike – that's democracy', in *Tender Comrade* (1943). More influential friendly witnesses included Jack L. Warner, Louis B. Mayer, Walt Disney, Gary Cooper, Robert Montgomery, Ronald Reagan, George Murphy, Robert Taylor and the self-appointed Hollywood expert on communism, Adolphe Menjou.

Jack L. Warner, eager to explain away a handful of pro-Soviet movies made during the war years, warned that communist writers were 'poking fun at our political system' and picking on rich men. Adolphe Menjou alerted the Committee to 'communist acting', which made propaganda, he said, 'by a look, by an inflection, by a change in the voice'. Walt Disney told how he had been pressured by 'communists' (in the unlikely guise of the League of Women Voters) to accept a cartoonists' union, which he regarded as communist-inspired. His evidence, however, was such manifest and damaging nonsense that it had to be retracted by cable.

After six months of psychological pressure within the industry, the public hearings were held in October. They lasted only two weeks, with testimonies from 23 friendly witnesses, and ended after 10 of the 19 unfriendly witnesses had been called before the Committee. These became known as the Hollywood Ten.

The Committee for the First Amendment was formed to organize the film industry's protest against the trial's infringements of the rights and freedoms of the American constitution. The chairman, John Huston, William Wyler and Philip Dunne organized a plane-load of stars, including Humphrey Bogart, Lauren Bacall, Danny Kaye, Gene Kelly, June Havoc and Jane Wyatt, to go to Washington and see that their people had a fair hearing. They arrived in a blaze of publicity and it was partly because of the row they caused that the hearings came to an abrupt, though temporary halt.

The Mississippi congressman John Rankin, a man whose vocabulary depended on the words 'kike' and 'nigra', delightedly discovered that the protesting liberals had something to hide. 'One of the names is June Havoc', he reported. 'We have found that her real name is June Hovick. Another is Danny Kaye, and we found that his real name is David Daniel Kaminsky.'

The Hollywood Ten were John Howard Lawson, Dalton Trumbo, Lester Cole, Alvah Bessie, Albert Maltz, Ring Lardner Jr, Samuel Ornitz, Herbert Biberman, Edward Dmytryk and Adrian Scott. Writers were predominant among them. At that time, Lawson and Trumbo were the most prominent figures. Lawson had edited a paper in Rome for many years, and had also held the post of publicity director for the European division of the American Red Cross, before achieving success as a Broadway playwright. After a spell as a contract writer at MGM, he freelanced for Wanger, Goldwyn and 20th Century-Fox, working on anti-fascist and/or anti-Nazi films like *Blockade* (1938), *Sahara* (1943) and *Counter-Attack* (1945), as well as melodramas such as *Smash-Up* (1947). He was a founder member of the Screen Writers' Guild.

Trumbo was a former reporter and editor, who graduated from cheapies like *Road Gang* (1936) to become the highest-paid scriptwriter in Hollywood by the mid-Forties; *Tender Comrade*, *A Guy Named Joe* (1943) and *Thirty Seconds Over Tokyo* (1944) were among his best-known credits.

Lester Cole was a freelancer who is probably best remembered for *Objective, Burma!* (1945). Bessie, who scripted *Northern Pursuit* (1943) and worked with Cole on *Objective, Burma!*, and Maltz, who scripted *This Gun for Hire* (1942) and *Cloak and Dagger* (1946), were successful contract writers. Ring Lardner Jr had been a reporter and publicity writer for David O. Selznick before achieving recognition as a scriptwriter. Among the films he worked on were *Woman of the Year* (1942), *The Cross of Lorraine* (1943), *Tomorrow the World* (1944) and *Cloak and Dagger*. Samuel Ornitz was the least known of the Ten, with *Three Faces West* (1940) as his only major credit.

There were also two directors and one producer. Herbert Biberman came to Hollywood from the New York theatre. He was a founder member of the Hollywood Anti-Nazi League, and the Academy of Motion Pictures Arts and Sciences. He directed and/or scripted minor action films – *One Way Ticket* (1935), *The Master Race*, *Action in Arabia* (both 1944). Dmytryk joined Paramount in 1923, while still at school, spending the Thirties as an editor until he started directing B films in 1939, but he was well established at RKO by the mid-Forties, having worked on *Hitler's Children* (1943), *Murder, My Sweet* (1944), *Back to Bataan*, *Cornered* (both 1945), and *Crossfire* (1947). Adrian Scott also had stage experience before starting as a scriptwriter in 1940, and settling at RKO as a producer, where he made *Murder, My Sweet*, *Cornered* and *Crossfire*, all with Dmytryk.

Led by John Howard Lawson, the Ten persistently refused to answer the question 'Are you, or have you ever been, a Communist?' and were cited for contempt of Congress. Rather than refuse to testify on the grounds that they might incriminate themselves (according to the Fifth Amendment), they regarded the Committee itself as unconstitutional. All were suddenly suspended without pay; actually firing them could have led to lawsuits.

The Committee for the First Amendment now felt obliged to issue statements dissociating itself from Lawson and the Ten's belligerent stance. According to Abraham Polonsky, one of

the unfriendly 19, who was not called to the stand in 1947: 'General Beadle Smith was sent to Hollywood and he met the important Hollywood owners. A policy was laid down to call these actors and directors off – the important ones. Pressure was put on them through their agents and the whole thing melted in about two weeks.'

There was no help for the victims from the industry as a whole. On November 24, 1947, the Association of Motion Picture Producers met at the Waldorf-Astoria Hotel in New York to discuss their attitude to the Ten and formulate their policy for the future. The Association declared that, since the Ten had 'impaired their usefulness to the industry', they would not be employed again until they had purged themselves of the contempt and sworn under oath that they were not Communists. They pledged that the industry would 'Not knowingly employ a Communist or a member of any party or group which advocates the overthrow of the Government of the United States by force, or by any illegal or unconstitutional method'. They asked for the support of the law, 'since the absence of a national policy, established by Congress with respect to the employment of Communists in private industry, makes our task difficult'. The declaration also said: 'There is the danger of hurting innocent people. There is the risk of creating an atmosphere of fear.' Hurt and fear followed. The ban on ten men became a general blacklist, informally applied and therefore beyond challenge. To escape the list, a suspect had to name his 'undesirable' contacts before some self-appointed rightist like the projectionist Roy Brewer, head of the craft union IATSE. The unions joined the moguls and, as the Korean war escalated, polarizing the issue of communism, their all-industry council denounced those who refused to tell all (or invent all) for the House Committee.

There were exceptions to the capitulation of the moguls. In his book, *The Hollywood Tycoons*, Norman Zierold tells how Sam Goldwyn, who loathed Russia and communism, 'watched the proceedings . . . with increased dismay because he felt this was not the American way of doing things; no Congressional committee should be the arbiter of a man's right to work.'

Goldwyn then sent a telegram explaining his views to J. Parnell Thomas and stating that he wished to appear before the Committee to elaborate his views personally. He threatened to make his views public if he did not get a reply from Thomas. Goldwyn's stand has been credited as a factor in Thomas' dropping his investigation.

Legal proceedings dragged on for more than two and a half years before any of the Ten actually served time in prison. John Berry produced and directed a short film in 1950 in their defence, entitled *The Hollywood Ten*. But, during this period, there was constant pressure from groups such as the Motion Picture Alliance for the Preservation of American Ideals to reopen the hearings, and 'clean up' Hollywood.

HUAC capitalized on the fact that, during the Thirties and Forties, there had been some card-carrying members of the Communist Party in Hollywood (including several of the Ten), and that a number of household names had contributed to liberal causes and funds, some of which had proved to be Communist 'front' organizations. These names formed the basis of the lengthening blacklist.

In 1950, the conclusion of the Alger Hiss trial, American involvement in the Korean War, but above all, the rise to prominence of Senator Joseph McCarthy, who repeatedly threatened to name names of Communists serving in the State Department, produced a hysterical right-wing paranoia that built up in the public mind the supposed influence of 'Reds under the beds' out of all proportion. Trash sheets like *Red Channels* began publishing the names of people in the media. The people concerned were put on the spot by their employers, and the HUAC hearings reopened in 1951 to examine those on the blacklist.

The 'grey' list was also set up by the American Legion, listing names of suspected Communists or sympathizers. Every artist was by now afraid of being on somebody's 'list'. Workers in Hollywood always faced the risk of being named by cooperative witnesses, for those on the list could 'buy' themselves off it. The 'cleaning' process required them not only to admit their own guilt, but to list publicly all their friends and colleagues who had ever shown the slightest left-wing sympathy. Clearance letters then had to be begged from the American Legion and other patriotic groups.

An estimated 320 people suffered directly as a result of this cleansing process. A few brave individuals like Trumbo, Polonsky and Howard Da Silva refused to compromise or cooperate, but one of the Ten, Dmytryk, even went as far as naming John Berry, who had made the film *The Hollywood Ten* in his defence! Elia Kazan, Sterling Hayden, Robert Rossen (another of the original 19) and others paraded through the witness box, and employment ended for John Garfield, Larry Parks, Zero Mostel, Gale Sondergaard, Marsha Hunt, Jeff Corey and many others. Actors and actresses remained out of work. Writers and directors like Berry, Joseph Losey and Carl Foreman, who had been named but refused to testify, left for Europe.

But for those writers who stayed in America, like Trumbo and Polonsky, business carried on. Producers and directors still went to the writers they knew were competent. A writer could use the name of a friend, which often created problems. Or he could use a pseudonym. Dalton Trumbo wrote *The Brave One* (1956) under the pseudonym Robert Rich, and even received an Oscar for it. Another Oscar went to the screenplay for *The Bridge on the River Kwai* (1957), written by Carl Foreman and Michael Wilson but attributed to Pierre Boulle, the French author of the original novel.

In the Sixties, some of the Ten had their own names back on the screen. Trumbo was the first to come out of the wilderness in 1960 when Otto Preminger gave him screen credit for *Exodus*. Herbert J. Biberman had directed the independent film, *Salt of the Earth* (1954), but did not re-emerge until *Slaves* (1969). Lardner had to wait until 1965 for his official screen credit on *The Cincinnati Kid*, and then went on to script *M*A*S*H* (1970). Lawson had retreated to Moscow.

J. Parnell Thomas himself ended up joining the Ten in prison, when he served a sentence for fraud. Yet HUAC continued its investigations until it was formally wound up in 1975, after having been renamed the Internal Security Committee in 1969. It had cast a blight for years over the film industry, radio, television and, to a lesser extent, the theatre. It had curtailed the string of social melodramas that followed the war years. Had it uncovered any subversive elements? If there was 'subversion' in Hollywood in the post-war years, it was either implicit in the pessimism of the *film noir* or explicit as in the social-problem movies that dealt with racialism and allied subjects.

Edward Dmytryk's *Crossfire*, for example, originally intended as an examination of homosexuality, changed its focus to anti-Semitism. The subject of Mark Robson's *Home of the Brave* (1949) was changed from hatred of the Jews to hatred of blacks. In more sentimental form, oppression of Jews surfaced in Elia Kazan's *Gentleman's Agreement* (1947), which was mostly concerned to show that Jews are exactly like everybody else. Race also formed the dramatic problem in Kazan's *Pinky* (1949), a tale of a black girl (Jeanne Crain) trying to pass for white.

The idea that it might be hard to adjust to peace, a thought utterly taboo in wartime, came to the surface in *The Best Years of Our Lives* (1946). Political corruption, once completely forbidden as a topic by the Production Code, was shown in Robert Rossen's *All the King's Men* (1949) and also formed the subject of Kazan's *Boomerang* (1946).

Essentially, this revival of interest in social conscience had minimal political content. It was an extension of the black mood of crime melodramas and was perhaps equally romantic in nature. These films reflected a pervasive pessimism rather than activism; they spoke of subjects rather than analysed them. The Production Code would not be softened until the Fifties: in the American remake of Marcel Carné's *Le Jour se Lève* (1939, *Daybreak*) – featuring Jean Gabin's poignant depiction of a doomed fugitive – entitled *The Long Night* (1947), the criminal is obliged to surrender himself rather than commit suicide as he does in the original.

Top: Home of the Brave *depicted the abuse suffered by a black soldier confronted with racism in the US Army. Above:* Al (Fredric March) returning from the war in The Best Years of Our Lives, *cannot adjust, and turns to drink.*

Above: John Garfield, A HUAC victim, starred in and produced Force of Evil *(1949), an offbeat racketeering drama.*

Certain subjects had, however, been opened by the war. Psychosis, induced by the strain of war, became a respectable subject because it had a visible cause. Social strain in the wake of the war was also discussed in films. This apparent liberalization was a fine illusion; it assimilated some of the uncertainties produced by the war but was swiftly reversed by the black-and-white moral certainties of the Cold War.

Other Blacklisted Directors Although Edward Dymtryk was the only well-known director to go to prison among the 'Hollywood Ten' prosecuted by the House Un-American Activities Committee (HUAC) investigating Communist influence in Hollywood, in the late Forties and early Fifties several careers were disrupted, either temporarily (Robert Rossen) or permanently (Joseph Losey, Jules Dassin, Abraham Polonsky). Rossen (1908–1966) escaped the first round in 1947 and, after a decade as a distinguished scriptwriter, made a reputation with *Body and Soul* (1947), a boxing drama scripted by Polonsky and starring John Garfield, himself also a later victim of HUAC. *All the King's Men* was an impressive adaptation of Robert Penn Warren's novel of political corruption in Louisana, based on the life of former Governor Huey Long with Broderick Crawford as the proto-fascist dictator. In 1951 Rossen was blacklisted and, although he broke down and named names in 1953, he thereafter worked abroad or on the East Coast. His films of the Fifties did not restore his reputation, although *The Hustler* (1961) was a bit hit.

Polonsky (b. 1910) directed a single, brilliant thriller, *Force of Evil* (1949), starring Garfield and Beatrice Pearson, before he was exiled to pseudonymous scriptwriting for television. He re-emerged as scriptwriter for Don Siegel's *Madigan* (1968) and directed two films, the complex pro-Indian Western *Tell Them Willie Boy Is Here* (1969) and the little-seen *Romance of a Horsethief* (1971) before sinking back into obscurity.

Joseph Losey (1909–1984) was a left-wing theatre director in the Thirties, made a few short films and, after war service, staged the famous production of Bertolt Brecht's *Galileo Galilei* with Charles Laughton in Hollywood and New York (1947). He then directed his first feature, an allegorical fantasy, *The Boy With Green Hair* (1948), following it with four thrillers, *The Lawless* (1950), *The Prowler, M* and *The Big Night* (all 1951), which he endowed with his social consciousness and awareness of human isolation. In 1951, while making a disastrous Italian co-production, *Imbarco a Mezzanotte* (1952, *Stranger on the Prowl*), with Paul Muni, he was summoned by HUAC; returning later to Hollywood he found himself blacklisted. He then established an international reputation in England before moving to France.

Britain

The British film industry entered the post-war period in a spirit of optimism. Annual attendances at British cinemas in 1946 climbed to 1635 million, a figure which was to be an all-time high. The statistic is all the more remarkable since, out of 5000 cinemas, as many as 230 remained closed owing to bomb damage and, because the limited supply of building materials was reserved for more essential uses, no new cinemas could be built.

It was not until April 1949 that cinemas were allowed to switch on their front-of-house display lighting once again. But despite a certain dinginess, the cinema was still an attractive escape from the austerity of post-war Britain with its fuel crises, rationing and various other shortages.

The major cinema circuits – Odeon and Gaumont (both controlled by J. Arthur Rank), and the rival ABC (Associated British Cinemas) – were prevented from further expanding their share of the market by the Board of Trade. It was a time for smaller companies like Granada, Southan Morris and Star to expand by taking over independent cinemas. The biggest single growth, however, occurred in Sol Sheckman's Essoldo circuit which more than tripled in size between the end of the war (26 cinemas) and the end of the decade (89).

The traditional low esteem accorded to home-produced films by British audiences had vanished. J. Arthur Rank (1888–1972), an established producer in the late Thirties, was encouraged by the popularity of such pictures as *Madonna of the Seven Moons* (1944) and *A Place of One's Own* (1945) and embarked on a great crusade to put British films on an equal footing with Hollywood product throughout the world. There were new markets to be won in the formerly occupied countries, long deprived of Hollywood and British films, and Rank's salesmen were there, trying to earn money vital to Britain's post-war economy.

Rank also had his eye on the lucrative North American market. In 1944, he bought a half-interest in the circuit of 80 Odeon cinemas in Canada, and a year later he was contemplating building a new Odeon to seat 2500 people in New York's Times Square (he eventually settled for leasing the Winter Garden Theatre).

Rank was the largest shareholder in Universal and set up a new company in partnership with them to distribute eight Rank pictures a year in North America. These films were block-booked with new Hollywood films to make a package acceptable to the American circuits. But the US government had for some time been opposed to the system of block-booking and Rank was forced to change his plans. He eventually persuaded the five major American circuits to book British pictures on their own merits.

Britain could not afford to let all the money earned by Hollywood films in the UK leave the country – unless British films could earn more money in the USA to help redress the balance. At the same time the British market was vital to the American studios. In 1946, for example, it was worth $87 million and provided 60 per cent of their foreign income. The American circuits were controlled by the big Hollywood companies who realized that they would have to play their fair share of British films in order to keep their side of the bargain. Expensive and prestigious Rank productions like *Henry V* (1944) and *Caesar and Cleopatra* (1945), as well as the more modestly budgeted *The Seventh Veil* (1945), were already making inroads into the American market.

In 1946, six British pictures shared 11 Academy Award nominations. Among the Oscar winners were Laurence

Olivier, with a special award for *Henry V,* Clemence Dane for the story of *Perfect Strangers* (1945) and Muriel and Sydney Box for their original screenplay for *The Seventh Veil.* Success in America continued into 1947 when Rank's production of *Great Expectations* (1946) played at the mighty Radio City Music Hall in New York, and *Odd Man Out* (1947) appeared at another important Broadway cinema. The following year *Hamlet* (1948) won the Oscar for Best Picture and Best Actor, marking further triumphs for Olivier. *The Red Shoes* (1948) was also nominated for Best Picture. Hollywood smarted under charges that it was losing its artistic initiative.

Rank built up his British studio on Hollywood lines. He established an animation unit with David Hand, a recruit from Disney; he started a two-reel documentary series, *This Modern Age,* to rival the *March of Time;* he founded the 'charm school' at his Highbury studios to develop new talent.

As an exhibitor, Rank extended his empire. By the end of 1947, he had an interest in 725 overseas cinemas with more than a hundred in each of five countries – New Zealand, Canada, South Africa, Italy and Australia – and strong representation in Eire, Ceylon, Holland, Egypt, Jamaica and Singapore. In Britain, his two cinema circuits formed the prime outlet for the Hollywood majors (except Warners and MGM who had distribution ties with the ABC circuit) and at the same time Rank was programming British cinemas with his own films.

ABC had no overseas cinemas and were, therefore, a smaller concern than Rank. Furthermore they were substantially owned by Warner Brothers and had no-one of J. Arthur Rank's drive and zeal at the helm.

The only potential opposition to Rank's dominance of the British film industry was Alexander Korda, but he did not have the benefit of a cinema circuit. During 1943–5, Korda worked in association with MGM but he produced only one picture, *Perfect Strangers,* and the chance to curb Rank's power was lost. MGM called off their deal with Korda; he re-established London Films as a separate company and took over Shepperton studios.

Korda never became a prolific producer on the scale of J. Arthur Rank. In 1948, he was in severe financial difficulties following losses on two very expensive pictures, *An Ideal Husband* (1947) and a new version of *Anna Karenina* (1948). His extravagant spending on *Bonnie Prince Charlie* (1948), filmed over nine months, only made matters worse.

Fortunately, productions like *Mine Own Executioner* (1947) and *The Winslow Boy* (1948) were more economically filmed and Korda's company made some profit from distributing several of the upper-class romances that Herbert Wilcox produced and directed, starring his wife, Anna Neagle, and Michael Wilding. These films – *The Courtneys of Curzon Street* (1947), *Spring in Park Lane* (1948) and *Maytime in Mayfair* (1949) – reflected Wilcox's opinion that audiences were sick of 'gloomy horrors' and 'wanted films about nice people'.

Associated British had some successes with the Boulting Brothers' *Brighton Rock* (1947) and *My Brother Jonathan* (1948). The first of these was adapted from Graham Greene's crime thriller and starred Richard Attenborough as the teenage gangster Pinky; and the second film had Michael Denison playing an ambitious young doctor in a northern industrial town.

Rank also backed the independent producers' company Cineguild, formed in 1942 by David Lean, Ronald Neame, Anthony Havelock-Allan and Noel Coward. It was this team that produced *This Happy Breed* (1944), *Blithe Spirit* and *Brief*

Above: the man with the gong – Rank's famous trademark. Above right: J. Arthur Rank and some of the starlets from his 'charm school', among them Sally Grey and Jean Kent. Right: Laurence Olivier's award-winning Hamlet. *Below: a diamond merchant's niece (Anna Neagle) falls for her footman (Michael Wilding) in* Spring in Park Lane, *only to find he is really an impoverished lord.*

Above: a woman gets a piece of grit in her eye; a stranger kindly removes it – the start of a Brief Encounter. *Right:* Oliver Twist *(John Howard Davies) and Bill Sikes (Robert Newton). Below right: sexuality suppressed in a convent in* Black Narcissus. *Below: Margaret Lockwood as a high-born highwaywoman in* The Wicked Lady.

Encounter (both 1945). David Lean directed all three films and went on to make his two celebrated adaptations from Dickens, *Great Expectations* and *Oliver Twist* (1948), under the Cineguild banner.

Gainsborough, the production company of the Gaumont empire, specialized in costume melodramas about gypsies, bandits and brutality featuring such stars as Margaret Lockwood, James Mason and Stewart Granger. Despised by the critics, films like *They Were Sisters* and *The Wicked Lady* (both 1945) and *Caravan* (1946) were adored by the public. Thereafter, Gainsborough appeared to lose its popularity and eventually the company ran into financial losses with *Christopher Columbus* (1949), a tedious historical drama starring Fredric March as the intrepid explorer.

Michael Powell and Emeric Pressburger, one of the most prolific production teams of the period, formed their own company, The Archers, which was also backed by Rank. It was Rank that released their idiosyncratic, widely discussed films: *I Know Where I'm Going* (1945), *A Matter of Life and Death* (1946), *Black Narcissus* (1947) and *The Red Shoes*. Frank Launder and Sidney Gilliat's Individual Pictures company (also linked to Rank) made a number of accomplished films

that brought credit to the parent company: *The Rake's Progress* (1945), *I See a Dark Stranger* (1946) and *The Blue Lagoon* (1949). The last of these was handicapped by interference on the part of Rank who insisted that it be shot in the studio rather than on location, thus forcing the film beyond its budget.

One of the fiercest critics of Rank's monopoly was Michael Balcon, the production chief and head of Ealing Studios, but even he was obliged to turn to Rank for distribution from 1944 onwards. The immediate post-war period was not a notable time for Ealing despite the critical successes of *Dead of Night* and *Pink String and Sealing Wax* (both 1945) and the acclaim given to *Hue and Cry* and *It Always Rains on Sunday* (both 1947). But in 1949 the company brought out *Passport to Pimlico*, *Whisky Galore!* and *Kind Hearts and Coronets* in rapid succession. The era of Ealing comedy had truly arrived at last.

Rank was making headway as an independent businessman selling his films in the USA when the British government intervened and placed a 75 per cent *ad valorem* tax on American films imported after August 1947. The result of this measure was twofold: Hollywood stopped sending new films to Britain, and American circuits were no longer disposed to show British films. The overseas sales that Rank was pursuing became harder to achieve. In Britain, cinemas were soon reduced to playing reissues of old films and to extending the runs of new British films. By the spring of 1948 the film business was in a bad way.

Rank's response to the crisis was to launch a crash programme of production at a cost of over £9 million, drawing on the spare funds of his highly profitable Odeon circuit for the first time. But the new Rank pictures spread the available talent too thinly and the quality of these films was not high enough to guarantee profits. At the same time, the Chancellor of the Exchequer, Sir Stafford Cripps, arranged for the original import tax on Hollywood films to be repealed in May 1948 in exchange for an agreement on the part of the Americans to limit the amount of earnings removed from the country to an annual figure of $17 million. The remainder of this revenue was to be reinvested in British film production. Hollywood, not surprisingly, unleashed a backlog of 265 pictures and the new British films were swamped under the competition.

Once again the government tried to take remedial steps. It raised the quota of British features to be shown in cinemas throughout the land from 20 to 45 per cent. The new figure made impossible demands on the British film industry even though Rank kept up production in an attempt to fulfil the quota. Hollywood was once again handicapped as the various studios scrambled for the limited playing time the new British law left them.

In the summer of 1949, Rank's £86 million empire had a £16.25 million overdraft and had lost £3.35 million in production, resulting in an overall year's trading loss of £750,000. J. Arthur Rank ordered savage cut-backs. No future film was to cost over £150,000. Rank stopped making cartoons, terminated *This Modern Age*, closed the studios at Highbury (and the 'charm school'), Islington and Shepherd's Bush and cut back on production activity at Denham. Pinewood was to be the main base for production. The economies forced many film-makers away, most of them joining up with Korda, a popular and cultured figure with whom artists felt at home.

Investment in production was no longer the attractive gamble it had been to financiers in the Thirties. Instead the government of the day created the National Film Finance Corporation which began in October 1948 with £5 million to loan to producers who proposed safe-looking projects for films. Rank made no attempt to borrow NFFC money, not wanting to increase his organization's debts, but Korda seized the opportunity and borrowed £3 million for a variety of productions.

The money gave Korda a new lease of life. He engaged Carol Reed to make *The Fallen Idol* (1948) and *The Third Man* (1949). The latter film was partly financed by the Hollywood producer David O. Selznick who supplied Joseph Cotten and Alida Valli from his roster of stars. Selznick also collaborated with Korda on Powell and Pressburger's *Gone to Earth* (1950), a melodrama set in the Shropshire countryside with spectacular hunting scenes. This film prompted an argument between Korda and Selznick over the quality of the close-ups of Jennifer Jones and Selznick had the scenes featuring Jones re-shot in the United States before releasing the film as *The Wild Heart*.

Associated British responded to Rank's cut-back with the announcement of a major production programme in association with Warner Brothers. One of the products of this

collaboration was *The Hasty Heart* (1949) starring Richard Todd. The film was directed by Vincent Sherman from a script by Ranald MacDougall and co-starred Patricia Neal; all three were Warners stalwarts from Hollywood. Associated British also drew on Hollywood talent for their lavish, American-style musical *Happy-Go-Lovely* (1951): the film was directed by H. Bruce Humberstone and starred David Niven, Vera-Ellen and Cesar Romero.

Other Hollywood companies were actively involved in British production, using up some of the frozen assets created by governmental restrictions. 20th Century-Fox made *Escape* (1948) and *Britannia Mews* (1949), a period romance written by Ring Lardner Jr. In 1949, MGM filmed *Edward My Son* and the Cold War thriller *Conspirator*, as well as establishing its own studio at Borehamwood.

At the end of the decade, the British film industry was badly battered. The high hopes of the post-war revival were dashed. In 1949, the government set up the British Production Fund which has always been known as the Eady Plan after Sir William Eady who devised the scheme. Briefly, the fund was the product of a levy on the price of cinema admission which would be returned to producers in direct proportion to the performance of their films at the box-office. The Eady levy placed a premium on financial success and British film producers felt it keenly. In the same year as the Eady Plan was introduced, the government reduced the quota of British films exhibitors were obliged to play to 40 per cent. This move may have eased the pressure on British production but the industry would never again enjoy the financial stability of the mid-Forties.

While Rank and Korda were undoubtedly the pre-eminent executives of the post-war years, creatively the period was dominated by the producer Michael Balcon at Ealing and the three outstanding directors David Lean, Carol Reed and Michael Powell (with Emeric Pressburger).

Michael Balcon and Ealing Balcon's connection with Ealing dated back to 1938, when he took over from Basil Dean, who had built the studios in 1931. Ealing under Balcon had little to do with the eminently respectable kind of cinema Dean liked to promote, yet the two regimes still had many similarities and points of continuity. Both men were con-

Above: the homely frontage of Ealing Studios was a far cry from the magnificence of its Hollywood counterparts.

cerned to make the studio's product characteristically British. The words of the plaque erected on the studio buildings in 1955, when they were sold to the BBC, put the matter in a nutshell:

'Here during a quarter of a century were made many films projecting Britain and the British character'.

Dean projected Britain largely through the pictorial image of the country. Balcon never neglected the country's pictorial image either: *Hue and Cry,* the film that ushered in the classic comedies, strikingly explored the blitzed landscapes of London, while one semi-documentary feature, *Painted Boats* (1945), was completely given over to canals. Yet his projection of Britain went considerably deeper than the details of urban and country landscapes. The best of Balcon's films use national characteristics as a springboard for their stories of community endeavours, of quirky individuals tilting at unwieldy officialdom.

Another link between the two periods is the importance given to comedy. By 1938 Gracie Fields had been lured with the offer of a higher salary to an American company, 20th Century, which produced her last three British films, concluding with *Shipyard Sally* (1939); thereafter three Hollywood films in the later years of the war terminated her screen career. The Lancashire tradition of comedy was sustained at Ealing by the production of George Formby films up to *Turned Out Nice Again* (1941), after which he succumbed to Columbia British, maintaining his position as Britain's top box-office star from 1938 right through to 1944, a unique record. The popular tradition of low-brow, low-budget moneymakers was then taken over by Will Hay, who had worked for Balcon at Gaumont-British and transferred his activities to Ealing from 1941 until 1943, when ill-health curtailed his career.

With the end of the war, however, Ealing's conception of comedy changed decisively. Instead of producing films shaped round comic stars with permanently established personalities, Balcon started to make films designed for a motley collection of versatile performers superbly adept at comedy: Alastair Sim, Alec Guinness, Margaret Rutherford, Joan Greenwood and Cecil Parker. Ealing comedies were now created by a team for a team.

Balcon continued and intensified Dean's tradition of benevolent paternalism. Signs with legends like 'The studio with team spirit' hung from the walls. Balcon was also careful to encourage the individual talents within his team. Future producers and directors began as editors (Robert Hamer, Charles Crichton), assistant editors (Seth Holt), writers (Alexander Mackendrick), art directors (Michael Relph). Monja Danischewsky rose from publicist to writer and associate producer.

The studio, in fact, became exactly the kind of isolated community it loved to celebrate in its films. It was populated by a closely-knit group of talents all proudly united in a common goal and somewhat suspicious of outsiders or anyone 'different'. Once established at Ealing, people tended to stay there. Certainly those who moved away, such as Henry Cornelius and Robert Hamer, were very much the exceptions.

Balcon's team was drawn together during the war years, when, in common with British films of the period, Ealing's output testified to a new strength, character and sense of purpose. *Convoy* (1940) was one of the most popular films of its time – a sturdy drama of life on board a convoy ship. Its publicity slogan was 'Entertainment with authenticity'. But at this early stage of the war the authenticity in *Convoy* lay chiefly in its location footage. The director Pen Tennyson

Above left: the sinister gang of The Ladykillers, *one of Ealing's finest comedies. Left:* Kind Hearts and Coronets, *an exquisitely subversive comedy about a young man determined to revenge his relatives' rejection of him. Above:* Passport to Pimlico, *quintessentially English in its whimsical individualism and defiance of authoritarianism.*

(killed in an air crash the following year) shot so much background material on the high seas that subsequent Ealing directors constantly returned to his footage to fill out their own maritime features and shorts. The attitudes of Tennyson's characters were, however, less authentic: the officer class paraded on deck with binoculars while the humble workers stoked the fires and checked the gauges down below, both social groups carefully keeping each other at a respectable distance.

But the pull of the war's events – and the influx of documentary-trained talent, like the director Harry Watt – helped Ealing films reflect Britain's new spirit of comradeship, all layers of society working together with courage and good humour. By the time of *San Demetrio, London* (1943), authenticity of emotional content was plainly considered more important than authenticity of location.

With the war drawing to a close, Ealing prepared for peacetime production. A deal with J. Arthur Rank's empire in 1944 gave the company security for the future and a guaranteed release in Rank's cinema chain for all their films. But what kind of films would these be? Balcon made an extravagant statement about this in the trade magazine *Kinematograph Weekly* in January 1945:

'British films must present to the world a picture of Britain as a leader in Social Reform, in the defeat of social injustices and a champion of civil liberties . . . Britain as a questing explorer, adventurer and trader . . . Britain as a mighty military power standing alone and undaunted against terrifying aggression.'

One could just about squeeze *Scott of the Antarctic* (1948) into that scheme, but it hardly accounts for Ealing's anthology of supernatural stories *Dead of Night* (1945), the rural romance of *The Loves of Joanna Godden* (1947) or the rush of comedies that followed in the post-war period.

It is not in the British character, despite Balcon's declaration in 1945, to use films to confront big issues and to conquer all and sundry. Ealing realized this and instead settled for small issues, small communities and characters too humble to stride anywhere, except in their dreams.

In comedies and dramas, Ealing kept the community spirit of the war still burning brightly: London's East End was featured in *It Always Rains on Sunday*, Paddington Green in *The Blue Lamp* (1950). Other films looked at a cross-section of society: the varied frequenters of a London dance hall in *Dance Hall* (1950), a group of seamen on weekend leave in *Pool of London* (1951). Post-war Ealing opened up other new areas to British cinema, literally in the case of *The Overlanders* (1946) and the other Australian and African films, such as *Eureka Stockade* (1949) and *Where No Vultures Fly* (1951).

This was unquestionably Ealing's richest period. The famous comedies emerged, three of them in 1949 (*Passport to Pimlico, Whisky Galore!, Kind Hearts and Coronets*), all subtly different in tone. Robert Hamer's *Kind Hearts and Coronets*, in which Dennis Price undertook the disposal of the d'Ascoyne family, was distinguished by its black humour, highly literate script and a visual elegance unique in Ealing's output. Alexander Mackendrick's *Whisky Galore!* provided a caustic look at human foibles as Hebridean islanders and a pompous British resident (played by Basil Radford) clashed over a consignment of whisky rescued from a wrecked boat. Henry Cornelius' *Passport to Pimlico*, with a script by the Ealing stalwart T.E.B. Clarke, presented a boisterous picture of another community eager to abandon constraints and portrayed the London district of Pimlico as an independent, ration-free state after a dusty document had revealed the area to be an outpost of the once-powerful Duchy of Burgundy.

Ealing's dramas of the period, like *The Blue Lamp*, also celebrated community life, although the population and officialdom were now seen working together to combat the anti-social elements that threatened its smooth running. Jack Warner played P.C. Dixon, a personification of the British bobby – cheerful, homely, fond of his darts and his garden plants. When he is fatally wounded during a bungled robbery, even the underworld fraternity unite with the authorities to trap the killer (played by Dirk Bogarde) among the happy crowds at a greyhound stadium.

As the Fifties moved on, however, Ealing's projection of British life began to falter. Comedies and dramas repeated the familiar formulas with diminishing returns. Comedies became increasingly pallid with *The Titfield Thunderbolt* (1953) and *The Maggie* (1954), and reached the height of whimsicality in *Barnacle Bill* (1957) when a sea captain, played by Alec Guinness, kitted out a rundown pier as an ocean liner. At least *The Ladykillers* (1955), where Mackendrick and his writer William Rose made a virtue of Ealing's obsession with the quaint and decrepit, was fully up to standard. The Ealing dramas turned equally limp: *Dunkirk* (1958) presented all the emotions and situations of the past war in a manner so cold that they instantly congealed into clichés.

After Ealing's home studio was sold to the BBC in 1955, production continued at MGM's Borehamwood studios. Their final film was *The Siege of Pinchgut*, released in August 1959.

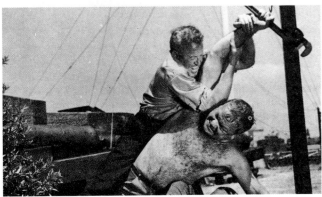

Left: The Siege of Pinchgut, *about a convicts' riot, was chiefly made on location in Australia. It was Ealing's last film. Top left: Diana Dors in* Dance Hall.

Deprived of a base, Balcon's central principles of production, continuity and community no longer obtained. Stressing the importance of common purpose and free exchange of ideas, he had once described a production unit as 'a sort of soviet'. His witty and well-loved colleague Monja Danischewsky characterized Ealing, with a different emphasis, as 'Mr Balcon's Academy'. There is no contradiction: that there was a genuine exchange of ideas, without regard to hierarchy, under Balcon, is undoubted; that the headmaster had the last word no less so.

Although Balcon's career did not end with the passing of Ealing, his later years were largely taken up with the politics of survival for independent production in Britain.

Key Directors   The films of **David Lean** (b. 1908) were frequently concerned with the conflict between discipline and individualism, between a peculiarly British emotional reticence and Romantic excess. The widely contrasting locales of his later films – the jungle in *The Bridge on the River Kwai* (1957), the desert in *Lawrence of Arabia* (1962), the icy wastes of *Doctor Zhivago* (1965), the wild Irish coastline in *Ryan's Daughter* (1970), the teeming subcontinent of *A Passage to India* (1984) – were no mere pictorial backdrops. Lean's characters were shaped by their social and physical environments and were constantly in conflict with them. They were placed in necessarily alien, inhospitable and challenging landscapes that appeared to offer a source of escape and self-discovery.

Running parallel to these assertive and tragic characters were the precisely delineated societies founded on class barriers, discipline, traditional values and moral complacency, all of which were challenged yet remained indomitable. Lean's was a deeply pessimistic vision, as evidenced by the fates of his characters: Laura, in *Brief Encounter*, renouncing love for drab security; Pip finding disillusionment in *Great Expectations*; Mary, in *The Passionate Friends* (1949), driven, like Laura, to near-suicide and then a living death; *Madeleine* (1950) ostracized and condemned by the courts to spiritual limbo; Ridgefield, in *The Sound Barrier* (1952), sacrificing a son for an obsession; Jane, in *Summer Madness* (1955), slipping back to her grey life; Nicholson, in *The Bridge on the River Kwai*, realizing, at the moment of his death, that the very quality that made him such a good leader – his iron fixedness of purpose – has made him a traitor to his country; Lawrence, in *Lawrence of Arabia*, destroyed by his own legend; Lara and Zhivago, in *Doctor Zhivago*, frozen into anonymity; Rosy Ryan ostracized and damned in *Ryan's Daughter*, with a suicide and several shattered lives on her conscience. The few happy endings were equivocal, undermined by the compromises which make such endings possible.

Lean's films were pessimistic, but never grim. He was first and foremost a master story-teller, an entertainer with a fine sense of drama and humour, an ironist – a poet and imagist, as his frequent collaborator the playwright and screenwriter Robert Bolt called him.

In the immediate post-war period Britain had no film director more highly regarded than **Carol Reed** (1906–1976). For three successive years the British Film Academy singled out his films as the best native product: *Odd Man Out* in 1947, *The Fallen Idol* in 1948, *The Third Man* in 1949. He was knighted in 1952, a rare honour for a director working full-time in the cinema. His adaptation of F.L. Green's novel *Odd Man Out* was not like *The Stars Look Down* (1939) where Reed was uncommitted to Cronin's hero: the fate of Johnny (James

Above: Alec Guinness as Colonel Nicholson in the first of David Lean's super-productions, The Bridge on the River Kwai. *Above right: Lean at work. Above far right:* Lawrence of Arabia *(Peter O'Toole) leads his Bedouins into battle.*

Mason), the Irish revolutionary wounded in a robbery to secure funds for the IRA, interested the director deeply. This is reflected in the film's visual conception: vertiginous camera angles and masterly shadow effects create a baroque world of disordered perception, fear and nightmare. (Indeed, tilted camera angles were so much a part of Reed's style in this film and its successors that the American director William Wyler jokingly gave him a spirit level to put on top of his cameras.) Johnny totters about helplessly, dripping blood and bandages, from air-raid shelter to house, to horse cab, to builder's yard, to pub, to inevitable death.

With *The Fallen Idol*, Reed began a fruitful collaboration with the distinguished writer Graham Greene, who as a film critic had praised Reed's work in the Thirties.

Most of their work together also reveals a fondness for exotic or eccentric locations – Vienna in *The Third Man*, Cuba in *Our Man in Havana* (1959). The action of *The Fallen Idol*, however, takes place in London. The boy Felipe (Bobby Henrey) lives in an unidentified embassy and idolizes the butler Baines (Ralph Richardson), whose tall stories of derring-do turn sour when his wife is found dead. Once again Reed uses distorted camera angles and bizarre spatial compositions to suggest the disordered perceptions of the main character – an odd boy out, isolated in an adult world he

Far left: Johnny McQueen (James Mason), IRA gang-leader in Carol Reed's award-winning Odd Man Out. *The film's message – violence only destroys – is still relevant. Left: Wendy Hiller and Trevor Howard in the moody* Outcast of the Islands. *Right: Carol Reed directs the action of* The Third Man, *with Joseph Cotton (centre) and Orson Welles (back to camera).*

cannot properly comprehend. Greene's own script, from his story *The Basement Room,* is strikingly witty.

The hero of *The Third Man,* filmed from an original Greene script, is another odd man out – a hack writer of Westerns, Holly Martins (Joseph Cotten), who stumbles naively around a post-war Vienna criss-crossed with zones and black markets, trying to uncover the truth about the death of his friend and meal-ticket, Harry Lime (Orson Welles). The quest brings many dilemmas for Martins, for he finds Lime is a murderous racketeer and not dead at all but slinking about the city's doorways and sewers. Once again Reed's camera tilts crazily, fashioning strange landscapes from the bombed Vienna exteriors; Anton Karas' zither music and Orson Welles' appearances, tantalizingly delayed until the last third of the film, are both haunting and enigmatic.

But for all the film's distinction there now seems something strained about Reed's direction; the effort that went into his visual effects is all too apparent. Perhaps Reed sensed this at the time, for his subsequent films look positively staid by comparison, though *Outcast of the Islands* (1951) bristles with tension – generated less by camera tricks than the fevered tempo of acting and editing. This film took him away from Graham Greene into the world of Joseph Conrad, another writer who loved making his characters' lives as morally

complex as possible. The outcast – one more odd man – is Willems (Trevor Howard), an arch-sensualist who is given control of an East Indian river village by his protector Captain Lingard (Ralph Richardson) only to fall victim to tribal jealousies and the attractions of the native girl Aissa (Kerima). Reed documents his decline into complete depravity with dogged skill.

Reed made ten more films before his death but none reached the level of this post-war quartet.

Our Man in Havana, however, reunited him with Graham Greene, who supplied a script from his own novel about yet another muddled innocent wading into deep water – a salesman-cum-British spy (Alec Guinness) who sends his superiors drawings of imaginary missiles closely resembling the vacuum cleaners sold in his shop. The one complete success of Reed's last years was *Oliver!* (1968). Reed filmed Lionel Bart's musical about Oliver Twist with bracing élan. His clinical style of directing, with its strong emphasis on editing, may have been old-fashioned by the late Sixties, when more free-wheeling styles were in vogue, yet it proved exactly right for the subject: Bart's songs and routines were put across with all their excitement and charm still intact. And at last Reed won another award – an Oscar for Best Director.

Above: the film-maker as voyeur in Powell and Press-burger's Peeping Tom *(1960), a film that was critically loathed when first shown but is now regarded as a classic. Right: Moira Shearer in* The Red Shoes.

Michael Powell (b. 1905) was the most extreme and the most elusive director in the English cinema. It was the war that enflamed Powell's imagination and brought him his vital collaborator, **Emeric Pressburger** (b. 1902). Pressburger was a Hungarian who had worked as a screenwriter in Europe. He came to Britain in 1938 and was introduced to Powell by another Hungarian, Alexander Korda. Powell and Press-burger began working together on *The Spy in Black* (1939), about Germans trying to penetrate the British naval base at Scapa Flow, with Conrad Veidt as Powell's first study of German decisiveness. They worked together until 1956, usually sharing credit for writing, direction and production. Powell's films around 1945 were personal reactions against the new socialist tide in Britain. Although *I Know Where I'm Going* and *A Matter of Life and Death* are love stories, they are also political statements wilfully set against the grain of the time. Their unruliness shows the difficulty Powell has had in being a man for his own time; but their spirit proclaims his loyalty to gentlemanly values, values buried in his sense of English tradition. The post-war love stories depict desire lurking within a restraining code, the lovers tossed about between common sense and irrational lyricism. Women are nuisances, helpmates or familiars who intuit the power of spell and fantasy. The films move violently yet serenely from reality to hallucination. *A Matter of Life and Death* has a bomber pilot 'killed' in action. But he claims a reprieve in heaven because he fell in love with a radio operator just before dying. Reality is given gorgeous colour, and the socialist utopia of heaven is insipid black-and-white. Although David Niven as the pilot is chatty and matter-of-fact, he is a poet too. Peace probably frustrated Powell. Instead of a splurge of joy and release in Britain, there were ration books and shortages. He responded with the exotic *Black Narcissus*, made in a studio re-creation of Nepal, about the thunder of denied sexuality in a convent. It was picturesque, fevered and half-crazy: Gothic romance has often beckoned Powell. The sensual potential of David Farrar, Deborah Kerr, Kathleen Byron and the young Jean Simmons is

viewed with flinching ecstasy. David Farrar and Kathleen Byron play the couple in *The Small Back Room* (1949). He is a crippled, alcoholic bomb expert who nonetheless is given the task of dismantling a new German weapon. Farrar is an ideal Powell hero: passionate but introverted. *The Small Back Room* is a remarkable *film noir* love story. Sexual longing hides in every shadow. *The Red Shoes* on the other hand, is an explosion of colour – garish, undried, and vibrant with emotion. Revered by ballet lovers, *The Red Shoes* was the demonstration of Powell's craze for total cinema – colour, story, design, music, dance – impressive for its relentless artiness, for its cinematic equivalent of the Andersen fairytale and its rapture with art. *The Red Shoes* captivates young people because its zeal is so close to nightmare: the ballerina (Moira Shearer) cannot stop dancing, and the impresario (Anton Walbrook) urges her to perform at the cost of her life and the love he cannot even admit to himself. *The Red Shoes* is theatrical and fanciful, but Walbrook's rendering of the Diaghilev figure reflects Powell's conception of the artist as outcast, scold, and prophet to an indolent world. The artist's dedication is close to destructiveness: his vision is never more romantic than when it refuses to yield to real obstacles; he is most tender and wounded when he cannot share the sentiments of other people. For all its rainbow dazzle, *The Red Shoes* glorifies the pained but magnificent – even necessary – isolation of the artist in modern society.

Italy

Neo-Realism When the great Italian director Roberto Rossellini was asked to define neo-realism, he said:

'For me it is above all a moral position from which to look at the world. It then became an aesthetic position, but at the beginning it was moral.'

To understand both the moral and aesthetic position which informed neo-realism, as well as the forces that helped destroy it, it is necessary to begin with the economic, political, and social context in which it was born.

There were, of course, harbingers of a 'new realism' before

Rossellini's *Roma, Città Aperta* (1945, *Rome, Open City)*, which portrayed the efforts and agonies of the underground Resistance. But when that film burst upon the international cinema scene in the immediate post-war years, neo-realism proper can be said to have begun. *Rome, Open City* was a direct product of the 'War of Liberation' taking place in Italy in 1945.

During 1943 and 1944, Italy had been torn apart, Mussolini's government had fallen, the new Badoglio government had surrendered to the invading Allied armies in the South while the Germans had occupied the North: anti-fascist Italians of every political and religious persuasion had been involved in the fighting to liberate their country and had been united by the struggle against fascism.

To film-makers and all other artists of the period it was clear that if the lies and empty rhetoric of the Mussolini government had brought Italy to agony, then a confrontation with reality, an encounter with 'truth' would save Italy. In terms of the cinema this meant the rejection of what had gone before, for although there were few blatant propaganda films made under the Fascist regime, the films that were produced in Italy during the war years had little to do with Italian reality.

Some long-term benefits emerged from the Fascist government's control of the film industry. The huge studio complex of Cinecittà had been built and the Italian film school, the Centro Sperimentale di Cinematografia, had already trained many important Italian film-makers. Not every film made under the Fascist regime was poor but none of them came close to touching the social reality of Italy; for the most part, they were the slick, glossy, vacuous melo-dramas made entirely in the studios and featuring upper-middle-class characters, known as 'white telephone' films.

Inspired by the 'War of Liberation', film-makers rejected the old cinema and its conventions. Their belief in showing 'things as they are' was placed in the service of the construction of a new Italy. In this way the moral and aesthetic principles of neo-realism were united. The manner and style of the new cinema was to be as much a statement as its subject-matter.

The theory of neo-realism was formulated in part from basic assumptions about the nature of cinema and its function in society, and in part from the early films of the movement. Theory and practice rarely coincided in one film and many were only superficially neo-realist films. Some astute Italian critics decried the use of neo-realist mannerisms to disguise purely commercial ventures (usually exploitative sexual melodramas) and the forcing of material that cried out for a different treatment into a neo-realist style.

Cesare Zavattini, the writer of Vittorio De Sica's major films, formulated the theory of neo-realism: cinema's task was no longer simply to 'entertain' in the usual sense of the word, but to confront audiences with their own reality, to analyse that reality, and to unite audiences through a shared confrontation with reality. The most disheartening thing for the neo-realist film-makers must have been that this basic goal was not achieved, simply because Italian audiences remained indifferent or hostile to the films, preferring instead pure escapism. They had no desire to confront on the screen the depressing reality of their everyday lives.

If cinema was to present things 'as they are', it meant that fiction, particularly that derived from novels and plays, would have to be replaced by looser, rather open-ended narratives, based on real experience familiar to the film-makers or, perhaps, found in newspapers. Zavattini cited the example of a woman buying a pair of shoes to show how simple such narratives could be and how social problems – poverty, unemployment, poor housing – could be illustrated within a fiction film.

Although most of the problems depicted in neo-realist films were susceptible to political solution, the neo-realists never presented a clear political programme. Their party affiliations were, after all, quite diverse: a number of writers and directors were Marxists but just as many were Christian Democrats, or held various other political ideas.

The theorists, especially Zavattini, insisted that there was a natural affinity betwen the cinema and 'reality', despite the fact that a camera will record whatever is in front of the lens and that the processed film will then (depending upon the skill of the film-maker) convince a spectator of the 'reality' of what he is seeing. But it was never quite so simple and Zavattini frequently made it clear that, for him, the entire question remained ambiguous, that cinematic 'realism' was merely a convention, and that the neo-realist method was only one possible approach to cinema.

Inevitably audiences become accustomed to cinematic conventions, even those as initially 'shocking' as open-air shooting on real streets with non-professional actors. In *Rome, Open City* real locations were used for most of the film but no-one has complained (and very few people even knew) that the priest's room, the Gestapo headquarters and one apartment were constructed entirely in a studio and therefore broke the rules of authenticity. Similarly, the theoretical principle that roles be played by 'real people' – which was partly an over-reaction to the artificiality of movie stars – became a convention in itself. Besides, several leading roles in *Rome, Open City* itself were acted by professionals, including Anna Magnani.

In De Sica's *Umberto D* (1951), the non-actor playing the role of the retired government official was in real life an elderly professor. He was highly praised for the 'reality' of his performance, but it was a performance; the professor had nothing in common with the character except age.

One of the few neo-realist films which followed the theory by having the entire cast made up of non-professionals was Visconti's *La Terra Trema* (1948, The Earth Trembles). In that film, however Visconti rehearsed his village fishermen over

Above: Rome, Open City *was a direct and authentic portrait of the time and place in which it was made.*

and over again until they delivered the performances he wanted. They were effective, not so much because they were fishermen, but rather because they had been formed into good actors.

For some critics and film-makers, 'reality' meant 'social reality' and in particular the representation of the conditions of the poor and unemployed. Later, when directors like Rossellini and Visconti moved away from the working classes, they were denounced as 'betrayers of neo-realism', as if the middle classes were not a part of 'social reality'.

Social criticism was hardly lacking in neo-realist films, but it was rarely their major thrust. In De Sica's *Ladri di Biciclette* (1948, *Bicycle Thieves*) the camera pans along rows of pawned sheets while the protagonist attempts to pawn those belonging to his wife. Throughout the film we are made aware of the thousands of people like him, all seeking work. Yet the problem of unemployment is never analysed. Instead the story takes a dramatic turn as the protagonist steals a bicycle to replace the one he has lost and is thus criminalized by his poverty. He is subsequently humiliated and finally 're-deemed'. At the end of the film we are moved by the man's plight, but we are no closer to an understanding of his social reality.

Visconti's *La Terra Trema,* comes closest to being the perfect neo-realist film: it achieves a clear understanding of how the fishermen are exploited and of how this 'social reality' works to oppress people generally. Ironically, while the theory of neo-realism was fulfilled by *La Terra Trema,*

Visconti violated one of Zavattini's fundamental tenets by basing the film on a novel, *I Malavoglia,* by the nineteenth-century writer Giovanni Verga, who is often mentioned by critics and film historians as one of the possible sources of Italian neo-realism.

Most of the arguments and polemics surrounding neo-realism had already been rehearsed in the nineteenth century. At that time the novelists, of the literary movement known as *Verismo* ('truthlikeness' or realism) concerned themselves primarily with the lower classes and their problems. One of the stated goals of the verist writers was the social education of their readers. Such work, however, rarely reached the class that might have drawn benefit from it. Most verist novelists, like several neo-realist directors, sought to increase their popularity by recounting routine shop-girl fantasies, cloaked in the mantle of realism. Verga remained the most distinguished exception.

In tracing the origins of Italian neo-realism, 'realist' film styles can be detected in the early Italian cinema: even the historical spectaculars which gave Italian cinema its international reputation contain a vividly realistic streak.

The American cinema may also be evidenced as an antecedent of Italian neo-realism; it is clear, for example, that everyone working in Italian cinema of the Forties was familiar with such 'realist' classics as Vidor's *The Crowd* (1928) and Stroheim's *Greed* (1924). Also influential was the so-called 'poetic realism' of Jean Renoir and his fellow film-makers in France during the Thirties. Visconti's own training as an

Above: fishermen's wives await the return of their menfolk in La Terra Trema. *Right: Vittorio De Sica was a star of Italian cinema prior to the war. His partnership with the writer Cesare Zavattini was central to the development of Italian neo-realist film. Far right above: Montgomery Clift in* Indiscretions of an American Wife. *Far right below:* Ossessione, *with the lovers Giovanna and Gino locked into the fatal compulsion of adultery and murder is often termed the first neo-realist film.*

assistant on *Une Partie de Campagne* (1936, *A Day in the Country*) and his close study of Renoir's films is echoed in films like *Ossessione* (1942, *Obsession*) and *La Terra Trema*.

The 'War of Liberation' may have temporarily united Italians of diverse political beliefs and provided an inspiration for the neo-realists but the honeymoon was short-lived. After the liberation, anti-communist propaganda took root in Italy.

Although the social criticism of neo-realist cinema was essentially mild and non-Marxist, the films did illuminate problems in Italy that remained unsolved. In the immediate post-war climate, 'anti-fascist' had come to mean much the same thing as 'communist' and the government did not take too kindly to the image of the country that the neo-realist film-makers were projecting. For its part, the Church claimed that such films were unsympathetic to the clergy and even blasphemous.

Some neo-realist films had great success at the box-office, but for the most part they depended on foreign receipts to cover the costs of even the small budgets involved. The huge popularity of American films all but destroyed whatever financial basis the domestic market had for Italian films, neo-realist or otherwise. Gradually the producers, too, became hostile to the neo-realist style,.

When the government appointed Giulio Andreotti as the head of the Direzione Generale dello Spettacolo (an agency for overseeing the performing arts), he was given wide-ranging powers over the cinema. Andreotti controlled bank loans: he restricted them to 'suitable' films and vetoed loans on films

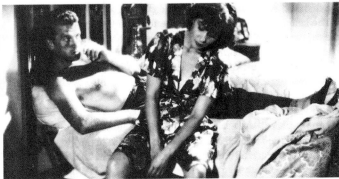

which were 'infected with the spirit of neo-realism'. His powers went even further: Andreotti could, and often did, ban public screenings of films that he decided were 'not in the best interests of Italy'. Even more harmful were the bans on the exportation of films that maligned Italy. And it was these moves as much as anything else that brought about the demise of the neo-realist movement.

The immediate inheritance of the neo-realist movement was to be evidenced in the Fifties, the decade that also saw the break up of the original core of directors – Rossellini, Visconti and De Sica. As their careers diverged and the political realities of Italy in the Fifties went through several changes, the Italian cinema gradually shed its mantle of neo-realism.

Key Directors   **Vittorio De Sica** (1902–1974) was born in the Ciociaria region half-way between Rome and Naples, the setting for *La Ciociara* (1961, *Two Women*), but he was Neapolitan in origin. His first film role was in 1918 and he also acted on the stage from 1923, specializing in musicals and sophisticated comedy. He became a film star with *Gli Uomini, Che Mascalzoni!* (1932, *What Rascals Men Are!*) and began directing himself in 1940, though he mostly kept his acting and directing careers apart once he established himself as a serious director with *I Bambini ci Guardano* (1943, *The Children Are Watching Us*), which dealt with the effects of parental adultery on the life of a small boy. This was his first official collaboration with Cesare Zavattini, who had previously helped him on the script of *Teresa Venerdì* (1941, *Doctor Beware*). Despite rifts and tensions, the partnership was to last another 30 years. Children also featured in their next two films, *Sciuscià* (1946, *Shoeshine*), the story of two shoeshine boys who turn to crime, and *Bicycle Thieves*, in which a young boy helps his father to search for the stolen bicycle which he needs to retain his precarious job as a bill-sticker. *Miracolo a Milano* (1951, *Miracle in Milan*), based on Zavattini's own novel, was a lively fantasy about the poor of a Milanese shanty town, led to paradise by a young man of totally virtuous simplicity. *Umberto D*, a searing portrait of an old man existing in genteel poverty and almost driven to suicide, was followed by a David O. Selznick co-production, *Stazione Termini* (1953, *Indiscretion of an American Wife*), with Jennifer Jones and Montgomery Clift, and *L'Oro di Napoli* (1954, *Gold of Naples*), an episodic comedy that helped to make Sophia Loren an international star. She won an Oscar as a mother who, along with her daughter, is victimized by war in *Two Women*; De Sica later directed her in several successful comedies and dire dramas. Increasingly a commercial director, as well as actor, De Sica regained some critical reputation with a visually striking study of Jews in Ferrara under Fascism, *Il Giardino dei Finzi Contini* (1970, *The Garden of the Finzi–Continis*), on which, for a change, Zavattini is not credited. But De Sica's contribution belongs essentially to the few years of the neo-realist triumph.

Luchino Visconti (1906–1976) was the Duke of Modrone and came from one of the most illustrious families of the Milanese aristocracy. Though a professed communist, he lived in sumptuous splendour; and he disdained to conceal his homosexuality at a time when it was far from socially acceptable. Having worked as an assistant to Jean Renoir, Visconti co-scripted with him and Carl Koch a version of *La Tosca* (1940) mostly directed by Koch, and planned to make his own debut with a Verga adaptation. When this was forbidden by the authorities, he decided to cast Anna Magnani, whom he had admired in De Sica's *Teresa Venerdì*, as the treacherous wife in a sombre story of lust, adultery and

et la Bête (1945, *Beauty and the Beast*) and *Les Parents Terribles* (1948), adapted from his own play.

René Clément's *La Bataille du Rail* (1946, The Battle of the Railway Workers), portrayed railway workers fighting for the Resistance and suggested, through its spare shooting style, that French films might have developed a neo-realist movement similar to that of Italian cinema in the post-war years. Clément himself followed this film with another war subject in the realist mode, but *Les Maudits* (1947, *The Damned*) did not find favour with audiences and Clément's example was not followed by other film-makers.

French directors seemed, in fact, more inclined to take up where they had left off, resuming the fatalistic style of pre-war films like Marcel Carné's *Le Quai des Brumes* (1938, *Port of Shadows*) and *Le Jour se Lève* (1939, *Daybreak*). Carné made *Les Portes de la Nuit* (1946, *Gates of the Night*), a drama set in the wartime black market. Clément added to the melancholic mood with *Au Delà des Grilles* (1949, Beyond the Gates), and several other films echoed the 'noir' atmosphere – doomed lovers playing out their lives in gloomy surroundings; these included: Duvivier's *Panique* (1946, *Panic*) and Clouzot's *Quai des Orfèvres* (1947, *Jenny Lamour*).

Of the French directors who came to the fore in the immediate post-war years, the most notable was Jacques Becker. His first success was a light-hearted, unsentimental film, *Antoine et Antoinette* (1947), about a lost lottery ticket. This was followed by *Rendez-vous de Juillet* (1949, Rendez-vous in July), in which Becker examined post-war youth through the interwoven stories of several young actresses. *Edouard et Caroline* (1951) portrayed a Parisian, bourgeois marriage and confirmed Becker's reputation as an expert maker of everyday comedies.

The documentary film-maker Georges Rouquier made a single feature-length dramatized documentary, *Farrebique* (1946), about the life of a farming family in the Massif Central. The film owed much to the style of the American documentarist Robert Flaherty, and the same tendency was perceptible in the post-war work of Roger Leenhardt – *Les Dernières Vacances* (1948, Last Holidays) – and Louis Daquin, whose outstanding film *Le Point du Jour* (1949, First Light) dealt with the lives of the miners of northern France.

However progressive these films may have been, the popular fare was bourgeois comedy in which stars like Fernandel, Bourvil and Noël-Noël were consistently popular. Alongside such traditional offerings, the debut of Jacques Tati in *Jour de Fête* (1949, Day of the Fair) – combining the influences of Chaplin, neo-realism and French rustic comedy – was a singular and welcome innovation.

Germany

Germany was defeated, destroyed, demoralized and artificially divided into zones under the control of the British, American, French and Soviet conquerors. By the end of the war the number of operative cinemas had dwindled to a fraction. But, as the occupying powers realized the value of cinema in the rehabilitation of a defeated people, they set about reopening movie houses and promoting production.

In the American zone the entertainment permitted to the Germans was strictly limited to Hollywood escapism. There was little reminder or re-examination of the recent war. Production, too, was closely supervised by the military government, which was rigorous in excluding suspected ex-Nazis. In 1947 production was licensed at the Geiselgasteig studios in Munich and at the old Tempelhof studios in Berlin. Apart from some footage shot for Hollywood films like *Berlin Express* and *A Foreign Affair* (both 1948) and a notable success with Robert Stemmle's *Berliner Ballade* (1948, *The Ballad of Berlin*), a satire on post-war Germany, no truly distinguished films emerged from the Berlin studios in this period.

The British Control Commission was more relaxed about the film entertainment permitted the defeated people. Old German films were allowed, if they were thought to be clean of Nazi content. Foreign films, too, were reintroduced after their long wartime absence and were shown in both subtitled and dubbed versions; among them were British war pictures like *The Foreman Went to France* (1942) and *San Demetrio, London* (1943).

A number of German productions dealt frankly with recent history and contemporary problems. Wolfgang Liebeneiner, who had been an active director during the war years, portrayed a young woman's gradual disillusionment with Hitler in *Liebe '47* (1947, Love '47): she falls in love with a man suffering from war wounds and her faith in humanity is restored. Helmut Käutner's *In jenen Tagen* (1947, In Those Days) depicted life under Hitler's rule from 1933 to 1945 in the episodic story of a car. Rudolf Jugert's *Film ohne Titel* (1948,

Far left: François (Jacques Tati) the village postman in Jour de Fête, *Tati's first feature-length film still often considered to be his masterpiece. It was a blend of neo-realism and French rustic comedy. Centre: the desolation of Berlin just after the German defeat in World War II in* Germania, Anno Zero. *Left: the legacy of the Nazi regime was shown in* Stronger Than Night, *a film that revealed how communists were interned in concentration camps.*

Film Without a Title) adopted a humorous approach by posing the question of how to make a comedy for German audiences who were suffering the tribulations of the post-war period. On the other hand, Eugen York's *Morituri* (1948, Those About to Die) confronted the reality of the death camps.

Although these films used plenty of location footage and adopted a straightforward shooting style, they were never part of the mainstream of neo-realism. One German-Italian co-production, however, can be properly termed neo-realist: Rossellini's *Germania, Anno Zero* (1947, Germany, Year Zero).

The Eastern zone, under Soviet control, began with considerable advantages. The newly formed Defa (Deutsches Film Aktiengesellschaft) inherited the old UFA organization, the Neubabelsberg and Johannistal Studios and the Agfa laboratories along with the Agfacolor process. Everything received full state backing. In the immediate post-war years some of the best and most progressive German directors were attracted to work for Defa. Wolfgang Staudte's *Die Mörder sind unter uns* (1946, The Murderers Are Amongst Us) examined varying attitudes to former war criminals and was perhaps the best of the group of films set in the ruins of Berlin that earned the generic name *Trümmerfilme* ('rubble films'). Other notable examples were Gerhard Lamprecht's *Irgendwo in Berlin* (1946, Anywhere in Berlin), a film about the plight of children in the aftermath of defeat, and Kurt Maetzig's *Ehe im Schatten* (1947, Marriage in the Shadows), based on the story of the famous actor Joachim Gottschalk who, together with his Jewish wife, committed suicide in Nazi Germany.

Slatan Dudow, who had directed *Kuhle Wampe oder Wem gehört die Welt?* (1932, Whither Germany?), from a Brecht scenario, before fleeing from Nazi Germany, returned to make *Unser täglich Brot* (1949, Our Daily Bread), a somewhat schematic film about socialist reconstruction. Dudow was later to direct a striking feature, *Stärker als die Nacht* (1954, Stronger Than Night) about Nazi oppression of communists.

Defa was now headed by the Moscow-trained Sepp Schwab. Bureaucracy took root and the best of the directors, who had provided a brief renaissance in East Germany, crossed to the West: Arthur Maria Rabenalt, Gerhard Lamprecht, Erich Engel (who later went back) and finally – after completing three more films for Defa – the gifted Staudte. Even after the death of Stalin in 1953, the revival of East German cinema was to be slow and reluctant.

The USSR

The developments in East Germany, paralleled throughout the whole of socialist Europe, were primarily the result of the strengthening influence of the Soviet Union. In the USSR the ending of the war brought a renewal of the grim repressions that had marked Stalin's domination in the Thirties. A.A. Zhdanov, a prominent member of the Politburo, had become Stalin's mouthpiece and led the campaign to bring art and artists into order, making them serve the precise and immediate needs of the Party. A Resolution of the Central Committee in September 1946 condemned the second part of Leonid Lukov's film *Bolshaya Zhizn* (1946, released 1958, A Great Life) for its realistic treatment of the people of the Donbas coal basin during the war. What was now officially required was an idealized image of Soviet history.

Other films came under attack: Kozintsev and Trauberg's *Prostiye Lyudi* (1945, released 1956, Plain People) was alleged to have dealt too frankly with the war, and V.I. Pudovkin suffered criticism for his historical biography of *Admiral Nakhimov* (1946, released 1947). Eisenstein, too, was a victim of the prevalent ideology. In *Ivan Grozny II: Boyarskii Zagovor* (1946, released 1958, Ivan the Terrible, Part II: The Boyars' Plot) his portrait of the Tsar as an iron ruler surrounded by a secret army was evidently too close to being a likeness of Stalin. The film was suppressed and the intended third part was finally abandoned. Eisenstein never worked again and died, at the age of 50, in 1948.

No subject now seemed safe. Dovzhenko's film about the life of the gentle biologist *Michurin* (1947, released 1948) became embroiled in the controversy about Lysenko's genetic theories, and had to be radically revised without Dovzhenko's cooperation. It was his last completed work also, though he survived until 1956. Even such an officially favoured director as Sergei Gerasimov ran into trouble with his two-part adaptation of a Stalin Prize-winning novel about a youthful Resistance group in German-occupied Krasnodon, *Molodaya Gvardiya* (1947, released 1948, The Young Guard), which also emerged only in a much altered form. Sergei Yutkevich's *Svet nad Rossiei* (1947, Light Over Russia), based on a successful play about Lenin's electrification scheme, was destined never to appear at all.

The films that did meet with official approval were, for the most part, heroic historical fabrications, particularly those which deified Stalin, like Mikhail Chiaureli's appallingly servile *Klyatva* (1946, *The Vow*), his two-part *Padeniya Berlina* (1949, *The Fall of Berlin*) and the eminently forgettable *Nezabyvayemyi 1919 God* (1951, *The Unforgettable Year 1919*). The Cold War spirit entered the cinema in such films as Mikhail Romm's *Russkii Vopros* (1948, *The Russian Question*) and his *Sekretnaya Missiya* (1950, *Secret Mission*), which depicted the attempts of an American intelligence agent and a senator to effect a separate peace with Hitler in 1945; the film ends with the Americans preparing to launch a new offensive against the Soviet Union. Abram Room's *Sud Chesti* (1948, *Court of Honour*) exposed a network of Russian scientists passing secrets to the Americans, while Grigori Alexandrov's *Vstrecha na Elbe* (1949, *Meeting on the Elbe*) revealed more of the anti-Soviet policies of US forces in post-war Germany. Mikhail Kalatozov's *Zagovar Obrechennykh* (1950, *Conspiracy of the Damned*), in a plot of bizarre imagination, unmasked a conspiracy between the Vatican and CIA to undermine communism in Eastern Europe. All these films vigorously attacked the American character and US imperialist ambitions, as well as 'cosmopolitanism' in general.

Although Zhdanov himself died in 1948, the fear and the tight bureaucratic control that he had helped to establish continued to take their toll. Production dropped by 1952 to the incredible low of five feature films in the year. The preference was more and more for apparently 'safe' subjects, and this explains the output of idealized historical biographies, direct records of stage plays (favoured by Stalin, who liked the theatre but had become increasingly paranoid about appearing in public), children's films and technical novelties like a version of *Robinson Crusoe* (1946) made in 3-D. The Soviet cinema's revival could not begin until after the death of Stalin in 1953.

Poland

The Polish cinema was nationalized in November 1945, with Aleksander Ford, a notable pre-war director, as head of the new organization called Film Polski. The first post-war Polish feature, Leonard Buczkowski's *Zakazane Piosenki (Forbidden Songs)* did not appear until 1947 but fast became a great hit at the box-office. The film popularized folk ballads that had been banned under the Nazis and is still one of the most successful films ever made in Poland.

Buczkowski followed it with a contemporary story of post-war reconstruction. *Skarb* (1949, *The Treasure*). This film, starring Danuta Szaflarska, who had appeared in *Forbidden Songs*, dealt in a gently humorous manner with the acute housing shortage in post-war Poland. Aleksander Ford, himself a Jew, made *Ulica Graniczna* (1948, *Border Street*) about the solidarity of Jews and Poles which culminated in the Warsaw ghetto uprising in 1943.

Wanda Jakubowska drew on her own recent memories of Auschwitz for *Ostatni Etap* (1947, *The Last Stage*). This small group of films was a remarkable start for a new-born industry, but in 1949 the Polish Workers Party assumed power and a congress of film-makers at Wisla laid down the new, strict dogmas of socialist realism: interest in imaginative and stylistic devices was condemned along with the portrayal of introspective characters; instead 'the positive hero of the new Poland' was to be made the subject of films that dealt with everyday life in the new socialist state. Those who could not make dutiful tracts escaped into historical biographies, such as Jan Rybkowski's *Warszawa Premiera* (1951, *Warsaw Premiere*) and Ford's *Młodość Chopina* (1952, *Young Chopin*).

Hungary

In Hungary the path of cinema history, from euphoria to reconstruction and from reconstruction to disillusion, was very much the same, if more complex. Production had continued in Budapest during the war, though by 1945 it had fallen to only three films a year. The oustanding film of that time was *Emberek a Havason* (1942, *People on the Alps*), written and directed by István Szőts, a marvellous evocation of a forest landscape as well as an indignant attack on

Left: cold-war politics prompted a number of anti-American films, like the Soviet Meeting on the Elbe. *Above: resistance fighters in* Border Street, *a re-creation of the Warsaw ghetto uprising in 1943.*

exploitation of the workers by a landowner, centring on a woodcutter and his wife. Hungary had been somewhat ambiguously and reluctantly involved in the war on the German side, but now it fell under Soviet influence. The great Russian films were screened there for the first time, alongside the American films excluded during the war. After a quarter-century of exile in Austria, Germany and the USSR, the famous film theorist Béla Balázs came back to teach at the Academy of Dramatic and Film Art, only just founded. At first a few films were made by private companies, but from 1947 only the main political parties were given production permits. Szőts was able to complete a project first planned during the war, *Ének a Búzamezőkről* (1947, *Song of the Cornfields*), written by László Ranódy, who himself became a director in the Fifties (though his first film in 1950 was never released). More pessimistic in tone than *People on the Alps*, it was hardly shown and Szőts later moved permanently to Austria. Balázs, an artistic consultant on *Song of the Cornfields*, worked on the script of Géza Radványi's *Valahol Európában* (1947, *Somewhere in Europe*), in which a gang of delinquent war orphans are reformed and protected by an elderly musician, much as the teacher tried to help the boys in Nikolai Ekk's early Soviet film *Putyevka v Zhizn* (1931, *The Road to Life*).

In March 1948 the film industry was nationalized for the second time – in 1919, under Béla Kun's short-lived communist Republic of Councils, it had briefly become the world's first nationalized film industry. The initial films produced by the state were decidedly auspicious. Frigyes Bán's *Talpalatnyi Föld* (1948, *The Soil Under Your Feet*) was a rural tale of love and exploitation in the manner of Szőts, who was originally to have directed it. Imre Jeney's *Egy Asszony Elindul* (1949, *A Woman Makes a New Start*) dealt with the position of middle-class women, while Félix Máriássy's *Szabóné* (1949, *Anna Szabó*) concerned a woman supervisor in a factory; both examined compassionately the problems of adjustment to a new society. But the Rákosi regime soon put into effect the most repressive Stalinist policies, including the strict propa-gandist demands of socialist realism. Scripts had to be approved in advance and rigidly followed – any variation was supposed to risk the sin of formalism. Balázs lost his job at the Academy and died in 1949 in Prague. Pudovkin was sent from Moscow as an 'adviser' on film affairs in 1950 and again in 1951. Hungary had moved into the most sterile period of its long film history.

Czechoslovakia, Rumania, Yugoslavia

No other Eastern European cinema began the post-war period with greater optimism than that of Czechoslovakia. A well-established film industry had survived the war and was nationalized in August 1945. A body of expert and experien-ced directors was assembled, among them Otakar Vávra, a specialist in historical and literary subjects. Jiří Weiss returned from London, where he had worked with the Crown Film Unit, and made his first feature film *Uloupená Hranice* (1947, *Stolen Frontier*). The Czech cinema was given a great moral boost when Karel Steklý's *Siréna* (1947, *The Strike*) won the top prize at the second post-war Venice Film Festival.

1948 brought to an end all hope of the country's self-determined road to socialism and with it the optimism of the Czech cinema. Alongside the political repressions of the Stalinist era came the usual Zhdanovite criticism and dogma; for instance, Alfréd Radok's stylistically innovative first film, *Daleká cesta* (1949, Distant Journey), which dealt with Nazi persecution of the Jews, was suppressed. The Czech cinema followed the rest of Eastern Europe into the dead lands of dutiful Cold War socialist realism. In Czechoslovakia, how-ever, there was one glimmer of light – the brilliant work in animation of Jiří Trnka and Karel Zeman, which was hard for bureaucrats to supervise and no less difficult, in consider-ation of the international prestige it earned, to suppress.

Similar patterns evolved in the Romanian cinema (nat-ionalized in 1948 but barely past the stage of primitive comedy and socialist morality films) and the Bulgarian film industry, also nationalized in the same year.

Above left: Somewhere in Europe, *about a band of homeless Hungarian children. Left: Yugoslavia's aspirations were often expressed in films about youth, as in* The Boy Mita. *Above:* Stolen Frontier, *a Czech film of the German occupation.*

In post-war Yugoslavia it had been necessary to create a national cinema from scratch - rather as the state itself had been established. The separate republics that made up Yugoslavia had their own languages and their own cultural character. In the summer of 1945 a state film enterprise was established. Promising young people were sent abroad to film schools, and film centres were established in Belgrade and in the major cities of the six republics.

The first productions of this newly-formed industry were documentaries, but in 1947 a feature film, *Slavica* (dir. Vjekoslav Afrić), was released. The film dealt with the partisans' struggles against the Nazis and this theme remained a dominant preoccupation of Yugoslav cinema. Similar partisan films included Vojislav Nanović's *Besmrtna Mladost* (1948, Immortal Youth) and Radoš Novaković's *Dečak Mita* (1951, The Boy Mita). Despite the break with the Soviet Union in 1948, Yugoslavia itself evolved a dogma of socialist realism, though here it was defined as 'national' realism. Whatever the name, the image of Eastern European cinema in the late Forties was one conditioned by the political situation — namely the Cold War.

Japan

The dropping of the atomic bombs on Hiroshima and Nagasaki in August 1945 brought an already weakened Japan to its knees. Within a few days the American occupying forces under the leadership of General MacArthur had accepted Japan's surrender and commenced the process of 'democratizing' what the Allies regarded as an essentially feudal state.

Japan had tended to depict its long tradition of highly structured, feudalistic society very firmly in its films. Prior to the war many films had been made which roused and reinforced the people's loyalty to the Emperor and the ideals of the nation. During the war such movies had become more overtly propagandist, and it was these to which the new American censors turned their attention. Of the 554 films from the war years, 225 were judged to be feudal or anti-democratic and were ordered to be destroyed.

At the start of the war all Japanese film companies had been amalgamated, but afterwards they were allowed to start up production as independent studios again. Censorship control was handed to the Civil Information and Education Section (CI & E) of MacArthur's Supreme Command Allied Forces in the Pacific (SCAP) in March 1946. Japanese films were subject to its rulings for the next four years but, freed from this yoke, production exploded in the Fifties and Sixties. Another reason for this boom was the physical rebuilding of the industry, especially the cinemas. In October 1945 there were only 845 cinemas in operation. By January 1946 the number had increased to 1137 cinemas; this rate of building continued so that by 1957 it had reached the astonishing total of 6000.

Meanwhile, the democratization process (which gave workers the initiative to seek greater powers), coupled with a colossal, crippling tax on the box-office returns, caused terrible strife in the studios and strikes resulted. Few films were produced during this period and it was not until 1949 that a balanced pattern emerged with four major companies carving up the market between them; these were Toho, Shochiku, Daiei and Shin Toho. Toho, for example, became the main distributors for period films. Daiei had previously specialized in military films, so obviously, in the post-war climate, had to seek new material in sex and violence.

Shochiku survived on domestic comedies, but in the Fifties these lost favour with audiences and the studio suffered a few lean years until it developed its enormously popular *yakuza* or gangster films. In 1951, a merger created an important new company, Toei; and in 1954 the oldest company, Nikkatsu, resumed production after a 12-year gap. With these new trends, Japanese film production expanded from 67 films in 1946 to the staggering total of 547 in 1960, by which time 18 companies were in business (the six majors plus a series of small independent companies).

After the war, all the precepts by which the Japanese had lived were being questioned, and writers, artists and film-makers had to cope with new ideas imposed by the West. Some indulged in recrimination; some, like Yasujiro Ozu, retreated to the conservatism of what might be called an essentially Japanese view of life; while others, like Akira Kurosawa, sought to find a balance between old and new values.

Whereas before and during the war the predominant mode of thought in Japan was of group identity (nation, family or company), the post-war turmoil generated what was for the Japanese an unfamiliar concept: that each person had to work out his or her own future. Film-makers started to examine the new ideologies, and the radical importance of this can only be fully appreciated in realizing the strength of the traditionalist views of parental power in Japan, of the obedience of children and the veneration of the family as a unit.

Ozu acknowledged the fragmentation of the traditional group ethic in *Nagaya Shinshi Roku* (1947, *The Record of a Tenement Gentleman*) in which a boy, roaming the streets amongst physical and moral disorder, seeks and finds his father. The failure of the family to provide the virtues of stability are exemplified in the boy's rejection of his father and the foster-mother's 'un-Japanese' reaction to the loss of the boy (in setting up a home for war orphans she moves outside the accepted family support structure). *Kaze no Naka no Mendori* (*A Hen in the Wind*), made the following year, is a melodramatic story of a mother, awaiting the return of her husband from the war, who is compelled to become a prostitute to support her sick child. It was not until 1949 with *Banshun (Late Spring)* that Ozu returned to the narrative style that he had begun to develop before the war. His best films have little or no story but examine a quality that has been termed *mono-no-aware* — an acceptance of things as they are. This view of life is not fatalistic but depends rather on a calm belief in a world that changes slowly around one. At the end of *Late Spring*, a daughter has gone to be married and her father is left alone, resigned but content.

Part of the search for new ideas - some of which bordered on the anarchic - led to the reconsideration of the woman's place in Japanese society. Directors such as Kenji Mizoguchi had long been concerned with the plight of women, but few had dared to make honest exposés of their subservient position. The new post-war freedom encouraged the fight for women's liberation. Mizoguchi in *Joyu Sumako no Koi* (1947, *The Loves of Actress Sumako*), and Teinosuke Kinugasa, in *Joyu* (1947, *The Actress*) both celebrated the heroic figure of Sumako Matsui, an actress who had earlier struck a major blow for the emancipation of women by playing Ibsen heroines.

Already famous before the war for his studies of women in such films as *Naniwa Ereji* (1936, *Naniwa Elegy*), *Gion no Shimai* (1936, *Sisters of the Gion*) and *Zangiku Monogatari* (1939, *The Story of the Last Chrysanthemums*), Mizoguchi also

Right: the story of the artist Utamaro and his unique art of body painting as told in Kenji Mizoguchi's Five Women Around Utamaro. *Below: in Ozu's* Late Spring, *a woman nearing the end of a marriageable age resists the attempts of her widower father to arrange a marriage for her. He implies that he himself wishes to remarry and she finally accedes to him. But he has no intention of remarrying and is left alone. Below right: a political prisoner in* My Love Has Been Burning, *a study of women by Mizoguchi. Below far right: prostitutes in* Women of the Night.

made *Josei no Shori* (1946, *Women's Victory*), a long-promised film about women fighting for and gaining professional posts with the law courts, and *Waga Koi wa Moeru* (1949, *My Love Has Been Burning*), dealing with the part played by women in active politics. The competence and strength of women is a subject that threads its way through many of Mizoguchi's films, particularly those with a modern setting. Even his *Utamaro o Meguro Gonin no Onna* (1946, *Five Women Around Utamaro*), the story of a famous artist set in feudal times, deals with the way in which women are exploited, and his most famous film of this period, *Yoru no Onnatachi* (1948, *Women of the Night*), is an unsentimental portrayal of the life of post-war prostitutes – a film largely instrumental in changing the laws governing prostitution.

Kurosawa, after an apprenticeship with Kajiro Yamamoto, directed his first film, *Sugata Sanshiro* (1943, *Judo Saga*), during the most nationalistic period. Immediately after the war he made a series of films each of which concentrated on an individual having to work out a course of action for him or herself. Kurosawa's greatest gift, supporting his narrative strength, is his psychological insight into character. It is rare to find clearly defined 'good' or 'bad' people in his films. *Waga Seishun ni Kuinashi* (1946, *No Regrets for Our Youth*) looked back to the political turmoil that had preceded the war and centred on a young woman who, when her illusions of

people are shattered and the man she loves dies in prison, chooses to live the life of a peasant with the man's parents. The villagers turn out to be as harsh and unjust as those people she had known in politics, yet she makes a conscious choice to stay and carry out what she sees as her duty. *Yoidore Tenshi* (1948, *Drunken Angel*) tells the story of a gangster (the first starring role for Toshiro Mifune) befriended by an alcoholic doctor who tries to cure him of his tuberculosis; the action centres round a festering pond that symbolizes the rotting heart of the lower depths of society. *Shizukanaru Ketto* (1949, *The Quiet Duel*) is about a doctor (Mifune) who, during an operation, becomes infected with syphilis from a patient. From this point his own life has to be reassessed as he turns away from the woman he loves and tracks down the infected man. *Nora Inu* (1949, *Stray Dog*) is based on a true story of a detective (Mifune again) whose gun is stolen. With his section chief (Takashi Shimura), he follows a chain of clues deeper and deeper into the criminal underworld. After a fight in a paddy field the detective eventually captures the thief but, by this time, they are all so covered with mud that 'good' and 'bad' are indistinguishable. This fine film, with its questions about who is really on the side of law and justice, was a precursor to *Rashomon* (1950), the film with which Kurosawa entered a new decade and thrust the Japanese cinema before a worldwide public.

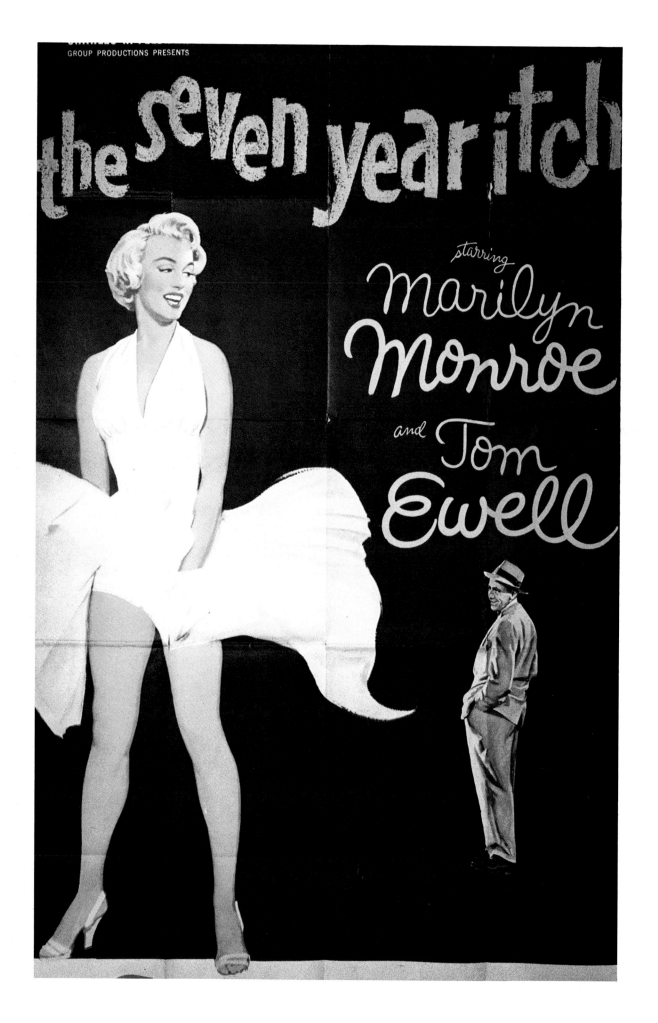

CHAPTER 13
Hollywood in the Fifties

Afterwards, the victims of the late Forties and early Fifties in Hollywood remembered the panics. They remembered Jack Warner screaming into the studio, pointing to contract artists one by one, bellowing, 'I can do without you! And you! And you!' They also remembered that the columnist Hedda Hopper, in a moment of uncharacteristic shrewdness, had warned in the *Hollywood Reporter* (May 1950):

'Television is the one medium that I don't believe Hollywood can give the old run-around; so we might as well take the TV producers by their hot little hands and cooperate.'

They remembered the obdurate studio heads, and the long process of convincing them that Hollywood was really changing, that the studio machine had cracked, that television mattered, both as a rival and as a potential source of revenue for the film industry, and that new and damaging forces were abroad.

The adjustment was painful, and the studios managed to mask it and evade it for a while by introducing wide-screen processes and big, splashy hits. But the industrial structure of Hollywood, already rocked in the Forties by the antitrust laws and by social changes, was radically altered in the Fifties by a declining demand for movies and the increased independence of stars, directors and writers, all striking out on their own to save on income-tax bills.

In place of the comfortable process of making assembly-line product for tied houses, uncertainties abounded. A movie might disappear soon after shooting or make a wholly unexpected profit. Nobody knew. The panic of men like Jack Warner may have reflected the more visible threat of television, but it also testified to an informed awareness that the industry was becoming a game of chance.

The simplest reason for the panic was the steady but inexorable decline in audience figures since the astonishing highpoint of 78 million weekly in 1946. Hollywood managed to fool itself about the true extent of America's loss of interest in regular moviegoing. Official estimates from within the film industry had proved too pessimistic, by tens of percentage points. The economic panic of the Forties came largely from banks and boardrooms where financiers believed the movies were doing even worse than they actually were. In the Fifties the movie industry gained resilience because those figures had been discredited as a result of closer analysis.

As movies slipped, television grew, but that is very far from the whole story. Film attendances declined from 1947, long before most American cities had television. For a while,

TV expansion was frozen while manufacturers solved problems of interference. By 1948, a million TV sets had been sold in the USA, but the average weekly cinema attendance showed a decline to 66 million. America was losing the filmgoing habit before television became an established substitute.

By 1951, the decline in movies and the rise of television were indissolubly linked in Hollywood's panicky mind. Cities that were part of TV networks were losing their movie audience – by as much as 40 per cent. Cinemas began to close down: 51 in New York since the war, 64 in Chicago, 134 in Southern California. Yet the moguls ignored some other factors which might have made them take a less simple view of the phenomenon. Cities receiving TV tended to be the expanding cities, the fattest markets.

After the Depression and its necessary, if hysterical, emphasis on work, the post-war years brought a kind of liberation. As the home and the immediate community became more and more important, two things happened. Physical barriers came between Americans and the movies – many lived in suburbia and the big cinemas were in the downtown areas; young children made demands on young parents and the new affluence meant that the big Saturday-night escape was less of an event than it had been during the Depression. Cinema was becoming an occasional diversion.

Such social changes meant that Hollywood's emphasis on battling TV with bigger, better pictures would not work in the long run. Drive-in theatres and, in the next decade, cinemas in suburban shopping malls were much more important in bringing back audiences.

As far as Hollywood was concerned, something had to be done about TV. One film from 1959 *(Happy Anniversary)* even showed David Niven kicking in a television set, and Jack Warner forbade the sight of a TV set in a single frame of Warners film.

For all their fundamental differences, however, movies, radio and TV had a long history of alliance. Radio Corporation of America, founder of the NBC networks, helped found RKO Radio Pictures; in 1929 it was Paramount's money which staked the struggling radio company CBS; in the Forties 20th Century-Fox agreed to release its Movietone News on TV five nights a week; even MGM, the most conservative of the majors, bought into a Los Angeles TV station. In 1949, Columbia established Screen Gems, a subsidiary that would handle films for television. By the early Fifties, the first important deal between a studio and a network took place: Disney sold a family-entertainment series called *Disneyland* to ABC-TV.

Left: an archetypal image from the Fifties – Monroe caught unawares by a gust of wind from a sidewalk ventilator.

The terms and the publicity surrounding the Disney deal finally convinced Jack Warner to join the game. He sold *Warner Brothers Presents,* a series of 50-minute dramas to which were attached 10-minute trailers for Warners stars and movies currently on release. The Warners series contained shows entitled *Casablanca, Kings Row* and *Cheyenne.* The latter was perhaps the most influential series ever. Warners made a profit on the $75,000 spent on each show, plus a bonus of $37,500 for each summer re-run. Jack Warner got publicity and ABC-TV came out of the deal with 40 hours of guaranteed glossy programmes for the year 1955–6.

The new TV movies bore a reassuring resemblance to the old product of Poverty Row. Films were made on low budgets with five-day schedules and limited ambitions. These were industrial products, pre-sold (as movies had been to chains of cinemas) with a built-in profit margin. They did not require huge publicity budgets, since the TV habit guaranteed their audience. Other studios joined the rush: *MGM Parade* and *20th Century-Fox Hour* followed the Warners lead in mounting TV shows with some of their top contract players in 50-minute featurettes.

Then in 1955, the unthinkable happened. RKO was in grave financial trouble. The corporation had suffered grievously as a result of being divorced from its cinema circuits. The bankers looked at the books and discovered that RKO's movies made only thirty cents in every dollar of company profit. The rest of the revenue came from the cinemas – huge assets that were barely maintained and cheap to run. RKO without their cinemas were a bad bet. Their bankers lost confidence and RKO needed cash. They earned it by selling out their movies (shorts and features alike) to television.

Significantly the deal was struck not with a TV network, but with an intermediary company that was in business to distribute movies for TV. The total price of the RKO package of films was $15 million – an average per feature film of barely $20,000.

The deal opened up the lucrative territory of screening old movies on TV. In time, TV sales came to constitute a source of revenue that was the salvation of the film companies. Television determined the basis of whole production programmes and was considered a kind of fail-safe device. Sales of movies to TV inevitably gave rise to contractual problems with artists, writers and directors who claimed fees for the rescreening of their work.

Anyone distributing movies to TV made a fortune, and television companies suddenly saw how they could fire most of their staff, run movies round the clock and have guaranteed audiences for minimal effort. The TV deals by major studios probably did more than any other single factor to boost the uninventiveness of American TV. They discouraged the evolution of a tradition of TV drama: movies for TV provided the networks with easy programming and gave the studios an illusion of a business that had found its stability again.

Between 1948 and 1959, all the major studios were forced by antitrust law to enter into 'consent decrees' whereby film-production companies were required to sell their cinema chains, and to stop block-booking. They could no longer rent all their movies to some rural cinema with the implicit threat that the cinema would get all or nothing at all. These decrees had radical effects: they reinforced Hollywood's post-war emphasis on the notion of hit films. Instead of gearing their studios to assembly-line production, the moguls aimed for single, one-off successes. Darryl F. Zanuck declared this policy for 20th Century-Fox in 1946; Columbia and Universal followed suit. MGM talked about economizing on budgets by trimming the length of their movies. Theirs was the most traditionally organized studio, but by 1958 MGM had also switched to a 'single hit' policy.

It had become clear that a movie with certain key elements which augured success was more likely to be booked by independent cinema owners and could be sold at higher prices. Big stars, thousands of Nubian slaves and a Cole Porter score – or any combination of the above – became the means of selling films to choosy cinema owners as well as to the public.

In the course of the Fifties, the studios realized that the cost of maintaining staff contracts for high-volume production was uneconomic in the face of declining revenue. Furthermore, once the cinema chains had been divorced from the major production companies, the hidden subsidies (whereby profits from cinemas had been channelled into productions) were no longer available. Stripped of their cinema assets and the profits that accrued from them, the studios were themselves less bankable and needed formulas for success that would convince accountants and loan officers. Suddenly, big screens and spectacle were promoted and helped make cinema movies the sort that 'Can never be seen on TV'.

At this point in Hollywood's history, the tested formulas of the Thirties (star-teaming, series, serials and so on) were thrown aside and movies became a chance game. The industry needed only a slight setback to topple into serious trouble although it could still be wildly successful. Hollywood remained cheerful. The optimism of the mid-Fifties was derived from gimmicks and single hit films. In this new climate, talent was no longer automatically contracted to one studio, although Universal and MGM were reluctant to give up their roster of stars. Actors went freelance and agents were beginning to exploit the fact. American tax laws made it sensible for the stars to appear to be independent; rather than sell their services and their labour, it suited actors better to be associated with completed movies. In this way they would pay 25 per cent tax on a sum which, had it been paid as salary, would have been subject to 90 per cent (from 1964, 70 per cent). The big talent agencies like MCA (Music Corporation of America) and William Morris encouraged the artists they represented to form their own production companies. The big banks now took over much of the financing of individual pictures: they did not, however, have an expert eye for scripts and so relied on the established drawing power of the stars, giving these luminaries more influence than ever before. As a result, the stars quickly escalated their salaries as much as ten times the amount they had earned working for a major studio under long-term contract. The agencies set about creating film packages: they would link up the author of a best-seller or hit play, a screenwriter to adapt it for the screen, a director and leading stars to make it, and then offer the project to several different studios to get the best deal on distribution and money.

The studios rapidly lost their distinctiveness, since now the stars determined what kind of films were made. Some had a deep interest in all aspects of film-making and were overjoyed to be able to produce and even direct their own work; others simply went into independent production for tax advantages and because all the stars were doing it. But either way they now had to take decisions.

Hollywood majors were becoming dependent on independent productions. In 1949 for example, only 20 per cent of the

Above left: by 1959 Hollywood's somewhat desperate attitude to TV was typified in this scene with David Niven from Happy Anniversary. *Above: a typically humorous opening to the* Alfred Hitchcock Presents *TV series. Hitchcock was one of the very few big-name film-makers to realize the commercial potential of TV. Left: Burt Lancaster and Deborah Kerr in – what was for Hollywood in the Fifties – a scene of steamy passion in* From Here to Eternity.

movies released were made independently of the major studios; in 1959, almost 60 per cent of American movies were made by independent companies. Of course, independence is an equivocal term; major studios still put up large sums of money – and sometimes all the money – for independent films, thereby exerting a powerful influence over what was made. But the fact remains that the movie marketplace had become disorganized. The passion for hits meant that 'name talent' (leading stars) placed a high premium on their skills. As the demand for movies continued to drop, production costs began to soar. Agent power supplanted studio power. The majors became increasingly passive.

Among the big companies, power balances had already shifted. Once the antitrust laws had finally divorced cinemas from film production, the smaller studios could compete in the market to produce main features. Columbia released *From Here To Eternity* (1953), United Artists put out *High Noon* (1952), Universal, once a studio dominated by serial and sequel production, produced *The Glenn Miller Story* (1953) and *Magnificent Obsession* (1954). The position of the older, undisputed majors (MGM, Paramount, 20th Century-Fox and Warner Brothers) was less solid. The most spectacular success story of Hollywood in the Fifties was the turn-around in the fortunes of United Artists. In the late Forties, United Artists

had been torn apart by disputes among the stockholders, but after reorganization during 1950–51 it thrived in its new role as a financing and distribution arm for independent movies.

Independent producers grabbed a new power in Hollywood and seemed to make films more efficiently, possibly because they did not have studio overheads to worry about. Hal Wallis, Norman Krasna and Jerry Wald survived brilliantly as producers, even after they had been fired or encouraged to leave by panicky studio bosses. Thoughtful movies from Stanley Kramer, and his quieter partners Carl Foreman and Richard Fleischer, and brasher stuff from Wallis and his peers, all kept the Hollywood distribution machine at work. A new structure was established in which the independent producers still had to sell their product through the existing networks of the Hollywood majors. The strict discipline of the old studio system was undermined by greed and wilfulness on the part of stars and producers. But the consent decrees did not bring an end to the oligopoly the majors operated in film distribution and exhibition, nor did they put an end to the restrictive practices of the huge cinema chains.

Hollywood's new customers were fickle and highly selective about what they went to see, but a single hit could keep a major studio financially safe for a year. Studio economics had changed radically but studio structures had not. The majors were still major.

As Hollywood entered the Sixties, the film business had such basic problems that the studios would not even think about them. In short, the studio system made less and less sense. If Hollywood gambled and lost, the industry might dissolve. That story is for the Sixties. But its roots were in the Fifties – the decade when the production of motion pictures went from an industry to a gamble in a mere ten years.

The Political Climate

In February 1946, after only nine months of 'peace' in Europe, demobilization of the Soviet army was halted and the emphasis in the current five-year plan was switched from consumer goods back to armaments. The Cominform (Communist Information Bureau) was established in 1947 to replace the Comintern (an earlier international organization of Communist Parties) and the spy system in the western world was significantly strengthened. The Cold War had arrived.

The war was fought not only in Europe and Asia, but also on the home front where the House Un-American Activities Committee (HUAC) continued its work. It is possible to measure the change in temperature of the Cold War by comparing HUAC's work in Hollywood in 1947 with its investigations into the film industry three or four years later.

After the Ten were jailed, a certain amount of witch-hunting in Hollywood was apparent. In the early Fifties the practice became enshrined in an actual blacklist, but in 1947 the vetting was negative rather than positive. The trade paper *Variety* reported quite openly that Katharine Hepburn had been discarded as a possibility for the lead in Leo McCarey's *Good Sam* (1948). McCarey told *Variety's* reporter that in view of Miss Hepburn's political sympathies, he would offer the role to Ann Sheridan. Similarly, unconfirmed reports that Dalton Trumbo was working on a script for Sam Goldwyn, and that John Howard Lawson was writing one for Walter Wanger, were quickly denied by the respective producers. In 1947–8 the atmosphere in Hollywood, as in the country at large, was fiercely anti-communist but not yet paranoid.

In the autumn of 1949 came the announcement that the Russians had closed the missile gap by exploding their first nuclear bomb. The triumph of the Berlin airlift, which only six months previously had persuaded the Russians to call off their blockade of the city, now seemed futile. Fear of communism spread like a contagion.

In the wake of the unpalatable investigations conducted by HUAC in 1947, the American film industry had already decided to show how clean its hands were by producing anti-communist films. The disease which gripped the country in 1949 served only to strengthen that resolve. Darryl F. Zanuck, produced the prototype of the burgeoning genre: *The Iron Curtain* (1948), based on the real-life story of Igor Gouzenko, a code clerk in the Russian embassy in Ottawa who defected to the West. Neither Dana Andrews (as Igor) nor Gene Tierney (as his wife, Anna) attempted Russian accents, but their Hollywood personae clashed badly with the efforts of the producer, Sol Siegel, and the director, William Wellman, to make a film similar to Louis de Rochemont's documentaries.

MGM followed 20th Century-Fox's lead with *The Red Danube* (1949). It starred Walter Pidgeon as the agnostic British officer, who gets involved in a pointless and vacuous theological debate with a nun (Ethel Barrymore) over the fate of a beautiful ballerina (Janet Leigh) whom the Russians are trying to recapture in Vienna. In *Conspirator* (1949) MGM sold its loveliest symbol of American virginity (Elizabeth Taylor) into communist bondage when she married Robert Taylor who, it transpired in the course of the film, was a Soviet spy. RKO's *I Married a Communist* used up writers and directors like paper towels. The picture, which starred Robert Ryan and Laraine Day, was finished at the end of 1949, but Howard Hughes, RKO's then owner, waited a further year before releasing it under the title *The Woman on Pier Thirteen*. After all the controversy the film turned out to be a tame story of trouble on the San Francisco docks.

In 1950 the Republican congressman Richard Nixon secured the conviction of the former State Department

Below: The Iron Curtain, *starring Dana Andrews, was one of the first anti-communist propaganda films.*

Below: Senator Joseph McCarthy used television to further his fanatical purges of alleged American communists.

official, Alger Hiss, on a charge of perjury arising out of his alleged Thirties espionage, and politicians of both major parties were convinced that America's major institutions were swarming with communist traitors. A primary list seemed to include Roosevelt and Truman, the labour unions, Alger Hiss, Secretary of State Dean Acheson and the entire State Department. The rising tide of anti-intellectualism was also useful to the witch-hunting factions. HUAC was the most publicized aspect, but the years 1949–50 saw the mushrooming of various committees dedicated to the elimination of all communist propaganda. Mostly they concentrated on stalking local libraries and bookstores for books they considered to be pro-communist. *The Grapes of Wrath* was one of the first books designated for burning.

Simultaneously, reports reached the West that the John Ford film *The Grapes of Wrath* (1940) was doing wonderful business behind the Iron Curtain. Performances were preceded by a lecturer who pointed out that the picture of dispossessed Okies was an accurate portrait of general conditions in the present-day USA. Zanuck modified the story somewhat when he told *Variety* that the Russians had re-dubbed and re-edited a print of *The Grapes of Wrath* to prove that the Okies were typical Americans, but when the print reached Yugoslavia it had to be hastily withdrawn from circulation because the living standard of the Joad family was seen to be better than that experienced by the Yugoslavian people at the time.

One US politician benefited from the hysteria even more than Richard Nixon. On February 9, 1950, Senator Joseph McCarthy, the junior and almost unknown senator from Wisconsin, delivered a speech to the Women's Republican Club in Wheeling, West Virginia, in which he claimed to have a list of 205 employees of the State Department who were known to Dean Acheson (the Secretary of State) as being members of the Communist Party.

McCarthy never managed to make any of his charges stick – but then he did not need to. He was talking to a country that was seemingly desperate to prove him right. In Wheeling, West Virginia, where it all began, a violent controversy started when it was discovered that inside packets of US bubble gum were certain give-away cards informing unwary children that the USSR, with its population of 211 million, had its capital in Moscow and was 'the largest country in the world'. The corrupting cards were removed from circulation. Mrs Thomas J. White, a member of the Indiana State Textbook Commission, charged: 'There is a communist directive now to stress the story of Robin Hood . . . because he robbed the rich and gave it to the poor. That's the communist line. It's just a smearing of law and order'.

The incidents piled on each other, progressing from the comic and the bizarre to the sinister and the tragic. Fearing the wrath of the new HUAC investigations, Monogram Pictures cancelled a projected 'biopic' on Henry Wadsworth Longfellow on the grounds that Hiawatha's peace activities might be construed as propaganda for a communist peace initiative. HUAC, now under the chairmanship of John Wood, was even more iniquitous than it had been under the rule of J. Parnell Thomas. This time the Committee headed mainly for the actors. The climate of fear and suspicion these investigations engendered in the film business led to a near-fatal sterility of ideas in Hollywood in the Fifties.

Meanwhile the anti-communist films continued to roll off the production line.

The Warner Brothers offering was *I Was a Communist for the FBI* (1952), the story of a man (played by Frank Lovejoy) who pretends to be a Communist, despite the whips and scorns of his family and close friends, in order to give the FBI vital information on the native Communist Movement. *My Son John* (1952), an appalling piece of anti-intellectual snobbery, was conceived, co-written, produced and directed by Leo McCarey. It wasted the talents both of Robert Walker, in his last film, as a middle-class, well-educated young man who works for the federal government, and of the distinguished stage actress Helen Hayes, as the mother who discovers that he is a communist spy. The selfless work of HUAC brought a unique tribute from John Wayne whose *Big Jim*

Below: Frank Lovejoy as the patriotic double agent in the simplistic I Was a Communist for the FBI.

Below: Red Planet Mars *was an absurd propaganda piece in which Martians played a part in overthrowing the Soviet Union.*

McLain (1952) was formally dedicated to the Congressmen of the House Un-American Activities Committee who, ran the text, continued to pursue their anti-subversive enquiries 'undaunted by the vicious campaign of slander launched against them'. Supreme in the genre, however, was *Red Planet Mars* (1952), an amazing collection of pseudoscientific, religious and political mumbo-jumbo. Peter Graves stars as an electronics expert who makes contact with Mars. When the messages from Mars assume a spiritual nature, the West pulls up its socks and the Russian peasants are inspired to overthrow their tyrannical Soviet rulers. The plot of Samuel Fuller's *Pickup on South Street* (1953) revolves around a piece of microfilm which a habitual pickpocket (played by Richard Widmark) steals from a spy. His conversion from apathy to patriotism, however, is motivated principally by self-interest and the film's success is due to the interplay of characters rather than to its political line.

The comic-book approach of such films gives only a faint indication of the suspicion and hysteria aroused by the Cold War. It should be remembered that McCarthy had warned of a North Korean invasion months before it happened in June 1950 and that General MacArthur had been proved wrong when the Chinese entered the war six months later.

Though it took considerable time for the American public to accept the fact, the two superpowers to emerge after 1945 were of fairly equal strength. If the USA claimed nuclear superiority, the Russians could point to the increasing spread of communism around the world. World War II had neatly labelled the two warring sides 'Right' and 'Wrong' and ensured the correct result. In the Cold War of the Fifties, the Americans re-labelled the opposing sides. The battleground for this war of propaganda was now on the airwaves and in the media, and film would continue to play its influential role in the conflict.

Nuclear Fears   The speed of the Allied victory against Japan was only made possible because of the success of the Manhattan Project, the operation based at Los Alamos, New Mexico, which manufactured the first atomic bombs. The capture of Iwo Jima, less than eight square miles of volcanic ash, had cost the lives of 6000 US marines with a further 17,500 wounded. The casualty list at Okinawa ran to 49,151. If the Japanese decided to defend their five principal islands with that sort of tenacity, the American Joint Chiefs of Staff estimated that Japan could probably hold out until well into 1948. America would, therefore, incur losses greater than the sum total of those killed since Pearl Harbor.

In the event two A-bombs were enough. On August 6, 1945, one bomb containing the equivalent of 20,000 tons of TNT was dropped on Hiroshima. In one minute a thriving city was obliterated; over 70,000 people were killed. On August 9, 39,000 people died in a second nuclear explosion at Nagasaki. Five days later, in the face of extreme opposition from fanatical militarists, the Emperor Hirohito publicly announced Japan's capitulation.

Far from being a 'war to end all wars', World War II had been terminated in a manner that everyone acknowledged could prove merely the harbinger of a future holocaust. By February 1947, Norman Taurog's *The Beginning or the End?* had been released – a tendentious pseudo-scientific semi-documentary about the Manhattan Project, and the first feature-length film on the subject of nuclear power, ushering in a long and more or less dishonourable line of bastard children, most of which have totally failed to come to grips with the nuclear issue.

Whether nuclear films constitute an independent genre is questionable – clearly many can usefully be regarded as being science-fiction or horror films, whilst others can be placed under the broad headings of comedy: Leslie H. Martinson's *The Atomic Kid* (1954); Stanley Kubrick's *Dr Strangelove, or How I Learned to Stop Worrying and Love the Bomb* (1964); documentary: Peter Watkins' *The War Game* (1965); *film noir*: Robert Aldrich's *Kiss Me Deadly* (1955); and crime film: Dick Powell's *Split Second* (1953). In Stanley Kramer's *On the Beach* (1960) the survivors of nuclear war await the inexorable drift of the radioactive clouds. Concentrating as it does on the lives of a few characters, the film has the effect of personalizing the entire situation, and manages to ignore or evade the true potential causes of war: the political struggle between the superpowers. The few cogent arguments against nuclear weaponry are considerably weakened by being put into the mouth of an ineffectual alcoholic, whilst the rest of the characters are simply vehicles for vapid sloganeering.

Other post-holocaust films include Arch Oboler's *Five* (1951), Ranald MacDougall's *The World, the Flesh and the Devil* (1959) and Ray Milland's *Panic in Year Zero* (1962). *Five* and *The World, the Flesh and the Devil* explore the possibilities of social reconstruction on a microcosmic level. In *Five* the group of survivors is decimated by radiation sickness and personal conflicts (including racial ones) until finally only a young couple is left to give the world a second chance, suggesting, with the help of biblical quotations, that mankind will survive, no matter what. Again there are no real explanations for the initial holocaust, and the film ends up as a facile version of the Adam and Eve story. Much the same applies to *The World, the Flesh and the Devil* in which two young people (he black, she white) find themselves alone in post-holocaust New York. Again racial problems intervene, and these are further exacerbated by the arrival of a white man. The film ends, however, with reconciliation and all three walking off hand in hand while the closing title reads 'The Beginning'. But if *Five* and *The World, the Flesh and the Devil* are examples of naive and misplaced idealism, *Panic in Year Zero* is fundamentally fascist. Here the destruction is not total (it being a so-called Limited General War) and Ray Milland and his family, who have taken to the hills outside Los Angeles, are represented as having to defend themselves primarily from attacks by looters, killers and rapists. Like America itself, presumably, Milland is never the aggressor – his violence is always retaliatory. Significantly he endorses precisely those ideals (militarism, territorialism, etc.) which, on a wider scale, lead to global wars in the first place.

A further category is the warning film, one of the best examples being the British *Seven Days to Noon* (dir. John Boulting, 1950), in which an atomic scientist becomes disgusted by his work, and threatens to destroy London unless all atomic research by Britain is stopped. The dissident scientist and his arguments are portrayed with unusual sympathy and understanding, and the sense of impending doom is conveyed with almost unbearable tension. The impact of the film gains greatly from its locations.

An allegorical variation on the theme is provided in *Kiss Me Deadly*, one of several films based on Mickey Spillane's thick-ear thrillers. The obnoxious private eye Mike Hammer (Ralph Meeker) tracks down a radioactive box that then explodes in the face of the murderous Pandora who dares to open it; he is led by a dreamlike trail of poetic clues that culminates in the nightmare of mushroom-cloud catastrophe.

Sidney Lumet's *Fail Safe* (1964) concerns a disaster sparked

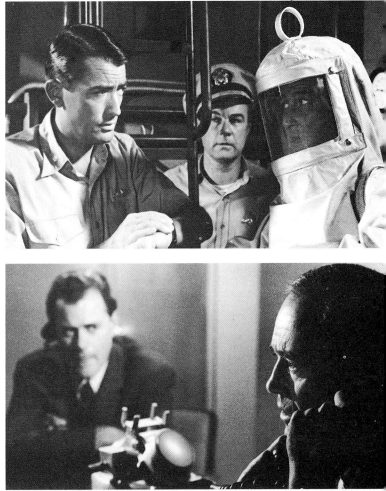

Above left: fears about atomic warfare were exacerbated by the Cold War and the concomitant witch hunts at home. The Beginning or the End? *was the first 'serious' consideration of atomic war. Top: submarine Commander Dwight Towers (Gregory Peck) sends Lieutenant Sundstrom (Harp McGuire) ashore in* On the Beach. *Above: Henry Fonda as the US President in* Fail Safe, *a film in which the question of human culpability is evaded and blame for the decision to use the bomb is shifted on to computers. Left: Major 'King' Kong (Slim Pickens) about to ride the bomb in Kubrick's* Dr Strangelove.

off 'by mistake' – a mechanical malfunction triggers an American nuclear attack on Moscow, and the President agrees to order the bombing of New York in return. Like *On the Beach* – a Grim Warning writ large – *Fail Safe* suggests neatly but unconvincingly that in international power politics two wrongs *do* in fact make a right. *Dr Strangelove* has an almost identical plot to *Fail Safe*, except here the American bombing triggers off a 'Doomsday Device' which destroys everything. However, Kubrick's approach is totally opposed to Lumet's – portentous seriousness is replaced by truly nightmarish humour which, like all true satire, comes closer to the heart of

the matter than any number of weighty treatises. Through excess, parody and caricature, Kubrick illustrates the kind of 'thinking' that makes the holocaust possible. No-one would suggest that he has produced a work of rich analysis; rather, he makes his points by means of fable, allegory and a blackly imaginative vision. Although *Dr Strangelove* may be less immediately obvious than its predecessors, it is nonetheless more profound, trenchant and hard-hitting. But it was not until *The War Game* that anyone produced a serious *political* analysis of the buildup to and results of atomic war, and combined this with a truly horrifying depiction of its effects.

War Films   Films about conventional warfare continued to be produced on a considerable scale. Whether its origins were American, British or Soviet, the classic combat movie tended to be characterized by the following features: the inclusion of several scenes in which large-scale combat is presented; a focus in the narrative on the platoon as the central group, with half a dozen figures pre-eminent within it; concentration on a single or small series of specifically military engagements (the attack on a hill, a farmhouse, a bridge): the absence of any critique of the war *per se* – although individual soldiers may have problems of fear or breakdown; and the almost total absence of the enemy except as a faceless, amorphous opposing force – something 'foreign' that we are not permitted to 'know' in the film.

These features were common to the combat films of all the participant nations that were producing films during World War II. In the altered moral and political climate of the Fifties and in the light of the very different experience of war shared by the various participants, film-makers were able to shape their subjects around an established framework.

Any number of films might serve as illustrations. In Britain *Cockleshell Heroes* and *The Dam Busters* (both 1955), dealing respectively with the attacks on blockade-running German ships and the strategy for knocking out vital industrial water supplies, celebrated heroic achievements in the field of conflict. For the USA, *The Young Lions* (1958), an account of US Army campaigns in Europe, and *The Steel Helmet* (1951), an expedition behind enemy lines in the Korean war, were similar tributes to successful military actions. Films which dealt with defeat – like Joseph H. Lewis' *Retreat Hell!* (1952), set in Korea, and the British film *Dunkirk* (1958) – were rare in Fifties cinema and though the latter film chronicles the military evacuation of the port of Dunkirk, the film construes the action as a victory for the ostensibly British quality of strength in adversity.

The overwhelming optimism that characterized the films of all the participant nations made during the war does, however, begin to crack in the war movies of the Fifties, though in ways peculiar to the culture in which they were made. Thus, while the commitment to victorious action remained strong in British and American films, the themes of suffering and divisiveness are not completely ignored.

This undermining of the confidence and complacency so long characteristic of the war film is intriguingly revealed in Robert Aldrich's *Attack!* (1956) in which the commanding officer (Eddie Albert) loses his authority as a result of his own fear and is supplanted and subsequently shot by an officer from his own company (Jack Palance). In the British film *The Bridge on the River Kwai* (1957) class conflicts conspire to lower the morale of officers and men in a Japanese prisoner-of-war camp.

Gradually notions of physical breakdown and psychosis became more common. Lewis Milestone's *Halls of Montezuma* (1950) analyses group neurosis and combat fatigue through the character of a company commander (Richard Widmark) with a narcotic addiction. Similarly, *The Caine Mutiny* (1954) challenged the authority of an inefficient commanding officer and, in its court-martial scene, raised vital questions about military conduct.

Certain of the contradictions that were papered over in Forties war movies began to be exposed in the Fifties. The ambiguous role of American blacks serving in the US armed forces while engaged in their own struggle was broached in *Home of the Brave* (1949), while *Go for Broke* (1951) focused on the treatment of American-born Japanese who had been drafted into the army. Under the guidance of their commanding officer (Van Johnson), a platoon of these men is put through basic training and each distinguishes himself in action in Italy. Towards the end of the Fifties the changing politics of international alliances exerted an influence over the way the movies told the history of the war, and by the time *The Guns of Navarone* (1961) was released, important distinctions were being made between Germans and Nazis in the film's narrative.

Science-Fiction   The upgrading of science fiction from its children's serial associations was largely motivated by the atmosphere of political anxiety coinciding with rapid technological advance. The film that changed the face of science-fiction cinema was *Destination Moon* (1950), George Pal's production was pure technology, the giant leap for mankind, prestaged as simple, stirring prophecy. There was nothing trivial about *Destination Moon*, with its majestic space-flight and super-spectacular lunar surface. It made science fiction on the screen respectable, even if the magazines persisted in disguising themselves as lurid nonsense. Derived from a Robert Heinlein story, designed by the space-artist Chesley Bonestell, advised by rocket expert Hermann Oberth, the film proclaimed its authenticity in every detail. It even avoided the extremes of Heinlein's original (in which Nazis are discovered plotting away on the moon), by translating his precocious schoolboy astronauts into average American adults, all courage and good humour.

The three classic science-fiction films of 1951 were *The Thing*, *The Day the Earth Stood Still* and *When Worlds Collide*, and they demonstrate how quickly the film-makers and their public recognized that a simple moonshot would do little to restore domestic security. The ending to *The Thing*, with its famous warning, 'Watch the skies!', illustrated that teamwork and wisecracks can burn one bloodthirsty alien but there are plenty more available, ready to propagate their seed-pods at the drop of a severed hand. And if they don't arrive as chilly foreign agents, they'll turn up as Michael Rennie in *The Day the Earth Stood Still*, accompanied by his giant robot, ready to burn *us* to a crisp by way of chastisement. Mankind must learn its lesson, or God will surely intervene once more; the gospel according to Philip Wylie's script for *When Worlds Collide* shows a new Ark leaving for a Technicolor Eden.

The late Fifties and early Sixties saw the world brought to an end with increasing frequency – most depressingly with *The World, the Flesh and the Devil* and *On the Beach* and most intriguingly with *The Last Woman on Earth* (1960) and *Rocket Attack USA* (1961). The Cuban missile crisis was just around the corner, and for students of science fiction it would be no great surprise.

The most consistent message of the period, as we now look back on it, was one of helplessness. William Cameron Menzies' *Invaders From Mars* (1953) was an early example: a melancholy account of a small boy's discovery that his parents have been taken over by aliens. The takeover theme returned in the mid-Fifties with the British *The Quatermass Experiment* (1955), *1984* (1956) – two very different sides of the same coin – Don Siegel's *Invasion of the Body Snatchers* (1956) and Roger Corman's trilogy of compulsion: *It Conquered the World*, *Not of This Earth* and *Attack of the Crab Monsters* (all 1956).

Each film shows society being eaten away from within. In dramatic terms, a few individuals gradually become aware of the developing cancer and make futile attempts to arrest its progress, often sacrificing themselves in the process.

More complex fears are exposed by the films dealing with changes in size. Jack Arnold's *The Incredible Shrinking Man* (1957) was an almost Orwellian exercise in paranoia that was promptly echoed by *Amazing Colossal Man* (1957), *Attack of the Puppet People* and the matrimonial melodrama *Attack of the Fifty-Foot Woman* (both 1958).

The three greatest science-fiction films of the decade date from the mid-Fifties. They had widely different origins, but were alike in the care with which they were produced and their excitingly successful special effects. Coincidentally, they illustrate the same theme of disenchantment. In Disney's *20,000 Leagues Under the Sea* (1954) Jules Verne's volatile recluse, Captain Nemo (James Mason), cruised bitterly into the twentieth century to demonstrate that the perpetual struggle between nations was a meaningless waste of planetary resources and a neglect of the magical powers that science could reveal to men.

In Joseph Newman's *This Island Earth* (1955), the fragility of our own planet is demonstrated through the story of a bright young scientist recruited to save the distant world of Metaluna from destruction by interplanetary warfare.

With *Forbidden Planet* (1956), the triptych is completed. Jules Verne's Nemo character becomes Shakespeare's Prospero, alias Morbius, a castaway on Altair-4. This planet contains, in mile upon mile of storage chambers, the accumulated knowledge of the Krell race, long since disappeared. Again mankind is offered scientific wealth that could bring, if anyone is interested, the key to the universe. Again mankind proves incapable of looking further than his immediate hungers, and Morbius is unable to prevent himself from using the Krell power simply to attack his fellow creatures. It wasn't a lesson to take too seriously at the time. The hit of the film was Robby the Robot, not the star, Walter Pidgeon, and while critics made passing allusions to *The Tempest*, it was overlooked that Shakespeare's play had also dealt with disenchantment and the collapse of a once-stable system.

Below: Klaatu, an alien who arrives from another planet, is shot in The Day the Earth Stood Still. *Bottom: mutants played an important role in films of the period – here a scientist falls victim to the* Attack of the Crab Monsters.

Below: Invasion of the Body Snatchers *was about alien 'pods' which take over the minds and bodies of the citizens of a small Californian town. Bottom: bizarre images of female dominance are present in* Attack of the Fifty-Foot Woman.

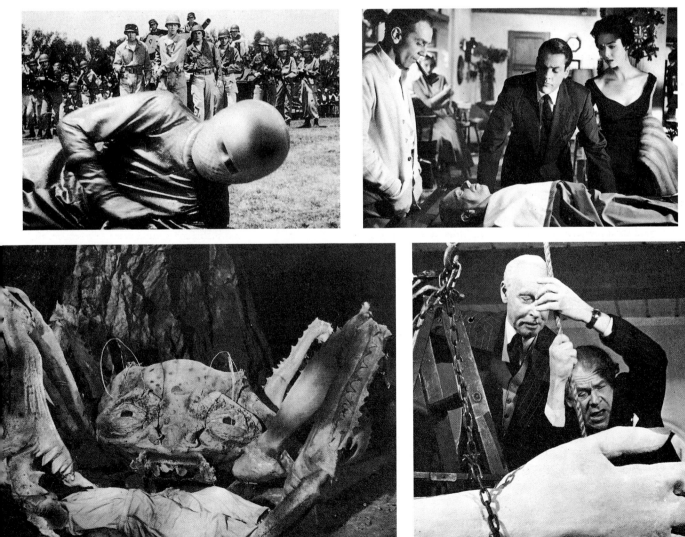

New Techniques

Big Screens and Epics   In the face of declining audiences and the threat posed by television, the film industry sought to make the big-screen film as different as possible from the tiny image on the tube in the corner of America's living rooms. TV in the early Fifties had two clear drawbacks: it was in black and white and the moving pictures it showed were on a small scale.

Most crucial among these economic measures to win back cinemagoers were the various technical experiments and processes designed to change the shape of the screen to a much wider, panoramic format beyond the reach of television. Cinema returned to the wide-screen experiments of the Twenties. In the Cinerama process, three 35mm cameras were used to shoot a scene and three projectors beamed the final films side by side on a huge curving screen that took up almost all the audience's field of vision. *This Is Cinerama* (1952) was the spectacular launching film for the new process, premiered on September 30, 1952, in New York. This two-hour travelogue also featured stereophonic sound from speakers positioned behind the screen and around the auditorium; sequences like the famous rollercoaster ride seemed frighteningly real. Eventually most of the movie theatres equipped for Cinerama switched to a single-projector system when the more workable 70mm gauge became available and did the same job of filling the enormous screens.

Late in 1952, 20th Century-Fox decided to take up CinemaScope. This process had been evolved from Henri Chrétien's experiments of the Twenties and Thirties and its advantage in the Fifties was that it provided a means of bringing wide-screen pictures to ordinary cinemas.

Films are always shown in one of several available 'aspect ratios' (the ratio of width to height); the standard or 'Academy' ratio was – and still is – 1.33:1 (roughly four units broad for every three units high) but in the early Fifties many so-called panoramic screens had been erected to present films in a broader 1.66:1 ratio. CinemaScope, however, was an altogether different ratio (2.55:1), and the first film to be screened in this new size was *The Robe* (1953), a biblical epic about the aftermath of the crucifixion. The public response to *The Robe* convinced the studios that CinemaScope had a future, and by 1954 the demand for big-screen pictures was so great that Warners halted the shooting of *A Star Is Born* (1954) and re-started it in the CinemaScope process.

Since 20th Century-Fox held the rights to CinemaScope and leased its use to other film producers, some studios preferred to adopt the other systems that suddenly appeared on the market. Around this time the term 'Scope' came into usage to cover all wide-screen processes of differing makes both in the USA and abroad.

The biggest challenge to CinemaScope's dominance of the wide-screen game was VistaVision, a system developed for Paramount which used a larger negative area to achieve better definition of the image. VistaVision films could be shown in a variety of ratios from the old-fashioned 1.33:1 to 2:1. The usual aspect ratio for VistaVision was 1.85:1. *White Christmas* (1954) was the first film to be shot in this process. In the long run, however, VistaVision proved too expensive and fell into disuse. Marlon Brando's visually arresting Western *One-Eyed Jacks* (1961) was perhaps the final demonstration of the process at its best.

It became clear that one way of broadening the picture was to use wider film stock. The Todd-AO process used 65mm film along with a special camera (developed by American Optical

for the producer Mike Todd) and was chiefly responsible for the visual splendour of *Oklahoma!* (1955) and *Around the World in 80 Days* (1956). Fox came up with CinemaScope 55, a process that depended on the use of 55mm film for shooting, from which would be struck the standard 35mm prints for distribution. Technicolor developed a system called Tech-nirama which involved the use of a 70mm negative for the filming thus providing crisper, better defined images when the 35mm release prints were made from it. *The Big Country* (1958) and *Spartacus* (1960) both owed their exceptionally sharp focus and visual clarity to this method.

The same impetus that led to this proliferation of wide-screen systems also encouraged movie technicians to re-investigate the early experiments with 3-D pictures. Once again there was nothing new about the idea of 3-D motion pictures but the notion of making them widely available to the viewing public was a challenge that the rise of television made more acute. The big studios quickly took up 3-D, and Warner Brothers enjoyed a huge success with *House of Wax* (1953). In the wake of this hit nearly twenty 3-D features were

Above left: filling the new CinemaScope screen was a new challenge to Hollywood cameramen: Jean Simmons and Richard Burton in 20th Century-Fox's The Robe, *an epic tale of the struggles of the early Christians. Far left: the slaying of a tiger in the Circus Maximus in* Demetrius and the Gladiators. *Left: in* Hercules Unchained, *Hercules (Steve Reeves) is urged to remember his past glories and recover his self esteem. Above: Peter Ustinov ran the gamut of nasty peculiarity as the mad Emperor Nero in* Quo Vadis?

released in 1953. It must be admitted that 3-D was very effective as a means of enhancing films with spacious settings – the deserts of *Inferno* and *Hondo* (both 1953), the South Seas of *Miss Sadie Thompson* (1953) or the valley over which a cable-car is suspended for the tense climax of *Second Chance* (1953). All too often, however, 3-D was used as a gimmick which sometimes became the sole *raison d'être* of the film. Finally, as well as earning a reputation for being somewhat contrived for the sake of their effects, 3-D films also suffered from the major disadvantage that the audience had to wear special spectacles to see them. Screens had to be specially treated and occasionally the synchronization lapsed between the two projectors operating to give the 3-D image. By the mid-Fifties, audiences were gripped in the excitement of CinemaScope which offered both depth and breadth, and did not require glasses.

The various wide-screen processes that were perfected and used in the Fifties caused directors and cameramen more than a few problems. The new oblong shape imposed its own personality on the screen and the broader space had to be

satisfactorily filled. The letter-box shape of CinemaScope was perfect for two-shots, rolling landscapes and casts of thousands but could be less accommodating for single close-ups, intimate moments, or anything of vertical stature. In the early days of the application of wide-screen processes, cinemas were reluctant to re-equip for the new system. As a consequence, most audiences saw the films in an ordinary 35mm format. When CinemaScope and the other wide-screen systems began to be more universally appreciated, there was a sudden demand for new visual stylists with a fresh eye for composition.

When 20th Century-Fox released *The Robe*, it was clear that the director, Henry Koster, had failed to exploit the potential offered by the 2.55:1 aspect ratio, although Delmer Daves, who directed the concurrently-shot sequel *Demetrius and the Gladiators* (1954), showed greater flexibility and was later to become one of the top artists in the medium of CinemaScope.

The wide screen was put to a variety of uses, but there was one genre with which it became particularly associated: the epic. Just as silent cinema had sought to present bigger and

Above left: El Cid *(Charlton Heston, left) does battle with the Moorish enemy. Above centre: Gina Lollobrigida as the Queen of Sheba in* Solomon and Sheba. *Her leading man was to have* been Tyrone Power, but when he died during filming in Spain the role was given to Yul Brynner. Above right: Heston in, arguably, the finest epic ever – Ben Hur.

better spectacle through historical epic films, so the cinema of the Fifties turned to ancient history for inspiration to find subject-matter that would do proper justice to the elaborate filming techniques recently perfected.

The impetus came from Italy where the development of neo-realism gave way to demands for a new, grander look to Italian films. The flamboyance of the historical epic fitted the bill. Alessandro Blasetti's *Fabiola* (1949) was made on a lavish scale and recalled the silent cinema epics. The genre had a good run. French critics, as usual, found a word for it: *peplum* (from the Latin version of the Greek word *peplos*, meaning a woman's shawl or long hanging dress). The *peplum* gained international notice with *Le Fatiche di Ercole* (1958, *Hercules*), but its origins reached back to the early Fifties. Riccardo Freda's *Spartaco* (1953, *Spartacus the Gladiator*), Pietro Francisci's *La Regina di Saba* (1952, *The Queen of Sheba*) and *Atilla Flagello di Dio* (1955, *Attila the Hun*), Mario Camerini's *Ulisse* (1954, *Ulysses*) and Guido Brignone's *Le Schiave di Cartagine* (1957, The Slave Women of Carthage) showed the emergence of certain stylistic points: basic concepts like freedom and equality were expressed in avowedly popular terms; moral and sexual stereotypes were placed in remote historical eras; and there was a move away from the spectacle of Hollywood towards a smaller-scale sensuality. As entertainment, they exuded a sheer energy that walked a perilous tightrope between tattiness and vitality.

Pietro Francisci provided the missing element which completed the equation of success. In search of a new gimmick, some Italian producers had hired Steve Reeves, the American bodybuilder who had been doing cabaret work in the USA on the strength of his Mr Universe title. His first film was the quickie *Hercules* and his two co-stars were Sylva Koscina and Gianna Maria Canale. The resulting film was bought cheaply by American producer Joseph E. Levine and heavily promoted in the USA, where it took $5million. The Francisci/Reeves/Koscina follow-up, *Ercole e la Regina di Lidia* (1959, *Hercules Unchained*), also crashed through the box-offices. The musclemen had arrived to complement the flimsily-clad, pneumatic heroines, thus providing the basic formula for the success of the *peplum*.

As the Italian cinema developed its native epic genre, Hollywood companies set up massive productions in Europe and brought large casts and crews to Italy and Spain. Mervyn LeRoy's successful remake of *Quo Vadis?* (1951) provided the definitive impetus for a spate of costume pictures.

There was a world of difference between the Italian *peplum* and the Hollywood epic. The first was made quickly and cheaply and the second was shot on a grand scale over a long period with a seemingly limitless budget. *Quo Vadis?*, *Knights of the Round Table* (1953), *Helen of Troy* (1955), *Alexander the Great* (1956), *The Vikings* (1958) and *Ben-Hur* (1959) all exploited European facilities such as the easier tax rates, the relative cheapness of labour and the opportunity to release the once-frozen capital that Hollywood companies had amassed in Europe.

At the end of the decade an American producer named Samuel Bronston expanded on these principles by convincing several business cartels, with money tied up in Spain, to invest their capital in a series of historical pictures which he would then sell on a world-wide basis. The first film in this programme was *King of Kings* (1961), which required a financial subsidy from MGM, but Bronston went on to finance *El Cid* (1961), *55 Days at Peking* (1963), *The Fall of the Roman Empire* (1964) and *Circus World* (1964) by pre-selling the distribution rights throughout the world.

The climactic period of the American historical epic was inaugurated right at the end of the Fifties with the appearance of *Ben-Hur*, William Wyler's triumphant blend of spectacle and psychological drama which will probably never be surpassed. The first few years of the Sixties were rich in films that explored different facets of the epic; Nicholas Ray's *King of Kings*, Stanley Kubrick's *Spartacus*, Anthony Mann's *El Cid*, Richard Fleischer's *Barabbas* (1962) and, finally, Joseph L. Mankiewicz's *Cleopatra* (1963).

Thematically the historical epic film is dominated by the message of personal and political freedom. In American cinema this notion frequently emerged in the form of Christianity or Judaism triumphant. The Italian *peplum* was less dogmatically concerned with religion and more inclined to explore areas of (pre-Christian) history in which the Hollywood film-makers showed little interest. The American epics invariably championed a cosy bourgeois life-style and showed an inordinate fascination with the grosser parallels between modern America and Ancient Rome.

The huge mass of Christian homilies which form the bulk of Hollywood's output are generally dramatized in the form of pious martyrs vs callous Romans, with appropriate Judaic interpolations. Both Fleischer's *The Vikings* and King Vidor's *Solomon and Sheba* (1959) make play with their Christian or Judaic vs pagan themes but the latter film (undoubtedly the better of the two) settles for a glib final conversion to monotheism of the idolatrous queen (played by Gina Lollobrigida in a commanding performance of electrifying sexuality).

When dealing directly with the story of Christ, the epic cycle produced two fascinatingly opposed portraits: *King of Kings* conceals a complex restructuring of the main biblical characters and a specifically Zionist ideology beneath its colourful, Sunday-school appearance, while *The Greatest Story Ever Told* (1965) is structured like a majestic symphony with Christ as the prime mover and central focus in a devout, almost funereal atmosphere.

Curiously, for the greatest works in this genre one must look to those stories in which the central protagonist functions as a mixture of the Christ-figure and pragmatic hero. *Barabbas* evokes *film noir* in its portrait of a man moving towards a destiny only half-perceived and from which he originally appeared to escape. *El Cid* presents an intense portrait of a medieval proto-Christ who is, at the same time, a knight redeemer. Finally, king of them all, is *Ben-Hur* where the protagonist progresses from nobility through oblivion to final redemption. It is a film that stands as a testament to the entire epic genre.

The Influence of Television   *Marty* (1955), the first film by television writer Paddy Chayefsky and television director Delbert Mann, was an extremely low-budget ($350,000) production, shot in New York City in black and white and the traditional screen size. It covered not years and miles but two days and several city blocks, and it told a simple story about drab people. Most astonishingly, it had originally been done as a play on, of all things, television.

Set in the Bronx, *Marty* is about a homely, 34-year-old, Italian-American butcher (Ernest Borgnine) who, after many rejections by women, has resigned himself to bachelorhood, aimless male cameraderie and loneliness. He meets a plain but sweet teacher (Betsy Blair) at a dance-hall, falls in love and expects some day to marry her – despite the objections of his petulant best friend, who thinks she's a 'dog', and his Old World mother, who suddenly fears being abandoned.

Marty's surprising critical and commercial success (it was reportedly intended as a tax write-off) led movie-makers to look at television in a new way. Hollywood began turning out other low-budget, black-and-white, small-screen adaptations of television plays, and hiring television's major writers (Reginald Rose, Rod Serling, Gore Vidal, Robert Alan Aurthur, Tad Mosel, Horton Foote, J.P. Miller, Abby Mann) and directors (Arthur Penn, Sidney Lumet, Martin Ritt, Robert Mulligan, John Frankenheimer, Franklin J. Schaffner, George Roy Hill, Fielder Cook, Ralph Nelson). These men learned their crafts during television drama's 'Golden Age', which lasted from about 1948 to 1958, when there were many 'anthology' series – presenting live, usually original, plays every week. This gave them an extraordinary opportunity to experiment and led to a new form of dramatic expression that combined the live performance of theatre with the visual techniques of movies.

Most of their early films were offspring (or at least close relatives) of *Marty*. Three were based on television plays by Chayefsky: *The Catered Affair* (dir. Richard Brooks, 1956),

which depicts an Irish-American family's arguments over wedding plans; *The Bachelor Party* (dir. Delbert Mann, 1957), a portrait of five unhappy men spending a disillusioning night on the town; and *Middle of the Night* (dir. Delbert Mann, 1959), the story of a May-December romance between Jewish-Americans, which Chayefsky had also adapted for Broadway. Along with *Marty,* these are archetypal 'clothesline dramas': modest little slices of modest little people's lives, filled with naturalistic dialogue and behaviour and emphasizing (like their television forbears and in distinct contrast to the epics of the era) character and psychology over action, everyday crises over earth-shattering events, claustrophobic spaces over spectacular expanses. Abandoning the usual Hollywood WASP types, they concentrate on urban, lower-to-middle class ethnic groups and individuals – on the ambitions, frustrations and small achievements of ordinary city people who learn to accept, even rejoice in, their very ordinariness, as in Vittorio De Sica's *Ladri di Biciclette* (1948, *Bicycle Thieves*), a formative Italian neo-realist work and a film Chayefsky acknowledged as an influence.

Unlike De Sica's film, *Marty* is not centrally concerned with economic hardships, although Marty's dreams of social improvement are important. The film does, however, emulate

Below: ordinary people – Ernest Borgnine as Marty, *seeking a soul-mate in Clara (Betsy Blair). Bottom: Don Murray (bridegroom-to-be) and E. G. Marshall, as one of his buddies, 'enjoy' themselves in* The Bachelor Party.

Above: husband and wife (Jack Lemmon and Lee Remick) drift into alcoholism in Days of Wine and Roses. *Right:*The Rack,*with Paul Newman and Lee Marvin, from a TV play.*

neo-realism's location shooting – Mann opens up the action by moving it onto Bronx streets – and its concentration on typical moments in typical lower-class lives. *Marty* succeeds in evoking a time, a place and a people. At the same time, the urban-ethnic accents and dialogue often sound forced, self-conscious. Chayefsky also seems condescending towards the 'common' people. Perhaps one reason for the film's appeal was not that moviegoers could finally identify with people on the screen, but that they could feel comfortably *superior* to characters who were somewhat stupid as well as homely.

Mann, who had directed the television version of *Marty*, approached his camera placements and the editing of the film as if he were still bound by the limitations of a television studio. He also telegraphed emotions and meanings through close-ups and extensive dialogue explanations; these were common on a ten-inch television screen, where pictorial subtlety was neither necessary nor desirable, but on the movie screen they make the material heavy-handed and visually dull. Despite the location work, Mann's *mise-en-scène* is largely inexpressive.

Many of *Marty's* faults and strengths can be found in the other Fifties films scripted by Chayefsky, and also in other screenwriters' adaptations of their own television plays, including Reginald Rose's *Crime in the Streets (*dir. Don Siegel, 1956), *Twelve Angry Men* (dir. Sidney Lumet, 1957) and *Dino* (dir. Thomas Carr, 1957); Rod Serling's *Patterns* (dir. Fielder Cook, 1956), *The Rack* (dir. Arnold Laven, 1956) and *Requiem for a Heavyweight* (dir. Ralph Nelson, 1962); Robert Alan Aurthur's *Edge of the City* (dir. Martin Ritt, 1956); Sidney Dozier's *The Young Stranger* (dir. John Frankenheimer, 1956); and J.P. Miller's *Days of Wine and Roses* (dir. Blake Edwards, 1962). Although all these films do not fit exactly into the Chayefsky mould, they share the television-influenced approach to structure, visual style and performance, as well as the tendency to blend humanism with condescension and

slices of life with large pieces of overcooked drama. They have generally liberal attitudes towards social issues but – perhaps because of lingering McCarthyism – ultimately uphold traditional American values (Chayefsky's work suggests that small but meaningful victories can be won within modest limitations).

In their time, *Marty* and the rest were praised as honest alternatives to Hollywood escapism, but they have not worn as well as many of their less 'realistic', more interestingly stylized contemporaries, such as *The Searchers, Bigger Than Life, Written on the Wind* (all 1956), *Vertigo, Touch of Evil* and *Some Came Running* (all 1958). Still, they left some memorable character studies and individual moments of affecting drama, and they are important historically as concrete reflections of an era's social concerns. They were also responsible for introducing a group of former television directors to the cinema, men like Penn, Frankenheimer and Mulligan who became major forces in American films during the Sixties.

Method Acting   In 1912, the Russian actor and drama theorist, Constantin Stanislavsky, set up the First Studio at the Moscow Art Theatre to develop and teach a radical new approach to acting. His early experience coincided with the growth of realism in the Russian theatre, exemplified by Anton Chekhov and Maxim Gorky. Stanislavsky had worked with both playwrights, who represented the two poles of the realist theatre, psychological realism (Chekhov) and social realism (Gorky).

Stanislavsky placed the actor at the centre of dramatic creativity. In his elaborate system, involving deep imaginative study of the psychologies of characters, the actor was almost required to become the role. His actors lived communally so that they could rehearse and improvise freely. Stanislavsky tried to systematize, through arduous exercises, the ability of great actors to convince an audience in their roles. The aim was an authenticity that transcended mere mimicry.

Several of Stanislavsky's students moved to America between 1917 and 1939. Maria Ouspenskaya and Richard Boleslavsky helped persuade Lee Strasberg, Stella Adler and Harold Clurman to set up the Group Theatre, founded 1931. This combined Stanislavskian techniques of psychological realism with a belief in theatre's social mission. Actors who graduated from the Group Theatre to Hollywood included Elia Kazan, Lee J. Cobb. John Garfield and Franchot Tone. Michael Chekhov, Anton's nephew, came to live in America in 1939; his studio theatre productions featured, among others, Yul Brynner and Hurd Hatfield. Moving to Hollywood, he taught and also acted, for example in Hitchcock's psychiatric thriller *Spellbound* (1945), until his death in 1955.

Before 1945, the impact of Stanislavskian techniques in Hollywood was minimal. The very newness of Stanislavsky's ideas and the conflicting interpretations of them seemed alien and difficult. All exponents of Stanislavsky's system in America agreed in opposing the commercial establishments of Broadway and Hollywood. Besides, Hollywood's self-image at first militated against new acting techniques. While the boom lasted, the film industry had no need of radical ideas, or of the intimacy and versatility of the Stanislavsky-trained actor. Such actors, in their screen assignments, usually ended up as character actors or, worse still, caricature actors.

The post-war period brought changes. Efforts to pull Hollywood out of its doldrums included low-budget productions using new talent and relying on the documentary-type realism so successful in Europe. Their ingredients preferably

Top: Marlon Brando, the moody Method hero, in A Streetcar Named Desire. *Above: the teenage wife (Carroll Baker) in* Baby Doll.

Top: James Dean as Jim Stark, the Rebel Without a Cause. *Above: Maggie (Elizabeth Taylor) with neurotic husband Brick (Paul Newman) in* Cat on a Hot Tin Roof *(1958).*

were a good script, a small cast, small sets or lots of location work and a small theme eschewing grandiose ideas. Contemporary social life and psychological drama were perfect subjects, and the theatre provided suitable raw material.

In 1947, Elia Kazan, by then turned stage and screen director, with Cheryl Crawford and Robert Lewis, formed the Actors' Studio in New York (Lewis left shortly and was replaced in the teaching trio by Lee Strasberg). The Actors' Studio was mainly an advanced study centre for experienced actors. The techniques of improvisation, 'affective memory'

and character building practised at the Studio were by Stanislavsky out of the Group Theatre, although Michael Chekhov in Hollywood and Stella Adler in New York had developed divergent interpretations, stressing imagination over immersion in the character's being. The Studio called its training a 'Method' out of deference for the irreplaceable role Stanislavsky's own practice played in the development of his theories. Despite the dissent of other Stanislavskian disciples, a new orthodoxy grew up as the so-called 'Method' school of acting.

Theoretically, there was no Method acting as such – only a flexible and informal rehearsal process aimed at psychological realism. In practice, through association with particular actors, writers and directors, the Method became identified with a brooding intensity suggestive of dark neurotic emotions. Marlon Brando typified the Method hero – surly, dishevelled and contemptuous of established values. His appearance in Kazan's 1951 film of Tennessee Williams' play, *A Streetcar Named Desire,* provided the perfect image of the Method. Hollywood loved it. It was scandalous, sexy, raw and compelling. It fitted the doom-laden, youth-centred mood of the time. Above all, it was economical to produce.

Kazan's professional stock went up when he testified before HUAC the following year, recanting his youthful Communist Party beliefs and naming names. He nurtured Brando's rebellious image and gave employment to several Actors' Studio members. The Studio soon became the hub of a new creative movement, involving a whole generation of actors: James Dean, Paul Newman, Geraldine Page, Carroll Baker, Eli Wallach, Rod Steiger, Eva Marie Saint, Ben Gazzara, Marilyn Monroe and Jane Fonda, among them.

During a time of Hollywood crisis, the stage seemed to reassert its originality and seniority. But Hollywood's version of the Method had eventually little to do with Stanislavsky's bold experiments. The unambiguous radical ambitions of the defunct Group Theatre vanished. The Actors' Studio, on the ascendant, dropped any pretensions to social realism and busied itself in a crude but politically uncontroversial psychologizing. Hollywood continued to condemn the youthful rebelliousness, violence and amorality of its new heroes and themes while profiting greatly from a string of films portraying them. *The Wild One* (1953), *On the Waterfront* (1954), *East of Eden, The Blackboard Jungle, Rebel Without a Cause* (all 1955), *Baby Doll* (1956) and a number of the film versions of Williams' plays all followed *Streetcar* into the territory of moral uncertainty, sexual promiscuity and brutal violence. The films were influenced by Italian neo-realism, and the performances invariably resonated against their settings and period. But the authenticity for which the Method had striven now conveyed only a subjective mood rather than a social reality.

New Styles, Old Genres

Teenage Films The Fifties saw the full integration of popular music into an evolving youth culture. It was a culture of full-blooded consumerism. In the public mind, the adjective 'teenage' referred to leisure, pleasure and conspicuous consumption. The teenagers' new music, rock'n'roll, symbolized a world of youth, caught up momentarily in hedonism and unrelated to adult interests. Rock'n'roll also brought with it a host of concepts and images that fired the public's ideas of youth: delinquency, adolescent gangs, motorcycle worship, ballroom-dance halls, jazz clubs, Melody Bars, Teddy Boys and similar phenomena.

Parents feared that the uncouth 'jungle' music meant an end to the civilized order as they knew it. Of course, they were to be proved wrong as rock'n'roll became big business and, later, show business. Through its stars and principals, however, early rock'n'roll was aggressive in providing ideas of style that were exclusively teenage.

The young had always worshipped idols: Frank Sinatra, Johnnie Ray, sports heroes and films stars. But now they had idols whose backgrounds, ages and interests they perceived as similar to their own. They sensed a whole culture of their own with a codified set of values clearly different from those of older generations. Participating in such a culture seemed a fitting rebellion against unreasonable, or merely conventional, ideas of how things should be experienced.

The aggressive manner in which teenagers identified with one another, and the singularity and exclusivity of the teenage cult, quickly became bracketed with deviancy and delinquency in the view of the scandal-hungry media. The teenagers' deliberate gestures of individuality, therefore, were interpreted as stances of defiance, aimed at their elders.

But in opposition to this view of the teenager there was the image of the pre-packaged teenager ready to be served up on the screen, in paperbacks and record stores. The motion picture – which might appear to be a series of typical teenage happenings, but which was always framed, directed and marketed by adults – provided the mechanism for resolving the problems of being a teenager. Anticipation of everything that was new gave way to acceptance of things as they were – conformity. If young people could be assimilated in this way they could be tacitly absolved from questioning the *status quo.*

The thrill of the star-vehicle musical remained undeniable: proof that the star could be fitted into an ordinary social perspective and could be sold at the box-office as a commodity to America's consumer class. The advent of the teenage idols of the Fifties – James Dean, Elvis Presley, Sandra Dee – heralded youth's yearning to see the rite of stardom enacted again and again. They symbolized the individual's rise not to riches – as might have been the case for the idols of the previous generation – but to popularity, social mobility and that state of absolute self-knowledge characterized by the adjective 'cool'.

Teenage idolatry had its origins in the pre-rock'n'roll era when jazz clubs, coffee bars and motorcycle gangs acted as a focus for the emerging teenage sensibility. In 1953 Marlon Brando appeared as Johnny, leader of the motor-bike gang, the Black Rebels, in *The Wild One.*

Two years later, *The Blackboard Jungle* featured Glenn Ford as a vocational schoolteacher trying to 'get through' to his New York City charges. The kids refer to him as 'Daddy-O' – one of the earliest commercial usages of the teenagers' 'heptalk' – and in the same year youth confronted adult incomprehension in *Rebel Without a Cause.*

The first big burst of rock films came in 1956 with *Rock Around the Clock,* produced by Sam Katzman and starring Bill Haley and the Comets. Katzman was to become a prolific producer of 'teenpix', none of which ever lost money. In 1961, less than a month after Chubby Checker hit the top of the record charts with 'The Twist', Katzman opened his movie *Twist Around the Clock* (1961) which starred Dion and The Marcels. Before the craze faded, he also managed to churn out *Don't Knock the Twist* (1962), featuring Chubby Checker again, this time with The Dovells and Gene Chandler.

Speed was the essence in the manipulation of the 'teen market'. *Don't Knock the Rock* (1956), a sequel to *Rock Around the Clock,* was on the screen the same year as its predecessor. So was Frank Tashlin's trail-blazing *The Girl Can't Help It* (1956) in which Fats Domino, Little Richard, Eddie Cochran and Julie London lent incidental support to a plot that revolved around Jayne Mansfield's attempts to become a pop star.

Then, at the height of his celebrity, Elvis Presley made the classic *Jailhouse Rock* (1957), in which he played a good-kid-gone-wrong in a rags-to-riches saga. Here was real rock drama

Left: by the mid-Fifties teenage sex and drugs and rock 'n' roll had become hot issues. The Black-board Jungle with Glenn Ford was one of the better exploitation films. Below: Jailhouse Rock provided Elvis Presley with one of his grittiest roles – as an ex-convict pop singer.

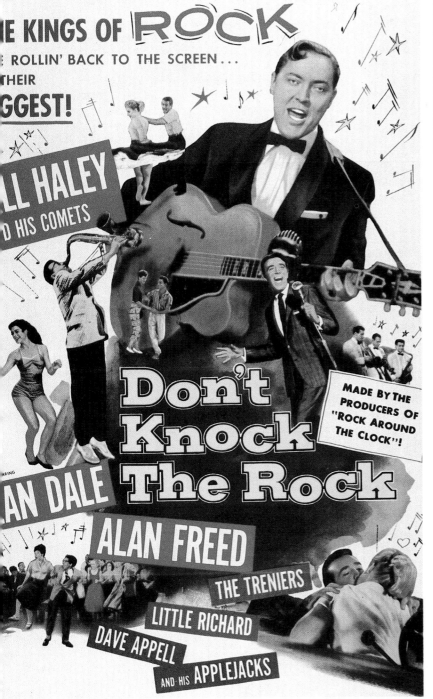

Left: a sequel (released in the same year) to the better known Rock Around the Clock, *this Bill Haley vehicle was designed to thrill the kids but was wholesome enough not to worry parents. Above:* Gidget *launched two new phenomena – Sandra Dee (centre), who became the first teen-queen idol, and beach-party movies filled with spills and thrills.*

as Elvis, rehearsing in a recording studio, spontaneously decides to cut an upbeat number for a change.

Towards the end of the decade, the wilder side of youth's aimlessness was being commercially cultivated by studios like American International Pictures. Two producers, Samuel Z. Arkoff and James H. Nicholson, had founded AIP with the aim of mounting 'teen appeal' packages which would portray American youth as decent rather than delinquent. The closely knit, family-style unit of directors, producers, writers and actors enabled AIP to minimize costs and production time on films. These movies were shot for next to nothing but their production costs were always equalled or surpassed by the amount poured into their promotion and for this reason they became known as 'exploitation movies'.

Of the many AIP producers and directors, the most brilliant was Roger Corman who produced for AIP *The Fast and the Furious* (1954), a road-racing epic with plenty of heptalk. Corman's most important youth movie of the period was, however, made for Allied Artists. Entitled *Teenage Doll* (1957), it was a moody picture with a well-paced plot and sympathy for teenage alienation. On a rainy street one night, the Black Widows (a girl gang) are cornered by the police; most of them flee, but a few walk rebelliously into the glare of the squad cars' headlights. The mood of the scene perfectly matches the mean and moody spirit of the Shangri-Las' hit singles like 'Leader of the Pack'.

Similarly aggressive in tone were AIP's *Dragstrip Girl* and *Motorcycle Gang* (both 1957) which both featured teen–parent conflicts, heroines torn between bad boyfriends and good boyfriends, plenty of hep jargon and high-speed motorbiking.

Katzman did not rule the teenage movie market alone: with *High School Confidential* (1958), Albert S. Zugsmith whipped up his own brand of hysteria. The film was notable for the introduction of the dope issue and for bosomy blonde Mamie Van Doren. Zugsmith coined some 'jive talk' especially for the occasion and added plenty of scenes with hot-rod automobiles just for good measure. Soon 'reefer madness' became a hot theme in movies. In *The Cool and the Crazy* (1958) a kid who has served time in a state institution sells some dope to his classmates and even kills 'Eddie the Pusher' before himself dying in a flaming car wreck in the middle of the desert.

Tragedies were becoming the very stuff of teenage movies. AIP's *Dragstrip Riot* (1959) culminated in a free-for-all between two warring gangs of fast-living youths. There was, of course, a lighter side. In *Summer Love* (1958), starring Jill St John and Rod McKuen, the Daley Combo make a guest appearance at a summer camp with their hit song 'To Know You Is to Love You'. The same formula also lingered on in similar blends of rock and romance like *Juvenile Jungle* and *Let's Rock* (both 1958).

Eventually television supplied the movies with fresh teenage idols: Ed 'Kookie' Byrnes appeared in Katzman's dreadful *Life Begins at 17* (1958). Cliff Richard was the British hipster in *Expresso Bongo* (1959) and the music business continued to provide performers for films like *Go Johnny Go* (1959) which starred Richie Valens, Eddie Cochran, The Cadillacs, The Flamingoes and Chuck Berry. The appearance, in 1959, of *Gidget* announced the arrival of the 'teen queen' – Sandra Dee.

By the end of the decade, serious considerations of teenage problems gave way to a tidal wave of beach and beat movies. *College Confidential* (dir. Albert S. Zugsmith, 1960) presented Mamie Van Doren as 'the student body', only this time the emphasis was equally on her professor, the well-known comedian Steve Allen. *Date Bait* (1960), a cheap and colourful 'exploitation' movie gave filmgoers a 'good' young couple who have to fight both their folks and her dope-crazy ex-boyfriend in order to marry.

The trend towards wholesomeness continued with *Because They're Young* (1960), where the TV actor Dick Clark played an ex-football star turned teacher, battling with youth problems in a high school in the style of *The Blackboard Jungle*. Finally, a film like *Where the Boys Are* (1960) demonstrates where the Fifties teenager had ended up. He or she was no longer a threat to civilized life, however many hi-jinks they might perpetrate. By the beginning of the Sixties, the movies saw the teenager as an energetic creature in need of advice and guidance, but meaning no real harm to society.

Comedies and Musicals   Television began to rival the cinema as a purveyor of original and inventive comedy with Sid Caesar's *Your Show of Shows* (a cradle of later film talent) and *The Phil Silvers Show*. These were complemented by more conventional programming derived essentially from radio formats but enriched with visual elements, such as slapstick, drawn from vaudeville and the movies themselves.

Lucille Ball, who had been a star of fairly modest stature around Hollywood for a decade or so, but then went on to television in a family situation-comedy series, *I Love Lucy*, with her real-life husband Desi Arnaz, instantly found fame and success far greater than anything she had ever dreamed of in the movies. When she went back to the cinema, it was on her own terms, as a visiting celebrity. This she did most notably in *The Long Long Trailer* (1953), in which Vincente Minnelli gave polish and sparkle to what was basically an extended *I Love Lucy* episode, and *The Facts of Life* (1960), in which she co-starred with Bob Hope, in a comic variation on *Brief Encounter* (1945). Bob Hope was rather a different matter. He was a veteran from the Thirties and had been big in films throughout the Forties. But in the Fifties he mostly made either sequels to his earlier successes, such as *Son of Paleface* and *Road to Bali* (both 1952), or films in which his special gift for quick-fire, stand-up comedian gags was less suited to the more relaxed comic style of the decade. With the solitary exceptions of *That Certain Feeling* (1956) and *The Facts of Life*, he seemed to have difficulty playing a character instead of merely playing Bob Hope. Things fared better for the other important survivor from wartime comedy, Danny Kaye. Kaye managed to keep his own brand of zany, frenetic comedy going in films like *Knock on Wood* (1954), *The Court Jester* (1956) which was, perhaps, his best film, and *Merry Andrew* (1958).

It was characteristic of the Fifties that Danny Kaye could peacefully co-exist with the biggest new challengers in comedy, Dean Martin and Jerry Lewis. They were to the Fifties what Laurel and Hardy had been to the Thirties and Abbott and Costello to the Forties. Martin and Lewis somehow brought to perfection a sort of lowest common denominator in comedy, and so built their popularity up from a solid base of mass appreciation on the part of unsophisticated audiences.

The films Martin and Lewis made together between *My Friend Irma* (1949) and *Hollywood or Bust* (1956) were among the most reliable box-office champions of their day, and after the team split up each individually went on to become a major star in his own right.

Comedy in the Fifties tended to be pretty unsophisticated. But even glossy comedy had a heart of pure candy-floss. This was certainly true of the comedies and lightweight dramas to which Doris Day graduated when she gave up musicals towards the end of the decade. Though some of them, like *Pillow Talk* (1959) and *That Touch of Mink* (1962), might seem to feature mildly risqué situations, it was from the outset a foregone conclusion that the heroine's virtue, faintly endangered though it may have been, was going to remain impregnable.

Not all comedy during the Fifties was quite so toothless. There was a little cycle all on its own which harked back in a fresh way to the splendours of the Thirties. In collaboration with the husband-and-wife team Garson Kanin and Ruth Gordon (who worked as writers, either separately or together), George Cukor made a series of sparklingly witty and sometimes surprisingly tender comedies with Spencer Tracy and Katharine Hepburn and a distinctive new discovery – the zany comedienne Judy Holliday. The three-way partnership

between Tracy, Hepburn and Holliday began with *Adam's Rib* (1949), a battle between rival lawyers who just happen to be married to each other. Tracy and Hepburn were then teamed (without Judy Holliday) as athlete and trainer in *Pat and Mike* (1952). Tracy then played the unwilling father of *The Actress* (1953) and Judy Holliday portrayed several variations of her lovable kooky character who turns out to be somehow wiser than the rationalists around her in *Born Yesterday* (1950), *The Marrying Kind* (1952) and *It Should Happen to You* (1954).

Once Marilyn Monroe had arrived as a superstar in Hawks' gloriously garish musical *Gentlemen Prefer Blondes* (1953), her energies were most happily channelled into comedy rather than drama, and in Billy Wilder she found a director who knew how to display her qualities to perfection. *The Seven Year Itch* (1955) and *Some Like It Hot* (1959) captured unforgettably – and hilariously – her innocent sexuality.

Below left: monkey business in My Friend Irma, *the first Dean Martin (left) and Jerry Lewis film. Below right: Spencer Tracy and Katharine Hepburn, with Judy Holliday between them, as rival (but married) lawyers in* Adam's Rib.

Bottom left: Doris Day on the line to Rock Hudson in Pillow Talk. *Bottom right: another bathing beauty – Tony Curtis with Marilyn Monroe in* Some Like it Hot, *about two men who join an all-girl band to escape from gangsters.*

Above: Audrey Hepburn as the charming Sabrina, *the chauffeur's daughter who falls for the playboy son (William Holden) of her father's millionaire boss. Above right: Esther Blodgett (Judy Garland) is discovered by the alcoholic movie star Norman Maine (James Mason) who does his best to see that* A Star is Born. *Right: wholesome values are foremost in* Oklahoma!: *Gordon Macrae sings 'Oh What a Beautiful Morning!'*

The Motion Picture Straight from the Heart of America!

With *Sabrina* (1954) and *Love in the Afternoon* (1957) Billy Wilder also created ideal vehicles for the very different charms of another brand-new star, Audrey Hepburn, and made the definitive transition from his image as a hard-hitting scourge of the world's follies to that of Hollywood's most brilliant comedy director, a role he was to revel in throughout the Sixties.

Not that he had so much competition. By the end of the Fifties, his were just about the only comedies not suffering from terminal softening of the brain. The musical too, which entered the decade at some kind of peak, left it a faded, overblown remnant. Judy Garland achieved some sort of apotheosis in *A Star Is Born* but great musical stars were few and far between in the Fifties. Gene Kelly danced in films like *Invitation to the Dance* (1956), *Brigadoon* (1954), *It's Always Fair Weather* (1955), his final collaboration with Stanley Donen, and *Les Girls* (1957), which included Cole Porter's last original score for the screen. The high points of the Fifties for Fred Astaire were *The Band Wagon* (1953) and *Silk Stockings* (1957), in both of which he partnered the statuesque Cyd Charisse. There were also two May-September matings, first with the elfin Leslie Caron in *Daddy Longlegs* (1954) and then with the ineffable Audrey Hepburn in *Funny Face* (1957). Stanley Donen went on to direct two more musicals at Warners, *The Pajama Game* (1957) and *Damn Yankees* (1958), before transferring his allegiance to dramatic films. Gene Kelly went on to direct non-musical films too. Many of the musicals that were made in the latter half of the Fifties were

safe, faithful transcriptions of recent Broadway successes: *Oklahoma!* (1955), *The King and I* (1956) and *South Pacific* (1958). Original creations for the screen like *Seven Brides for Seven Brothers* (1954) and *Gigi* (1958) were, by and large, considered too risky in a Hollywood reeling at the onslaught television had made on its public.

Westerns By the early Fifties the Western was flourishing as it never had before. High-quality Westerns, mainly in Technicolor, were produced by all the major studios alongside the last of the cheapie programmers in black and white (soon to be killed off by television), while Westerns from the small independent companies like Republic, Monogram and United Artists often exploited the new, cheap, two-colour processes like Cinecolor and Trucolor. There were still 'serious' pictures in black and white like *The Gunfighter* (1950) and *High Noon*. A new respect for the Indian was a feature of 20th Century-Fox's *Broken Arrow* (1950) and MGM's *Across the Wide Missouri* (1951). The more traditional action film also continued to flourish, as represented by the Audie Murphy cycle of Westerns from Universal. The contribution of veteran directors like Ford and Hawks was matched by experienced men like Anthony Mann, Delmer Daves and John Sturges, who had begun their careers during the Forties, along with a group of younger directors coming to maturity, including Robert Aldrich, Budd Boetticher and Nicholas Ray. The film audience was more sophisticated than before and demanded a greater complexity and maturity in Western themes and characterization.

The decline of the old studio system coincided with a greater emphasis on location filming of major features in colour making use of authentic settings; the B feature was virtually abandoned. And many leading directors chose a Western for their first venture into colour, including Delmer Daves' *Broken Arrow,* Anthony Mann's *Bend of the River* (1952) followed by *The Naked Spur* (1953) – both starring James Stewart; Don Siegel's *Duel at Silver Creek* (1952, starring Audie Murphy) and George Stevens' *Shane* (1953). Sets and costumes were generally less expensive than for other types of period picture, while the colourful landscapes and settings were coveniently close to Hollywood.

Established Western stars such as John Wayne, Gary Cooper and Randolph Scott appeared in many of their best roles. James Stewart suddenly emerged as a major Western star, after appearing in only one previous Western, *Destry Rides Again* (1939). Veteran character actors like Walter Brennan and Andy Devine were much in demand, along with a new generation of 'heavies' including Dan Duryea, Richard Boone and Jack Elam. Marlene Dietrich totally dominated Fritz Lang's *Rancho Notorious* (1952). Joan Crawford gave a suitably larger-than-life performance as the tough owner of a gambling saloon in Nicholas Ray's *Johnny Guitar* (1954). But

Below left: Gregory Peck as The Gunfighter, *a man desperately trying to live down his unwanted reputation. Below: political allegory, suspensful psychological Western, or apotheosis of nervous heroism,* High Noon *remains a work of enduring excellence. Bottom left: saloon-keeper Vienna (Joan Crawford) faces a lynch mob whipped up by cattle boss Emma Small (Mercedes McCambridge) in* Johnny Guitar. *Bottom right: Jessica Drummond (Barbara Stanwyck), the boss of* Forty Guns.

Above: Joey (Brandon de Wilde) and his father (Van Heflin) greet the stranger (Alan Ladd) who will change their lives in Shane. *Top: John Wayne as Ethan Edwards, one of* The Searchers *who, having found the abducted girl he was looking for*

and reunited her with her family, wanders off alone. Top right: Wayne as John T. Chance in a showdown with Feathers (Angie Dickinson) in Rio Bravo. *Above right: James Stewart as a trigger-happy cowboy in* The Far Country.

for toughness and self-reliance no-one could rival Barbara Stanwyck, who emerged as a leading Western star during the mid-Fifties in such pictures as *Cattle Queen of Montana* (1954). *The Violent Men* (1955), *The Maverick Queen* (1956) – and, most impressive of all, as the ruthless ranch boss of *Forty Guns* (1957), Sam Fuller's much underrated Western, atmospherically filmed in black-and-white CinemaScope.

In the landmark year of 1950 there was a major upgrading of the Western genre. John Ford directed *Rio Grande* (the last of his cavalry trilogy) and *Wagonmaster*. This superb tribute to the pioneers who travelled west in wagon trains drew on Ford's stock company of favourite actors, including Ward Bond, Jane Darwell, Russell Simpson, Ben Johnson and Harry Carey Jr.

Another veteran director, Henry King, produced an unexpected bonus from his collaboration with Gregory Peck. The theme of the gunslinger unable to live down his past has often been dealt with since, but never more effectively than in *The Gunfighter*.

The year 1950 also marked the debut of a number of new

Western stars, and directors such as Anthony Mann and Delmer Daves. Mann directed his first three Westerns in 1950: *The Furies,* at Paramount, starring Barbara Stanwyck and Walter Huston; *Winchester '73,* at Universal, with James Stewart in his first mature Western role; and, at MGM, *Devil's Doorway,* in which Robert Taylor played an Indian fighting for the rights of his people. In Delmer Daves' *Broken Arrow,* Stewart played an Indian-scout who falls in love with and marries an Indian girl; Jeff Chandler played Cochise in this first modern Western to portray the Indians with human stature and dignity. William Wellman's *Across the Wide Missouri* (1951), with Clark Gable, presented an intelligent treatment of the theme of a white trapper and his Indian wife. However, the claim for a new respectability for the Western was firmly established in 1952 with the phenomenal success of *High Noon*. But *Shane* was the biggest Western hit of the decade. The fine cast was headed by Alan Ladd, Jean Arthur, Van Heflin and Brandon de Wilde, with Jack Palance as the villainous hired gun brought in to intimidate the homesteaders.

Among the many Westerns filmed in the new processes, Robert Aldrich had a big hit in 1954 with *Vera Cruz*, one of the first films in SuperScope. And although Anthony Mann proved in *The Far Country* (1954) that it was still possible to get excellent results from the old format, he finally made the transition to CinemaScope with *The Man From Laramie* (1955), the last of his films with Stewart; all of his subsequent Westerns were in 'Scope. Similarly, John Ford's masterpiece, *The Searchers*, benefited from the superior photographic quality of VistaVision. The picture presents a harsher, more bitter and sophisticated view of the West than is found in his earlier films.

On a more unassuming level, the revenge theme that largely motivated *The Man From Laramie* and *The Searchers* was also powerfully developed in several among a remarkable series of low-budget Westerns from the late Fifties, starring Randolph Scott and directed by Budd Boetticher: *Seven Men From Now* (1956), *The Tall T, Decision at Sundown* (both 1957), *Buchanan Rides Alone* (1958), *Ride Lonesome* (1959) and *Comanche Station* (1960). John Sturges' output included the modern Western thriller *Bad Day at Black Rock* (1955) and the more traditional *Gunfight at the OK Corral* (1957).

The black-and-white picture made a temporary comeback during the late Fifties with Delmer Daves' *3.10 to Yuma* (1957) and Arthur Penn's *The Left-Handed Gun* (1958), starring Paul Newman. Both films presented sophisticated and realistic treatments of traditional themes – the lone lawman bringing an outlaw to justice, the story of Billy the Kid – with a modern emphasis on character and relationships on a small scale. The moments of violence develop naturally out of the intensity of personal conflict.

The end of the decade saw one outstanding Western, Howard Hawks' *Rio Bravo* (1959). On the surface, the picture may appear conventional; yet the characters and relationships are observed with great insight and wit while retaining the kind of vitality and spontaneity found in Hawks' earlier pictures. Hawks neatly built on the juxtaposition of old, established Westerners like John Wayne and Walter Brennan with a newer generation represented by Dean Martin and Angie Dickinson. Unfortunately, as the decade drew to a close, the studios increasingly turned to the overblown, blockbuster Western in the style of William Wyler's *The Big Country*.

The Gangster Revival In the Fifties the gangster movie produced three new strains, one of which took its impulse directly from the reality of American crime at the time. In this first strain there are two characteristic images: one is of a figure, very often a racketeer, testifying, amid considerable media coverage, before a Senate sub-committee; the other is of a group of elderly, sober-suited men sitting around a boardroom table and voting on whether an erstwhile colleague should be murdered. The real events to which both these images relate are the hearings and conclusions of the Senate Special Committee to Investigate Crime in Interstate Commerce, usually called the Kefauver Committee after its chairman. It was the findings of this committee which gave rise to the cycle of gangster movies in which 'the Syndicate' (sometimes city-wide, sometimes state- or nation-wide) figured so prominently.

In many respects *The Enforcer* (1951) is *the* transitional crime film between the Forties and the Fifties. Dealing with the activities of 'Murder Incorporated', it has some of the features of the so-called 'semi-documentary' film of the Forties but sounds the note which was to dominate the Fifties,

Top: Sam Fuller's vicious tale of revenge fought out in the streets of America's cities. Above: Marilyn Maxwell and Broderick Crawford in New York Confidential, *the story of a crime boss who comes to a violent end.*

the existence of an all-embracing crime conspiracy modelled on legitimate business activity. This cycle includes *Hoodlum Empire* (1952), *New York Confidential* (1955), *The Brothers Rico* (1957) and *Underworld USA* (1960). This motif, more than any other, should have provided the means of offering explanations of crime in terms of social structure rather than personal disposition; but the form of the classical narrative movie, with its emphasis on individual characters, is not well suited to posing questions and explanations in other than personal terms. The Syndicate is usually defeated in this cycle of movies, but almost always through the action of one man motivated by vengeance. The two central recurring scenes of testimony and conspiracy, however, take on a different political dimension if interpreted as a quasi-unconscious means of dealing with an unmentionable, repressed topic: the hearings of HUAC and, in the Senate, of McCarthy, together with the consequential blacklisting.

The second strain which appeared in the Fifties indicated that Hollywood was beginning to have a conscious sense of its own history. This type consisted of a series of films set in the

Prohibition and Depression periods, the time of the early gangster movies. Very often they took the form of a biography of a notorious criminal. This cycle includes *Baby Face Nelson* (1957), *The Bonnie Parker Story, Machine Gun Kelly* (both 1958), *Al Capone* (1959) and continues into the Sixties with *The Rise and Fall of Legs Diamond, Pay or Die!* (both 1960), *Portrait of a Mobster* (1961), *Bonnie and Clyde, The St Valentine's Day Massacre* (both 1967) and *Bloody Mama* (1970). These consciously stylized films often made use of music evolving a sense of period.

The third strain which came to the fore in the Fifties had its origins to some extent in the big-robbery films of the Forties, such as *Criss Cross* and *White Heat* (both 1949). But *The Asphalt Jungle* (1950) was unique in American cinema for the attention it gave to the preparation for and execution of the robbery. The form which it initiated – the 'caper' movie – is in many respects a celebration of the narrative process of cinema itself. Within this form, a group of disparate individuals comes together to pull off a robbery. The cycle in the Fifties includes *The Killing* (1956), *Odds Against Tomorrow* (1959), *Seven Thieves* and *Ocean's Eleven* (both 1960).

If the thriller and *film noir* were less frequently made in Fifties Hollywood, their spirit lived on. Nowhere was this more apparent than in the realization of particular acts of violence in the Fifties. In the classic gangster movie of the Thirties, violence tended to be swift, unritualized, unmarked by specific cinematic effects (such as close-ups) and usually executed by firearms. Violence in the thriller and *film noir* of the Forties involved beating, crushing, burning, cutting, disfigurement, pushing from high buildings and poisoning. This more tactile sense of violence is evident, primarily in the Fifties gangster movie and thriller, but also in other Fifties

Above far left: Bonnie (Dorothy Provine) and Clyde (Jack Hagan) in The Bonnie Parker Story. *Above centre: stern warnings accompanied publicity for* Baby Face Nelson, *one of the early hits of the revived gangster genre which ushered in a stream of biopics. Above: Debbie Marsh (Gloria Grahame), face bandaged after having had scalding coffee thrown in her face in* The Big Heat, *a film typical of Fifties crime movies in its concern with the spread of organized crime and police and judicial corruption. Above right: the gang (Sam Jaffe, Anthony Caruso and Sterling Hayden) in* The Asphalt Jungle, *perhaps the first really influential heist movie. Below right: a dance of death in Roger Corman's* The St Valentine's Day Massacre, *a detailed retelling of Al Capone's most famous crime. Below left: seedy hotels, deserted gas stations and sleazy bars – home to Charles Bronson and Susan Cabot as the criminal couple in the violent* Machine Gun Kelly.

genres such as the Western and the war movie. An example which excited much comment at the time was the shooting of James Stewart's gun hand in *The Man From Laramie*. Among the most disturbing acts of violence in the Fifties gangster movie are those enacted (actually or potentially) on women, such as the disfigurement with boiling coffee suffered by Debbie (Gloria Grahame) in *The Big Heat* (1953), and the threat of acid to the face of Vicki (Cyd Charisse) as she is slowly unbandaged in *Party Girl* (1958).

It may be that highly stylized genres like the gangster movie, the thriller and the suspense movie in the Hitchcock mould offer a better guide retrospectively to the mood of a particular society at a given time and to its hidden stresses and strains than films with an overt, contemporary social message. When viewed today, Fifties thrillers and suspense movies seem to have lost little of their high drama and human interest.

What Price Stardom?

It has often been observed by film critics and sociologists that if you look at the history of Hollywood stardom, you can see a fundamental shift in ideas about what a star is. In the silent period and continuing on into the Thirties and Forties, stars were like gods and goddesses – they were not just gifted, popular, hard-working actors and actresses but people of a different kind from the ordinary run. Even Mary Pickford and Charlie Chaplin, and certainly Greta Garbo or Rudolph Valentino, however much you might care about them, were not the sort of people you would expect to meet in your own life. Yet gradually through the Thirties and Forties, and moreso since the Fifties, the stars have come down to earth.

There are exceptions; but the gods-to-humans direction has essentially been that taken by the stars' images. The first stage in this secularization of the stars reached its apogee in the Fifties, the great period of the star-as-ordinary-person. They were no longer the special beings of the past but straightforward, uncomplicated, average humans. In retrospect it may be hard to understand this. Doris Day's hard-edged, peppy virginity, Rock Hudson's towering, soft hunkiness, June Allyson's almost-swallowed burr of a voice and wig-like coiffure, Gregory Peck's elegant eyebrows and somnolent performance style – to those who were not around at the time, seeing the films as they were released, these attributes must seem as baroque as those of Mae West or Ramon Novarro. Yet at the time such stars stood for the idea of normality; and 'normality' was the predominant reigning idea of the time. What this meant was that all the ideals of human behaviour that societies of the past had striven for, however unsuccessfully or hypocritically, had finally been abandoned. For now it was not the best that society encouraged its members to strive for, but the average – to work at being typical, ordinary, acceptable. If stars like Greta Garbo, Fred Astaire, Lillian Gish and Douglas Fairbanks Sr had shown that there were other, more marvellous ways of being alive than the merely everyday, stars like Doris Day, Rock Hudson, June Allyson and Gregory Peck insisted that the everyday was best. They were stars who represented the result of the chilling pressure to conformism of the Fifties.

This is in no way to underestimate their abilities, their charm or the complexities of their images. Doris Day, for instance, was actually much spunkier than the normal passive image of women in the magazines of the Fifties, while big, manly Rock Hudson was at times almost 'feminine' in his gentle and sensitive bearing and expressions. Some films were built up on these aspects of the stars' images. Doris Day is a splendidly stroppy shop-steward in *The Pajama Game*, while a film such as *Pillow Talk* painfully exposes the pressures on businesswomen of the period. Rock Hudson is a virile yet oddly ineffectual presence in Douglas Sirk's melancholy meditations on the emptiness of contemporary American values: *Magnificent Obsession, All That Heaven Allows* (1955) and *The Tarnished Angels* (1957). Yet for all that, Day and the others – to say nothing of Mitzi Gaynor, Donald O'Connor, Dorothy McGuire or Dana Andrews – represented Mr and Mrs Nice Guy, Norman and Norma Normal. Their off-screen image was frequently confused with their film roles.

Significantly, only a handful of the 'ordinary' stars were really big – the other giant names were much less comfortable figures, expressing a very different truth about how people were feeling in the period. Beneath the plastic, antiseptic, streamlined conformity of the Fifties, there was a un-articulated but widespread sense of dissatisfaction, a realization, though still as yet unformulated, that the *status quo* was not the best way things could or should be. This undertow of discontent gathered momentum in the Sixties in the wave of political and cultural protests that so characterized that decade; but in the Fifties we have to detect it in disguised, covert forms, unknown even to itself. The chief sign of this buried unease, as far as the image of stars goes, was the role of scandal.

This was a remarkable feature anyway. It was as if the less godlike, the more mortal the state of stardom became, the more rotten it turned out to be. The Fifties and Sixties were the period in which a star's faults and sins, far from being something to be hushed up, could become their strongest selling point. This marked a major change from earlier periods. Fatty Arbuckle's trial on rape and manslaughter charges, even though he was eventually acquitted, destroyed his career. Yet Lana Turner and Elizabeth Taylor, for instance, thrived on the many scandals of their lives. As a publicity man of the period put it:

'The stars are losing their glamour. It's next to impossible to get Burt Lancaster into columns these days. He's too serious. The public prefers its stars to behave a little crazy. Look what that dope party did for Bob Mitchum! Look how Deborah Kerr's divorce troubles sent her price way up! Who wants to form a fan club for a businessman?'

These scandals were a disruption of the image of normality, and the fascination of the stars who were the subject of them was precisely that they were stepping outside of the cosy, stifling atmosphere of the mainstream. It would be wrong to see this as being directly political, but it had an implicit political direction. Politics as such was itself a taboo in the Fifties – this was the age of consensus, when 'of course' everyone agreed, within the marginal differences between Republican and Democrat, Labour and Conservative, that the way society was going on right now was pretty well along the right lines. McCarthyism, which made such a devastating impact on Hollywood, saw to that. Stars who had dallied with any other line of thought – and all such lines were 'commie' to McCarthyism – were out. Being smeared by HUAC ruined the careers of John Garfield, Betty Garrett and Larry Parks; even Marlon Brando and Marilyn Monroe risked jeopardizing their position by their apparent friendliness towards the Left.

If direct politics was not possible, a sort of indirect protest was. This was most evident in the so-called 'rebel' stars: Montgomery Clift, James Dean, Marlon Brando as well as stars from other countries such as Zbigniew Cybulski in Poland, Jean-Paul Belmondo in France and Albert Finney in Britain. They were 'angry' – their acting was heavy on scowls and pained looks; they played parts of misfits, delinquents and tearaways; off-screen they were difficult with the press and uncooperative with the studio's publicity machine. Yet it would be hard to say just what they were angry *about* – their characteristic inarticulateness (Clift's piercing silences, Brando's mumbling delivery, Belmondo's throwaway style) was an expression of the very unfocused nature of their discontent. Brando, in *The Wild One*, is asked what he is rebelling against and replies with another question: 'What have you got?' Albert Finney, at the end of *Saturday Night and Sunday Morning* (1960), throws a stone at the housing estate, a symbol of everyday conformity, but it is really no more precise than that. The rebel stars were 'anti-', but as a lifestyle rather than as a political position.

All the rebels were men. However inarticulate and unfocused it might be, male stars could at least register protest.

Above: Ingrid Bergman's love affair with Italian director Roberto Rossellini severely harmed her career and was a major scandal of the Forties. Top: in 1949 Robert Mitchum was sentenced to 60 days for possession of marijuana.

Discontent emerged in more distorted ways with women stars. Women, far more than men, were the centre of the scandals concerning the stars. There were exceptions, notably Robert Mitchum's conviction for possession of drugs; but even when the scandal concerned couples, as with the on-off relationships of such as Ava Gardner and Frank Sinatra, or Elizabeth Taylor and Richard Burton in the Sixties, it was the women who attracted attention. The first really big scandal was Ingrid Bergman's affair with Roberto Rossellini, by whom she had a child. No matter that they were subsequently married – Ingrid Bergman brought down the wrath of Hollywood upon herself and seemed to be defying the whole moral order in breaking her own previous 'virtuous' off-screen image. Yet only seven years later she was welcomed back to Hollywood with the plum role of *Anastasia* in Anatole Litvak's 1956 film about the alleged survivor of the Russian royal family; and she got the Oscar for it. Her scandalousness only made her ultimately more an object of interest and sympathy. A similar result attended Lana Turner's ambiguous involvement in the murder of underworld figure Johnny Stompanato, which was reflected in her film, *Portrait in Black* (1960).

Elizabeth Taylor's string of marriages was likewise publi-

Above: a scandal larger than life – Lana Turner's lover Johnny Stompanato (centre), a small-time gigolo/crook, was stabbed to death by her daughter Cheryl (right). Above right: Eddie Fisher and Debbie Reynolds, seen together in a popular fan magazine of

the period, were parted by Elizabeth Taylor. Top: smiling one minute, fighting the next, Frank Sinatra and Ava Gardner had a particularly stormy marriage. Right: Monroe – the image of male sexual fantasy.

cized, particularly what was felt to be her heartless breaking-up of that nice, normal couple, Debbie Reynolds and Eddie Fisher. The mixture of disapproval and envy in the response to the actions of these and other women stars is unmistakable, and it is parallel to the response to the male rebel stars. For in an unconscious way the likes of Ingrid Bergman, Lana Turner and Elizabeth Taylor could be taken to be rebelling against their conditions of servitude as women.

There was another aspect to female stardom: sex. More directly than ever before, stripped of the mystique of a Gloria Swanson or a Marlene Dietrich, women stars embodied sexuality. This was often caught in particular images: Jane Russell in her widely publicized cantilevered bra, lying on a heap of straw in *The Outlaw* (1943): Carroll Baker in a cot, thumb in mouth, in *Baby Doll*: Brigitte Bardot, bare shoulders, hair falling over her face, in numerous pin-up shots. This emphasis often led to grotesquerie, as in the exaggeratedly form-fitting dresses and almost deformed walk of Jayne Mansfield, and the Fifties' 'mammary madness' as Marjorie Rosen, the feminist critic, has put it. These strange, distorted expressions of sexuality are of a piece with the increasing emphasis on sex, and sexual variety, in the cinema and can also be seen as part of the underground unease of the period.

Throughout the Fifties and since, the idea that sexuality held the key to all human problems was urged by such otherwise disparate figures as Alfred Kinsey and Hugh Hefner (of *Playboy*), Betty Friedan, in her brilliant analysis of the situation of women in the Fifties, *The Feminine Mystique* (published in 1962), shows how much stress was being put on sexuality as *the* source of fulfilment for women.

Perhaps the reason why Marilyn Monroe is the most significant star of the period is that she combined this belief in the absolute centrality of sexuality to human existence with a sense of rebellion at the way women were so relentlessly and reductively seen in terms of sex. With the other women stars this contradiction came out in twisted forms; but with Marilyn there was a much clearer sense of actually questioning the role of sexuality in modern life, and especially in the treatment of women. The confusions and contradictions of Monroe – she seemed both to push herself as sex-object and to resent being trivialized for this emphasis – were never resolved, just as the wider problems of the tensions between nice 'n' normal and a deep-seated discontent could not yet be brought to the surface.

Besides, Marilyn died in 1962. And James Dean had died in 1955, and Judy Garland would die in 1969. Prosaically, these deaths were a reminder that the stars were indeed mortal. Gods, after all, do not die. There is more to it than that. Whatever the truth of the matter, these three deaths seemed to symbolize a crumbling of the faith and optimism that Hollywood, and American culture, had for so long peddled. Dean could be taken as having died at the frustration of his rebelliousness, Monroe as a human being crushed by the social dehumanization of women, Garland as a victim of the supreme example of capitalist-style artistic production, Hollywood. They seemed to die of the very things – youthfulness, sexuality, showbiz – that had made them stars. From having once represented ideals of human happiness and aspiration, by the Sixties stardom almost came to represent the defeat of those ideals.

Key Directors

Born in 1906 to a well-off Austrian Jewish family and educated in Vienna, **Billy Wilder** went to Berlin in 1926 as a journalist and established himself as a scriptwriter from 1929 until his hasty departure for Paris in 1933. He co-directed a film there before moving to Hollywood in 1934. From 1938 he collaborated as a scriptwriter with Charles Brackett, mostly on comedies such as *Midnight, Ninotchka* (both 1939) and *Ball of Fire* (1941). From 1942 he also directed a whole series of successes, including *The Major and the Minor* (1942), with Ginger Rogers (aged 30) masquerading as a 12-year-old to travel at half-fare, *Double Indemnity* (1944, co-scripted with Raymond Chandler), the archetypal *film noir* of adultery, murder and betrayal, *The Lost Weekend* (1945), with Ray Milland as a desperate alcoholic, *A Foreign Affair* (1948), confronting Marlene Dietrich and Jean Arthur in Berlin, and *Sunset Boulevard* (1950), with Gloria Swanson as the fading silent film star and William Holden as her scriptwriting gigolo. From 1951 Wilder produced nearly all of his own films and from 1957 he began a new scripting collaboration with a Romanian-born New Yorker, I.A.L. Diamond.

However thoroughly Wilder may have assimilated the atmosphere of the USA, especially California and New York, many of his films have been set in Europe, notably Paris and Berlin. His evocations of Europe are tinged with melancholy, the humour being a safeguard against emotional indulgence; in his Parisian films the tone is always romantic, whereas in the Berlin films it is astringent; but both are nostalgic. He shows Americans humanized by contact with Europe: Gary Cooper as a playboy in *Love in the Afternoon*, Jack Lemmon as a harrassed businessman in *Avanti!* (1972). Stay-at-home Americans are victims of greed and sexual enslavement, and either wind up dead (as in *Double Indemnity* and *Ace in the Hole,* 1951) or renounce material values for subjective moral principles; having to choose between money and happiness, they demonstrate their maturity in selecting the humanist option, as in *The Apartment* (1960), *Kiss Me, Stupid* (1964) and *The Fortune Cookie* (1966).

Frank Tashlin (1913-19) was a magazine cartoonist, a film animator (of Merrie Melodies and Looney Tunes), a gag-writer (for Laurel and Hardy and the Marx Brothers, among others), a story director (for Disney cartoons) and, from 1944, a writer for live-action features.

Beginning with *The Lemon Drop Kid* (1951), which he co-directed (receiving no screen credit) with Sidney Lanfield, he directed fairly prolifically until 1968, but most Anglo-American critics have tended to dismiss his career as an appendage to the work of Jerry Lewis, who starred in eight of Tashlin's movies. Apart from the fact that two of Tashlin's

most inspired films – *The Girl Can't Help It* and *Will Success Spoil Rock Hunter?* (1957) – have nothing to do with Lewis, such judgements clearly undervalue his contribution to Lewis' career. Tashlin made the finest of all Dean Martin-Jerry Lewis films, *Artists and Models* (1955) and wrote and directed six of Lewis' solo vehicles between 1958 and 1964.

He brought distinct innovations to Hollywood comedy. His greatest feat was the consistent turning of 'reality' into a cartoon caricature of itself – his films are littered with visual and aural gags derived from animation. He relentlessly parodied the crassness and power of the media; most notably television (especially in his Fifties films), but also advertising, rock'n'roll, publishing and other movies, not least his own. And he was the first director to take up the challenge issued

Below: Billy Wilder and Marilyn Monroe at a party for Some Like It Hot, *co-scripted by I.A.L. Diamond. Bottom: Jack Lemmon as a clerk and Shirley Maclaine as the elevator girl sleeping with his boss in Wilder's* The Apartment.

by *Hellzapoppin'* (1942) – by destroying the illusion of cinema and building jokes from an exposure of the film-making process itself.

Samuel Fuller (b. 1911) says: 'A film is like a battleground. Love . . . hate . . . action . . . violence . . . death. In a word – emotion!' Seven of his twenty-plus films are war movies: *The Steel Helmet*, the first Korean War movie; *Fixed Bayonets* (1951); *Hell and High Water* (1954); *China Gate* (1957), the first Vietnam film and Angie Dickinson's first leading role; *Verboten!* (1958); *Merrill's Marauders* (1962); and, most personal of all, *The Big Red One* (1980), commemorating the US First Infantry Division, in which he served from North Africa to Czechoslovakia. His Westerns, crime films and newspaper movies are scarcely less violent, both in subject-matter and in

their shocking, jagged, abrupt style. His aim has always been to force America into awareness of its problems (racial tensions, organized crime, runaway self-interest, war memories, war guilt) and its possibilities (as melting pot, as dynamic society, as nation with nostalgia and pride in its rich and vital history). Fuller's cinematic style thrives on the audaciousness of its contrasts. Static, talky shot set-ups give way – sometimes without a cut – to bravura displays of camera mobility. Startling ruptures of narrative continuity occur – through the insertion of printed 'headlines', the clash of studio footage with film-within-a film newsreel or travelogue material, the intercutting of moving and non-moving shots. Writing and often producing his own films, Fuller seemed to the French *nouvelle vague* directors an authentic

Below: Wilder's Sunset Boulevard, *a film about the grandeur, greed, dreams and nightmares of Hollywood, with Gloria Swanson as forgotten silent star Norma Desmond. Bottom: Fuller's* The Steel Helmet *pulsates with war's mad energy.*

Below: Frank Tashlin directs Dean Martin and Jerry Lewis in Artists and Models, *regarded as their best film. Bottom: Elia Kazan's* Splendour in the Grass *starred Natalie Wood and the then unknown Warren Beatty.*

and courageous *auteur* who boldly confronted socio-political issues in the most direct terms. Without much honour in his own country until recently, he was relatively inactive after 1963 until his comeback in the Eighties with *The Big Red One*, *White Dog* (1981), a curious anti-racist parable, and *Les Voleurs de la Nuit* (1984, *Thieves After Dark*).

Elia Kazan (b. 1909) directed films from 1945 and even won an Oscar for *Gentleman's Agreement* (1947), though the location shooting and naturalistic acting of his social thrillers *Boomerang* (1946) and *Panic in the Streets* (1950) were more promising. Arguably his best work of the Forties was in the theatre, co-founding the Actors' Studio and directing the early (and, as it turned out, best) plays of Tennessee Williams and Arthur Miller (whom he introduced to Marilyn Monroe in 1950). With *A Streetcar Named Desire* he transferred to the screen both Williams' masterwork and the brutally powerful performance of Marlon Brando. Vivien Leigh was the neurotic Blanche DuBois, a role originally written for Lillian Gish, but never played by her. Following Kazan's cooperation with HUAC in 1952, *On the Waterfront* came to be seen as a defence of informers as well as an attack on dockland corruption and union gangsterism. Certainly it was a vindication of the Actors' Studio (and indeed the Group Theatre) in the acting of Brando, Eva Marie Saint, Rod Steiger and Lee J. Cobb. The script was by Budd Schulberg, who also wrote *A Face in the Crowd* (1957), a denunciation of television demagoguery. The Williams connection continued with *Baby Doll*, more obviously cinematic but less poetic than *A Streetcar Named Desire*. The Actors' Studio supplied James Dean for his first big role in *East of Eden,* from a novel by John Steinbeck, who had written *Viva Zapata!* (1952) for Kazan and Brando. *East of Eden* was Kazan's first film in colour and wide screen, both of which he easily mastered, as was apparent in *Wild River* (1960), a more lyrical and romantic view of the South than in his earlier films, set in the Thirties at the time of TVA river control projects, with Lee Remick as a wistful, vulnerable young widow and Montgomery Clift as an apparently ineffectual federal agent. *America, America* (1963) and *The Arrangement* (1969) were based on his own novels.

Of Danish origin, Detlef Sierck (b. 1900) established himself in Germany in the Twenties and early Thirties as an innovative left-wing theatre director. He switched to the

Above: Marlon Brando as the boorish Stanley Kowalski – a role he had successfully played on stage with Vivien Leigh as Blanche Dubois, desperately clinging to the last vestiges of her beauty and respectability in Kazan's version of Tennessee Williams' A Streetcar Named Desire. *Above right: James Dean and Julie Harris, with Raymond Massey, in* East of Eden. *Above far right: Vicki Gaye (Cyd Charisse) and Thomas Farrell (Robert Taylor) make a grisly discovery in Nicholas Ray's* Party Girl *(1958). Far right: urban nightmare seen through the eyes of Anthony Mann in* T-Men. *Right: Rock Hudson and Jayne Wyman in Sirk's* Magnificent Obsession.

politically safer area of film melodramas in 1934 but fled in 1937. His American career as **Douglas Sirk** began with the low-budget anti-Nazi *Hitler's Madman* (1942) and ended with Universal's biggest box-office hit to that date, *Imitation of Life* (1959). He worked at Universal from 1950 in a variety of genres including musicals and comedies, but it was with a run of colourful family melodramas that he made his commercial and, much later, critical reputation: *Magnificent Obsession, All That Heaven Allows, Written on the Wind, The Tarnished Angels* (in black and white) and *Imitation of Life*. (All but the last starred Rock Hudson, who also played four other roles for Sirk.) The social milieu depicted is quite often that of the well-off middle class, inevitably emotionally crippled within the parameters of home, family and country club, frequently resorting to alcohol for ineffectual relief.

In his films Sirk seems to have consciously intended both to deliver all the most satisfying elements of the 'weepie' – glossy bourgeois settings, handsome heroes, suffering heroines – and to operate a critique of that ethos (and thus of bourgeois America itself) by dismantling the form from within. This dismantling – rooted in Sirk's refusal to align

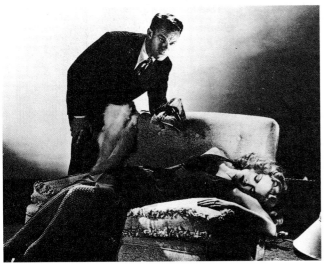

himself, as director, with the sentimental responses that the story-lines of his films demand – is achieved in a variety of ways: artifice in acting, framing, use of colour, mirror shots, and especially his relentless insistence on the *fabricated* quality of the films. The emotional intensity typical of melodrama is often pushed to a point of delirious excess that evokes the highly stylized forms of the German Expressionist cinema. Music and objects are made to carry an unusual emotional weight, as in the stunningly lavish funeral of the black maid at the end of *Imitation of Life,* with gospel singer Mahalia Jackson delivering 'Trouble of the World' – a fitting conclusion to Sirk's American career.

The 'Hollywood' directorial career of **Nicholas Ray** (1911–19) occupied a limited segment of his life, 1947–62; indeed, *Ombre Bianche* (1959, *The Savage Innocents*) and the Sixties epics *King of Kings* and *55 Days at Peking* were shot in Europe. A student of architecture and American folklore, he worked in the theatre, radio and television before his debut film, *They Live by Night* (1948), was released in late 1949. It established Ray's favourite theme of the loner, the outsider at odds with society, seeking some tenuous, even tender, human relationship of love or friendship. 'I'm a stranger here myself', says the gunfighter (Sterling Hayden) in *Johnny Guitar;* and other examples include the troubled teenagers (James Dean, Natalie Wood, Sal Mineo) in *Rebel Without a Cause;* the rodeo rider (Robert Mitchum) in *The Lusty Men* (1952) and the Eskimo (Anthony Quinn) in *The Savage Innocents*. The latent violence in man is a major isolating factor in *Knock on Any Door* (1949), *In a Lonely Place* (1950) – both starring Humphrey Bogart – and *On Dangerous Ground* (1951). Even the women (Joan Crawford, Mercedes McCambridge) are violent to the edge of murder in *Johnny Guitar*, while a harassed teacher (James Mason) is driven to paranoia by drug abuse in *Bigger than Life* and nearly kills his own son. Ray drew unusually sensitive and nervy performances from a diversity of stars, and embedded these in a dynamic visual style that even mastered the cumbersome screen ratio of CinemaScope. His extraordinary compositions, both of form and colour, were not just masterly craftsmanship but counterpoints of the actions, emotions and psyches of his characters. Difficulties of temperament and health led to his withdrawal from commercial film production, severely limiting his output in later years; but his critical reputation, particularly in Europe, continued to rise.

Anthony Mann (1906–1967) forged a darkly dramatic visual style in his *films noirs* of the late Forties, notably *T-Men* (1947) and *Raw Deal* (1948), before turning to the Western in 1950 with *Devil's Doorway*, a sombre epitaph to the Indian; *The Furies,* a drama of intense family conflicts recalling the world of Greek tragedy with Freudian overtones in which a rancher's daughter struggles to prove herself worthy of her tough father; and *Winchester '73*, the first of five Westerns with James Stewart, elemental revenge dramas played out against an epic Western landscape which functions as a protagonist in the action, providing a visual correlation of the characters. In Mann's Westerns, Stewart generally plays an isolated, almost schizophrenic hero, propelled at once by violent inner forces and a desire for peace. In *The Naked Spur* he becomes a bounty hunter largely in order to exact revenge upon *himself* for being too human and vulnerable in the past. Often the charming villain – Robert Ryan in *The Naked Spur*, Arthur Kennedy in *Bend of the River* and *The Man From Laramie* - functions as a reflection of the hero, as his more or less unbalanced alter ego. This is what gives their confront-

Top: James Stewart as Will Lockhart, the lonely avenger in The Man From Laramie, *faces his enemy (Arthur Kennedy). Above: Laura (Gene Tierney) encounters detective Mark McPherson (Dana Andrews) in Preminger's chic murder mystery.*

Top: Otto Preminger, Viennese exile and autocratic producer-director, prepares a scene for Advise and Consent. *Above: Frank Jessop (Robert Mitchum) is drawn into a web of murder by Diane Tremayne (Jean Simmons) in* Angel Face.

ations such epic power. Like all legends, Mann's Westerns revolve around the family – the hero of *Winchester '73* remorselessly pursues the brother who has murdered their father. In *The Man From Laramie* an engaging usurper kills the weakly evil legitimate heir to a cattle kingdom, and both are guilty of murdering the hero's brother. In *Man of the West* a reformed outlaw (Gary Cooper) kills his adoptive father (Lee J. Cobb) and grotesque 'family' so that he may continue to live a new life. Such films are spectacular in the true sense – Jean-Luc Godard called *Man of the West* 'an admirable lesson in cinema – in modern cinema'. Whereas Nicholas Ray was comparatively restricted by the impersonal trappings of the epic, Mann gravitated naturally to the grand gestures of *El Cid* and *The Fall of the Roman Empire*.

Of prosperous Viennese–Jewish origin, **Otto Preminger** (b. 1906) went to America in 1935, working on Broadway and in Hollywood as a director and actor. His first big hit was *Laura* (1944), a *film noir* in which a detective (Dana Andrews) falls in love with a beautiful girl (Gene Tierney) believed to be dead – an early study in obsession, one of Preminger's recurrent themes. *Fallen Angel* (1945) and *Angel Face* (1952),

with Jean Simmons, were again brooding murder mysteries that subordinated conventional suspense to a mood of perverse romanticism, while *Where the Sidewalk Ends* (1950) featured Dana Andrews as an even more off-beat policeman than in *Laura*. Preminger varied his routine with comedies, 'women's pictures' and the trashy but colourful historical epic *Forever Amber* (1947), with Linda Darnell. As an independent producer, he challenged the censors with the sex comedy *The Moon is Blue* (1953) and *The Man With the Golden Arm* (1956), which dealt with the forbidden topic of drug addiction. He experimented with the CinemaScope frame in *River of No Return*, with Marilyn Monroe and Robert Mitchum, and the all-black musical *Carmen Jones* (both 1954), with Dorothy Dandridge and Harry Belafonte. He discovered Jean Seberg for *Saint Joan* (1957) and used her limitations to depict an impulsive, uncontrolled girl ruining the lives of her irresponsible father (David Niven) and his fiancée (Deborah Kerr) in *Bonjour Tristesse* (1958). He went on to a series of grandiose films based on popular bestsellers, including *Anatomy of a Murder* (1959), *Exodus* (1960), *Advise and Consent* (1962) and others, dealing with public themes –

Top: Carmen Jones *(Dorothy Dandridge) seducing Joe (Harry Belafonte) in Preminger's all-black update of Bizet's opera. Above: tennis star Guy Harris (Farley Granger) and the suave Bruno (Robert Walker) meet as* Strangers on a Train.

Top: James Stewart as a temporarily crippled photographer who is witness to a murder through The Rear Window. *Above: Roger Thornhill (Cary Grant) on the run from a crop-dusting plane in Hitchcock's* North by Northwest.

justice, politics, government, war, religion – in a vigorously superficial manner but with plenty of narrative skill. Sympathetic critics have praised his objectivity of style, often expressed in long takes in which the character may be hysterical but the camera remains detached. He concluded the Seventies with *The Human Factor* (1979), an oddly under-played version of Graham Greene's espionage novel.

Alfred Hitchcock specialized in the mechanics of suspense. The central figures of his films often have everyday occupations – a tennis player (Farley Granger) in *Strangers on a Train* (1951), a priest (Montgomery Clift) in *I Confess* (1952), a temporarily crippled news-photographer (James Stewart) in *Rear Window* (1954), an advertising man (Cary Grant) in *North by Northwest* (1959), a spoiled society girl (Tippi Hedren) in *The Birds* (1963) – which collapse under their feet, tumbling them into the most nightmarish situations. These nightmares do not have a *social* basis; they are not concerned with the characters' relations with the outside world. Rather, they are concerned with the fragility of the characters' own person-ality and identity and with the horrors that may lie in the depths of their own psyches. Thus the priest of *I Confess,* the

tennis player of *Strangers on a Train* and the ad-man of *North by Northwest* effectively take on the appearance of guilty men. The girl in *The Birds* is accused of being a witch, responsible for the deadly plague of attacking birds. The temporary invalid of *Rear Window* becomes a voyeur, while the policeman (James Stewart) of *Vertigo* seems an emotional necrophiliac, as he morbidly tries to remake a shopgirl he picks up (Kim Novak) into the image of his (as he supposes) dead love. In *Marnie* (1964) the hero (Sean Connery) per-versely tries to rape a pathological liar and thief (Tippi Hedren) into normality. In Hitchcock's bleakest film, *The Wrong Man* (1957), an unassuming bass player (Henry Fonda) is wrongly identified as an armed robber; slowly and deliberately the judicial process locks him into this role, his family disintegrates under the experience and his wife (Vera Miles) retreats into madness. Most famously and shockingly of all, in *Psycho* (1960), a girl (Janet Leigh) who steals for love is hacked to death by a maniac (Anthony Perkins) who finally assumes the catatonic role of his mummified mother. Hitch-cock, the jokey master of suspense, cut deep into anxieties and fantasies no more remote than a newspaper's headlines.

CHAPTER 14
Worldwide Visions

The Fifties was a time of major revolutions in world cinema. Partly due to the influence of television, audiences everywhere were diminishing, though in some countries (e.g. Britain) the decline had begun some years earlier. Yet the film industry remained buoyant in France, Italy and Japan, among others, as a new period marked by increased international exchange got under way. The international development of art-houses, film societies and major film festivals brought about a degree of awareness of new developments in cinema unknown since the easy interchange of the silent era. The growth of film archives was indicative of a need for increased knowledge and preservation of the cinema's past and present. On the production side, American film personnel became aware of Europe's artists and technicians as many American movies came to be made abroad.

France
In commerical terms, French cinema in the Fifties was the healthiest in Europe. Production was maintained at a steady and relatively high rate in comparison with other major film-making countries outside of the USA. Although the market was virtually restricted to domestic and French-speaking territories (thereby limiting the amount of money French films could earn), careful budgeting on the part of the producers, along with an efficient and well-established star system and reliable attendance figures, guaranteed profits.

Only towards the end of the decade did the threat of television make itself felt; this new distraction, together with the burgeoning French obsession with cars, holidays and other leisure pursuits, would cause annual attendances to plummet from 411 million to 232 million between 1957 and 1966. Consequently some 4000 cinemas went out of business.

In the meantime, however, French audiences appeared well pleased with their national cinema. The staple diet was Hollywood-influenced thrillers, 'naughty' sex comedies and period pieces along with perennial vehicles designed for such local superstars as Jean Gabin, Fernandel and Martine Carol. More significantly the cinema had, almost since its inception, enjoyed intellectual respectability in France and was soon to become a positive passion among the educated young. In this way it was possible for a 'difficult' film, like Robert Bresson's *Un Condamné à Mort S'Est Echappé* (1956, A Man Escaped), to chalk up excellent returns at the box-office.

This respectability was encouraged by unusually energetic governmental measures to aid the industry at its frequent

Left: Orphée *(Jean Marais) vainly attempts to follow the mysterious princess through the mirror.*

moments of crisis. In the immediate post-war period, the number of domestically made films had declined to the point where numerous cinemas risked closure through lack of product. This situation was aggravated by a quota system (instituted long before World War II) that limited the importation of dubbed American films to 120 a year. In 1946 a pact between France and the USA known as the Blum-Byrnes Agreement replaced the quota by another regulating the number of French films that cinemas were compelled to screen. The authorities settled on a figure of 37 per cent, even though French film production could have easily exceeded such a quota.

Those sectors of the industry engaged in distribution and exploitation benefited enormously from the Blum-Byrnes Agreement and flooded the market with dubbed Hollywood films. The effect on the production side of the business, however, was disastrous. After concerted protests from the industry and the press, the Agreement was revoked in 1949; the domestic quota was revised upwards and the level of imported American films re-established at 120. Furthermore, a surtax was levied on cinemas from which a fund was set up to help finance the industry. This proved a major boost to production until the system was changed again in 1959.

Artistically, however, the picture was less sanguine. Viewed with hindsight, the Fifties appears as an undistinguished interim period between the glories of pre-war cinema (and the isolated miracles effected under the occupation) and the rise of the *nouvelle vague* in the early Sixties.
Key Directors Many of the film-makers who had dominated the Thirties — Jacques Feyder, Julien Duvivier, René Clair, Jean Renoir — were only now returning to France from self-imposed exile. Although the last three (Feyder died in 1948) were to continue working irregularly all through the Fifties, only the youthfully inquisitive Renoir was really able to adapt to changing conditions and evolving techniques.

Clair had some success at first through collaboration with Gérard Philipe, who was to become and remain one of France's leading male stars until his premature death in 1959. *La Beauté de Diable* (1949, Beauty and the Devil) was based on the Faust legend and also starred Michel Simon; since Faust and the Devil exchange bodies, each actor played both roles. In *Les Belles de Nuit* (1952, Beauties of the Night) Philipe was a music teacher who dreams of beautiful women in various historical epochs. In *Les Grandes Manoeuvres* (1955, Summer Manoeuvres) he played a philandering young officer in a provincial garrison town who woos a divorcée (Michèle Morgan) for a wager and discovers, too late that he has fallen in love with her. It was a bitter-sweet comedy of errors.

Tout l'Or du Monde (1961, *All the Gold in the World*) deals with a simple farmer who refuses to sell his land to a real-estate promoter seeking to turn the village into a holiday camp. The film was notable for the performance of Bourvil, cast as a father and his two sons. But Clair was clearly less at ease with rustics than with his beloved Parisians.

Les Fêtes Galantes (1965, The Love Parties) was a Franco-Romanian co-production filmed in Romania and featuring Jean-Pierre Cassel. Clair had wanted for some time to make a film about the stupidity of war – he set this in the eighteenth century to avoid the kind of organized massacre he felt characterized his own century. The film was unsuccessful, and terminated his career. In 1960 Clair had become the first film artist as such to be elected to the French Academy (Cocteau had gained his place primarily for his literary work). He died in 1981.

The pre-war style of 'poetic realism' lingered on in post-war films like Marcel Carné's *Les Portes de la Nuit* (1946, *Gates of the Night*) but after the dream-like *Juliette, ou la Clé des Songes* (1950, *Juliette, or the Key of Dreams*), Carné, who together with his scenarist Jacques Prévert had been the architect of this style, found himself driven into a career of crass commercialism.

For the three most notable mainstream directors who had come to prominence during the Occupation – Jacques Becker, Henri-Georges Clouzot and René Clément – the Fifties saw the consolidation of their talents. If Becker, the most original, is largely forgotten today, it is doubtless due to the slightly disconcerting diversity of his work, almost all of it in a minor key. He was a modest creator, unconcerned with uttering grand statements and it was this that endeared him to young directors, such as François Truffaut, later in the decade.

The work of **Jacques Becker** (1906–1960) is marked by a meticulous, though never oppressive, sense of detail and a precise rendering of time and place, whether in the register of intimate comedy-drama like *Edouard et Caroline* (1951), the thriller *Touchez Pas au Grisbi* (1954, *Honour Among Thieves*), the 'biopic' *Montparnasse 19* (1958, *The Lovers of Montparnasse*) in which Gérard Philipe played the painter Modigliani, or the prison-escape movie *Le Trou* (1960, *The Hole*). In a period when French cinema was balefully devoid of human warmth, it was especially refreshing to encounter Becker's characterizations and the bemused affection which he contrived to extend, even to the most minor among his characters.

Becker died in 1960 at the age of 54. If he left behind no undisputed masterpiece, he will perhaps be most fondly remembered for *Casque d'Or* (1952, *Golden Marie*), a tragic love-story set in turn-of-the-century Paris and enshrining a magnificent performance by Simone Signoret.

The cinema of **Henry-Georges Clouzot** (1907–1977) could hardly be more opposed to that of Becker. His reputation for absolute rigour and perfectionism was often more applicable to his notoriously finicky shooting methods than to the results he achieved on the screen. Clouzot's films are shot through with a blackness verging on nihilism. *Manon* (1949), his version of the Abbé Prévost's novel *Manon Lescaut*, updated to the twilight, post-war world of black-marketeers and clandestine refugee ships bound for Palestine, has at its centre what must be the last sympathetic pair of young lovers in cinema history.

The work that established Clouzot internationally, *Le Salaire de la Peur* (1953, *Wages of Fear*) concerned four dead-enders paid to transport a cargo of nitro-glycerine over the bumpy, deeply rutted roads of South America, and ended up with the violent deaths of all four.

Except for *Le Mystère Picasso* (1956, *The Picasso Mystery*), a fascinating and straightforward study of the artist in the throes of creation, Clouzot's films were less artistically successful, although *Les Diaboliques* (1955, *The Fiends*) was a huge commercial hit both in France and abroad. *Les Espions* (1957, The Spies) was a confused and pretentious spy thriller, obviously intended to be Kafkaesque and even more obviously failing. *La Vérité* (1960, *The Truth*), a court-room drama, revealed the growing *nouvelle vague* influence in its choice of theme (the amorality of modern youth) and star (Brigitte Bardot), but was otherwise stamped with Clouzot's own stolid if efficient technique. After this box-office triumph his career went into decline until his death in 1977.

René Clement (b.1913), who had served his apprenticeship as Jean Cocteau's assistant on *La Belle et la Bête* (1945, *Beauty and the Beast*) and made one of the rare French contributions to neo-realism, *La Bataille du Rail* (1946, The Battle of the Railway Workers), was the quintessential craftsman, crucially dependent on his scripts and not noticeably animated by a passion to explore the boundaries of his chosen medium. Clément's greatest success was *Jeux Interdits* (1952, *Forbidden Games*) which dealt with the secret universe created by two small children in wartime. His subsequent career included a British film, *Knave of Hearts* (1954), an Ealing-like comedy set in London; *Gervaise* (1956), the obligatory adaptation from a classic novel with Maria Schell as the heroine of Zola's tale of alcoholism in nineteenth-century France; and *La Diga sul Pacifico* (1958, *The Sea Wall*), a turgid international co-production based on a novel by Marguerite Duras.

Among Clément's more interesting work is *Plein Soleil* (1959, *Blazing Sun*), an adaptation of one of Patricia Highsmith's Ripley thrillers. Its fluid, versatile camerawork by the cinematographer Henri Decaë (later to become a major stylist in the *nouvelle vague*), the predominantly young and attractive cast (including Alain Delon, Maurice Ronet and Marie Laforêt) and a clearly perceptible influence from Hitchcock, further underlines the inroads which the young directors were making into mainstream cinema.

To these names should be added that of **Claude Autant-Lara** (b.1903) who started as a set-designer with the painter Fernand Léger and the architect Mallet-Stevens on Marcel L'Herbier's silent film *L'Inhumaine* (1934, *Futurism*). From the lending-library adaptations that comprise Autant-Laras' post-war work (ranging from Stendhal, Dumas and Dostoevsky, to Feydeu, Colette and Simenon) we might single out *La Traversée de Paris* (1956, *A Pig Across Paris*), a black comedy about two men involved in the black-market meat trade. Though marred by a complacent reliance on studio sets and lighting, when the material cried out for location shooting, the film is distinguished by a quite subtle modulation from comedy to tragedy.

From the point of view of subject matter, French cinema was very tightly controlled during this period. Government aid was withheld from any film seeking to reflect the contemporary political reality of the country, plagued in these years by two colonial wars – in Indo-China and Algeria. Indeed the only French film by a major director treating, even indirectly, the Algerian war was Jean-Luc Godard's *Le Petit Soldat* (1960, *The Little Soldier*), and that was banned from exhibition for three years.

The prevailing political climate may explain the critical

favour then enjoyed by **André Cayatte** (b.1909), a barrister turned film-maker. In four widely discussed films: *Justice Est Faite* (1950, *Let Justice Be Done*), *Nous Sommes Tous des Assassins* (1952, *Are We All Murderers?*) *Avant le Déluge* (1954, *Before the Flood*) and *Le Dossier Noir* (1955, *The Black Dossier*) Cayatte and his scenarist Charles Spaak tackled a variety of social and legal problems such as euthanasia, capital punishment and juvenile delinquency. The films are, however, very flatly shot: André Cayatte's penchant for the basic shot/reaction set-up ideally suited the dramatic confrontations in which his films traded. Dry and schematic, they frequently resorted to loaded arguments and special pleading. The issues are developed in terms of right versus wrong, sympathies are engaged according to the charismatic qualities of the actors playing the roles, the condemned man whose fate hangs in the balance invariably turns out to be innocent, and so on.

These were the directors most violently attacked by a group of up-and-coming critics (François Truffaut, Jean-Luc Godard, Eric Rohmer) who wrote in *Cahiers du Cinéma* and who, as directors themselves, were to revitalize French cinema towards the end of the decade. A celebrated polemical piece by Truffaut entitled 'Concerning a Certain Tendency in French Cinema' was a St Valentine's Day Massacre of what he derisively referred to as 'le cinéma de papa'.

Only a handful of film-makers survived the massacre. Renoir was one, and in the Fifties he completed a trio of what might loosely be termed 'musical comedies'. *Le Carosse d'Or* (1952, *The Golden Coach*) was a bitter-sweet meditation on the interrelation of theatre and life centred on a Commedia dell'arte troupe touring in eighteenth-century Peru; *French Cancan* (1955) emerged as a lovingly detailed homage to La Bell Epoque, which his father (the impressionist painter, Auguste) had immortalized. *Eléna et les Hommes* (1956, *Paris Does Strange Things*) took the form of a witty 'spoken operetta' about General Boulanger's attempted *coup d'état* in the 1880's.

In his austere manner, **Robert Bresson** continued his lonely pursuit of cinematic Grace in *Le Journal d'un Curé de Campagne* (1951, *Diary of a Country Priest*), tracing the career of a priest from his arrival in the village of Ambricourt through his sufferings to his death from cancer. *Diary of a Country Priest*, adapted from Georges Bernanos' novel, took the unprecedented step of retaining the author's first-person narration while neither strictly illustrating nor complementing it with images in any conventional manner. Instead the commentary is used as part of a complex dialectic. *Diary of a Country Priest* also launched a series of Bresson features built around the spiritual progression of a confined and solitary individual towards freedom. This individual was embodied (rather than 'played') in each case by a non-actor – Claude Laydu in *Diary of a Country Priest*, François Leterrier (now a film director himself) in *A Man Escaped* – one of Bresson's masterpieces and a film no doubt inspired by his own prisoner-of-war experiences – Martin Lasalle in *Pickpocket* (1959) and Florence Carrez in the title role of *Le Procés de Jeanne d'Arc* (1962, *The Trial of Joan of Arc*). *Au Hasard, Balthazar* (1966, *Balthazar*) was a contemporary rural fable that chronicles the life of a donkey while detailing all the instances of human failing and corruption that he passes through almost in the manner of a medieval allegory. Perhaps for the first time in his work, Bresson expressed some of his rage against the modern world – focused, in this case, on a cruel teenager named Gérard whose motorbike and transistor

Right and below: in The Wages of Fear, *bored adventurers Jo (Charles Vanel) and Mario (Yves Montand), stranded in South America, agree to transport high explosives over mountain roads to put out a blaze at a nearby oil well.*

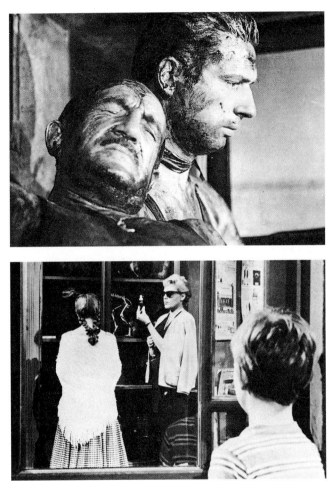

Above: Simone Signoret in Clouzot's macabre Les Diaboliques, *in which an invalid is eventually frightened to death. Critic David Thomson has described Clouzot's body of work as a 'cinema of total disenchantment'. Right: Balthazar the donkey is a pet of Marie (Anne Wiazemsky) in Bresson's contemporary rural fable* Au Hazard, Balthazar. *Both are victimized by young thugs when Marie falls for their leader.*

radio seemed to make him as emblematic as the bikers in Cocteau's *Orphée* (1950). It is a rage that can be felt, indeed, to greater and lesser extents in all six of Bresson's subsequent films, and which forms the very substance of *Le Diable, Probablement* (1977, *The Devil, Probably*).

Bresson again used a rural setting for *Mouchette* (1967), from another work by Georges Bernanos, which resumed the theme of heroic inner struggle in the figure of a friendless 14-year-old girl (Nadine Nortier). Following this harsh tragedy, Bresson made a belated – and seemingly permanent – shift from black and white to colour, starting with adaptions of two short stories by Dostoevsky which he filmed on location in present-day Paris: *Une Femme Douce* (1969, *A Gentle Creature*) and *Quatre Nuits d'un Rêveur* (1971, *Four Nights of a Dreamer*), the latter taken from the story *White Nights* that Luchino Visconti had already filmed in 1957.

The remarkable *Lancelot du Lac* (1974) comes across as peculiarly modern. Bresson, pushing some of his elliptical measures to their most extreme limits (framing figures from the waist down, encasing most of them in armour and largely using their rattling movements to establish their on and off screen presences), turned this 20-year-old project into an anguished statement about the loss of idealism and faith. Beginning and ending with anonymous, indifferent slaughter in a dark forest, it depicts the fragile love between Lancelot and Guinevere as the only remaining spark in an otherwise dying culture.

The Devil, Probably – which might be regarded as an angry, impassioned postscript to *Lancelot du Lac* and *Four Nights of a Dreamer* – takes up the theme of pollution as a summary of what Bresson hates most about the world today. Returning to contemporary Paris, he becomes more of a pamphleteer with this film than with any previous one, depicting such horrors as the clubbing to death of seals, the desecration of churches, the money-grabbing of psycho-analysts and the felling of beautiful trees – the destruction, in short, of all he holds sacred – while following the despairing progress of his youthful hero, the student Charles (played by Antoine Monnier), towards suicide. Paradoxically, as the possibility of an ultimately transcendent vision becomes less and less likely in Bresson' work, the increasing, sharpening materiality of his sounds and images creates a world of stunning presence.

This was no less true of *L'Argent* (1983, Money), based on a Tolstoy story, about the destruction wrought by a forged banknote: an ordinary young worker loses everything and becomes an axe-murderer, killing even the elderly woman who gives him shelter.

The supreme stylist of the Fifties was the German-born **Max Ophuls** (1902–1957). His long, intricately plotted tracking and dolly shots in *Le Plaisir* (1952, Pleasure) and in *Madame de . . .* (1953) embellished these fine adaptations, respectively from Maupassant and Louise de Vilmorin. Ophul's masterpiece, *Lola Montès* (1955), an account of the nineteenth-century courtesan told within the framework of the circus-ring setting, was hacked to pieces by its producers but virulently defended by the young critics: Truffaut compared the humiliation of Martin Carol's Lola to that of Joan of Arc at the stake.

Above right: Tina Irissari as Alberte (left) and Antoine Monnier as Charles (second from right) in Bresson's sympathetic study of youthful alienation, The Devil Probably. *Right: Jacques Tati in characteristic pose in* Mon Oncle, *a gentle satire of modern consumer society.*

In the Fifties, **Jacques Tati** (1908–1982) laid claim to being the most original creator of comedies France had ever produced. *Les Vacances de Monsieur Hulot* (1953, *Monsieur Hulot's Holiday*) became an instant world-wide favourite. Once again as in *Jour de Fête* (1949, Day of the Fair) using an authentic background, that of St. Marc-sur-Mer in Brittany, the film satirized the universal holiday-maker and introduced the frightening and endearing character of Hulot, who charged into the peculiarly brittle fabric of seaside society with all the gusto and misapprehension of a three-year-old. Despite his air of desperate improvisation, Hulot's mishaps were meticulously planned. Hulot has remained on view in all Tati's subsequent work. He has echoes of many screen clowns, primarily in his embarrassment at the problem of what to do with himself in a world patently ill-suited, not only to his physical awkwardness, but also to his inner remoteness. Hulot works twice as hard as anybody else at the task of integration – the tennis match in *Monsieur Hulot's Holiday* and the garden party in *Mon Oncle* (1958, My Uncle) show him at his most frenzied in the battle to keep up appearances – but a certain jauntiness in the angle of pipe and umbrella, a natty style of hat, and a private choreography of walk in which he seems to choose his own confident road along invisible stepping stones, imply that secretly he does not care too desperately that the world is hell-bent on progress. He is a gentle anarchist, too polite and affectionate to shake the nonsense out of his contemporaries; if they cannot be contented, at least he can find his own kind of peace in isolation.

In *Mon Oncle* – which appeared after nine months of shooting and a year of cutting and dubbing – Hulot often seems withdrawn, a hermit in his own cosy part of town,

although his struggle to be a part of everything continues.

Mon Oncle proceeded to a quietly biased, irresistibly sentimental comparison between the old and the new and the widening gulf between them.

Hulot the charming recluse was the model for a decade of drop-outs, but his unswerving kindness and imperturbable good manners were an archaic and quixotic armour in an era of computerized dehumanization.

Playtime appeared after a long interval in 1968. Tati had spent three years constructing it with a massive £1 million budget, but it had nothing to add. Hulot wanders around the glass boxes of the modern Paris, an aimless ghost in a procession of repetitive and only mildly amusing incongruities. Like Antonioni, Tati strengthened his anti-urban argument by making the architecture a dominating force, but went a stage further by building his own studio city, spotless and soulless, like a maze enclosing experimental mice. And like the holiday-makers of *Monsieur Hulots' Holiday*, the mice are recognizable 'types' – the American tourists, the German salesmen, the little old-ladies who need someone to mend a simple electric lamp but find that such expertise is not available in today's sophistication, the fussing married couple, the waiters who never get around to serving anybody. Hulot strikes up a tentative friendship with an American girl and gives her a present to take back home – a small bunch of plastic flowers. International or not, it provides a melancholy symbol for the film as a whole; precise, well-meant, a spectacular piece of craftsmanship but not much of a substitute for reality.

With *Traffic* (1970, *Traffic*), Tati was on happier ground. Hulot is a driver in a convoy of new cars *en route* from Paris to an international motor show in Amsterdam. More prominent

as a character than in *Playtime*, but still a model of detachment, he has come to terms with progress to the extent that he tends to have the solution to such problems as breakdowns, traffic-jams, and car crashes, offering good sense while his contemporaries swarm about in counter-productive distraction. Tati satirizes all the less lethal driving habits, stringing together an amiable line of sight-gags – like a squashed shape under a car-wheel that could be either dead dog or discarded jacket – which have an edge to them that is discreetly blunted to avoid the shedding of blood. Discretion, after all, had always been the essence of Tati's humour.

Although **Jean Cocteau** (1889–1963), made only two films in the decade – *Orphée* (1950, *Orpheus*) and *Le Testament d'Orphée* (1959, *Testament of Orpheus*) – the spidery watermark of his signature could be traced through the whole decade and even more visibly in the one that followed. In *Orphée*, myth is so firmly rooted in everyday life that Cocteau's poetic exploration of the creative imagination also functions, simultaneously and seamlessly, as a superb *film noir* thriller.

These great artists, always considerably more than regents waiting for the young princess of the *nouvelle vague* to come to age, kept French cinema alive until Francois Truffaut's *Les Quatre Cents Coups* (*The Four Hundred Blows*) and Alain Resnais' *Hiroshima Mon Amour* (Hiroshima My Love) became the *succès de scandale* at the 1959 Cannes Film Festival.

Indeed the rigid structure of the industry had already been dented by the work of a few younger directors, notably Roger Vadim, whose Bardot vehicles have often been confused with *nouvelle vague* cinema but were rather the frothy foam on its crest, and Jean-Pierre Melville. But it was in the field of short films that the first tangible signs of aesthetic renewal

Above: a typically stylish shot from Ophuls' Le Plaisir. *Right: Cocteau wanders through the landscapes of his imagination in* Le Testament d'Orphée.

emerged. Shorts were generously subsidized by the state and provided an exceptionally fruitful training ground for apprentice directors.

Georges Franju (b.1912) who was subsequently to pursue his career in feature films, made his reputation with a series of shorts that transformed the mundane format of 'information films' into coolly poetic indictments of justice. *Le Sang des Bêtes* (1949, The Blood of Animals), a documentary on abattoirs, made an unforgettable impression by the surreal juxtaposition of its placidly banal treatment and narration and the elemental horror of its imagery.

Franju's *Hôtel des Invalides* (1952) contrasted the pomp of military glory recorded in the nation's military museum with the reality of the battered victims of two world wars. Other themes subjected by Franju to similar demystification were salmon breeding, stray dogs, and the cathedral of Notre Dame. At the end of the Fifties, Franju began his career as a features director with *La Tête Contres les Murs*, about a young man wrongfully confined in a mental hospital; and *Les Yeux Sans Visage* (1959, *Eyes Without a Face*), a horror movie about a surgeon who 'steals' young girls' faces to graft onto that of his badly disfigured daughter.

Alain Resnais (b.1922) also started with short films, which were graced by a painterly sense of composition and a musical sense of editing. His first were studies of artists and their work and included Gauguin, Van Gogh, Picasso's *Guernica*, and African sculpture and statuary. His masterpiece in the short film was *Nuit et Brouillard* (1955, *Night and Fog*) in which touristy colour film of the concentration camps in 1955 was juxtaposed with newsreel and Nazi 'home movie' footage of the camps in operation, thus producing a document of great emotional power. In his following film, *Toute la Mémoire du Monde* (1957, The Whole Memory of the World), Resnais depicted the labyrinthine French national library as a concentration camp where books were incarcerated.

A more literary approach to film-making was evident in *Le Rideau Camoisi* (1953, *The Crimson Curtain*) by the former critic **Alexandre Astruc** (b.1923). A somewhat academic director, Astruc was of greater significance to film history as the author of an influential essay 'Le Caméra Stylo' (the movie

camera as pen), in which he argued persuasively that films should be composed by their 'authors' in the same way that novels are – that the camera, in short, was the director's pen. It was this article together with the iconoclastic writings of the *Cahiers du Cinéma* critics and the theories of André Bazin that championed the work of those half dozen maverick French film-makers and prepared the way for the infinitely more bracing decade to come.

Meanwhile, at the level of popular cinema, the liveliest developments were in crime films and comedies.

The first screen appearances of Peter Cheyney's 'hero' Lemmy Caution was in 1952 in an episode of Henri Verneuil's film *Brelan d'As* (Three Aces) entitled *Je Suis un Tendre* (I'm a Nice Guy). *La Môme Vert-de-Gris* (1953, *Gun Moll*) marks the historic fusion of Lemmy Caution with Eddie Constantine, the actor and crooner who was to become synonymous with Caution in *Cet Homme est Dangereux* (1953, *This Man is Dangerous*), *Femmes s'en Balancent* (1954, *Dames Don't Care*) and most notably in Jean-Luc Godard's *Alphaville* (1965). By 1953 the indigenous thriller was fairly well established, and produced a succession of the following years' major works. The first of these was Becker's *Touchez Pas au Grisbi* which is both the study of an ageing criminal (played by Jean Gabin, now familiar to the point of being emblematic) and a meditation of friendship.

Razzia sur la Chnouf (Chnouf) also appeared in 1954 – a location-shot thriller by Henri Decoin concerning police infiltration of a gang of drug smugglers. But *Razzia sur la Chnouf* is less a picture of police work than of the drug underworld and of the seamier side of Paris-by-night, unrestrained by Anglo-Saxon puritanism and censorship. Needless to say, the film was heavily cut in Britain. The police are notable by their absence in Jules Dassin's *Du Rififi Chez les Hommes* (1955, *Rififi* or *Rififi Means Trouble*) which, like *Razzia sur la Chnouf*, is based on a book by Auguste le Breton, and like *Touchez Pas au Grisbi*, is very much concerned with human relationships and the mores of the criminal world. Dassin's film also contains one of the most famous of all robbery sequences and some finely orchestrated chases. The long robbery scene, apart from creating suspense, illustrates

the down-to-earth, material nature of crime, and thus helps to strip away the false glamour and mystique which has accrued to it through its representation in films and literature.

Jean-Pierre Melville's first crime film *Bob le Flambeur* (1956, Big Deal Bob) was the story of an ageing criminal and compulsive gambler. Like Melville's later masterworks, such as *Le Doulos* (1963, Stool Pigeon) and *Le Deuxième Souffle* (1966, Second Breath) it is an intense, intimate, almost microscopic examination of a shifting web of friendship, loyalty and betrayal, in which every gesture and word is of significance. At the same time he creates an extraordinarily mesmeric, poetic though never simply picturesque vision of night-time Montmartre – an attempt to recapture the flavour of pre-war Paris.

In 1957 Arsène Lupin came to the screen in Becker's *Les Aventures d'Arsène Lupin* (The Adventures of Arsène Lupin), scripted by Albert Simonin, author of *Touchez pas au Grisbi* and of the Parisian thriller *Une Balle dans le Canon* (1958, *A Slug in the Heater*) filmed by Charles Gérard and Michel Deville. In 1959 Claude Sautet combined with Jean Redon to write the script of *Le Fauve Est Lâché* (Beast on the Loose) for Maurice Labro. Sautet wanted to create a role for Lino Ventura, whom he had admired in *Touchez Pas au Grisbi*, and *Le Fauve Est Lâché* increased Ventura's popularity immensely. Later that year he went on to star with Belmondo in Sautet's first feature – *Classe Tous Risques* (1960, *The Big Risk*); the film's cinematic purity and efficacy recall Hawks, Sautet's strongest influence. He has even called *Classe Tous Risques* 'a Western in business suits' in that, like many Westerns, it focuses primarily on simple relationships and elementary characters caught up in a train of events beyond their comprehension or control.

Italy

The years 1950–60 were the most exciting ever for Italian film-makers witnessing a remarkable and sustained dominance of European film culture by a group of writers and directors whose work astonished the world. Rossellini, Visconti, Fellini, De Sica, Antonioni and the unjustly neglected Pietro Germi destroyed the complacent image of the Italian cinema which had flourished under Mussolini. Their mastery of the medium was immediate, their talent acknowledged both at home and abroad, and their output prolific.

By 1952, films such as Renato Castellani's *Sotto il Sole di Roma* (1948, Under the Roman Sun) and *Due Solde di Speranza* (1952, *Two Pennyworth of Hope*), Luciano Emmer's *Domenica d'Agosto* (1950, *Sunday in August*) had led to the coining of a new phrase to describe a branching-out from neo-realism to *neorealismo rosa*, or realism through rose-tinted spectacles.

The films of Pietro Germi, whatever their ostensible backgrounds, were invariably preoccupied with questions of personal honour and commitment to codes of behaviour. Although he had never been to Sicily before making *In Nome della Legge* (1949, *In the Name of the Law*), he frequently returned to the island, with its brooding ambience of fearful independence, its tribal suspicions and its perverse moralities. Marcello Mastroianni's restlessly comic wife-murderer in *Divorzio all' Italiana* (1961, *Divorce – Italian Style*) is a prisoner of the same society as Sarò Urzi's honest carabiniere of *In the Name of the Law* and the tragic heroine of *Sedotta e Abandonata* (1964, *Seduced and Abandoned*), a Sicilian girl (Stefania Sandrelli) whose life is ruined because of the rigid code of honour which prevails in the mafioso-riddled island.

The largest studios at Cinecittà, had resumed production in 1947 with a programme of five films. In ten years from 1950, total Italian film production rose to an average of 140 films per year. Box-office admissions reached 819 million in 1955 compared with 662 million in 1950 and 745 million in 1960 (falling to 319 million in 1978).

Much of the production activity reflected the peculiar and perennial preoccupation with the *peplum* and historical adventure films. The direct Hollywood involvement, from *Quo Vadis?* (1951), directed by Mervyn LeRoy, through to *Ulisse* (1954, *Ulysses*), *Atilla Flagello di Dio* (1955, *Attila the Hun*) and Robert Wise's *Helen of Troy* (1955), complemented and encouraged local initiatives.

The key factor was money. The America studios had millions of dollars trapped in Italy by post-war exchange controls. They could not take their earnings back home in cash without offering some advantage to the Italians. They could either use the blocked funds on the spot, as MGM did with *Quo Vadis?* or they could enter into co-production deals. United Artists signed with Rizzoli to produce DEAR Films, MGM went to Titanus to produce such spectacles as the Mario Lanza picture *Arrivederci Roma* (1957, *Seven Hills of Rome*), and Carlo Ponti and Dino De Laurentiis (partners until 1957) joined with Paramount for epics like the Kirk Douglas *Ulysses*. In 1951 the Italian government and the American industry agreed that the studios could take half their blocked money home – provided the other half stayed in Italy as short- or long-term finance for Italian movies.

Production in Italy was cheap. Hollywood studios were still smarting from the effective unionization of the Screen Actors' Guild, whereas in Rome there were no limits on how many hours an actor could work, and an actress for a speaking part need earn no more than five dollars a day. The studios had craftsmen and technicians from the grander pre-war days, and location filming was cheaper than anywhere in Europe. American stars were happy to work in Rome, since

Right: Totò as the tutor in safe-cracking to an incompetent gang in Persons Unknown. *Opposite page: the full-bosomed, fiery sexuality of some Italian leading ladies helped make them international stars. (From left to right) Gina Lollobrigida, here in* La Donna Più Bella del Mondo *(1955,* Women Are Dangerous); *Anna Magnani; Sophia Loren, here as a prostitute in* Marriage, Italian Style *(1964); and Silvana Mangano, femme fatale of the paddy field, in the neo-realist* Bitter Rice.

their agents told them that working 18 months outside the country would save them from US income tax.

From the early Fifties, Rome became Hollywood-on-Tiber. The main product was the so-called 'epics' – lengthy movies devoted to an equal mixture of apparent culture and flesh. Italian movie-makers, with American participation either before or after production, turned out sagas of Aphrodite, Barabbas, Barbarossa, Byzantium, Constantine the Great, Coriolanus, Herod, Hannibal, 'My Son Nero', and even Sappho of Lesbos.

Although more public and critical attention has been paid to the epics and historical-mythological *peplum* films, the cape-and-sword melodramas were not entirely devoid of interest. They lacked the budgets and the lightness of touch of their Hollywood cousins, but often their disturbing mixture of juvenile plot development and blatant sadism echoed a recurrent theme in Italian popular culture. Two films directed by Mario Soldati and starring Mai Britt, a would-be Garbo who never reached the heights, are clear examples: *Jolanda la Figlia del Corsaro Nero* (1952, Yolanda, Daughter of the Black Pirate) and its simultaneously shot sequel, *I Tre Corsari* (1953, *The Three Pirates*). Bloody revenge, flogging, transvestism and torture embellish the threadbare plots of these swash-buckling melodramas. The later so-called 'spaghetti' Westerns and increasingly perverse comic books, or *fumetti*, of the late Sixties and the Seventies amply illustrate developments of these themes.

Film series, in Italy as elsewhere, usually degenerated in quality as each succeeding film reworked the material of the original. Occasionally, a subsequent film in a series could equal the first. Both Julien Duvivier's *Il Piccolo Mondo di Don Camillo* (1952, *The Little World of Don Camillo*) and his *Il Ritorno di Don Camillo* (1953, *The Return of Don Camillo*) were exceedingly funny and faithful to Giovanni Guareschi's tales of unholy discord between the wily priest (Fernandel) and the communist mayor, Peppone (Gino Cervi), of a small village in the Po valley. Later Don Camillo films, however, increasingly caricatured the pair, becoming unfunnier in the process, and failed to repeat the international success of the originals.

The 'Bread, Love and . . .' series which also had wide distribution abroad, began with two films directed by Luigi

Comencini, *Pane, Amore e Fantasia* (1954, *Bread, Love and Dreams*) and *Pan, Amore e Gelosia* (1954, *Bread, Love and Jealousy*), both featuring Vittorio De Sica and Gina Lollobrigida at their most appealing. But it was the third in the series, Dino Risi's *Pane, Amore e . . .* (1955, *Scandal in Sorrento*), with Sophia Loren, which achieved the greatest success.

The Totò films were the most enduring series: low-budget comedies which were rarely exported but were churned out by the dozen from 1948 to 1964. Totò (Antonio de Curtis Gagliardi Ducas Comnuno di Bisanzio) was a clown in the classic mould, even though he was born of a ducal house in Naples in 1898. Overcoming the objections of his aristocratic family, he was on the stage before he was twenty, and by the Twenties was already a favourite comedian of *café-concerts*. By the Thirties he had his own revue company, and remained a major star until his death in 1967. A diminutive figure, he moved with the epileptic jerks of a marionette, and had all the dignity of a penguin at a trot. His face, however, with its vast eyes and permanently raised eyebrows, never yielded its look of hurt pride, whatever the circumstances.

The main international selling point of Italian movies was sex. A lickerish, lip-smacking barrage of publicity sold Italian actresses. Even *Roma Città Aperta* (1945, *Rome, Open City*) was promoted on sex. The publicity fuelled itself: serious newspapers debated whether the rather innocent orgy scene of Fellini's *La Dolce Vita* (1959, The Sweet Life), could pass Customs. Less serious journals talked of Gina Lollobrigida's 'justly famous anatomical assets', and *Vogue* pronounced her 'creamy as a mauve bonbon'. Paris slang for a brassière was 'les Lollos'. Sophia Loren's remarkable talent was almost buried – despite Carlo Ponti's best efforts – in her early reputation as 'Europe's Number One Cover Girl'. This arrant sexism was hugely important in promoting Italian movies during an era when American studios in particular were eager for more suggestive material to distribute, and reluctant to incur the moral opprobrium of producing it.

Film production companies in Italy rarely specialized in particular genres, and individual producers were far more adventurous than their British and American counterparts. Carlo Ponti and Dino De Laurentiis formed Ponti-De Laurentiis Productions in 1950, and in the seven years they were together they worked on projects as diverse as Toto films, Rossellinis' *Europa '51* (1951 *The Greatest Love*), *Jolanda, la Figlia del Corsaro Nero*, *Le Notti di Cabiria* (1957, *Nights of Cabiria*), Germi's *Il Ferroviere* (1956, *Man of Iron*) an epic Hollywood co-production such as King Vidors' *War and Peace* (1956).

Carlo Ponti's earlier involvements had included neo-realist films by Germi, Alberto Lattuada and Luigi Zampa; and after the break-up of Ponti De Laurentiis he continued with great success to produce a wide variety of films, often starring his wife, Sophia Loren. De Laurentiis was the more ambitious of the duo. After a number of unremarkable low-budget features he had achieved great success with *Bitter Rice*, and worked steadily to increase his international affiliations.

Old and new producers responded to the excitement of the booming Fifties. Angelo Rizzoli had started in films in 1934, but been inactive for many years when, in 1950, he produced Rossellini's *Francesco, Giullare di Dio* (*Flowers of St. Francis*). For the rest of the decade he was very active indeed, often setting up French co-productions including René Clair's *Les Belles de Nuit* (1952, *Beauties of the Night*) and *Les Grandes Manoeuvres* (1955, *Summer Manoeuvres*) as well as the first two Don Camillo films and Fellini's *La Dolce Vita*.

Franco Cristaldi was only 30 when he produced his first three films in 1954. His early films were routine romantic dramas which did reasonably well at the box-office. Following greater success with Steno's *Mio Figlio Nerone* (1956, *Nero's Weekend*), starring Alberto Sordi and Vittorio De Sica, he showed himself willing to take chances by producing Visconti's *White Nights*. He backed Francesco Rosi's first two features as director, *La Sfida* (1958, The Challenge) and *I Mahliari* (1959, The Swindlers) and was later to finance the same director's politically sensitive examination of the myth of the Sicilian bandit, *Salvatore Giuliano* (1961). He also produced the two best Italian comedies in *Persons Unknown* and *Divorce – Italian Style*.

The Fifties were years of enthusiasm and manic energy; geniuses and hacks rubbed shouders in a crowded, jostling film factory. An industry which had been virtually wiped out in 1944 was back and booming.

Key directors Born in 1920 in Rimini on the Adriatic coast, **Federico Fellini** first began to show signs of the autobiographical preoccupations which predominated in many of his later films with *I Vitelloni*. The film is also interesting in that it hints at the cynical and despairing representations of male sexuality that featured in his later work, culminating in *Il Casanova di Federico Fellini* (1976, *Casanova*).

However it was with the international success of his fourth film, *La Strada* (1954, The Road) that Fellini staked his claim for serious critical attention. The film stars Fellini's wife, Giulietta Masina as Gelsomina, a simple girl who is bought by Zampano (Anthony Quinn) as his assistant in his travelling strong-man act. *La Strada* is basically concerned with Gelsomina's uncomprehending love for Zampano, her ultimate abandonment and death, followed by his gradual recognition of his loss of and need for her. The film is crucial to Fellini's avowed sense of man needing to be more than a creature of lust, and of woman as his potential redeemer. In addition, the role of Gelsomina crystallized Masina's image in Fellini's films as one of vulnerability, sensitivity and purity of heart, if not in deed.

Il Bidone (1955, *The Swindlers*) and *Le Notti di Cabiria* (1957, *Nights of Cabiria*) maintained critical and public interest in his work. The basic tension that forms *Il Bidone* is between a world of basic drives and ugliness and its alternative, the world of beauty and the spirit – again symbolized by women. *Le Notti di Cabiria* (on which Bob Fosse based *Sweet Charity*, 1969) stars Giulietta Masina as a prostitute. Although she is twice robbed by her lovers, her simplicity and basic innocence give her the moral strength to carry on.

It was with *La Dolce Vita* that Fellini once again took the world by storm. The film is concerned with the descent of Marcello, a journalist (Marcello Mastroianni) into a modern Roman world of idleness, debauchery and *ennui*.

Fellini's next two films were to put the seal on his reputation as a 'personal' and 'auto-biographical' film-maker. *Otto e Mezzo* (1963, $8\frac{1}{2}$) deals with the artistic crisis of a film director, Guido (Marcello Mastroianni) who is also having problems with his wife (Anouk Aimée) and an affair with a young woman.

Juliet of the Spirits, immediately raised the assumption that it was based on his marriage with Masina; the character of Giulietta remains constant to Fellini's theme of women as essentially healthy in spiritual terms. Where Marcello in *La Dolce Vita* succumbs totally to the alienation of modern, urban man, Giulietta, faced with a personal crisis centred around her home, realizes that life has no meaning without personal or moral codes.

Fellini Satyricon (1969) and *Roma* (1972, *Fellini's Roma*), show a change of emphasis and direction away from the autobiographical elements of his previous work. Despite their visual spectacle, they are more cerebral in theme. Based on Petronius' text *Fellini Satyricon* is clearly the director's vision of Roman society before Christ. In the amoral world of the film, the sole drive that animates society is sexual fulfilment; its totem is the hermaphrodite. The range of bizarre characters that inhabit it are embodiments of sensual appetite, at times beautiful in their joyful, unashamed sense of themselves. Although *Roma* includes recollections of Fellini's young manhood in the Fascist period, its stress is mainly on the city, its history and its people.

Amarcord (1973), dialect for 'I remember', is a very personal work, re-creating a Rimini of the Thirties with a boy, who can be interpreted as a young Fellini, as the main character.

Casanova brings to its ultimate conclusion the preoccu-

Above: Monica Vitti in L'Avventura.
*Above centre: Federico Fellini directs
a scene from* Fellini Satyricon, *a vision
of Roman Society before Christ. Top:
Giulietta Masina and Anthony Quinn
(left and centre) in* La Strada. *Top
right: Anita Ekberg as Sylvia, a sexy
American actress, in* La Dolce Vita.
*Above right: Donald Sutherland in the
title role of* Casanova. *Right: the boxer
(Renato Salvatori) stabs the woman he
loves in Visconti's* Rocco and His
Brothers.

pation which had informed very nearly all Fellini's films – directly in *I Vitelloni*, *La Strada* and *La Dolce Vita* and indirectly in his other films – male sexuality. The film offers a particularly bleak view of it as Casanova journeys through the bodies of women, going nowhere. The visual imagery is extravagant but stringently allied to the theme of the sexual anxieties upon which male identity is constructed.

Fellini's greatest strength is not simply his extraordinarily vivid visual imagination, but his phenomenal cinematic mastery. One can revel in his imagery – surreal, ironic, comic as it may be; wonder at the freakish characters with which he fills his films (he interviews thousands of non-professionals to get the right look, usually dubbing another's voice to get that right too); ponder over his thematic preoccupations; identify his specifically Italian love-hate relationships with the Church and its members; analyse his symbolic and metaphoric use of the sea, roads, clowns and circuses; but overriding all these is the fact that he has a control of the film-making process which has probably never been surpassed.

The major successes of **Michelangelo Antonioni** came in the Sixties with *L'Avventura* (1960, *The Adventure*) and its successors, including the British-made *Blow-Up* (1966). His main films of the Fifties were *La Signora Senza Camelie* (1953, *Woman Without Camellias*), which recounts the rise and fall of a film star from a humble background; *Le Amiche* (1955, *The Girl Friends*), from a story by Cesare Pavese, about the complex relationships of a group of middle-class women and their various lovers; and *Il Grido* (1957, *The Cry*), an uncharacteristic attempt to deal with working-class life, culminating in the suicide of its depressed hero.

Visconti followed the excellent historical film *Senso* (1954, *The Wanton Counters*) with a Dostoyevsky adapation, *White Nights*, which posed the aesthetic question of a choice between reality and fantasy within the narrative of a man attempting to woo a woman away from her romantic dreams of an absent lover. The women's dream comes true with his return and the 'realistic' lover is rejected. Visconti heightens the film's preference for romanticism through the purposely artificial sets. At the start of the Sixties, Visconti made a partial return to his earlier social concerns in the melodramatic *Rocco e i Suoi Fratelli* (1960, *Rocco and His Brothers*), concerning the misadventures of a Sicilian family come to Milan to find work.

Sweden

The fifteen years between 1925 and 1940 are usually dismissed by critics as a Dark Age in the history of Swedish cinema. Films were turned out with prolific haste, but success at the box-office, rather than quality, was the touchstone. Domestic comedies ruled the roost, and few directors attempted to use the cinema for genuine artistic purposes or for anything other than earning quick profits.

One director, however, did pursue a competent career throughout the entire period, and on even into the Sixties. Gustaf Molander (1888–1973) started as an actor in Stockholm in 1911, and worked as a screenwriter on such early Swedish classics as *Terje Vigen* (1917). His first significant film as a director was *En Natt* (1931, One Night), a drama involving two brothers who join different sides at the outbreak of the Finnish revolution. Sound and lighting were particularly sophisticated. In *Intermezzo* (1936), Molander yielded somewhat to the prevailing mood of the time, telling an intense and melancholy love story against the backdrop of European cities and resorts. The film introduced Ingrid Bergman to the outside world (she later remade the film in Hollywood), and her performance as the young piano teacher entranced by a famous (but married) violinist has a freshness and spontaneity that challenge the *kitsch* of the period.

Six years later, Molander made a laudable screen version of the novel by Vilhelm Moberg, *Rid i Natt!* (1942, *Ride Tonight!*). Set during the aftermath of the Thirty Years War, *Ridi i Natt!* denounced the feudal dominance exercised over the common folk by a group of robber barons in Sweden. Both Moberg and Molander stressed the parallels with Nazi Germany and the war that was threatening to engulf even traditionally neutral Sweden. The occupation of Norway provided the background to Molander's *Det Brinner en Eld* (1943, There Burned a Flame) and *Ordet* (1943, The Word). The latter film was based on a play by the Danish writer Kaj Munk, who was shot by the Nazis.

The turning point in the fortunes of the Swedish cinema came in 1942 when Carl Anders Dymling was appointed head of Svensk Filmindustri, the country's largest film company. One of Dymling's first acts was to name Victor Sjöström, then over sixty, as production supervisor. Now at last talent was able to assert itself. Alf Sjöberg won attention with *Himlaspelet* (1942, *The Road to Heaven*), a morality play by

Left: Anders Henrikson and Rune Lindström in Road to Heaven. *Above: one of the boys rescues a young otter in Arne Sucksdorff's superb film* The Great Adventure.

Rune Lindström, and *Hets* (1944, *Frenzy*), based on an original screenplay by the young Ingmar Bergman, and introducing a bright new star, Mai Zetterling. For the next decade, Bergman and Sjöberg would be the guiding lights of Swedish film, although Sjöberg was the senior by nearly fifteen years.

The Swedish cinema of the Forties was marked by a kind of undeveloped guilt in the face of the war in Europe. Sweden's neutrality worried the intellectuals and artists of the period, especially when both Denmark and Norway were overrun by the Nazis. This anxiety emerged in the visual style of many films, in which the characters seemed oppressed by their environment and menaced by an incomprehensible fate.

Molanders' *Kvinna Utan Ansikte* (1947, *The Woman Without a Face*) scripted by Bergman, showed the world in a cruel light as a young man strays from his marriage into a doomed liaison. *Frånskild* (1951, *Divorced*), again directed by Molander and written by Bergman, contained a moving performance by Inga Tidblad as the deserted wife for whom the lure of suicide is strong.

Arne Sucksdorff (b. 1917) was, meanwhile, following his personal line of exploration through film. His ethnographic and animal documentaries remain classics of their genre; they are specifically Swedish in their preoccupation with the passage of the seasons and in their meticulous technique. His most acclaimed achievement is the feature *Det Stora Äventyret* (1953, *The Great Adventure*), but *En Sommarsaga* (1941, *A Summer Tale*), *Trut!* (1944, The Gull), *Gryning* (1944, Dawn), *Människor i Stad* (1947, People of the City) and *En Kluven Värld* (1948, A Divided World) are all worthy of note.

Bergman's reputation, even in Sweden, would not reach the heights until the mid-Fifties. Sjöberg, with masterpieces like *Bara en Mor* (1949, *Only a Mother*) and *Fröken Julie* (1951, *Miss Julie*), was regarded as pre-eminent in his field and for a short period between 1951 and 1955 it appeared as though Arne Mattsson (b. 1919) would equal his accomplishment. Mattsson was much influenced by the work of Hitchcock and Ford and yet drew on the inspiration of Sjöström in his depiction of bucolic life in Sweden. *Hon Dansade en Sommar* (1951, *One Summer of Happiness*) provoked controversy when it was released. Its story of young love in the countryside was nothing new, but its frankness of expression certainly was — at least in one brief scene beside a lake. *One Summer of Happiness*, however, was by no means the best of Mattsson's films. *Kärleckens Bröd* (1953, The Bread of Love) unfolded in the snowbound forests of Finland during the Russo-Finnish war of 1939, and focused with relentless accuracy on the behaviour of a small patrol of men trapped in a minefield by their Soviet enemy. Mattsson, deploying an elaborate time structure (the film consisted of interlocking flashbacks) with the most elegant of camera movements, built up a psychological suspense that would become the hallmark of his work.

Mattsson's *Salka Valka* (1954) was drawn from a novel by the Icelandic author Halldór Laxness. It recounted how a mother and her young daughter come to a fishing community and survive on a combination of wits and energy.

Apart from Ingmar Bergman, whose work attracted worldwide acclaim but failed to break box-office records in his own country, none of the established directors made significant progress during the decade. After 1955 no worthwhile film reflected the true state of life in Sweden at the time. Escapism was once again the order of the day.

As the Fifties drew to a close, conditions in the domestic industry worsened and the Swedish cinema would be saved only by the foundation in 1963 of the Swedish Film Institute

which encouraged a new generation of film-makers, among them Bo Widerberg, Vilgot Sjöman and Jan Troell, to pursue their distinctive careers in the cinema.

Ingmar Bergman   Bergman was born on July 14, 1918 in the Swedish university city of Uppsala where, as he has since recalled, a number of influences came to bear upon him so vividly that they have recurred throughout his work. The bells of Uppsala Cathedral, the heavy furniture in his grandmother's flat which 'in my fantasy, conversed in a never-ending whisper', the nursery blind which, when lowered, somehow unleashed a horde of menacing shadows — these recollections continue to echo in Bergman's mind. Fifty years later, for example, they are combined to create the hallucinatory atmosphere of *Ansikte mot Ansikte* (1975, *Face to Face*), in which a woman (Liv Ullmann), visiting her grandparents, sleeps fitfully among the shadows, cries and whispers of her nursery room. More crucially, *Face to Face* also restages a particular trauma from Bergman's childhood, the severe punishment administered on occasion by his father: the boy would be locked in a cupboard containing, it was asserted, a creature that would bite off his toes. Not surprisingly, the characters in Bergman's films have often been subjected to confinement, sudden outbursts of violence, and almost casual torture.

At the time he escaped from the parental tyranny in 1937,

Far left: Ulf Palme and Anita Björk in Fröken Julie, *based on Strindberg's play about a headstrong aristocrat's hopeless love affair with one of her servants. Left: Harriet Andersson and Åke Grönburg as ill-matched lovers in* Sawdust and Tinsel. *Below: Max Von Sydow as the tortured artist in* Hour of the Wolf. *Below left: the first appearance of Death (Bengt Ekerot) in* The Seventh Seal. *Below far left: a smiling Ingmar Bergman chats with Bibi Andersson and director-actor Victor Sjöström, the stars of* Wild Strawberries.

to study literature and art at the University of Stockholm, the only panacea he could find for the pain of agnosticism was the theatre. His first public success was with a stage production of *Macbeth* in 1940, and for two years he was assistant director at the Royal Dramatic Theatre, writing and producing plays. Although Svensk Filmindustri tempted him into screen playwriting in 1942, and then into film direction, Bergman's theatrical work has continued ever since, in startling parallel to his cinema career. His earliest films demonstrated more of a theatrical energy than a cinematic awareness, but by 1947 this had begun to take shape. *Musik i Mörker* (1947, *Night Is My Future*), although written by somebody else, clearly anticipates Bergman's later work not only in its cast (which includes Birger Malmsten, Naima Wifstrand and Gunnar Björnstrand) but also in such assertions as 'Pain and suffering are part of God's design'. With *Fängelse* (1949, *Prison*) his agnostic irony was at its most poisonous: 'Life is only a cruel, meaningless journey from birth to death', stated the film, illustrating its theme with the wrist-slashed suicide of a defeated girl. The Devil rules the world, churches are his allies and God is his own invention.

Fortunately the darkness begins to lift almost immediately, and by the time of *Sommarlek* (1951, *Summer Interlude*), a fine, delicate, complex elegy of a film, Bergman's affection for overstatement has been tempered with subtlety. For the

ballet-dancer, the stage is the only compensation for the lover she has lost after one perfect (and very Swedish) summer, but in the course of the film she shows signs of being resurrected from beneath the mast of greasepaint. Himself divorced in 1950, Bergman seemed able to study the processes of love and marriage with a more varied perspective from this point onwards – affectionately in *Sommaren med Monika* (1953, *Summer With Monika*), sensitively in *Gycklarnas Afton* (1953, *Sawdust and Tinsel*), humorously in *En Lektion i Kärlek* (1954, *A Lesson in Love*) and with elegant and memorable irony in *Sommarnattens Leende* (1955, *Smiles of a Summer Night*), which marks the end of the cycle.

Det Sjunde Inseglet (1957, *The Seventh Seal*) and *Smultronstället* (1957, *Wild Strawberries*) were two journeys through the wasteland that led Bergman's restlessness to a temporary haven. In both films, the only certainty is death, in both the only compensation is the family unit, in both the only unknown is God's ultimate purpose, if any. In *The Seventh Seal*, the knight (Max von Sydow), trying to discover something of value in the plague-swept country he is about to leave, realizes that the clown's family, eating wild strawberries in the afternoon sun, has found the only available peace of mind. In *Wild Strawberries*, the aged professor (Victor Sjöström), pursuing a solution to his 'death-in-life' problem on a pilgrimage through the territory he knew as a

Left: Alma (Bibi Andersson), nurse to a neurotic actress, Elizabet (Liv Ullmann), dreams that her charge has come to her room in Persona, *Bergman's mature examination of identity and reality. Above right: Matti Kassila's* Harvest Month *was an attack on alcoholism, telling the story of a drunken lockkeeper torn between two women; a sub-plot of young love relieves the gloom. Right: Astrid Henning — Jensen directed her young son in the short fantasy* Palle Alene i Verden, *about a boy who dreams he is in a world that exists without other people.*

young man, discovers in the evocation of the family birthday party and in the memory of his parents beside a lake in summer the love that slipped so long ago out of his own marriage and left it empty. Fascinated since childhood by the element of illusion in cinema, Bergman has described the film-maker as a conjurer. The key film in the confrontation between conjurer and analyst is *Ansiktet* (1958, *The Face*), in which von Sydow plays a melancholy travelling showman who may or may not have genuine magical powers and is dissected by the merciless Björnstrand, scalpel in hand.

Since *The Face* there have been a number of harrassed illusionists in Bergman's films: the painter in *Vargtimmen* (1968, *Hour of the Wolf*), the violinist in *Skammen* (1968, *Shame*), the forger in *En Passion* (1969, *A Passion*) – all played by von Sydow. All have been savaged by their environment, their ultimate fate uncertain; in the case of *A Passion*, the central figure is actually pulled apart by the celluloid itself, processed so that his shape is no more than a mass of colour dots on the screen. It is an ending which reaffirms Bergman's apology; he is using deceit to portray deception, yet the inexplicable magic remains.

The question of the artist's place in society is one of Bergman's most familiar themes. It can be traced from the broken-hearted ballet-dancer in *Summer Interlude* to the unemployed tight-rope walker in *Das Schlangenei* (1977, *The Serpent's Egg*) with some particularly emphatic outbursts represented by *För att inte Tala om Allà Dessa Kvinnor* (1964, *Now About These Women*) and *Riten* (1969, *The Rite*). In such films as *Persona* (1966) dealing with a mentally disturbed stage actress, and *Shame* (musicians) and *Herbstsonate* (1978, *Autumn Sonata*) (concert pianist), the art-in-society debate can, however, be seen as part of a more general discussion about the predicament of the average human being in a collapsing environment.

The sense of helplessness refers back to films which are Bergman's best known, like *The Seventh Seal* and forward to

perhaps his most disregarded film, *Nattvardsgästerna* (1962, *Winter Light*), and again it is linked with his childhood. The search for God – or some acceptable equivalent – haunted the Bergman career up the point at which, with the trilogy of *Såsom i en Spegel* (1961, *Through a Glass, Darkly*), *Winter Light* and *Tystnaden* (1963, *The Silence*), he appeared to exorcize it. If God insisted on remaining silent, to pursue Him was at worst to risk insanity (the Harriet Andersson character in *Through a Glass, Darkly* claims to see God as a giant spider) and at best futile (the priest in *Winter Light* is unable to deflect one of his parishioners from suicide). Although hints of both can be found in the later films, particularly in *Viskningar och Rop* (1972, *Cries and Whispers*), with its central character on the brink of death, and in the despondent priest in *The Serpent's Egg* from *The Silence* onwards Bergman begins to favour a different kind of comfort found, despite all the difficulties in relationships, in mutual human compassion. Little hope was evident in *The Silence*, with its despairing illumination of the obstacles confronting *any* kind of communication between generations, between sexes or between nations. The political events of the Sixties and Seventies increasingly touched upon in his work, even when it was centred on his island home of Fårö, have seemed to support his argument – culminating in his own flight from Swedish tax authorities into a cathartic exile. But in *Cries and Whispers, Scener ur ett Äktenskap* (1973, *Scenes From a Marriage*), *Face to Face* and (if perhaps less convincingly) *Autumn Sonata*, he seemed to find the same small crust of comfort. However there was precious little to cheer the viewer – apart from Bergman's unique film-making skills – in *Aus dem Leben der Marionetten* (1980, *From the Life of the Marionettes*), a hypnotic, violent, study of sexual obsession and madness. As if to confound deliberately critical accusations of terminal misanthropy, Bergman then created his most optimistic work, *Fanny and Alexander* (1982). It was made in two versions – one for television, running for 300 minutes and one for the cinema, running for 180 minutes. For

Above right: in Dreyer's Ordet, *an old Jutland farmer (Henrik Malberg) is disappointed to learn that his crazy son (Preben Lerdorff Rye) is only unconscious, not dead. Right: danger threatens for Lisbeth Movin in the war-film* De Røde Enge.

this tale of a theatrical family in turn-of-the-century Sweden, Bergman brilliantly blended domestic comedy, period drama and expressionistic fantasy, with the adroitness of Cocteau and something of the humour and humanity of Renoir. Its joyous assertion of the magical power of art and illusion to exorcize the demons of the past and make life bearable showed the director at his most positive and expansive.

Finland, Denmark, Norway

Film is, and always has been, a cottage industry to Finland. To achieve success a feature must attract nearly half a million filmgoers to the box-office – and the country's population is a mere 4.7 million, spread over 130,000 square miles.

During the Thirties and Forties, between 15 and 25 features were completed annually. Feather-light comedies, literary adaptations and rural romances were commonplace. Risto Orko and T.J. Särkkä were the leading personalities in this middle period.

Orko's gift for effervescent farce in an upper-class milieu was shown to good effect in *Siltalan Pehtoori* (1934, The Steward of Siltala), which his rousing sense of melodrama was at its best in a flamboyant war film – set in 1916, with Finnish soldiers returning from Germany after fighting for the Kaiser – entitled *Jääkärin Morsian* (1938, The Infantryman's Bridge). Särkkä's picaresque *Kulkurin Valss* (1941, The Vagabond's Waltz) is one of the few Finnish films to have been seen by more than one million spectators in its own land.

Nyrki Tapiovaara, who was killed at the age of 28 behind Russian lines just before the end of the Winter War, has acquired a posthumous reputation on the strength of just five features. *Varastettu Kuolema* (1938, Stolen Death) is the most intriguing and imaginative of them, and takes place in the grey, dubious years at the start of the century when 'activists' were engaged in an underground campaign to thwart the expansionist designs of Tsarist Russia.

War has frequently been the inspiration for imposing films from Finland. None more so than *Tuntematon Sotilas* (1955, The Unknown Soldier) directed by Edvin Laine from the famous novel by Väino Linna. It captured the peculiar blend of joviality and bitterness that characterizes the Finnish people's attitude towards the Soviet Union, and the wars of attrition that have engaged both nations.

During the Fifties other names came forward for consideration in the history of Finnish film: Erik Blomberg, for his searing and visually exhilarating saga *Valkoinen Peura* (1952, The White Reindeer); Matti Kassila for *Sinien Viikko* (1954, Blue Week) which described, in an idiom very similar to that of Bergman, a clandestine affair between a young man and a married woman during the summer holidays. Kassila was also highly regarded for *Elokuu* (1956, Harvest Month) which attacked the evils of alcoholism in a rural environment. The film was based on a novel by F. E. Sillanpää, one of Finland's greatest writers.

Denmark has produced a single great director – Carl Theodor Dreyer (1889–1968). His career spanned almost six decades and yet his work never caught the public imagination in the way that Bergman's did. His finest film of this central period was *Vredens Dag* (1943, Day of Wrath), a grim and haunting study of a man's inhumanty to man in the face of witchcraft. Danes suffering under the Nazi occupation could perhaps see more in this film than was apparent to the casual viewer. *Ordet* (1955, The Word) was a remake of Molander's 1943 film from Kaj Munk's play. Dreyers' version is less naturalistic than Molanders' and ends on a mystical note with the awakening from the dead of the young wife Inger, rising from her coffin in the ghostly light of a bare white room at the farm where she lives.

A husband-and-wife team of outstanding talent in Denmark were Astrid and Bjarne Henning-Jensen, who between 1940 and 1960 made some twenty films. Their collaboration was particularly fruitful in respect of the films they made on childhood and adolescene. *Palle Alene i Verden* (1949, Palle

Alone in the World) and *Paw* (1960, *Paw – Boy of Two Worlds*) were among the most rewarding of their works. Denmark made an impression at the first Cannes Film Festival in 1946 with *De Røde Enge* (1945, The Red Earth) dealing with the wartime Resistance movement.

Norway lacks a continuous film tradition, although the government has long been involved in the industry and maintained a greater influence over film-making than is common in other Scandinavian countries. The nation's first film studio was built at Jar, in the Oslo suburbs in 1936, but the Kristiania Film Company had been producing features on a steady scale for a decade or so prior to this. Tancred Ibsen, who had worked in Hollywood for MGM, returned to Norway to earn fame as the director of *Den Stora Barnedåben* (1931, The Great Baptism), which was Norway's first talkie. Lief Sinding's *Fantegutten* (1932) was the first Norwegian screen musical. Rasmus Breistein was active throughout the period with films like the seafaring adventure *Jumfru Trofast* (1921, Miss Faithful), and romances such as *Liv* (1934, Life) and *Gullfjellet* (1941, The Golden Mountain). Sinding elected to work under the Germans as director of the Norwegian Film Industry, and for a long while after the war he was unable to practise his craft owing to this collaboration. In the wake of the liberation, Arne Skouen emerged as one of the promising Norwegian directors on the strength of his feature film debut, *Gategutter* (1949, *Street Children*), adapted from his own screenplay.

Spain, Mexico, Greece

Under the Franco regime, Spanish cinema was severely censored and it was rare to find films dealing with the problems, social or otherwise, of ordinary working people. Notable exceptions, however, occurred in the work of Juan Antonio Bardem and Luis García Berlanga. Bardem's *Muerte de un Ciclista* (1955, *Death of a Cyclist*) described the callousness of a couple of middle-class lovers who fatally injure a cyclist on the way to a party. His subsequent feature, *Calle Mayor* (1956, *Main Street*) recounted the cruel trick played on a village spinster who is led to believe she is engaged to be married. Berlanga, on the other hand, was noted for the satirical tone he used to such effect in *Bienvenido, Mr Marshall* (1953, *Welcome, Mr Marshall*), a critique of the way a poor rural village spends money it receives under the Marshall Aid plan.

The greatest Spanish director, Luis Buñuel (1900–1983), was known mainly for his early Surrealist works, made in France: *Un Chien Andalou* (1928, An Andalusian Dog), a short film on which he collaborated with the Spanish painter Salvador Dali, and *L'Age d'Or* (1930, The Golden Age).

L'Age d'Or is like no other film before or since. With its extraordinary images revealing the bizzare and horrific in the everyday, its anti-clericalism, anti-authoritarianism, anti-bourgeoisism, sadism, blasphemy, celebration of *l'amour fou*, above all its humour and irony, it is the definitive declaration of Buñuel's credo (or anti-credo) and was to provide a continuous source of reference for his subsequent films. After a documentary and some uncredited co-directing on several features that he produced in Spain, he went into exile at the end of the Civil War and spent a barren time in New York and Hollywood.

Buñuel did not resume feature-film direction until 1947 when he began a series of lightweight, low-budget, popular films in Mexico, which culminated in *Los Olvidados* (1950, *The Young and the Damned*), a melodrama about delinquent boys in Mexico City – distinguished by Buñuel's characteristic blend of documentary and surrealism. When the film won the Official Jury Prize for direction at Cannes in 1951, Buñuel was definitively restored to the ranks of the great international film artists.

He has called *Los Olvidados* a social film, but it is one of the few of its genre to transcend those limitations of intent – it is not exploiting what it sees in order to make some glib comment. Buñuel is merciless and direct in his treatment of the young gangsters observed in Mexico City. They bully a blind man and take a legless cripple off the trolley on which he propels himself. Jaibo (Roberto Cobo), the vicious leader of the gang, is at once the director's conception of the 'free man' and one who is shackled by his own urges. He is hero-worshipped by the younger Pedro (Alfonso Mejia), whose mother (Estela Inda) sleeps with Jaibo. Sent to an outdoor farm-reformatory, Pedro is trusted by the governor, but – out on an errand – again comes under the violence of Jaibo. Both boys are killed. Buñuel not only infiltrated his own spectacular brand of surrealism into the film – notably a mother-loving dream sequence – but imposed on the whole a ruthless logic which precluded sentimentality. The kindly governor who sends Pedro on an errand is typical of the wishy-washy liberalism which Buñuel, the anarchist, despised. Liberal kindness leads to Pedro's death. And the blind man for whom we feel initial sympathy is eventually shown to be as cruel as his environment. About all the young, he screams: 'Tomorrow, tomorrow, we'll be finished with the lot of you!'

Right: Silvia Pinal as a beautiful novice nun in Buñuel's subversive Viridiana. *Above: the teen-age gang bully a blind man in* Los Olivadados. *Above right: the saintly Simon (Claudio Brook) meditates on top of a pillar in* Simon of the Desert. *Far right:* Stella *introduced Melina Mercouri and confirmed the reputation of director Michael Cacoyannis.*

An impeccable craftsman who liked to work fast and efficiently, Buñuel never spurned purely commercial chores and he poured his own personality and preoccupations into them. He succeeded in making films that appealed to a popular audience, without in any respect compromising his own distinctive and essentially austere view of the world. From the Mexican period came such masterworks as *Él* (1953, *This Strange Passion*), a marvellous study of pathological jealousy; his intelligent, heretical *Robinsón Crusoe* (1954); and the great black comedy *Ensayo de un Crimen: La Vida Criminal de Archibaldo de la Cruz* (1955, *The Criminal Life of Archibaldo de la Cruz*). The climax of the Mexican period was *Nazarin* (1958), an ironic and yet touching fable on the impossibility of leading a truly Christian life in an imperfect world.

This theme was developed further in *Viridiana* (1961), made in Spain after he had been invited back as a distinguished and honoured son. Buñuel — always convinced that you should bite the hand that feeds you — set the Spanish establishment by the ears with his joyous blasphemy and indecency in a film which, having had its first showing at the Cannes Festival where it won the Palme d'Or, defied subsequent attempts to suppress it. He made only two more films in Mexico: *El Angel Exterminador* (1962, *The Exterminating Angel*) which returned to purely surrealist themes with the utmost gaiety and humour in a story of a group of bourgeois trapped by some inexplicable force in a *salon*; and the mischievous little moral tale *Simón del Desierto* (1965, *Simon of the Desert*), about a saint dedicated to such abstract

works of devotion as sitting atop pillars in the desert. Though he continued to be a Mexican resident and citizen, most of Buñuel's later films were to be French — made sometimes with Spanish connections.

The films made in Greece during the Fifties by the young Greek-Cypriot director Michael Cacoyannis (b. 1922) showed great feeling for simple, working-class townsfolk or peasant people. His first international success was with a comedy *Kyriakatiko Xypnima* (1954, *Windfall in Athens*) and this enabled Cacoyannis to secure finance for a couple of tougher, 'social comment' films: *Stella* (1955), starring Melina Mercouri in her first screen role, as a woman seeking to liberate herself from a state of virtual enslavement in Greek society, and *To Koritsi Me Ta Mavra* (1956, *A Girl in Black*), a tale of murder and persecution in the aftermath of the overthrow of a village's petty nobility. *To Telefteo Psemma* (1958, *A Matter of Dignity*), Cacoyannis' fourth feature, starred Ellie Lambetti, who had appeared in two of his earlier films and become a firm favourite with international audiences. In the Sixties, Cacoyannis turned his attention to the classics of ancient Greek drama, filming them with Lambetti and Irene Papas as his star actresses. But it is for *Zorba the Greek* (1964), an international co-production, that he will perhaps be best remembered.

Britain

In some senses the Fifties in Britain did not really begin until the winter of 1951–52, when the country underwent great political and constitutional changes. In October 1951 the Labour government, much weakened after hard years battling to establish its post-war reforms, was replaced by the Conservatives who continued in office throughout the decade, their majority rising with each successive General Election.

In February 1952 King George VI died, and Britain had a new, young, female monarch, crowned with all possible pomp the following year. Journalists called it the 'New Elizabethan Age' and looked forward to solid achievements in trade, industry and the arts to rival those in the sixteenth century. Stability and prosperity in many areas were certainly achieved: the last remnant of wartime rationing vanished in July 1954, the country grew towards full employment, and the newly affluent public found an increasing range of items to spend their wage packets on. There were television sets, washing machines, new American imports like nylon shirts and do-it-yourself kits. And there was hire-purchase to make the consumer's life even easier.

People could also spend their money at their local Odeon or ABC cinema, where double bills of predominantly family entertainment were shown, sprinkled with the occasional X-certificated pictures. But statistics show that fewer and fewer people chose the cinema for entertainment. Attendance figures for 1950 were 1,396 million — already a decline from the post-war peak. By 1959, the figure had shrunk further to 600 million. As the years went by there were also fewer cinemas to visit. By 1959 over a thousand of the 4,500 cinemas proudly standing at the start of the decade had made way for supermarkets, office blocks, garages and new roads.

It is customary to point an accusing finger at television for this slump. The BBC's broadcast of the Coronation ceremony in June 1953 (watched by an estimated 20,400,000 people — nearly half the country's population) had given the new medium a terrific boost. Then in 1955, commercial television was introduced and made its appeal particularly to working-

Above: British film starlets Dinah Sheridan, Kay Kendall, Kenneth More and John Gregson in the hit comedy Genevieve. *Above right: Joyce Grenfell, Alastair Sim and a few of* The Belles of St Trinians. *Right: Laurence Olivier as the hunch-backed, hook-nosed* Richard III. *Opposite page, above: Dr Frankenstein on the receiving end of his Monster (Christopher Lee) in Hammer's* The Curse of Frankenstein. *Below: Christopher Lee as the blood-sucking* Dracula.

class audiences who may have been deterred by the establishment image of the BBC. And television not only acquired audiences from the cinema; it also acquired technicians, performers and whole studios (both Gainsborough's Shepherd's Bush studios and Ealing were converted for television use by the BBC).

Yet clearly there were other reasons for the drift of regular customers away from cinemas. Britain's relative prosperity did not remove the necessity for economy in the home, particularly in a home financed through hire-purchase schemes. More and more people settled in new suburbs and estates some distance away from circuit cinemas. The rigid attitudes of the film industry and the booking policies of the cinemas also made the choice of available films distressingly limited.

Too often British cinema in the Fifties gives the impression of an industry left to its own devices, content to re-work well-established formulas and genres. In fact the industry was given much consideration from the government who were anxious to keep this branch of entertainment alive. The National Film Finance Corporation, which began operations in 1949, offered support to many film-making groups, including Alexander Korda's London Films. There was also the British Film Production Film, financed by a levy on the sale of cinema tickets. The levy was a product of the Eady Plan, introduced in 1949 as a 'temporary' measure for generating finance and operated by the film industry for the next 35 years.

The Production Fund specifically helped the work of the Children's Film Foundation (aimed at Saturday-matinée audi-

ences) and the generally tepid feature films of Group Three, a production company headed by John Grierson, Michael Balcon and the producer/director John Baxter.

The industry was given encouragement and finance, but there was little incentive to experiment; in the struggle to combat declining audiences and the growth of television, only safe, reliable, well-proven material found favour. Consequently World War II came back on the screen. Kenneth More, John Mills, Jack Hawkins and Trevor Howard seemed to spend half the decade parading with binoculars and gold braid on ships' bridges, contemplating the wives they left behind as they faced up to the next clash with 'Jerry'.

There was *The Cruel Sea* (1953, with Jack Hawkins battling against the elements in an Atlantic corvette); there was *The Dam Busters* (1955), with the bouncing bombs of Barnes Wallis destroying the Ruhr in 1943; there was *Reach for the Sky* (1956), with the legless figher pilot Douglas Bader portrayed by Kenneth More. Other films saluted the courage of the French Resistance (*Carve Her Name With Pride*, 1958) and the inmates of prisoner-of-war camps (*The Colditz Story*, 1955).

The decade's other major genre was comedy. It offered a different kind of reassurance to the war film's memories of Britain's heroic past. In a country steadily becoming more uniform in appearance and taste, British comedy looked fondly on all things traditional and quaintly eccentric – old railways (*The Titfield Thunderbolt*, 1953) old boats (*The Maggie*, 1954), old flea-pit cinemas (*The Smallest Show on Earth*, 1957), old landladies and lodging houses (*The Lady-*

killers, 1955). One of the period's biggest successes was *Genevieve* (1953) which concerned the rivalry between Kenneth More – certainly the decade's most ubiquitous star – and John Gregson in the annual veteran-car race from London to Brighton. Henry Cornelius, the film's director, was a former Ealing man; the writer, William Rose, worked at the studio afterwards. Ealing's influence in the genre was all-pervasive. Ealing itself gradually ran out of steam during the decade and finally closed down in 1959. But in films like Alexander Mackendrick's *The Man in the White Suit* (1951) and *The Ladykillers* Michael Balcon's team proved they could still produce original comedy with a bite.

The writer-producer-director team Frank Launder and Sidney Gilliat also provided a variety of comedies that avoided the conventional formulas. *The Belles of St Trinian's* (1954) ushered in a series of farces based on Ronald Searle's cartoons of schoolgirl horrors. Subsequent films offered gentle whimsy (*Geordie,* 1955), sophisticated high comedy (*The Constant Husband,* 1955) and high jinks in the world of politics (*Left, Right and Centre,* 1959).

Other film-makers gratefully fell back on the current successes of the West End stage and the past library of English classics for source material. Laurence Olivier followed his Shakespeare films of the Forties with boldly theatrical but satisfying *Richard III* (1956). On a less spectacular level, Anthony Asquith consolidated his reputation as a careful transformer of stage plays. Oscar Wilde's *The Importance of Being Earnest* (1952) offered some superb comic performances and an enjoyable Technicolour display of Victorian bric-a-brac, while the film of Terence Rattigan's play *The Browning Version* (1951), and *Carrington VC* (1954) – adapted from a courtroom drama by Dorothy and Campbell Christie – probed the English characteristics of moral and emotional reticence.

Some stable commodities of British cinema were considerably less respectable, such as the desperately routine crime thrillers produced by small studios like Merton Park and intended purely to prop up the main attraction in double bills. The titles often gave hints of the exotic and the bizarre – *The Strange Case of Blondie* (1954, for example, and *Night Plane to Amsterdam* (1955) – but they generally contained nothing more exciting than Scotland Yard detectives in gaberdines and Wolseley cars hotly pursuing jewel thieves at 30 miles per hour. The films at last provided a resting place for imported American male leads of limited charisma as well as a training ground for young directors – both the aforementioned films were directed by Ken Hughes, who finally graduated to more ambitious projects in the Sixties.

Yet even those directors firmly established in the industry at the start of the Fifties had mixed fortunes. Attempts by Michael Powell and Emeric Pressburger to repeat the dazzling success of *The Red Shoes* (1948) resulted in a series of films top-heavy with classical music, ballet and determinedly lavish decor. Without a simple plot to hang on to, audiences found themselves lost and gasping for air in the artistic clutter of *The Tales of Hoffmann* (1951), adapted from Offenbach's operetta, and *Oh, Rosalinda!!* (1955), a version of Johann Strauss' *Die Fledermaus.* The Powell and Pressburger team returned to conventions in *The Battle of the River Plate* (1956), where they enlivened the British war film with their characteristic eye for colour and visual design.

David Lean put his craftsman's skills to work on some bewildering varied subjects. *The Sound Barrier* (1952) celebrated a scientist's dogged determination to perfect the jet plane; in *Hobson's Choice* (1954), he abandoned RAF types for

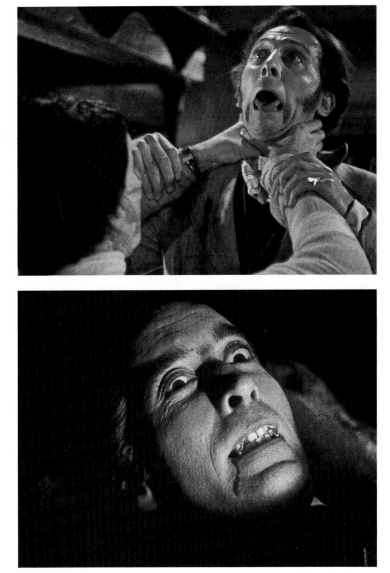

homely Lancashire folk in an excellent version of Harold Brighouses' venerable comedy, in which Charles Laughton gave one of his finest performances. Then, after *Summer Madness* (1955), a flimsy story of an American spinster's Venetian romance, Lean ascended into the realm of the blockbuster. *The Bridge on the River Kwai* (1957) was yet another war film but one of great tension and some moral ambiguity; Alec Guinness finally escaped his Ealing comedy niche with his brilliant performance as the captured British officer increasingly obsessed with the bridge he is ordered to build for the Japanese.

Despite the decade's debilitating passion for past traditions and habits, some new blood was pumped into cinema's mainstream. In the case of Hammer films the blood was clearly visible up on the screen, very often gleaming and dripping in full colour. *The Curse of Frankenstein* (1957), the first of the studio's revivals of the Universal horror classics, shocked critics but delighted audiences, for Hammer films not only had violence, perpetrated by such icy gentlemen as Christopher Lee (Count Dracula) and Peter Cushing (Dr Frankenstein), they also offered a touch of sex, with their succession of sweet maidens struggling to avoid the blandishments of marauding monsters.

In 1954, the husband-and-wife team of John Halas and Joy Batchelor created a genuine masterpiece in the field of animation. They produced and directed the first full-length animated film made in Britain and the first animated feature to

Top: the animals of Animal Farm *decide to rebel against cruel, drunken Farmer Jones. Above: Peter Sellers (centre) as the workers' strike leader in* I'm All Right, Jack, *the Boulting Brothers' satire on industrial relations.*

be made on an adult theme – *Animal Farm*, based on George Orwell's satirical novel.

There were also fresh developments in comedy. The Boulting brothers, previously associated in the public eye with worthy entertainments on serious subjects, launched into a series of satirical comedies, starring, Ian Carmichael, that explored and occasionally exposed British Institutions. *Private's Progress* (1956) looked at the army, *Brothers-in-Law* (1957) at the legal profession; *Lucky Jim* (1957) – a diluted version of Kingsley Amis' comic novel – took the bumbling Carmichael character to university, while *I'm All Right Jack* (1959), the most pungent of all, dealt with factory life and trade unions. Compared with the satirical product of the Sixties, the Boultings' approach may seem pretty conventional but the broadness of their comedy style, their acute observations and their ability to lampoon all sides of an issue gave the series tremendous popular appeal.

The decade also saw the first film vehicles of Norman Wisdom, first popular on television, who provided a stream of comedies balancing slapstick with sentimentality. The Carry on series, beginning officially with *Carry on Sergeant* (1958), looked at more British institutions – the police, hospitals, schools – from a defiantly low-brow angle. And *Doctor in the House* (1954) introduced audiences to a clutch of high-spirited medical students wearing the brightly checked shirts and V-neck pullovers then considered the uniform of youth. Dirk Bogarde, the brightest and best of Rank's contract artists, found new popularity in the role of Simon Sparrow.

But soon film producers were made to realize that there

were other kinds of youth in Britain – the people who frequented the newly popular espresso coffee bars and jazz clubs, who either formed skiffle groups or stormed the cinemas brave enough to exhibit the American film *Rock Around the Clock* (1956) with Billy Haley and his Comets. In the latter half of the Fifties, the smooth pattern of British life was finally receiving a few jolts. Young people now had enough buying power to demand their own entertainment. Film and television and record producers began to fall over themselves trying to provide it. Television's *6.5 Special* was rushed to the screen in 1958 with its contemporary delights like Lonnie Donegan and Don Lang and his Frantic Five. Pop Singer Tommy Steel found himself the subject of a screen biography called *The Tommy Steel Story* (1957) when he was not yet twenty-one, and then rock'n'roller Cliff Richard began his career in movies with *Serious Charge* (1959).

In other areas Britain was being stirred up for the better. In 1956 occured the political débâcle of the Suez crisis. There was also the first performance at London's Royal Court theatre of John Osborne's *Look Back in Anger,* which achieved instant notoriety through the passionate tirades of its main character Jimmy Porter. Journalists dubbed Osborne and other newly popular authors' Angry Young Men'.

But whatever label one cared to attach to it, there was a new critical spirit abroad, a willingness to break with tradition, slowly began drifting into feature films. A new breed of performers, too, began to come to films with their regional accents untouched by the classical diction of the Rank Charm School of the Old Vic Theatre. The reawakening of British cinema was just beginning.

Eastern Europe

After Stalin's death in March 1953, the Cold War atmosphere progressively eased. Simultaneously the circumstances of film-making in Eastern Europe began changing almost at once. The first impulse was in Hungary: films by Félix Máriássy and Zoltán Fábri symbolized their faith in the possibility of speaking in a freer language. They included Máriássy's *Budapesti Tavasz* (1955, Spring in Budapest) and *Egy Pikoló Világos* (1955, A Glass of Beer), and also Fábri's *Körhinta* (1955, Merry Go Round), a socially aware story of young lovers at a fairground, and *Hannibál Tandár Úr* (1956, Professor Hannibal), about a teacher who defies official criticism of his book on Hannibal, the classical hero who challenged Rome's military power – a touchy subject just before the Soviet invasion.

These directors, along with the young Károly Makk and Imre Fehér, looked back for models to the Soviet avant-garde of the Twenties and, still more to Italian neo-realism and the ideas of scriptwriter Cesare Zavattini. Italian neo-realist films had previously been banned in the Eastern bloc. Films such as *Professor Hannibal* were like the first breezes of a fresher air in the heavy atmosphere so characteristic of Eastern Europe in general, and in particular of its cultural life and had an enormous influence throughout the area. But unfotunately the suppression of the Hungarian revolution in 1956 destroyed the promising 'Hungarian school' before it could really establish its own independent aesthetic line. The Hungarian cinema took almost a decade to recover and to start rebuilding on the foundations laid during the 1954–6 period.

In the Soviet Union, a huge increase of output was projected, radically changing the moribund condition into which film production had sunk under Stalin's control. The new party line called for a target of as many as 150 films annually. In 1954, 49 films were actually completed. To achieve this, the studios were opened to new generations of film-makers, and to the older artists who had been denied any continuity in their careers by the sheer paucity of films out in Stalins' last years. The rapid increase in production led incidentally to the easing of censorship and supervision in the various republics.

The first landmark was a tragic yet lyrical wartime romance, *Letyat Zhuravli* (1958, *The Cranes Are Flying*). Its director, Mikhail Kalatozov, and director of photography, Sergei Urusevski, had both once belonged to the Twenties avant-garde – Kalatozov directed the classic *Sol Svanetii* (*Salt for Svanetia*) in 1930. Yet for years they had been putting their names on films that adhered strictly to the Stalinist political and aesthetic creed. Now they revived what was best in their past experience, creating a film that was a recapitulation of the avant-garde theories and an anthology of its directional styles. The film's main impact was in the emotive power of the black-and-white image and the power of montage (already proven in the films of Eisenstein and Pudovkin), when used to describe certain tragic aspects of Soviet life that had been banished from the screen for years. As one Soviet critic put it:

'It was as if the wall between art and living life had fallen ... Hundreds of international awards could not equal the tears with which people purged their emotions after this film ... Our tears "unlocked the door".'

The important newcomers included Grigori Chukhrai, *Ballada o Soldate* (1960, *Ballad of a Soldier*); the co-directors Lev Kulidzhanov and Yakov Segel, *Dom v Kotorom ya Zhivu* (1957, The House I Live In); Marlen Khutsiev, *Vesna na Zarechnoi Ulitse* (1956, Spring in Zarechnaya Street); the Georgian Tengiz Abuladze, *Lurdzha Magdany*, Magdana's Little Donkey; and Sergei Bondarchuk, *Sudba Cheloveka* (1959, *Destiny of a Man*). Bondarchuk was subsequently better known for his heavy-handed epics, *Voina i Mir* (1965–7, *War and Peace*) and *Waterloo* (1970).

Not all of these directors were young; some had spent years in expectation of a first opportunity. Likewise, some of the old masters had long been waiting to work in the way they wanted, with some freedom of subject-matter and artistry. among them was Grigori Kozintsev, who moved quickly to the forefront with his *Don Kikhot* (1957, Don Quixote), though he is best remembered in the West for his Shakespeare adapations, *Hamlet* (1964) and *Kovol Lir* (1970, *King Lear*), often considered to surpass the English versions by Laurence Olivier and Peter Brook respectively.

Other classic adaptations were Josif Heifitz's version of Chekhov's *Dama s Sobachkoi* (1959, *Lady With a Little Dog*); Ivan Pyriev's *Idiot* (1958, The Idiot), after Dostoyevsky; and Sergei Yutkevich's *Othello* (1955) and *Banya* (1962, The Bath House), from Mayakovsky's famous satirical comedy.

Yulia Solntseva, the widow of the great director Dovzhenko, brought to the screen several of his unfilmed scenarios, including *Poema o Morye* (1958, *Poem of the Sea*) and *Povest Plammenykh Let* (1961, *The Flaming Years*); unfortunately their quality did not make up much for the destruction, years before, of Dovzhenko's career by Stalin's personal hostility. Mikhail Romm, who had been the first to present an adulatory image of Stalin on the screen in *Lenin v Oktyabre* (1937, *Lenin in October*), became one of the fiercest post-Stalin reformers of the Soviet cinema, to which he contributed such important films as *Devyat Dnei Odnogo Goda* (1961, *Nine Days of One Year*), concerning the work and love problems of nuclear physicists.

Top to bottom. *Mari Tõrõcsik and Imre Sós as a village Juliet and Romeo in* Körhinta; *Ernö Szabó as Professor Hannibal, a persecuted teacher; Alyosha (Vladimir Ivashov) and Shura (Shanna Prokhovenko) have to part in* Ballad of a Soldier; *Ya Savina as* The Lady With a Little Dog.

The hopes of Soviet film-makers during the late Fifties remained mostly unfulfilled. The liberalization under Khrushchev did not go far enough to allow for truly personal expression, really individual styles or subjective approaches. It soon became all too clear that the bulk of mainstream production would have to continue serving the purposes of state propaganda and indoctrination of the masses, although in a more sophisticated and subtle way than before.

The most important reaction against the Stalinist and Cold War years, and against socialist realism, occurred in Poland, which had been struggling against Russian domination for centuries. The first breakthrough was by the veteran Aleksander Ford, with *Piątka z Ulicy Barskiej* (1953, *Five Boys From Barska Street*), about the rehabilitation of a group of young delinquents; the film was stylistically influenced by the French cinema of the period. Ford's later and better-known *Krzyzacy* (1960, *Knights of the Teutonic Order*), which commemorated the fourteenth-century battle of Grünwald, was a colourful patriotic epic, made primarily to appeal to the nationalism of Polish audiences, but with an eye on the popular international market.

But three younger directors, Andrzej Munk, who died prematurely, Andrzej Wajda and Jerzy Kawalerowicz, were mainly responsible for creating the 'Polish School'. They were concerned with analysing, criticizing and, quite often, de-romanticizing Polish history, particularly the recent war years.

Andrzej Munk (1921–1961) in his memorable *Człiek na Torze* (1956, *Man on the Track*), told of a simple engine-driver who is attacked and persecuted because he is old and resistant to change. He becomes a hero, however, when he perishes on the tracks while preventing a train crash. Poland was in a state of political crisis, with public demonstrations and a change of government; and the film became symbolic of the tragic years that preceded its production. It also introduced the subjective perception of a disintegrating world of reality, which would have been impossible in the Stalinist cinema, since it emphasized the viewpoint of the individual.

Until his accidental death in 1961, Munk continued his examination of the Polish past: *Eroica* (1957) was a two-episode feature film consisting of a comedy set in wartime Warsaw and an ironic tragedy in a prisoner-of-war camp; and *Zezowate Szczęście* (1960, *Bad Luck*) was a satirical portrait of a dedicated but unsuccessful follower of political fashion, who is always out of step with the march of time. His last film was the unfinished *Pasażerka* (1961, *Passenger*) completed and released in 1963, about two women, a prisoner and a guard, in a concentration camp. With his deep and almost grotesque sense of irony and contradiction, Munk was convinced that thorough demystification of the past liberated both society and individuals.

One of the keys to understanding the work of **Andrzej Wajda** (b. 1926) is an awareness of the tradition of Polish Romanticism, of the extent to which Wajda surrenders to its bleaker aspects, and the extent to which he tries to transcend it. The denial of full nationhood to Poland from the eighteenth to the twentieth century created a tradition in its art of doomed foreboding, of heroic martyrdom in the nationalist struggle, and a sometimes delirious cultivation of style and elegance.

Andrzej Wajda, as the son of a serving cavalry officer, would have been particularly exposed to this tradition. On the other hand, he came to maturity during World War II, served briefly in one of the Resistance groups, and received his higher education in post-revolutionary Poland, the ideology of which was adamantly opposed to all the things the Polish Romantic tradition stood for.

The tension between the two ideologies is very evident in Wajda's first feature, his diploma film at the State Film School in *Lódź Pokolenie* (1955, *A Generation*). Its theme of the growth to personal and political maturity of a young working-class layabout was a common one in socialist realist art since the Thirties. It is an extremely good film at every level and one can easily understand its wide appeal to politically committed critics in the West: its obvious socio-political theme; its assured handling of the resources of cinema; the superb playing of its actors; and its obvious 'poetry' and unashamed simplicity of feeling. But perhaps it is more interesting in its contradictions, the central of which is its veering between socialist realism, rational, progressive, optimistic, on the one hand, and on the other, Polish Romanticism, regressive and pessimistic.

The scale of Wajda's second film *Kanał* (1957, *They Loved Life*) is much more ambitious and marks a significant advance in his handling of the medium. It features a large number of characters and relationships and has a bolder *mise-en-scène* – for example, the very lengthy opening tracking shot within which the members of the military unit are introduced. At the same time, however, the commentary over this shot – 'Look at these men and women. We are going to watch them die' – indicates the extent to which the film will surrender to the atavistic Romanticism which is held in balance in *A Generation*.

Nevertheless, despite its Romantic excesses (recurrent images of doomed, young people dying heroically for Poland in the sewers of Warsaw), *Kanał* is a film of undeniable power. *Popiół i Diament* (1958, *Ashes and Diamonds*) is generally considered to be Wajda's most considerable early work. In it he explicitly brings into collision the two traditions which shaped his artistic growth. The film is set during the last day of World War II and the first day of peace. Its central figures are two young nationalist underground fighters who are on a mission to kill a visiting Communist leader. By mistake they kill two workers, and then hang around the visiting leader's hotel until the younger of the two gets a chance to kill the old man. He is himself subsequently killed.

A bare outline gives little indication of the complexity of *Ashes and Diamonds*, of how it weaves together its complex narrative, bringing the large cast of characters into relationship with each other so that a complete cross-section of Polish society is presented.

Thus Szczuka, the visiting Communist, is the brother-in-law of the aristocratic lady who harbours the leader of the right-wing assassination squad; Szczuka's own son is a member of the same movement as his young assassin. *Ashes and Diamonds* shows a nation conceived as a family, tearing apart. The ending of the film particularly articulates this theme. Drawing on a famous Polish stage play, Wyspianski's *The Wedding* (which Wajda was to adapt for the screen in 1973), Wajda shows his cross-section of Polish society dancing a sad polonaise while outside the hotel the old Communist, having been shot by the young terrorist, staggers forward into his assassin's arms in what looks for a moment like a filial embrace. The national dimension is present in the terrorist's own death. Attempting to find cover among the billowing white sheets on a washing line, he is shot; the blood stains one of the sheets which drape him. Even though the film is shot in black and white, the symbolism of red on

Far left: Zbigniew Cybulski as Maciek, the Resistance fighter turned terrorist of Ashes and Diamonds. The role made him a world star – 'the Polish James Dean'. Above left: Tadeusz Lomnicki and Tadeusz Janczar in Five Boys From Barska Street, which examines the 'Western' attitudes of a young labourer. Above: fugitives from the ghetto hide in the sewers in Kanal. Left: the wife of a disillusioned worker hero leads a patriotic parade in Wajda's dissection of Polish contemporary history, Man of Marble.

white (the colours of the Polish flag) would be unmistakable to a Polish audience. *Lotna* (1959) marked Wajda's last direct engagement with this tradition although it recurred (albeit from the much more sceptical and distanced point of view) in later films such as *Wszystko na Sprzedaż* (1968, *Everything for Sale*) and *Krajobraz po Bitwie* (1970, *Landscape After Battle*). His output, (not to mention his work for television) has been very diverse: *Polowanie na Muchy* (1969, *Hunting Flies*) is a study of contemporary manners; *Brzezina* (1970, *The Birch Wood*) and *Panxiy z Wilka* (1979, *The Young Ladies of Wilko*) are elegiac looks at the period between World War I and II; and *Ziemia Obiecana* (1974, *Land of Promise*) is an ambitious adaptation of a famous novel about the emergence of capitalism in nineteenth-century Poland.

However the film to prove most popular with Western audience in the Seventies was *Człowiek z Marmur* (1976, *Man of Marble*). The film, concerning an aggressive young woman film-maker seeking to make a documentary about the emergence and disappearance of a worker hero of the Fifties, brings together the two areas in which Wajda seems to function productively – discussions of Polish history and discourse about the cinema itself. Its sequel was the much more controversial *Człowiek z Żelaza* (1981, *Man of Iron*), which dealt directly with the decade leading up to formation of solidarity and even featured Lech Wałęsa as himself. In France, Wajda made *Danton* (1982) in France with a Franco-Polish cast, adapting a Polish play about the French Revo-

lution and in particular the fatal clash of Danton and Robespierre.

Jerzy Kawalerowicz (b. 1922) made an early impression with such films as *Celuloza* (1954, A Night of Remembrance) and *Pod Gwiazda Frygijska* (1954, Under the Phrygian Star), about the growth of a young peasant's consciousness. But he is mostly remembered for an artistically successful version of the 'Devils of Loudun' story, *Matka Joanna od Aniołow* (1961, *Mother Joan of the Angels*). In his hands the story became an aesthetically beautiful metaphor for intolerance and dogmatism – the destroyers of both inquisitors and victims.

Despite occasional later successes, and Wajda's continuing struggle for his artistic identity and relevance to the changing times, in general the first manifestation of the Polish school, died as quickly as it had emerged. It was repressed in the 'restoration of order' which, in the early Sixties, succeeded the agitated and relatively liberal post-Stalin years. The best of a later generation, such as Roman Polanski and Jerzy Skolimowski, mostly went abroad to develop their talents – Polanski is best known for *Rosemary's Baby* (1968), *Chinatown* (1974), and *Tess* (1979), Skolimowski for *Deep End* (1970) and *Moonlighting* (1982). The two most brilliant Polish animators of the Fifties, Jan Lenica and Walerian Borowczyk, also left their native country for the West.

Czechoslovakia after World War II inherited a long cinematic tradition and intact production facilities, including the Barrandov Studios in Prague. Yet it did not emerge into

Above: a bizarre scene from Dušan Vukotić's Surogat, *winner of an animation Oscar in 1961.*

the mainstream of post-Stalinist film-making as quickly as Poland, and not as impressively until the Sixties. The 'first thaw' around 1956 brought renewed life to such established directors as Jiří Weiss and Jiří Krejčik but belong mainly to the younger Zbyněk Brynych, formerly Weiss's assistant, whose first film was *Žižkovská romance* (1958, A Local Romance) and Votjěch Jasný, whose poetic, four-episode film, *Touha* (1958, Desire), was the most radical denial of the restrictive philosophy and aesthetics of the preceding years. Jan Kadár had collaborated with Elmar Klos since 1952; but their four features of the Fifties were little-known abroad compared with their Academy Award-winning *Obchod na Korze* (1965, A Shop on the High Street).

Shortly after the 'first thaw' had been brough to a halt in the late Fifties, a deep economic and political crisis undermined the repressive cultural policy of the establishment and provided an unexpected degree of freedom for Czechoslovak art and culture in the Sixties. Similarly, the fresh revival of the Hungarian cinema after the crushing of the Revolution in 1956 did not come until seven or eight years later. In Yugoslavia, film-making had to start again from scratch after World War II and, slowly developing over the years into an original culture, did not achieve a period of great blossoming until the latter half of the Sixties.

An exception was the development of animation, especially following the establishment of the Zagreb studio in 1956. **Dušan Vukotić** (b. 1927) was the leading light; even from his first film, in 1951, he made a clean break from the Disney style and content then internationally prevalent. It was appropriate that a decade later his *Surogat* (1961, *Ersatz*) won the Academy Award for Cartoons, the first non-American film to do so and indeed Yugoslavia's first Oscar winner.

The film is typical of the dazzling crystallizations of satirical or ironic ideas that poured forth from the group of talented young film-makers who became known as 'the Zagreb school'. Most of them were graduates from the Zagreb Academy of Arts and had started as newspaper cartoonists. Working closely together, discussing and criticizing each other's work, they dedicated themselves to the development of new graphic styles and animation techniques and to the

exploration of adult contemporary themes. They were all, in their separate ways concerned with the conflicts between simplicity and pretentiousness, the natural and the fake, peace and war. Music and sound effects were important elements in their films but there was little or no dialogue, which made them easily accessible to the six nationalities within Yugoslavia as well as to foreign audiences.

The grotesque, bizarre and sometimes surreal elements in the work of the Zagreb animators had links with the longstanding Eastern European tradition of black humour and satire that had already found new forms of expression in newspaper caricature and cartoon strips. The development of the cartoon film as a medium for contemporary satire could be seen as a natural next step. The death of Stalin had particular implications for Yugoslavia, fiercely proud of its independence from Moscow, and for the country's artists, who were strongly protective – sometimes in the face of severe difficulties – of their own right to freedom of expression.

East Germany built up its post-war film industry on the ruins of the Nazi-controlled Ufa company. In the early years of the new nationalized film organization, Defa, there was a brief revival of early German expressionist and realist trends to challenge the tradition, still predominant as in the Nazi period, of film as an instrument of propaganda and indoctrination. Though the ideology was now communist, the same strict surveillance as before rapidly prevailed, even over simple love-stories and films for children. Film in East Germany, uniquely in Eastern Europe, has never allowed for the emergence of individual styles, a subjective approach to reality or untamed and ironic laughter.

The major exception, **Konrad Wolf** (b. 1925), son of a leading German anti-fascist writer, spent his childhood in Moscow and returned to Germany with the Soviet army in 1945. Because of his model personal history and the strength of his talent. Wolf alone was able to create in the years after 1955 an individual body of work, rarely sinking into the lower depths of Defa-type conformism. The best of his early films included *Lissy* (1957) and *Sterne* (1959, *Stars;* a co-production with Bulgaria), both set in the Nazi era. *Stars* was a tragic love-story, which attacked anti-Semitism, and became an international prize-winner.

The twin Cinderellas of the East European cinema have been Romania and Bulgaria. After 1945 they had to start building up industrial facilities for film-making and also to learn basic crafts. Romania's first international impact was with the animated films of Ion Popescu-Gopo, prize-winners in the Fifties. But such outstanding talents as Liviu Ciulei and especially Lucian Pintilie, did not emerge until the Sixties and have since been exiled from the studios and confined to working in theatre. Otherwise almost nothing of interest came out of the technically well-equipped Bucharest studios.

In Bulgaria, by contrast, the lesson of modern film-making was learned rather well, despite periodic crackdowns on nonconformists directors and consequent lack of continuity in their careers. The first internationally important film was Rangel Vulchanov's *Na Malkya Ostrov* (1958, On the Little Island). Under the combined influence of the Polish school and the French *nouvelle vague*, Vulchanov, who had also worked on Wolf's *Stars*, did much to pull the Bulgarian cinema out of its provincialism. Bulgaria's biggest international success was to come in the Sixties with Vulo Radev's *Kradetsat na Praskovi* (1964, *The Peach Thief*), a romantic story of doomed love separated by national barriers during World War I.

Japan

By and large Western recognition and appreciation of Japanese films can be said to have dated from the appearance of key movies at Venice and Cannes Film Festivals. Akira Kurosawa's *Rashomon* (1950) won the Golden Lion at Venice in 1951; Kenji Mizogouchi followed this up with a hat-trick of lesser prizes – for *Saikaku Ichidai Onna* (1952, *The Life of Oharu*), *Ugetsu Monogatari* (1953, *Tales of the Pale and Silvery Moon After the Rain*) and *Sansho Dayu* (1954, *Sansho the Bailiff*). By the time that Teinosuke Kinguasa's *Jigokumon* (1953, *Gate of Hell*) was awarded the Cannes Film Festival's Golden Palm in 1954, *Rashomon* and *Gate of Hell* had both won Academy Awards. Japanese cinema had clearly become a cultural force to be reckoned with.

All five of these prize-winners were in the *jidai-geki* or historical genre. Before World War II, period dramas comprised almost half of the total film production in Japan. After the war, owing to the guidelines laid down by the American occupation forces, attempts were made to discourage *jidai-geki* films in view of their feudal backgrounds and anti-democratic tendencies. During the period of the Occupation *gendai-geki* (films about contemporary life) comprised roughly two-thirds of Japanese film production. A number of distinct genres developed within this category that dealt with family roles and questions of social class.

Rumpen-mono are films about the lumpen proletariat. The more mainstream genre of *shomin-geki*, on the other hand, depicts lower middle-class life. At its most sophisticated stages of development, this genre was a starting point for the films of Yasujiro Ozu, Heinosuke Gosho and Mikio Naruse.

The most prominent genres based on familiar roles are undoubtedly the *haha-mono* and the *tsuma-mono* – 'mother films' and 'wife films' respectively. Both of these categories could be considered as subdivisions of *kachusha-mono*. Named after the heroine of Tolstoy's late novel *Resurrection*, these films feature self-sacrificing women. In the *haha–mono* mothers suffer and sacrifice everything for their children.

For the most part, the *tsuma-mono* is a post-war phenomenon and is best exemplified by Ozu's *Kaze No Naka No Mendori* (1948, *A Hen in the Wind*), about a wife becoming a prostitute in order to pay for her child's hospital bills while waiting for her husband to be demobilized. Elements in Japanese cinema can be traced back to certain literary and theatrical forms. The medium who speaks for the dead samurai husband in *Rashomon*, for instance, is essentially a figure from the classical, lyric Noh theatre (a dramatic form played out on a bare stage by male actors using carefully restrained and measured gestures). Kurosawa's remarkable version of Shakespeare's *Macbeth*, *Kumonosu-Jo* (1957, *Throne of Blood*), utilizes other Noh elements for the strange makeup style of Lady Macbeth and the background music. In general, however, the influence of Noh theatre on cinema has been minimal. Kabuki theatre, on the other hand, has furnished a certain number of *jidai-geki* (including the sub-category known as the *chambara*, or sword-fight films) with numerous themes and plots. Most notable of these is the story of the *Loyal 47 Ronin* of which many film versions have been made. On a more experimental level the cinematic uses of Kabuki theatre in Keisuke Kinoshita's *Narayamushi-Ko* (1958, *The Ballad of the Narayama*) are quite explicit. His sets drop or slide out of the frame when they are no longer required; the lighting is dimmed at the end of certain sequences in deliberate imitation of Kabuki stage techniques. The best-known development of Kabuki influence is, however Kon

Above: a son carries his mother to die on a mountain-top, in accordance with local custom, in The Ballad of the Narayama.

Ichikawa's *Yukinjo henge* (1963, *An Actor's Revenge*) in which Kazuo Hasegawa plays the same double role (small-time gangster and Kabuki actor of female roles) that he had played in Kinugasa's 1935 version of the same story.

Key directors With the worldwide acclaim that greeted Japanese cinema in the early Fifties, **Kenji Mizoguchi** (1898–1956) found that he was an honoured master abroad, and was accordingly afforded greater facilities and wider financial freedom than he had received during the impoverished late-Forties. The major films that resulted were divided between modern stories – usually on the recurrent theme of the fate of geishas – and recreations of legends and historical epochs but often with a contemporary relevance (for example, the ravaging effects of war, the fate of fallen courtesans, the intrigues of a ruling class against lovers of a lower social order). Among these films were *The Life of Oharu*, *Ugetsu Monogatari*, *Sansho the Bailiff* and *Chikamatsu Monogatari* (1954, *The Crucified Lovers*).

The Life of Oharu, despite some awkward plot contrivances, has some claim to be the strongest film in the group: in Jonathan Rosenbaum's phrase 'the most powerful feminist protest ever recorded on film', Mizoguchi pursues his thesis with a polemical and narrative rigour that encompasses a wide variety of moods as Oharu (Kinuyo Tanaka), the beautiful young daughter of a samurai, falls in love with a commoner, is exiled to the country and descends into poverty and prostitution. The script by Yoshikata Yoda, Mizoguchi's favourite writer, delineates this decline in a way that continually stresses Oharu's exploitation by men. Integrated into Oharu's personal story is a sumptuous, panoramic view of court life in Kyoto in the seventh century, expressed through Mizoguchi's elegant directorial style. The films ends, as it began with the aged heroine, now reduced to street-begging, silently shuffling down a street and past a pagoda.

Women also suffer in *Ugetsu Monogatari* when war disrupts their lives. A potter's wife (Kinuyo Tanaka) is killed while her husband is being led astray by an evil spirit in the form of a beautiful aristocratic lady (Machiko Kyo); a farmer's wife becomes a prostitute when her husband goes seeking glory as a fake samurai. The element of fantasy and the supernnatural is effectively integrated with the vivid re-creation of sixteenth-century life. In *Sansho Dayu* a whole aristocratic family is disrupted, but finally the son finds his mother (Kinuyo Tanaka) again – she has become a superannuated prostitute, blind and crippled. In *The Crucified Lovers* a bourgeois woman is falsely accused of adultery with a servant, but then falls in love with him before they both die.

Mizoguchi's last phase took in a new creative experiment – the use of colour in *Yokihi* (1955, *The Empress Yang Kwei-Fei*) and *Shin Heike Monogatari* (1955, *New Tales of the Taira Clan*). The former, despite a fine performance by Machiko Kyo, has a slightly uncertain tone (perhaps due, in part, to Mizoguchi's difficulties with the film's Hong Kong co-producers), but *Shin-Heike Monogatari* is a major achievement. A complicated study of the filial loyalties and religious conflict, its fine images – shot by Mizoguchi's regular cameraman, the great Miyagawa – make it regrettable that he never lived to continue experimenting with colour, wide screens and 70mm film. The movie also proves Mizoguchi's ability, when required, to be a swift, economical action director.

Mizoguchi was, in the best sense, the most aristocratic of directors: easy, facile effects played no part in his artistic make-up. He was constantly exploring, refining and developing a cinematic language to which he alone held the key.

The impact of *Rashomon*, directed by **Akira Kurosawa** (b. 1910), at the 1950 Venice Film Festival was shattering; only the Japanese were surprised when it won the Golden Lion. Japanese critics had never rated *Rashomon* highly, declaring that it lacked the social commitment of Kurosawa's earlier films and ignoring its basic theme of the subjective nature of truth. In the film four contradictory versions of the same incident – the violent encounter of a bandit (Toshiro Mifune) with a married couple (Masayuki Mori and Machiko Kyo) in a forest – are related via flashbacks from the perspective of the three participants (the murdered samurai husband, the woman and the bandit) and a passing woodcutter. The unconventional narrative structure was in many respects as challenging to Japanese audiences as it was to those in Europe and America. Many key aspects of Kurosawa's genius emerge from *Rashomon*: his masterly control of a complex narrative; his direction of his actors; and the film's dazzling use of light and shade. No one could forget the bandit's race through the glinting forest, or the rape scene when the camera makes a 360° revolution around the tree tops to suggest an orgasm (a device that was subsequently much imitated).

It is certain that the foreign success of *Rashomon* gave Kurosawa great artistic freedom; the immediate result of this was *Ikiru* (1952, *Living*), which must rank among his finest works. The main character is a middle-aged bureaucrat (superbly played by Takashi Shimura) who learns that he is suffering from terminal cancer. This stirs him to take stock of his life, which he realizes has been sterile and empty. Two years later, Kurosawa made his greatest world success, *Shichinin no Samurai* (1954, *Seven Samurai*). He has always claimed that John Ford was one of his inspirations and *Seven Samurai* does have affinities with the Western. Each of the samurai is impeccably characterized, and Mifune as a jokey braggart, a would-be samurai and a hanger-on to the sternly dedicated band of warriors, reveals an unsuspected gift for comedy. In 1957 Kurosawa filmed two adaptations from foreign sources: *Kumonosu-Jo* (*Throne of Blood*), based on Shakespeare's *Macbeth*, and *Donzoko* (*The Lower Depths*), from Gorky's play.

Having plumbed the depths of human depravity, treachery and greed in these films, Kurosawa made three period films over the next five years which dealt with the less lethal, even comic, aspects of evil. The first was *Kakushi Toride no San Akunin* (1958, *The Hidden Fortress*), a kind of action-packed fairy-tale. The other two were *Yojimbo* (1961) and *Tsubaki Sanjuro* (1961, *Sanjuro*). All three starred Mifune, his formidable presence and athletic prowess still undiminished. Underlying the comic approach to the traditional violence however, was a thread of something akin to desperation; a suggestion that the human condition was so irretrievably base that the only thing to do was to mock at it.

In *Akahige* (1965, *Red Beard*) Kurosawa plunged once again into deeper waters. The film traces the growth of a strong emotional relationship between Red Beard, a doctor (Mifune) and his young disciple (Yuzo Kayama). The doctor convinces the young man that only by dedicating himself wholly to the service of the needy can his life become meaningful. Yet the final implications have a bleak edge.

By the early Seventies Kurosawa's career had hit the doldrums. In 1970, aged 60, he made his first colour film *Dodesukaden* (*Dodeskaden*) the title of which is onomatopoeic, evoking the sound of a train running along the tracks. It dealt with low life in a large city and is a stylized variant on *The Lower Depths*. A proposal that he would co-direct the American account of the Japanese attack on Pearl Harbor, *Tora! Tora! Tora!* (1970) aborted in disagreeable circumstances. In addition, the Japanese film industry was at a low ebb; finance for anything but routine subjects was well-nigh impossible to find. These factors may well have contributed to the depression that led him to attempt suicide. Happily Kurosawa rallied and found new inspiration in the USSR.

The Soviet-sponsored story he embarked on, *Dersu Uzala* (1975), is set in the nineteenth century and once more explores a relationship between two men, this time from vastly different cultural backgrounds, that changes both their lives. The eponymous hero is a hunter whose life is inextricably linked with his surroundings; he is at one with nature. Dersu is hired by Arseniev, the leader of an expedition to survey the wastes of Siberia. The guide reveals the ways of nature to the party; Arseniev thus discovers through Dersu the true meaning of life.

When Kurosawa succeeded in setting up *Kagemusha* (1980, *Shadow Warrior*) ten years had elapsed since he had worked in his own country. The directors Francis Ford Coppola and George Lucas helped to persuade 20th Century-Fox to invest in the production. Set in the latter part of the sixteenth century, the film concerns a poor thief who is spared on account of his resemblance to a powerful warlord. When this leader is wounded in battle and dies, the thief is ordered to impersonate him to keep the warlord's clan together and its enemies at bay. He grows more and more accustomed to the role of clan leader, but is exposed when he is unable to ride the warlord's horse. Thrown out, he watches helplessly as the clan he regards as his own clan is overwhelmed by enemy forces.

Kagemusha, budgeted at $6.5 million, was the most expensive Japanese film ever made. At the Cannes Film Festival in 1980, where the film shared the Grand Prix with Bob Fosse's *All That Jazz* (1979), some critics found the battle scenes magnificent but protracted. This was not surprising as, in the rush to make the film available for the Festival Kurosawa had left himself no time to trim these scenes as he had envisaged. For years he has favoured a multi-camera

Bottom far left: a poster for Ozu's Living, *featuring its star, Takashi Shimura, as the dying civil servant Watanabe. Below far left: a young warrior in Mizoguchi's* New Tales of the Taira Clan. *Left: Kinuyo Tanaka as a gentle potter's wife in* Ugetsu Monogatari. *Below left: poster of Kurosawa's version of Macbeth,* Throne of Blood, *starring Isuzu Yamada and Toshiro Mifune.*

Above: Tatsuya Nakadai as a poor thief, whose facial resemblance to a powerful clan chieftain enables him to impersonate the leader when the latter dies, in Kurosawa's magnificent epic of the sixteenth-century Japanese clans at war, Kagemusha.

Left: Kyoko Kagana as Kyoko and Chishu Ryu as her elderly father in Tokyo Story *which, like many of Ozu's later films, is a moving meditation on the decline of the family as an institution in twentieth-century Japanese society. Above left: rich boy meets poor boys in* I Was Born, But ... *Ozu's last silent feature, a sad-funny film about the problems of moving to a new city. Above: Tatsuya Nakadai in Ichikawa's* The Key, *a powerful study of modern, urban alienation.*

technique of shooting which, while ensuring the spontaneity that he feels may become lost in repeated takes, naturally calls for a longer period than usual in the cutting room.

Apart from the popular silent film *Umarete wa Mita Keredo* (1932, *I was Born, But ...*), the reputation of **Yasujiro Ozu** (1903–1963) in the West is principally based on the work of the last period of his career – the 15 films completed between 1947 and his death in 1963.

The backdrop to all these simple tales was the aftermath of the occupation of Japan and the influence of American values. But it was the impact of this change of the ordinary individual within the family unit that obsessed Ozu. *Ochazuke no Aji* (1952, *The Flavour of Green Tea Over Rice*) is a simple story about a marital crisis experienced by a middle-aged couple, whereas in *Soshun* (1956, *Early Spring*), the marital crisis strikes a young couple after the husband – an officer worker bored with his job and frustrated by lack of prospects – has a brief affair. He then accepts a job transfer out to the country, where he is rejoined by his wife, and they agree to start again. But though the films are based on close observation of real people and real-life details, they are not simply fictionalized documentaries. There is an intensity which springs from the autobiographical aspect of his work. Ozu's father was rarely at home when he was growing up; the boy became devoted to his mother and spent his adult life looking after her, rather than marrying. Ten of Ozu's fifteen post-war films concern the difficulties posed by the death (or absence) of a parent, or uncertainty about a child's marriage. Ozu scripted all of the films of this period in close collaboration with Kogo Noda, a writer with whom he felt particularly sympathetic. The obsessive aspect of Ozu's work is emphasised by his reliance on the same actors and actresses, to such an extent that they practically constituted a personal company. Chishu Ryu, the actor most closely identified with Ozu, claims to have

appeared – in major or minor roles – in all but two of Ozu's films. Towards the end of Ozu's career, Ryu virtually became the director's on-screen alter ego.

Ozu's characters are so typical, and the contexts in which he places them so timely, that the films easily meet Western standards of 'realism'. Without exception they are convincing and moving. Yet Western recognition of Ozu's achievement has been slow. The magnificent *Tokyo Monogatari* (1953, *Tokyo Story*) was not released for general distribution in the West until 12 years after it was made. This is the result of Ozu's committedly Eastern style, grounded in Japanese culture. The most obvious manifestation of this is his consistent use of the low-angle shot, averaging only 40mm (16 inches) above the floor in medium shots and not much more in most long shots and exteriors. At the same time, the usually static camera allows for detached observation of the events unfolding before it, the beautifully composed images offering themselves for contemplation.

Another strikingly Japanese trait is Ozu's use of repetitive 'establishing' shots which are considered unnecessary by Western standards. For example, a carefully composed shot of the passage-way in a middle-class house recurs throughout *Samma no Aji* (1962, *An Autumn Afternoon*). Not only does Ozu's repeated use of this re-establish the locale of the action, it also affirms the familiar sameness of the space (identical camera position) and points to subtle changes in the quality of daylight, in the blues and browns of approaching autumn. In addition, the shot also operates as punctuation for the action, a point of reflection on the development of the plot, which concerns the eventually successful effort of a widower to marry off his reluctant daughter. And by the end of the film it becomes apparent that this shot of a passage-way symbolically embodies the themes of 'passage' and 'change' which distinguish the film.

Ozu's films achieve enormous power through the combination of ordinariness and Zen awareness. He observed the trauma of change in Japan through a filter of traditional aesthetics and philosophy. And though the importance of his contemplative vision is at last recognized by many Western viewers, a critical dispute still rages about whether Ozu's attitude is one of resignation or acceptance. The later films are suffused with a sadness and pessimism which contrast with the optimism of the pre-war *shomin-geki*. Perhaps the answer lies in the Zen concept of *mono no aware*, which means something like balance and contemplation, a sad but total acceptance of the way things are.

A contemporary of Akira Kurosawa and Keisuke Kinoshita, **Kon Ichikawa** (b. 1915) made his directorial debut in the immediate post-war period. His appreciation of American comedy technique and his successful application of it to Japanese subjects earned him a reputation as a Japanese Frank Capra. Ironic comedies dealing with the frustrations of the ordinary working man became his stock-in trade, but, with hindsight, it can be seen that his concern was already for the outsider, the one who elects to drop out of organized society, even oppose it.

As the director's talent matured, the vision darkened. *Biruma No Tategoto* (1956, *The Burmese Harp*) came as a major surprise to everyone, including the Japanese, and it established Ichikawa's reputation in the Western world. In the same year his *Shokei No Heyea* (1956, *Punishment Room*) with its savage rape scene, was to give the Japanese public a further insight into the darker side of the film-makers' imagination. But whereas *Punishment Room* fitted a cycle of films popular at the time, dealing with juvenile delinquency, *The Burmese Harp* was a unique and haunting work, owing no allegiance to any category.

The hero of *The Burmese Harp* – Mizushima – is an army scout in a Japanese unit who plays a harp to warn his fellow soldiers when they are in danger of being ambushed. When the war ends he decides to carry out the vocation he now knows to be his – to bury or burn the thousands of Japanese dead he has come across during his journeyings. Refusing repatriation, he roams the devastated countryside disguised as a monk, obsessed with his grim task, showing that an individual can make a stand against the futility of war.

In *Enjo* (1958, *Conflagration*), the hero, Mizoguchi – an acolyte in a glorious temple in Kyoto – becomes increasingly oppressed by the sordidness of the human life around him: his selfishly demanding mother, the lascivious, hypocritical head of the temple, the climate of American-occupied Japan. Nothing can equal the beauty of the temple, which so obsesses the acolyte that he wishes to destroy it.

The year 1959 was a particularly creative one for this prolific director. He achieved two works of startling individuality: *Nobi* (1959, *Fires on the Plain*) and *Kagi* (1959, *The Key*) also released as *Odd Obsessions*. With the exception of the maid, everyone in the bizarre household in *Kagi* is literally obsessed with sex – and sex, moreover, of a repellently seamy order. Sex is equated with death and corruption; a mordant, oppressive sickness prevails; the viewer is made to feel like a voyeur in a den of iniquity. Perhaps this microcosm of depraved life is meant to imply, by extension, that the whole of modern society is rotten and ripe for extinction.

The other film of the same period, although totally different in subject, would seem to underline the message. *Fires on the Plain* must rank as one of the most devastating war films ever made. Astonishingly bold in its conception and its deliberate,

grindingly slow pace, it pushes its depiction of tragic human folly to the very brink of grisly farce. The film's awesome presentation of the total degradation that war engenders shows cannibalism as the ultimate denigration of the human condition, yet within the potential of the average man when hell-bent on survival.

Ichikawa found a readier international audience with his stylish film *An Actor's Revenge*, whose hero is a female impersonator on quest for self-identification. The eminent actor Kazuo Hasegawa here plays a dual role as a female impersonator in the Kabuki theatre and a small-time gangster determined to avenge his parents.

Tokyo Orimpikku (1965, *Tokyo Olympiad*), his film of the 1964 Tokyo Olympics, found Ichikawa once more at odds with his producers. A far cry from Leni Riefenstahl's lyrical celebration of the athletes in the Berlin Games, Ichikawa concentrated on the personal concerns of contenders and spectators. The producers would have preferred a more joyous reportage of the Games with less emphasis on their strain and anguish. They doubtless changed their minds when the film became one of Japan's biggest moneyspinners.

India

In 1947 India was freed from British colonial rule. The British administration left behind a clumsy system of rationing raw film stock, severe censorship of films established in order to control the nationalistic sentiments of patriotic Indians during the struggle for independence, and heavy taxes of up to sixty per cent on film-makers. Much of this heritage survived the departure of the British, as did the system of illicit payments to avoid taxation.

Bombay was the main centre for the production of films in Hindi (the most widely-spoken of India's many languages). By now there was a fixed formula for the success of any film – one or two stars, six songs, three dance sequences, a bit of crying, a bit of laughter, extremes of emotion – but in 1948 S.S. Vasan's *Chandralekha*, made in the Tamil and Hindi languages and the biggest extravaganza of its time, started a successful new trend with its chorus-dance sequences.

Mehboob Khan made many multi-star films such as *Aan* (1952, *Savage Princess*) and *Bharat Mata* (1957 *Mother India*), which were unprecedentedly successful at the box-office, yet established a precedent by combining sensitivity and commercial ingredients, and always including some reference to the oppressed classes of society. On the other hand, Raj Kapoor was involved in making entertainment films, such as *Awara* (1952, *The Vagabond*), that were basically musicals and showed the sublimity of love, Bimal Roy was meanwhile making offbeat films such as *Do Bigha Zamin* (1953, *Two Acres of Land*) and *Sujata* (1960) about subjects like poverty, money-lending and untouchability. K.A. Abbas scored international critical success with *Munna* (1954, *The Lost Child*), the story of an orphan.

In the South, where Madras was the main production centre, films were similar in theme and treatment of those of Bombay. Madras films were usually musicals, melodramas and stories about the problems of the joint family system. Though Tamil was the language of the region, many films in Telugu were also produced in Madras.

Films for the Sri Lanka (formerly Ceylon) market were shot in the studios of the South. Only the dialogue was written by the Sri Lankans in the Sinhalese language; the rest of the production was done entirely by the South Indians. Most of these films were carbon copies of typical Tamil and Hindi films. Then Lester James Peries made *Rekava* (1957, *The Line of Destiny*) on location, using a neo-realist style – the first truly national film to appear from Sri Lanka. His third film *Gamperaliya* (1963, The Changing Village) won the Grand Prix at the third International Film Festival of India, the first Sinhalese film to gain an international award.

Satyajit Ray Ray (b. 1921) is universally regarded as India's foremost film-maker, in addition to being a notable artist, journalist, composer and novelist. His background and middle-class orientation are the two most important factors behind his talent for perceiving the reality around him and rendering it with simplicity. He comes from an extremely gifted family of writers and artists.

In 1948, while Ray was working as a commercial artist for an advertising company, he and his friends formed the Calcutta Film Society. This gave him a chance to view many of the world's finest films and to meet various celebrities, in particular Jean Renoir. Renoir came to India in 1950 to make *The River* (1951) and was to be an early and dominant influence on Ray's work.

Ray became increasingly determined to make a film himself and decided to adapt for the screen a novel by Bibhutibhushan Bandapaddhaya called *Pather Panchali* (which Ray had been asked to illustrate some years earlier). Ray did not want to lose the security of his job, so became a part-time filmmaker, devoting Sundays and holidays to shooting *Pather Panchali*. He pawned his wife's jewellery and sold his precious books and records in order to buy raw stock and hire a camera.

Ray would have been unable to afford to finish the film without the help of a friend of his mother-in-law, who persuaded the Bengali government to provide financial assistance. *Pather Panchali* (*Song of the Little Road*), completed in 1955, was shown at the Cannes Film Festival the following year and won worldwide acclaim. Its success resulted in many offers for Ray to make films abroad; yet, though he speaks excellent English, he has said that he feels incapable of making films in any language other than his own, Bengali.

He followed up this story of a boy, Apu, growing up in a village, with two sequels: in *Aparajito* (1956, *The Unvanquished*) Apu moves to Benares, where his father dies, and then to university in Calcutta, during which time his mother also dies back in the village; in *Apur Sansar* (1959, *The World of Apu*) he marries but his wife dies in childbirth and several years go by before he is reconciled with his son. The Apu trilogy secured Ray's worldwide reputation.

Speaking of the issues raised in some of his other films, Ray said:

'*Devi* (1960, *The Goddess*) was against superstition and dogmatism. *Jalsaghar* (1958, *The Music Room*) tried to show the inevitability of the old being replaced by a new (not necessarily better) system. But my commitment is not to a particular political system. I am certainly not interested in power politics'.

The portrayal of women in Ray's work differs from film to film; sometimes they are one step ahead of and sometimes they are subservient to men. In *The Goddess*, Dayamoyee (Sharmila Tagore), deified as the result of a vision seen by her father-in-law, eventually rebels against being an object of worship. In *Kanchenjunga* (1962) Ray's first film about contemporary society, the women assert themselves and their

independence in a so-called man's world. In *Mahanagar* (1963, *The Big City*), Arati Majumdar (Madhabi Kukherji) not only fights against the conventions of making women homebound but also becomes the financial supporter of her family.

Pratidwandi (1970, *The Adversary*) was close to the political climate of Indian in the late Sixties. But here, Ray concentrates on the pursuit of security (the perennial problem of an Indian youth) undertaken by the hero, Siddhartha; the uncompromising political activism of Siddhartha's brother is kept in the background. In *Ashani Sanket* (1973, *Distant Thunder*) a man-made famine (brought about by the requisiton of food for military requirements), leads to the death of five million people. Only the events up to the calamity are shown. The film's last, lingering shot of starving villagers makes no comments but raises questions about the human values and priorities of civilization. These themes are also explored in *Seemabadha* (1971, *Company Limited*), in which a young married couple struggle to adjust to the competitive business ethics of the Western capitalist system.

An exception to his standard practice of filming in Bengali was *Shatranj Ke Khilari* (1977, *The Chess Players*), which he made in Hindi-Urdu. The film is based on a short story by the most prominent Hindi author. Munshi Premchand, and concerns two chess players who are so obsessed with their game that they are totally unaware of the important political developments taking shape around them. Ray interwove Premchand's story with details of the annexation of the state of Oudh by the British in 1856, a major factor behind the Indian Mutiny of the following year.

In 1984 Ray fulfilled a long-cherished ambition to film Rabindranath Tagore's *The Home and the World*, though in the last stages the production was prejudiced by Ray's severe illness, which prevented him from editing it with his usual precision and economy.

Ray has strong feelings about children. He has not only made four films for children, but has also created much of his fiction and illustrative work for the young.

Ray uses the term 'artless simplicity' to describe his style. Though he has made a number of films in colour, he believes that colour can never be realistic as it has a tendency to make things look attractive whatever the context. Ray operates the camera himself and leaves the technical aspects of shooting to his cameraman – a post usually held by Subrata Mitra. Ray knows how much to take in a shot and where to cut while he is filming, although he is open to improvisations by the actors which might add extra depth to the finished film. The dialogue tends to be strictly functional, though in *Charulata* (1964, *The Lonely Wife*), which he considers his best film, he resorted to dialogue in order to probe the psychology of his characters.

Right: Apu (Soumitra Chatterjee) and his son set off in search of a better future at the end of The World of Apu. *Above right: Sarbojaya (Karuna Bannerjee) and her children Durga and Apu in* Pather Panchali. *Top right: the actress Natan and her leading man Sunil Dutt in Bimal Roy's* Sujata, *an example of social commitment from the Indian cinema. Top far right: a young wife (Shabana Azmi) tries to convince her husband (Sanjeev Kumar) that there is more to life than chess in* The Chess Players. *Far right: Soumitra Chatterjee and Madhabi Mukherjee in Satyajit Ray's* Charulata.

CHAPTER 15
New Directions

The initial triumph of the French *nouvelle vague* ('new wave') was at the Cannes Film Festival of 1959. This was the year in which François Truffaut, banned from attending as a critic because he had savagely derided the standard of the French entries in his magazine column, returned as a film-maker to take the Best Direction prize with *Les Quatre Cents Coups* (1959, *The 400 Blows*), a down-to-earth tale of a delinquent boy. Not all of the forty or so young directors given the opportunity to make their first films over the next year were noticeably talented. Some, like Roger Vadim and Edouard Molinaro, were even then making films indistinguishable from the commercial norm, except that the directors came from a younger generation. Even this last categorization did not always apply. Marcel Camus won the Festival's Grand Prix with *Orfeu Negro* (1958, *Black Orpheus*), a slice of picturesque exoticism that could have been made at any time during the previous ten years. He was 47 at the time.

Nevertheless, there *was* a *nouvelle vague*, given a tenuous identity and unity only because the sudden influx of new directors was the result of inexorable critical pressure that had been brought to bear on the French film industry over a number of years; and because when the dam of tradition and box-office caution finally gave way, the most talented newcomers – Jean-Luc Godard, François Truffaut, Claude Chabrol, Jacques Rivette and Eric Rohmer – also happened to be critics collaborating on *Cahiers du Cinéma*, the magazine which had articulated and applied most of that pressure.

The first rumblings of discontent were given influential expression in 1948 by Alexandre Astruc in an article called 'The Birth of a New Avant-Garde: *Le Caméra Stylo*', which fulminated against the assembly-line method of producing films which the French industry had inherited from Hollywood.

The great film-makers, Astruc argued, directors such as Renoir, Welles and Bresson, were using the camera much as a writer uses a pen (*stylo*), to make a personal statement or to describe a personal vision. In the early Fifties *Cahiers du Cinéma* took Astruc's argument a stage further in a series of close critical analyses of the work of outstanding film-makers such as Hitchcock and Hawks who had worked mostly within the Hollywood studio system. Similar articles and reviews drew attention to Samuel Fuller, Robert Aldrich, Don Siegel and Jacques Tourneur who had hitherto been disregarded as mere studio journeymen. All these critiques amounted to a

Left: Rita Tushingham, epitome of the adventurous innocence of the Sixties, in The Knack.

demonstration of how a creative personality could surface even if the script was uncongenial to the director or had to be shaped to fit box-office preconceptions.

These ideas were formulated as what later came to be known as the '*auteur* theory', after a cautionary article by the critic André Bazin, '*La Politique des Auteurs*', published in 1957. *Cahiers du Cinéma*'s concepts were unique in the history of the cinema's avant-garde movements in that they accepted the realities of the film industry and the need to keep an eye on the box-office. Even so, the argument ran, a true film-maker could shape characters, situations and attitudes in order to impose a distinctive personal style. He should infiltrate his personal preoccupations and, if necessary, transform alien material into his own.

Godard began with *A Bout de Souffle* (1960, *Breathless*), a casually jokey gangster story. Now the dust has settled and audiences barely notice – to cite the most obvious example – the jump-cuts once hailed with critical jubilation as the most radical new departure offered by *Breathless*. As a number of older film-makers somewhat tetchily pointed out at the time, there was nothing new about jump-cutting: the technique had been familiar in Hollywood for years, and little or no critical excitement had been noticeable when, six years before Godard and *Breathless*, Kurosawa used it every bit as systematically in *Shichinin no Samurai* (1954, *Seven Samurai*).

But where Kurosawa used the jump-cut in its traditional role as a purely technical means towards an end – speeding up the action, keeping things constantly on the move – Godard lent it an additional, metaphorical dimension. In *Breathless* the jump-cutting does indeed keep the film racing along in amiable pastiche of the Monogram B movies; but, acquiring an undertone of insolence through being identified with Belmondo's raffishly but ineffectually Bogartian Michel Poiccard, the technique *also* implies a parody-appraisal of the Hollywood thriller genre as a whole.

Looking back, it is apparent now that the *nouvelle vague* films – Godard's in particular – generated so much electricity because they comprised a critique of both the cinema's past and its present, rejecting what was worthless in film history, sifting out what remained valid, raising signposts for future exploration. As Godard remarked in an interview in 1962:

'Criticism taught us to admire both Rouch and Eisenstein. From it we learned not to deny one aspect of the cinema in favour of another. From it we also learned to make films from a certain perspective, and to know that if something has already been done there is no point in doing it again. A young author writing today knows that Molière and Shakespeare exist. We were the first directors to know that Griffith exists. Even

Carné, Delluc and René Clair, when they made their first films, had no real critical or historical background. Even Renoir had very little; but then of course *he* had genius.'

The insistence of traditional film-makers on continuity was fundamental to the practice of both making and viewing movies. They believed that to break the 'rules' which temporal and spatial continuity demanded would confuse, disorientate and even offend the audience. But that was precisely what had begun to happen in the films of Godard, Alain Resnais and, in Italy, Antonioni. Just how the 'rules' of temporal and spatial continuity were broken in innovatory French and Italian films of the early Sixties has been the subject of thorough analyses by such theorists as Noël Burch and Peter Wollen.

In his book *Praxis du Cinéma* (Paris, 1969; English translation, *Theory of Film Practice*), Burch proposes five categories within which film time operates. The first is that of absolutely continuous action from one shot to the next, the most obvious way that time is seen to pass in film; the second is where the action is abbreviated or truncated, in the interest of economy of expression, by cutting, for example, from the beginning of an action to its conclusion without slavishly depicting each step on the screen. It is this thoroughly familiar narrative technique that Godard pushes to extremes in *A Bout de Souffle*, as Resnais had less notoriously done in *Hiroshima, Mon Amour* (1959, Hiroshima, My Love). The result is a sensation of action 'quoted' rather than properly represented.

Burch's third category concerns films where some period of time has been omitted from the story-telling process and the viewer must find clues in a clock, a line of dialogue, a change of dress and so on in order to determine where in time the movie is. Such ellipses of time are common in the work of Resnais but particularly played upon in *L'Année Dernière à Marienbad* (1961, Last Year in Marienbad).

Finally Burch lists two categories of time reversal in film: the first, which is fairly rare, involves the repetition of a small part of a film's action by means of an overlapping cut to gain a deliberate effect, as in the scene of the bridge being raised in Sergei Eisenstein's *Oktyabr* (1927, October). The other category is the infinitely more common reversal called the flashback. Unless, however, the dates of the flashback are clearly designated, the viewer is unlikely to be able to measure the time spanned by the flashback or even to be certain whether it is not a flash-forward. This complex juggling of different tenses – movements *elsewhere* in time rather than specifically backwards or forwards – is what makes *Last Year in Marienbad*, for instance, such a remarkable and influential film.

If memory is not to be trusted, runs the argument of *Hiroshima, Mon Amour* and *Last Year in Marienbad*, then perhaps the past is a tissue of illusions; and since the past largely determines the present, how 'real' can the present be? Certainly, *Last Year in Marienbad* offers no answers; its purpose is to raise the questions, suggesting that memory, if not a lie, is at best only a partial truth. The fascination of this film resides almost entirely in its form and structure; that is why it is a key work of modernist cinema where formal and structural concerns are at least as important as aesthetic and thematic ones.

Directors of the *Nouvelle Vague* François Truffaut (1932–1984) was born in Paris. His turbulent childhood was reflected in his much-praised first feature *The 400 Blows*, the story of a boy, Antoine Doinel (Jean-Pierre Léaud) neglected and mistreated by his parents, teachers and the police. Truffaut returned to the character of Doinel (whom Léaud continued to portray), describing his continuing search for love and happiness in an episode of *L'Amour à Vingt Ans* (1962, *Love at Twenty*) and the features *Baisers Volés* (1968, *Stolen Kisses*), *Domicile Conjugale* (1970, *Bed and Board*) and *L'Amour en Fuite* (1979, *Love on the Run*).

Truffaut had become passionately interested in cinema in his teens. A meeting with the editor of *Cahiers du Cinéma*, André Bazin, lead to a career as a film critic after Truffaut's dishonourable discharge from the army in 1953.

As a critic, Truffaut was one of the key figures responsible for the establishment of the *'auteur* theory', expounded most clearly in his 1958 manifesto: studios were to be abandoned in favour of location shooting; dialogue was not to be based on literary adaptation but on conversational speech verging on improvisation; stars were not vital and the only qualification that was needed in order to direct a film was the desire to make a personal statement with the camera as directly as a writer does with the pen.

Many elements from Truffaut's later features can be traced back to his short *Les Mistons* (1957, *The Mischief Makers*), about the first sexual stirrings of a gang of boys and the girl who becomes the object of their desires: the impossibility of prolonged happiness, the role of fate, the bitter-sweet tone,

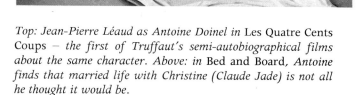

Top: Jean-Pierre Léaud as Antoine Doinel in Les Quatre Cents Coups – *the first of Truffaut's semi-autobiographical films about the same character. Above: in* Bed and Board, *Antoine finds that married life with Christine (Claude Jade) is not all he thought it would be.*

the importance of women and the intoxication with cinema.

The concept of the evanescence of happiness runs through the whole of Truffaut's cinema. The idea occurs intensely in an idyllic scene at the lakeside chalet in *Les Deux Anglaises et le Continent* (1971, *Anne and Muriel*), fleetingly in *Jules et Jim* (1962) and on isolated occasions like the fairground outing or when Antoine's parents take him to the cinema in *The 400 Blows*. Happiness for Truffaut's characters may be enjoyed briefly before it degenerates into the boredom of marriage, as in *Bed and Board*, or is terminated by death, as in *Tirez sur le Pianiste* (1960, *Shoot the Pianist*), *Jules et Jim*, *La Mariée Etait en Noir* (1968, *The Bride Wore Black*) and *La Chambre Verte* (1978, *The Green Room*).

Women feature strongly in Truffaut's films and fall into three major categories – dream goddesses, mother figures or whores. The last group usually provide consolation when the first two have failed as in *Stolen Kisses* and *Bed and Board*. The man is vulnerable, liable to rejection (as Truffaut's own mother rejected him) and therefore prone either to despise or to idealize women – which leads to an inability to involve himself in the fluctuations and imperfections of a long-term relationship.

Bernadette (Bernadette Lafont) is an idealized sex-object in *The Mischief Makers*, inaccessible and therefore desirable; Catherine (Jeanne Moreau) is initially merely an enigmatic smile in *Jules et Jim*, in the pursuit of which a close male friendship is destroyed and two deaths ensue; Julie (Jeanne Moreau) is literally a man-killer in *The Bride Wore Black* as is Julie/Marion (Catherine Deneuve) in *La Sirène du Mississippi* (1969, *Mississippi Mermaid*).

There is clearly a great deal of solitariness in Truffaut's universe, despite his attempts to people it with substitute families, a gallery of warm stock-characters, and despite the recollection by Madame Tabard (Delphine Seyrig), in *Stolen Kisses*, that her father's final verdict on life had been 'People are fantastic'. Yet at crucial moments in their lives most of the characters are alone or else return to solitude.

Even so grounds for hope seem to exist. There is the simple existence of children and their presence in most of Truffaut's films. From survival in *The 400 Blows* to civilization in *L'Enfant Sauvage* (1970, *The Wild Child*) and the indulgent celebration of childhood in *L'Argent de Poche* (1976, *Small Change*), Truffaut seems to protect and defend the innocence and purity of childhood and adolescence on the screen almost as a form of compensation for the neglect and unhappiness he himself experienced.

Another compensatory factor in Truffaut's world is the very existence of the cinema – 'The cinema reigns supreme', as he says in *La Nuit Américaine* (1973, *Day for Night*), his affectionate film about film-making at the old Victorine studio

Above: poster for Jules et Jim, *featuring Jeanne Moreau as the captivating, capricious Catherine. Above right: Catherine Deneuve and Jean-Paul Belmondo in* Mississippi Mermaid. *Far right: Truffaut with Jacqueline Bisset in* Day for Night. *Right:* L'Enfant Sauvage.

in Nice. His philosophy is that films reflect life, films are life and in watching, making and talking films one is never alone. The actors and crew make up an ideal family, writing, shooting and editing being part of the conception and gestation process. The film is born and the next one begins. Just like life, or better than life, for films never die.

In the Eighties, Truffaut's career seemed to gain fresh impetus through his personal and professional association with the actress Fanny Ardant. She starred in two successful films – the bitter-sweet love story *La Femme d'à Cote* (1981, *The Woman Next Door*) and the thriller *Vivement Dimanche* (1983, *Finally Sunday*), which proved to be his last film. Truffaut's sudden death in his early fifties robbed French cinema of one of its most articulate and subtle film-makers.

As a critic for *Cahiers du Cinéma*, Parisian **Claude Chabrol** (b. 1930) was known less for his aggressiveness than for the humour and diversity of his cinematic tastes. To create his first movie he needed money. So he had the idea of making another very low-budget film put together so as to obtain a *prime à la qualité* (an official grant awarded to certain 'intellectual' films). With the money from the bursary he was able to make the other film on which he had set his heart.

But that film, *Les Cousins* (1959, *The Cousins*), was a commercial failure, as were the films that followed it. Chabrol has been accused of black gloominess, of misogyny, even of fascism. Admittedly the characters in his early films are for the most part stupid, feeble or even repugnant, but through them Chabrol conveys both a deep-seated pessimism, only alleviated much later in his career, and a fascination with stupidity – a fascination that does not preclude pity.

The lack of success of these ambivalent films forced him for a few years to direct any commercial assignment he could get, notably a series of spy-films shot as parodies of the James Bond films – for example, *Marie-Chantal Contre le Dr Khâ* (1965, Marie-Chantal Against Dr Khâ). On his return to serious subjects, particularly with *Les Biches* (1968, *The Does*), public taste had altered. The outrages of the *nouvelle vague* had become acceptable, and Chabrol's qualities could be seen in their true light; he is actually a humorist with a touch of tenderness. The cruelty of some of his portrayals is the product of a clear-sighted and lively intelligence – a quality Chabrol shared with Alfred Hitchcock, who was a major influence on his work. (Chabrol co-wrote an important analysis of Hitchcock with Eric Rohmer in 1957.)

His chosen subjects have a realistic surface, somewhat in the tradition of Jean Renoir or Julien Duvivier: couples threatened by adultery, impulsive passions leading to crimes committed by respectable members of the bourgeoisie – more often than not set in the provinces. What is more, the 'moral' of these stories is eminently rational: *La Femme Infidèle* (1968, *The Unfaithful Wife*), for example, is a homage to fidelity.

So Chabrol presents a seemingly comforting portrait of contemporary France. Of course he depicts it in a corrosive, even vicious, fashion: silliness, meanness, pettiness abound. But this picture corresponds in the eyes of the average spectator to a well-established literary tradition of realistic studies of Parisian and provincial life as in classic authors. Moreover the satirical aspects of his work are balanced out by

Below: Jean-Luc Godard in 1980. Right: his first feature, Breathless *starred Jean-Paul Belmondo as a car thief turned killer and Jean Seberg as the girl who eventually gives him up to the police. Far right: Belmondo shortly before he blows himself up at the end of the avant-garde gangster film* Pierrot Le Fou. *Below right: Raoul (Sady Rebbot) with Nana the prostitute (Anna Karina, Godard's former wife) in* Vivre Sa Vie.

the true sympathy in his representations of women or children.

If Chabrol is fascinated by stupidity, it is not simply because 'there are no limits to it', as he himself has pointed out, but also 'because it is dangerous'. More often than not his characters avoid stupidity only to fall prey to another danger – madness. This is something more fascinating, less mediocre than stupidity. Often it is the fruit of a frustrated passion or of a totally unreasonable demand. Even when it is caused by a neurotic trauma, the sufferer (in Chabrol's eyes no madman can be happy) is an object worthy of our compassion.

Possibly Chabrol's most successful film from this point of view is *Le Boucher* (1970, The Butcher). It is essentially a drama with only two important characters, whom it brings face to face: a schoolteacher, Hélène (played by Stéphane Audran, Chabrol's second wife and frequent star in the late Sixties and Seventies), and a butcher, Paul (Jean Yanne), both equally possessed of passionate desires despite all appearances to the contrary. Paul conceals a terrible neurosis which periodically leads him to murder young girls. Since he realizes that he is suspected by the woman he loves, his suicide in her presence becomes an act of love.

Similar flashes of insanity recur in many of Chabrol's films. In *A Double Tour* (1959, Web of Passion) a father hopes to 'tear the eyes out' of an unknown murderer, who is eventually discovered to be his own son. A husband who has gone violently mad is the starting point for *La Rupture* (1970, The Break-Up): the behaviour of the normal characters, who then put the blame on the heroine, his wife, also looks as if it stems

from some mental instability. In *Les Innocents aux Mains Sales* (1975, *Innocents With Dirty Hands*) the heroine at the end of the film sinks into a kind of premeditated insanity as the only means to regain her integrity. It is this sort of obsession that ensures the unity of Chabrol's work, since it is found as often in the films with a strict dramatic structure as in those which are less carefully worked out or even botched.

Chabrol's later films included a detailed reconstruction of a real-life murder case, *Violette Nozière* (1978), *Le Cheval d'Orgeuil* (1980, *The Proud Ones*), *Les Fantômes du Chapelier* (1982, The Hatter's Ghosts) and *Le Sang des Autres* (1984, *The Blood of Others*).

Born in Paris in 1930, **Jean-Luc Godard** was first educated in Switzerland and went on to the Sorbonne to study ethnology. It was during his university days that he discovered his passion for cinema and, like Louis Delluc, his Twenties predecessor, he began his film career by writing about it.

From the very beginning he considered himself an essayist rather than a storyteller. 'I write essays in the form of novels or novels in the form of essays. Instead of writing criticism, I now film it,' he wrote, and it is true that conventional narrative – the backbone of most cinema – has never been the most important element in his films.

As a story, *Breathless* (written by Truffaut originally) is not much different from any of the American thriller novels Godard was later to adapt – Dolores Hitchens' *Fool's Gold* for *Bande à Part* (1964, *The Outsiders*), and Lionel White's *Obsession* for *Pierrot le Fou* (1965, Pierrot the Fool). Even when he adapted literary works of a higher level – Moravia's *A Ghost at Noon* in *Le Mépris* (1963, *Contempt*) – he always transformed the original material with a massive injection of documentary material. This was even true of *Alphaville* (1965), a *film noir* set in the future which sustained the commercial appeal of previous films.

His films before *La Chinoise, ou Plutôt à la Chinoise* (1967, *The Chinese Girl*), in which a group of students sets up a Maoist cell during their holidays, were less overtly political than those which followed, and yet *Vivre Sa Vie* (1962, *It's My Life*) was in fact already as much a study of prostitution as the story of its heroine, Nana; *Le Petit Soldat* (1960, *The Little Soldier*) was the first French film to attempt to deal with the Algerian war – and it was banned by the French government until 1963 as a result. Even the more intimate films – *Une Femme Mariée* (1964, *A Married Woman*) or *Contempt* – could be called studies in micropolitics, the politics of the couple, the politics of sex. And a film like *Deux ou Trois Choses Que Je Sais d'Elle* (1967, *Two or Three Things I Know About Her*) was in many ways a sociological essay.

All Godard's films – even *Masculin-Féminin* (1966), which on the surface looks as casually put together as a TV film – reveal a very complex formal substructure under scrutiny. At the same time as being insistent on 'realism' – direct sound, filming on location – Godard was equally concerned in taking these pieces of direct reality and abstracting them. He takes a moment of real life, a moment in time, and transforms it into art through his editing.

But if there was not such a total break between his films of the Sixties and those of the Seventies, it is true that in the Seventies – or even as early as *Un Film Comme les Autres* (1969, *A Film Like the Others*) – Godard gave up both stories and stars. He deliberately attempted to make unpopular films, and succeeded.

But in so doing he successfully suppressed most of his talents as a film-maker. Although he was not a storyteller, his earlier films allowed his talent for the lyrical full rein; and although he often cast his stars against the grain – drawing out extraordinary performances, such as Mireille Darc's in *Weekend* (1967) – they did contribute a great deal to his films.

In his post-1968 period of total asceticism, he masochistically would not allow himself to do what he could do best. If proof be needed, compare *Tout Va Bien* (1972, *All Goes Well*) with others of the period: there, the presence of Jane Fonda and Yves Montand again allowed him to display his talent for directing actors. Although the film was austerely made, his genius for the staggering image, and his unique sense of sound and editing were very much in evidence. And he went back to fiction – although only as a support – with a large injection of documentary material. It was precisely the dialectics between reality and fiction that made *Tout Va Bien* a more successful film than his other films at that time.

Tout Va Bien was not the commercial success Godard had hoped for and he abandoned Paris and the world of commercial film-making, retiring to Grenoble to set up his own company, Sonimage, making films for cassette and television.

Godard returned to feature-film making with *Sauve Qui Peut (La Vie)* (1980, *Slow Motion*) and the film achieved a greater success and wider audiences than any of his films since *Weekend*. *Slow Motion* is an encapsulation of all his previous work, both of his Sixties' feature films and his Seventies' documentary essays. He followed it with *Passion* (1982) in which a film director (Jerzy Radziwiłowicz) attempts to re-create classic works of art with live models, while a factory girl (Isabelle Huppert) stands up for her rights against an oppressive industrialist (Michel Piccoli). The director becomes emotionally involved with both the girl and the factory owner's wife (Hanna Schygulla). The next year, after this fascinating commercial failure, Godard won the top prize at Venice with *Prénom: Carmen* (1983, *First Name, Carmen*), this time himself playing the film-maker whose documentary is used as a cover-up for a kidnap attempt by his criminal niece Carmen (Maruschka Detmers). To some extent, this film represents a return to Godard's Sixties practice of structuring events and meditations around a popular or literary piece of storytelling, particularly in the thriller genre, but usually involving a more or less unhappy love affair, which ends in death or separation. He followed this in 1984 with a version of the nativity story, *Je Vous Salue, Marie* (Hail, Mary).

Above: a bourgeois couple (Jean Yanne and Mireille Darc) get stuck in a traffic jam before being involved in a series of horrific events in Weekend. *Right: the young prostitute (Isabelle Huppert) with a client in* Slow Motion.

Bottom: the guests of the vast hotel, from the opening of Resnais' Last Year in Marienbad. *Below: the inmates of Auschwitz concentration camp in the short documentary* Night and Fog. *Right: Emmanuelle Riva in the Cannes prize-winner* Hiroshima, Mon Amour. *Below right: Ellen Burstyn and David Warner in* Providence. *The film was not a great success.*

Alain Resnais was born at Vannes, Brittany, in 1922. Though he made his breakthrough to feature film-making at the same time as Godard, Truffaut and Chabrol, Resnais was ten years older and the shaping forces on his life and work were quite different.

Resnais studied acting, began a course in film-making at the Institut des Hautes Etudes Cinématographiques (IDHEC), the French film school and worked professionally as a film editor.

It was out of a series of studies of painters undertaken in 16mm that Resnais' career as a professional director grew. In 1948 he was commissioned to remake in 35mm a study of *Van Gogh* (1948) initially shot in 1947. He followed this with *Gauguin* and a masterly account of Picasso's *Guernica* (both 1950).

Together with Georges Franju, he became a dominant figure in French documentary at a time when it far surpassed French feature film-making in its commitment, intelligence and originality.

The five short films completed by Resnais between 1950 and 1958 were on totally divergent subjects: colonization and native art in *Les Statues Meurent Aussi* (1953, Statues Also Die), co-directed with Chris Marker; the Nazi concentration camps in *Nuit et Brouillard* (1955, *Night and Fog*); the French

National Library in *Toute la Mémoire du Monde* (1957, The Whole Memory of the World); industrial safety in *Le Mystère de l'Atelier 15* (1957, The Mystery of Workshop 15); and the manufacture of polystyrene in *Le Chant du Styrène* (1958, The Song of the Styrene). In these short films he developed the particular approaches that would characterize all his early feature-film work – a separation and re-fusion of the elements of image, music and text – and perfected a working method which involved collaboration on equal terms with writers of real literary quality, such as Paul Eluard for *Guernica* and Raymond Queneau for *Le Chant du Styrène*.

Alain Resnais' debut as a feature film-maker in 1959 was *Hiroshima, Mon Amour*, scripted by the novelist Marguerite Duras. Four further features followed in the Sixties, and in each he collaborated with a novelist who had little or no previous experience of feature-film scriptwriting: with Alain Robbe-Grillet on *Last Year in Marienbad*; with Jean Cayrol on *Muriel, ou le Temps d'un Retour* (1963, *Muriel*); with Jorge Semprun on *La Guerre Est Finie* (1966, *The War Is Over*); and with Jacques Sternberg on *Je T'Aime, Je T'Aime* (1969, I Love You, I Love You). It is a measure of Resnais' influence that his first four collaborators all went on to direct feature films of their own.

Though all are highly original, these five films have a considerable stylistic homogeneity. There is a constant return to the problems of time and memory. In *Hiroshima, Mon Amour* past and present come together as two love affairs, 14 years apart, are fused in a woman's mind. By contrast, *Last Year in Marienbad* refuses all chronology. The attempt to separate real and imaginary, this year and last year, is merely one of the many traps set by the writer, Alain Robbe-Grillet; he was a pioneer of the *nouveau roman* ('New Novel') and, like Duras, went on to become a leading French film-maker of the Sixties and Seventies. In *Muriel* (the writer of which, Jean Cayrol, had previously scripted *Night and Fog*), the focus is again different. Here the strangeness of the film stems from a strict adherence to chronology – even when two simultaneous actions are described – and an openness to the chance occurrences and hazards of shooting.

La Guerre Est Finie, a look at the life of a Spanish Communist activist in exile, makes extensive use of what can only be called the 'flash-forward' shots that anticipate events that may or may not unfold in the way the hero, Diego, expects. Perhaps the most original of the films in this respect is *Je T'Aime, Je T'Aime*, a pseudo-science-fiction story in which logic and chronology are almost totally abandoned in favour of an apparently random interweaving of levels of time and reality, actually reflecting an emotional logic that leads inevitably to the hero's death.

His two films of the Seventies, *Stavisky . . .* (1974), from another script by Jorge Semprun, and *Providence* (1977), an English-language production from a script by the British dramatist David Mercer, are works which display to the full Resnais' meticulous control of every aspect of film-making. There is, however, a certain loss of force. Immaculately shot where the earlier films had been radically inventive, they seem cold and unapproachable, and are marred by a certain shallowness of conception.

No such reservations are needed about *Mon Oncle d'Amérique* (1980, *My American Uncle*), scripted by Jean Gruault, which was Resnais' freest film since *Je T'Aime, Je T'Aime*. The film interweaves the story of three disparate characters – two men and a woman who has contacts with both – with an exposition by the French biologist Henri Laborit of his theories about human and animal action and aggression, and with crucial reference points from Forties films starring such memorable performers as Jean Gabin, Jean Marais and Danielle Darrieux.

La Vie Est un Roman (1983, *Life Is a Bed of Roses*), though in many respects a follow-up, with an elaborate time-structure reminiscent of the early films, was greeted with bewilderment and even dismay. Resnais returned to form with *L'Amour à Mort* (1984, *Love Unto Death*), an intimate study of two loving couples confronted by the death of one of their number.

A number of other directors came to prominence under the aegis of the *nouvelle vague* in the late Fifties and early Sixties. **Jacques Rivette** (b. 1928), a former critic for *Cahiers du Cinéma* and assistant of the directors Renoir, Becker, Rohmer and Truffaut, made his first feature, *Paris Nous Appartient* (1960, *Paris Belongs to Us*), in the late Fifties. It concerned a production of Shakespeare's *Pericles* and an imaginary world conspiracy and contained several deaths; it was thus an appropriate debut for a director who has never ceased to be experimental, literary, theatrical and uncompromising. *Suzanne Simonin, la Religieuse de Diderot* (1965, *La Religieuse/The Nun*), starring Anna Karina, ran into censorship difficulties but proved to be Rivette's only major

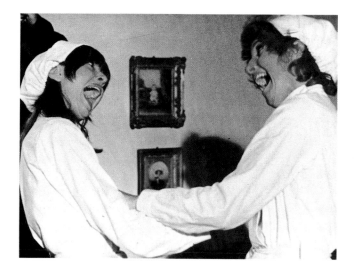

Above: Juliet Berto and Dominique Laborier in Rivette's dream-like Céline and Julie Go Boating.

commercial hit in the decade. The long and difficult, *L'Amour Fou* (1968), and *Out One* (and its shortened form, *Out One: Spectre*, 1974) were succeeded by the charming, dreamlike fantasy of *Céline et Julie Vont en Bateau* (1974, *Céline and Julie Go Boating*), the success of which increased Rivette's standing, especially in the English-speaking world. After the disappointing *Noroît* (1976, *Northwest Wind*) and *Duelle* (1976, *Women Duelling*), Rivette returned to critical favour with *L'Amour par Terre* (1984, *Love on the Ground*).

Another one-time film critic, **Eric Rohmer** (b. 1920), pursued his own independent line while achieving consistent box-office success with *Ma Nuit Chez Maud* (1969, *My Night With Maud*), *Le Genou de Claire* (1970, *Claire's Knee*) and *L'Amour l'Après-Midi* (1972, *Love in the Afternoon*). These films formed part of a series, Six Contes Morales (Six Moral Tales) – sophisticated, witty portrayals of modern relationships whose male protagonists are all torn between fidelity to a long-standing relationship and finding romantic fulfilment in a new one. After two decorative period films, *Die Marquise von O* (1976, *The Marquise of O*) and *Perceval le Gallois* (1978, *Perceval*), Rohmer began a new series, Comédies et Proverbes, purporting, in the style of the Romantic writer Alfred de Musset, to be moral illustrations of popular proverbs. The anecdotes were rich in humour and human observation. The series included *La Femme de l'Aviateur* (1981, *The Aviator's Wife*), *Le Beau Mariage* (1982, *A Good Marriage*), *Pauline à la Plage* (1983, *Pauline at the Beach*) and *Les Nuits de la Pleine Lune* (1984, *Full Moon in Paris*). Rohmer has proved one of the most consistent, satisfying, individual and perceptive of French film-makers in the Seventies and Eighties.

Jacques Doniol-Valcroze (b. 1920), co-editor with Bazin of *Cahiers du Cinéma* until Bazin's death in 1958 and chief editor until 1963, contributed to the *nouvelle vague* as occasional actor, scenarist and director. His *L'Eau à la Bouche* (1960, *The Game of Love*) caused some censorship problems in the USA, but of his later films only the Franco–Swedish co-production *Le Viol* (1967, *A Question of Rape*), with Bibi Andersson, made much international impact. He collaborated as co-writer and actor with another *Cahiers* critic turned director, Pierre Kast (1920–1984), on *Le Bel Age* (1959, *Love Is When You Make It*) and *Vacances Portugaises* (1963, *Portuguese Holiday*) though not on Kast's best-known film, *La Morte-Saison des Amours* (1960, *The Season for Love*).

Above: Anouk Aimée and Jean-Louis Trintignant in Lelouche's romantic A Man and a Woman.

Jacques Demy (b. 1931) brought grace and charm to the *nouvelle vague* with the romantic *Lola* (1961), the almost Bressonian *La Baie des Anges* (1963, *Bay of Angels*) and the lyrical *Les Parapluies de Cherbourg* (1964, *The Umbrellas of Cherbourg*). But even the most likeable of his later films, *Peau d'Ane* (1970, *The Magic Donkey*), with Catherine Deneuve as a lovely fairy-tale princess, did not quite recapture his early spontaneity. His wife, **Agnès Varda** (b. 1928), made a precocious debut with the short *La Pointe Courte* (1955) and, after several personal documentaries, followed it with *Cléo de 5 à 7* (1961, *Cleo From 5 to 7*), two hours in the life of a pop-singer (Corinne Marchand) who fears she may be dying of cancer. *Le Bonheur* (1965, *Happiness*) was a beautifully made film about a man who loves both wife and mistress; when the wife commits suicide, the mistress takes her place.

In 1969 Demy and Varda tried their luck in Hollywood, when they made, respectively, *Model Shop* and *Lions Love*. Both films were unsuccessful, but in 1977 Varda was back in France and on form with the feminist *L'Une Chante, l'Autre Pas* (*One Sings, the Other Doesn't*).

The field of comedy proper, as distinct from the decidedly mixed offerings of Truffaut, Rohmer, Chabrol and Godard, was mostly left to comparatively minor directors. **Philippe de Broca** (b. 1933) followed his *Les Jeux de l'Amour* (1960, *Playing at Love*), essentially the same story – of a girl who wants a baby and a man who does not – as Godard's *Une Femme Est une Femme* (1961, *A Woman Is a Woman*), with several similar lightweight comedies and the popular spoof-adventure film *L'Homme de Rio* (1964, *That Man from Rio*), starring Jean-Paul Belmondo. But his later work was less successful. The actor-director **Jean-Pierre Mocky** (b. 1929) also made most impact with his early films, the social satires *Les Dragueurs* (1959, *The Young Have No Morals*), *Un Couple* (1960, *A Couple*), scripted by Queneau, and *Snobs* (1961). Though contemporary with, rather than properly part of, the *nouvelle vague*, **Michel Deville** (b. 1931) deserves mention for keeping up the tradition of French comedy with *Ce Soir ou Jamais* (1960, *Tonight or Never*), *Adorable Menteuse* (1961, *Adorable Liar*) and *A Cause, à Cause d'une Femme* (1962, *Because of a Woman*); but only the untypical period piece *Benjamin ou les Mémoires d'un Puceau* (1967, *Benjamin, or The Diary of an Innocent Young Man*) achieved much international showing.

The traditional comedy of mime, in the vein of Tati, was explored by actor-writer-director **Pierre Étaix** (b, 1928), in the short films *Rupture* (1961, *Break-Up*) and *Heureux Anniversaire* (1962, *Happy Anniversary*) and then in the features *Le Soupirant* (1963, *The Suitor*) and *Yoyo* (1965).

Among the older directors admired and certainly imitated by the *nouvelle vague* directors were **Jean-Pierre Melville** (1917–1973) and the ex-documentarist Georges Franju (b. 1912). Melville occasionally returned to the literary adaptations with which he had started his career, as in *Léon Morin, Prêtre* (1961, *Léon Morin, Priest*) with Belmondo as the priest and Emmanuelle Riva as an atheist, communist widow; but mostly he pursued his favourite line of crime films. These became increasingly abstract as he turned to colour in *Le Samouraï* (1967, *The Samurai*), with Alan Delon, and *Le Cercle Rouge* (1970, *The Red Circle*). Franju was also much involved in adaptations, sometimes of very literary material. *La Tête Contre les Murs* (1959, *The Keepers*), from Hervé Bazin's novel, deals with themes of delinquency and madness in a restrained style, contrasting with the wild lyricism of his poetic horror-film *Les Yeux Sans Visage* (1959, *Eyes Without a Face*). *Thérèse Desqueyroux* (1962, *Therese*), based on François Mauriac's novel, featured Emmanuelle Riva as the erring wife. *Judex* (1963) was a witty and magical re-creation of Feuillade's silent serial. *Thomas l'Imposteur* (1965, *Thomas the Impostor*) was a critically praised adaptation of Cocteau's novel, mixing reality and fantasy in a war setting; less well-received was *La Faute de l'Abbé Mouret* (1970, *The Sin of Father Mouret*), based on Emile Zola's novel. In his later years Franju mostly made documentaries and features for television.

Two notable novelists – former Resnais scriptwriters – subsequently became film directors: **Alain Robbe-Grillet** (b. 1922) and **Marguerite Duras** (b. 1914). Robbe-Grillet's *L'Immortelle* (1963, The Immortal Woman) was a tedious tale of an ambiguous affair with a mysterious woman sparked off by mixing *Last Year in Marienbad* with *film noir*. *Trans-Europ Express* (1967), however, juggled wittily with levels of reality in its story of some film-makers and the scenario they are inventing about a criminal brought down by his sadistic sexual obsessions. After that the tide of fashion turned against Robbe-Grillet, though he remained quite productive. Marguerite Duras, who started later, has had only a cult following but she has managed to make films regularly since 1966 in a way that would hardly have been possible outside France. Films like *Détruire Dit-Elle* (1967, *Destroy She Said*) and *India Song* (1975) are the cinematic equivalents of her abstruse yet romantic novels.

Finally, **Claude Lelouch** (b. 1937) must be mentioned, though his *nouvelle vague* debut, *Le Propre del'Homme* (1960, *The Right of Man*) virtually disappeared without trace. After several flops he made a popular documentary on the Tour de France cycle race, *Pour un Maillot Jaune* (1966, *For a Yellow Jersey*) and the enormously successful glossy love story *Une Homme et une Femme* (1966, *A Man and a Woman*), with Anouk Aimée in a leather coat and Jean-Louis Trintignant in a fast car. *Vivre Pour Vivre* (1967, *Live for Life*), with its starry lineup of Yves Montand, Annie Girardot and Candice Bergen, was a similar hit. Lelouch's fondness for experiment with time-shifts, colour and camera movement is the only remaining trace of the *nouvelle vague* in his subsequent commercial confections – *Le Voyou* (1970, *Simon the Swiss*), *Un Autre Homme, une Autre Chance* (1977, *Another Man, Another Woman*), *A Nos Deux* (1979, *An Adventure for Two*), and *Les Uns et les Autres* (1981, *Bolero*).

Britain

When *Room at the Top* was released in 1959, it signalled the beginning of one of the most exhilarating bursts of creativity in the history of British cinema. During the following five or six years new film-makers with fresh ideas brought to the screen a sense of immediacy and social awareness that had people queuing again after nearly a decade of decline.

These dynamic film developments sprang from the political and social agitation of the period. British imperialism had been dealt a severe body blow by the failure of the 1956 Suez venture in alliance with France against Egypt. Thousands of young people had gathered in London's Trafalgar Square to demand the withdrawal of British troops from Egypt. Thousands more were flocking to join the annual anti-nuclear Aldermaston marches in order to campaign for unilateral nuclear disarmament.

It was a time of protest and demonstrations. Ideas were in the melting pot. Young people no longer accepted that their elders were necessarily their betters, and in the process of re-examining basic principles gained a new sense of collective identity, which in turn transformed books, plays and popular entertainment.

Singers like Tommy Steele, Cliff Richard and Lonnie Donegan spurned traditional showbiz glamour in favour of a jeans-and-T-shirt image. Authors ultimately as different as John Braine, Alan Sillitoe and Stan Barstow all wrote grittily from working-class and lower-middle-class experience. On the London stage, the 'kitchen sink' era had begun. At the Royal Court Theatre in 1956, John Osborne had created the concept of the 'angry young man' in *Look Back in Anger*; Arnold Wesker then faced West End audiences with East End problems, and Joan Littlewood, creator of Stratford Theatre Royal and Theatre Workshop, brought a whole new generation of playwrights, actors and actresses into being, to express the questing, socially critical spirit of the times.

Things moved more slowly in the film industry. The measures it took to counter the catastrophic drop in cinema attendances, caused largely by the upsurge of TV, were mainly commercially opportunist and gimmicky, and thus only succeeded in driving more people back home to watch television.

The first hint of change in feature production came from a modest suspense drama, *The Man Upstairs* (1958), tautly directed by Don Chaffey for ACT Films (the production company of the film technicians' union). Set in a London boarding house, it touched upon many of the vital issues of the day and challenged conventional, cosy attitudes to class relationships and the role of the police. It was a straw in the wind. But it was completely overshadowed by the smash-hit success of *Room at the Top*, released early the next year.

Directed by Jack Clayton, and based on the John Braine best seller – a key book in the new-style literature – *Room at the Top* was, in fact, a transitional film. Its starry cast, its steamy sex scenes and its depiction of life at the top belonged to the past. But its Northern setting and its candid exploration of the social barriers, corruption and palm-greasing of class-divided Britain signposted the future. Its enormous popularity at home and abroad brought fresh confidence to the film industry and helped to shake some of its more entrenched notions of what draws people to the cinema.

Room at the Top showed how under the existing systems a working-class boy with the desire to succeed could only do so at the cost of his self-respect, peace of mind and personal happiness. The forces ranged against Joe Lampton ('I'm

working class and proud of it') are epitomized by the characters of Jack Wales, Mr and Mrs Brown and his own aunt and uncle. Jack Wales, Susan Brown's boyfriend, is an icily patronizing, upper-crust ex-squadron leader, who never loses an opportunity to put Joe in his place. He is the symbol of everything the British 'New Wave' disliked in the old order. But he has allies in the Browns, Susan's parents.

Brown, a self-made millionaire from humble origins, now a Tory and a councillor, shows the tendency of those who escaped from the working class to join the establishment. This point is reinforced in the portrayal of his wife, a mercilessly caricatured snob, who, on being introduced to Joe, observes: 'Curious names some of these people have'. On the other hand, Joe has to face the conservatism and apathy of the working class itself in the face of entrenched privilege; his aunt and uncle, old-fashioned, decent, hard-working folk, urge him to stick to his own class and not try to rise above his appointed place.

His brief affair with a foreign and therefore perhaps comparatively classless woman (Simone Signoret in an Oscar-winning performance) only temporarily diverts him from his project of marrying Susan and getting to the top, at whatever cost, including the death of the woman he really loves.

Meanwhile, back at the National Film Theatre, a group of youngish, independent film-makers, including Karel Reisz, Tony Richardson, Lindsay Anderson and cameraman Walter Lassally, were showing each other and young audiences the documentary films they had made with small grants from the

British Film Institute or at their own expense, in a series of programmes they called Free Cinema.

The stated aim of the group was, by adopting far more personalized styles, to break away from the approach to documentary film-making established by John Grierson in the Thirties. Most of their films were free-flowing observations of work and play among young working-class people; and in retrospect they are more striking for their continuity with the Grierson tradition than for their rejection of it. Anderson looked at a Margate amusement arcade in *O Dreamland* (1953); at life in a school for deaf children in *Thursday's Children* (co-directed with Guy Brenton), which won an Oscar in 1954; and at the people of Covent Garden market in *Every Day Except Christmas* (1957).

With Tony Richardson, Reisz co-directed *Momma Don't Allow* (1955), a short documentary about a London jazz club. He followed this with a longer and more ambitious documentary about a south London youth club, *We Are the Lambeth Boys* (1959).

Crucially, Reisz (along with Richardson and the other Free Cinema film-makers) shared with Grierson, Paul Rotha, Arthur Elton and Edgar Anstey the aim of realism. Where the Free Cinema films tend to differ from those of the Thirties is in their subject matter. The earlier documentaries were concerned with the world of work, especially its transformation by technical innovation. Apart from Anderson's, the Fifties documentaries dealt with the world of leisure, especially that of young people.

The 'personalized' view was sometimes patronizing or snobbish. The standard of the films was uneven; but the best of them had a freshness and sense of urgency which was a taste of things to come. They stimulated discussion in the pages of the serious film journals; Lindsay Anderson argued for the recognition of the relationship between art and society in his much-discussed article, 'Stand Up! Stand Up!', published in *Sight and Sound*, Autumn 1956. The enthusiasm generated by the group in its search for contemporary styles to match contemporary attitudes helped to open up new possibilities for feature production.

First to the starting post was **Tony Richardson** (b. 1928), who had produced John Osborne's plays on the stage, and joined with him to form Woodfall Films with a view to adapting them for the screen. This initiative and Richardson's personal drive were crucial to the establishment of a British 'New Wave'. Neither *Look Back in Anger* (1959), with Richard Burton as Jimmy Porter, the original 'angry young man', nor *The Entertainer* (1960), with Laurence Olivier as the has-been stand-up comic, was as successful on film, largely, perhaps, because Osborne had been addressing himself to middle-class theatre audiences.

It was not until Woodfall linked up with a working-class writer, Alan Sillitoe, that it was able to launch the cinematic equivalent of the theatre's 'kitchen sink' revolution, with the screen version of Sillitoe's bestseller, *Saturday Night and Sunday Morning* (1960), directed by Karel Reisz.

Despite the ripples made by *Room at the Top*, Woodfall had

Bottom: Danny (Albert Finney) ingratiates himself with the wealthy Mrs Bramson (Mona Washbourne) in Night Must Fall. *Below: David Warner as the anarchic hero of* Morgan, a Suitable Case for Treatment. *Right:* Saturday Night and Sunday Morning *was the first British film to realize the box-office potential of depicting the realities of modern working-class life.*

Above: Tom Courtenay as the hero of The Loneliness of the Long-Distance Runner.

a long and difficult struggle to raise the finance for a film with a factory worker as 'hero'. Few believed that it could succeed. In the event, it beat all former box-office records for a British film and proved that there need be no contradiction between artistic integrity and commercial success. The ripples then grew into a flood-tide; and for the next few years British cinema rode on the crest of the 'New Wave' which, for a time, freed a section of it from Hollywood financial and cultural domination.

'New Wave' Style and Subjects The new film-makers, like the pioneers of the 'Grierson school' before them, rejected studio sets in favour of location shooting in the back streets, waterways and working-class homes of industrial cities. The black-and-white photography, mainly with natural lighting, gave rise to the 'grainy realism' which was the typical visual style, and the influence of recently developed TV techniques helped achieve a sense of immediacy.

The star system was abandoned, and leading roles were taken by new or up-and-coming players (Albert Finney, for example, was virtually unknown outside London theatre circles before *Saturday Night and Sunday Morning*). The characters they played were close to life, complex – like real people rather than standard 'heroes' and 'heroines'.

Most 'New Wave' films were based on books and plays by authors with personal experience of working-class life in the provinces (very few were made from original scripts). This contrasted with the rather condescending view of working-class life that had been adopted in earlier feature films.

Woodfall Films, with the backing of the British Lion subsidiary, Bryanston Films, continued to lead the field. Tony Richardson brought Shelagh Delaney's Theatre Royal play, *A Taste of Honey*, to the screen (1961), with Rita Tushingham as the pregnant schoolgirl and Murray Melvin (from Theatre Workshop) as the lonely homosexual with whom she shares a brief spell of contented domesticity. Richardson followed it with *The Loneliness of the Long Distance Runner* (1962), based on Alan Sillitoe's remarkable short story, with Tom Courtenay as the young delinquent in Borstal who demonstrates which side he is on by deliberately losing the race that, if won, would have brought great prestige to the Borstal authorities. Much underrated by critics at the time, it has proved to be among the most enduring films of the period. Both these films gained much from Walter Lassally's brilliant camerawork.

Woodfall also launched Desmond Davis (b. 1928) as a director; his two films based on Edna O'Brien stories – *The Girl With Green Eyes* (1964) and *I Was Happy Here* (1966) – were late contributions to the no-longer-new trend.

The young Canadian director, Sidney Furie (b. 1933), probed current social issues among working-class youngsters in *The Boys* (1962) and *The Leather Boys* (1963). He injected a crisp, contemporary style into British musicals with *The Young Ones* (1961) and *Wonderful Life* (1964), both featuring Cliff Richard.

Saturday Night and Sunday Morning, directed by **Karel Reisz** (b. 1926), was a key film for British cinema. It marked, first, the emergence of a new generation of film-makers; second, through the performance of Albert Finney, the emergence of a new generation of film actors; and thirdly, and most importantly, the refurbishing and up-dating of the tradition of realism within British feature cinema, which by the late Fifties had become coy and archaic. To gain a proper historical perspective on *Saturday Night and Sunday Morning* it should be seen with a film like Ealing's *The Titfield*

Thunderbolt (1953), for example. Through its acknowledgment of sexuality and violence, and through its careful observation of a working-class world being transformed by increased wealth, *Saturday Night and Sunday Morning* destroyed the coyness and showed it was possible for the cinema to be responsive to contemporary social developments.

Although Reisz had moved from documentary to feature films, *Saturday Night and Sunday Morning* belongs in many ways with *Momma Don't Allow* and *We Are the Lambeth Boys*. All three films were part of the Free Cinema struggle to revitalize realism: all three deal sympathetically with young people in the context of the social change that was coming to be known as the 'affluent society'; and all three are careful to avoid sensational effects.

Reisz's next three films, *Night Must Fall* (1964), *Morgan, a Suitable Case for Treatment* (1966), and *Isadora* (1968), can also be conveniently grouped together. Although they reveal the same interest in the observation of social context, the central characters are more dominant in the narrative. Their behaviour is also more extravagant and unconventional. The hero of *Night Must Fall* is a murderer; Morgan in *Morgan, a Suitable Case for Treatment* leads an anarchic and uncontrolled social life; the dancer Isadora Duncan, the heroine of *Isadora*, is disastrously ambitious in both her artistic and her personal life.

Along with this change in the conception of the central figures went a change in film-making technique. The technique of *We Are the Lambeth Boys* and *Saturday Night and Sunday Morning* is sensitively orthodox. Generally the editing is unobtrusive and its rhythms controlled, the lighting is balanced and camera positions unspectacular. This orthodoxy, if not completely overthrown in the later group of films, was considerably loosened up.

In accordance with one of the central tenets of realism – the artist should be a neutral observer – the presence of the director was not made obvious in Reisz's earlier films. In his later films the director's presence was more discernible. This development in Reisz's work highlighted one of the contradictions in the Free Cinema position. A central demand was that the cinema should be a medium where personal expression was possible; a film director should have the same creative scope that novelists, poets, composers and painters were supposed to have. But the demand for realism limited that freedom since the director was necessarily constrained by the nature of the world he was trying to represent.

Where the realist commitment had been dominant in Reisz's earlier films, the commitment to authorial freedom became dominant in the succeeding ones. Reisz was responding to the changed character of film-making brought about by the work of the *nouvelle vague*.

Of Reisz's films, *Morgan, a Suitable Case for Treatment*, with its speedily paced narrative, over-exposed photography and intercut clips from old Tarzan films, most obviously shows the signs of the *nouvelle vague* influence. Because of the change in technique, *Morgan, a Suitable Case for Treatment* was considered representative of the 'swinging London' era. Reisz has always been sensitive to changes in cultural atmosphere.

The Gambler (1974) and *Who'll Stop the Rain?* (1978), known in Britain as *Dog Soldiers*, indicate another change in his career. Both of these films were financed by American companies, are set in the United States, and deal with subjects rooted in American life. Both films have aspects in common with the American thriller, yet they seem closer to the 'kitchen sink' drama of *Saturday Night and Sunday Morning* than to that of *Morgan, a Suitable Case for Treatment*: the central characters are not so dominant, the film-making technique is less obtrusive and there is the same kind of careful observation and presentation of the social contexts in which the action takes place.

He returned to England to make *The French Lieutenant's Woman* (1981), an adaptation of John Fowles' novel scripted by Harold Pinter. Instead of looking at the Victorian events through the eyes of a sophisticated modern narrator, as in the novel, Pinter invented a modern frame involving the making of the film itself and an affair between the two stars (played by Meryl Streep and Jeremy Irons) which parallels their illicit relationship in the film-within-a-film. Whether this casts any light on the heroine, a sort of early feminist born out of her time, is open to question. The tight, controlled quality of the film is in marked contrast to Reisz's previous historical venture, *Isadora*, and *The French Lieutenant's Woman* remains largely within the British tradition of historical re-creation and realistic evocation of setting (mainly Lyme Regis in Dorset).

Reisz clearly has a place in the history of the British cinema for his work in revitalizing realism in the late Fifties and early Sixties. Even if that revitalization was shortlived within the British cinema it had an important effect on television, helping to create the climate out of which came the work of Ken Loach and Tony Garnett, a television series like *Z Cars* and the plays of David Mercer, Dennis Potter and Trevor Griffiths.

As the leading light of the Free Cinema movement, **Lindsay Anderson** (b. 1923) remained committed primarily to documentary for a dozen years (1948–59), and even later he returned occasionally to this area – for instance, as narrator of Kevin Brownlow's *Abel Gance – The Charm of Dynamite* (1968) and David Robinson's *Hetty King – Performer* (1970). Many of his early documentaries were quite functional treatments of work and of social problems, though he took every opportunity to develop his topics with energy and imagination. His last English documentary was a propaganda film co-directed anonymously for the Campaign for Nuclear Disarmament (CND), *March to Aldermaston* (1959). Meanwhile he had tried his hand at several episodes of *The Adventures of Robin Hood* for television in 1955–6.

It was not until 1962 that Lindsay Anderson made his first feature film. *This Sporting Life* (1963), based on a David Storey novel. At one level, it explored a miserably stormy relationship of two lovers (Richard Harris and Rachel Roberts); at another, it exposed the corruption and commercialism of Rugby League as a business. It was highly acclaimed by most critics; but its fragmented flashback structure and rather heavily emphatic symbolism – a departure from typical 'New Wave' directness – operated against commercial success; it was six years before Anderson was able to make his second and more successful feature film, *If . . .* (1968). This was the English public school story to end all public school stories, culminating in revolution and the shooting of the headmaster and most of the governors. Almost by chance, it caught the mood of that traumatic year, achieving more success in Europe and America than in Britain, where student rebellion had been little more than token. The hero of *If . . .*, Mick Travis (Malcolm McDowell), who inevitably lacked A-Levels and testimonials, went on to become a coffee salesman in *O Lucky Man!* (1973), a panoramic, heavily stylized view of the state of the nation, ranging from a sinister secret research

station to City financial speculation and international diplomatic corruption. On a more modest level, Anderson filmed a David Storey play, *In Celebration* (1975), about three sons returning North for their parent's wedding anniversary. This formed part of Anderson's continuing involvement, mainly in the theatre and on television, with Storey's plays. His other television work included a controversial studio version of Alan Bennett's play, *The Old Crowd* (1979). He resumed his large-scale and increasingly negative commentary on British life with *Britannia Hospital* (1982), using the collapse of the National Health Service as a metaphor for the country's decline and imminent fall.

Another of the key directors of the period was **John Schlesinger** (b. 1926) who, after gaining attention with his Waterloo Station documentary, *Terminus* (1961), teamed up with the Italian producer Joseph Janni to make *A Kind of Loving* (1962).

Below: Mia Farrow and Nick Nolte in Who'll Stop the Rain? *Bottom: Jeremy Irons and Meryl Streep as guilty, Victorian lovers in* The French Lieutenant's Woman.

In most of his films Schlesinger has been concerned, in one way or another, with the difference between the way people would like to behave and the patterns of behaviour forced on them by the moral, social and cultural values of their specific environments.

In *A Kind of Loving* the inhibiting force is Northern working-class Puritanism which, combined with the housing shortage, cripples the relationship between a disorientated young couple (Alan Bates, June Ritchie) who are more or less forced into marriage. In *Billy Liar* (1963) popular images of romance and heroism dominate the mind of a mixed-up lad (Tom Courtenay) frustrated by small-town life. A casual encounter with a free-spirited young woman (Julie Christie) offers him a genuine, single chance of escape.

This was Julie Christie's first important screen role, and Schlesinger again provided her with a fine showcase with *Darling . . .* (1965) as a young model fecklessly climbing the social ladder in search of new experiences and finding emptiness at every level.

Although Schlesinger's first three films belonged firmly to the Sixties trend for socially critical realism, he stood a little apart from the other key directors of the period – Karel Reisz, Lindsay Anderson, Tony Richardson. His characters were victims of society rather than rebels against it. There was, in fact, a kind of fatalism about his work – which is probably why he was drawn to the novels of Thomas Hardy.

Bathsheba (Julie Christie), the central character in *Far From the Madding Crowd* (1967), is a typical Schlesinger heroine: an impoverished but high-spirited country girl enters the male-dominated world of business when she inherits a farm, but she is unable to resolve the conflict between her own sexual and emotional desires and her received notions of 'womanly' behaviour.

For his first Hollywood film, the Oscar-winning *Midnight Cowboy* (1969), Schlesinger shone his keen observational light on an alien scene – the streets, hotels, cafés and back-alleys of New York – revealing an undercurrent of corruption and violence. The two main characters can be seen as opposite sides of down-beat American life. Joe (Jon Voight) is a thick-headed Texan youth in flash cowboy gear who has a totally deluded image of himself constructed from the macho heroes of Westerns and commercialized culture. Ratso (Dustin

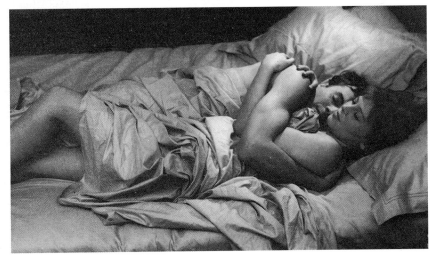

Above: Mick (Malcolm McDowell) arrives back at school in If . . . *Top: Richard Harris in* This Sporting Life. *Above right: Alan Bates as Vic, June Ritchie as his pregnant girlfriend in* A Kind of Loving. *Right: Dirk Bogarde and Julie Christie in* Darling.

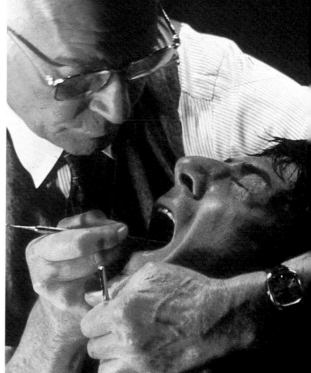

Below left: Donald Sutherland as the wealthy, pathologically shy Homer in Day of the Locust. *Left: the protagonists in the three-way affair of* Sunday, Bloody Sunday *– Peter Finch, Murray Head and Glenda Jackson. Below: Laurence Olivier and Dustin Hoffman in* Marathon Man.

Hoffman), who offers Joe back-street shelter when his plans to make his fortune as a stud go violently and pathetically awry, is a gutter realist dying of consumption.

In *Sunday, Bloody Sunday* (1971), perhaps his most personal and deeply felt film, the key symbol is the telephone – the disembodied voice substituting for physical contact among people cut off from normal London suburban life by the nonconformist nature of their sexuality. Delightfully observed episodes of middle-class conformity under its various guises run counterpoint to a complex emotional drama between a trendy, bisexual sculptor (Murray Head), a gentle homosexual doctor (Peter Finch) and an independently minded heterosexual (Glenda Jackson). The film remains one of the very few to have treated the theme of homosexuality in a calm, unsensational manner.

Schlesinger and his American co-producer Jerome Hellman had to fight hard to set up *The Day of the Locust* (1975). This Nathanael West novel about Hollywood in the Thirties offered the basis for yet another variation on the Schlesinger theme; a young artist/designer arrives at the film city full of hopes and illusions which are gradually shattered by the realities behind the Hollywood dream.

His next two American films were *Marathon Man* (1976), a taut political thriller, and *Yanks* (1979), about Americans in wartime Britain. In both films, however, there are signs of deviation from the straight line between *Terminus* and *The Day of the Locust*. *Yanks*, with its underlying themes of conflicting loyalties and clashing life-styles provoked by a British/American romance, reflects the changes in Schlesinger's own life – the pressures and problems faced by

an international film-maker commuting between two cultures.

Honky Tonk Freeway (1981) – a costly all-American comedy-fantasy with 14 principal characters, 103 speaking parts and a veritable army of cars, lorries and zoo animals – was financed by the British company EMI. It was a total flop, but Schlesinger redeemed his artistic reputation with a small-scale television film, *An Englishman Abroad* (1983), based on actress Coral Browne's encounter in Moscow with the upper-class ex-spy Guy Burgess, played by Alan Bates.

From 'New Wave' to 'Swinging Sixties' In the main, the 'New Wave' films were produced by small independent companies, raising money where and how they could – from National Film Finance Corporation loans, from deferred fees, from small American investments.

An example was the enterprising Beaver Films of **Bryan Forbes** (b. 1926) and **Richard Attenborough** (b. 1923). Forbes and Attenborough perfectly exemplified the new method of film financing when they took no salary for producing *The Angry Silence* (1960), the controversial but highly praised film about the ostracism of a lone worker by strikers. Later they joined forces with Michael Relph and Basil Dearden, Jack Hawkins and Guy Green to form Allied Film-Makers, pooling their talents to produce a polished and popular 'caper' thriller, *The League of Gentlemen* (1960). Under this banner, Forbes and Attenborough went on to produce a series of sensitive, meticulously crafted off-beat dramas which brought them deserved critical acclaim – *Whistle Down the Wind* (1961), *The L-Shaped Room* (1962) and *Seance on a Wet Afternoon* (1964).

But when Woodfall proposed a colour film of *Tom Jones*, Henry Fielding's classic eighteenth-century novel of a young man's growth to maturity, the director Tony Richardson and scriptwriter John Osborne were unable to raise the money from British backers and approached an American company, United Artists, for financial support. United Artists' decision to invest in the film and the enormous international success of *Tom Jones* (1963) were to change the face of British film-making. Bawdy, funny, uninhibited, *Tom Jones* celebrated a previous permissive age of gusto, gourmandizing and joyous free-living. It caught the mood of the moment. The Labour election victory in 1964 ended 13 years of Conservative rule with the promise of '100 days of dynamic action'. Censorship, prudery and convention were in retreat. Swinging London was born. It was a frenzied saturnalia, a cult of the new and the now, a world of colour supplements, pirate radio, glamorous television commercials, 'dolly birds', discos and boutiques, exciting music and freedom of thought and expression.

In the early Sixties United Artists also backed the desire of producers Harry Saltzman and Albert R. ('Cubby') Broccoli to bring Ian Fleming's chic spy thrillers to the cinema screen. The result was *Dr No* (1962). This film and its immediate follow-ups, *From Russia With Love* (1963) and *Goldfinger* (1964), all starring Sean Connery, created another cult hero — secret agent 007, James Bond, 'licensed to kill'. The Bond films (which enjoyed continued success in the Seventies and Eighties) were an unbeatable blend of conspicuous consumption, brand-name snobbery, colour-supplement chic, comic-strip sex and violence, and technological gadgetry. Above all, the films were cool, stylish and knowing, and these were the prized characteristics of the Sixties.

The almost simultaneous success of Connery as James Bond and Albert Finney as Tom Jones with American and international audiences helped convince American film companies that a bonanza awaited them in the United Kingdom. Britain had become the music and fashion centre of the world and, with the young, 'Britishness' was in. Overhead costs were lower in Britain than in the United States and there were reserves of acting, directing and technical talent to be tapped too. So American companies began to announce big British production programmes. Paramount, Columbia, Warner Brothers, Universal and the other major studios poured money into their British operations and were joined by leading American independents, including Joseph E. Levine's Embassy Films and Martin Ransohoff's Filmways. The independent British companies which had characterized the 'New Wave' were simply unable to compete.

By 1966, 75 per cent of British first-features were American-financed; in 1967 and 1968 that proportion had risen to 90 per cent. The last gasp of the native industry came with the sale of British Lion, the company which had released the bulk of the 'New Wave' films. Since the National Film Finance Corporation had a controlling interest in it, the government decided to sell off the company in 1964. After an unsavoury scramble by a variety of groups, a consortium headed by Michael Balcon acquired it, aiming to launch a viable programme of film-making independent of the American companies. But the lack of guaranteed circuit release, difficulties in raising capital and boardroom squab-

Bottom left: Susannah York, Hugh Griffith and Albert Finney in Tom Jones. *Below left: Alan Bates, Diane Holgate and Hayley Mills in* Whistle Down the Wind. *Below: James Bond (Sean Connery) encounters Honey (Ursula Andress) on the beach in* Dr No, *the first of the Bond films.*

bles combined to defeat the venture and British Lion never became the projected 'third force' in British film-making.

The 'New Wave' had spent itself by 1964. Swinging London was now the theme, encouraged and financed by the Americans. Sober realism and earnest social comment gave way to fantasy, extravaganza and escapism; black-and-white photography and north country locations were superseded by colour photography and the lure of the metropolis. Stars and directors who had made their names in 'New Wave' films forsook grim industrial landscapes and the pressures of working-class living.

Just as Richardson, Reisz, Anderson and Schlesinger had been the characteristic directors of the 'New Wave', so the celebrants of the new style were Richard Lester, Clive Donner and Michael Winner.

The style of **Richard Lester** (b. 1932), fragmented and breathtakingly fast-moving, was an amalgam of influences from television commercials, comic-strips and Goon Show surrealism. He was at his best in *A Hard Day's Night* (1964) and *The Knack* (1965), both of them photographed in black and white and set in highly stylized, dazzlingly designed decors. *A Hard Day's Night* – a jokey, fictionalised documentary that parodied the *cinéma-vérité* style – enshrined the myth of the decade's greatest cult figures, the Beatles.

Although *A Hard Day's Night* made the American-born Lester's name, the film's bursts of visual virtuosity and its sly, absurdist sense of humour had been foreshadowed two years earlier in a humble low-budget quickie directed by him. This was *It's Trad, Dad!* (1962), made to cash in on a brief vogue for Dixieland jazz and featuring an assortment of then popular bands and singers.

It might not be stretching a point to say that 1965 was 'Lester Year' in the popular cinema. At the Cannes Film Festival, his movie *The Knack*, starring Michael Crawford, Rita Tushingham and Ray Brooks, carried off the top prize; this sharp, affectionate fantasy about young London flat-dwellers had the metropolitan sophistication denied to Lester's previous projects without sacrificing any of their vitality. However rapidly the term may have become a stale cliché, *The Knack* helped put the 'swing' in Swinging London.

Hard on its heels came the second Beatles movie, *Help!*. Filmed in colour and in a variety of locations, this was a considerably more lavish undertaking than its predecessor. It was completely of its time in genially spoofing the gimmick-ridden spy sagas which, as the James Bond craze got into full swing, were then all the rage.

Lester attempted a full-scale Broadway musical adaptation, *A Funny Thing Happened on the Way to the Forum* (1966), before returning to satire with an anti-war comedy, *How I Won the War* (1967). The relative commercial failure of this film and of its immediate successors, *Petulia* (1968) and *The Bed Sitting Room* (1969) severely dented Lester's reputation. However he bounced back with two comic swashbucklers – *The Three Musketeers: the Queen's Diamonds* (1973) and *The Four Musketeers: the Revenge of Milady* (1974). He flopped again with *Royal Flash* (1975) only to redeem himself with *Robin and Marian* (1976), which was sustained by the charm of its stars (Sean Connery and Audrey Hepburn). In the Eighties Lester moved into comic-strip sci-fi with *Superman II* (1980) and *Superman III* (1983).

Nothing But the Best (1964), directed by **Clive Donner** (b. 1926), was the new era's equivalent to *Room at the Top*, redone as a black comedy in lavish colour. This time working-class aspirant Jimmy Brewster (Alan Bates) jokily cons and

Top: *the Beatles on the run from Beatlemania in* A Hard Day's Night. Above: *Michael Crawford, Rita Tushingham and Donal Donelly in* The Knack.

murders his way to the top, in stark contrast to the earnest and painful ascent of Joe Lampton in the earlier film. *Here We Go Round the Mulberry Bush* (1968) took up the theme of *The Knack*, that of an inexperienced youth trying to lose his virginity. But this time the story was filmed in colour, set in Stevenage New Town and told with engaging humour and charm. Rather more in the Sixties mainstream was the frantic knockabout of *What's New Pussycat?* (1965).

Donner's career suffered a severe setback with the failure of *Alfred the Great* (1969). In the doldrums during the Seventies he made a creative comeback in the following decade with the Dickens adaptation *A Christmas Carol* (1984).

The films of **Michael Winner** (b. 1935), particularly *You Must Be Joking* (1965), *The Jokers* and *I'll Never Forget What's-'is-Name* (both 1967) encapsulated the remorselessly flip humour of the day. Winner later carved out a successful American career, cynical violence being the key characteristic of his films, several of which – *Chato's Land, The Mechanic* (both 1972), *Death Wish* (1974) and *Death Wish II* (1982) – starred Charles Bronson.

Above: Christopher Reeve in Superman II. *Right: Paula Prentiss and Peter O'Toole get down to basics in the 'swinging'* What's New, Pussycat?

Above left: Oliver Reed in I'll Never Forget What's-'is-Name. *Above: Jane Asher, Michael Caine and Julia Foster in* Alfie. *Above right: David Hemmings in* Blow-Up.

Two highly popular films that artfully combined elements of the social realism of the British 'New Wave' with the new, mid-Sixties explicitness in matters of sex were both American-backed – Paramount's *Alfie* (1966), directed by Lewis Gilbert, which charted the amatory progress of a cockney Casanova (Michael Caine) and Columbia's *Georgy Girl* (1966), directed by Silvio Narizzano, which concerned the romantic misadventures of an awkward provincial girl (Lynn Redgrave) in London. Less flashy were Ken Loach's documentary-style feature debut *Poor Cow* (1967), about a young, working-class mother (Carol White) with a criminal husband, and Bryan Forbes' *The Whisperers* (1967), a haunting study of loneliness and old age.

European directors produced some distinctive work in British studios. François Truffaut's *Fahrenheit 451* (1966), a science-fiction fantasy about a book-burning society of the future, was accounted one of the less successful efforts. But Antonioni's *Blow-Up* (1966) utilized the contemporary London scene and one of its key icons, the fashion photographer, played by David Hemmings, for a characteristically opaque and multi-layered study of the relationship between illusion and reality. Roman Polanski, the Polish director, also found Britain a congenial setting for his powerful and disturbing visions of sexuality and instability – *Repulsion*

(1965) and *Cul-de-Sac* (1966).

A significant figure, **Joseph Losey** (1909–84), working independently in Britain, remained distanced from both the British 'New Wave' and the 'Swinging Sixties' scene. This expatriate American director had been in England since the early Fifties, a victim of blacklisting by HUAC. At first he wrote scenarios for shorts, directed countless advertising commercials and finally two full-length features – *The Sleeping Tiger* (1954), accredited to the producer Victor Hanbury, and *The Intimate Stranger* (1956), accredited to the obvious pseudonym Joseph Walton (Walton being Losey's other forename).

In 1957 some young British independent producers enabled him to make *Time Without Pity* under his own name. Whereas the two preceding films were notable as sketches or 'roughs' for his later work, *Time Without Pity* was a key film in his development. Although the film is a melodramatic suspense story in which a father (Michael Redgrave) tries to save his son (Alec McCowen) from hanging, it allowed Losey to comment on capital punishment and alcoholism.

Losey based his cinema on the reconciliation of two opposing principles: observation of externals and determined concentration on the most violent and innermost emotional dramatic moments.

His was essentially a cerebral cinema. Although he managed to include emotion and even a straightforward perception of the surrounding physical world, whatever the subject he dealt with – excepting *Modesty Blaise* (1966), a folly which shows no trace of the Losey touch – the predominating factor in his cinema was, at first glance, the 'seriousness' of a man concerned with general concepts – concepts of social critique and even of metaphysics. This does not mean that Losey was at pains to prove theories or propose solutions. For him, as with all the great American directors, a film was essentially the spectacular presentation of character conflicts. Therefore his taste for debating ideas rarely spilled over into the schematic development of the film.

Losey's finest films, all scripted by the playwright Harold Pinter – *The Servant* (1963), the story of a weak, rich young man exploited and humiliated by his manservant, *Accident* (1967), which uncovers a web of frustrations, lies and deceit beneath the superficial tranquility of Oxford academic life, and *The Go-Between* (1971), a lavish adaptation of L.P. Hartley's novel about a lower-middle-class boy's traumatic holiday with a rich, upper-class family – carefully and sensitively probe the repressions and resentments inherent in the British class system. In addition to his mature understanding of complex relationships and painstaking attention to details of decor – which tended to overwhelm his last films, *Mr Klein* (1976), *Don Giovanni* (1980) and *La Truite* (1982, *The Trout*) – Losey will be remembered for revealing the untapped potential of the actors Dirk Bogarde, Stanley Baker and James and Edward Fox.

Another American who chose to base himself in Britain was **Stanley Kubrick** (b. 1928), an obsessive artist with the ambition and daring of a Griffith, Stroheim or Welles. Temperamentally unsuited to working within the Hollywood studio system of the time, he immediately sought creative autonomy, making his first feature, *Fear and Desire* (1953) with money borrowed from relatives. Only on *Spartacus* (1960) did he lack total control and he now disowns the film. In the early Sixties he moved to England to make *Lolita* (1962) and *Dr Strangelove, or How I Learned to Stop Worrying and Love the Bomb* (1964), and remained there. As his power and meticulousness increased, his output slowed down – *2001: A Space Odyssey* (1968), *A Clockwork Orange* (1971), *Barry Lyndon* (1975) and *The Shining* (1980) were long-gestating projects of unusual ambition and technical challenge.

The turning point in Kubrick's career was *2001: A Space Odyssey*. Until then he had maintained a sardonic distance from the human folly he had charted; he had shown himself to be a moralist with a vivid sense of humour that safeguarded him against indulgence. *Lolita*, from Nabokov's novel, is a merciless satire on American matriarchy and philistinism and also an intensely felt study of sexual obsession. *Dr Strangelove* is a brilliantly structured 'nightmare comedy' about nuclear paranoia and political disenchantment. These are Kubrick's most satisfying films, tightly plotted with sharp characterizations and technically unobtrusive. His earlier films are less impressive: *Killer's Kiss* (1955) and *The Killing* (1956) are modest crime pictures; *Paths of Glory* (1957) and *Spartacus* (1960), despite their humanitarian top-dressing, are enthralled with the mechanisms of power, revealing only token concern for the victims of military might and conniving.

After destroying the world at the end of *Dr Strangelove*, Kubrick turned to outer space for the wholly figurative *2001*. The sardonic wit is there but, despite its clever use of classical music to emphasize or undercut the action, it is a chilling film – its human characters made banal by the sophistication and ascetic beauty of technology.

Human feeling in his later films has been virtually banished. *A Clockwork Orange* delineated a society in which art and beauty have been corrupted (for example, the protagonist, played by Malcolm McDowell, uses Beethoven to gear himself up for a bout of 'ultra-violence'). Kubrick offers no critical distance from the ugliness he photographs so imaginatively – only a patronizing disdain.

Traditional institutions – the home, family, trust and leadership – do not work in Kubrick's universe. *A Clockwork Orange* and *Barry Lyndon* show the erosion of civilization; Jack Torrance (Jack Nicholson) in *The Shining* wields an axe rather than a bone (like the apes of *2001*) because it is the heritage of the species. When Torrance freezes to death, he becomes alive again in the past. The timelessness of evil is a concept that has come to haunt Kubrick's work.

In 1975 the critic David Thomson asserted that 'Kubrick is the most significant and ornate dead end in modern cinema'. While an unequivocal endorsement of that view would deny many of Kubrick's achievements, his work since *2001* has shown that those elaborate tracking shots through those extraordinary sets are rapidly heading into a blind alley.

From Boom to Bust   The British boom could not last. The bubble eventually and inevitably burst. Universal poured some £30 million into Britain in three years, 1967–9, producing a dozen films, few of which made any profit at all, and some of which were simply expensive fiascos. Despite the involvement of such directorial talents as Jack Gold, Joseph Losey, Peter Hall, Karel Reisz and even Charlie Chaplin, Universal produced failure after failure: *A Countess From Hong Kong* (1967), *Charlie Bubbles, Work Is a Four Letter Word* (both 1968), *Three Into Two Won't Go* (1969) and, to cap it all, the ludicrously titled *Can Hieronymus Merkin Ever Forget Mercy Humppe and Find True Happiness?* (1969), arguably the last word in self-indulgence. But more conventional film titles also failed at the box-office, including such hugely expensive British-made musicals and epics as *Dr Dolittle* (1967), *Star!* (1968), *Goodbye Mr Chips* (1969), and *Alfred the Great* (1969).

By 1969, almost all the Hollywood film companies were heavily in debt, the taste for 'Britishness' had passed and the films that were making money were such all-American works as *The Graduate* (1967) and *Butch Cassidy and the Sundance Kid* (1969). Their remedy was simple. They pulled out, virtually altogether and virtually all at once. By 1970 only Columbia had any sort of production programme in Britain at all. The British film industry collapsed. Symptomatic of its plight was the rapid dashing of the attempt to fill the vacuum when EMI took over Associated British Pictures in 1969, appointed Bryan Forbes as production chief and announced an ambitious production schedule. But the first three films released almost simultaneously failed and although *The Railway Children* (1970) and *Tales of Beatrix Potter* (1971) proved successful, Bryan Forbes had by then resigned and the experiment had been abandoned. With the Seventies, London stopped swinging, the butterfly culture of the Sixties flew away and, as economic recession, stagnation and unemployment loomed, there was a return to traditional values with the re-election of a Conservative government. The British film industry meanwhile lay flat on its back.

Top to bottom: a foreboding moment from The Servant; Alan Bates as a farmer involved in a secret love-affair, Dominic Guard as his 'postman' in The Go-Between; Stanley Kubrick films the ritualistic rape scene (featuring Adrienne Corri) of A Clockwork Orange.

Top to bottom: Dirk Bogarde, Michael York and Vivien Merchant in Losey's Accident; James Mason as Humbert Humbert, Sue Lyon as his beloved nymphet in Kubrick's Lolita; Jack Nicholson as Torrance, a homicidal maniac prone to hallucinations in The Shining.

The USA

In the USA a new spirit was also abroad by the Sixties; but it manifested itself outside mainstream cinema, in the almost unknown tradition of the American avant-garde. The dominance of Hollywood had been so thoroughgoing as to obscure the existence of this late offshoot of the European experimentalism of the silent era. 'Underground film' was a term the press coined to describe the independent film activity that reached its peak in the Sixties in the United States and particularly in New York. Until the end of the Sixties, most states and cities had direct censorship of all films that were publicly exhibited, and often charged film-makers heavily for viewing and judging their work. This system was not changed until all film censorship was declared unconstitutional by the United States Supreme Court in the late Sixties.

The Underground movement was not united by one type of film-making but by the necessity for film-makers to stand collectively against the harassment of police raids and the mockery of the press. This togetherness provided the very essential social relationships which made up an audience, as well as the physical exchange of film-making equipment and even actors – many film-makers acted in each other's films. Most of them came to film from other art disciplines; the essential motivating force was self-expression and the use of film was another, and new, medium in which to express and explore individual concerns. In this they followed the example of the Dadaists and Surrealists, some of them also film-makers, who had shocked the established European art world of the Twenties.

The new forms, images and content appeared as a sort of rebellion that was confronted by the usual reaction against the new, as well as the more political confrontation with the censorship that made it 'illegal' to have public showings of uncensored films or to charge admission. Working on and showing films had to function much as the 'underground' resistance did during the war – signs and markings on lamp posts, word of mouth in the new film-making community and empty warehouses as cinemas. An additional factor was that after the war years, film material and equipment became cheaper and accessible to more people, so it was suddenly easier for an artist to acquire a camera and make films.

Prior to the many Underground films of the Sixties, there were individual attempts to free cinema expression, notably by **Maya Deren** (1908–61), a dancer, whose first film, *Meshes of the Afternoon* (1943), attempted to express her own personal sense of duality, sometimes by showing two images of herself simultaneously on the screen. Deren also began to lecture and write about the personal or individual film. She hired a small theatre, the Provincetown Playhouse in downtown New York City, to show her films and with the money received from the screenings helped other independent film-makers, including Stan Brakhage and Kenneth Anger.

In 1958 the California film-maker Robert Pike decided to distribute his own films, since no other distributor would handle them. He also distributed the films of other West Coast film-makers, including the Whitney brothers' 'motion graphics', Jordan Belson's new animation, Bruce Conner's film collages made from 'found footage' and Curtis Harrington's filmic drama poems.

These attempts, small as they might seem, laid the groundwork for the most important initiative for the presentation and distribution of independently made films, the formation of the New York Film-Makers Cooperative. This cooperative

Above: Jack Smith's Flaming Creatures *featured an orgy involving transvestite men and a few women. Top: the Pre-Raphaelite face of Maya Deren in her otherwise Surrealistic* Meshes of the Afternoon.

was the gathering together of many film-makers, not only for film production but also to handle the exhibition of their work. For its time, the unity and the collective policy of the New York cooperative were unique, for it not only challenged the censorship laws but also introduced a policy allowing all films, of any content or style, to be supported, screened and distributed without bias. There was no pre-selection policy and the organizational matters and labour were handled by film-makers themselves.

Its moving spirit, **Jonas Mekas** (b. 1922), was a poet, writer and film-maker. His own films were in a free diary-like style: *Circus Notebook* (1966) or *Reminiscences From a Journey to Lithuania* (1972). Mekas also wrote for the widely read and influential newspaper *The Village Voice* and his weekly column, reviewing the new independent films, drew considerable attention to the new film movement. Along with his brother Adolfas, also a film-maker, Jonas Mekas founded in 1955 the first serious magazine to deal with all aspects of cinema, *Film Culture*.

By the Sixties, the break from conventional Hollywood film became clearer. The battle had begun when the Underground films began to be shown by the New York Film-makers Cooperative. One of the most memorable film screenings was the first showing of Jack Smith's *Flaming Creatures* (1963), a film of fantasy in a dream-like transvestite orgy, in a warehouse in downtown Manhattan. *Flaming Creatures*

Left: Kenneth Anger. Top: a sailor's penis turns into a Roman candle in Fireworks. *Above: Scorpio relaxes with a comic-book in* Scorpio Rising.

became so notorious that the United States Customs and the New York police destroyed any prints they could find. Years later it was the same film, brought before the United States Supreme Court, that finally led to the abolition of censorship.

The films of **Kenneth Anger** (b. 1930) inhabited the same arena of homosexual concerns and the same frustrations of a suppressed group as *Flaming Creatures*.

Fireworks (1947), which he made at the age of 17, marked one of the most incandescent debuts of the post-war cinema. It is a psycho-drama – a form introduced to art and film circles in California by Maya Deren – framed as a violent fable of homosexual initiation. Anger himself plays the lead, a young man who dreams of a rough encounter with a group of sailors, and emerges from the nightmare with a longed-for lover in his bed.

It was *Fireworks* which also introduced what was to become Anger's most enduring theme: the relationship between an individual and a group – often phrased as a fantasy of some sort – with the group ultimately being assimilated into the individual by some uniquely cinematic osmosis. This theme reappears in Anger's two best-known films, *Inauguration of the Pleasure Dome* (first version, 1954; second version, 1959; third version, 1966) and *Scorpio Rising* (1963). *Pleasure Dome* is an extended fantasia about a party, where the polysexual host adopts a different persona (and costume) to welcome each of the guests.

Scorpio Rising, on the other hand, begins as a quasi-documentary on a Brooklyn motorcycle gang, and gradually turns into a bizarre Hallowe'en ritual which rhymes hero-worship with blasphemy, and speed with death.

The strong currents of fantasy and eroticism that run through these films come together in Anger's fascination with the 'sex Magick' of the English occultist Aleister Crowley.

Anger is half aesthete, half maker of popular culture. At their best, his films subversively tease out undercurrents in the society around him, while at the same time marking daring advances in film aesthetics. *Scorpio Rising* finds all manner of disquieting implications in its soundtrack of 1962 pop songs and its images of comic-strips, pin-ups and leather fetishism. *Kustom Kar Kommandos* (1965) has the last word on car fetishism with its images of a Californian blond polishing his prized hot-rod with a powder puff.

Although consistently innovative, the films are never obscure: each is designed to work first and foremost as a sensual experience, articulated through colour, surreal juxta-position and, above all, humour.

Film as Film   Most Underground films were made without any assistance from grants or large public funding bodies. Personal expression was allowed in painting and poetry, but in terms of film it was highly criticized as not being properly film at all, much less serious cinematic expression. On another level, film was considered a mass medium used for communication, entertainment and propaganda, and was predominantly used as such. The notion of film in the hands of individuals or political groups presented a threat to the control of any establishment in society.

The films made moved across many terrains. More than thirty years after Maya Deren's *Meshes of the Afternoon* attempted to express the role of a woman in society, Yvonne Rainer continued the theme in her *A Film About a Woman Who . . .* (1975). Another area seriously explored by film-makers was the formal notion of 'film as film', in which the film material itself or the physical presence of film and light became the subject.

Tony Conrad's *The Flicker* (1966) simply consisted of clear and dark frames, arranged in patterns, causing the sensation of a changing but calculated strobe-effect. In a similar vein, in which the metric rhythm becomes an essential ingredient along with light and dark, is the Viennese Peter Kubelka's *Arnulf Rainer* (1960), but instead of a strobing effect, a greater rhythmic beat is created. Kubelka pursued this metric effect mainly through the editing process – Conrad did it through the camera process – and this rhythmic editing is best exemplified in *Unsere Afrikareise* (1966, *Our Trip to Africa*) which uses images rather than pure black-and-white frames. Another scrutiny of the filmic material can be found in *Tom, Tom, the Piper's Son* (1969) by Ken Jacobs, in which an old short film based on the nursery rhyme, made by D.W. Griffith's cameraman Billy Bitzer in 1905, was subjected to a process of reframing, slowing down and other effects, to make up a whole new film in which every primary element of the cinema is explored.

Structuralism was a movement in French thought that emphasized the structure of relationships between parts rather than the parts themselves. *Wavelength* (1967), made by the Canadian **Michael Snow** (b. 1929), was unquestionably most influential in establishing the notion of structuralism in film. The film had the power to embrace filmic time, movement, colour and sound into a single unit, and those same elements were the content of the film itself. Snow, being both a sculptor and a musician, was able to bring into film in a pure state the ingredients of these other arts. Snow continued to explore these concepts in his films *Back and Forth* (1969) and *La Région Centrale* (1971, *The Central Region*), shot on a mountain in Quebec. *Wavelength*, however, remained the most influential; viewers attributed to the film the notion of 'real time' (the length of time a film takes to view being equal to the time in which it was shot) because the film appeared to be a continuous zoom through a large room when, in fact, it was not continuous and often the 'real time' was broken.

Underground Directors   It was the pop artist **Andy Warhol** (b. 1928) who actually used 'real time'. This is best seen in *Empire* (1964), eight hours from dusk to dawn of the Empire State Building in New York.

One of the main radical moves of Warhol's early cinema is a re-investigation of the basics of the film apparatus. No sound and one camera set-up emphasize the apparatus by the very insistence of avoiding editing, avoiding camera and lens movement, avoiding narrative, avoiding synchronous sound to fill in the meaning of the image. Essentially the early work is a cinema of negation. It functions simply and ineluctably to question the illusionist mechanisms of dominant cinema, whilst at the same time forming a different – an avant-garde – cinema of its own.

In normal Hollywood cinema – as in the 'high' art cinema of

Europe – the labour process, the film process, the mechanisms used, are always effaced or suppressed to create the 'suspension of disbelief' that is the basic tenet of such cinema involvement. But Warhol's is a cinema that makes cinema as illusionistic experience problematic, while at the same time dealing materialistically with problems of representation, realism, truth, narrative: showing the mechanics of the whole process, the material qualities of film-making.

By 1965 Warhol had begun working with sound film: in *Kitchen*, with its tableaux shot with static camera for two half-hour segments, the actors have a basic script by Ronald Tavel, who wrote many plays for Warhol's middle-period films (1964–6).

In *The Chelsea Girls* (1966), a $3\frac{1}{2}$ hour double-screen film – probably Warhol's best-known and most important – the usage of the machinery is different from the early period. A set of instructions comes with the film, and the first 5 minutes with sound come up on one screen, while the other reel is being laced onto the projector, then a switch and 25 minutes with sound on the other, and so on. The half-hour reels are all single takes, and within the given duration the camera takes up a position and varies wildly from scene to scene in the way it is operated: constant zooming, focusing, swivelling (both of the camera and the microphone) create an effect of equalizing the weight of the given subject matter and the apparatus which is supposedly communicating this subject matter. A radical requestioning is taking place, even in the way the viewer is here positioned. There is no narrative; when any does occur, it does not last long enough for the viewer to identify or involve him- or herself (even unconsciously) as in a conventional narrative with its seamless flow of images.

The constant emphasis in Warhol's work is on sexuality. Sexuality is always given as produced, as an ideological position, and not as some preordained biological necessity. Stereotypes of femaleness and maleness are always challenged. When a woman overacts, camping it up as Edie does in *Kitchen*, or when a man in drag camps it up in *The Chelsea Girls*, or when in *Women in Revolt* (1972) women and transvestites enact other people's fantasies of what 'the feminine' is, then we, as viewers, are always placed in a position of non-acceptance of the dominant cultural archetypes. These gestures, these ways of speaking, these enactments are always seen as precisely that – enactments.

Since 1968 Paul Morrissey's work – *Flesh* (1968), *Trash* (1970), *Andy Warhol's Flesh for Frankenstein* (1973) and *Andy Warhol's Dracula* (1974) etc – has attempted to cash in on the fame which society accorded to Warhol's persona. Produced by Warhol, they are more or less straightforward high-art films – some, like *Heat* (1972) very funny, others merely pretentious, with a 'Warhol style'. Morrissey films are thus a different genre in all respects.

The distinguishing feature of the American avant-garde film-makers of the Sixties was the range of their individual imagery, output and attitudes. The work of **Stan Brakhage** (b. 1933), made over many years, includes *Dog Star Man* (1964), in which a man chopping down a tree is haunted by visions of his own past, *The Art of Vision* (1965) and a series called *Songs* (completed in 1969) as well as a relentless array of other films dealing with his own life, the world of nature, birth and death, and with the very nature of film and seeing.

For many the Underground became a temporary shelter from the chilly cross-winds blowing outside the Hollywood citadel. They drew sustenance from the alternative strategies of distribution and exhibition it offered, and were warmed by the unaccustomed glow of media attention. Only in the aftermath of the Sixties cultural storm could confident distinctions begin to be drawn between the true 'subterraneans' and those film-makers who were more than relieved to surface.

It is these latter figures, exemplified by John Cassavetes, who are generally omitted from subsequent anthologies of the avant-garde, but whose work of the period remains crucial to an understanding of any wider history of American independent cinema.

The long involvement of **Lionel Rogosin** (b. 1924) with independent cinema goes beyond his own film-making

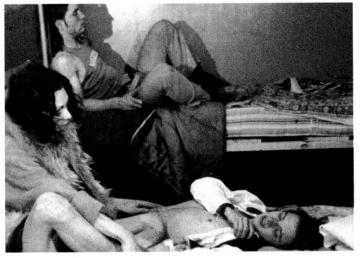

Andy Warhol (top), high priest of camp, is now more famous as a cult hero than as a film-maker. However his creative output has exerted a strong influence on avant-garde artists of all kinds.

Most of his later films, including Flesh *(left),* Trash *(above left) and* Heat *(above), which were all heralded by their Underground notoriety, were directed by Paul Morissey.*

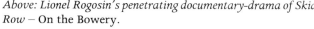

Above: Lionel Rogosin's penetrating documentary-drama of Skid Row – On the Bowery.

Above: Shirley Clarke's stark depiction of black-ghetto life in The Cool World.

practice. His establishment of New York's Bleecker Street Cinema as a showcase for Underground work and his activities in international distribution – initially supplying much material for ventures like the pioneering New Cinema Club in London – combined to sustain the wide interest he had first attracted for alternative American film-making with the prize-winning reception of his *On the Bowery* (1955) at the 1956 Venice Film Festival.

On the Bowery is a gritty, powerful narrative about a drifter's encounters with street-life alcoholism and dereliction in New York's lower depths, and uses non-actors from that actual environment. *Come Back, Africa* (1959) was shot in much the same way, though in large measure clandestinely, among black South Africans oppressed by apartheid. Rogosin's subsequent films have largely focused on the black experience in America, but the growing radicalism of their content – *Black Roots* (1970) traces developing militancy – has been accompanied by an increasing conservatism of form.

By the time the Underground was identified as such, **Joseph Strick** (b. 1923), like Rogosin, was a relative veteran. He had been a wartime US Army Air Force cameraman and in 1948 co-directed an influential short, *Muscle Beach*, with Irving Lerner. Following a spell in television, he joined fellow documentarists Ben Maddow and Sidney Meyers to independently produce and direct *The Savage Eye* (1959). This semi-documentary odyssey through the more sensational, saddening and seedy aspects of American life, as undertaken by a young divorcee (Barbara Baxley), was castigated for its cheap-shot cynicism and condescension.

Strick's subsequent career has consisted largely of adaptations from the more risqué products of the literary avant-garde. A version of Jean Genet's *The Balcony* (1963) was followed by censor-baiting attempts to transpose novels by James Joyce and Henry Miller, but the resultant flurries around the films of *Ulysses* (1967) and *Tropic of Cancer* (1969) centred more on morals than movies.

Some of his tarnished radical credibility was restored by the harrowing short, *Interviews With My Lai Veterans* (1970), shot in the aftermath of the infamous Vietnam War massacre, but after the commercial failure of *Janice* (1973), his contribution to the Seventies road-movie cycle, he again retreated to the modern classics library for a dull adaptation of Joyce's *A Portrait of the Artist as a Young Man* (1977).

Shirley Clarke (b. 1925) successively focused on three areas of, and approaches to, ghetto sub-culture. *The Connection* (1961) is an intriguing film version of Jack Gelber's off-Broadway play about black junkies who, while waiting for their fix in a white 'dude's' loft, kill time by improvising jazz and jive-talk as a caricatured 'documentary' film-maker 'directs' them.

Documentary and fiction again collided creatively in Clarke's next features. *The Cool World* (1963) is a worthy melodrama about adolescent crime and survival in Harlem. *Portrait of Jason* (1967), a Warholian camera-stare at a black homosexual prostitute, documents nothing less than a full-scale 'performance' by its subject, in the process of inventing an entertaining autobiography for himself.

Unable to raise finance for further projects, Clarke bared her frustrations on film when playing herself as a suicidal film-maker in Agnès Varda's *Lions Love* (1969). She then virtually disappeared, only re-emerging on the festival circuit ten years later with a new dance film, *Four Journeys Into Mystic Time*.

The famous still photographer **Robert Frank** (b. 1924) made the first and only authentic 'Beat' film, *Pull My Daisy* (1959). In collaboration with painter Alfred Leslie he adapted a single inconsequential act from Jack Kerouac's unproduced play *The Beat Generation*; cast counter-culture gurus like Allen Ginsberg, Larry Rivers and Gregory Corso opposite a pseudonymous Delphine Seyrig (in her first screen role); and over the resultant laid-back mayhem got Kerouac to record an improvised commentary that includes all the film's dialogue. In its poetic exuberance and incoherence, *Pull My Daisy* is the epitome of frenetic 'cool'.

Frank went solo for his next film, *The Sins of Jesus* (1960), and followed it in 1968 with the chaotically complex *Me and My Brother*, ostensibly a portrait of Julius Orlovsky, the catatonic schizophrenic brother of poet Peter Orlovsky. As much a fantasy as a documentary, the film includes sections where an actor plays Julius, and ends with the real Julius regaining his powers of speech.

In 1972 Frank accompanied the Rolling Stones on an American concert tour, but the footage contained in the resultant feature, *Cocksucker Blues* (1973), was intensely disliked by Mick Jagger who eventually placed legal restraints on its distribution and exhibition.

Above: the midget President and First Lady (centre couple) get advice in Putney Swope.

The novelist **Norman Mailer** (b. 1923) was an even greater celebrity than Frank when he briefly discovered an enthusiasm for film-making. Of his three films the last two, *Beyond the Law* (1968) and *Maidstone* (1970), represent fascinating advertisements for himself' and characteristically betray an egotistically idiosyncratic approach to the medium. Mailer's first effort, *Wild 90* (1968), shot with the help of *cinéma-vérité* pioneer D.A. Pennebaker, was all but unpresentable on account of the poor quality sound recording – a mortal handicap for a film composed around static, mock-mafioso conversations. *Beyond the Law* is similarly – though audibly – wordy: a consequence of the unscripted, improvisatory approach to portraying one night in a New York police precinct. Mailer plays an Irish lieutenant and everyone around him, seemingly, shares a taste for philosophical wit, sharpened insults and casual violence.

The violence which climaxes *Maidstone*, however, is much less casual. The character played by Rip Torn, irritated by the egocentric campaign exploits of Mailer's porno-film-maker-cum-presidential-candidate, mounts a *very* convincing assault with a hammer on the director/star. Torn's action cuts through the self-indulgent play with reality and illusion, and effectively closes Mailer's entertainingly dilettantish film career.

The first film made by **Robert Downey** (b. 1936), *Babo 73* (1964), a vulgar satire on the government of the United Status (sic), broadly marked the course his erratic career would follow. *Chafed Elbows* (1966) prompted Jonas Mekas to make a typically polemical comparison between Downey and Lenny Bruce. However *Putney Swope* (1969) won Downey a wide audience.

Opening with the board of a smart advertising agency accidentally electing their token black member to the chair, and continuing to log the consequent corporate history of 'Truth and Soul Inc', *Putney Swope* offers ample scope for Downey's satire, and the outrageousness escalates as his targets range way beyond consumerism and racism. In the trend for overblown, bad-taste comedy Downey was able to get his foot in the Hollywood door with the *Mad Magazine* presentation of *Up the Academy* (1980).

A career as erratic as Downey's awaited **Jim McBride** (b. 1941) after he produced *David Holzman's Diary* (1967), one of the enduring highlights of the Underground era; a clever, gently subversive and good-humoured gag on 'personal cinema'. David Holzman, apparently both director and star of his own home-movie diary (the film the audience actually watches), is in fact a fictional character, played by actor – and later screenwriter – Kit Carson. But so closely did the character's self-obsession and cinephilia reflect the spirit of the time that many viewers were completely taken in.

Once sown, such doubts as to whether McBride's cinema was truth or lies confused the response to his next film – a straight(ish) documentary on an admittedly absurdist event. *My Girlfriend's Wedding* (1969) was exactly that; the marriage of convenience to a virtual stranger of McBride's former English girlfriend. After this his post-apocalyptic science fiction fantasy *Glen and Randa* (1971) suffered major distribution problems and was little seen. *Hot Times* (1974), a bizarre high-school sex-movie satire much altered by censors and distributors, emerged from amidst several unrealized projects. McBride was responsible for the commentary added at a late stage to Samuel Fuller's 1980 war movie, *The Big Red One*. He finally made a commercial feature in 1983 with *Breathless*, an unhappy remake of Godard's first film, starring Richard Gere.

Of course, there were other film-makers who emerged from this broad Underground grouping whose reputations were made elsewhere.

The explicitly politicized cinemas of Robert Kramer (*Ice*, 1970) and Emile De Antonio (*In the Year of the Pig*, 1969) had Underground roots, while the early work of Brian De Palma – culminating in his first two freewheeling features, *Greetings* (1968) and *Hi, Mom!* (1970) – stands as a concrete link between the Underground and the 'movie brat' generation of Seventies Hollywood.

John Cassavetes (b. 1929), who is still better known as an actor than as a director, has always placed actors and acting at the centre of his film-making concerns. His experimental 16mm feature *Shadows* (1960) grew out of the improvisations at an acting class he taught, and centred on a black family of two brothers and a sister. Their varying skin tones – the younger brother (Ben Carruthers) is light and the girl (Lelia Goldoni) can pass as white – crucially affect their destinies and relationships. Cassavetes then tried his luck as a Hollywood director with the jazz film *Too Late Blues* (1961) and *A Child is Waiting* (1963), about retarded children. He returned to 16mm in *Faces* (1968), exploring the sexual frustrations of the suburban middle class. His wife, Gena Rowlands, played a call girl and has starred in most of his subsequent films. *Husbands* (1970), however, concentrated on macho high jinks as a trio of New York suburbanites (Cassavetes, Ben Gazzara and Peter Falk) extend a post-funeral drinking spree as far as London. *Minnie and Moskowitz* (1971) is a romantic comedy with Rowlands as a museum curator and Seymour Cassel, another Cassavetes regular, as a Los Angeles parking-lot attendant. *A Woman Under the Influence* (1974) traces the nervous breakdown of a working-class wife. *The Killing of a Chinese Bookie* (1976) jokily replays the violent gangster melodramas of Cassavetes' youth with the story of a strip-club owner (Gazzara) forced to repay a debt by murder. *Opening Night* (1977) is a direct if traumatic tribute to the theatre, while *Gloria* (1980) is another gangster melodrama with Rowlands as a tough broad saving a little boy from the Mafia. Cassavetes, after subsidiary parts in *Minnie and Moskowitz* and *Opening Night*, finally took the lead opposite Rowlands in *Love Streams* (1984), though they played brother and sister rather than husband and wife. After doing his own original

Above: beerguts go on proud display during the making of John Cassavetes' bitter-sweet Husbands.

Above: Gena Rowlands as the indomitable protector of a boy (John Adames) from the Mafia in Gloria.

scripts since *Faces*, Cassavetes adapted a play for *Love Streams*, which was also his first return as director to the commercial cinema since *A Child Is Waiting*.

Documentary

New approaches to the problems of film realism were especially evident in the USA in the field of documentary. These came to be collectively known by the French title of *cinéma-vérité*. This term, also applied to the work of Jean Rouch and even Chris Marker, was a literal translation, 'cinema-truth', of the Soviet documentarist Dziga Vertov's newsreel title *Kino-Pravda*, originally intended to suggest a cinematic equivalent or parallel to the national party newspaper *Pravda*, as well as a challenge to the predominant form of the fiction film. The Americans also used the term 'Direct Cinema' to suggest the relatively unmediated quality of what they were trying to achieve, a direct view of real rather than fictitious or enacted events. This required the film-maker to be present when things actually began to happen, taking chances and therefore needing a whole new kind of apparatus.

That apparatus was just beginning to appear: portable tape recorders; faster film stock; lenses that allowed for shooting in natural light; and, an almost overlooked development, the zoom lens. This lens allowed the cameraman to get rid of the turret full of lenses that he formerly had to carry, and to use one that could be adjusted to anything he wanted. It could move objects closer or further away. It could begin to suggest that peculiar flexible quality of the human eye, which combines peripheral vision and the equivalent of telephoto, overlapping and intermingling constantly, unlike the fixed view of a normal camera lens. It meant that a scene could be filmed in real time with successively different eye perceptions, and not require editing afterwards except perhaps for shortening. With the zoom the cameraman could select the material as he shot, in a continuous camera-edited take, without changing the real-time sequence of events.

A film-maker could take a hand-held camera and sound recorder almost anywhere. As people discovered their own subjects and made films about them, the role of the film-

maker began to emerge as no longer the one-way glass through which an audience watched unobserved; the relationship between filmer and filmed began to take a part in the film. Unlike all previous forms of communication, film had the ability to show what had happened at a particular event, even show simultaneous views that no one participant could have seen. The documentary, unlike the narrative film, could show a real world without the necessary pre-arrangements of the screenplay-writer's mind. The documentary was still a work of the imagination. But it was to develop its own 'playwrights' and its own regulations as it moved forward gathering momentum. Often the initial concept was laid down in the camera, intact and in full heat. Editing further intensified it. The visual language of this kind of film was unique in its immediacy.

Among the first of the new documentaries was *Primary* (1960). It was made by *Life* magazine as part of an experiment, soon dropped, to help programme their newly purchased television stations. The film depicted John F. Kennedy and Hubert Humphrey squaring off for the Democratic nomination in the 1960 presidential campaign. It was the first released film of the *Time-Life*/Drew Associates series and was made by Robert Drew, Richard Leacock, Albert Maysles, Terence Macartney-Filgate and D.A. Pennebaker. In *Primary* Kennedy emerges as a reality and not a machine-made politician. Actually, much of *Primary* is the same old commentated voice-over documentary that had been around for years. But such was the vitality of the real Hubert Humphrey arranging his own television show and of Kennedy strategizing in his hotel room that the unfamiliar bits were taken for the whole, and the film was immediately seen as something new. The French called it *cinéma-vérité* when it appeared at the Pagode cinema in Paris.

The new material for this kind of film drama would be events and persons of the real world, who were in principle available free of charge and required no written script. The Drew unit went on to make a large number of such films. Some, including *Yanki No* (1960) about Cuba, went on network television. Others, such as *Eddie* (1960), concerning a racing driver, and *Jane* (1962), a portrait of Jane Fonda in a stage play, had a minor cinema release; and the rest – *David* (1961), *The Chair, Susan Starr* (both 1962) and others – fell into limbo and were syndicated throughout the United States on various television stations.

The idea of a camera operating unobtrusively within a delicate situation seemed impossible. Yet it was discovered that there was almost nowhere that a camera could not be taken, provided the operators were sufficiently sensitive to the complex psychological dynamics involved and the subjects were truly willing – not simply bought or pressured into a mood of camera acceptance.

Showman (1962), an early film by Albert and David Maysles, was a touching but superficial portrait of movie impressario Joseph E. Levine; Levine did not wholeheartedly accept the freedom of the film-makers to depict him and refused permission for the film to be shown in the United States. The Maysles brothers' later *Salesman* (1969) resulted from a year-long engagement with four Bible salesmen, the least successful of whom is particularly featured. *Salesman* demonstrates the greater depth possible when the film-makers can genuinely enter the lives of the protagonists. It was one of the first *cinéma-vérité* films to crash the barrier of cinema distribution and ran for 12 weeks in a New York first-run house.

By then, too, independent distributors had emerged, often motivated by social conscience as much as by profits. Bruce Brown's California surfing film *The Endless Summer* (1966) appeared at a long-established porno house and ran for six months. Documentary was no longer a dirty word when it came to the box-office. Another film produced by Drew Associates, *Crisis: Behind a Presidential Commitment* (1963), which concerned the integration of the University of Alabama

under pressure from President Kennedy and Attorney General Robert Kennedy, despite the opposition of Governor Wallace, had opened at the New York Film Festival in 1963, and might have played in cinemas had not the ABC network decided to run a slightly censored version on the air. This was the last time for a decade that an independently produced political-confrontation film was allowed to go out on network television.

Richard Leacock's incisive portrait of a small Midwestern town agonizing over the birth of quintuplets, *Happy Mother's Day* (1963), was intended for cinemas but it came too early and the film was too short. As a result it has never had much exposure in the United States although it ran on BBC television in Britain. What became apparent by the middle of the Sixties was that the only outlets for independents were cinemas, colleges and film groups. Films made both money and reputation in cinemas; but it was necessary to rid the cinema owners of a long-term bias against 16mm film.

When *Dont Look Back* was completed in 1966 it was shown to every cinema distributor in the United States. It was in black and white, about a singer with then only a cult following, Bob Dylan, and mainly shot in 16mm, so it aroused no interest. A few years later, the audience for rock music had grown enormously; the popular interest in rock helped ensure Richard Leacock's and D.A. Pennebaker's concert film, *Monterey Pop* (1969) and the Maysles Brothers' controversial film of the Rolling Stones' ill-fated Altamont concert, *Gimme Shelter* (1970), wide distribution despite the fact that, like Michael Wadleigh's rock documentary, *Woodstock* (1970), they had been initially shot in 16mm.

The films of **Frederick Wiseman** (b. 1930) are less concerned with entertaining a mass audience. A former

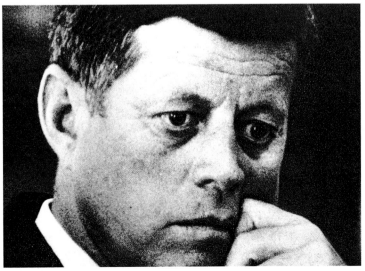

Below left: D. A. Pennebaker, one of the principal pioneers of the cinéma-verité *style in American documentary. Left: Bob Dylan cues the words of his 'Subterranean Homesick Blues' in* Don't Look Back, *Pennebaker's record of the singer's 1965 British tour. Below: President Kennedy is forced to take stock of the situation when his power is challenged by a State Governor in* Crisis.

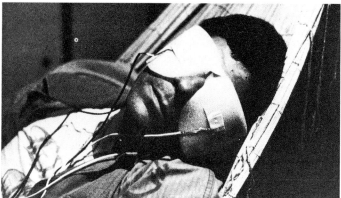

Bottom left: the elderly await a hearing in Welfare. *Left: a scene from Wiseman's* Basic Training, *about the difficult life of regimental draftees in the US army.*

lecturer in law at Boston university, Wiseman produced Shirley Clarke's *The Cool World*, then directed his first, and still his most controversial film, *Titicut Follies* (1967), a devastating study of the Bridgewater, Massachusetts, State Hospital for the Criminally Insane. Wiseman thus embarked on his almost obsessive cycle of documentaries about American institutions – social, military and governmental – which comprises an unparalleled social history (or 'natural history' as he prefers to call it) of America in the Sixties and Seventies. Nowhere in Wiseman's films is there a hint of the lyricism, artiness or didacticism of the traditional documentary. His exclusive aim is to gather information, and to impart it, by the most faithful and unobtrusive means possible. His films are stripped bare of artifice, acting, false situations, narrative, dramatic structure and overt polemic. He uses no commentary, music or sound-effects to distract, influence or manipulate the viewer, and there is not even the visual seduction of colour, but rather a deliberate austerity induced by shooting in a grainy monochrome. They are, as he puts it, voyages of discovery painstakingly structured to present a balanced view of the situation he is investigating, in which the viewer is expected to become an active participant and to draw his or her own conclusions from what is on the screen. Condemnation of an institution may be implicit in the visual

Above: newsreel footage of an anti-war demonstration from Far From Vietnam. *Top: with the aid of drugs a man manages to travel back in time through his own memories in Chris Marker's* La Jetée.

material, as in *Titicut Follies, High School* (1968) or *Basic Training* (1971), but it is not the result of intentional editorializing by the director.

His *Law and Order* (1969) documents the routine activities of the Kansas City Police Department in Missouri and explores the complexity of the police role in American society.

In *Hospital* (1970), *Juvenile Court* (1973) and *Welfare* (1975), there is as much sympathy for the staffs of the institutions under scrutiny – trying to cope with the social ills of their community in the face of bureaucracy and faulty communication – as there is for their patients, charges and clients. *Basic Training* is a possible exception simply by dint of the self-condemnatory nature of what it reveals. It shows civilians being battered into soldiers by the Army Basic Training Program. There are echoes of this theme in *Primate* (1974), about the activities of an animal research centre concerned with primate behaviour (notably aggressive and sexual behaviour) which Derek Malcolm, film critic of the *Guardian*, neatly summarized as being 'essentially about one set of

Above: Borinage – *Ivens' and Storck's disturbing portrait of a Belgian miners' strike. Top: a kaleidoscope of umbrellas – a typically atmospheric, impressionistic shot from Iven's short, silent documentary* Rain.

primates who have power, using it against another who haven't'. By contrast, *Essene* (1972), a moving and sympathetic look at life in a Benedictine monastery, has none of the latent outrage of Wiseman's other documentaries from this period.

As his work has progressed, Wiseman has seemed to take an increasingly dispassionate view of his chosen subject-matter, aligned with an obdurate persistence with repetitive and mundane detail. There are signs of this in *Meat* (1976) – a study of one of America's largest feed lots and packing plants – despite its unflinching abattoir scenes, and even more so in his trio of films about the activities of American military and governmental agencies abroad, *Canal Zone* (1977), *Sinai Field Mission* (1978) and *Manoeuvre* (1979). They are important and revealing, nevertheless, in their unmasking of individual behaviour and their questioning of American social values.

Model (1980) is entertaining in its portrait of the fashion and advertising business and no less interrogatory than his previous work of the value Western society has placed on

itself. With its 'showbiz' concern, it was a prelude to his first feature, *Seraphita's Diary* (1982), virtually a solo performance by a non-professional actress. Wiseman then made his first documentary in colour, *The Store* (1983), a study of the Neiman-Marcus department store in Dallas.

France In the early sixties, the work of a group of documentarists became known as *cinéma-vérité*. A leading pioneer was **Jean Rouch** (b. 1917), a research ethnographer specializing in Africa. In *Chronique d'un Eté* (1961, *Chronicle of a Summer*), made in collaboration with the sociologist Edgar Morin, he turned his attention to the people of Paris. The four cameramen included Michel Brault, whose skill in hand-held camerawork with new lightweight equipment was crucial. Rouch later returned mainly to African themes.

Chris Marker (b. 1921), a radical writer/director and later the founder of a film-making cooperative, was an accomplished political essayist in print as well as on film. He collaborated on a couple of Resnais' documentaries and made his own in many parts of the world. But his best-known film was the unique science-fiction short *La Jetée* (1962, *The Pier*) which consists, except for one shot, entirely of freeze-frames, stills taken from movie film, and tells a compelling story of time travel and impossible love after the nuclear holocaust. Simultaneously Marker was making his somewhat uncharacteristic contribution to the *cinéma-vérité* study of Parisian life in *Le Joli Mai* (1963, *The Lovely Month of May*). Later he initiated and supervised *Loin du Vietnam* (1967, *Far From Vietnam*), a protest against the war by six directors, Godard, Resnais, Agnès Varda, Lelouch, the American William Klein and the veteran Joris Ivens. Marker's Seventies films – *Les Mots Ont un Sens* (1971, Words Have a Meaning) and *Le Fond de l'Air Est Rouge* (1977, The Bottom of the Air Is Red) – were little seen abroad. However, he regained international prominence with *Sans Soleil* (1983, *Sunless*).

The veteran Dutch communist film-maker **Joris Ivens** (b. 1898) had been making documentaries since 1927, though his early experimental films, *De Brug* (1928, *The Bridge*) and *Regen* (1929, *Rain*), had then been thought of as contributions to the realist wing of the avant-garde, studies in form. These led to an invitation from Pudovkin to the Soviet Union, and on a second visit he made *Komsomol* (1932, *Song of Heroes*) with the workers of Magnetogorsk. On his return, he collaborated with Henri Storck on *Borinage* (1932), a militant study of Belgian miners which chrystallized his political views, and *Nieuwe Gronden* (1934, *New Earth*). He went on to America, where left-wing writers sponsored him to go to Spain to make *Spanish Earth* (1937) for the Republican cause, with a commentary written by the novelist Ernest Hemingway. Then came his first trip to China for *The 400 Million* (1939), which attempted to rally support for the Chinese in their struggle against the invading Japanese. Back in the USA he made *Power and the Land* (1940), about electric power being brought to a farming family, and several films for the war effort with John Grierson in Canada and Frank Capra in the USA. But his contribution to the *Why We Fight* series, *Know Your Enemy, Japan* (1945, co-directed with Capra) was uncredited and the film was not distributed since its attack on Japanese imperialism and its treatment of the Emperor as a war criminal did not fit in with US policy for its post-war handling of Japan. Appointed film commissioner for the Dutch East Indies, he soon resigned to make a film, *Indonesia Calling* (1946), which supported the liberation movement against his own government. For much of the Fifties he taught and made films in Eastern Europe. In the early Sixties he was in Cuba and Chile. Then he moved to the major trouble spot, South-east Asia, where he made *Le Ciel, la Terre* (1965, *The Threatening Sky*) about American intervention in the Gulf of Tonking. He was one of the collaborators on *Loin du Vietnam* where his footage was used to link the episodes of other directors. Soon after this he began his collaboration with Marceline Loridan, whose particular expertise was in sound. Their first films were made in Vietnam and Laos, but their major enterprise was a 12-part film about daily life in revolutionary China, *Comment Yukong Déplaça les Montagnes* (1976, *How Yukong Moved the Mountains*), made between 1972 and 1975, mostly using direct sound so that the people of China could speak for themselves (with voice-over translation).

Britain The dominant British documentary traditions established by Grierson in the Thirties, the Crown Film Unit in the Forties and Free Cinema in the Fifties were followed up in the Sixties mostly on television, principally the BBC and Granada, the Manchester-based programme company. Indeed, the most original film-makers, Denis Mitchell and Philip Donnellan, owed much to radio documentary in their use of wildtrack recording and ballads respectively. Mitchell collaborated with the producer Norman Swallow to nurture a generation of young documentarists, several of whom (Michael Apted, John Irvin) later made cinema features. Other film-makers (John Boorman, John Schlesinger, Jack Gold) also cut their teeth on personal documentaries made for TV. Their observational essays had elements in common with American Direct Cinema, but they tended to be less rigorous in method and less concerned with crisis situations. Occasionally they pioneered new techniques – Mitchell's *Sharon*, about faith-healing, and Swallow's *A Wedding on Saturday* (both 1964) were shot on videotape. Increasingly both Mitchell and Donnellan felt the need to intervene personally in their films, to break the mystique of objectivity – for instance, by talking to the subject, more in the manner of French *cinéma-vérité*.

From the mid-Sixties, British television was moving over to colour. By the early Seventies, colour film was fast enough to encourage a revival of fly-on-the-wall techniques, similar to those used by the Americans in the early Sixties, in such BBC-produced series as Paul Watson's *The Family* (1974, dir. Franc Roddam) about the Wilkins family in Reading, and Roger Mills' *Sailor* (1976, prod. John Purdie) which concentrated on the *Ark Royal*. The most committed practitioner was an American resident in Britain, Roger Graef, who made *The Space Between Words* (1972), a five-part series on communications problems in public, working and private life for the BBC. His main interest, like that of Wiseman in America, was in society's institutions. His three-part *Decision* (1976, Granada) examined decision-making in the British Steel Corporation, the council of the London Borough of Hammersmith and a major oil company. The sequel, *Decision: British Communism* (1978), was a three-part study of the British Communist Party. Returning to the BBC, he made his most ambitious series, *Police* (1982), in collaboration with his regular cameraman, Charles Stewart. A detailed portrayal of the Thames Valley police at work, its 11 parts included the controversial *A Complaint of Rape*.

This area of documentary had proved surprisingly resilient, despite frequent criticism of its methods and rationale, mainly on the grounds that the presence of the film-makers changes the situation they are trying to record. However, during the Sixties and even into the Seventies, more critical interest and controversy were concentrated in the areas,

allied to each other, of dramatized documentary and documentary drama, both of which might borrow stylistic devices from *cinéma-vérité*, but only in the interests of fictitious verisimilitude. Both also found their main outlet in television, particularly at the BBC, rather than in cinemas. The dramatized documentary, pioneered by Humphrey Jennings and Ralph Bond, found its best-known practitioners in Ken Russell and Peter Watkins. Russell made arts documentaries, of which *Elgar* (1962) was the most popular, though *Song of Summer* (1968) was much more thoroughgoing in its dramatic re-creation of Delius' last days. Watkins' *Culloden* (1964) was a powerful evocation of the Scottish battle of 1746, and its bloody aftermath, but the claims of the house of Stuart were no longer controversial. By contrast, *The War Game* (1965), which forecast the devastation of a nuclear war and incidentally highlighted the inadequacies of civil defence, was banned from broadcasting by the BBC until 1985, but it was made available to cinemas and also in 16mm for film societies and other organizations, as well as being seen in the USA, where it won an Oscar. Watkins continued his attack on authoritarianism with two commercially unsuccessful features (including *Privilege*, 1967) and then made *Punishment Park* (1971) in the

USA. This depicted an imaginary America of the near future in which dissidents are set an almost impossible endurance test and then killed or imprisoned even if they succeed, their ordeal being recorded by two television crews.

Documentary drama was well over the borderline of fiction and tended, like much of Russell but unlike Watkins, to use professional actors, at least for the main roles. Tony Garnett, as producer of the BBC Wednesday Play series, was able to present several socially conscious films, often directed by Ken Loach, including *Up the Junction* (1964), about the problems of working-class girls in London, and *In Two Minds* (1967), about a schizophrenic girl. Written by David Mercer, *In Two Minds* was later remade by Loach as a cinema film in colour, *Family Life* (1971).

Canada In 1967, Allan King with Dick Lieterman in Toronto made *Warrendale*, an institutional film about emotionally disturbed children which was particularly interesting in that King, an ex-CBC documentarist, broke with the time-honoured tradition of putting all possible information into the commentary and instead opted for a narrationless drama, with much of the medical aspect unexplained. King's *A Married Couple* (1969) dealt with family problems in a direct

Below far left: After her back-street abortion goes wrong, Rube (Geraldine Sherman) is helped by friends Sylvie (Carol White) and Eileen (Vickery Turner) in Up the Junction. *Far left: a terrifying image of the nuclear holocaust from the BBC drama-documentary* The War Game. *Left: War-rendale concerned a treatment centre for young people. Below: Paul Anka with fans in* Lonely Boy.

and forceful manner. One of his most intriguing later productions is an object-lesson in anarchy, *Who's In Charge?* (1983, dir. Sig Gerber). A group of unemployed people were called to a meeting which had no chairman: the *cinéma-vérité* cameras recorded the progressive frustration, anger and breakdown of this un-directed group.

The Canadians were busy all through the Fifties and Sixties – the existence of the National Film Board had given them a big start over other countries in developing documentary imaginatively. In the Sixties the French section of the Board, relatively quiet throughout the earlier years, began to show more and more energy. With works like *Pour la Suite du Monde* (1964, *The Moontrap*) by Michel Brault and Pierre Perrault, a study of Quebec rural life, the French-Canadians began to match in style and passion such earlier *cinéma-vérité* films as Terence Macartney-Filgate's *Blood and Fire* (1958), about the Salvation Army, and *The Back-Breaking Leaf* (1960), about the tobacco harvest in southern Ontario. A forerunner of *Dont Look Back* was Wolf Koenig and Roman Kroitor's *Lonely Boy*, a *cinéma-vérité* portrait of the Canadian pop-singer Paul Anka, made in 1961.

Animation

There are many tributaries flowing into the mainstream of animation. The four basic techniques are based upon drawing on cel (the acetate original) and paper; cut-out and hinged figures; models and puppet figures; and special effects. All these methods involve frame-by-frame shooting, but require different skills in handling, so are usually considered as separate fields.

Feature animation – like most entertainment shorts – uses drawn animation, as this is best suited to production-line techniques. The larger animation studios, now mostly defunct, used a team consisting of director, designer, animators, assistant animators, inbetweeners, tracers, painters and checkers. The drawings were refined stage by stage, with the animator doing the key positions.

This system worked well enough, but the original drawings lost much of their personality by the time they had gone through the process. With the coming of television commercials and series, the deadlines became tighter, and attempts had to be made to speed up the production. Cel animation is also very expensive, so new techniques were devised to make it cheaper: by animating directly onto cel with wax pencil, or photocopying the pencil drawings onto the cel, the tracing stage was cut out. With the short television commercials, it became practical for the team to be brought down to designer, director/animator, painters and a checker, and this is typical of studios today.

Television led to changes in other aspects of animation: it was a quite different market from cinema; it required animation for titles, effects, education, inserts and entertainment fillers; it also created the long children's series; and it proved an outlet for ideas and talents frustrated by the big-studio system. The UPA (United Productions of America) group of ex-Disney animators created a 'TV style' with cartoon figures having large heads and small bodies. Characters were often unsympathetic and certainly not cute. Stories were often satires or comments on society, and particularly the 'confused little man' trying to find meaning and purpose in the world.

The pioneer Ernest Pintoff – actually a musician, not an animator – made films like *The Critic* (1963) and *The Old Man and the Flower* (1962), which allowed the story to unfold rather than using clichéd characters and situations familiar in earlier cartoons. Around this time – the late Fifties – artists from outside animation were becoming aware of the medium. Animation is not restricted to drawings on cel or paper: Norman McLaren had scratched drawings directly onto film, and Alexandre Alexeieff of France had a board of tightly packed pins that enabled pictures to be created by depressing the pins to produce tonal variations from the shadows they cast on the board.

One artist, who was both an accomplished oil painter and animator, made a film that radically changed many people's idea of what animation was all about. The artist was a Canadian, Richard Williams, and the film was *The Little Island* (1958). Williams, who was only 26 at the time it was completed, had tackled a philosophical subject: three men, representing truth, beauty and goodness, share an island. When each tries to dominate, the result is conflict and war, demonstrating that virtues cannot exist absolutely. It showed animation in another application as the ideal medium for conceptual ideas. But in spite of winning great acclaim, it was not a commercial success. Cinema audiences had come to expect animation to be entertainment on a fun level. The time was 1958, and years had to pass before attitudes changed.

Williams worked in London. He was part of a new studio set up to meet the anticipated demand for television commercials. This was TVC (Television Cartoons), the first major company in Britain for television advertising, run by George Dunning, who had formerly worked for both UPA and the National Film Board of Canada. TVC was to play a vital part in establishing British animation.

The development in Britain was helped by some fortuitous events. The large American studios had split up into smaller studios to serve television, education and advertising, leaving them spread over a wide area with little contact between groups. This promoted the individual style that was now becoming dominant, but prevented the interaction that brings new concepts into being. In Britain, such a service industry already existed to serve the film industry as a whole, which was centred around Wardour Street in the heart of London. With the animation studios being in the same area, there was considerable exchange of ideas, further increased by both Americans and Canadians passing through London and working a while. Also, those artists in Europe who saw the potential of television for animation, but had no commercial network of their own, came to London where the genre in the early Sixties took off in a quite spectacular way.

A string of successful experimental films came from TVC with *Wardrobe* (1960), *The Apple* and *The Flying Man* (both 1962) being typical of the output. *The Flying Man*, about a man who can fly and another who envies him, had used the technique developed by Dunning, where figures are painted directly onto cel without the cartoon outline. The texture of the paint strokes makes the figure 'live' and adds visual interest. The technique was not new. Way back in the Twenties, artists like Oscar Fischinger had inspired Disney to use this approach in visualizing music in *Fantasia* (1940). The technique was just not suitable for production-line animation, so had not been pursued, but now the individual artist was able to explore the method more fully, and even Picasso in *Le Mystère Picasso* (1956, *The Picasso Mystery*) animated a painting.

The Sixties saw great scope for progress. The surrealist humour of BBC radio's *The Goon Show* provided the inspiration for, in particular, the work of Bob Godfrey, who created such films as *Do It Yourself Cartoon Kit* (1959), *The Rise and Fall of Emily Sprod* and *Alf, Bill and Fred* (both 1964). Richard Williams set up his own studio and produced commercial shorts like *Love Me, Love Me, Love Me* (1962) – the story of two men, one liked by all and the other universally hated – in which Charles Jenkins started developing optical effects. These were later exploited in credits for films such as *What's New, Pussycat?* (1965) and *Casino Royale* (1967).

The National Film Board of Canada explored philosophical ideas in *Universe* (1960) and *Cosmic Zoom* (1969). Walerian Borowczyk – a Polish animator – experimented with new techniques. He exploded a doll's house with its contents, and made it appear to reassemble itself slowly, frame by frame, in *Renaissance* (1963). Disney was winning Academy Awards with time-lapse photography, showing flowers blooming and the processes of nature speeded up by single-frame shooting. Computer experts like Ken Knowlton of Bell Laboratories were pioneers in computer animation. It did not take long for avant-garde artists like the Whitney brothers and Stan Vanderbeek to see the potential of this medium and explore the patterns and movements that could be created in this way.

By the mid-Sixties, the idea of 'animated films' was a long way from the moralistic cartoons of the past with their good guys and bad guys fighting it out in a series of crazy situations. International festivals just for animation were established. They attracted new audiences and offered a market for films that might never otherwise have been made. Animation itself is perfectly suited for dealing with subjects too incongruous or fantastic for live action, and while zany violence had always been part of animation, now sex started to become a regular theme.

In 1970 Bob Godfrey's vision of a bored office-worker's exhausting sexual daydreams – *Henry 9 till 5* – was given an X certificate, yet was only a mild satire on men's fantasies. It was Ralph Bakshi's *Fritz the Cat* (1972) that brought the subject into the open and made sex, if not respectable, at least established in the medium.

Pop songs – and the Beatles in particular – created one more field for animation to stretch its legs. George Dunning produced *Yellow Submarine* (1968) and introduced a whole range of innovative visual ideas – especially his animation of pop poster design – to feature-film animation.

By the early Seventies another era was beginning to dawn. Cameramen had for a long time been required simply to shoot animation as prepared by the studios. The new automated and computerized cameras, however, enabled effects to be done that were not based on drawn artwork but on existing films. Although these techniques had been around for a long time, in most cases they were too expensive to be used generally. Multiple exposures, back projection and complex mattes all contributed enormously to improving the quality of science-fiction and catastrophe films. *Autobahn* (1979), based on the song by the rock band Kraftwerk, and the space fantasy *Heavy Metal* (1981) are both partly computerized.

Feminism also found a place in animation, expressing subtle viewpoints on feelings and relationships that get scant recognition in most cartoons. Animators like Thalma Goldman and Caroline Leaf were among a number of newcomers in the Seventies to use animation in a very personal way. Leaf, for example, through animating with sand on a lightbox or painting on glass, has achieved a sensitive fluidity in such films as *The Owl Who Married a Goose* (1974) and *The Street* (1976).

Another trend is the seemingly obvious one of animating

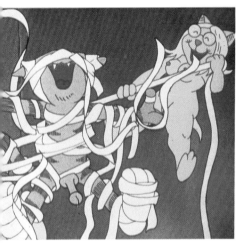

Above: Fritz frolics in the X-rated Fritz the Cat. *Right: the Beatles in the Sea of Holes in* Yellow Submarine. *Far right: an example of Terry Gilliam's work for BBC-TV's* Monty Python's Flying Circus.

famous paintings: this has been done with works by Leonardo da Vinci, Rembrandt, Toulouse Lautrec, Hokusai, and even the complex geometric shapes of M.C. Escher have been given movement to add to the optical illusions he created. The American-born Terry Gilliam employed a kind of animated collage technique, mixing up iconographic images to grotesque, often very funny effect in BBC-TV's *Monty Python's Flying Circus.*

With the dominance of rock music in the Seventies, the pop culture displayed itself in several ways, giving birth to comics, magazines, record-cover designs and, of course, animation. Quite a few of the rock groups originated in art schools, and it had become common to use visual displays of lights and backgrounds of film with live performances. A leading animator in this field is Ian Eames, who has made several films for groups, and even the caricaturist Gerald Scarfe took to animation, his work being the most exciting feature of Alan Parker's *Pink Floyd – The Wall* (1982).

The notion of visualizing music and animating painting had been tried out by Disney in the early Forties. Such ideas had then become commonplace, but no-one had actually repeated or developed the idea of *Fantasia* (1940) as a classical form. However, *Allegro non Troppo*, made in 1976 by Bruno Bozzetto, was a beautifully satirical version along the same theme.

Although entertainment features on the classical fairy stories were still being made, new areas of development were constantly sought. The popular Charlie Brown comic strip *Peanuts* with Snoopy the dog was featured in two films by the Bill Melendez studio. Popular books became animated features – Martin Rosen directed *Watership Down* (1978) and Ralph Bakshi had *The Lord of the Rings* (1979). After *Fritz the Cat*, Bakshi had turned in other directions with *Coon Skin* (1975) – a mixture of live action and animation, dealing with drugs and trafficking – and *Wizards* (1977), a mythological story close in feeling to his *The Lord of the Rings*.

Recent experiments with computers and video effects now offer animators completely new fields to explore. One line of research involves the creation of shape and movement by machine. The 'animator' then becomes the person who operated the machine. This method is particularly suited to computer-generated animation where the shape and move-

ment can be controlled frame by frame and displayed on a screen before being shot on film. Once it is on film it can be coloured in the laboratories and superimposed on itself (or on live-action film) to create 'other world' effects.

Another possibility is to use the computer to control normal animation equipment such as an animation-camera rostrum, articulated models or stands that models are mounted on. Special effects can thus be created that, though possible by normal techniques, would generally take so long or cost so much that it would not be practical. The titles of *Superman, The Movie* (1978) were made on a computer rostrum, and many of the special effects using spacecraft in *Star Wars* (1977) were shot on a computer-controlled model stand.

The third area of innovation is with computer-aided animation, where the computer is integrated with normal techniques. One example is with electronic colouring. A cartoon drawn in black and white lines is transferred to video, enabling an artist to view it on a television monitor. The artist points an electronic pen to an area – such as the sky – and selects the colour from a palette on the screen. The area is immediately coloured in.

The computer can also help the artist check timing and movement by recording directly onto video tape so that the images can be played back immediately against the soundtrack. If it is wrong, the artist simply erases it and tries again. A very advanced system developed in Japan even allows the drawings to be played back at any speed, reversed and edited. With such a machine, the artist can produce long cycles (like walks and runs) with only a few drawings by letting the machine do all the repeats. By being able to rehearse the animation sequence in rough drawings first, it is possible for a complete film to be worked out and checked before the first frame is shot on film.

Animation was once synonymous with crazy cartoons. It now means just about anything that is recorded frame by frame, and that includes special effects in science-fiction films, horror movies, disaster films and the whole range of fantasy films. The combined effect of film, video and computer techniques opens up realms that are only just being touched upon. Techniques have caught up with the imagination. It now only needs imaginative people to use them.

CHAPTER 16
Hollywood in the Sixties

The Sixties was a decade of immense change for the American cinema as it was for American society as a whole. After the time-marking of the Fifties, when the widespread post-war prosperity combined with fear of the blacklist to produce a period of relative artistic stagnation, the Sixties was a time of revolution in Hollywood. Only in the Twenties, with the transition from silent movies to sound and all the problems consequent upon that change, was there havoc comparable to that wreaked in Hollywood during the Sixties.

Television's rising importance had led Hollywood to experiment with various forms of wide-screen projection in order to combat the domestic competition but the nature of the movies had not significantly altered. In the early Sixties Doris Day was America's Sweetheart, riding high on the crest of a wave of films such as *Pillow Talk* (1959), *Lover Come Back* (1961) and *That Touch of Mink* (1962). By the end of the decade Day's star was firmly eclipsed by the new style of violent, sensational, youth-orientated movies represented by *Easy Rider* and *The Wild Bunch* (both 1969).

One element that hastened the inevitable change in movieland was the death or retirement of so many key figures from the golden years of the American film industry. Two of the Marx Brothers, Chico and Harpo, died. So did Clark Gable, Marilyn Monroe, Charles Laughton, Judy Holliday, Buster Keaton and Judy Garland. Producers or directors Michael Curtiz, Jerry Wald, David O. Selznick, Robert Rossen, Leo McCarey and Josef von Sternberg all died within a few years of each other; Louis B. Mayer had died back in 1957. Jack L. Warner made only a few productions after buying the stage success *My Fair Lady* for screen adaptation. However, Darryl F. Zanuck achieved an important success as an independent producer with *The Longest Day* (1962) and then took over 20th Century-Fox again, running it with his son Richard until increasing losses at the end of the decade forced Richard's resignation in 1970 and Zanuck's own in 1971.

Sam Goldwyn no longer made films; and MGM, under the guidance of Kirk Kerkorian, appeared markedly less successful in the late Sixties; Universal headed for television and the tourist industry; Paramount was cheaply bought by the conglomerate Gulf + Western in 1966; Warner Brothers was absorbed into the Kinney group. United Artists, which started life as an attempt by four independent film-makers (Mary Pickford, Douglas Fairbanks Sr, Charles Chaplin and D.W. Griffith) to free themselves from the shackles of studio

Left: Vincent Price as the psychopathic Roderick, with Myrna Fahey in Fall of the House of Usher, *the first of the Edgar Allan Poe series of gothic horror movies produced by Roger Corman.*

interference, ironically found new salvation under the corporate umbrella of Transamerica Corporation. The jailers had relieved the inmates of control of the asylum.

Blockbusters

Indeed, perhaps the kindest way to approach the shambling, dinosaur-like movies of the Sixties is with a clear understanding that the industry that produced them had gone mad. Hollywood was on a spending spree – investing twice as much each year as it could possibly hope to get back from the box-office worldwide. Cold-eyed bankers saw the seeds of destruction, but the studios could not afford to pause. They owed too much money and made too little profit.

The logic of making supermovies – of spending $12 million on a thin slapstick comedy such as Blake Edwards' *The Great Race* (1965) at Warners, for example – was threefold. Big movies, at big ticket prices, might earn big money fast. Sometimes the theory worked: for instance, MGM stayed afloat in the late Sixties largely on the high earnings of David Lean's *Doctor Zhivago* (1965) and the reissue profits from *Gone With the Wind* (1939). Big movies at high ticket prices, with deals that made cinemas send back a high proportion of their take, would probably bring back a big cash flow, so staving off problems with the banks – at least there would be money passing through which, with a little creative accounting, could be represented as a real business asset. And big movies were supposed to have international appeal – bloody wartime action, broad comedy, parades of stars, a sense of gloss and luxury.

Other, more general factors pushed the studios towards making megamovies. It was easier to borrow money for a relatively accessible, explainable project than for smaller stories which bankers might not understand; it was easier to borrow to make another big gamble than to find the cash to service existing debt. The studios, to stay credible, had to keep borrowing – and the big movies were often the easiest way.

During this period, Hollywood, for the first time in its history, was drawing more than half of its income from outside America. Movies for all the globe, so Hollywood thought, were the necessary product in the Sixties.

Their international character was partly a question of markets and partly a matter of production costs. The moguls had seen labour costs in California rise alarmingly, and they felt they could drive a harder, better bargain outside America. They could also use the movie subsidies in more than one country. This logic led to such films as *Cleopatra* (1963): by 1964 it was lying fourth in the list of America's all-time top-grossing movies, and it was still nowhere near turning a penny of profit – an international, glossy, money-spinning disaster.

The success of *Around the World in 80 Days* (1956), produced by Mike Todd, helped convince Hollywood, not only that big movies spelt big business, but that speculation on a grand scale resulted in accumulation on an even grander one. When the movie opened, Todd's cheques were bouncing in spectacular fashion. Much of United Artists' investment went to settle payrolls on which Todd was about to default. Once released, though, the movie coined money. Its production costs were around $6 million, twice the original budget – it is difficult, more with Todd even than with other producers, to be exact. By 1968, that $6 million had earned United Artists $23 million in American rentals and $18 million in the rest of the world.

Darryl F. Zanuck, making his black-and-white *The Longest Day* (1962), was asked by his staff how the public would know the movie was not a newsreel. 'We'll have a star,' he said, 'in every reel.' Routine products such as *The VIPs* (1963) and *The Yellow Rolls Royce* (1964), both well-crafted and sluggish movies by Anthony Asquith that belied the high intelligence of his *Orders to Kill* (1958), were among the top ten movies of their respective years when they appeared in America, and sold largely on their stellar casts. The formula owes something to such earlier MGM star vehicles as *Grand Hotel* (1932) and Cukor's *Dinner at Eight* (1933), but with this twist: stars were no longer required to act, but were introduced into a film like bright, shiny sixpences in a stodgy, indigestible Christmas pudding.

High budgets and production values made commercial sense only when they were entrusted to a director with a geuine fascination with epic themes, such as David Lean. His *The Bridge on the River Kwai* (1957) was hugely successful, both critically and commercially; his *Lawrence of Arabia* (1962), which involved ten months' shooting in the Jordanian desert and nineteen months of work for its star Peter O'Toole, was also hugely successful. *The Bridge on the River Kwai* was shot on difficult locations, with the centrally important bridge built simply to be blown up and a train hauled across jungle terrain for its starring role. At the time such devices seemed extravagant, and yet the total production cost was barely $3 million; the film was sold to US television in 1966 for $2 million, after its highly profitable career in cinemas.

Lean's triumph – although there is room for debate about its quality – was *Doctor Zhivago*, shot on location in Spain at an approximate cost of $15 million. The film's resounding success was the salvation of MGM during its most difficult years.

Less distinguished than Lean was Ken Annakin, journeyman director of *Those Magnificent Men in Their Flying Machines* (1965) and *Quei Temerari Sulle Loro Pazze Acatenate Scalcinate Carriole* (1969, *Monte Carlo or Bust!*), known in America, inevitably, as *Those Daring Young Men in Their Jaunty Jalopies*. Annakin's solid, professional, characterless output was utterly without distinguishing themes or viewpoint. Such thin entertainments were successful because Annakin allowed his star turns to perform effectively. The only characterization permitted was casting according to type: a Germanic villain, played by Gert Fröbe, brought overtones of every other villain Fröbe had ever played; a cad played by Terry-Thomas was exactly like every other Terry-Thomas cad. Nonetheless, enthusiastically backed by Darryl F. Zanuck, Annakin's films did make money.

Stanley Kramer's *It's a Mad, Mad, Mad, Mad World* (1963) was less successful. Kramer had assembled stars from the silent era and later, all for the purpose of denouncing human greed. The result made much less money than expected.

The megamovies left a legacy. Although the financial logic of the early specimens had involved the availability of subsidies in certain countries, and varied sources of finance, encouraging co-productions on a grand scale, one of the most successful was *Airport* (1970), made by a full-time studio employee, Jennings Lang, one-time head of the talent agency MCA's television film company and later a major figure at the MCA-owned Universal studios. When it appeared, *Airport* seemed heavy-handed, literal, old-fashioned. With *Airport*, Lang revived the old-style narrative movie, creating a hoax drama full of easily recognizable, cardboard characters.

There were danger signs in all this megalomania. Little movies grossed almost as much as the big ones: *Easy Rider* (1969) in its first year almost squelched *Chitty Chitty Bang Bang* (1968) in the American top ten; Mark Rydell's botched version of a D.H. Lawrence story *The Fox* (1967) almost matched *2001: A Space Odyssey* (1968) at the box-office. The profits, of course, except with such a long-lived classic as *2001: A Space Odyssey*, were infinitely greater from the smaller movies. Hollywood's sense of spectacle seemed to be eroding its sense for business.

Spectacle was hardly likely to be a useful response to the odd turbulences of the late Sixties, when the heroic and mass-produced stereotypes of warfare turned into the angry music-hall routines of Richard Attenborough's *Oh! What a Lovely War* (1969) and Richard Lester's black comedy *How I Won the*

Top, left to right: MGM was saved from bankruptcy by Dr Zhivago, *made by David Lean, one of the most 'bankable' directors of the Sixties; a music-hall singer (Maggie Smith) entices young men to take the King's shilling and enlist for World War I in* Oh! What a Lovely War, *Britain's contribution to Sixties spectacle; Darryl F. Zanuck, who ran 20th Century-Fox almost single-handedly for over 20 years; Robert Mitchum (as Brigadier-General Norman Cota) was just one of the stars of Zanuck's* The Longest Day. *Above: in Corman's* The Trip, *Paul Groves (Peter Fonda), dissatisfied with his work and marriage, tries the drug LSD with mixed results. Above left: Despite a glorious Queen of Egypt (Elizabeth Taylor), and despite the fact that it was one of the highest grossing movies at the time,* Cleopatra *turned into a $40 million disaster that nearly brought 20th Century-Fox to its knees.*

War (1967); or when drug experience became commercial in such movies as *The Trip* (1967); or when political unrest required some reflection, some resonance in movies.

By that time the Hollywood studios owed too much money to listen to the world. Instead, they listened to the banks — who dreamed, as did the moguls, of the great hit that would heal all the fundamental problems of the movie industry. The great hit never came; the problems took over; Hollywood changed, and the violence of the change was largely due to the ill-founded optimism that megamovies had generated for a few mad, mad years in the mid-Sixties.

The Violent Years

From 1960's *Psycho* and *Spartacus* to 1969's *The Wild Bunch* and *Easy Rider*, the Sixties can be regarded as the period when screen violence not only became respectable but even 'art'. Contemporary viewers of 1960 would simply have been shocked by the brutal shower murder in Hitchcock's *Psycho*. A few years later various critics exhorted audiences to appreciate the director's technical virtuosity in creating this sequence — and to treat as a side issue the ethical and moral implications of scenes of violence, even sexual violence. However, *Psycho*'s shower murder lasted less than a minute; violent death in Peckinpah's *The Wild Bunch* was attenuated into a grisly combination of underwater ballet and 'action replay' by the technically obvious device of showing it in slow motion.

Peckinpah claimed that the long-drawn-out deaths in his film were supposed to 'make violence so repulsive as to turn people against it'. Other Sixties film-makers argued that a high degree of violence was merely what their movies' subject-matter demanded – most notably, in war films such as Fuller's *Merrill's Marauders* (1962), Aldrich's *The Dirty Dozen* (1967), and in such critiques of the war picture as Godard's *Les Carabiniers* (1963, *The Soldiers*) and Peter Watkins' TV film *Culloden* (shown by the BBC in 1964).

Crucial to the new trend for violent films were the action-packed 'spaghetti' Westerns and the James Bond thrillers, both of which appealed to large international audiences. Their jokey, 'life is cheap' approach to killing showed the stylizing influence of Japanese cinema, and specifically the films of director Akira Kurosawa and actor Toshiro Mifune: *Shichinin no Samurai* (1954, *Seven Samurai*), *Kumonosu-Jo* (1957, *Throne of Blood*), *Yojimbo* (1961) and *Tsubaki Sanjuro* (1961, *Sanjuro*). The heady brew of international influences at work in one of Hollywood's most violent and most profitable late-Sixties movies, *Bonnie and Clyde* (1967), was particularly complex. It involved the French *nouvelle vague*'s inventive use of camera angles, European cinema's fad for soft-focus colour photography and romantic nostalgia, Hollywood's own special gift for wisecracks and showmanship (particularly evident in the glamorous casting of Faye Dunaway and Warren Beatty) and a helping of Kurosawa (in the film's slow-motion killings).

As far back as 1954, the critic Robert Warshow had noted: 'The two most successful creations of American cinema are the gangster and the Westerner: men with guns.' When a few real-life robberies of the late Sixties seemed to have been modelled closely on those in *Bonnie and Clyde*, the question was again raised as to how seriously screen violence could affect public behaviour. Subsequent studies of mass responses to violence, most of which have concentrated on TV, have suggested that a great deal depends on the extent to which audiences identify with a violent character, whether a

gangster or (a particularly common trend in movies from the Sixties onwards) a law enforcer. In the Sixties, for the first time, film audiences were exposed to extremely attractive heroes, whose status was bound up with a special ability to kill people, such as the 'spaghetti' Western hero The Man With No Name and James Bond, 'licensed to kill'.

As the decade progressed, so its political mood became darker, with Western society increasingly split into factions and pressure groups, often violently opposed. The Establishment's opposition to the younger generation and vice versa was manifested by the violence inherent in such hits as *Wild in the Streets, If....* (both 1968), *Easy Rider* and *Joe* (1970). With violence increasingly accepted as a fact of everyday life, films like *In Cold Blood, Targets* (both 1967) and *The Boston Strangler* (1968) belatedly attempted to discover the motivations behind particularly nasty mass murders. But whether its causes were psychological or socio-political, there was no denying that violence became big box-office in the Sixties. By the next decade it would become virtually an essential ingredient for commercial success.

The Alternative Hollywood

There could be no greater contrast between the history of Hollywood's major studios during the Sixties and that of AIP (American International Pictures). Throughout the decade it was run by Samuel Z. Arkoff and James H. Nicholson, as it had been since its inception in 1954. Their policy was also unchanging: cheaply produced double-feature bills (an average total of about twenty movies per year) made specifically for the ever-buoyant market of independent and drive-in cinemas that were unable to show major studio output, which went to the circuit cinemas in towns. They were also aimed squarely at the 16-25 age group which made up 80 per cent of the filmgoing population. AIP followed fashions, occasionally created them and exploited any subject that was even remotely filmable. The only difference from the Fifties was that, with eventual sales to television in mind, the movies were now all in colour.

The black-and-white teenage-delinquent dramas of the late Fifties were replaced by the plastic colourfulness of the Beach Party movies, inspired by the musical success on records of the Beach Boys and Jan and Dean. After the establishing formula of *Beach Party* (1963) itself, only the titles changed in the eight movies that followed. Whether they were called *Bikini Beach* (1964), *How to Stuff a Wild Bikini* (1965) or *Beach Blanket Bingo* (1965), the formula was the same: sun, sea, sand and surfing; no drinking, no smoking and no real love-making; antiseptic heroes and heroines (usually played by Frankie Avalon and Annette Funicello); adults such as Robert Cummings and Basil Rathbone always treated as figures of fun; and the depiction of a life-style that seemed to be totally dedicated to all-day surfing and all-night parties.

By the late Sixties, AIP was depicting a more realistic, although still fantasized, life-style. American involvement in Vietnam dominated the air-waves and newspapers, and it was once again a time when young people were disillusioned. But it was no longer just a question of broken families leading to juvenile delinquency. There was now a mood of open warfare against the whole of established society, and it was organized on a grand scale. AIP reflected the growth of this rebellion and of what was to become known as the alternative society. *The Wild Angels* (1966) was the precursor of a seemingly endless series of motorbike-gang movies. The drug culture which became an accepted part of the alternative society was explored in *The Trip* and *Maryjane* (1968). The arrival of the hippies of Haight-Ashbury and the dawn of Flower Power in San Francisco was celebrated in *Psych-Out* (1968). In the ultimate youth fantasy *Wild in the Streets*, a millionaire pop star and drug pusher actually becomes President of the United States after the voting age is lowered to 14. Yet, to their credit, AIP never over-exploited the violence and drug themes of

these movies, although this was perhaps due as much to Samuel Z. Arkoff's business acumen as to any degree of social conscience. After the shootings at Kent State University, in which real students were killed by real national guardsmen, AIP withdrew from making youth-revolt pictures. Arkoff thought that the subject had become much too serious to be used simply as entertainment. This same acknowledgement of public outcry had earlier in the decade resulted in AIP's most

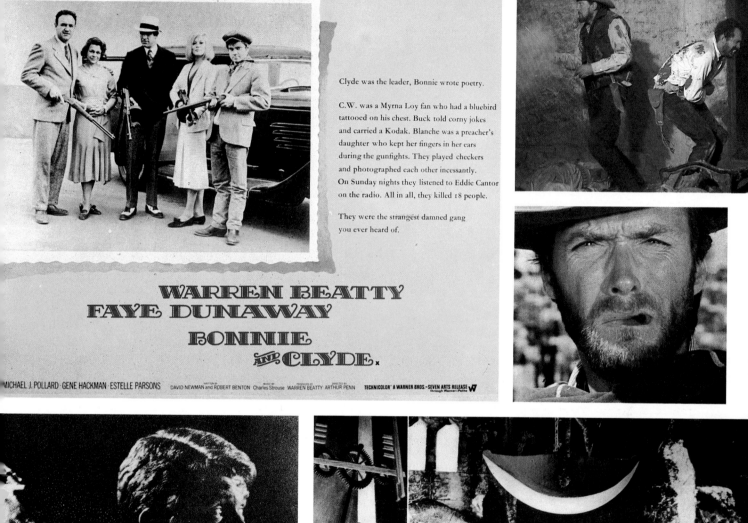

Clyde was the leader, Bonnie wrote poetry.

C.W. was a Myrna Loy fan who had a bluebird tattooed on his chest. Buck told corny jokes and carried a Kodak. Blanche was a preacher's daughter who kept her fingers in her ears during the gunfights. They played checkers and photographed each other incessantly. On Sunday nights they listened to Eddie Cantor on the radio. All in all, they killed 18 people.

They were the strangest damned gang you ever heard of.

**WARREN BEATTY
FAYE DUNAWAY
BONNIE and CLYDE**

MICHAEL J. POLLARD · GENE HACKMAN · ESTELLE PARSONS · DAVID NEWMAN and ROBERT BENTON · Charles Strouse · WARREN BEATTY · ARTHUR PENN · TECHNICOLOR® A WARNER BROS.-SEVEN ARTS RELEASE

Top: setting the vogue for late-Sixties violence, Bonnie and Clyde *opened to critical indignation and audience acclaim. Top right: the bloody end of Sam Peckinpah's* The Wild Bunch. *Above right: chief icon of the spaghetti Western – Clint Eastwood as the 'good' in* The Good, the Bad and the Ugly. *Right: Roger Corman came to prominence with his Edgar Allan Poe adaptations for AIP. He was subsequently able to foster younger talent. Above: Peter Bogdanovich, a critic and Corman disciple, directed* Targets.

AMERICAN INTERNATIONAL PRESENTS **EDGAR ALLAN POE'S THE PIT AND THE PENDULUM** IN PANAVISION AND COLOR

STARRING **VINCENT PRICE · JOHN KERR · BARBARA STEELE · LUANA ANDERS** · SCREENPLAY BY **RICHARD MATHESON** · PRODUCED AND DIRECTED BY **ROGER CORMAN** · MUSIC BY **LES BAXTER**

enduring contributions to the list of outstanding independent productions of the Sixties, Roger Corman's Edgar Allan Poe cycle. The company had received criticism about the cheap exploitation of sex and violence in such films, now seemingly harmless, as *I Was a Teenage Werewolf* (1957), concerning an aggressive youth subjected to dangerous experiments, and *The Cool and the Crazy* (1958), which examined the drugs problem in high schools. Arkoff's answer was a series of intelligent, literate and almost-respectable movies based on classics of American literature – the short stories of Edgar Allen Poe. The first, *Fall of the House of Usher* (1960), became AIP's highest-grossing picture up to that time and resulted in further Poe adapations – *The Pit and the Pendulum* (1961), *The Masque of the Red Death* and *The Tomb of Ligeia* (both produced in England in 1964). The films established the director Roger Corman as a major film-maker and made a popular star of Vincent Price. Arkoff had no doubt as to

why the Poe adaptations proved so lastingly popular with young audiences: 'They go on the basis that they're campy – campy fun.'

Corman (b. 1926) joined AIP in the mid-Fifties and became their leading director in the following decade. However his importance in Hollywood history goes beyond his considerable talents as a film-maker. Just as important as the 23 movies he directed in the Sixties and the many he subsequently produced is what has become known as 'The Corman Connection'. This consists of a group of film-makers, later to make important contributions to American cinema, whose earliest work is represented in the credits of undistinguished AIP productions. Thomas Colchart, for example, was listed as the director of *Battle Beyond the Sun* (1963). In fact, this was *Nebo Zobyot* (1959, The Sky Calls), a Russian space movie Americanized by dubbing and the shooting of additional scenes; and 'Thomas Colchart' was actually Francis

Below: J. R. (Harvey Keitel), prevented by his Catholic conscience from making love to his girlfriend, has a dream about an imaginary nude in Who's That Knocking at My Door?

Below: Jack Nicholson as Bobby Dupea, a disaffected musician turned drifter in Five Easy Pieces. *Bottom: love among the sand dunes of Death Valley in* Zabriskie Point.

Above: murderous zombies lay siege to a house in Night of the Living Dead.

Ford Coppola, a 24-year-old UCLA graduate who served his apprenticeship with Corman as sound man, dialogue coach, assistant director and second-unit director. His reward was *Dementia 13* (1963), a horror movie he made in Ireland using the resources and left-overs of Corman's own *The Young Racers* (1963). Others who learned their craft at AIP had their enthusiasm similarly rewarded.

A notable example, Monte Hellman, had already made his directorial debut in 1959 with the Corman-produced *Beast From Haunted Cave*; but by 1963 he was still helping Corman to shoot *The Terror* in three days by taking charge of second-unit filming. He was more than adequately rewarded three years later when Corman produced the two movies on which Hellman's high, although not widespread, reputation is largely based, *The Shooting* and *Ride in the Whirlwind* (both 1966), two rough, violent, mythic Westerns shot simultaneously in the Utah desert and featuring Jack Nicholson, until

Below: Easy Rider, *a low-budget motorcycle movie, was the first of a long line of 'road' films. Bottom: students, sex and revolution in* The Strawberry Statement.

then an undistinguished Corman juvenile lead. They have been little seen, unlike *Targets* (1967); this was the first movie directed by the critic Peter Bogdanovich, who reputedly had fuelled the motorbikes on Corman's *The Wild Angels*. Other important figures who gained useful experience with Corman were the directors Martin Scorsese, Dennis Hopper, John Sayles, Jonathan Demme, Stephanie Rothman, Paul Bartel and Jonathan Kaplan, while, in addition to Jack Nicholson, the list of actors who first came to public notice in his films includes Bruce Dern, Robert De Niro, Ellen Burstyn, Peter Fonda and David Carradine.

If the combination of Roger Corman and AIP was the most successful of the Sixties, it was not without competitors. Joe Solomon's Fanfare Corporation, for example, was modelled on much the same lines as AIP; its huge success with *Hell's Angels on Wheels* (1967) not only furthered the career of the director Richard Rush, the star Jack Nicholson and the cameraman Laszlo Kovacs, but also pointed directly ahead to *Easy Rider*.

There were stirrings, too, on a truly independent level. Brian De Palma was planning to become the American equivalent of Jean-Luc Godard with mixtures of political documentary, improvisation and irreverence such as the commercially successful *Greetings* (1968), a portrait of the young, aware and liberated Vietnam generation, and *The Wedding Party* (1967), which was co-directed with Cynthia Munroe and Wilford Leach and featured Jill Clayburgh and Robert De Niro in a story of a couple who marry after doubts and hesitations. At about the same time, Martin Scorsese was struggling to complete his first feature, *Who's That Knocking at My Door?* (1968), similarly influenced by *nouvelle vague* techniques and portraying a young man's growing up in New York's Little Italy. In deepest Pittsburgh, George A. Romero had completed his tale of menacing resurrection, *Night of the Living Dead* (1968), financed by a local advertising agency. Yet this most influential of modern horror movies was described by the trade paper *Variety* at the time as 'amateurism of the first order'. Nevertheless, the so-called amateurs were poised to take over Hollywood itself, just as Romero's zombies took over in his memorably scary movie.

The clearest indication of that can be seen in the early history of Raybert Productions, set up by independent entrepreneur Bert Schneider and writer/producer Bob Rafelson in 1965 to produce a television series that was inspired by the example of the Beatles and the zany, almost surrealist style that Richard Lester had created in their first feature film *A Hard Day's Night* (1964). The totally manufactured group featured in the series was the Monkees, who were a great success in their own right, but of greater importance is that of the first 32 of their shows, 29 were made by new directors, including Rafelson himself. This success was also the base on which Raybert launched into feature-film production, at first with the heavily satirical *Head* (1968), directed by Rafelson, written by Jack Nicholson and starring the Monkees in a series of film parodies in which they ridiculed themselves. Then came *Easy Rider*, and the floodgates opened.

Easy Rider cost $400,000 and earned $19 million in North America alone for Columbia, who bought it for distribution. Its success gave rise to a range of picaresque 'road films', such as Monte Hellman's *Two-Lane Blacktop*, Richard Sarafian's *Vanishing Point* (both 1971), Jerry Schatzberg's *Scarecrow* and Joseph Strick's *Janice* (both 1973). Rafelson and Schneider formed BBS Productions with aid from Columbia to make feature films. As a result, such movies as Rafelson's *Five Easy*

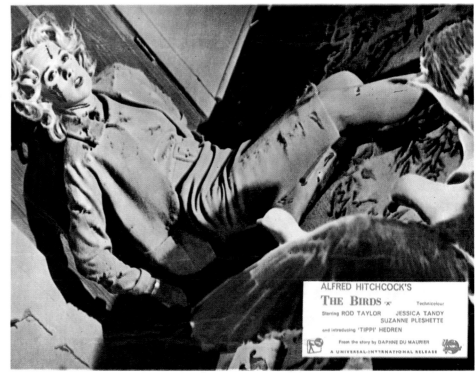

Pieces (1970) and Bogdanovich's *The Last Picture Show* (1971) would soon be forming an intelligent and talent-filled base for the Seventies, and one that would eventually create a whole new audience for Hollywood movies.

Yet all this seemed very distant in 1970, when the major studios were simply reacting to the great success of *Easy Rider* in the traditional, and equally traditionally disastrous, way of emulating their independent teachers. Columbia was employing Richard Rush for a satirical look at campus unrest in *Getting Straight*, while MGM was treating the same subject seriously in *The Strawberry Statement* and trying to understand the failure of Michelangelo Antonioni's curious contribution to the rebellious-youth cycle *Zabriskie Point* (all three 1970). Dennis Hopper, the director of *Easy Rider*, was in Peru making *The Last Movie* (1971) for Universal, who never gave it a general release.

Only slowly would the major studios begin to understand that, as the independent producers of the Sixties had so clearly shown, the key to survival was new talent working in a new structure on original and not necessarily expensive projects that with intelligent marketing could create a new movie-going audience.

Key Directors

During the Sixties, Hollywood struggled to keep abreast of the social and economic changes sweeping the Western world, changes that had a profound effect on the cinema-going public's notions of what constituted 'entertainment'. Having lost much of its formerly reliable family audience to television, Hollywood found that it had to appeal to an 18-30 age group. This young audience's speedy growth in superficial sophistication during the decade demanded more graphic realism in the depiction of sex and violence. It also wanted to see characters it could easily identify with on screen (i.e. drawn from a similar age range), and films that mirrored its own attitudes and concerns or that held up to ridicule or otherwise exposed parental ideals and assumptions.

Not surprisingly, many of Hollywood's old-established directors, themselves fast-ageing members of the older generation, were unable or unwilling to adapt to these requirements. Others, however, contrived particularly notable successes. **Alfred Hitchcock** began the decade with the archetypal modern horror film *Psycho* a harrowing black comedy with a grotesque psychopathic villain riddled with Freudian neuroses, and some of the most terrifying sequences of violence (notably the shower murder) ever filmed. Having set standards in horror and suspense that would heavily influence film-makers in the Seventies and Eighties, Hitchcock then prefigured the later vogue for 'disaster' epics with *The Birds* (1963). *Marnie* (1964) was a psychological thriller

Top left: Marion Crane (Janet Leigh) is slashed to death in Hitchcock's Psycho *– not only a box-office success, but a social phenomenon. Top right: Melanie Daniels (Tippi Hedren), a victim of* The Birds. *Above far left: Robert Aldrich gives Ursula Andress direction in* Four for Texas. *Above centre: Charlotte (Bette Davis) who goes mad in* Hush . . . Hush, Sweet Charlotte. *Above right: Laurel-and-Hardy fancy dress for 'Childie' (Susannah York) and her domineering lover (Beryl Reid) in* The Killing of Sister George. *Far left: Sidney Lumet's* The Pawnbroker, *about a concentration camp survivor, was condemned for its images of women's breasts. Left: Jack Crabb (Dustin Hoffman) in* Little Big Man.

that hinged in then-risqué fashion on its heroine's repressed sexuality, while *Torn Curtain* (1966) and *Topaz* (1969) were trendy spy thrillers, enlivened by Hitchcock's technical panache. His final films, *Frenzy* (1972) and *Family Plot* (1976), while lacking the originality of his earlier work, still proved popular.

Another experienced film-maker who flourished in the new climate of the Sixties was **Robert Aldrich** (1918–1983); his films were characterized by an ambiguous (and therefore appealingly modern) attitude to violence. His Westerns, war and crime films of the Fifties appeared to offer moral critiques of violence, while later films were disturbingly amoral. The horror high-camp of *What Ever Happened to Baby Jane?* (1962) and *Hush . . . Hush Sweet Charlotte* (1964) proved especially popular with Sixties audiences, as did the brutality of *The Dirty Dozen* (1967) and the lesbian theme of *The Killing of Sister George* (1968). Cynical but darkly humorous tales of death and destruction formed the bulk of his subsequent work – *The Grissom Gang* (1971), *Ulzana's Raid* (1972), and *Hustle* (1975). He also made occasional, rather heavy-handed comedies – *The Longest Yard* (1974), *The Choirboys* (1977) and *. . . All the Marbles* (his last film, made in 1981).

The new directors that would figure large in the revival of American cinema in the Sixties and early Seventies were in the main transplanted from the New York theatre and the world of television – Sidney Lumet, Arthur Penn, Mike Nichols, John Frankenheimer, Norman Jewison, William Friedkin, and Sam Peckinpah.

In the Fifties, **Sidney Lumet** (b. 1924) had directed some of the best plays networked on live television from New York. A similarly claustrophobic style was evident in his early features, such as *Twelve Angry Men* (1957) and *Long Day's Journey Into Night* (1962). With *The Pawnbroker* (1965), he ignored the Production Code by showing explicit nudity. Released without a Seal of Approval, the film was nevertheless acclaimed by critics and public. The best of Lumet's subsequent films – *Serpico* (1973), *Dog Day Afternoon* (1975), and *Prince of the City* (1981) – were characterized by their careful examination of naturalistic, violent, urban themes. However, he achieved his biggest popular successes with a classy adaptation of Agatha Christie's *Murder on the Orient Express* (1974) and a bitter satire about television, scripted by Paddy Chayefsky, *Network* (1976).

Arthur Penn (b. 1922) had achieved a solid reputation on Broadway before an adaptation of William Gibson's *The Miracle Workers* (1962), his second film, brought him success as a movie director. *Bonnie and Clyde* established him and its stars, Warren Beatty and Faye Dunaway, in the new Hollywood Establishment. However, success did not lead Penn to compromise his very personal vision of the individual's often doomed struggle against repressive social forces. *Alice's Restaurant* (1969) was the most affectionate and telling picture of the aspirations of late-Sixties American youth; the satirical *Little Big Man* (1970) brilliantly exposed the white man's systematic cruelty to the Red Indian. The private-eye thriller *Night Moves* (1975) and the Western *The Missouri Breaks* (1976) reflected the widespread loss of social idealism in the mid-Seventies and exploded traditional genre conventions of plot and character. But a second attempt to analyse the Sixties, *Four Friends* (1981, GB: *Georgie's Friends*) was indifferently received and failed commercially, putting its director's future in doubt. Though his output has been relatively small, Penn can be regarded as one of the most important contributors to American cinema since the Fifties.

Mike Nichols (b.1931), Oscar-winning director of 1968's biggest hit, the satirical sex comedy *The Graduate*, had earlier established himself in the theatre, at first as a performer in collaboration with Elaine May and then as a director, before turning to films with *Who's Afraid of Virginia Woolf?* (1966). He followed *The Graduate* with the anti-war black comedy *Catch-22* (1970), and *Carnal Knowledge* (1971), another sex comedy, more bitter and nihilistic than *The Graduate* and scarcely less so than *Who's Afraid of Virginia Woolf?*. After five years of remarkable success, Nichols' career suddenly declined with *The Day of the Dolphin* (1973) and *The Fortune* (1975). He returned to the cinema in the Eighties with a critically praised study of nuclear 'martyr' Karen Silkwood, (played by Meryl Streep), *Silkwood* (1983).

Like Lumet, **John Frankenheimer** (b.1930) spent much of the Fifties directing live television drama. His film career began in earnest with *The Young Savages* (1961), a hysterical study of juvenile delinquency. This began a five-picture association with Burt Lancaster, who drafted him as replacement director for *Birdman of Alcatraz* (1962) and *The Train* (1964). The early Sixties was Frankenheimer's most successful period, yielding a number of films with a distinctly contemporary edge – *All Fall Down* (1962), which returned to the teenage theme with a side-swipe at American maternal possessiveness (personified by Angela Lansbury); *The Manchurian Candidate* (1962), which starred Lansbury as a communist agent who uses her son (Laurence Harvey) in a plot to assassinate the President and take over the White House; and *Seven Days In May* (1964), which portrayed a right-wing military coup. Frankenheimer's career then declined with an over-long motor-racing film, *Grand Prix* (1966) and *Seconds* (1966) a futuristic vision of the consumer society. A thoughtful adaptation of Eugene O'Neill's *The Iceman Cometh* in 1973 was arguably the best of his later films, which included the disappointing *French Connection II* (1975), an above-average thriller, *Black Sunday* (1977), a pretentious horror film, *Prophecy* (1979) and a late addition to the martial-arts genre, *The Challenge* (1982).

Canadian-born **Norman Jewison** (b.1926) initially worked in television in Britain, Canada and the USA, where he specialized in musical spectaculars. He began his film career with a sentimental comedy, *40 Pounds of Trouble* (1962), and a Doris Day vehicle, *The Thrill of It All* (1963). His career began to gather momentum with *The Cincinnati Kid* (1965) and he then hit the jackpot with *In the Heat of the Night* (1967), in which an intelligent black cop (Sidney Poitier) has to overcome the bigotry of a white Southern sheriff (Rod Steiger). Jewison achieved further success with the flashy Steve McQueen vehicle *The Thomas Crown Affair* (1968), then produced and directed two overblown stage-musical adaptations, *Fiddler on the Roof* (1971), and *Jesus Christ Superstar* (1973). The futuristic violence of *Rollerball* (1975) revitalized his career. *F.I.S.T.* (1978), was an uncharacteristically punchy Union film, while ... *And Justice for All* (1980) marked something of a return to liberal social concerns.

The film career of ex-TV director **William Friedkin** (b.1939) began in particularly auspicious style with the film version of Harold Pinter's *The Birthday Party* and a riotous period comedy set in a burlesque theatre, *The Night They Raided Minsky's* (both 1968). Friedkin subsequently scored two of the Seventies' biggest smashes with *The French Connection* (1971) and *The Exorcist* (1973), which spurred other film-makers to cash in on the public's ghoulish fascination with demonic possession among children.

Perhaps the most significant director to move from TV to film in the Sixties was **Sam Peckinpah**, (1925–84) who outraged his producers with *Major Dundee* (1965) and large sections of the public with the slow-motion slaughter of *The Wild Bunch*. Peckinpah's subsequent films obstinately idealized the loner, the misfit, the outmoded and the outsider and were characterized by long sequences of brooding atmosphere punctuated by scenes of grotesque carnage and machismo. The rape scene in *Straw Dogs* (1971) intensified his critical notoriety. He then made two successful films starring Steve McQueen, the uncharacteristically gentle *Junior Bonner* and a violent thriller, *The Getaway* (both 1972), before beginning an epic, elegiac Western, *Pat Garrett and Billy the Kid* (1973), perhaps his finest, most thoughtful film. His career then lost impetus, the long-winded nastiness of *Bring Me the Head of Alfredo Garcia* (1974) being succeeded by a routine

Below far left: Richard Burton and Elizabeth Taylor as a professor and his wife parade their marital discord before guests (George Segal and Sandy Dennis) in Who's Afraid of Virginia Woolf? *Far left: Benjamin (Dustin Hoffman) with Mrs Robinson (Anne Bancroft) in* The Graduate. *Left: Steve McQueen and Faye Dunaway in* The Thomas Crown Affair. *Below left: Sidney Poitier and Rod Steiger in* In the Heat of the Night. *Below centre: Gene Hackman in* The French Connection. *Below: a rebel officer (Richard Harris) battles with an Apache in* Major Dundee.

crime-thriller, *The Killer Elite* (1975), a blood-soaked war epic, *Cross of Iron* (1977) a country-and-western, *Convoy* (1978) and a final thriller, *The Osterman Weekend* (1983).

Unlike Peckinpah, the Polish-born **Roman Polanski** (b.1933) is a director who generally prefers to keep violence bubbling just under the skin of his work. Having achieved a healthy critical reputation as a master chronicler of obsession and abnormal sexuality with *Nóz w Wodzie* (1962, *Knife in the Water*), *Repulsion* (1965) and *Cul-de-Sac* (1966), Polanski arrived in Hollywood in the late Sixties. He achieved immediate mainstream commercial success with the influential horror film *Rosemary's Baby* (1968), based on Ira Levin's bestseller, which convincingly combined the archaic mumbo-jumbo of black magic with a modern, urban setting. The following year his pregnant wife, the actress Sharon Tate, was murdered with several others by the psychopathic Manson

Above left: in Polanski's Repulsion, *Carol (Catherine Deneuve), out of her mind alone in a London flat, kills innocent male visitors whom she believes to be rapists. Above centre: La private-eye J. Gittes (Jack Nicholson) is attacked by hoods, who slit his nose to scare him off a case in* Chinatown. *Above: Tess (Nastassja Kinski in her first major role) with her ailing, illegitimate baby.*

'family'. Despite this appalling tragedy, Polanski soon returned to the screen, with *Macbeth* (1971) and an excellent latter-day *film noir*, *Chinatown* (1974). He then left the USA to avoid possible imprisonment on a charge of statutory rape, and settled in France, where he made a typically bizarre horror film, *Le Locataire* (1979, *The Tenant*) and *Tess* (1979), a visually stunning but somewhat sterile adaptation of Thomas Hardy's *Tess of the D'Urbervilles*.

CHAPTER 17
New Film in Europe

Britain

The Seventies was a fairly disastrous decade for British production. Anglo-Amalgamated and British Lion, which had at times been lively sources of quality pictures, were absorbed into EMI, which had taken over the Associated British Picture Corporation (ABPC) in 1969. The new owners of ABPC had the creditable notion of putting a film-maker, Bryan Forbes, in charge of production at Elstree. Some films well-rooted in the British scene followed, ranging from Lionel Jeffries' charming *The Railway Children* (1970) to Andrew Sinclair's unreleased *The Breaking of Bumbo* (1971), the story of a rebellious National Service guardsman, and Forbes' own *The Raging Moon* (1971), about a romance in a home for the physically handicapped. EMI and Forbes parted in 1971, and the company eventually moved to a policy of making films with international appeal, mostly in America, including *Convoy* and *The Deer Hunter* (both 1978). *The Deer Hunter* went way over budget, but was a box-office success. EMI's home-based Agatha Christie adaptations – *Murder on the Orient Express* (1974), *Death on the Nile* (1978) and *The Mirror Crack'd* (1980) – were also packed with starry casts of worldwide appeal. EMI fell foul of production crises and runaway budgets with the remake of *The Jazz Singer* (1980) and with *Honky Tonk Freeway* (1981), which reached a negative cost of £11 million. But the company had not entirely turned its back on low-budget indigenous production, partnering the National Film Finance Corporation on *Memoirs of a Survivor* (1981), after the director David Gladwell had spent four years looking for backers.

Rank made a determined return to production that was blighted by lack of a clear policy and failure to tie up a strong enough American release. Remakes of *The Thirty-Nine Steps* (1978) and *The Lady Vanishes* (1979) showed a paucity of imagination; and *The Lady Vanishes* was compromised by its American stars Elliott Gould and Cybill Shepherd, who were not popular enough to ensure the film's success abroad. A period adventure, *The Riddle of the Sands*, and a Western, *Eagle's Wing* (both 1979), were not the sort of films audiences were yearning for, even in Britain, while the children's film *Wombling Free* (1977) did not get a general release. With *Bad Timing* (1980), Rank completed a programme of eight pictures costing £10 million, and then withdrew from film-making entirely.

Lord Grade, the colourful television tycoon, linked his ATV company with American exhibitors General Cinema to

Left: Isabelle Huppert and Gerard Dépardieu, two of France's leading young film stars of the Eighties, in Loulou.

form Associated General Films in 1975: but the lacklustre performance of such films as *Voyage of the Damned* (1976) and *March or Die* (1977) ended the partnership. In 1979, Grade joined forces with EMI to establish a new releasing company, Associated Film Distribution (AFD), to deal directly with the American market, as Rank had attempted in the late Fifties. Their efforts were hamstrung by a succession of box-office losers, most conspicuously with two expensive 1980 productions, *Can't Stop the Music* and *Raise the Titanic!* which cost £19 million to make. AFD's only real success was *The Muppet Movie* (1979). In 1981 the company had to turn over American distribution to Universal.

The British industry continued to survive thanks to the efforts of a few individualistic directors. Apart from the expatriate Americans, Kubrick and Losey (who subsequently moved to France), they included John Boorman, Ken Russell, Kenneth Loach, Nicolas Roeg and Derek Jarman. Towards the end of the decade, some promising newcomers emerged, including Ridley Scott with *The Duellists* (1977), based on a Joseph Conrad story, and the sci-fi horror film *Alien* (1979). Meanwhile the indefatigable independents Kevin Brownlow and Andrew Mollo followed up their quasi-documentary on the Nazi occupation of Britain, *It Happened Here* (1964), with *Winstanley* (1975), re-creating the Diggers' commune of 1649.

John Boorman (b. 1934), originally a documentarist, was among the group of television-trained directors who turned to the cinema in the Sixties. Since then, like Schlesinger, he has divided his career between Britain (or latterly, Ireland) and the USA. His first feature, *Catch Us If You Can* (1965), starring the Dave Clark Five, was one of several films that exploited the international success of British pop music. Much less frenetic than Lester's Beatles romps, it is a gentle satire on advertising. Its distaste for modern urban living and affectionate exploration of the British landscape suggested affinities with Ealing comedy. By contrast, *Point Blank* (1967), starring Lee Marvin, was a thoroughly American gangster movie with a strong narrative drive and forceful presentation of violence, e.g. the systematic wrecking of a car by its driver. Its elliptical presentation of the story and its visual experiments suggested European *nouvelle vague* influences, particularly Resnais. *Hell in the Pacific* (1968) was an unconventional war movie with only two characters, an American soldier (Marvin) and a Japanese (Toshiro Mifune) on an island. *Leo the Last* (1970) represented a return to Britain in its picture of racially mixed inner London, as seen by a European aristocrat (Marcello Mastroianni) who owns a large house set in a slum. However, it was a Felliniesque fantasy rather than a social-problem picture. His most successful film, *Deliverance*

(1972), was set in the Appalachian mountains, but otherwise recalled the vigorous narrative and bleak tone of *Point Blank* in its portrayal of four city-dwellers in grotesquely violent conflict with the primitive locals. After this, Boorman settled in Ireland and turned to fantasy with *Zardoz* (1974), a science-fiction movie, and *Exorcist II: The Heretic* (1977), a horror film. Both are uneven in quality, technically ambitious and hazy in ideas. In the Eighties, Boorman made *Excalibur* (1981), a visually beautiful adventure story based on the King Arthur legends; he also acted as executive producer for Neil Jordan's fine feature debut *Angel* (1983).

The fascination with, and irreverence towards, the arts and creative artists on the part of **Ken Russell** (b. 1927) is evident not only in the topics of his television and cinema films, but also in the film styles and forms he borrows and parodies from the directors he most admires – Eisenstein, Fellini, Truffaut, Orson Welles. He transformed the TV biopic, most controversially in *The Dance of the Seven Veils* (1970), a fantasia that charged Richard Strauss with Nazi sympathies. Russell had already established his cinema credentials with a seaside comedy, *French Dressing* (1964), and an original spy story, *Billion Dollar Brain* (1967). His passion for freedom – personal, sexual, political or cultural – was declared in the D.H. Lawrence adaptation *Women in Love* (1969) and in *The Devils* (1971), retelling the story of French nuns allegedly possessed by the devil in seventeenth-century Loudon and the subsequent execution of their sensual chaplain. Russell's own obsessions, as a convert to Catholicism, also emerged in the first of his cinema biographies, *The Music Lovers* (1970), which depicted Tchaikovsky as a guilt-ridden homosexual. In more mellow vein, he brought together the themes of freedom

and artistic creativity in *Savage Messiah* (1974), which concerned the relationship between the middle-aged writer Sophie Brzeska and the talented young sculptor Henri Gaudier, killed in World War I. Russell plunged further into fantasy in the extraordinary *Mahler* (1974), with its welter of cinematic, musical and Freudian references. But with *Lisztomania* (1975) he temporarily worked out the vein of musical biographies in an incoherent mix of Nazi theatricals and pop-music parallels, casting the Who's Roger Daltrey as Liszt. Daltrey was more at ease in *Tommy* (1975), based on Pete Townshend's rock opera about a blind, deaf and dumb pinball-machine player. Russell's previous musical, *The Boy Friend* (1971), a backstage version of Sandy Wilson's Twenties pastiche, had relied heavily on the charm of ex-model Twiggy. After surveying so many of the orthodox and popular arts, Russell turned to the cinema itself in *Valentino* (1977), casting the dancer Rudolf Nureyev as the Twenties star. His first American film was a science-fiction horror story, *Altered States* (1980), concerning drug experiments in psychic and physical regression. Meanwhile, he had returned to television with a patchy, two-part film about the poets Wordsworth and Coleridge, *Clouds of Glory* (1978). This was followed in 1984 by a study of the composer Ralph Vaughan Williams, which provoked unfavourable critical comparisons with the recently reshown *Elgar* (1962).

Nicolas Roeg (b. 1928) first made his mark in the film industry as a cinematographer. This phase of his career, which included credits on *The Masque of the Red Death* (1964), *Fahrenheit 451* (1966) and *Far From the Madding Crowd* (1967) – for Corman, Truffaut and Schlesinger respectively – culminated in *Petulia* (1968, directed by Richard Lester). This

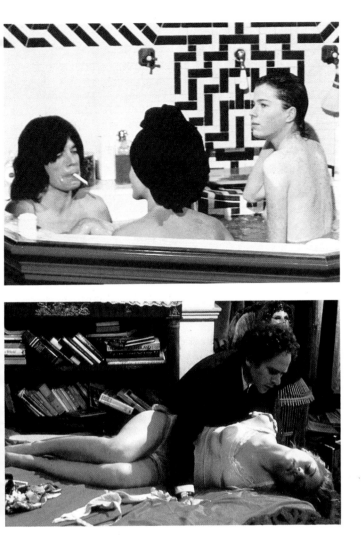

film anticipated Roeg's own directorial style — characterized by a rapid and fragmented kaleidoscopic cross-cutting between diverse strands of narrative, creative meaning largely through unexpected juxtapositions. He co-directed *Performance* (1970) with its writer, Donald Cammell, and also photographed it. This and his following three films concerned one or more characters fleeing from a native culture associated with death into an alien environment that profoundly challenges their former identities. In *Performance* a small-time gangster (James Fox) on the run from his boss invades the home of a retired rock star (Mick Jagger) and mysteriously exchanges personalities with him. In *Walkabout* (1971), also photographed by Roeg, an adolescent girl (Jenny Agutter) and her young brother (Lucien John, Roeg's own son), lost in the Australian outback, are saved by an Aboriginal youth (David Gulpilil) who kills himself when the girl rejects his ritualized wooing. *Don't Look Now* (1973) concerns a couple (Donald Sutherland and Julie Christie) who go to out-of-season Venice after the accidental drowning of their daughter; she believes that she has made psychic contact with the dead child, while he, denying this possibility, is murdered by a psychopathic female dwarf — a hideous parody of the daughter. In *The Man Who Fell to Earth* (1976), pop-singer David Bowie plays an exile from another planet whose extraordinary powers are blighted in the corrupt environment of the USA. Yet another rock star, Art Garfunkel, portrayed an American psychiatrist living in Vienna in *Bad Timing* (1980); his obsessive relationship with another American (Theresa Russell) is almost matched by that of a police inspector (Harvey Keitel) investigating his involvement in the woman's suicide attempt. *Eureka* (1982) set in the

Caribbean, also involves an investigation, since it is based on a famous real-life unsolved murder case of the Forties, that of Sir Harry Oakes, around which it weaves an elaborate web of symbolism and cross-references.

Derek Jarman (b. 1942) is a fantasist at heart. His influences include the directors Jean Cocteau, Michael Powell, Kenneth Anger and Hollywood B-feature science fiction. His cinema career began when Ken Russell invited him to design the lavish and imaginative sets for *The Devils* and *Savage Messiah*.

Jarman's is a cinema of magic and spectacle, and the real wonder is his gift for achieving such seductive results on very slim budgets. Thematically, his movies are connected by a preoccupation with groups of characters isolated by a bleak setting — the desert-like Sardinian landscape in *Sebastiane* (1976), the devastated urban sprawl of *Jubilee* (1978), and the island-bound decaying mansion in *The Tempest* (1979). The emphasis is thus placed upon the interaction of characters, especially upon power relationships, both political and sexual.

Sebastiane, based upon the explicitly erotic Renaissance paintings of the famous martyr, is remarkable for the fashion in which Jarman's panning camera dwells upon the naked male form and renders even the landscape sensual. Co-directed with Paul Humfress, the film is possibly unique in having its dialogue in Latin.

Jubilee, the most extravagant and bizarre of Jarman's features, is the least endearing of his works. It is a vision of the decadence and decay of modern society, situated in some future London where a group of punk terrorists prey remorselessly on a culture they see as unredeemable. The movie certainly helped launch Toyah Willcox and Adam Ant as vivacious luminaries of the late Seventies pop world.

Toyah herself went on to star (as Miranda) in Jarman's third feature, a typically quirky adaptation of Shakespeare's *The Tempest*. If *Sebastiane* is Jarman's most erotic film, then *The Tempest* is his most human. It is also the most visually ravishing of his movies. There is a density to the images – decorated with patterns of shadow and sensuous fabrics – reminiscent of the work of Josef von Sternberg, and the boldly stylized use of colour reminds one of Vincente Minnelli's films. Jarman has also made many shorts in the Super-8mm gauge and a number of pop videos – modest though inventive offerings.

Kenneth Loach (b. 1936), in contrast to Boorman, Russell, Roeg and Jarman, is very much in the British social-realist tradition. His first cinema film, *Poor Cow* (1967), though made in colour, was a development from his television films *Up the Junction* (1965) and *Cathy Come Home* (1966). Beneath its close-to-life surface lies a carefully designed structure that emphasizes the gap between life as it is and life as it should be, as it deals with a young working-class mother rising above the grimness and deprivation of her circumstances through the memory of a short-lived, idyllic romance. *Kes* (1969), the story of a scraggy little Yorkshire schoolboy who finds self-fulfilment through the rearing and training of a bird of prey, a kestrel, is a purer and more poetic development of a similar theme. In scene after scene – engaging, funny, exhilarating or sad – Loach shows how home, school and future prospects are totally at odds with the boy's aspirations. *Family Life* (1971) was not only a plea for a more humane and environmental approach to the treatment of mental illness but also a bitter attack on both the destructiveness of conventional family morality and on the ethics of society. During the Seventies Loach continued to make controversial television films, notably the four-part *Days of Hope* (1975), about family and political loyalties in the ten years leading up to the General Strike. His children's adventure film, *Black Jack* (1979), about

Below: the unloved Billy (David Bradley) with his only solace, the kestrel he tends and trains, in Loach's Kes.

a young apprentice and a highwayman, presented a de-glamorized portrayal of eighteenth-century town and country life. Both *The Gamekeeper* (1980) and *Looks and Smiles* (1981) were made with TV support and were scripted by Barry Hines, the author of *Kes*. *The Gamekeeper* sympathetically studies a man trapped in the ideologies of class and male dominance, while *Looks and Smiles* probes deeply and sadly, but with great affection, into the lives of three unemployed Northern youngsters.

The Eighties Revival British films experienced a remarkable resurgence in the early Eighties, despite falling production and attendances. This revival was signalled by a sudden flush of Academy Awards for Hugh Hudson's *Chariots of Fire* (1981), produced by David Puttnam, and Richard Attenborough's big-budget epic *Gandhi* (1982).

The groundwork for these successes had been laid in the late Seventies with the emergence of several creative, independent producers, some of whom (Puttnam, Leon Clore) had been in the business for some time, while others (Michael White, the team of Davina Belling and Clive Parsons) were newcomers. The public sector was represented by Mamoun Hassan and Simon Perry at the National Film Finance Corporation (NFFC) and Peter Sainsbury at the British Film Institute (BFI). Among new production companies, the most notable was HandMade Films, established by ex-Beatle George Harrison to make *Monty Python's Life of Brian* (1979). It maintained the Python comedy connection, and also branched out into drama.

Television came to play an increasingly large part in financing films, blurring the distinctions between those made for the cinema and those made for TV. Scottish Television helped finance Bill Forsyth's highly successful *Gregory's Girl* (1980), a teenage school comedy set in Scotland about an awkward young romantic and a football-playing girl. The advent of Channel Four gave rise to a group of films intended for screening by the channel but also receiving exposure in cinemas, both at home and abroad. This included Peter Greenway's stylized, intellectual 'thriller' *The Draughtsman's Contract* (1982), an erotically spiced murder mystery set in a country house in the late seventeenth century; Polish director Jerzy Skolimowski's *Moonlighting* (1982), a wryly witty tale of four Polish workmen clandestinely renovating a house in Kensington while the military are taking over in their native land; novelist Neil Jordan's debut film *Angel* (1982), an oblique comment on the violence of Northern Ireland; and Richard Eyre's *The Ploughman's Lunch* (1983), a comprehensively cynical *Room at the Top* for the Eighties, scripted by novelist Ian McEwan.

Ex-critic Christopher Petit, a disciple of Wim Wenders, managed to establish a marginal yet fairly consistent career with the road-movie *Radio On* (1979), the P.D. James detective story *An Unsuitable Job for a Woman* (1981) and the Anglo-German quasi-thriller *Fluchtpunkt Berlin* (1983, *Flight to Berlin*), with assorted backing from the BFI, NFFC, Channel Four, the independent Boyd's Company and even Wenders' own organization.

Meanwhile the traditional 'commercial' cinema was producing films as varied as Alan Parker's *Pink Floyd—The Wall* (1982), based on a best-selling rock LP; Peter Yates' *The Dresser* (1983), a backstage tragi-comedy adapted from Ronald Harwood's play; veteran Lewis Gilbert's *Educating Rita* (1983), based on Willy Russell's play about a working-class woman who yearns for education; *Heat and Dust* (1983) from the established team of writer Ruth Prawer Jhabvala,

Top left: director, stars, writer and producer of Chariots of Fire *at Cannes in 1981 (from left: Hugh Hudson, Ian Charleson, Nigel Havers, Colin Welland and David Puttnam. Top: Dorothy (Dee Hepburn) supported by Gregory (Gordon John Sinclair) argues her way into the school soccer team in* Gregory's Girl. *Above: rock star Sting, as rock'n'roll-loving petrol-pump attendant, plays Eddie Cochran's 'Three Steps to Heaven' to David Beames in* Radio On. *Above left: Eric Idle, Terry Gilliam and Michael Palin in* Monty Python's Life of Brian. *Left: Christopher Lambert as Tarzan in* Greystoke. *Below left: David Lean's epic of the British Raj,* A Passage to India. *Below: Richard Burton in his last screen role as O'Brien from the Ministry of Love with John Hurt as the victimized Winston Smith in* 1984.

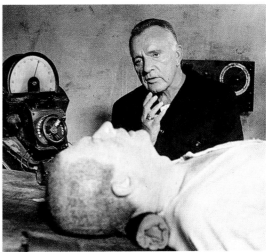

producer Ismail Merchant and director James Ivory; and Hugh Hudson's lavish *Greystoke: the Legend of Tarzan, Lord of the Apes* (1984), which claimed to be the most faithful film adaptation of Edgar Rice Burrough's novel.

1984 appeared a particularly promising year with Marek Kanievska's *Another Country*, from Julian Mitchell's play, James Ivory's *The Bostonians*, based on Henry James' novel, Roger Donaldson's historical epic *The Bounty*, Pat O'Connor's *Cal*, a modern love story set in Northern Ireland, Clive Donner's Dickens adaptation *A Christmas Carol*, Bill Forsyth's comedy-drama *Comfort and Joy*, Neil Jordan's horror-fantasy *Company of Wolves*, Steven Frears' off-beat thriller *The Hit*, Malcolm Mowbray's comedy *A Private Function*, scripted by Alan Bennett, Jerzy Skolimowski's *Success Is the Best Revenge*, Michael Radford's film version of George Orwell's novel *1984*, and Roland Joffé's *The Killing Fields*.

By the mid-Eighties, a mixture of high-budget international productions, medium-budget cinema movies of some international potential and low-budget films destined primarily for TV seemed to allow more scope than at any other time since the 'New Wave' heyday of the early Sixties for the development of a flourishing cinema of national character.

West Germany

To see the New German Cinema of the Seventies in context, it is necessary to review briefly key developments within the film industry since the end of World War II. The Allied Control Commission's policy, dominated by the Americans, was ideological and economic rather than cultural in motivation. Production was decentralized to Berlin, Munich, Hamburg and even Wiesbaden; small independent producers were forbidden by law to merge. This meant that there was a constant lack of finance for feature films. So German films could not compete internationally and the industry became oriented to films for the local market.

During the Fifties, production consisted mostly of sex films, musicals, leaden comedies or historical romances, aimed at local audiences. Income from the export of German films was therefore always low. The federal and state governments tried to encourage film production with guaranteed bank credits, tax relief, subsidies and cash prizes. Most of these attempts were abandoned or sharply modified throughout the Fifties and Sixties as the results were seen to favour the distributors, and the producers of low-quality, but politically acceptable, films.

Inspired in part by the *nouvelle vague* in France, 26 young film-makers who had been involved in short films – some of which had won prizes at international festivals – signed the Oberhausen Manifesto in 1962. Although vague and general in its proposals, it assumed the 'death' of the established industry and maintained that the hope of German cinema was in a new generation of directors 'who speak the international language of the cinema'. Through intense lobbying (led by Alexander Kluge, who is a lawyer as well as a film director), the Kuratorium Junger Deutscher Film (Board of Curators of the Young German Film) was established in 1965 to provide interest-free loans for first films. Between 1965 and 1968, DM 5 million was invested in a number of short films and 20 features, including Kluge's *Abschied von Gestern* (1966, *Yesterday Girl*) and Werner Herzog's *Lebenszeichen* (1968, *Signs of Life*), and the New German Cinema had begun.

Having previously ignored the all-important distribution area of the industry, several young directors (Wim Wenders, Werner Herzog, Rainer Werner Fassbinder and others) founded the Filmverlag der Autoren (Authors' Film Publishers) in 1971 for the distribution and international sales of their films. While the organization had some success, especially in getting films sold outside Germany, it never managed to deal with more than four hundred cinemas within West Germany and West Berlin.

In addition to various small subsidies and cash prizes which still existed for serious directors, there was also television. If the introduction of the small screen in Germany in the Fifties helped to kill the box-office for cinema, it also provided the means by which many young directors made their films. Volker Schlöndorff has claimed that with television '70 per cent of the German cinema is subsidized'. Many directors, including Peter Lilienthal, Hans Jürgen Syberberg and Wolfgang Petersen, began in television and have continued to work directly for it. Werner Herzog produced most of his earlier films on a combination of small subsidies, prizes and television money. Fassbinder also worked directly or indirectly for television; probably more Germans have seen his own successful television series, *Acht Stunden sind kein Tag* (1972–3, Eight Hours Are Not a Day) and *Berlin Alexanderplatz* (1980), than all of his cinema films put together.

While television has allowed many directors to keep working and others to begin careers, the situation has not necessarily been ideal. Syberberg, for example, has commented that: 'All the (political) parties are represented by television and they would never finance a film which really treated seriously, for example, atomic power or terrorism.'

Television did finance and show a number of films that touched these subjects obliquely, such as *Die verlorene Ehre der Katharina Blum* (1975, *The Lost Honour of Katharina Blum*), *Vera Romeyke ist nicht tragbar* (1976, *Vera Romeyke: Not Acceptable*), and *Messer im Kopf* (1978, *Knife in the Head*). However these films remained studies of specific cases rather than general statements.

At times the difficulties of finding the money to make a film have been overwhelming for directors of the New German Cinema. Some, like Syberberg and Wenders, left to work in America for a while. Some, like Reinhard Hauff and Schlöndorff, have managed to alternate between 'personal' and 'commercial' projects. Others, particularly Fassbinder, have become successful on the international market, so that producers know that budgets can be recouped abroad. In the Eighties the New German Cinema continued to experience difficulty in distribution and in finding production funds, but has remained prominent among national cinemas, with about ten established directors and another two dozen or so minor but interesting directors actively working. Among those with international reputations were Alexander Kluge, Rainer Werner Fassbinder, Jean-Marie Straub, Werner Herzog, Reinhard Hauff, Volker Schlöndorff, Hans Jürgen Syberberg, Wim Wenders and, to a slightly lesser extent, Werner Schroeter and Daniel Schmid.

Alexander Kluge (b. 1932) began with a strong admiration for the work of Jean-Luc Godard which was reflected in his shorts and his early features *Yesterday Girl* and *Die Artisten in der Zirkuskuppel: ratlos* (1968, *Artistes at the Top of the Big Top: Disorientated*). In *Gelegenheitsarbeit einer Sklavin* (1974, *Occasional Work of a Female Slave*), the story of an ex-abortionist who become politically active, he continues to use Godardian devices, such as a fragmented narrative, printed quotations and deliberately shaky hand-held-camera images; but its very cool intellectual analysis of a woman's position in a male-dominated society marks it as clearly a Kluge film. Since then it has become apparent that Kluge's interests are indeed social and political. Even in *Der starke Ferdinand* (1976, *Strongman Ferdinand*), where he reveals both a sense of the comic and a sympathy for his unpleasant protagonist, the chief security officer of a factory, this final interest is in an analysis of how a passion for 'security' develops into a fascist mentality. Kluge was later involved in straight political analysis in group-directed films, *Deutschland im Herbst* (1978, *Germany in Autumn*) and *Der Kandidat* (1980, The Candidate), which concerns the ambitions of Franz-Josef Strauss for the Chancellorship.

Jean-Marie Straub (b. 1933), who collaborates closely with his wife Danièle Huillet, must be mentioned for his early films, though he left Germany for Italy after the Sixties and no longer works regularly in the German language. *Nicht versöhnt* (1965, *Not Reconciled*) united memories of anti-Nazi resistance in the Thirties with the story of an architect's son who becomes a demolition expert in World War II and blows up his father's masterpiece. *Chronik der Anna Magdalena Bach* (1968, *Chronicle of Anna Magdalena Bach*) was a costume piece, structured around the imaginary journal of Bach's second wife and containing performances of a couple of dozen extracts from Bach's music. *Geschichtsunterricht* (1972, *History Lessons*) was based on Brecht's novel about Julius Caesar, while *Moses und Aron* (1975, *Moses and Aaron*) was a version of Schönberg's opera. Straub's elliptical style makes few concessions to the viewer and his critical repute, especially in left-wing circles, is far in advance of his popular impact.

Reinhard Hauff (b. 1939) is one of the more varied of the New German directors in both style and subject-matter, having moved from the glowing antique colours of the historical tale about the hero-bandit *Mathias Kneissl* (1971), through a strong case-study of a prisoner, *Die Verrohung des Franz Blum* (1974, *The Brutalization of Franz Blum*), to the more personal *Der Hauptdarsteller* (1977, *The Main Actor*), in which he examines his own relationship with a youngster he had used as the main actor in an earlier film. *Knife in the Head* was a return to the case-study, concerning an amnesiac accused of being a terrorist. In *Der Mann auf der Mauer* (1982, The Man on the Wall) he tackled the difficult subject of the Berlin Wall.

Volker Schlöndorff (b. 1939), like Hauff, is a careful craftsman, without the personal style and vision of a Herzog or a Fassbinder. While he has made such purely commercial films as the bourgeois tale of adultery *Die Moral der Ruth Halbfass* (1972, The Morals of Ruth Halbfass), he is obviously intelligent and serious enough to be more at ease with subjects like the amateur criminals of *Der plötzliche Reichtum der armen Leute von Kombach* (1971, *The Sudden Fortune of the Poor People of Kombach*), in which he side-stepped every trap of romanticizing and sentimentalizing poverty-stricken farmers. His adaptation, with author Günter Grass, of *Die Blechtrommel* (1979, *The Tin Drum*) is particularly thought-provoking and well-made. *Die Fälschung* (1981, *Circle of Deceit*) is about a journalist in war-torn Beirut. In *Un Amour de Swann* (1983, *Swann in Love*) Schlöndorff finally brought Proust to the screen after more eminent directors, Visconti and Losey among them, had failed to do so. Schlöndorff's wife and former scriptwriter, Margarethe von Trotta, meanwhile established herself as a director of films about political issues and women's roles in society, most notably with *Die bleierne Zeit* (1981, *The German Sisters*).

Hans Jürgen Syberberg (b. 1935) has moved with the times, beginning with fairly realistic motorcycle and sex dramas and moving on to his stylized trilogy about power and the German past: *Ludwig II – Requiem für einen jungfräulichen König* (1972, *Ludwig II – Requiem for a Virgin King*), *Karl May* (1974) and *Hitler* (1977, *Hitler – a Film From Germany*). Although he has said that his back-projected decors and his use of other non-realistic devices came originally from a lack of production funds, he subsequently stuck to them, in-

Below: Harry Baer as the last King of Bohemia in Ludwig II – Requiem for a Virgin King.

Above: Alexandra Kluge, the director's sister, in Yesterday Girl. *Right:* The Tin Drum *concerns a boy who decides to stop growing at the age of three.*

trigued by their dramatic effectiveness. In 1982 he made a startlingly psychoanalytical version of Wagner's opera *Parsifal*.

Because of an extensive involvement in Munich fringe theatre, by the time **Rainer Werner Fassbinder** (1946–82) began making feature films he had not only experience, but, crucial to his methods of working, a sort of stock company of actors around him who were used to his ways, able to take his lightning changes of direction in their stride, and to work as complete collaborators in the evolution of new works, whether on stage, screen or – later on – television.

Hence the alarming statistic that once Fassbinder had embarked on a career in films, he made in the first three years (1969–71) no fewer than *ten* features. Most of them had a wild, improvisatory quality which Fassbinder never wholly shook off, and indeed, when he tried to, he seemed in danger of falling into the opposite trap of mandarin pretentiousness. The products of this period inclined towards Godard as the primary influence, both in their rough-and-ready shooting style and in their general commitment to a critique of bourgeois society. He also had a passion for the Western and for overheated Hollywood melodrama, particularly as directed by Douglas Sirk. Thus it should have come as no surprise to find him, amidst his tributes to Godard, suddenly veering towards Samuel Fuller in *Der amerikanische Soldat* (1970, *The American Soldier*). In the more than usually bizarre *Whity* (1971) he is to be found pastiching a whole range of American Westerns and steamy tales of the Old South, with the mulatto hero darkly brooding on vengeance against the white master-race, represented here by a bunch of sadists and dribbling half-wits.

In 1971 Fassbinder began the series of films which were to make him an important international figure. These were interspersed from 1972 with films and series intended wholly or partly for television, some of which – *Acht Stunden sind kein Tag* and *Berlin Alexanderplatz* – are very extensive. The first of the theatrical movies was *Der Händler der vier Jahreszeiten* (1972, *The Merchant of Four Seasons*), chronicling the economic rise and personal decline of a greengrocer in a sober style illuminated from time to time with flashes of bravura melodrama.

The second, *Die bitteren Tränen der Petra von Kant* (1972, *The Bitter Tears of Petra von Kant*), is the story of a spoilt fashion designer who has a brief lesbian affair, and following a series of highly-charged meetings with her mother, her daughter, her best friend and most of the important people in her life, is finally deserted by them all and left alone.

The next to appear was *Angst essen Seele auf* (1974, *Fear Eats the Soul*) – an unexpectedly cheering view of a marriage between an elderly, widowed German char and a Moroccan immigrant worker younger than herself. Fassbinder treated his subject in a minutely realistic manner, making it readily approachable by general audiences. With hindsight one may see that in the fourth, *Fontane Effi Briest* (1974, *Effi Briest*), a conspicuously well-upholstered adaptation of Theodor Fontane's famous turn-of-the-century novel about a dissatisfied wife and a fatal liaison, Fassbinder was already moving over, through a concern for surface polish and 'style', towards affectation and stuffiness.

In *Faustrecht der Freiheit* (1975, *Fox*) he plays a rough, homosexual fairground-worker who wins a lottery, is taken up by supposedly grand homosexuals and then eventually cast aside by his elegant businessman-lover once his money has run out.

Its success seems to have had a slightly disorienting effect on Fassbinder, or perhaps merely confirmed him in a direction he was already going. *Mutter Küsters Fahrt zum Himmel* (1975, *Mother Kuster's Trip to Heaven*) resumed the theme of *Fox* – the betrayal of the proletariat by the bourgeoisie – in another form, with the ruthless exploitation of a working-class heroine by perfidious middle-class politicos. But *Chinesisches Roulette* (1976, *Chinese Roulette*), *Satansbraten* (1976, *Satan's Brew*) and particularly *Despair* (1978), pursued an extravagant aestheticism to the exclusion of much else: *Chinese Roulette*, a melodramatic family tragedy exploring emotional sterility among the promiscuous rich, is at least foolish but fun. But *Despair*, though enlivened by a fine study in suppressed hysteria by Dirk Bogarde as a chocolate manufacturer slowly going mad, suffers from Fassbinder's relative insecurity directing in English. The film was already overloaded with a plot taken from a Nabokov novel and an over-literate script by Tom Stoppard.

Die Ehe der Maria Braun (1979, *The Marriage of Maria Braun*), however, courageously took in 30 years of German history in its (part-allegorical) story of a wife (Hanna Schygulla) who reluctantly uses her sexual attractiveness to survive and then achieve success in business, all for the love of her absent husband. *Lili Marlene* (1981) told the story of a popular singer (Hanna Schygulla) initially going along with and then rejecting the Nazis. *Lola* (1981) combined elements from both films in the person of a cabaret singer who highlights provincial corruption by vamping a civic official and ends up owning the town brothel. *Die Sehnsucht der*

Above: Margit Carstensen as the self-pitying heroine of The Bitter Tears of Petra Von Kant. *Above right: Fassbinder with Emmi Kurowski in his* Fear Eats the Soul. *Right: Bruno S as the innocent protagonist of Herzog's* The Enigma of Kaspar Hauser. *Far right: in* Aguirre, Wrath of God, *Klaus Kinski plays the power-hungry Aguirre who assumes leadership of a group of Conquistadores looking for El Dorado in the South American jungle and finding instead sickness and death.*

Veronika Voss (1982, *Veronika Voss*) concerned a faded film star addicted to drugs and death. After these often absorbing and lively studies of women, Fassbinder returned to homosexual themes in *Querelle* (1982), adapted from a Jean Genet novel, with a sailor as the vamp. His death in 1982, from a mixture of drink and drugs, was a profound loss to world cinema.

The films of **Werner Herzog** (b. 1942) tend to be historical in their setting and metaphysical in their concerns as against a general tendency towards the contemporary and the political.

In his work, Herzog is preoccupied with situations at the limits of human existence: at points where it is hard to separate human from animal life; where the normal, everyday world is undermined by fantasies, superstitions, obsessions, premonitions. In *Jeder für sich und Gott gegen alle* (1975, *The Enigma of Kaspar Hauser*), for example, the difference between human beings and animals has been eroded because Kaspar (Bruno S) has been kept in complete isolation during his early life, and as a consequence cannot use or understand language properly. In *Aguirre, der Zorn Gottes* (1973, *Aguirre, Wrath of God*) an obsessive quest pits the hero against both the hostility of nature and that of other human groups until he is reduced to an animal-like level and destroyed.

As well as this interest in extreme situations, the character of Herzog's film-making is most clearly defined by its awareness of the physical world. Frequently nature is presented in terms of a hostile grandeur – jungles, volcanoes or deserts – whereas the human physical world is presented rather differently. The German and Dutch towns that provide the environment in a number of his films are seen as exquisite, untouched by time, museum-like, but the external world is never less than a strong dramatic presence.

Since he began directing in the early Sixties, Herzog has worked on a regular basis, having made many feature films as well as five substantial documentaries. Despite this output he is, in an important sense, not a professional film-maker. Rather like the long, spiritual journey through sixteenth-century South America of *Aguirre, Wrath of God*, film-making is for him an obsessional activity designed to test his energy, courage and resourcefulness. Nowhere was this more true in his work than in his filming of *Fitzcarraldo* (1982), a marathon Amazon trek. The film's story concerns a heroic but eccentric figure (Klaus Kinski) who dreams of building an opera house in the heart of the Amazon jungle.

Herzog's cinema is very much in the romantic tradition – anti-bourgeois and anti-rational. In keeping with his romantic outlook, it is animated by a spirit of pathos, stressing the beauty and hostility of the natural world, the mystery and insecurity of human existence. However, it is a cinema that is also open to strong critical objections. It can be argued that it represents the worst of art cinema, and that the films draw upon associations from the traditional established arts to claim a quality that they do not intrinsically have.

Some of Herzog's films are difficult to defend from criticisms of this kind. *Herz aus Glas* (1976, *Heart of Glass*), for instance – based on a simple story about the disappearance of a formula for making a special kind of glass – is so full of long-held shots and grotesque, unexplained behaviour that

Above: ageing goalkeeper Josef Bloch (Arthur Brauss) and one of the girls he encounters on his aimless flight from the scene of a murder he has committed in The Goalkeeper's Fear of the Penalty. *Top right: nothing is ever the same for easy-going picture-framer Jonathan after he encounters the unscrupulous Ripley in* The American Friend. *Convinced that he is suffering from an incurable disease, Jonathan allows himself to be bribed into assisting the raffish Ripley in his murderous intrigues. Above right: father and son get to know each other – Harry Dean Stanton and Hunter Carson in Wenders'* Paris, Texas.

the story is unable to take the weight of its treatment. The result becomes both tiresome and unconsciously funny. In *Nosferatu: Phantom der Nacht* (1979, *Nosferatu the Vampyre*) the traditional vampire story is treated in a similar fashion, making unavoidable the ever-present danger in the horror genre, namely the risk of tipping over into the ridiculous.

Oddly enough, despite Herzog's seeming preference for historical contexts, one of his most attractive and successful films, *Stroszek* (1977), has a contemporary setting. It opens in a milieu more reminiscent of Fassbinder – an underworld of petty criminals, pimps and prostitutes – before moving to the present-day United States, where an immigrant German worker encounters unbearable hardships. What the film emphasizes is how important a part innocence plays in Herzog's film-making. It is the ability to be an 'innocent eye' that allows him to create striking images: the simplicity with which the arrival of a mobile home is observed suggests charm and freshness, and the construction of innocent central characters allows Herzog to enrich the film with a gentle humour.

Humour also coloured *Wo die grünen Ameisen träumen* (1984, *Where the Green Ants Dream*), set in Australia and depicting a fictional conflict between big mining interests and Aboriginal rights and customs.

The phenomenon of how post-war German culture and society has been colonized by the Americans is a key theme in the work of **Wim Wenders** (b. 1945).

Born in Düsseldorf, Wenders is a child of the American Occupation. His cultural conditioning, through Hollywood and rock'n'roll, gave him an image and myth of America which could be both sterile and seductive at the same time. His first feature, *Summer in the City* (1970), was completed as his film-school graduation movie. Employing a deliberately unstructured story about a man coming out of prison and trying to pick up his old friendships in Munich and Berlin. Much of Wenders' later work is summed up in this film and the themes within it – isolation, the urban blues, the hope expressed in rock music.

Equally important and formative is *Summer in the City*'s use of the journey – here, Munich to Berlin and finally to Amsterdam – not simply as a narrative device, but as a way of looking at the world (out of aircraft windows, through car windscreens, and so on). With the exception of *Der scharlachrote Buchstabe* (1973, *The Scarlet Letter*), an unsatisfactory costume movie (of which Wenders mockingly remarked, 'the Puritans had no pinball machines, so I lost interest'), all Wenders' subsequent films are based around journeys in which the landscapes are almost always as important as the characters. In *Die Angst des Tormanns beim Elfmeter* (1972, *The Goalkeeper's Fear of the Penalty*), adapted from a novel by Peter Handke, Wenders' interest lies in his protagonist's aimless wanderings in the border country between West Germany and Austria.

Still working under the banner of the Filmverlag der Autoren, Wenders made *Alice in den Städten* (1974, *Alice in the Cities*) in which a German photographer helps nine-year-old Alice, abandoned by her mother at an American airport, to find her grandmother's house in the Ruhr valley. The result is a film at once brutally honest in its portrait of contemporary

Germany and delightfully amusing in its tale of two worldly travellers playing at private detective.

Wenders' next film, *Falsche Bewegung* (1975, *Wrong Movement*), continues the same journey of exploration, drawing a parallel between Germany in 1975 and the Germany of 1795 when Goethe wrote the novel *Wilhelm Meister*, on which *Wrong Movement* is loosely based. A despairing perspective on the problems of creativity in the Seventies, *Wrong Movement* graphically illustrates its theme through the cunning shooting of the journey of the central character (a writer unable to write).

By the mid-Seventies the Wenders journey had reached epic proportions, and in *Im Lauf der Zeit* (1976, *Kings of the Road*) he elevates the 'road' movie to classic genre status. This three-hour film is simply an account of two men who meet on the road, after one has spectacularly ditched his Volkswagen, and travel together in a pantechnicon truck. Exquisitely photographed in black and white by Robby Müller, *Kings of the Road* echoes certain American 'road' movies like *Easy Rider* (1969) and *Two-Lane Blacktop* (1971). The film stands as a challenge to the 'two-buddies-hit-the-road' kind of film popular in Hollywood at this time. It questions the American cinema's assumptions of male self-sufficiency by presenting a portrait of two men without women failing to come to terms with themselves.

The theme of male friendship is pushed to testing limits in Wenders' next film *Der amerikanische Freund* (1977, *The American Friend*), in which an 'innocent' Hamburg picture-framer, Jonathan, is led into a nightmarish adventure of murder and Mafia revenge through his tentative friendship with Ripley, an enigmatic American.

Wenders collaborated with his own 'American friend', the director and occasional actor Nicholas Ray, just before Ray died in May 1979, on a film about an ageing art dealer (played by Ray) trying to regain his lost reputation. Over the two months they worked together, *Lightning Over Water* (1980) became more like a documentary on the incipient death of its main protagonist.

Wenders' first wholly American feature, *Hammett*, was finally completed in 1982 after principal photography in early 1980 and late 1981. An imaginary episode in the life of thriller-writer Dashiell Hammett, it distanced its complex *film noir* tale of treachery and murder not so much by parody as by its studio settings and exploration of how the material of 'life' is transformed by imagination into 'art'. *Der Stand der Dinge* (1982, *The State of Things*), a return to low-budget black and white, was thematically related to *Hammett* in its depiction of the making of a sci-fi film impeded by financial skulduggery. Appropriately, it was shot (in Portugal and Los Angeles) during the intermission on *Hammett*.

Wenders then achieved a major critical and commercial success with *Paris, Texas* (1984), which won the Golden Palm at the 1984 Cannes Film Festival. Dazzling in pictorial effect, with a screenplay by Sam Shepard, the film combined a brooding love story with the 'road' film, telling how an amnesiac loner (Harry Dean Stanton) sets off in search of his estranged wife (Nastassja Kinski) along with their young son.

France

In the aftermath of the student riots of May 1968, French radicals felt that freedom of expression, discovered by the *nouvelle vague* earlier in the decade, had softened into a smoother, blander style that flattered the bourgeoisie's image of itself as fashionably left-wing and liberated. Certain film-makers were still determined to tackle the country's social problems: Marin Katmitz's *Camarades* (1970, *Comrades*) challenged the whole basis of trade unionism as a means of workers' power; Jean-Luc Godard's *Tout Va Bien* (1972, All Goes Well) was a bitter commentary on the compromises that had resulted in the downfall of the students' and the workers' frail alliance in May 1968; and *Coup pour Coup* (1972, *Blow for Blow*) made by a collective directed by Marin Karmitz, criticized the trade unions in its story of a workers' occupation of a textile factory.

However, the most consistent effort to open up political questions and re-create France's recent past belonged to a director born in Greece of half-Russian origins, **Costa-Gavras** (b. 1933). After coming to France to study at the Sorbonne, he switched to IDHEC and by the early Sixties was an assistant director to Clair, Demy, Clément and others. His debut was a slick thriller, *Compartiment Tueurs* (1965, *The Sleeping Car Murders*) but it was his third film, *Z* (1969), that established his characteristic brand of 'political thriller'. Based on the real-life assassination in 1963 of a left-wing Greek politician, it starred Yves Montand, then associated with the communist left. Montand next played a defendant at the Stalinist show trials of 1952 in Czechoslovakia in *L'Aveu* (1970, *The Confession*). In *Etat de Siège* (1973, *State of Siege*) he appeared as an American CIA 'advisor' kidnapped and killed by the Tupamaros in Uruguay. Having upset several bands of the political spectrum, Costa-Gavras turned his attention to wartime France with *Section Spéciale* (1975, *Special Section*), again dramatizing a historical event, the framing of four Frenchmen for the murder of a young German, with the complicity of the French judicial system. After *Clair de Femme* (1979, *Womanlight*), a psychological study of a woman who loses her husband and child in a car crash, he returned to politics and South America for his first American film, *Missing* (1982). Set in the aftermath of the 1973 military coup which toppled the Allende government in Chile, it recounted the unsuccessful search for a missing American writer by his

Below: police and demonstrators clash after the assassination in Costa-Gavras' political thriller Z.

father (Jack Lemmon) and wife (Sissy Spacek). Emphasizing humane and moral values rather than political commitment, accessible and even conventional in form and style, *Missing* was garlanded with prizes and achieved some commercial success.

This film confirmed Marxist critics in their opinion that Costa-Gavras was a liberal purveyor of compromised entertainment movies rather than a serious political film-maker. However, Costa-Gavras has inspired a whole sub-genre of political thrillers that combine messages for contemporary audiences with all the suspense of action movies. Modishly nostalgic films such as Louis Malle's *Lacombe Lucien*, Alain Resnais' *Stavisky . . .* (both 1974), François Giraud's *Le Trio Infernal* (1974, *The Infernal Trio*), Joseph Losey's *Mr Klein* (1976) and Claude Chabrol's *Violette Nozière* (1978) were a strong draw at the box-office while offering more than mere period charm. They suggested through their re-examination of *causes célèbres* that all was far from well beneath those carefully authentic period costumes and sets. For the first time since the war, it could be admitted that France was not so anti-fascist as all that and the myth of the Resistance – so sacred to the Gaullists – was a deception that had kept people from understanding the truth about their nation.

It was in this context that such a film as *Lacombe Lucien*, with its account of how a peasant youth is refused entry to the Resistance and joins the Nazi secret police instead, could be produced and become a *succès de scandale*. The floodgates were actually opened by the documentarist Marcel Ophuls, whose film *Le Chagrin et la Pitié* (1970, *The Sorrow and the Pity*) released many memories and feelings that had been repressed since the Occupation. Other documentaries that evoked similar responses included *Français, Si Vous Saviez* (1973, *Frenchmen, If You Knew . . .*) and *Chantons Sous l'Occupation* (1976, *Let's Sing Under the Occupation*). It became clear that the real struggle in French cinema was to be fought over the question of popular memory – how the people understood their history.

Other subjects were taken from earlier, well-documented cases, such as René Allio's *Moi, Pierre Rivière, Ayant Egorgé Ma Mère, Ma Soeur, Mon Frère . . .* (1976, *Moi, Pierre Rivière*), a young nineteenth-century peasant's account of how and why he killed his mother, sister and brother, or Bertrand Tavernier's *Le Juge et l'Assassin* (1976, *The Judge and the Killer*), which dealt with a perversion of justice in the pursuit and prosecution of a mass-murderer in rural France. Several 'historical' films, among them Robert Bresson's *Lancelot du Lac* (1974) and Franck Cassenti's *La Chanson de Roland* (1978, The Song of Roland), sought their subjects in medieval legend or in the period before the French Revolution – René Allio's *Les Camisards* (1971, The Camisards), Bertrand Tavernier's *Que la Fête Commence . . .* (1975, *Let Joy Reign Supreme*) and Ariane Mnouchkine's *Molière ou la Vie d'un Honnête Homme* (1978, *Molière*). These films tended to be more lavish and spectacular than the scrupulously documented case histories like *Moi, Pierre Rivière*, but essentially all the films favoured analysis of history over mere story-telling with period backdrops.

Both Malle and the veteran Spaniard Luis Buñuel, while touching on fashionably political topics, stood essentially apart from the general run of French cinema, developing their own interests. **Louis Malle** (b. 1932) is that phenomenon relatively rare since the days of Alice Guy-Blaché and Maurice Tourneur, a French director who has become an American director. He started as a documentarist, co-

directing Jacques-Yves Cousteau's underwater feature *Le Monde du Silence* (1956, *The Silent World*), and returned intermittently to documentary, sometimes for television, in his later career. His solo debut, the psychological thriller *Ascenseur Pour l'Echafaud* (1958, *Lift to the Scaffold*), brought him the Louis Delluc prize at the age of only 25. He established his *nouvelle vague* credentials and also caused a scandal with *Les Amants* (1958, *The Lovers*), in which Jeanne Moreau played a bourgeoise succumbing to *l'amour fou* with a young student. *Zazie dans le Métro* (1960, *Zazie*) played visual tricks in seeking the equivalent of novelist Raymond Queneau's verbal pyrotechnics. *Vie Privée* (1962, *A Very Private Affair*) was a semi-biographical extravaganza around the iconic figure of Brigitte Bardot, while *Le Feu Follet* (1963, *A Time to Live and a Time to Die*) explored the last days of a suicidal alcoholic, played by Maurice Ronet. Bardot and Moreau joined forces in a comedy of Latin American revolution, *Viva Maria!* (1965). Jean-Paul Belmondo played a rebel against society in *Le Voleur* (1967, *The Thief*). Rebelling himself against the French film world, Malle went to India to make controversial documentaries, *Calcutta* (1969) and a TV series. He caused more shock and horror with his sympathetic presentation of an adolescent son's incestuous sexual initiation in *Le Souffle au Coeur* (1971, *Dearest Love*) and a young collaborationist's involvement with the occupying Nazis in *Lacombe Lucien*. Moving to the USA, Malle ran into censor-

Left: Rose (Isabelle Huppert) with her lover, the hypocritical Judge Rousseau (Philippe Noiret), who is determined to send an insane killer to the guillotine in Le Juge et l'Assassin, *set in provincial France at the turn of the century. Below left: knights prepare for battle in* Lancelot du Lac, *Bresson's version of the Arthurian legand. Below: Jeanne Moreau as a wife with two lovers in Malle's* The Lovers. *Right: an improbable relationship flowers briefly between an ageing former gangster (Burt Lancaster) and a would-be croupier (Susan Sarandon) in* Atlantic City. *Below right: Catherine Deneuve as Séverine in* Belle de Jour, *who is frigid with her husband but uninhibited in her fantasies — which she subsequently lives out by becoming a prostitute in the day time.*

ship problems with *Pretty Baby* (1978), the story of a young girl growing up in a New Orleans brothel. With *Atlantic City USA* (1980), he was on safer ground, depicting gambling, crime, illusions and romance in a fading East Coast resort. *My Dinner with André* (1981) was a two-handed conversation piece about creativity and theatre, a surprising chic success in the USA. Malle returned to the mainstream with *Crackers* (1984), a remake of the Italian safe-cracking comedy *I Soliti Ignoti* (1958, *Persons Unknown*), which had been a hit in the USA under the title *Big Deal on Madonna Street*.

Never changing or compromising, **Luis Buñuel** always showed a remarkable capacity for renewal. After 1960 he announced each new picture as his definitive farewell to the screen. Yet, in 1964, well past sixty, he embarked on a new and triumphant phase in his career. That year he completed his adaptation of a subject Renoir had made in Hollywood some eighteen years before, Octave Mirbeau's *Le Journal d'une Femme de Chambre (The Diary of a Chambermaid)*. In Buñuel's hands the novel — almost romantic in Renoir's version — became a ferocious assault on the manners and political morals of the bourgeoisie. The film was the start of a long and happy collaboration with the producer Serge Silberman and the writer Jean-Claude Carrière that was to continue to provide Buñuel with ideal conditions in which to make films as and when he felt the inspiration. Silberman even provided special video equipment to minimize the

strains of directing — Buñuel was already 77 when he came to make his youthful and vigorous *Cet Obscur Objet du Désir* (1977, *That Obscure Object of Desire*).

The only French film made by Buñuel in this period and not produced by Silberman — although Carrière remained his co-writer — was the brilliant comedy of a woman's sexual fantasies, *Belle de Jour* (1967), which established the director — at 67 — as a major box-office attraction. It was the sort of irony he enjoyed; his subsequent films continued to maintain this reputation even when, as in *La Voie Lactée* (1969, *The Milky Way*) — a curious comic essay on the heresies of the Catholic Church — the subject matter was not obviously popular.

He returned to his native Spain to adapt a novel by Benito Pérez Galdós, author of *Nazarín*. This was *Tristana* (1970), in which the heroine (Catherine Deneuve) loses a leg but gains the upper hand in her relationship with her domineering guardian. *Le Charme Discret de la Bourgeoisie* (1972, *The Discreet Charm of the Bourgeoisie*) and *Le Fantôme de la Liberté* (1974, *The Phantom of Liberty*) were beautiful, absurdist comedies that, without altering the direction or the intensity of Buñuel's hatreds against his life-long targets, seemed to gain in gaiety and dexterity. *That Obscure Object of Desire* returned to a subject he had wanted to make more than twenty years before (when, instead, it went to Julien Duvivier), an adaptation of Pierre Louÿs' 'decadent' novel of the late nineteenth century, *La Femme et le Pantin (The*

Woman and the Puppet), in which the opposing aspects of a man's ideal woman are personified by two different actresses.

Buñuel must figure among the few undisputed giants of the cinema. In his intellectual austerity, moral intransigence, total integrity, unweakening anger, rich humour, and underlying humanism, he never faltered or compromised. In the use of the medium he always displayed the simplicity, directness, confidence and correctness of an impeccable craftsman. Buñuel's complex vision is expressed through means and images that are clean, classical, limpid; and it is the apparent transparency of the means through which his intense concerns and surreal vision find their outlet that gives his films their irresistible appeal.

In the Seventies and Eighties, the French cinema remained remarkably rich in *auteurs* who were able to express an individual vision or a minority ideology, if sometimes only intermittently and to limited audiences. Alongside this unquestionably artistic level of enterprise, there flourished a vigorous commercial cinema of popular comedies and thrillers. Both these aspects, apart from occasional successes, had only a partial and selective exposure in the English-speaking world. To give a single instance, **Maurice Pialat** (b. 1925), who had been making distinguished studies of personal relationships since the Sixties, did not become internationally known until *Loulou* (1980), a low-life drama starring Gérard Depardieu and Isabelle Huppert, and *A Nos Amours* (1983, *To Our Loves*), a sympathetic portrait of a confused girl (Sandrine Bonnaire) unable to cope with family and love problems; Pialat himself played her father.

Italy

The Sixties in Italy were marked not only by the increasingly ambitious works of Visconti, Fellini and Antonioni but also by the emergence of a new generation of directors. Some of them had been working in films since the Fifties (Pier Paolo Pasolini, Ermanno Olmi) or even the Forties (Francesco Rosi) in various capacities, while others were newcomers (Bernardo Bertolucci, Marco Bellocchio). Even in its decline, neo-realism gave them a common starting-point from which to reach out to more individual and personal modes of expression. Excepting Olmi, they also shared various brands of Marxism, in common with Zavattini/De Sica, Visconti and Antonioni (but not Rossellini or Fellini) among the established film-makers. Olmi and Rosi, in their very different styles, remained the most committed to the task of reporting the state of the nation, while Pasolini and Bertolucci sought poetic and experimental means of expression, but the two concerns frequently overlapped. Indeed their broad similarities emerge by contrast with the development of **Franco Zeffirelli** (b. 1923), who is probably more widely known abroad than any of them. Like Rosi, he had been an assistant of Visconti's; but it was the theatrical rather than the neo-realist aspect of Visconti that he manifested, initially as designer and director of operas and plays, but then as an international film director of the Shakespeare adaptations *The Taming of the Shrew* (1967) and *Romeo and Juliet* (1968). After a tribute to St Francis of Assisi, *Fratello Sole, Sorella Luna* (1972, *Brother Sun, Sister Moon*), he undertook the epic television series *Jesus of Nazareth* (1977) for Lew Grade; its star-packed opulence was

in striking contrast with the simplicity and directness of Pasolini's *Il Vangelo Secondo Matteo* (1964, *The Gospel According to St Matthew*), which had been shot in black and white, with non-professional actors. Following a couple of sentimental American films exploiting young people, *The Champ* (1979) and *Endless Love* (1980), Zeffirelli found his true niche with a sumptuous version of Verdi's opera *La Traviata* (1982, *The Fallen Woman*).

Luchino Visconti had begun the Sixties with *Rocco e i Suoi Fratelli* (1960, *Rocco and His Brothers*), in which he combined the surfaces of neo-realism with an operatic approach to character and drama. The film has a realistic base in the problems of Southern families seeking to better themselves in a hostile Northern city. But its power stems from the internal explosion of the family and the tension between fraternal fidelity and sexual obsession.

Il Gattopardo (1963, *The Leopard*) was a return to the *risorgimento* period of *Senso* (1954, *The Wanton Countess*), with the action removed to Sicily. Instead of centring on an obsessive love affair, however, the plot concerns the ageing prince Don Fabrizio (Burt Lancaster) attempting to come to terms with the inevitable disappearance of his class, the aristocracy, either through revolution or through inter-marriage. His nephew, Tancredi (Alain Delon), seems in his way the agent for both, first as a soldier for Garibaldi and then as the new husband of the daughter of the bourgeois Don Sedara. Like Visconti himself, the prince is an aristocrat, but his sympathies are with the revolution.

Burt Lancaster's performance as the prince was unequalled in his career until he played a similar role in *Gruppo di Famiglia in un Interno* (1975, *Conversation Piece*). This was Visconti's most personal film in a decade. The professor has locked himself away from life, collecting paintings of English family groups. Suddenly into his world break the wife of a fascist industrialist, her politically active leftist lover, her son, and her son's (and lover's) young mistress. At first horrified by their 'corruption' and 'bad taste', he learns to love Konrad, the activist, and to understand the others. He also learns finally to reject the past, and 'art', and to live in the present, with people.

Between *The Leopard* and *Conversation Piece* Visconti made five feature films of variable quality. *Vaghe Stelle dell'Orsa* (1965, *Of a Thousand Delights*) is again concerned with the break up of a family and the effect of the past on the present.

Lo Straniero (1967, *The Stranger*) perhaps came 25 years too late, based as it was on the novel *L'Etranger (The Outsider)* by Albert Camus, whose own existentialist ideas had subsequently developed further. The main character's 'uncinematic' passivity and indifference made for a dull film.

With *La Caduta degli Dei* (1969, *The Damned*), the themes of family disintegration, the fall of a class and sexual obsessions are set against the rise of Nazism in Germany. While many of the set-pieces are extremely well handled the constant hysteria in tone and the excesses of acting and decor ultimately tend to trivialize the film's political and social ideas. *Morte a Venezia* (1971, *Death in Venice*) succeeds mainly on the level of decor and historical recreation. The three-hour *Ludwig* (1973) suffers from an error in central casting. Ludwig (Helmut Berger) is made less a figure of grand and glorious madness with a vision too grandiose for even a king to make real than a rather pouty young man who likes fancy dress, his cousin, big castles and young artists.

Visconti returned to full creative power with *Conversation Piece*, but his health then rapidly declined. He had almost

Above: in Antonioni's La Notte, *a crisis in the marriage of Lidia (Jeanne Moreau) and Giovanni (Marcello Mastroianni) leads them both to attempt extra-marital love affairs. Below left: Visconti recreated the sumptuous surroundings of the Sicilian aristocracy in* The Leopard.

finished *L'Innocente*, (1976, *The Innocent*), based on Gabriele D'Annunzio's novel, when he died, and the film was finished by other hands. Still, what there is of Visconti is impressive and the central themes of sexual attraction and family disintegration are treated with typical panache and style.

The career of **Michelangelo Antonioni** underwent a change in the middle Sixties. Having worked in Italy on a series of meticulously observed, angst-ridden love-affairs, which had brought him wide critical acclaim, he left his native country and began to travel – to England, to the USA, to China and to the several countries depicted in the scene shifts of *Professione: Reporter* (1975, *The Passenger*).

However, the change was less far-reaching than first appeared. His films continued to explore the communication-gaps between people and the relations and discrepancies between the outside world and his protagonists' personal outlook and concerns. Made in England, *Blow-Up* (1966) provides an insight into Sixties 'swinging' London life, but is primarily concerned with the way a photographer behaves when he comes to believe that his pictures have accidentally uncovered a murder in a quiet, suburban park.

Antonioni's characters are wistful dreamers, torn between their search for satisfaction and awareness of encroaching decline, and sometimes unable even to look at one another because of the pain attendant upon seeing and being seen. In the early Sixties especially he was treated as the studiously forlorn poet of pessimism and dismay. However this overlooks the real significance of detachment in his work, and the way that this quality subsequently grew into something like mystical exhilaration.

Born in Ferrara in 1912, Antonioni recalled it as a 'marvellous little city on the Paduan plain, antique and silent'. Already he had an intuition of the decor of his films; reality becoming an evocative model, like the deserted city in *L'Avventura* (1960, *The Adventure*).

The emblematic significance of an environment or space is crucial to many of his films: the lift-shaft in his first feature, *Cronaca di un Amore* (1950, *Chronicle of a Love*); the sense of fraud that hangs over the film-set in *La Signora Senza Camelie* (1953, *Woman Without Camellias*); the frontier of the beach in *Le Amiche* (1955, *The Girlfriends*); the grey wasteland of *Il Grido* (1957, *The Cry*) . . . and so on, to the tumult of the stock exchange in *L'Eclisse* (1962, *The Eclipse*), the cramped orgy room with boats looming up in the mist outside in *Deserto Rosso* (1964, *Red Desert*), the photographer's studio in *Blow-Up*. Finally, the African hotel, the London house, the Gaudí buildings and the Hotel de la Gloria in *The Passenger*.

In the Eighties Antonioni again worked in Italy, making *Il Mistero di Oberwald* (1980, *The Oberwald Mystery*), an experimental video version of Cocteau's 1946 drama of love and death, *L'Aigle à Deux Têtes (The Eagle Has Two Heads)*. With *Identificazione di una Donna* (1982, *Identification of a Woman*), dealing with a film director's frustrated search for the ideal woman, he returned to some of the preoccupations of his earlier Italian films.

Ermanno Olmi has often been called a pessimist because he depicts the bleakness of life so vividly and implies that Christian resignation will console the sufferer for everything he must bear in this world. However, this is a very schematic and indeed dogmatic way of looking at the content of his cinema. Olmi is really an optimist; he believes that life's mystery lies with the old and the very young.

He was born in 1931 in one of the most clerical regions of Northern Italy – the Bergamasco, the frontier between Lombardy and the Veneto. His first job was as a clerk with the Edison-Volta electrical firm in Milan, where eventually he made 16mm shorts, at first about company outings and activities, and then documentaries which gradually won him a reputation. He then persuaded his employers to let him make a long documentary that turned into a feature. This was *Il Tempo si è Fermato* (1959, *Time Stood Still*), made in black and white but in 'Scope, about the human relationship between a mature man of mountain peasant stock and a young student from the city who spend a winter together as watchmen over a half-built dam.

His first fiction film was *Il Posto* (1961, *The Job*), a wry, semi-autobiographical comedy about a boy's first job in a dreary office, beautifully played by non-professionals – Olmi later married his leading lady.

Olmi established his professional reputation as a creative film-maker in Milan – only being tempted once towards the alluring Roman film scene. Even this was something very much according to Olmi's vision of things: a film about Pope John XXIII who, like Olmi, had been born in the Bergamasco peasant fringe. The film – *E Venne un Uomo* (1965, *A Man Named John*) – produced by Harry Saltzman, was not a success. Partly it was because Olmi let himself be convinced for the first and only time to use a professional actor, Rod Steiger, who was quite out of place, even if the idea of telling the Pope's story through a contemporary intermediary was interesting.

Olmi ventured south in only one film, his third feature *I Fidanzati* (1963, *The Engagement*). This was to Sicily where his hero, a welder from a Milan factory, had been transferred with a good contract, though obliged to leave behind his fiancée.

Olmi's most mature films before *L'Albero degli Zoccoli* (1978, *The Tree of Wooden Clogs*) were his trilogy on bourgeois Milan. The best of the three is *Un Certo Giorno* (1969, *One Fine Day*) – as delicate and sorrowful a film as *Il Posto* but with a much stronger feeling for characterization. Another of his non-professionals, Brunetto De Vita (on whom Olmi moulded the character), plays the advertising executive who is about to get a promotion. An accident – the man runs over a worker on the side of a street as he is speeding to the airport – causes him to stop and reassess his values and his relationships.

In *Durante l'Estate* (1971, *During the Summer*) Olmi allowed the whimsical in his nature to take the upper hand. Yet this story of a rather odd map designer with a passion for heraldry was full of charm and showed another aspect of Milan from that of the drudgery of work.

In 1974 he made *La Circostanza (The Circumstance)* – a cold and rather over-written story, again about a car accident that changes people's lives. Four years later Olmi was to make *The Tree of Wooden Clogs*. Thanks to Italian television he had been able to keep on working during the lean years between films. As well as the features produced for RAI (Italian state-owned television) he had made documentaries and series on young people's problems and on religious subjects. The success of *The Tree of Wooden Clogs* in winning the Golden Palm at Cannes gave him a wide audience in Italy for the first time.

Its epic vision of peasant life at the turn of the century is composed of small incidents lovingly depicted and reputedly based on stories told by Olmi's peasant grandmother. RAI also sponsored *Cammina, Cammina* (1983, Keep Walking, Keep Walking), an allegorical film about a group of travelling players re-enacting the journey of the Magi to Bethlehem, filmed in Tuscany. Far from orthodox, it was attacked by the Vatican and restricted by censorship from showing to under-14s. But its faith in innocence and humanity is entirely consistent with Olmi's other work.

The cinema of **Pier Paolo Pasolini** is deeply embedded in Italian cultural and political life with all its conflicting traits and elements, the most important of which is the opposition between the two commanding ideologies of Catholicism and Communism.

Born in 1922 in Bologna, northern Italy, Pasolini developed a visceral anti-Fascism and turned towards Marxism. After the war, his Marxist leanings were reinforced at the University of Bologna, and he actually joined the Communist Party briefly in 1947–8. However, he himself admitted that his Marxism was emotional, aesthetic and cultural rather than directly political, and was strongly linked to his attachment to the (largely Catholic) peasantry.

His first film, *Accattone* (1961), is the chronicle of a small-time hustler, which, for all its employment of seemingly neo-realist devices (fragmentary narrative, non-professional actors, seedy locations, etc.), is significant precisely for its departures from the genre.

Accattone, like so much of Pasolini's work, operates not on the level of the psychological and the social, but on that of fable and myth. His second film – *Mamma Roma* (1962) – is the story of an ex-prostitute who tries unsuccessfully to give her son a 'respectable' bourgeois background. It introduces another key Pasolini theme, and one that is exposed more fully in *Teorema* (1968, *Theorem*): the unacceptable face of the modern bourgeois and petit-bourgeois worlds.

With *Il Vangelo Secondo Matteo* (1964, *The Gospel According to St Matthew*) Pasolini took an already much mythologized subject. Clearly influenced by Rossellini's *Francesco, Giullare di Dio* (1950, *Flowers of St Francis*), Pasolini almost reverses the trajectory of *Accattone* by moving from the mythical and sacred to the everyday. Ultimately the film expresses a belief in the virtues of the people independent of social classes, while its view of history is too cloudy and romanticized to be considered properly materialist. In line with Pasolini's reverence for what he called the sacred, the miracles are allowed to retain their sense of mystery.

Coinciding with the upsurge in left-wing political activity in the late Sixties, Pasolini retreated increasingly into the creation of a largely mythical universe, with films such as *Edipo Re* (1967, *Oedipus Rex*), *Teorema*, *Porcile* (1969, *Pigsty*) and *Medea* (1970). It was hardly surprising that he should be attracted by the Oedipus legend, not only in *Oedipus Rex* but throughout many of his films in which its presence (though not always immediately obvious) acts as a structure of images and ideas informing the whole.

Like many Pasolinian figures, Oedipus inhabits a pre-moral world, obeying only his basic drives before eventually being forced to enter into knowledge, to understand the significance of his acts and to realize that certain desires are taboo. But by then it is too late and retribution inevitably follows, making many of Pasolini's films akin to pagan versions of the myth of the Fall, set in the realms of the universal and the mythic as opposed to the personal and the psychological. Indeed, his trilogy of tales – *Il Decameron* (1971, *The Decameron*), *I Racconti di Canterbury* (1972, *The Canterbury Tales*), *Il Fiore delle Mille e Una Ňotte* (1974, *Arabian Nights*) – celebrates a pre-lapsarian world, the invocation of an almost magical past in which innocence is still possible. *Arabian Nights* in particular is a paean to guiltless sexuality, to the naked human body and to frank sexual desire; a film in which, unusually, the male heterosexual vision does not dominate, and male and female beauty and desire are treated in an unconventionally equal manner.

After the relative innocence of the trilogy Pasolini plunged back into the horrors of a twentieth century in the grip of Fascism with *Salò o le Centoventi Giornate di Sodoma* (1975, *Salò or the 120 Days of Sodom*). Transposing the Marquis de Sade's eighteenth-century erotic tales to a castle in northern Italy during the last days of Mussolini, Pasolini presents an increasingly extreme series of orgies and tortures in order to demonstrate that sex is no longer a means of liberation but simply one more tool of oppression. The point may be debatable, but not the horrifying cruelty and pessimism of this uncannily valedictory work. Pasolini was battered to death by a teenage youth shortly after completing *Salò* on November 2, 1975, in circumstances that have yet to be fully explained.

The overriding film-making motives of **Francesco Rosi** are to portray the life of the nation, to analyse the forces at work in Italy and to present a debate of ideologies. When watching his films, the audiences may witness the development of Italy's history from World War I to the economic and political problems of the present. His work deals with such topics as Thirties fascism in a Lucanian village, the liberation of Italy, banditry in Sicily, local politics in Naples, the oil crisis and the Mafia.

Rosi was born in Naples in 1922, and most of his films centre on the problems of southern Italy – with that derelict

Top right: Olmi's The Tree of Wooden Clogs *revealed the desperate hardship of an Italian peasant's life at the turn of the century. Above right: Judas (Otello Sestili) gives the kiss by which Jesus (Enrique Irazoqui) is betrayed in Pasolini's* The Gospel According to St Matthew. *Right: a scene of sexual humiliation from* Salo.

and oppressed half of the country that is seen as part of the Third World by the rich North. But far from being provincial, his work illuminates one of the basic problems of 'modern' times, the growing gap between the underdeveloped countries and the technologically advanced ones.

For several years he worked as an assistant to both Visconti and Michelangelo Antonioni. His first two films as director were *La Sfida* (1958, *The Challenge*), about the power of the Neapolitan Mafia over the fruit business, and *I Magliari* (1959, The Swindlers), about the various shady deals of southern Italian salesmen in Hamburg.

The story of the investigation into the death of the famous Sicilian bandit, *Salvatore Giuliano* (1961), is a dazzling mosaic that probes the complexities of the Italian political system and shows the various powers of the police, the army, the Mafia and the law. It is far from being the biography of a historical character, and contrary to so many 'political' films, it has no message. Rosi does not draw conclusions, but juxtaposes points of view.

Different in structure, but employing the same methods, are the largely biographical *Il Caso Mattei* (1972, *The Mattei Affair*) and *Lucky Luciano* (1973). The former starts with the death in a plane crash (accident or murder?) of the Italian oil tycoon Enrico Mattei. If *The Mattei Affair* portrays the excitement, activity and rhetoric of the business and political world, *Lucky Luciano*, about the Mafia, is a film of silence and obscurity where things are implied but never fully stated.

Uomini Contro (1970, Men Against) and *Mani Sulla Città* (1963, *Hands Over the City*), with their linear narrative and clear issues, are films of greater simplicity. Rosi does not unnecessarily complicate the reality he is confronted with. World War I in the first case, and the corruption of housing speculators, together with the political intrigues of the Municipal Council in the second, offer a much clearer landscape to the observer.

Cadaveri Eccellenti (1976, *Illustrious Corpses*) is a detective story that leads an honest policeman looking for the truth about the murder of a public prosecutor into the labyrinth of Italian politics.

Rosi's next film, *Cristo si è Fermato a Eboli* (1979, *Christ Stopped at Eboli*), also took the form of a journey; the discovery of the poor, mystical world of a southern village by a rational, left-wing, northern intellectual who is sent into exile there by the Mussolini regime of the mid-Thirties.

Tre Fratelli (1981, *Three Brothers*) is the story of an old peasant who sends three telegrams urging his sons to attend their mother's funeral. The film shows the reality of the present, their past experiences and, through their confrontations, all the problems of present-day Italy. The brothers, in a way, also sum up Rosi's personality: one is rational, one utopian, the last angry and violent. In 1983 Rosi directed one of several new versions of *Carmen*.

Born in Parma in 1940, **Bernado Bertolucci** is the son of Attilio Bertolucci, the Marxist poet and film critic, who indirectly got him into films. He knew another Marxist poet who wanted to make a film and suggested his son as a knowledgeable assistant. The year was 1961 and the director was Pier Paolo Pasolini. The remarkable result was *Accattone*.

After *Accattone*, Pasolini gave Bertolucci a script to work on for himself. *La Commare Secca* (*The Grim Reaper* or, literally, 'the dry housewife', Roman slang for death) was screened in 1962. It was shot on location in Rome and tells the story of a prostitute's murder and the ensuing police investigation. Two years later, Bertolucci made *Prima della*

Rivoluzione (1964, *Before the Revolution*), set in his home town of Parma, about the clash between radicalism and tradition ten years after the Liberation.

Many people thought that here was the heir to Luchino Visconti, but much of Bertolucci's technique was derived from Jean-Luc Godard. His next feature, *Partner* (1968), loosely based on Dostoevsky's *The Double*, was clearly reliant on the new narrative techniques espoused by Godard. Though striking, *Partner* is uneven and puzzling in its attempt to marry art and politics. In 1970 he made *La Strategia del Ragno (The Spider's Stratagem)* for RAI-TV. This was also the *annus mirabilis* during which he made *Il Conformista (The Conformist)* with money raised internationally.

The Spider's Stratagem concerns a plot to muder Mussolini during a provincial performance of *Rigoletto*. A young man returns to his home in Tara to find out about his father, a hero of the Resistance; but the hero turns out to have had feet of clay since, in fact, he betrayed the man who attempted the assassination. Its use of music is superb, its *mise-en-scène* sumptuous and its atmosphere of mystery compelling.

The Conformist was based on a novel by Alberto Moravia. Once again, everything is imbued with a sense of the past as its story of hypocrisy and betrayal unfolds. It is about a civil servant (Jean-Louis Trintignant) who becomes a Fascist in 1938, perhaps to protect his job, and is sent on a dangerous assignment: he has to travel to Paris to assassinate his former

Far left: the bandits who lead the battle for Sicilian independence in Rosi's Salvatore Giuliana. Below far left: Don José (Placido Domingo) is torn between his duty to the army and his desire for Carmen (Julia Migenes-Johnson) who challenges him to stay with her in Rosi's version of Bizet's opera Carmen (production shot). Below left: Bertolucci's 1900 chronicles the desperate peasant struggle against their repressive landlords. Left: the murder of Professor Quadri (Enzo Taroscio), a political activist, by Italian Fascist hirelings in The Conformist. Below: Philippe Noiret, Marcello Mastroianni and Michel Piccoli as three friends intent on gorging themselves to death in Blow Out.

professor, an influential radical.

Bertolucci's next project was *Ultimo Tango a Parigi* (1972, *Last Tango in Paris*) – his most sexually-orientated film and also his most commercial. The film posits the impossibility of permanence in human sexual relationships; but however pessimistic, few could deny its power, aided by Marlon Brando's often-improvised central performance and Maria Schneider's sensuality.

1900 (1976), his next film, was his most ambitious – the longest and most expensive Italian film ever made. The alternative, and better, title is *Novecento*, which in Italian also means the twentieth century. Bertolucci was determined to cover the whole century in the film's philosophical span. It was to be 'a film about politics which everybody could understand, because it is couched in familiar story-telling terms.' Its sweep is undeniable, the majesty of individual sequences catch the breath, but somehow the whole does not make up the sum of its parts and it falls short of Bertolucci's intentions.

La Luna (1979, *Luna*) seemed to many a hollow and operatic study of modern malcontents, brilliantly filmed but obfuscated by psycho-drama. Even the controversy, which centred on the mother and son sex scene, paled in comparison with the furore created by *Last Tango in Paris*.

He returned to political themes with *La Tragedia di un Uomo Ridicolo* (1981, *The Tragedy of a Ridiculous Man*), about

the kidnapping of a rich man's son. A mystery without a solution and a study of terrorism that neither 'explained' nor totally condemned this phenomenon, it was ill-received in Italy, where terrorism on the extreme Left and Right has provoked such unresolved anxiety.

Bertolucci's central dilemma seems to be that he still wishes to be a Marxist film-maker but has become trapped by an industry that believes only in box-office success.

Marco Ferreri (b. 1928), having achieved some success in Spain with the black comedy *El Cochecito* (1959, *The Wheelchair*), worked in both Italy and France. His elegantly bitter reports on the battle of the sexes included *Dillinger è Morto* (1969, *Dillinger Is Dead*) and *L'Ultima Donna* (1976, *The Last Woman*). His critique of the bourgeois consumer society, implicit in the endless food preparations in *Dillinger Is Dead*, reached an extreme in *La Grande Bouffe* (1973, *Blow-Out*) in which four men eat themselves to death. His first English-language film was *Ciao Maschio* (1978, *Bye By Monkey*), with Marcello Mastroianni as a seedy, asthmatic professor in a decaying New York of the future. In *Storie di Ordinaria Follia* (1982, *Tales of Ordinary Madness*) Ben Gazzara played a drunken American poet in search of love. In contrast to the misogynistic overtones of some earlier films, *Storia di Piera* (1983, *Piera's Story*) portrayed a liberated working-class woman (Hanna Schygulla) and her daughter (Isabelle Huppert).

Marco Bellocchio (b. 1939) made a striking debut with *I Pugni in Tasca* (1965, *Fists in the Pocket*), a study of the destructive tensions within an epileptic middle-class family, set in a small provincial town with Lou Castel as the hyperactive, murderous brother. *La Cina è Vicina* (1966, *China Is Near*) again centred on a family, satirizing the political state of Italy and not even sparing the Maoists with whom Bellocchio's own sympathies lay. *Nel Nome del Padre* (1971, *In the Name of the Father*) used a Jesuit school to stand for the ills of society. *Salta nel Vuoto* (1980, *Leap Into the Void*) was another claustrophobic examination of family life, concentrating on the enigmatic relationship of a middle-aged brother and sister. *Gli Occhi, la Bocca* (1982, *The Eyes, the Mouth*) formed a long-delayed and unsatisfactory sequel to *Fists in the Pocket*.

Gillo Pontecorvo (b. 1919), also a Marxist, has been more concerned with the politics of public life. In *Kapò* (1960), a young Jewish girl becomes an overseer in a concentration camp. *La Battaglia di Algeri* (1966, *Battle of Algiers*) commemorated the early days of the Algerian fight for independence from the French, employing a semi-documentary style and making full use of massive co-operation from the Algerian government and the people of the Casbah, who had lived through the events re-created on screen. *Queimada!* (1969, *Burn!*) again depicted anti-colonialist struggle, this time set on an imaginary Caribbean island, with Marlon Brando giving an extraordinary performance as an aristocratic English *agent provocateur*.

Politics and Film In Liliana Cavani's *I Cannibali* (1970, *The Cannibals*), a latter-day Antigone is determined to bury the body of her rebel brother after a bloody revolution although the authorities have decreed that the dead will lie in the streets as an example to all. Somewhat over-schematic in its political allegory, the film is nevertheless a powerful moral tale for the Seventies and a chilling vision of the incipient

police state which was to provide the thematic basis for many of the finest Italian movies of the next five years.

Typical of such political parables, though distinguished from many by the ingeniousness of its plot and the rigour of Gian Maria Volonté's central performance, was Elio Petri's *Indagine su un Cittadino al di Sopra di Ogni Sospetto* (1970, *Investigation of a Citizen Above Suspicion*), in which a police officer apparently escapes detection for a crime he has committed because his seniority places him 'above suspicion'.

One of the most controversial figures to emerge in the early Seventies was **Lina Wertmuller** (b. 1928), who mounted a policy of populist cinema that would tackle the major issues of the past and the present. Foregrounding sex and politics in a bold and entertaining manner, Wertmuller was acclaimed in the USA as a cult figure. On the surface, her politics appeared to be left-wing – she professed herself a Socialist supporter in interviews – and her treatment of sex seemed progressive, with dominant, self-aware women calling the shots in the sex war. Her various films include *Mimi Metallurgico Ferito nell'Onore* (1972, *The Seduction of Mimi*), *Film d'Amore e d'Anarchia* (1973, *Love and Anarchy*), *Travolti da un Insolito Destino nell'Azzurro Mare d'Agosto* (1975, *Swept Away by an Unusual Destiny in the Blue Sea of August*) and *Pasqualino Settebellezze* (1976, *Seven Beauties*). The reaction against her films from the Left and from feminists was most vociferous in the USA, where they were breaking box-office records for Italian films. Depending on viewpoint, Wertmuller's ideas are either too broad to be confined in social or political labels, or so haphazardly thought-out as to be class-bound and sexist.

By contrast with what threatened to become a complacent bourgeois cinema in France, the revival of civil and political themes in Italian cinema was refreshing. Two notable films, Damiano Damiani's *Confessione di un Commissario di Polizia al Procuratore della Repubblica* (1971, *Confessions of a Police Commissioner to the District Attorney*) and *L'Istruttoria è*

Above: Gian Maria Volonté (left) as a police inspector who seems to have got away with murder in Petri's Investigation of a Citizen Above Suspicion. *Right: Dirk Bogarde as a sadomasochistic SS officer, Charlotte Rampling as his willing concentration-camp victim in* The Night Porter. *By a strange quirk of fate the couple encounter one another after the war and resume their relationship.*

Chiusa: Dimentichi! (1972, The Inquest Is Over: Forget About It!), exposed corruption in the judiciary and the prison system.

Questions of a serious nature about the relations of power to violence and sexuality were also hinted at in a number of Italian box-office hits of the period, including Liliana Cavini's *Il Portiere di Notte* (1974, *The Night Porter*), Lina Wertmuller's *Seven Beauties* and Tinto Brass' *Salon Kitty* (1976): but the treatment was so superficial – on the level of sex and jackboots – as to make no contribution to the understanding of Fascism.

Finally, it should be recalled that the debate about history and its representation on film brought to world recognition several directors who already had at least a decade's experience behind them but whose finest work to date was completed in the Seventies. Francesco Rosi has been mentioned but Ettore Scola (b. 1931) with two films – *C'Eravamo Tanto Amati* (1975, *We All Loved Each Other So Much*) and *Una Giornata Particolare* (1977, *A Special Day*) – and Paolo (b. 1931) and Vittorio (b. 1929) Taviani with *Allonsanfán* (1974), *Padre Padrone* (1977, *Father Master*) and *Kaos* (1984) all greatly contributed to the continuing commitment of their native cinema.

Sweden

By 1962, the decline in the Swedish film industry was at a drastic level, despite the international success of Bergman's productions. The following year, the government took the momentous step of founding the Swedish Film Institute; this was planned by Harry Schein, its first director, in recognition of the fact that, in a mixed economy like Sweden's, the native cinema could survive only with the help of subsidies. A punitive entertainments tax was replaced by a levy of 10 per cent on all box-office receipts. This sum, amounting initially to some £850,000 per annum, financed the Institute: 30 per cent was distributed to all Swedish productions in proportion to their earnings; 33·3 per cent was dispensed in the form of quality awards to Swedish films (valued by a jury of experts); and the balance was earmarked for the promotional, preservational and educational activities associated with more orthodox national film institutes. As a direct result, scores of films were made during the next decade. The prospect of an Institute award made producers willing to take risks.

The new directors who emerged, including Bo Widerberg, Jörn Donner and Vilgot Sjöman, were responsive to the influence of the French *nouvelle vague* and of American low-budget directors like John Cassavetes. Their first films had a raw, naturalistic texture; they dealt with social problems in modern Sweden, while Ingmar Bergman (as they claimed) was immured in his private heaven and hell. The talent of **Bo Widerberg** (b. 1930) was immediately clear in *Kvarteret Korpen* (1964, *Raven's End*), which studies a young author's revolt against his depressing home background during the late Thirties. He achieved world-wide acclaim for the beautifully filmed love story *Elvira Madigan* (1967), *Ådalen '31* (1969) and a feature shot on location in the United States, *Joe Hill* (1971), about the Swedish labour leader executed in dubious circumstances in Utah in 1915. The thriller *Mannen på Taket* (1976, *The Man on the Roof*), was hugely successful in Sweden; Widerberg then returned to romance with *Victoria* (1979). Widerberg's contribution to Swedish cinema consists of a lyrical style allied to an acute sense of social injustice.

In his time, **Jörn Donner** (b. 1933) has served as writer, critic, producer and administrator as well as directing films –

he was managing director of the Swedish Film Institute and then chairman of the Finnish Film Foundation. Of his own features, *Att Älska* (1964, *To Love*), a witty glance at contemporary sexual customs, *Anna* (1970), made in Finland, and *Män Kan inte Våldtas* (1978, *Men Can't Be Raped*) best demonstrate his dry, sardonic approach to life.

Vilgot Sjöman (b. 1924) is the most incorrigibly rebellious of this group. He began in comparatively staid fashion with *Älskarinnan* (1962, *The Mistress*), but in 1967 startled literally millions of people in Sweden and abroad with *Jag Är Nyfiken – Gul* (*I Am Curious – Yellow*), which interspersed an exuberant, lusty girl's search for personal liberty with a documentary inquiry into the shortcomings of Swedish democracy. The sex scenes were so overt that the film was banned in many states in the USA. Sjöman's inventive fire waned somewhat during the Seventies. Only *En Handfull Kärlek* (1974, *A Handful of Love*), a period piece set against the general strike in Sweden in 1909, and *Linus* (1979), about a crime in a mysterious brothel, confirmed his talent.

Jan Troell (b. 1931), a brilliant cameraman as well as director, brought to film the eye of a painter and poet. He captured the sights and sounds of the Swedish landscape – and the people within it – in such masterpieces as *Här Har Du Ditt Liv* (1966, *Here Is Your Life*) and *Utvandrarna* (1971, *The Emigrants*). Troell earned a high reputation overseas for this picture of nineteenth-century Swedish workers making a new home in the United States, even being compared with John Ford. *Nybyggarna* (1972, *The New Land*) was an equally poignant and effective sequel. Troell's ventures into English-language film-making did not prove successful; but *Ingenjör Andrées Luftfärd* (1982, *The Flight of the Eagle*) marked a return to the epic genre.

Below: a moment of carefree passion for the ill-fated lovers Thommy Berggren and Pia Degermark) of Elvira Madigan.

Below: hi-jinks in the woods in I Am Curious – Yellow *(production shot). Below right: location filming of* Hugo and Josephine, *with Marie Öhman as the little girl Josephine and Beppe Wolgers as Gudmarsson, her father's gardener. Right: Anna Godenius as a rape victim determined to take revenge on her assailant in* Men Can't Be Raped. *Below far right: Maria Schneider and Monique van der Ven making* Eeen vrouw als Eva, *in which a wife leaves her family for a girlfriend. Far right:* Blue Movie *was an independent box-office success in Europe and the USA.*

A second wave of film-makers followed swiftly during the later Sixties. Mai Zetterling came back to her native country to direct three scrupulously-made features from a feminist point of view, the most lasting of which will no doubt be *Älskande Par* (1964, *Loving Couples*), about some restless young society women during the period 1910–20. Jonas Cornell brought to the screen an ironic and detached vision of modern life in the comedy *Puss och Kram* (1967, *Hugs and Kisses*) and the social drama *Som Natt och Dag* (1969, *Like Night and Day*), both starring his wife, Agneta Ekmanner.

Kjell Grede made a splendid debut with *Hugo och Josephine* (1967, *Hugo and Josephine*), a children's film that appealed also to adults, and integrated the blithest and most touching of stories with the felicities of the summer landscape. Grede's subsequent films have grown more introspective, even mystical in tone, with *Harry Munter* (1969) the most rigorous and sensitive. By contrast, Jan Halldoff, starting in 1965, has kept his eye firmly on the everyday life and loves of young Swedes. His films are shot with authority, and often do well at the box-office, the most memorable being *Korridoren* (1968, The Corridor), about a young doctor. Johan Bergenstråhle has fiercely tackled social issues, dealing with capitalist corruption in *Made in Sweden* (1969), the problems of immigration in *Jag Heter Stelios* (1972, *Foreigners*) and the forcible repatriation of political refugees after the war in *Baltutlämningen* (1970, *A Baltic Tragedy*).

In 1972, the statutes of the Film Reform of 1963 were amended so as to give more active encouragement to produc-tion, with grants being advanced ahead of shooting. This led to the emergence of yet a third wave of directors, although quality and talent remained scarce. Gunnel Lindblom, an actress in Ingmar Bergman's films, made her debut as a director with *Paradistorg* (1977, *Summer Paradise*), which, despite a schematic scenario, included some engaging conversations and a persuasive picture of the Swedish family under stress. Another woman director, Marianne Ahrne, announced her own idiosyncratic style of movie-making with *Långt Borta och Nära* (1976, *Near and Far Away*), about a love affair in a mental hospital involving a young man psychologically unable to speak and a social worker, while Mats Arehn quickly showed himself deft at handling both drama and comedy with *Maria* (1975), *Uppdraget* (1977, *The Assignment*) and *Mannen Som Blev Miljonär* (1980, To Be a Millionaire).

Stefan Jarl has made two remarkable and disturbing documentaries, *Dom Kallar Oss Mods* (1968, *They Call Us Misfits*) and *Ett Anständigt Liv* (1979, *A Respectable Life*), describing the punitive attitude to drug-use in a so-called free society. More entertaining, and a boon for jazz lovers, was *Sven Klangs Kvintett* (1976, *Sven Klang's Combo*), which evoked the Fifties through music and was made by a team including members of the radical October Group and intelligently directed by Stellan Olsson.

Denmark

Denmark's establishment of the Danish Film Foundation, one year after its Swedish model, gave hope to new directors. Few

several kinds of film – comedy, science fiction, contemporary satire, social broadsheet – before being tragically killed in a road crash after the premiere of his finest film, *Jäniksen Vuosi* (1977, *The Year of the Hare*).

Two women directors should be noted. From Finland, Pirjo Honkasalo made, with Pekka Lehto, the striking epic *Tulipää* (1981, Firebrand); and from Norway, Anja Breien is best known for *Hustruer* (1975, *Wives*), a hilarious response to John Cassavetes' *Husbands* (1970), and for *Arven* (1979, The Legacy), dealing with guilt and rapacity in the archetypal Norwegian family.

The Netherlands

The documentary tradition inaugurated in the late Twenties and early Thirties by Joris Ivens was carried on by his collaborators, including John Fernhout (Ferno), cameraman-turned-director and eventually a Cannes prize-winner for *Sky Over Holland* (1967), and Helen van Dongen who edited Flaherty's *Louisiana Story* (1948). Meanwhile, as in the silent period, feature production continued on a small scale, not on the whole greatly improved by an influx of refugee directors from the German industry, including Max Ophuls, Douglas Sirk and Ludwig Berger.

After World War II, **Bert Haanstra** (b. 1916) became the leading documentarist with *Spiegel van Holland* (1951, *Mirror of Holland*), which showed the country as reflected in its lakes, rivers and canals. His many short films included the Oscar-winning *Glas* (1958, *Glass*) and the humorously observant *Zoo* (1962). His first feature, *Fanfare* (1958), was an Ealing-style comedy about rival brass bands in a country village, with script assistance from Alexander Mackendrick. It was a big hit, but its successor flopped and Haanstra turned to feature-length documentaries with *Alleman* (1964, *The Human Dutch*), a candid-camera look at his fellow-countrymen, *De Stem van het Water* (1967, *The Voice of the Water*) showing the Dutch relationship to the sea and the canals, and *Bij de Beesten af* (1972, *Ape and Super-Ape*), about man and the animal kingdom. He resumed making fiction films with the dark, obsessive *Dokter Pulder Zaait Papavers* (1975, *When the Poppies Bloom Again*) and a study of elderly businessmen, *Een Pak Slaag* (1979, *Mr Slotter's Jubilee*).

Other distinguished documentarists include **Charles Huguenot van der Linden** (b. 1909) and **Herman van der Horst** (1911–76). Van der Linden 'discovered' Audrey Hepburn for the semi-documentary *Dutch in Seven Lessons* (1948), financed by J. Arthur Rank, and has also made fiction shorts and features. His *Bouspelement* (1963, *The Building Game*) won a prize for Best Short at Berlin. He later won an Oscar for *Die Kleine Wereld* (1972, *This Tiny World*), about antique toys in a museum. Van der Horst depicted nature and the sea, as in *Het Schot is te Boord* (1952, *Shoot the Nets*), but he also encompassed the 'city symphony' tradition, as in *Amsterdam* (1965).

The most sustained career in feature films was that of **Fons Rademakers** (b. 1920). *Dorp aan de Rivier* (1958, *Doctor in the Village*) was a tragi-comic story of primitive rural life at the turn of the century. *Het Mes* (1960, *The Knife*) showed a boy coming to terms with adolescent traumas. *De Dans van de Reiger* (1966, *Dance of the Heron*), made in Yugoslavia, depicted a crisis in a troubled marriage and starred Gunnel Lindblom as the wife. *Mira* (1971), filmed in Belgium, was another rural tragi-comedy, with a sexy heroine contributing to its box-office success. Rademakers' most ambitious film was an epic of corruption in Java, *Max Havelaar* (1976).

Danish film-makers, however, have enjoyed more than intermittent success. **Henning Carlsen** (b. 1927) whose *Sult* (1966, *Hunger*) won the Best Actor Award at Cannes for Per Oscarsson, is the exception: he is unusually adroit at analysing the growth of relationships among people of disparate ages and backgrounds. Other directors of note include Jørgen Leth, whose films on cycle-racing are loved and admired in sporting circles; Henrik Stangerup, a novelist who made some sensitive features before leaving Denmark; and Morten Arnfred, with his humorous and perceptive studies of teenage development, *Mig og Charly* (1978, Me and Charly) and *Johnny Larsen* (1980).

Finland

Finland did not have a Film Foundation until 1969, and its inauguration by no means assured a renaissance. But four key figures (in addition to Jörn Donner) persisted with their personal films during the Seventies. Mikko Niskanen has worked for both television and the large screen, with *Kahdeksan Surmanluotia* (1972, Eight Deadly Shots) as his most trenchant accomplishment – an attack, like so many Finnish books and films, on the ravages of alcoholism and rural poverty. Rauni Mollberg is a painstaking artist who has brought the inhabitants of Lapland vigorously to life in three features, the best being *Maa on Syntinen Laulu* (1973, *Earth Is a Sinful Song*). Erkko Kivikoski has focused on social pressures and the interplay of domestic passions. The most significant Finnish *auteur*, Risto Jarva, had developed into a master of

The team of Pim de la Parra and Wim Verstappen founded Scorpio Films in 1965 and, taking turns as producer and director, turned out 15 films in a dozen years, frequently using English soundtracks for international sales. Martin Scorsese co-wrote de la Parra's thriller *Obsessions* (1969). Verstappen's debut film was *Minder Gelukkige Terugkeer van Joszef Katús naar het Land van Rembrandt* (1966, The Less Fortunate Return of Joszef Katús to the Land of Rembrandt), set in Amsterdam against the background of the anarchist Provo movement. His *Blue Movie* (1971) was a commercial hit, but *Dakota* (1974), about a hazardous transatlantic flight, and *Alicia* (1975), about a dissatisfied wife, did more for his reputation. After parting from de la Parra, he made *Pastorale 1943* (1978), concerning the fumbling efforts of the wartime Resistance in the Dutch countryside.

The most commercially successful director of the Seventies was **Paul Verhoeven** (b. 1931), who usually worked with the enterprising producer Rob Houwer and scriptwriter Gerard Soeteman. His early films, *Wat Zien Ik?* (1971, *Any Special Way*) and *Turks Fruit* (1973, *Turkish Delight*) trod a fine line between social comment and sexual exploitation. He turned to historical reconstruction in *Keetje Tippel* (1975, *Cathy Tippel*) and, more challengingly, in *Soldat van Oranje* (1977, *Soldier of Orange/Survival Run*), a wartime film that depicted Dutch anti-semitism and fascist sympathies as well as the heroism of the Resistance. *Spetters* (1980, *Wild Dreams*), concerned with motorbike racing, recapitulated the ambiguous stance of Verhoeven's first films; but *De Vierde Man* (1983, *The Fourth Man*), an ambitious thriller, consolidated his reputation.

Nouchka van Brakel (b. 1940) established herself as the top woman director with *Het Debuut* (1977, The Debut) about a young girl's first affair and *Een Vrouw als Eva* (1978, A Woman Like Eve), about a wife who leaves her family for a girlfriend. Her handsome period melodrama *Van de Koele Meren des Doods* (1982, The Cool Lakes of Death) chronicled the decline and fall of a bourgeois young woman. Other women film-makers include Lili Rademakers, Anette Apon, Mady Saks and Marleen Gorris. The best-known avant-garde director, depicting sex as ritual, is Frans Zwartjes (b. 1927), whose *Zeventig Minuten?* (1976, *It's Me*) spends over an hour examining an actress (Willeke van Ammelrooy) preparing for a date.

Belgium

Belgium, like Canada and Switzerland, is a country divided along linguistic lines, and this makes its already small population almost too fractional to support a native film industry. In effect, there was none until the Sixties. Top talents, such as director Jacques Feyder and writer Charles Spaak, emigrated to France; and it was left to the documentarists, notably Henri Storck, to keep Belgium's film reputation alive. Belgium's breakthrough year was 1967, when André Delvaux' *De Man Die Zijn Haar Kort Liet Knippen* (1966, *The Man Who Had His Hair Cut Short*) won the British Film Institute's Sutherland Trophy as the most original and imaginative film of the year, and Jerzy Skolimowski's *Le Départ* (1967, The Departure) won the Grand Prix at Berlin.

Harry Kümel (b. 1940) made an outstanding debut in 1968 with the Dutch co-production *Monsieur Hawarden*, a baroque fantasy of ideas. A similar approach worked less well in such later films as *Malpertuis: Histoire d'une Maison Maudite* (1972, *Malpertuis*) and *Het Verloren Paradijs* (1977, The Lost Paradise). **André Delvaux** (b. 1926) had more success with

his later films, working in both French and Flemish. His finest achievement was an epitome of poetic ambiguity, *Rendez-vous à Bray* (1971, *Rendezvous at Bray*); but he has continued to excel in such films as *Belle* (1973) and *Une Femme Entre Chien et Loup* (1979, *Woman in a Twilight Garden*).

The second wave of Belgian directors emerged from the avant-garde in the early Seventies, led by the highly original **Chantal Akerman** (b. 1950) whose *Jeanne Dielman, 23 Quai du Commerce, 1080 Bruxelles* (1975) was a deliberately paced but powerful piece of intensely feminist cinema, over three-and-a-half hours long. Her later films, including *Les Rendez-vous d'Anna* (1978, *Anna's Rendezvous*) and *Toute une Nuit* (1982, *All Night Long*), increased her reputation. Jean-Jacques Andrien made a strong impact in 1975 with his hallucinatory *Le Fils d'Amr Est Mor* (Amr's Son Is Dead). One of Akerman's associates, Samy Szlingerbaum, became a director himself in 1980 with the sensitive Yiddish-language *Bruxelles – Transit* (Brussels – Transit).

Switzerland

Swiss cinema hardly existed before the Sixties; its roots were in Fifties Britain – Alain Tanner and Claude Goretta were both associated with the Free Cinema movement and made the short *Nice Time* together in 1957. State finance and television money finally got the Swiss feature industry under way in the late Sixties and, as in Canada, it was the French-language film-makers who made the initial running, notably **Alain Tanner** (b. 1929) with *La Salamandre* (1971, *The Salamander*), Michel Soutter with *Les Arpenteurs* (1972, The Surveyors) and **Claude Goretta** (b.1929) with *L'Invitation* (1973, *The Invitation*). All were founding members of the Group of 5 production company, which helped to make the Swiss cinema a viable international force. Tanner was interested in socio-political investigation, especially in *Le Retour d'Afrique* (1973, *Return from Africa*) and *Jonas: Qui Aura 25 Ans en l'An 2000* (1976, *Jonah Who Will Be 25 in the Year 2000*), but turned mystical in the English-language *Light Years Away* (1981), filmed in Ireland. Goretta was the explorer of human frailty, especially in his masterpiece *La Dentellière* (1977, *The Lacemaker*).

The Geneva-based French-language directors had a rather delicate Alpine-airy quality in the films, a stark contrast to the heavier work of the German-language directors who emerged from Zürich in the middle of the decade. Thomas Koerfer was the most intellectual, with such intensely Brechtian films as *Der Tod des Flohzirkusdirektors oder Ottacaro Weiss reformiert seine Firma* (1973, *The Death of the Director of the Flea Circus*), highly theatrical in style, and *Der Gehülfe* (1976, *The Assistant*). Daniel Schmid was more operatic and style-conscious, as he demonstrated in *La Paloma* (1974) and *Schatten der Engel* (1976, *Shadows of Angels*). Rolf Lyssy put Swiss society under a critical microscope in *Konfrontation* (1975, *Konfrontation: Assassination in Davos*) and *Die Schweizermacher* (1978, *The Swissmakers*).

Spain

The biggest disappointment of the Seventies was the new Spanish cinema. At the beginning of the decade, a group of young film-makers headed by Carlos Saura seemed certain to give birth to a major new cinema as Franco's hold on Spain weakened. Good films were produced and new directors did appear but the expected breakthrough did not happen.

The obsessions of **Carlos Saura** (b. 1932) became central to Spanish cinema in such films as *La Caza* (1966, *The Hunt*),

Below left: Anna Torrent as the girl who believes she has befriended Frankenstein's Monster in The Spirit of the Beehive. *Far left: Delphine Seyrig in Akerman's* Jeanne Dielman. *Left: Bulle Ogier in* The Salamander. *Below: regret gnaws François (Yves Beneyton) when he visits his gentle former girlfriend (Isabelle Huppert), now an inmate in a sanatorium in* The Lacemaker.

Above: the actors arrive at a provincial railway station at the beginning of The Travelling Players.

Peppermint Frappé (1967), Cría Cuervos (1976, Raise Ravens) and Deprisa, Deprisa (1981, Quickly, Quickly). He also experimented with dance films, Bodas de Sangre (1981, Blood Wedding) and Carmen (1983), in which ballet was influenced by the flamenco tradition.

The best Spanish film of the Seventies was Victor Erice's El Espiritu de la Colmena (1973, The Spirit of the Beehive); few other films were able to reflect the psychological state of Spain with such accuracy and effectiveness.

Erice followed it a decade later with El Sur (1983, The South), another period piece, again revealing deep insight into the contradictions of the Spanish experience and an extraordinary gift for directing children.

Two new talents of the Seventies were José Luis Borau with Furtivos (1975, Poachers) and Jaime Camino with Las Largas Vacaciones del 36 (1976, The Long Holidays of 1936). Pilar Miró's El Crimen de Cuenca (1980, The Cuenca Crime) depicted the Civil Guard as being less than angelic; it was totally banned in Spain and a military court ordered all copies destroyed. The death of Franco had not changed Spain as much as had been hoped.

Greece and Turkey

Strict controls of content affected the young Greek film-makers in the Seventies as commercial production began to drop and audiences slipped away to television. The major film-maker who emerged was **Theodor Angelopoulos** (b. 1935), whose Anaparastassis (1970, Reconstruction) was a critical hit at the 1971 Berlin Festival. Angelopoulos seemed to have borrowed stylistically from Miklós Jancsó for his second, more overtly political film Meres Tou 36 (1972, Days of 36); but the borrowings were fully absorbed in his third film and masterpiece O Thiassos (1975, The Travelling Players), an updated left-wing version of Aeschylus' classical tragic trilogy, The Oresteia, spanning the years 1939–52, and perhaps the greatest film in the history of Greek cinema. His more recent films, also long and epic in style, are I Kinigui (1977, The Hunters) and O Megalèxandros (1980, Alexander the Great), mixing history and myth with political and cinematic awareness in long, continuous shots.

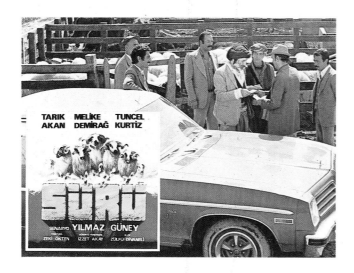

Above: Güney's brilliant The Herd *won the British Film Institute Award for 1979.*

Greece's neighbour, Turkey, produced nearly two hundred films in 1979, but is mainly known around the world for the work of **Yilmaz Güney** (1937–84) who began as a star actor and went on to writing and directing, taking his popular audience with him. His criticisms of injustice aroused the animosity of officialdom and he was imprisoned on political grounds. Later, he received a 19-year sentence for shooting a judge and had to make films from prison, directed on his behalf by his associate Zeki Ökten. *Sürü* (1979, *The Herd*) and *Düsman* (1980, The Enemy) were made in this way. *Yol* (1982), a harsh story of five men on brief compassionate leave from prison, directed this time by Serif Gören, was a surprising international hit, following its Grand Prix at Cannes. Having meanwhile escaped from prison, Güney was able to edit *Yol* himself and to direct as well as write *Le Mur* (1983, *Güney's The Wall*) in France. This re-created a revolt in 1976 by children held in an Ankara prison.

The USSR

Nikita Khruschev's revelation in 1956 of the Stalinist excesses that had led to death or imprisonment for so many in the preceding years awoke the need throughout Eastern Europe to tell the truth about other aspects of life and to discover reality, not least in the cultural sphere; and the cinema played its part in this general movement.

In the Soviet Union, the social and personal problems of the Stalinist period were shown in an important series of films, most of which have not been seen in the West. Increased production allowed younger film-makers, graduates of the Film School (VGIK), to break with the restrictive formulae of earlier years. But the official attack on culture that began in 1962–3 led to a tightening of control in the second half of the Sixties.

Grigori Chukhrai, who had already promised much with *Sorok Pervyi* (1956, *The Forty-First*) and *Ballada o Soldate* (1960, *Ballad of a Soldier*), directed *Chistoie Nebo* (*Clear Skies*) in 1961. The story of a pilot who becomes the victim of Stalinist persecution, it had a great impact in the Soviet Union. Alexei Saltykov's *Predsedatel* (1964, *The Chairman*) which discusses the problems of the collective farms in an open way never previously allowed, was personally supported by Khruschev, whereas Marlen Khutsiev's *Zastava Ilychi* (1961, Ilyich Square) had been the main focus of his attack on the film industry in 1963. A neo-realist-inspired story of three young people searching vainly for moral ideals in contemporary Moscow, it was substantially re-shot and re-edited and only released – as *Mne Dvadtsat Let* (*I Am Twenty*) – in 1964.

Despite pressures, the Sixties saw the emergence of some remarkable new film-makers who managed to establish an international reputation. Foremost among these were Andrei Tarkovsky, Andrei Mikhalkov-Konchalovsky and Sergei Paradzhanov.

Andrei Tarkovsky, however, has clearly not been at all times a source of comfort and satisfaction to the Soviet cultural establishment. His first feature film, *Ivanovo Detstvo* (1962, *Ivan's Childhood*), won the Golden Lion of the Venice Film Festival – and had, superficially at least, enough of the patriotic and heroic view of World War II to gain approval at home.

On the face of it, Tarkovsky's next subject looked safe enough: a re-creation of the world of the early fifteenth-century Russian icon painter Andrei Rublev. Completed in 1965, the film was not seen until 1969 when it appeared unheralded at the Cannes Film Festival. It took another three years for *Andrei Rublev* to be shown in the Soviet Union.

Solaris (1972), a science-fiction film based on a novel by the Polish writer Stanislaw Lem, is a haunting work – the story of scientists under the influence of a planet whose forces work to give their inner desires an illusory existence.

Zerkalo (1975, *Mirror*), an exercise in autobiography which like much of Tarkovsky's work freely manipulates time and space, the real and the surreal, was condemned as a 'film crossword puzzle' and shelved. Finally, after a year or so, it was released.

It is an over-simplification, though, to see Tarkovsky – for all the recurrent incomprehension and suspicion which his films have aroused in the Soviet Union – as a dissident martyr. He remains, above all, a *Russian* artist.

Tarkovsky was born in Zavrozhe in 1932. His father, Arseni Tarkovsky, a well-known poet, left his wife and child when Andrei was very small. The loss had a profound effect on him: the young boys in *Ivan's Childhood* and *Andrei Rublev* who are forced to abandon their childhood to assert their manhood, and adopt the roles of their own lost fathers, are the most memorable and heart-rending figures in his work. *Mirror*, in which the poems of Tarkovsky's father are read, and his mother plays her own real-life role, also reflects the pain at this early loss of a parent.

The compulsive, mystifying *Stalker* (1979) is set in an unspecified but not too distant future. The Zone is a space which, since some inexplicable interplanetary visitation, has remained shut off, forbidden, dangerous. The Stalker is one of a race of people who live by penetrating the Zone, guiding people there.

The central situation of the film, a quest, an adventure in search of confrontation with a man's own soul, is very much paralleled by *Andrei Rublev* and *Solaris* (each has the same actor, Anatoli Solonitsin, in a leading role).

No less durable than the metaphysical odysseys of Tarkovsky's films, however, is the visual magic of his cinema. Each film creates its own world: the beautiful birch woods of *Ivan's Childhood* concealing deathly menace; the violent, medieval chaos of *Andrei Rublev*; the contrasted worlds of cold technology and pantheistic nature in *Solaris*. The future universe of *Stalker* is formed out of the ruins, pollution and detritus of the modern world: poisoned landscapes, decayed buildings, foul mud, putrid water.

Tarkovsky made *Nostalghia* (1983, *Nostalgia*) in Italy. It was concerned with themes of exile, homesickness and ritual, as well as the difficulty and necessity of human contact. The following year he decided not to return to the Soviet Union and began to prepare a second production in Western Europe.

The feature debut of **Andrei Mikhalkov-Konchalovsky** (b. 1937), *Pervyi Uchitel* (1965, *The First Teacher*), co-scripted by Tarkovsky, met much the same reaction as *Ivan's Childhood*. Dealing with the establishment of Soviet rule in Kirghizia in 1923, it was ideologically acceptable but showed an unusual stylistic attack prompting comparisons with Wajda and Visconti. After working with Tarkovsky on the script of *Andrei Rublev*, Konchalovsky made *Istoriya Asi Klyachinoi, Kutoraya Lyubila, da ne Vyshla Zamukh* (1966, *Asya's Happiness*), a portrait of life in a contemporary village, done on location with a mixture of professional and amateur actors. It was promptly banned until 1969 and he retired to the safe area of the classics with versions of a Turgenev novel, *Dvorianskoye Gniezdo* (1969, *A Nest of Gentlefolk*) and a Chekhov play, *Dyadya Vanya* (1970, *Uncle Vanya*).

Below: the desolate, war-torn landscape of Ivan's Childhood. *Bottom: molten lead is prepared for pouring down a man's throat in* Andrei Rublev.

The Georgian-born Armenian director **Sergei Paradzhanov** (b. 1924) provided his own jolt to the status quo with *Teni Zabytykh Predkov* (1964, *Shadows of Our Forgotten Ancestors*), made in the Ukraine. He placed his emphasis on the visual elements of the film, drawing his inspiration from folklore and ethnography and holding to a very simple, naive storyline. His later film *Nran Gouyne* (1969, *The Colour of Pomegranates*), based on the life of the eighteenth-century Armenian poet Aruthin Sayadin or 'Sayat Nova', again focused on the beauty of imagery. However, its espousal of Armenian cultural and religious traditions, together with its extreme obscurity, presumably led to suspicions of nationalism and formalism. Re-edited and cut, it was released in the Soviet Union in 1973; but its export was restricted until 1983.

Paradzhanov was working on an adaptation of Hans Andersen's stories with the veteran writer and formalist critic Viktor Shklovsky when he was arrested and sentenced to a labour camp from 1974 to 1977.

Below: The Stalker *(centre) meets* The Writer *and* The Scientist *prior to leading them into the Zone. Bottom: Ivan Kikolaichuk in* Shadows of Our Forgotten Ancestors.

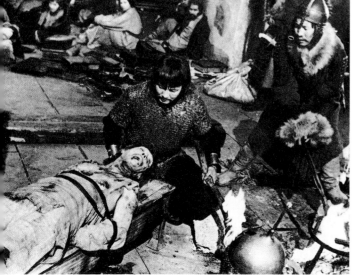

Right: Pirosmani *told the life story of the Georgian primitive painter who fled from his own wedding and eventually died penniless and alcoholic, in 1918.*

Paradzhanov's films were made in the Ukraine and Armenia and it is in the non-Russian republics that some of the most interesting films are being produced, drawing on very different cultural and historical sources. The Ukraine, Moldavia and Lithuania can be singled out but the films have been little seen outside of the Soviet Union. Georgian cinema has had a rather better exposure with such films as *Pirosmani* (1972), directed by Georgi Shengelaya, and Tengiz Abuladze's *Drevo Zhelanya* (1977, *The Wishing Tree*).

Poland

Although Polish cinema had attracted attention in the Fifties, the 'Polish school' was criticized for its negative tendencies and the Sixties marked a period of relative eclipse. The decade began well with Andrzej Wajda's *Niewinni Czarodzieje* (1960, *Innocent Sorcerers*) and Roman Polanski's *Nóż w Wodzie* (1962, *Knife in the Water*), the first a portrait of the disillusion of contemporary youth, the second a triangle drama involving conflict between the generations. But both were attacked politically in 1963 as the kind of films that should be avoided.

Jerzy Skolimowski (b. 1938) had collaborated on both scripts. His own feature films, *Rysopis* (1964, *Identification Marks: None*), *Walkower* (1965, *Walkover*), *Bariera* (1966, *Barrier*) and *Ręce do Góry* (1967, *Hands Up!*), revealed his characteristic interest in the myths and preoccupations of different generations coupled with a sense of the absurd and an innovative, surrealist technique. *Hands Up!*, which he regarded as the best of his Polish films, was banned for its symbolic criticism of Polish society. Since then, he has directed such features as *Deep End* (1970), *Moonlighting* (1982), *The Shout* (1978), and *Success Is the Best Revenge* (1984) in Western Europe.

Krzysztof Zanussi (b. 1939) was the only other major new talent to emerge in the Sixties. Zanussi, whose background is in physics and philosophy, eschews the visual pyrotechnics of many of his colleagues for a quiet and profound analysis of the situations in which his contemporary heroes find themselves. *Struktura Krysztatu* (1969, The Structure of Crystals), his first feature, analysed the clash between two scientists, each possessing a different attitude to life – urban ambition as against rural quietism. In *Życie Rodzinne* (1971, *Family Life*) the modern hero returns to his family home to confront the world in which he was raised, while *Iluminacja* (1973, *Illumination*) focuses on self-awareness in a more physical sense as its hero faces the onset of heart disease. *Constans* (1980, *The Constant Factor*) is a study of an intelligent young man who fails to attain his objectives in life when he refuses to go along with petty corruption and nepotism.

Towards the end of the Seventies, with the first murmurings of new political unrest in Poland, the cinema adopted an increasingly militant stance. Zanussi's *Barwy Ochronne* (1976, *Camouflage*), describing the relationships involved in a university seminar, brilliantly exposed and satirized the machinery of political manipulation and the survival of attitudes and personalities from the bad old days of 'Personality Cult'. The official displeasure attracted by this film was soon eclipsed by the offence given to the establishment by Wajda's *Człowiek z Marmuru* (1976, *Man of Marble*), a brilliant critique of recent Polish history through the central figure of a worker hero of the Fifties who became a victim of the repressions of the late Sixties. The film was held back; and Wajda's next, *Bez Znieczulenia* (1978, *Rough Treatment*), described feelingly the social humiliations and economic privations reserved for public figures who stepped out of line.

Wajda and Zanussi were both artistic heads of studios; and their influence was felt through younger disciples, like Agnieszka Holland, who had worked as scenarist with Wajda and made a notable directorial debut with *Aktorzy Prowincjonalni* (1978, *Provincial Actors*); and **Krzysztof Kieślowski** (b. 1947), whose *Amator* (1979, *Camera Buff*) laid bare the mechanisms of official half-truth and untruth. These were among the first films of a whole wave which now began to criticize social institutions and looked with a new frankness at recent history. This new wave coincided chronologically and spiritually with the great popular support for the Solidarity movement. Wajda and Zanussi remained in the forefront. Wajda's *Człowiek z Żelaza* (1981, *Man of Iron*), continuing the story of *Man of Marble* up to the present, chronicled the whole background and inspiration of Solidarity: Lech Wałęsa personally figures in the film; and much of the drama is set against documentary scenes of the turbulent history of that movement. Western-financed, Zanussi's *Z Dalekiego Kraju* (1981, *From a Far Country*), nominally the life story of Pope John Paul, was in fact an epic panorama of Poland's history.

The new spirit came to an end, inevitably, when the surge of Solidarity was finally restrained by martial law in December 1981. The films of the Solidarity epoch were withdrawn. Some film-makers, like Agnieszka Holland, emigrated. Of those who stayed, those who had been most outspoken were silenced and lost their official posts. To a large degree control of the cinema – gravely restricted by the economic difficulties of the time – fell into the hands of conformists and time-servers. Zanussi and Wajda worked abroad: in France Wajda directed a film version (1982) of the play *Danton*, which he had successfully staged in the theatre in Warsaw; he then directed a West German–French co-production about the tragic wartime love of a German woman and a Polish prisoner of war, *Liebe in Deutschland* (1984, *Love in Germany*). To prove that the new Polish cinema had not been entirely stifled, one of the youngest of the new directors,

Juliusz Machulski, who had earlier directed a witty 'caper' comedy *Vabank* (1981) made *Seksmisja* (1984, *Sex Mission*), which employed a superficially farcical science-fiction comedy to provide a sharp allegory on every kind of political terror. Zanussi resumed work in Poland with a West German co-production *Rok spokojnego slonca* (1984, *Year of the Quiet Sun*).

Czechoslovakia

In the late Fifties, a number of important films were produced which can be considered forerunners of the Czechoslovak 'New Wave'. Directors making their debuts included Vojtěch Jasný, František Vláčil, Karel Kachyňa, Zbyněk Brynych and Ladislav Helge. With older directors such as Václav Krška and the team of Ján Kadár and Elmar Klos, they produced a body of work that challenged the conventions of the Fifties. The challenge took two forms: an attempt to look honestly at contemporary society: and a revival of Czech lyricism applied to a basically humanist subject-matter. A number of the films were examined at a special conference in 1959, as a result of which five were banned and the head of the Barrandov studios sacked. But all of the directors went on to make a major contribution in the Sixties, notably Kadár and Klos with their *Obchod na korze* (1965, *A Shop on the High Street*).

The first breakthrough of the Sixties came with the Slovak film by Štefan Uher, *Slnko v sieti* (1963, Sunshine in a Net), a

Above: Krysztyna Janda as a sympathetic student in Wajda's Rough Treatment, *which traces the systematic persecution of a journalist by the authorities. Top: Jane Asher as a swimming-pool attendant and John Moulder Brown as her young admirer in Skolimowski's* Deep End.

Top to bottom: Jeremy Irons (second from right) in Moonlighting, *about a group of Polish builders working in Britain; the birth of the worker's union Solidarity in* Man of Iron; *Jozef Kroner and Ida Kaminska in* A Shop on the High Street, *the first Czech film to win an Oscar.*

Above: Andula (Hana Brejchová), the girl who is deceived by a young travelling pianist in A Blonde in Love. *Above right: Magda Vašáryová in the title role of* Markéta Lazarová, *with František Velocký as her seducer. Above far right: lesbian vampires from* Valerie and Her Week of Wonders. *Far right: Věra Chytilová's film had only limited distribution in the West. Right: Jack Nicholson as the rebellious, charismatic MacMurphy, imprisoned for rape in an insane asylum in Forman's multi-Oscar-winning* One Flew Over the Cuckoo's Nest.

complex, poetic account of the problems of contemporary youth which was accused of containing a coded political message. In 1963 a number of new directors made their first films and were stimulated by a desire to reflect society in a non-stereotyped fashion, to focus on the 'look' of everyday life and to examine the lives of non-heroes. They included **Jaromil Jireš** (b. 1935), whose debut film was *Křik* (*The Cry*), Miloš Forman and Věra Chytilová. All in different ways were influenced *cinémavérité*.

The one group which remained faithful to the realist tendencies of 1963 consisted of Forman and his two friends and script collaborators, Ivan Passer and Jaroslav Papoušek. Together they developed a recognizable style of film-making, with both Passer and Papoušek becoming directors in their own right. In their preference for non-actors, everyday themes, functional use of camera and casual approach to

Passer made one Czech feature of his own, *Intimní osvětlení* (1966, *Intimate Lighting*); but most of his films have been made in the USA, including *Born to Win* (1971) and the thoughtful post-Vietnam thriller *Cutter's Way* (1981). Papoušek's debut film was *Nejkrásnější věk* (1968, The Most Beautiful Age) and he then made the first of his comedies about a typical man, *Ecce Homo Homolka* (1969, Behold the Man Homolka).

Miloš Forman (b. 1932) studied drama at the Prague Academy and wrote several scripts before directing a couple of medium-length documentaries in 1963. Forman's first feature-length movie, *Cerný Petr* (*Peter and Pavla*), also appeared in 1963. Played by non-professional actors, and to some extent improvised, the film has a deceptive simplicity. The situation it describes – to call it a plot would be an overstatement – is the quintessential one of an adolescent boy coming to terms with his first job, at the same time putting up with his parents and making unsure advances to girlfriends.

In *Lásky jedné plavovlásky* (1965, *A Blonde in Love*), the central character is Andula (Hana Brejchová), a teenage girl whose infatuation with a young dance-band pianist leads her to mistake his casual affection for the start of a lasting relationship. Most memorable are two brilliant set piece sequences at the provincial dance-hall.

With his first colour film, *Hoří, má panenko* (1967, *The Fireman's Ball*), Forman moved on to different ground. The ostensible material is in much the same vein – the comic difficulties attached to holding the annual fire-brigade dance in a small Czech town. However, with an ambition that belies its modest scope, *The Fireman's Ball* can be read as a satirical allegory on the failings of Czechoslovakia's socialist bureaucracy.

When, in August 1968, Soviet tanks moved into Czechoslovakia to crush the reformists, Forman was in Paris. He opted to become an expatriate and the following year moved to the United States. His first American film was *Taking Off* (1971). The situation around which the film is woven is again of the utmost simplicity, and the central figure is again a teenager, a girl who runs away from home.

Taking Off belongs unmistakably to Forman in its idiosyncratic precision and command of tempo. Perhaps the movie's most ingenious device is to shift the emphasis away from Jeannie (Linnea Heacock) — the runaway seeking the bright lights of showbiz — to her well-to-do suburban parents (admirably played by Lynn Carlin and Buck Henry) who learn to loosen up a little.

Forman went on to the movie for which he is best known, *One Flew Over the Cuckoo's Nest* (1975), winner of five Oscars and a huge box-office success. Adapted from the Ken Kesey novel which achieved cult-status in the Sixties' counterculture, it tells of an unlikely rebel in even more unlikely surroundings — a state mental hospital — and the ultimate terrible revenge (lobotomy) that the system takes against him. Beginning as an almost realistic comedy — parts of it actually being shot at the Oregon State Hospital — the film escalates into tragic melodrama.

Forman's subsequent project represented a considerable change of pace although it too looked back to the Sixties, in fact to one of the most spectacular theatrical icons of the decade's latter half, the 'tribal rock' musical *Hair*. Sadly, however, Forman's 1979 movie version cannot be considered a success.

Forman then for the first time tackled a full-scale period piece. *Ragtime* (1981) is an adaptation of E.L. Doctorow's best-selling novel of the same name, an ambitious panorama of American life in the early years of this century. Dino De Laurentiis, its producer, claimed that he lost $10 million in making the film. Nevertheless, Forman returned to Czechoslovakia in 1983 to work on an adaptation of Peter Shaffer's play about Mozart and Salieri, *Amadeus* (1984), which proved to be his first critical and commercial hit in almost a decade.

Other directors worked alongside Forman's group, in a form derived from the tradition of critical realism. Although the approach to narrative was more conventional and professional actors were used, the criticism offered was frequently more analytical and overt. Films by Jireš and, particularly, **Evald Schrom** (b. 1931), can be placed in this category. In *Každý den odvahu* (1964, Everyday Courage), Schorm dealt with the consequences of Stalinism and provided a not unsympathetic portrait of a party dogmatist who ended up a lonely and bewildered man. Schorm's next film, *Návrat ztraceného syna* (1966, Return of the Prodigal Son), was a compelling study of alienation, the story of an intellectual contemplating suicide. His problems lie in a refusal to adapt and accept compromise even if it is 'consecrated by a great cause'.

The cultural revival of 1963–5 ushered in a new interest in literature and the avant-garde traditions of the Thirties. Notable films based on pre-war works included two adaptations from Vladislav Vančura: Vláčil's impressive historical epic *Markéta Lazarová* (1967), set in thirteenth-century Bohemia, and Jiří Menzel's bitter-sweet story of strolling players in a small town, *Rozmarné léto* (1968, Capricious Summer). Jireš made a late entry with his visually elaborate version of Nezval's surrealist vampire novel, *Valerie a týden divů* (1970, Valerie and Her Week of Wonders). The influence of the novelist Franz Kafka was apparent in a number of films, most notably Pavel Juráček's *Postava k podpírání* (1964, *Josef Kilian*), where the absurd was linked to a world of bureaucracy lost without its Stalinist supports. Perhaps the best films based on contemporary novels were Menzel's Oscar-winning version of Bohumil Hrabal's *Ostře sledované vlaky* (1966, *Closely Observed Trains*), a comic account of how a lovesick young station guard accidentally becomes a martyr during World War II, and Jireš' version of Milan Kundera's *Žert* (1969, *The Joke*), about the attempted revenge of a young man who had been sent to a labour camp for writing 'optimism is the opium of the people . . . long live Trotsky' on a postcard to his humourless Communist girlfriend.

The film-makers most interested in formal innovation were **Jan Němec** (b. 1936) and **Věra Chytilová** (b. 1929). Němec made three deliberately 'unrealistic' features, two of them almost without dialogue. In *Démanty noci* (1964, *Diamonds of the Night*), he portrayed the visions and hallucinations of two youths escaping from a Nazi death train, while his *Mučedníci lásky* (1967, *Martyrs of Love*) presented a dream world drawing heavily on pre-war traditions of Surrealism — a homage to silent films, sentimental ballads and sad heroes. The influence of absurdist theatre, such as the dramas of Ionesco and Beckett, can be found in his *O slavnosti a hostech* (1966, *The Party and the Guests*), the most politically controversial of all the Czech films. It is the story of a lakeside celebration or feast to which guests are escorted by an ominous assortment of secret police. The real subject is the process of accommodation and self-deception by which the guests adapt to an ideological tyranny.

Věra Chytilová's characteristic combination of feminism and experiment was already apparent in her first film, *O něčem jiném* (1963, *Something Different*). It juxtaposed the unrelated lives of an ordinary housewife (filmed as fiction) with that of a world champion gymnast (filmed as semi-documentary). In *Sedmikrásky* (1966, *Daisies*) she produced a complex, non-narrative film based on the destructive antics of two teenage heroines who decide that, since the world has been spoiled, nothing really matters. Her attraction, and that of her husband and cinematographer Jaroslav Kučera, to the visual in its own right was even more apparent in *Ovoce stromů rajských jíme* (1970, *The Fruit of Paradise*), an amazingly rich, beautiful film with a deliberately ambiguous narrative in which 'nothing is as it seems'. Chytilová's objectives were to make any single interpretation of her films impossible and to force a conclusion that what has been seen forms only part of the truth.

At the end of the Sixties, after so much development in the Czech part of the country, the focus again shifted to Slovakia, where a number of new directors made their first films. These included Juraj Jakubisko, Elo Havetta and Dušan Hanák. Before the shutters came down in 1969, Jakubisko made a notable impact with his apocalyptic and comic vision of the horrors of war, *Zbehovia a pútnici* (1968, *The Deserters and the Nomads*), which drew its inspiration from Slovak folk art and perhaps also from the example of the Armenian director Sergei Paradzhanov.

While the economic issues of the early Sixties played a key role in the crisis of the Novotný regime and the coming to power of the reformers, the cinema throughout the Sixties was concerned with the even more profound spiritual crisis. The examination of contemporary society or of personal morality characterized nearly all of the films, regardless of differences of approach.

1968 and After   The Warsaw Pact invasion of 1968 was a relatively swift reaction to the Prague Spring inaugurated by the reform leadership of Alexander Dubček. The proposal to introduce a 'socialist democracy' was seen as a threat to the leading role of the Communist Party and the division of Europe established by the Yalta and Potsdam agreements of 1945. Following the Soviet invasion, the degree of repression required under the policy of 'normalization' was not immediately apparent. Dubček remained in office until April 1969 and was not expelled from the Party until mid-1970. However, the 'expulsion' of 70,000 Party members and the 'removal' of a further 400,000 indicated the extent of the crisis. The film industry was relatively untouched until its reorganization in 1969 but, in mid-1970, ten films were banned and a number stopped in mid-production. The early Seventies saw an abject fear not only of honest comment but also of possibly dangerous allegorical themes.

Directors chose historical subjects and children's films while veterans produced some dire imitations of Fifties social realism. In this unpromising climate, Jireš turned out one of the few convincing 'committed' works, *A pozdravuji vlaštovsky* (1972, And My Love to the Swallows). The story of the unswerving convictions of a wartime resistance heroine, it caused a minor ripple since her relatives had supported the Sixties reforms. Forman, Passer, Kadár, Jasný, Němec and others left the country and most of the 'New Wave' filmmakers were unable to work.

It was not until 1976 that there was some sign of revival with the return to the studios of Menzel with *Na samotě u lesa* (1976, *Secluded, Near Woods*), Chytilová with *Hra o jablko* (1977, *The Apple Game*), Vláčil with *Dým bramborové natě* (1977, Smoke on the Potato Fields) and Hanák with *Růžové sny* (1977, Rose-tinted Dreams). While all the films were bland by the standards of the Sixties, *The Apple Game* became another *cause célèbre* and provided some abrasive feminist comedy, and *Růžové sny* used a fantasy framework to touch on the controversial issue of the treatment of gypsies. Vláčil's form of poetic humanism seemed best fitted to survive and his next film *Stíny horkého léta* (1978, The Shadows of a Hot Summer) was rewarded with the Grand Prix at the Karlovy Vary Film Festival in 1978.

Menzel went on to pay an amusing tribute to the earliest days of film production in Prague, *Báječní muži s klikou* (1979, *Those Wonderful Movie Cranks*), followed by another period piece, *Postřižiny* (1980, *Short Cut*). Jireš maintained his reputation with *Causa králík* (1980, *The Rabbit Case*), the story of an elderly lawyer who moves to a small country town, and *Neuplné zatmění* (1982, Partial Eclipse), about a teenage girl who goes blind. An outstanding Slovak production was Štefan Uher's *Pásla kone na betone* (1982, Concrete Pastures), concerning an unmarried mother whose daughter becomes pregnant. Notable newcomers included Karel Smyczek, Jaroslav Soukup and Vladimír Drha. Smyczek's *Housata* (1979, Goslings), Soukup's *Vítr v kapse* (1982, The Wind in My Pocket) and Drha's *Dneska přišel novy klúk* (1981, A New Boy Started Today) all dealt sympathetically with the problems of teenagers tackling their first job. New women directors included Marie Poledňáková, Ladislava Sieberová and the Slovak Eva Štefankovičová.

Hungary

Czechoslovakia excepted, the most interesting developments of the Sixties took place in Hungary, where freedom for formal innovation went hand in hand with an ability to offer criticism both of Stalinism and of contemporary society. In 1961 films began to appear from the Béla Balázs studio, in which young graduates of the Film Academy were given the chance to make their first films. In 1963 a deliberate policy of encouraging youth was started in both education and industry. In a period of five years, nineteen directors made their debuts.

Miklós Jancsó (b. 1921) was the first Hungarian director to achieve world-wide fame without permanently leaving his country. From 1951 he worked in newsreels and documentaries.

He directed his first feature film in 1958; but he prefers to forget about it. His first proper feature *Oldás és Kötés* (1962, *Cantata*) was about the self-searchings of a young surgeon.

Jancsó's transition from the private to the panoramic, from psychology to history, can be traced in *Így Jöttem* (1964, *My Way Home*), which tells of a young Hungarian soldier taken prisoner by the Soviet army at the end of World War II. (Since *My Way Home*, Jancsó's screenplays have been written in collaboration with Gyula Hernádi in Hungary and Giovanna Gagliardo in Italy.) With *Szegénylegények* (1965, *The Round-Up*) Jancsó revealed the full originality of his talent. Still shot

Above: in The Confrontation, *Catholic students are challenged by a group of Communist youths. Top: a criminal's girl is forced to submit to a public beating by soldiers in Jancsó's masterful* The Round-Up, *a story of Hapsburg oppression, and the resistance of heroic outlaws.*

in black and white, with the sharpest possible contrasts of sunshine and shadow, *The Round-Up* introduced many of the stylistic features which are characteristic of Jancsó, including long takes and sweeping camera movements.

A Jancsó film could be described as an analysis of oppression, revolution, counter-revolution and even the contentious idea of permanent revolution. Oppression is frequently shown as the outcome of a counter-revolution. In *The Round-Up*, the chief mechanism of oppression is treachery; in *Csend és Kiáltás* (1968, *Silence and Cry*), it is compounded by the complicity of a demoralized peasantry.

Revolution, in the broad sense of a popular uprising, appears in various historical settings. In his first colour film, *Fényes Szelek* (1969, *The Confrontation*), the young and rather crass idealists who resemble the Peoples' College groups of 1945–7 fall victim to manipulation by Party professionals. In *Még Kér a Nép* (1972, *Red Psalm*), Jancsó choreographs a peasant uprising of the 1890s, though as in all his films since *The Round-Up* time and place are abstract and notional. The strikers are butchered, but their spirit symbolically survives.

Counter-revolution has many faces. In *The Round-Up* reprisals were the aftermath of the unsuccessful 1848 revo-

lution against the Austrian Empire. Both *Csillagosok, Katonák* (1967, *The Red and the White*) and *Égi Bárány* (1971, *Agnus Dei*) take place after the Bolshevik revolution was attacked by freshly grouped counter-revolutionary armies, who were defeated in Russia but who conquered in Hungary.

The idea of permanent revolution infuses *Szerelmem, Elektra* (1975, *Elektreia*), in which Orestes persuades his sister Elektra to shoot him. But he springs up from his bier, resurrected: a Redeemer cannot die. As Jancsó's films became more stylized, moving from epic story-telling to choreographed ritual, his films became more poetic and ambiguous.

For instance, when an unarmed left-wing popular movement behaves more like a folk-group at a dance festival than a revolutionary force, as in *Red Psalm* or *Elektreia*, Jancsó's indulgence of their holiday mood is not without irony. Similarly, the counter-revolutionaries are always well-tailored, handsome young men, sometimes in love with death

Below: the victims of oppression abase themselves in Agnus Dei. *Below left: the dangerous fun of sexual freedom, as depicted in* Private Eyes, Public Virtues. *Below: Klaus Maria Brandauer in the Oscar-winning* Mephisto.

and destruction, but manipulated by wily politicians. This becomes almost exaggerated in *Magyar Rapszódia* (1979, *Hungarian Rhapsody*) and *Allegro Barbaro* (1979), two parts of an uncompleted trilogy, where instead of sweeping destructively through the countryside in vengeance, the White officers are shown at an orgy which ends in mass suicide.

While *Elektreia* was based on Greek myth, his fourth and best-known Italian film, *Vizi Privati, Pubbliche Virtù* (1976, *Private Vices, Public Virtues*) is a parody of a Viennese operetta, including even a court ball.

Like all his films, *Private Vices, Public Virtues* must be understood on several levels at once. The rebel prince is romanticized, but also shown as a naive fool; the beauty of sexual freedom is advocated, but shown to be an empty, childish charade when those who indulge themselves are manipulated and eventually destroyed by the authorities. The planned trilogy, ending in 1956, was loosely based on the biography of a Hungarian politician who changes from being a right-wing, nationalist officer to becoming a self-appointed leader of a disaffected peasantry.

But he abandoned the third part of the trilogy, *Concerto*, and went on to a Hungarian-Italian co-production, made in Hungary but scripted by Giovanna Gagliardo. *A Zsarnok Szíve avagy Boccaccio Magyarországon* (1981, *The Tyrant's Heart, or Boccaccio in Hungary*) is a claustrophobic historical drama of role-playing, echoing *Hamlet*, but finally opening out into a typically vast panorama of the Hungarian plain.

Jancsó's dream of human equality, which is the touchstone of his morality has nothing puritanical about it. Perhaps some of his ambiguity comes from showing even evil and destruction with seductive loveliness, while at the same time creating dream images of singing, dancing, sharing and loving communal Utopias.

Jancsó's films were inspired by key periods in the development of Hungarian socialism but the re-examination of history was also the preoccupation of many other directors of the same generation. András Kovács' *Hideg Napok* (1966, *Cold Days*), for instance, looked at the forgotten subject of Hungarian fascism in its portrayal of the Novi Sad massacre of 1942, while Sándor Sára's *Feldobott Kő* (1968, *The Upthrown Stone*) dealt powerfully with the injustices of the Rákosi era of the early Fifties. The Stalinist period was most penetratingly examined in the veteran director Károly Makk's *Szerelem* (1971, *Love*), which told of the wife and the mother of a political prisoner, both waiting for his return, the mother believing that he is pursuing a successful career abroad.

Another near-contemporary of this group, **Péter Bacsó** (b. 1928) began his career as a screenwriter, but later became a prolific director, at first specializing in contemporary, realistic dramas which often made use of non-professional actors. His best film, *Tanú* (1969, *The Witness*), a black comedy about life under the Rákosi regime, when imprisonment for almost undefinable 'political' offences was commonplace, was suppressed by the authorities until 1981.

With the Eighties, while Jancsó's international reputation waned, that of **István Szabó** (b. 1938) grew, following the American Academy Award for his *Mephisto* (1981) as Best Foreign Film of the year. Szabó's earlier films were patently autobiographical in inspiration, and influenced by the work of directors of the French *nouvelle vague*, notably Truffaut and Resnais. *Álmodozások Kora* (1965, *The Age of Daydreaming*), *Apa* (1967, *Father*) and *Szerelmes Film* (1970, *Love Film*) all told of the lives and sentiments of young people growing up in Budapest in the post-World War II era. Szabó passed to

more elaborate and allegorical approaches in the mid-Seventies, but returned to a direct narrative style in *Bizalom* (1979, *Confidence*), which described the troubled love story of two people hiding together from the Nazis during the war. After *Mephisto*, based on Klaus Mann's *roman à clef* about the life of the German actor Gustav Grundgens, Szabó collaborated with the same leading actor, Klaus Maria Brandauer, on *Redl* (1985, *Colonel Redl*), which dramatized a true incident of the years before World War I.

Szabó was the legal representative of a new generation of directors that came to the fore in the Sixties, their careers accelerated by a number of reforms of the cinema organization.

One of the most formally inventive directors was **István Gaál**. In the Sixties he made *Sodrásban* (1964, *Current*) about the feelings of youth at the time; *Zöldár* (1965, *Green Years*) about the political excesses of the Fifties; and *Keresztelő* (1968, *Baptism*) about the interaction between past and present. His later films, such as *Magasiskola* (1970, *The Falcons*) and *Holt Vidék* (1972, *Dead Landscape*), showed the formal influence of Jancsó integrated into a more realist context. Two women directors established an international reputation: Judit Elek with *Sziget a Szárazföldön* (1969, *The Lady From Constantinople*) and **Márta Mészáros**, who made her debut with *Eltávozott Nap* (1968, *The Girl*). Mészáros consolidated her reputation in the Seventies with several more films embodying her profound analysis of the situation of women, including *Kilenc Hónap* (1976, *Nine Months*) and *Ő Ketten* (1977, *The Two of Them*). After acquiring a cult popularity in France, Mészáros was misguided into a series of self-consciously 'aesthetic' international co-productions. In 1982 however she returned triumphantly to her best form, with *Naplo* (*Diary for My Children*), a sinewy reminiscence of her adolescence, which traces her return from the Soviet Union, where her father had perished during Stalin's purges, to Hungary in the first uneasy experience of socialism.

A large and gifted younger generation came to the fore in the Sixties and Seventies, revealing a wide range of temperaments and interests and a concerted determination to eschew the old literary traditions that had dogged the Hungarian cinema since its origins. The most visually creative of the generation was Zoltán Huszárik, whose extraordinary, visionary features *Szindbád* (1971, *Sindbad*) and *Csontváry* (1979) sought to reflect and express the respective geniuses of the writer Gyula Krudy and the painter Csontváry. **Zsolt Kézdi-Kovács** (b. 1936), who began his professional career as assistant to Jancsó, made a series of works which displayed a gift for cinema, a sternly intellectual approach, and a sharply accurate socio-political criticism which did not make him an establishment favourite. His films included *Mérsékelt Égöv* (1970, *Temperate Zone*), *Romantika* (1972, *Romanticism*), *Locsolókocsi* (1973, *The Orange Watering Truck*), *Ha Megjön József* (1977, *When Joseph Returns . . .*) and *A Kedves Szomszéd* (1979, *The Nice Neighbour*).

The films of **János Rózsa** (b. 1939) – *Bübájosok* (1969, *Charmers*) and *Álmodó Ifjúság* (1974, *Dreaming Youth*) – have most characteristically dealt with young people and society's persistent tendency to fail them where their need is greatest. Like Rósza, **Pál Sándor** (b. 1939) has benefited from association with the brilliant cameraman Elemér Ragályi, outstanding even among a whole generation of cinematographers of exceptional brilliance, including János Kende and Sándor Sára, a director in his own right. Pál Sándor's special gift for evoking period and his feeling for juxtapositions of tragic and grotesque appeared most strikingly in *Régi Idők Focija* (1974, *Old Time Football*), *Herkulesfürdői Emlék* (1977, *Improperly Dressed*) and *Szerencsés Dániel* (1982, *Daniel Takes a Train*). Pál Gabor's *Angi Vera* (1979) offered a fiercely critical view of the Stalinist period through its story of a good-natured girl moulded into a party conformist. An earlier film with a similar theme but a wider timespan was Ferenc Kósa's *Tízezer Nap* (*Ten Thousand Suns*), completed in 1965, but delayed for two years. After several features, Kósa (b. 1937) made a highly controversial documentary, *Küldetés* (1977, *Portrait of a Champion*), about the corruption and political exploitation associated with athletics. The partnership of **Imre Gyöngyössy** (b. 1930) and **Barna Kabay** (b. 1948) looked back to an ideal of peasant culture in films like *Meztelen Vagy* (1971, *Legend of the Death and Resurrection of Two Young Men*), *Szarvassá Vált Fiúk* (1974, *Sons of Fire*), *Várakozók* (1975, *Expectation*) and the documentary *Két Elhatározás* (1977, *A Quite Ordinary Life*).

A group of younger directors calling themselves 'The Budapest School' and led by **István Dárday** (b. 1940), struck out against the vestiges of literary and stage traditions with a group of films that employed a considerable degree of improvisation, and non-professional actors. The best of the series were Darday's *Jutalomutazás* (1974, *Holiday in Britain*), which still retained much of conventional narrative style and Béla Tarr's *Családi Tüzfészek* (1978, *Family Nest*).

Eastern Europe

In East Germany, interest remained primarily at the level of script content. The main controversy centred on the 'rabbit' films of the Sixties, so called after *Das Kaninchen bin ich* (1965, The Rabbit Is Me), directed by Kurt Maetzig. Some six feature films which attempted to look at society in a spirit of critical realism were withdrawn after Ulbricht, the East German leader, attacked 'the poison of scepticism and the negation of heroism and great emotions'. One of the 'rabbit' directors, Frank Beyer, again courted official disapproval when he filmed Jurek Becker's story of life in the Jewish ghetto under the Nazis, *Jakob der Lügner* (1975, *Jacob the Liar*), one of the few East German films to attract international attention when it did the rounds of the festival circuit.

Individual directors of note appeared in most East European countries: Khristo Khristov in Bulgaria; Lucian Pintilie in Romania; and, outside the Warsaw Pact countries, Aleksander Petrović and **Dušan Makaveyev** in Yugoslavia.

Born in Belgrade in 1932, Makavejev graduated in philosophy before enrolling in the Belgrade Academy of Film, Theatre, Radio and Television. A number of short student films already demonstrated his sharply ironic viewpoint. In 1966 he made his first feature, *Čovek Nije Tica* (*Man Is Not a Bird*), in which his use of *cinéma-vérité*, jokes investigative asides already showed his belief that: 'We can use everything that comes to hand, fiction, documents, actualities, titles. "Style" is not important. You must use surprise as a psychological weapon . . . We can even use material taken from the enemy.'

The same principles were developed in *Ljubavni Slučaj ili Tragedija Službenice PTT* (1967, *Switchboard Operator*) which originated in a newspaper story about a girl who was thrown down a well by her lover; and *Nevinost Bez Zaštite* (1968, *Innocence Unprotected*), a reworking, with additions and commentary, of the first Serbian feature film, a bizarre but touching primitive work made during World War II by a professional strong man, featuring himself and his stunts – the

kind of oddity irresistible to Makavejev's idiosyncratic humour.

His next film, *WR – Misterije Organizma* (1971, *WR – Mysteries of the Organism*) was a freewheeling tribute to the Austrian psychoanalyst and sex therapist Wilhelm Reich, who died in prison in Pennsylvania; it also involved a love story between a liberated Yugoslav girl and a repressed Soviet skating champion, in which, as in *Switchboard Operator*, the girl ended up dead – but, in this case, still volubly preaching sexual freedom.

With *WR – Mysteries of the Organism* the guerrilla activities of Dušan Makavejev's cinema reached their peak. It was, in its spirit, a supremely international film, and a film for its moment. At the time it was made the Vietnam War was still on, the events of 1968 in West and Eastern Europe were still vivid in the memory and the sexual revolution was at its height. Makavejev struck out wildly, gaily, poetically, philosophically in every direction, and made firm enemies on both sides of the Iron Curtain.

The film was banned for a while in Yugoslavia, and Makavejev went into exile, making *Sweet Movie* (1974) in France. He returned to international notice with a surrealistic black comedy, *Montenegro, or Pigs and Pearls* (1981), made in Sweden with an American actress, Susan Anspach, as a bored housewife who takes up with Yugoslav immigrants who run a sex club, murders her lover there and then poisons her entire family. This erotic comedy was based, like *Switchboard Operator*, on an actual murder case.

Below: a simple Yugoslavian country girl turned cabaret artiste puts on a decidedly erotic show for the patrons of the night club in Montenegro *(production shot).*

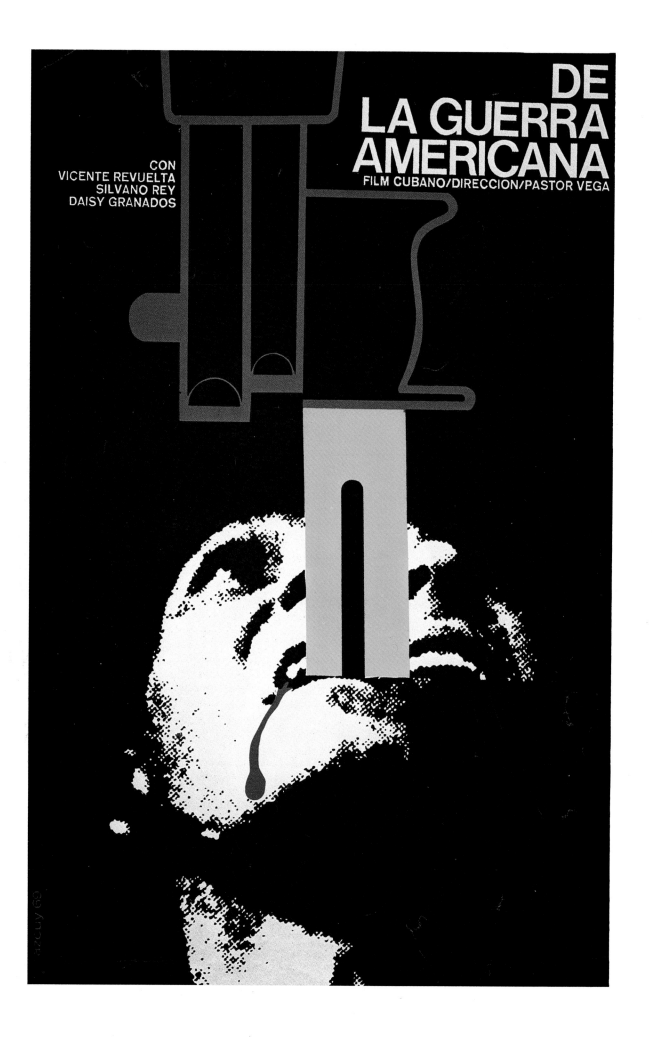

CHAPTER 18
The International Scene

Japan

In December 1963 Yasujiro Ozu died on his sixtieth birthday. In retrospect this date appears as the turning point in the evolution of contemporary Japanese cinema.

Ozu's death marked the beginning of Japan's cinematic 'decline' in the wake of the Golden Age of the Fifties. Of course, this is not to imply that there were no successful film-makers after that decade, for Akira Kurosawa continued his brilliant career with major commercial hits – *Yojimbo* (1961), a Western in samurai dress, and *Tengoku no Jigoku* (1963, *High and Low*), a kidnapping thriller – and with international prize-winning films such as *Dersu Uzala* (1975), in which progress is at odds with nature, and *Kagemusha* (1980), a tribal warfare epic in feudal Japan. Another important film-maker, though little known abroad, was Mikio Naruse, whose films dealt with various aspects of Japanese women – *Horoki* (1962, Lonely Lane), *Midareru* (1964, Desire). He died in 1969.

The late Fifties and beginning of the Sixties saw the emergence of a new generation of film-makers who believed that they should confront the many problems of post-war Japan. Without denying the dramatic heroism of Akira Kurosawa's films, without really objecting to the conservatism of Yasujiro Ozu's, the new film-makers were eager to deal with themes more closely allied to their daily lives, more directly voicing their concerns. To a greater or lesser extent they were all influenced by the works of the European and American film-makers of the period rather than by the heritage of their national cinema. These influences soon became apparent: social and political themes were more in evidence; sexuality and violence were increasingly obvious in the images.

Shohei Imamura (b.1926) who began his career as an assistant to Ozu in the Shochiku studios, and **Ko Nakahira** (1926–1978), who also started at the Shochiku studios but as assistant to other directors, were the first film-makers who voluntarily left their mentors in order to join the new Nikkatsu production company. Both Imamura and Nakahira were concerned with the problems of young people in post-war Japan – with their constricted energy, their anger, desires and hopes.

Shohei Imamura's *Buta to Gunkan* (1961, Pigs and Battle-ships) portrays the life of a young boy living in a city that has prospered because of the American military base there. The film follows him through his involvement with the city's mafia and his dreams of fleeing the city with his girlfriend, and accurately reflects the energy with which the younger generation dealt with the problems it encountered after World War II. *Buta to Gunkan* remains not only one of the most important films in Imamura's filmography, but also one of the most representative of contemporary Japanese films.

An interesting sidelight on the stag-film industry in Japan was cast by his *Jinruigaku Nyumon* (1966, *The Pornographer*). After devoting himself to television documentaries for most of the Seventies, he returned to the big screen with his study of a murderer, *Fukushu Suruwa Ware ni Ari* (1979, *Vengeance Is Mine*), which was followed by a politically motivated period piece set in 1867, *Eijanaika* (1980, *Why Not?*), and in 1983 he won the Golden Palm at Cannes with *Narayama Bushi-ko* (*The Ballad of Narayama*), a violent tale of primitive village life that questions the values of civilization.

Ko Nakahira's career declined as he became older – he died in 1978 – but in the late Fifties he was one of the foremost exponents of Japanese youth themes, dealing directly and strongly with violence and sexuality. His *Kurutta Kajitsu* (1958, *Juvenile Passion*) was the precursor of a series of films that dealt with 'angry juveniles'.

Yasuzo Masumura, one of the youngest disciples of Kenji Mizoguchi, joined the Daiei studios after a period studying in Rome. Less directly concerned with realistic problems, he depicts more sensual relationships between men and women, as shown by his films based on the novels of Junichiro Tanizaki – *Manji* (1964, *Passion*), *Chijin-no Ai* (1967, An Idiot in Love).

Around the end of the Fifties, the Shochiku studio, then still dominated stylistically by Ozu, with his taste for beautifully underplayed dramas of middle-class family life, decided to launch a *nouvelle vague* of youth films, stressing sexuality, violence and crime. The new young directors of these films, already working at Shochiku as assistants, were Nagisa Oshima, Masahiro Shinoda and Yoshishige Yoshida.

The single outstanding figure of this period was undoubtedly **Nagisa Oshima** (b.1932). He has been called the least inscrutable of Japanese directors. But as leader and chief theoretician of the 'New Wave' movement, which started in Japan at the same time as in France, he has also been thought difficult and inaccessible.

Despite a reputation as a prominent left-wing student activist at Kyoto University (where he studied law), Oshima gained a position as an assistant director at the Shochiku Film Company in 1954. As a fully-fledged director, he began by making gangster (*yakuza*) films – *Ai to Kibo no Machi* (1959, *A Town of Love and Hope*) and *Seishun Zankoku Monogatari*

Left: Pastor Vega's stark picture of war, De la Guerra Americana *(1969, On the American War) was a product of the flowering Cuban cinema in the Sixties and Seventies.*

(1960, *Naked Youth*) – but his work rapidly became increasingly controversial and critical of Japanese society. His first feature to be shown extensively in the West was *Koshikei* (1968, *Death by Hanging*), based on the true story of a young Korean in Japan who raped and killed two girls and was hanged years later, after he had confessed and reformed. *Shinjuku Dorobo Nikki* (1969, *Diary of a Shinjuku Thief*) and *Tokyo Senso Sengo Hiwa* (1970, *The Man Who Left His Will on Film*) combined pessimistic socio-political comment with anguished sex and showed the stylistic influence of Jean-Luc Godard and other *nouvelle vague* directors. Less self-indulgent was *Shonen* (1969, *Boy*) a moving story of a parasitic couple who train their small son to run in front of passing cars and pretend to be injured, so that they can gain financial compensation.

Following *Gishiki* (1971, *The Ceremony*), the chronicle of a wealthy provincial family and an off-beat, allegorical love story, *Natsu no Imota* (1972, *Dear Summer Sister*), Oshima amazed and scandalized world cinema with his powerful sex tragedy *Ai No Corrida* (1976, *Empire of the Senses*). Based on fact, the film concerns two lovers who embark on an obsessive quest for the ultimate sexual ecstasy. In Japan, in particular, the film was regarded as a blow for female equality. The film's heroine, Sada, overturns social and moral taboos, finally killing and castrating her willing partner.

Ai no Corrida's success gained Oshima an international reputation, persuading him to make films away from his native land. Perhaps as a result, the cutting edge of his work seems to have been dulled. *Ai no Borei* (1978, *Empire of Passion*) was a somewhat directionless thriller and the prestigious prisoner-of-war drama, *Merry Christmas Mr Lawrence* (1983), starring David Bowie, Tom Conti and Japanese pop star Ryuichi Sakamoto teetered perilously between high drama and high camp.

Like Oshima, **Masahiro Shinoda** (b.1931) also started with contemporary films on themes of crime and violence; but with *Shinju Ten no Amijima* (1969, *Double Suicide*), based on a Bunraku puppet play, he turned to period films, to which he gave a modern twist – in that case, by casting his own wife, Shima Iwashita, as both the wife and the obsessively loved courtesan. In *Yash-ga-ike* (1979, *Demon Pond*) both the leading female roles were played by a male Kabuki actor – an unexpected throwback to the conventions of Japanese silent film. Himself a former athlete, Shinoda diversified with a documentary, *Sapporo Orimpikku* (1972, *Sapporo Winter Olympic Games*).

Yoshishige Yoshida (b.1933) made his first film, *Rokudenashi* (1960, Good-for-Nothing) – dealing with sex and violence among students – in 1960 and made his name as one of the young leading lights of the Japanese 'New Wave'. His Sixties films included *Amai Yoru no Hate* (1962, Bitter End of a Sweet Night), *Mizu de Kakareta Monogatari* (1965, Forbidden Love) and *Eros + Gyakusatsu* (1969, *Eros and Massacre*), which caused something of a stir for its explicit sex scenes. In the Seventies Yoshida worked mainly in television, completing a 98-part series of documentaries on art, *Bi no Bi* (Beauty of Beauty).

Sexuality in the cinema of Sixties Japan was an important element that aided in the revelation of reality and the destruction of ancient myths, as well as being closely tied to social and political concerns. However, the sex ingredient eventually became indispensable. During the decline in the Japanese movie business, sex – and to a lesser extent violence – became necessary for commercial success; pictures without

sex no longer appealed to audiences. This is, of course, an argument that may well apply to all the movies of the world, but in Japan censorship in the sexual field had always been very strict and the exploitation of the subject through films became a major element of social development.

The sex-films of the later Sixties are referred to as 'pink films' and the type still occupies an important position in each year's production schedule. Made on extremely low budgets, and with no artistic ambition in evidence, they are usually shown to a faithful weekly following at special theatres.

In 1970 another phenomenon burst upon the scene, 'roman-porn' films – signifying either 'romanesque-porn' films or 'romantic-porn' films. To avoid bankruptcy the massive Nikkatsu studios had invented this genre of cheap soft-core porn film, and despite the limitations of censorship, Nikkatsu has continued to produce one or two 'roman-porn' films every month.

Hongkong

It was the flood of martial-arts films into western markets in 1972–3 that brought the Hongkong film industry to the notice of the West in a way that sporadic screenings of films from Hongkong at festivals had failed to do.

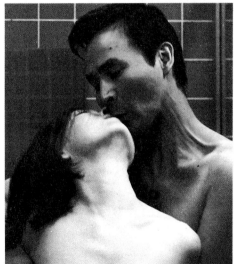

Above left: Kurosawa's Dersu Uzala *was a Soviet-sponsored film about two men from vastly different backgrounds. Above: after three years as his clan's chief in* Kagemusha, *the poor thief is banished. Far left: ultimate sexual ectasy – during passionate love-making in* Ai No Corrida, *the maid strangles the master, then castrates him. Centre: in* Tokyo Senso Sengo Hiwa *a woman masturbates as her dead lover's film is projected on her. Left: more explicit sex, this time in Yoshishige Yoshida's film,* Eros Gyakusatsu.

In general, the history of film-making in Hongkong had been intimately bound up with that of China. Genres structured around classical literary sources, stories from myth and folklore or from cycles of tales of knight-errantry, low-life comedies, melodramas, subjects drawn from opera, drama and history have been common to both since silent days. The key events in China's history – the marathon struggle that began in the late Twenties between the nationalist ruling party, the Kuomintang, and the Communist Party, the long and bitter war with Japan, the Communist victory in 1949 and the subsequent changes in political line – were equally decisive in the history of the colony island. For one thing, the disruption of China's film industry and of cultural production resulted, from the Twenties onwards, in an influx of intellectuals, performers and writers into Hongkong.

The first Hongkong production company was established in 1921. Ten years later, some five major companies were in operation, surrounded by a host of smaller ones. But Hongkong as a producer remained under the shadow of Shanghai – the Hollywood of the East – until that city was occupied by the Japanese in 1937.

The situation is complicated by the existence of two Hongkong cinemas. The arrival of sound in the late Thirties led to the development of a (northern Chinese) Mandarin-language cinema alongside the local Cantonese-dialect one. Mandarin cinema found its market – until 1954 – on the mainland and then increasingly in South-east Asia, eclipsing Cantonese cinema in the mid-Sixties. But it was within Cantonese cinema that Hongkong's first important and popular series of martial-arts films was produced.

During the Sino-Japanese War, Tianyi, one of Shanghai's major studios, moved to Hongkong. Its studio manager was one of the Shaw brothers, Runde Shaw. The company began turning out popular Cantonese genre films before switching to Mandarin around 1950 to enable it to service the chain of Shaw theatres in South-east Asia. Its main rival during the late Fifties and early Sixties was an offshoot of the Singapore-based Cathay Organization, Motion Picture & General Investment (MP & GI). By 1965, Shaws had comfortably overtaken MP & GI, after emerging as Shaw Brothers, a new company headed by Run Run Shaw, in 1957. They moved from their small Kowloon studio to Clearwater Bay, completing their legendary Movietown studio in 1961. Their aim seems to have been to maintain a large output, initially 50 films a year (dropping to something like half that in the Seventies) while establishing superior Shanghai-style production values.

Shaws made their push at exactly the right moment. By the early Sixties, Hongkong had recovered from the wartime occupation and the cinema was a boom industry. By the mid-Sixties, production on the mainland virtually ceased. Shaw Brothers turned out the romances and musicals that MP & GI had made a success of, and also began to make something of a speciality of the historical drama, a genre that Mandarin cinema, with its larger market and therefore larger budgets, could mount with some authenticity. Films were made in colour and then on widescreen. A number of important directors worked for Shaws during this period, including Hu Chin-ch'üan (King Hu) and Chang Cheh, whose several martial-arts films have achieved a measure of exposure in the cinemas of the West.

It was the sensuous sophistication of the films of **Li Han-hsiang** that provided Shaws with the money-spinners that helped seal their reputation. A graduate of the Peking Art Institute, Li was attracted to Hongkong in 1948, aware of the possibilities in the colony's fumbling attempts to rival mainland production, and signed on as a contract director at Shaws in 1955. He turned gradually from small-scale socially-orientated themes to more classic subjects, to which he gave increasingly epic and lavish dimensions. His major box-office success was *Liang Shan-po yü Chu Ying-t'ai* (1963, *The Love Eternal*), an opera adapted for the screen and co-directed with King Hu, who three years later was to revivify the martial-arts film with his *Ta tsui hsia* (1966, *Come Drink With Me*), also for Shaws.

The apogee of the historical drama was reached during Li's work for his own company in Taiwan after leaving Shaws in 1963. Taiwan's situation as a film production centre has been very much a direct function of its political situation with a very stringent code of production in operation, and equally stringent censorship. Production has been dominated by the output of the government-owned Central Film Studio. Escapist contemporary melodrama has been the most notable genre. But Taiwan has also operated as something of an offshoot of Hongkong, as in Li's case. Li returned to Shaws in 1971, but not before such films as *Hsi Shih* (1967, *Hsi Shih: Beauty of Beauties*) and the remarkable *Ti Ying* (1970, *The Girl Who Saved Her Father*), with their quite extraordinarily expressive use of landscape and performers, had revealed the limitations inherent in the studio system as it operated in Hongkong.

Although the martial-arts film dominated production from about 1966 for the next ten years, any list of key films of the Seventies must include the works of Li Han-hsiang. Undeniably the most ambitious films of the decade were those comprising his two-part epic, *Ch'ing-kuo ch'ing-ch'eng* (1975, *The Empress Dowager*) and *Ying-t'ai ch'i hsüeh* (1976, *The Last Tempest*). The two films examine the declining years of the Ch'ing dynasty and the rise of the Reform Movement; quite hypnotically powerful and enormously resonant, they draw beautifully modulated performances from a number of Shaws' key actors. Other central works, if in a more modest vein, are the two-part satire on power and corruption consisting of *Ta chün-fa* (1972, *The Warlord*) and *Ch'ou-wen* (1974, *Scandal*), and a number of compendia of erotic fables such as *Ch'in p'ing shuang yen* (1974, *Golden Lotus*), a seductive and entertaining version of the Chinese erotic novel, and *Feng hua hsüeh yüeh* (1977, *Moods of Love*). In the Eighties he made two more films on the Empress Dowager Tz'u-hsi, concentrating on her early life – *Chui lian ting zheny* (1983, *Reign Behind a Curtain*) and *Huoshao Yuanmingyuan* (1983, *The Burning of the Imperial Palace*) – both shot on location in mainland China as China–Hongkong co-productions.

Left: Bruce Lee, master of the martial arts movies in Fist of Fury, *the film that made him a superstar.*

Distinctive balletic interpretations of the martial-arts films appeared in the work of King Hu, including *Hsia nü* (1969, *A Touch of Zen*), *Ying-ch'un-ko-chih feng-po* (1973, *The Fate of Lee Khan*) and *Chung-lieh t'u* (1974, *The Valiant Ones*), or the superlative philosophical swordplay thrillers directed by Ch'u Yüan at Shaws.

The martial-arts films that are best known internationally star the charismatic Bruce Lee, who died in 1973. However, it was a series of three comedies that pointed to the development of a new and distinctive cinema for Hongkong. **Hsü Kuan-wen** (Michael Hui), a television personality and an ex-Shaw Brothers actor-turned-director, gave a fresh twist to the low-life Cantonese comedy in *Kuei ma shuang hsing* (1974, *Games Gamblers Play*), *T'ien-ts'ai yü Paich'ih* (1976, *The Last Message*) and *Pan-chin pa-liang* (1977, *The Private Eyes*), which centred humorously on the problems of survival in contemporary Hongkong.

Hui, with his studio experience, forms a bridge between the Hongkong cinema's veterans with their mainland backgrounds and a group of new film-makers, many of whom have both international film-school and television experience. These younger film-makers found that the stringent economic climate during the mid-Seventies and the concomitant unadventurousness on the part of the major studios blocked any hope of entry into the industry. Directors such as **Allen Fong**, with *Yüan-chou-tsai-chih ko* (1977, *Song of Yuen Chau-chai*) and *Fuzi Qing* (1981, *Father and Son*) and **Hsü An-hua (Ann Hui)**, with *Feng chieh* (1979, *The Secret*) and *T'ou-pen nuhai* (1982, *Boat People*) attempted films that spoke with some urgency to the situation of life in Hongkong while acknowledging both that island's legacy of Chinese culture and the lively grassroots industry where drug and embezzlement scandals become instant thrillers. As China opens up during the Eighties, the situation will again undoubtedly change.

China

Although film was introduced to China in 1896 and indigenous production started six years later, it was not until the Mingxing Company was founded in 1922 that Chinese cinema began to establish a firm base and an identity. Mingxing's greatest success was the martial-arts series *Huoshao honglian si* (1928–31, The Burning of the Red Lotus Monastery). Several episodes were banned by a government fearful of social unrest. Most companies had fallen into bankruptcy and China had become one of the world's biggest markets for American films. To counter the industry's escapism, the Communist Party established a base within Mingxing in 1932. The writer Xian Yen joined the studio, bringing with him a group of young radical talents from the theatre. The studio then produced more popular films: comedies and dramas modelled on Hollywood formulas but subverted by sharp social realism. The audience responded to seeing itself on screen in a realistic context for the first time. The financial success of these films encouraged other studios to experiment and this first flowering of a Chinese cinema established stars and directors who remained central to its development.

These advances ended abruptly with the Japanese bombing of Shanghai in 1937; the left-wingers dispersed to the countryside and the studios fell to the Japanese. The film-makers reconverged on Shanghai in 1946 and formed the Kunlun Film Company. For three years, as civil war raged, this studio produced the most outspoken films China had ever seen. After *Yijiang chunshui xiang dong liu* (1947, *The Spring River Flows East*) enjoyed massive critical and box-office success for its attack on opportunism and decadent luxury, censorship became even tighter and Kunlun had to toe the line. In 1948 it started to shoot *Wuya yu maque* (1949, Crows and Sparrows), a scathing picture of Shanghai slum life; but the film was so critical of the ruling Kuomintang, the Chinese nationalist party, that production was halted by force, and the film was completed only after the Communist victory. All film-making was soon brought under government control. The veterans of the Thirties were put in charge and film was encouraged by the government. The purpose of film now was to educate the masses in the need for and structure of the new society, and the cinema became subject to the vagaries of political policy. A brief freedom was enjoyed in 1956–7 during Mao's 100 Flowers Campaign and films like *Li Shizhen* (1956) treated unusual subjects – in this case, the life of a famous pharmacologist – with delicacy and grace. Despite the ensuing anti-rightist purge, the film industry recovered and by 1964 was producing works of real sophistication. Then the Cultural Revolution swept China in 1966 and all film production was halted for over four years.

The Cultural Revolution produced 'model' operas and ballets, full of static revolutionary tableaux, and a few features that tried, within strict limitations, to raise political debates. But almost all of the talents who had created a once-huge industry were imprisoned or sent to hard labour in the country. Only after the overthrow of the Gang of Four in the late Seventies could the film industry begin to re-establish itself.

The task is immense: the survivors of the Thirties are too old to re-create a truly Chinese cinema and the young have been for so long denied access to their own film history that everything must be learned anew. Recent films betray a level of naivety. However, there is no doubt that, in time, China will produce works as interesting and as accomplished as the films of its rich past.

Above left and right: periods of restraint alternating with periods of relative relaxation marked film-making activity on Mao's China. Shiwuguan *(1956, Fifteen Strings of Cash) and* Wutai jiemei *(1964, Two Stage Sisters) benefited from a brief freedom in matters of artistic style.*

India

India is the biggest film-producing country in the world – in 1983 over seven hundred and fifty films were released. Though outnumbered by films in the Tamil and Telugu languages of the South, many of these were still the traditional Bombay films – romantic musical melodramas made in the Hindi language (the traditionally dominant all-India language), and generally dismissed by serious critics as insipid, hidebound, hybrid, outlandish and escapist.

India has a long heritage of cinema. The first movies were shown in Bombay, the principal city of the West Coast, on July 7, 1896. Film production started in 1913, and early films often imitated Hollywood models. At the end of the silent era, the film pioneer Ardeshir Irani – inspired by Universal's *Show Boat* (1929) – produced and directed the first full-length talkie in Hindi, *Alam Ara* (1931, Beauty of the World). Audiences welcomed the changeover to sound, and new studios were set up in various parts of the country.

The growth of the studio system in India was similar to that in Hollywood. In 1929, V. Shantaram, S.Fatehlal, V.G. Damle, K.R. Dhauber and S.B. Kulkarni – five young film-makers of ambition and total dedication – formed Prabhat Film Company in Kolhapur, south of Bombay in the state of Maharashtra. In 1933 they were able to buy a sprawling estate on the outskirts of Poona, south-east of Bombay, and launch a regular studio with four stages and a number of outdoor locales, where they made films mostly in the Marathi language. The high quality of the studio's resources was responsible for the visual richness and realistic sound in their films. The use of spoken dialogue, which sound made possible, enabled the Prabhat film-makers to examine the psychological and social sides of their themes. It also helped them to bring out the contemporary relevance of traditional literature about saints – Damle and Fatehlal's *Sant Tukaram* (1937, Saint Tukaram) is one of the highest achievements of the early sound period, and won a prize at the Venice Film Festival.

Shantaram's first sound film *Ayodhyecha Raja* (1932, The King of Ayodhya) starred Durga Khote, a high-caste girl, making her debut. In the early silent period, no decent women appeared in films and most females were played by boys. In 1936 Shantaram made *Amar Jyoti* (Eternal Light) in Hindi – also shown at the Venice Film Festival. His other notable films were *Duniya Na Mane* (1937, The Unexpected), about the problem of a May-December marriage and the customs restricting the life of a widow, and *Admi* (1939, The Man), which challenged traditional attitudes about the prostitute's place in society.

Another prominent studio at the time was Bombay Talkies, founded by the husband-wife team of Himansu Rai and Devika Rani, who had learned about film production in England and Germany. One of their most respected social pictures was *Acchut Kanya* (1936, Untouchable Girl), about a girl from the lowest Hindu social group who falls in love with a Brahmin upper-caste youth. Most of the Bombay Talkies films were concerned with social reform.

In Calcutta, West Bengal (in the eastern part of the country) the producer B.N. Sircar recruited Dhiren Ganguly and Debaki Bose in 1930 to direct films for his newly-founded New Theatres company. Bose showed his talents in *Chandidas* (1932), the story of a poet-saint of the sixteenth century. It included songs based on the work of Chandidas, and also used specially-written background music for the first time in Indian cinema. Next he made *Puran Bhagat* (1933, The

Devotee) in Hindi, which brought New Theatres into a wider market than their previous Bengali features. In 1937 Bose's *Vidyapathi*, another film about a poet-saint, was released in both Bengali and Hindi versions. Also for New Theatres, P.C. Barua made *Devdas* (1935), attacking the arranged-marriage system in India; its quietly-performed songs, its realistic dialogue and its tragic ending were all new to Indian films.

From the late Thirties, as the war produced a boom economy, there was an influx of new independent producers who attracted the star actors as well as the top directors and technicians from the established studios by offering bigger money. The stars soon realized their crowd-pulling capacity and recognized the value of independence from the strict discipline of the studio system. Prithviraj Kapoor (the father of Raj Kapoor and Shashi Kapoor and the grandfather of today's star Rishi Kapoor) had already shown the way by making a great success of freelancing. Following the example of their stars, some of the leading directors broke away. V. Shantaram left Prabhat in 1941 to start his own company, Rajkamal Kalamandir. Mehboob Khan left Sagar Movietone to work under his own banner.

In 1947 India was freed from British colonial rule. The British administration left behind a clumsy system of rationing raw film stock, severe censorship of films in order to control the nationalistic sentiments of patriotic Indians during the struggle for independence, and heavy taxes of up to sixty per cent on film-makers. Much of this heritage survived the departure of the British, as did the system of illicit payments to avoid taxation.

By now there was a fixed formula for the success of any film – one or two stars, six songs, three dance sequences, a bit of crying, a bit of laughter, extremes of emotion – but in 1948 S.S. Vasan's *Chandralekha*, made in the Tamil and Hindi languages and the biggest extravaganza of its time, started a successful new trend with its chorus-dance sequences. In the same year Uday Shankar, brother of the musician Ravi Shankar, made a film on the classical dances, *Kalpana* (Imagination); but the film was not generally well liked, perhaps because of the growing popularity of light music and westernized themes.

Mehboob Khan made many multi-star films such as *Aan* (1952, Savage Princess) and *Bharat Mata* (1957, Mother India), which were unprecedentedly successful at the box-office, combining sensitivity and commercial ingredients, and always including some reference to the oppressed classes of society. On the other hand, Raj Kapoor was involved in making entertainment films, such as *Awara* (1952, The Vagabond), that were basically musicals and showed the sublimity of love. Bimal Roy was meanwhile making offbeat films such as *Do Bigha Zamin* (1953, Two Acres of Land) and *Sujata* (1960) about subjects like poverty, money-lending and untouchability. K.A. Abbas scored international critical success with *Munna* (1954, The Lost Child), the story of an orphan.

In the South, where Madras was the main production centre, films were similar in theme and treatment to those of Bombay. Madras films were usually musicals, melodramas and stories about the problems of the joint family system. Though Tamil was the language of the region, many films in Telugu were also produced in Madras.

Films for the Sri Lanka (formerly Ceylon) market were shot in the studios of the South. Only the dialogue was written by the Sri Lankans in the Sinhalese language; the rest of the production was done entirely by the South Indians. Most of these films were carbon copies of typical Tamil and Hindi films. Then Lester James Peries made *Rekava* (1957, *The Line of Destiny*) on location, using a neo-realist style; this was recognized as the first truly national film to appear from Sri Lanka. His third film *Gamperaliya* (1963, The Changing Village) won the Grand Prix at the third International Film Festival of India, the first Sinhalese film to gain an international award.

In the East, Calcutta showed promise when Satyajit Ray made *Pather Panchali* (1955, *Song of the Little Road*) with meagre resources. Ray was the first Indian director to win world-wide fame and esteem. *Pather Panchali* took the critics completely by surprise and led them to much fresh thinking by its truthful portrayal of village life. The film refused to fall into any familiar pattern or set category – Ray had rebelled against the prevailing styles of Indian cinema.

The S.K. Patil Committee, which inquired into the working of the film industry in the early Fifties, suggested many reforms, including the setting up of a government-sponsored institution for financing films. The Committee clearly saw that many of the worst ills of Indian cinema arose from the lack of institutional finance on reasonable terms. The Film Finance Corporation (FFC), which came into operation in 1960, was supposed to make money available to the film industry as a whole, not solely to art cinema or popular movies. In its early years it pursued a cautious policy, supporting experienced directors such as Shantaram and Ray, but still managed to lose money. It then changed its policy to encourage low-budget productions. In 1969 the FFC announced the completion of six films made by aspiring directors, including Mrinal Sen's *Bhuvan Shome*. These were regarded as representing a 'New Wave' in Indian cinema. Subsequently several first features were supported. Though the FFC was able to balance its annual budgets in the Seventies, its contribution was arguably marginal to the mainstream of Indian cinema.

The commercial cinema had its own ups and downs. The producer G.P. Sippy's *Sholay* (1976, *Embers*) has been the biggest blockbuster in the history of Indian cinema. An action-packed film, a mixture of the thrills of the Western with Indian music and emotions, the film started a new trend, the making of colossally-budgeted films. But the success of *Sholay* could not be repeated. In Bombay the film industry was caught in a vicious financial circle from which it was unable to extricate itself on its own, while the government swallowed as much as forty to fifty per cent of box-office income. The only hope for a better cinema lay in the increased sponsoring of production by the various states of India in their own regional languages.

Parallel Cinema   There is no way that the Indian Parallel Cinema movement – whatever its starting date – can be considered coherent either in style or content. And its tragedy is that, despite the emergence of many fine talents, there are still very few cinemas in its home country prepared to foster their work. That undeniable fact has caused much argument in a perennially argumentative nation. A young director has infinitely more chance of making a film in India today than his equivalent in England, but to get it effectively released means that he has to face very similar problems. The complications in India are perhaps even greater because of language: at least a dozen official tongues make widespread dissemination almost impossible.

The Bengali directors Satyajit Ray, Mrinal Sen and **Ritwik Ghattak** can be regarded as the forefathers of the Parallel Cinema. The young film-makers chose the veteran Ghattak to chair the first public meeting of their Parallel Cinema group, seeing him as a valued teacher and profound influence. Ghattak (1924–1977), whose work is hardly known in the West was a wayward and troubled genius; his career consisted of only six feature films, all of extraordinary inventive and visual qualities. Ghattak was deeply affected by the tragedy of Bengali Partition, and the themes of separation and rupture recur insistently throughout his films. Sadly, the young film-makers' organization proved short-lived: the man they had chosen as their chairman was soon to die of alcoholism.

Mrinal Sen (b.1923) remains the most controversial of Indian directors, variously vilified as a mediocre sensationalist or revered as an outspoken radical. Born in 1923 in East Bengal, now part of Bangladesh, Sen travelled to Calcutta in 1940, working as a sound recordist at a film studio, a tutor and a journalist. He also joined the Indian People's Theatre Association – the cultural wing of the Indian Communist Party – and developed an interest in the aesthetics of film.

His first films, *Raat Bhore* (1956, Night's End) and *Neel Akasher Neechey* (1959, Under the Blue Sky), betrayed his inexperience; however, with his third feature, *Baishey Sravana* (1960, Wedding Day), which depicted the breakdown of a marriage during the 1943 famine in East Bengal, Sen's reputation began to grow. Studies of relationships set against the complexities of city life formed the bases of his next three films, *Punascha* (1961, Over Again), *Abasheshey* (1962, And at Last) and *Pratinidhi* (1964, The Representative). 1965's *Akash Kusum* (Up in the Clouds) proved to be something of a turning point in Sen's career. The story of a boy who dreams of marrying a sophisticated, upper-class girl, the film did not conform to traditional Indian narrative styles and made ironical comments on the class system.

Sen's deepening concern with the plight of India's poor – the theme of *Matira Manisha* (1967, Two Brothers) – found expression in a series of historical documentaries commissioned by the Indian government. The opportunity to probe the causes and effects of India's political and social history

Below: the married couple in Baishey Sravana *are unable to break off or mend their unhappy relationship.*

caused Sen to revise and refine his approach to cinema. He subsequently emerged as his country's foremost political film-maker, with such films as *Interview* (1971), *Calcutta '71* (1972), and *Padatik* (1974, The Guerrilla Fighter). In these Sen attempted to 'provoke, confuse, shake up the masses and lead them to find the truth'. *Oka Oorie Katha* (1978, *The Outsiders*), concerning a father and son who refuse to work to enrich the wealthy and cut themselves off from society, is widely accepted as one of Sen's masterpieces. Other important films are *Ekdin Pratidin* (1980, *And Quiet Rolls the Dawn*), the story of a Bengali family both financially and emotionally dependent on their eldest daughter, *Akaler Sandhane* (1981, In Search of Famine) and *Khandar* (1984, *The Ruins*), an atmospheric romantic drama.

If Satyajit Ray and Mrinal Sen are the two most widely known Parallel directors, there is a third whose position has been pivotal over the last decade – **Shyam Benegal**.

Born in the Hyderabad area in 1934, Benegal moved early to Bombay and became a highly successful maker of commercials and documentaries. *Ankur* (1974, *Ankur – The Seedling*), his famous first feature, was financed by the advertising company for whom he worked, and was remarkably popular with middle-class audiences looking for more than the average Hindi spectacular could offer. The story is of a landlord's son sent to administer a rural estate and his love for a beautiful peasant girl, married to a deaf and dumb worker. The film shot the actress Shabana Azmi to stardom, and was generally admired for its sensitivity and social relevance.

Nishant (1975, *Night's End*), which came next, was again about the landlord class and the way gross injustice and

Far left: Mrinal Sen's Akaler Sandhane *(1981, In Search of Famine), a film about making a film about the wartime food shortage in India. Centre: landlord and exploited maid in* Ankur – the Seedling. *Left: mass violence erupts in* Night's End *when a man loses his wife to powerful landowners. Below left:* Kondura, *about a magic root which brings tragedy to superstitious peasants. Below centre: set during the mutiny of 1857,* Possessed *traces the love of an Indian for a British girl. Below: a scene from M.S. Sathyu's* Hot Winds.

even if highly successful in their careers – still had the odds stacked against them. But the censorship rating given to the film prevented men taking their wives to it, with the inevitable result that the very audience Benegal was seeking failed to see it in sufficient numbers.

Junoon (Possessed), which was made in 1979, caused no such restrictive practices. It was produced and acted in by Shashi Kapoor, the Bombay superstar, and its subject was the 1857 Sepoy Revolt. After seeing it, some felt that Benegal was selling out to the film establishment, while others thought that perhaps he was taking it over. What is certain is that Benegal is a technically assured film-maker, able to secure subtle performances and to use significant themes in his attempt to move the Parallel Cinema out of its tiny art-house ghetto.

At the other end of the spectrum are *auteurs* like Mani Kaul and Kumar Shahani who have a far greater concern about the films they make than the audiences that are attracted to them. Kaul has made five features, of which *Satah se Uthata Aadmi* (Rising From the Surface) – a film without formal plot, exploring reactions to Indian life – was shown at Cannes in 1981 and praised by several French critics. He has been clearly more influenced by European rather than Indian film-making and remains a fascinating if difficult talent, who is unfortunately received in India with little understanding. Shahani, who has worked with Robert Bresson, is a similar case, ploughing a lonely furrow within an art cinema dedicated so often to countering big-budget fantasyland with small-budget neo-realism. But *Maya Darpan* (1972), his non-narrative first feature, is still a considerable achievement.

Another highly original, if less difficult, director is G. Aravindan one of the leading figures of Malayalam (South India) culture. A cartoonist, painter, musician and devotee of the theatre, Aravindan has a wonderful eye for detail and a richness of imagination unequalled in the South Indian cinema. Two films, in particular, have been recognized in the West: *Thampu* (1979, The Circus Tent), about the effect of a travelling circus on the life of a faraway village, and *Kummatty* (1980, *Bogeyman*), a superb children's story.

One of the Parallel Cinema's greatest achievements – artistically if not commercially – was M.S. Sathyu's *Garm Hava* (1974, Hot Winds), the only major film set against the controversial political canvas following the 1947 Partition with Pakistan. About a middle-aged Muslim trader in Agra who refuses to leave for Pakistan despite the urging of his friends, it was at first banned for instigating communal dissension, though finally given an All-India award for its contribution to national integration.

Two other film-makers of note sprang up in the Seventies: Girish Karnad and B.V. Karanth, who had made movies both together and separately – with Karnad also pursuing a highly productive acting career, and Karanth doing much work for the theatre. Karanth's best film is almost certainly *Chomana Dudi* (1975, Choma's Drum) which has a fine performance from Vasudeva Rao as a harijan (untouchable) who dreams of owning land but whose hopes disintegrate as caste and class put up insurmountable barriers. Karnad's breakthrough was *Kaadu* (1973, The Forest) in which two warring villages are watched through the eyes of a child growing up. He also directed and co-scripted *Ondanondu Kaladalli* (1978, Once Upon a Time), an action-packed adventure set in medieval times and full of strong characterizations, that reminded many critics of the samurai films of the Japanese director Akira Kurosawa, to whom it was dedicated.

feudal customs overwhelm even those determined to end them until the revolutionary process intervenes. Benegal then made *Manthan* (1976, The Churning), which was produced by 500,000 Gujarat farmers who each invested two rupees (about 10p) in its making. The film is about a young vet who persuades farmers to start a cooperative and thereby to fight the landlords who had previously mulcted them of their profits. It is a stirring tale, with optimism in the final reel but no false hopes that this kind of organization could ever be easy in such a tradition-bound country.

Bhumika (1978, *The Role*) and *Kondura* (1978, The Boon) were less popular with the public and persuaded Benegal that to defeat a conservative industry meant being more thoroughly a part of it. *Bhumika* was a biography of a celebrated screen actress of the past; it was designed to show how women –

Above: the Seventies saw the emergence of some fine new Indian directors – Benegal, Karanth and Karnad among them. Vasudeva Rao (left) as an untouchable in Karanth's Chomana Dudi.

The latest wave of Indian directors – many obviously influenced by Benegal – is making strenuous attempts to reach wider audiences than in the past, often by appealing to specifically regional susceptibilities.

Three of these are particularly worthy of mention. The first is Saeed Mirza, whose polemical *Albert Pinto ko Gussa Kyon Aata Hai* (1981, What Makes Albert Pinto Angry?) provided a decisive change of gear from his somewhat elliptical first feature, *Arvind Desai ki Ajeeb Dastaan* (1978, The Strange Tale of Arvind Desai). Buddhadeb Dasgupta made *Dooratwa* (1979, Distance) about the emotional sterility of the Indian middle class, and followed this with *Neem Annapurna* (1980, Bitter Morsel), describing the fatal lure of the big city for the hopeful petit bourgeois. And Govind Nihalani – whose impressive *Aakrosh* (1981, Cry of the Wounded) shared the main award at the 1981 Delhi Festival – showed how much he has developed as a film-maker after years as Benegal's cameraman. It is directors such as these who look set to alter the face of the Indian cinema.

Merchant and Ivory   Since the Sixties, India has fostered the careers of one of the most supremely cosmopolitan partnerships in world cinema, Ismail Merchant and James Ivory. Merchant was born in India in 1936 and educated in the USA. Ivory was born in 1928 in California, graduated from the Film School of the University of Southern California, but made his first features in India. Their frequent collaborator and screenwriter, the author Ruth Prawer Jhabvala, was born in Germany in 1927 of Polish parents, educated in England, married an Indian and later moved to the USA. Hardly surprisingly a recurrent theme in their work is that of a group of people beached – in one way or another – on the shores of an alien culture.

The trio's first project was *Gharbar* (1963, The House-holder), adapted from Jhabvala's novel. They received great encouragement from Satyajit Ray, who re-edited the film, giving it a tighter structure. He also composed the music for this and for *Shakespeare-Wallah* (1965). A film of wistful charm and nostalgia, based on the true story of the Kendal family, *Shakespeare-Wallah* relates the adventures of a troupe of English actors touring Shakespeare around an India from which the British long ago disappeared. After the Paramount-financed *The Guru* (1969), which failed to match the critical and commercial success of *Shakespeare-Wallah*, Merchant and Ivory, undeterred by this setback, embarked upon *Bombay Talkie* (1970), a rich and comic panorama of the Indian commercial film industry.

Subsequent Indian subjects were an engaging documentary portrait of a well-loved local star, *Helen, Queen of the Nautch Girls* (1972) and *Hullabaloo Over Georgie and Bonnie's Pictures* (1978). An anecdote about the supposed theft of a collection of Indian miniatures, this is a typical blend of gentle character comedy, nostalgia for a lost past and reflections upon people's relations to art and to possessions.

All these Indian subjects were scripted by Jhabvala. After *Bombay Talkie*, however, Merchant and Ivory turned to America and to new writers, George Trow and Michael O'Donohue, for *Savages* (1972), a curious fable in which a single household is witness to the evolution from savagery to civilization and its eventual reversal.

Their next American venture, *The Wild Party* (1975) – a vision of Twenties Hollywood based on a ballad poem by Joseph Moncure March – proved a less happy experience as a

Above: love and despair in Paris in the Twenties for the beautiful, victimized heroine of Quartet. *The French actress Isabelle Adjani won the Best Actress award in 1981 at the Cannes Film Festival.*

Top: Felicity Kendal plays a member of her own real-life family's theatre company in Shakespeare-Wallah. *Above:* The Europeans *are two visitors to Boston in the 1850s who have to adjust themselves to suit their New World relatives.*

result of the vicious re-cutting by the distributors.

For the third project in America, Merchant and Ivory reunited with Jhabvala. *Roseland* (1977) is a triptych of stories about characters frequenting the famous New York ballroom of that name. The central story – of an intense young woman (Geraldine Chaplin) caught up in a pre-doomed love affair with a flippant young gigolo (an early performance by Christopher Walken) – dominates the two slighter anecdotes that flank it.

It was not surprising that Henry James – who so often wrote about the enquiring American in search of the stimulation of older cultures, generally European – should attract Ivory; and in 1978 the team found it possible to make a delicate and elegant adaptation of *The Europeans*. Six years later they made an ambitious film version of James' *The Bostonians*.

Jane Austen in Manhattan (1980) turned to quite different literary inspiration and a much more complex style. It deals with the rivalry of two opposed theatrical interpretations of the same text, a rediscovered play by Jane Austen. In 1981 it seemed that, with their stylish, evocative adaptation of Jean Rhys' *Quartet*, the team had found an author and a theme perfectly reflecting their own continuing paradox: the search for a balance between cosmopolitanism and a sense of rootlessness. An air of sophisticated assurance in the handling of a complex narrative was once more apparent in their fine film version of Jhabvala's novel of the British Raj, *Heat and Dust* (1983).

Australia

The sound movie made its debut in Australia with *The Jazz Singer* (1927), starring Al Jolson. Produced by Warner Brothers with Vitaphone sound-on-disc recording, it opened at the Lyceum Theatre, Sydney on December 26, 1928. The rights to the film had been secured in New York by Stuart F. Doyle, then managing director of Union Theatres. The rival Hoyts Theatres, headed by Frank W. Thring, opened with a Fox feature *The Red Dance* (1928), sound-on-film but with music-and-effects track only, at the Regent Theatre, Sydney. Both Stuart Doyle and Frank Thring were to become important names in Australian film production.

Early in 1930, Thring decided to sell all his interests in Hoyts Theatres to the Fox Film Corporation, thereby opening the door into the Australian exhibition field for the Americans – a lucrative position from which they have not retreated. Thring put much of the money from Fox into Australian film production, taking over a fire-damaged theatre in Melbourne and fashioning it into a film studio of sorts. He went to the USA and came back with all the equipment necessary to make first-class sound films; but never entirely achieved this goal. Certainly his Efftee Films made a sizeable contribution to early Australian sound production, completing eight features and several shorts, but all without much commercial success.

Thring's general failure to select the right subjects is hard to explain, since he was a man well versed in show business. Yet he must be credited with making the first fully professional sound film in Australia, a comedy entitled *Diggers* (1931), featuring Pat Hanna, a World War I concert-party comic. Hanna then broke with Thring, because he claimed to have disliked the way Thring had handled this film. Later he hired the Efftee studios independently so that he could personally produce and direct two moderately successful follow-ups, *Diggers in Blighty* and *Waltzing Matilda* (both 1933).

Efftee Films itself, with Frank Thring producing and directing, went on to make *The Sentimental Bloke* (1932), based on poems by local author C.J. Dennis about the adventures of a lovable Australian rogue; but it did not begin to match the quality or the success of the silent version made by Raymond Longford in 1919. Thring also made three comedies with George Wallace. However, with his death in Melbourne in 1936 Efftee Films, which had ceased production in 1934, finally closed down.

In the mid-Twenties, there had been keen competition among radio hams to find ways of getting synchronous sound on film or disc without infringing the seemingly watertight patents of the American companies. Eventually a young radio engineer from Tasmania, Arthur Carrington Smith, designed and built sound-on-film equipment that was to become a major factor in the upsurge of film production in Australia in the Thirties and after. He perfected it in 1931 and Stuart Doyle's assistant, Ken G. Hall, supported it enthusiastically. Doyle was finally won over to the new sound system and set up Cinesound as a subsidiary of Union Theatres. It was the very depth of the Depression, when the rate of unemployment in Australia was over thirty per cent of the work-force. The theatres were empty and the company was mortgaged to the banks. It seemed an impossible time to start anything.

But Doyle, with his strong showman instinct, wanted a feature film made of the comedy *On Our Selection*, which concerned a farming family and had been a stage hit for nearly twenty years. Without ever being officially designated as such, Hall found himself director of this first film as well as general manager of the company and also managing editor of the weekly newsreel *Cinesound Review* which Doyle wanted organized – while Hall was still on location actually making *On Our Selection* (1932). Despite being shot with antiquated lights and camera in a sound studio set in a skating rink, *On Our Selection* became an overwhelming box-office success, outgrossing any other film from whatever source released in Australia up to and well beyond that time. It was also released in England, as all the Cinesound features were to be; for English distribution it was retitled *Down on the Farm*.

It was this film that established Cinesound, because its profits were ploughed back into equipment and studio improvement. So were those of the two highly successful films immediately following, *The Squatter's Daughter* (1933), which was praised for its bushfire climax, and *The Silence of Dean Maitland* (1934), the story of a parson's passionate love affair. Stuart Doyle was reaping a three-way harvest from production, distribution and exhibition, particularly the last – the parent company controlled all three aspects of the industry. Cinesound became the firm base for Sydney production through the Thirties, serving its own needs and those of independents. It slowly built up a well-trained and skilful permanent crew which never had to face being laid off after each film finished production, as happened in America and elsewhere.

Among the independents was English-born producer-director Harry Southwell, who came in to make one of many pictures about the notorious Ned Kelly gang, *When the Kellys Rode* (1934), and later *The Burgomeister* (1935), an adaptation of the actor Sir Henry Irving's favourite play *The Bells*.

In Melbourne the indefatigable director A.R. Harwood turned out five quickies through the Thirties, including *Spur*

of the Moment (1931), about the disappearance of a domestic flight.

Beaumont Smith, who had been a successful producer-director as far back as 1917, used Cinesound facilities for *The Hayseeds* (1933), a rural comedy directed by Raymond Longford, and *Splendid Fellows* (1934), directed by Smith himself and featuring some actuality scenes shot in Melbourne.

Cinesound was also the studio where Charles Chauvel made his first sound film, the semi-documentary feature *In the Wake of the Bounty* (1933), in which Errol Flynn made his acting debut as Fletcher Christian. Chauvel returned much later to make his two hit films, the outstanding cavalry picture *Forty Thousand Horsemen* (1940) and *Sons of Matthew* (1949), the story of the pioneering O'Riordan family. Of course, Cinesound studios already had competition from Thring's Efftee Films in Melbourne. And more was to come.

John Bruce and Phil Budden, operating Commonwealth Laboratories, quickly set up a small production base to be used by the three McDonagh sisters (an actress, a writer and a director) and some other independents. In 1935, powerful newspaper interests, headed by Sir Hugh Denison of the *Sydney Sun* and with a board fairly glittering with knights, founded Pagewood studios a mile or so from the centre of Sydney – and, indifferent to the aircraft noise, half a mile from Sydney Airport. Denison entered into an association with Gaumont British, which advised on the studio design and building, and took control of the first film *The Flying Doctor* (1936). Gaumont British provided not only the director Miles Mander, but also the writer Jock Orton, the cameraman Derek Williams and additional production experts; the star was American Charles Farrell. But despite all the importations, *The Flying Doctor* failed to get off the ground.

Chauvel's Aboriginal story *Uncivilised* (1936) was also made at Pagewood. But that studio's most successful feature was *Rangle River* (1936), produced in association with Columbia; it featured Victor Jory and was directed by Clarence Badger, both Americans. The modern, well-equipped Pagewood studio had little or no success after that and gradually fell into disuse.

Cinesound made 17 feature films between 1932 and its close-down, enforced by the war, in 1940. All save one were commercially successful – a record not surpassed in Australia before or since its time. Ken G. Hall directed all but one of them, and even then produced the one he did not direct, *Come Up Smiling* (1939).

Noel Monkman, who won early acclaim for his microscopic and underwater photography in a series of shorts made in association with Frank Thring, attempted his first feature film with an adventure picture set in North Queensland, *Typhoon Treasure* (1938). While it suffered from story trouble, it indicated Monkman's promise as a director. This was enhanced with his next feature *The Power and the Glory* (1941), which concerned young pilots defending Australia in trainer planes.

In 1940 Ken Hall finished a comedy, *Dad Rudd, MP*, knowing that his production crew would then be laid off for the duration of the war. They were reprieved, however, by Charles Chauvel's re-entry into the studio to make his first big success *Forty Thousand Horsemen*, a tribute to the Australian Light Horse cavalry in World War I. After that it was newsreel and wartime propaganda for the small crew Cinesound retained. In 1943 Cinesound won an Oscar for a full-length newsreel subject *Kokoda Front Line* (1942). Hall holds the Oscar as producer-director-writer. It was photographed by the brilliant Damien Parer, later killed in action, and is the only Academy Award ever made to any newsreel.

Charles Chauvel's outstanding success with *Forty Thousand Horsemen* meant that he was able to continue his career with *Rats of Tobruk* (1944), a World War II film starring Peter Finch, Chips Rafferty and Grant Taylor, who all began their screen careers under Hall's direction. Location work for both films was at the sandhills of Cronulla, near Sydney.

Cinesound, despite its remarkable success in the Thirties, was permitted by its board to make no more feature films after the war. Ken Hall was commissioned by Columbia to make *Smithy* (1946), the story of the World War I fighter pilot Charles Kingsford Smith, the first man to fly the Pacific from San Francisco to Brisbane in 1928. Though shot at Cinesound

with Hall's old crew, the feature was completely financed by Columbia.

By this time Norman Bede Rydge, who succeeded Stuart Doyle as managing director of Greater Union when he was deposed in 1936, had sold a 50-per-cent share in the entire Greater Union group of companies to the rapidly expanding English company of J. Arthur Rank. The outlook for further feature production at Cinesound almost immediately became grim. The Rank policy, as later expressed in Australia by

Below left: the Cinesound newsreel lasted from 1931 to 1972. Below right: The Squatter's Daughter *was Cinesound's second feature film. Bottom:* Orphan of the Wilderness *was about a kangaroo's cruel treatment at the hands of a circus owner. The director, Ken G. Hall, is second from left.*

executive John Davis, was to make the pictures in England, which had the studios, equipment and talent, and to show them in Australia, among other places. Rydge accepted this because, as an accountant, he was nervous of the risks of the creative side of the film industry.

At this crucial time Harry Watt who had moved into Australia in 1945 with the backing of Michael Balcon of Ealing Studios, wrote and directed the immensely successful *The Overlanders* (1946), which portrayed an overland cattle-trek to Queensland during World War II. This film's world-wide earnings fixed English production eyes eagerly on Australia. But no help, or finance, was offered by the Australian half of the partnership, which had already restricted Cinesound to the newsreel, commercial and documentary field. Additionally, the Greater Union-Cinesound board was being considerably shaken by the fact that Charles Chauvel had been on location in Queensland for an almost fruitless six months in 1946 on the production of *Sons of Matthew*, which was backed by Greater Union in association with Universal.

It took Chauvel three years in all to get *Sons of Matthew*, a good but not outstanding film, on to the screen in 1949. He had exceeded his original budget by 500 per cent. This did nothing to steady the already shattered nerves of the Greater Union board and it did not back another Australian film for the next quarter of a century.

Harry Watt returned to make *Eureka Stockade* (1949), a historical film of a gold-miners' 'revolt' against authority in the early 1850s. The film featured Chips Rafferty, but he was not yet ready for the serious dramatic acting role he was given. He had no training as an actor and succeeded best, as so many Hollywood actors also did, when playing himself. Critically assailed, *Eureka Stockade* failed in the theatres.

A year later the Cinesound board made another shattering decision that was to seal the fate of the unit. It sold the Bondi studio property, laboratory and all, to a soft-drink company.

From 1949 onwards, Australian film production was in catastrophic decline. Apart from Chauvel's last feature *Jedda* (1954), an Aboriginal love story, and Cecil Holmes' trio of stories about friendship, *Three in One* (1956), not one genuinely Australian film of any significance was made in the next twenty or so years. It is true that the Cinesound building was taken over in 1956 and transformed back into a studio – at very considerable expense – by Southern International, a company formed by Chips Rafferty and director Lee Robinson and funded by public subscription raised largely on Rafferty's by-now-well-established name. They made three films: *Walk Into Paradise* (1956), filmed in New Guinea; *The Restless and the Damned* (1959), a co-production with Silver Films of Paris that never rated a showing in Australia; and *Dust in the Sun* (1959), based on Jon Cleary's novel and set in

Far left: Chips Rafferty strikes out in The Overlanders. *Left: pictures spoke more eloquently than words in* Walk Into Paradise. *Below far left: Paddy (Robert Mitchum) a sheep drover, and his wife Ida (Deborah Kerr) in* The Sundowners. *Below left: Peter Finch in* The Shiralee. *Below: Ava Gardner and Gregory Peck in* On the Beach.

Alice Springs. All three films failed and Southern International went into liquidation. The studio which had been a hive of industry through the Thirties – and still operative, though to a lesser degree, in the Forties – finally became one of a chain of merchandising discount houses.

In 1966 *They're a Weird Mob*, adapted from an Australian best-selling novel by John O'Grady about a new immigrant, was a big success in Australia but a failure elsewhere. With 50-per-cent English finance, Michael Powell as producer-director, an English screenplay, an English cameraman, an Italian star (Walter Chiari) and an Irish leading lady, it could hardly be hailed as an all-Australian film – though it was, of course, by an over-enthusiastic press, rarely accurate on film matters.

Films were being made in Australia during the period but all of the few successes – and some of the failures – were actually American or English films made on location. Some were star-studded – with overseas stars, naturally. The talents of Maureen O'Hara and Peter Lawford and of the director Lewis Milestone were invested by 20th Century-Fox in the expensive *Kangaroo* (1952), which failed; Milestone seemed astray and ill at ease in the Australian outback. On the other hand, the brilliant Fred Zinnemann went into the same kind of territory in 1960 and directed the very successful *The Sundowners*, with Robert Mitchum and Deborah Kerr as an

Australian sheepman and his wife, complete with 'authentic' – as against the usually exaggerated – accents.

Among the few other successes of that long, long drought were: Anthony Kimmins' two films about a boy's adventures, *Smiley* (1956) and *Smiley Gets a Gun* (1958); Ealing's *The Shiralee* (1957), with Peter Finch as a jolly swagman on the road with his young daughter; Stanley Kramer's apocalyptic *On the Beach* (1960), with Gregory Peck, Ava Gardner and Fred Astaire as temporary survivors in a post-nuclear world; and Hecht-Hill-Lancaster's *Summer of the Seventeenth Doll* (1960), with Ernest Borgnine and John Mills as Queensland cane-cutters on holiday having trouble with their girlfriends, played by Angela Lansbury and Anne Baxter. Michael Powell also made another film set in Australia, *Age of Consent* (1968), the love story of an ageing artist and a young girl, with James Mason and Helen Mirren.

After virtually twenty years of little real effort and no success, Australian feature-film production was apparently dead or, at best, dying as the Sixties drew to a close. Something really had to be done. Something was done – in the form of a life-giving injection of gold from the public purse – and, with the coming of the Seventies, the great revival of Australian cinema began.

The 'New Wave' In 1971 the Australian government began to make available money to support a feature film industry; a boom was thus created that brought unprecedented international exposure and critical praise to Australian features, directors and stars. The first films produced were almost all broad, 'ocker' comedies, such as Tim Burstall's *Stork* (1971), adapted from a play by David Williamson and featuring a tall, loudmouthed but sexually insecure hero caught up in a *ménage à quatre*.

Tim Burstall (b. 1929) proved to be the only one of the new directors of the Seventies to have made a feature film in the preceding decade – the ambitious *2000 Weeks* (1969). This was a semi-autobiographical plea to people of artistic talent to stay and work in Australia rather than flee to what at the time were seen as the greater cultural attractions of Britain. Although much criticized at the time, the film represented a worthwhile, if somewhat self-conscious, attempt to extend the frontiers of Australian cinema.

In the Seventies Burstall concentrated on making commercial entertainments. *Alvin Purple* (1973) merged 'ocker' comedy with soft-core sex, while *Petersen* (1974) was a comedy drama about a labourer (Jack Thompson) trying to improve his prospects with a belated education and becoming involved with the wife (Wendy Hughes) of his professor.

Less successful was *End Play* (1975), a somewhat predictable whodunnit scripted by Burstall himself, but he redeemed himself with *The Last of the Knucklemen* (1979), an excellent adaptation of a popular play by John Powers. Burstall's style is punchy and sometimes unsubtle, leading to frequent critical accusations of male chauvinism. However he is generally respected as a battler who, after a serious early reverse, has shown that he has his finger on the Australian public's pulse. During the Sixties, another 'ocker' hero, Barry McKenzie – that stereotypical, uncouth, lager-swilling Australian male – had been created by Barry Humphries in the British satirical magazine *Private Eye*. Two bawdy films, directed by **Bruce Beresford** – *The Adventures of Barry McKenzie* (1972) and *Barry McKenzie Holds His Own* (1974) – were based on the misadventures of this comic-strip character. Beresford (b. 1940) had made amateur films in Sydney before becoming film editor for the Nigerian government's production unit and, in 1966, head of film production at the British Film Institute.

As a result of the success of the first McKenzie film, Beresford was given the chance direct the screen version of one of David Williamson's sharpest and most popular plays, the satirical, sexy *Don's Party* (1976). Since then he has deliberately diversified: *The Getting of Wisdom* (1977) was a sensitive tale set in a girls' boarding school in 1900, while *Money Movers* (1978) was a fast-paced thriller. In 1980 Beresford made two very successful films – the award-winning Boer war drama *Breaker Morant*, starring British actor Edward Woodward and an amusing version of yet another Williamson play, *The Club*. He subsequently made *Tender Mercies* (1982) with Hollywood backing. Beresford prefers to work with a regular team of collaborators (including Don McAlpine as director of photography and Bill Anderson as editor) and is highly respected as an economical, conscientious film-maker with an astringent sense of humour.

Until the Seventies, Australian audiences had largely been denied seeing their history on film, and several directors set out to remedy the omission. Michael Thornhill's *Between Wars* (1974) was a key early example, following the fortunes of an outspoken non-conformist (Corin Redgrave) from the end of World War I to the outbreak of World War II. Philip Noyce effectively evoked the post-war period in his remarkable debut film *Newsfront* (1978), which explores the career of a newsreel cameraman (Bill Hunter) between 1948 and 1956, a time when Australia was becoming increasingly Americanized. With its witty script (by Bob Ellis) and skilful intercutting of vintage newsreel material, *Newsfront* was a huge success domestically though less so overseas; despite many excellent reviews, distributors felt it to be too Australian for general release.

In the mid-Seventies, **Peter Weir** (b. 1944) inaugurated a vogue for soft-focus nostalgia with the haunting *Picnic at Hanging Rock* (1975). With superb photography by Russell Boyd, this was the first Australian art film to win international recognition. Weir, who was to become one of the most consistent of the new Australian directors, made his first films to entertain his fellow employees at a Sydney television station during their annual Christmas party. His quirky sense of humour was much in evidence in his first feature – *The Cars That Ate Paris* (1974) – about the inhabitants of a small town who scavenge the passing cars they have deliberately caused to crash. However his subsequent films eschewed comedy for a brooding sense of unease. He and Boyd once more collaborated on the supernatural thriller *The Last Wave* (1977), starring Richard Chamberlain. Despite the film's success (particularly in the USA), during the next three years Weir was only able to make a television film, *The Plumber* (1979). He returned to the big screen in 1981 with *Gallipoli*, which viewed the disastrous Dardanelles campaign of World War I from the point of view of a generation of young Australians, only just discovering the concept of their own national identity. With 1983's *The Year of Living Dangerously*, a drama set in Indonesia at the time of the fall of Sukarno, Weir moved with qualified success into international production.

Turn-of-the-century Australia provided the evocative setting of *My Brilliant Career* (1979), directed by **Gillian Armstrong** (b. 1950), based on the autobiographical novel by Miles Franklin. The film was an enormous success all over the world with its sensitively told story of a young woman who chooses a career as a writer in preference to a safe marriage,

and made international stars of Judy Davis and Sam Neill. Armstrong then made an engaging pop musical, *Starstruck* (1983).

A director particularly concerned with social themes is **Fred Schepisi** (b. 1939), who entered the industry through newsreels, documentaries and commercials. His fine first film, *The Devil's Playground* (1976), is strongly autobiographical in its study of the repressive life of boys in a Catholic seminary in the Fifties. Schepisi also made one of the most important Australian historical films, *The Chant of Jimmie Blacksmith* (1978), an angry indictment of the mistreatment of the Aborigines; he then travelled to the USA to make a Western, *Barbarosa* (1982), and a study of alienation, *Iceman* (1984).

A neglected area of Australia's past was explored in *Break of Day* (1976), set at the time of the first Anzac Day in 1920 and concerning life in a small town decimated by the loss of its menfolk during World War I. The film's director, **Ken Hannam**, who had previously worked in radio and for BBC TV, started his feature film career with the excellent *Sunday Too Far Away* (1975), about the lives of sheepshearers. He had less success with subsequent films – *Summerfield* (1977), a thriller, and *Dawn!* (1979), a biography of swimming champion Dawn Fraser.

Donald Crombie (b. 1942), who scored an immediate success with his debut film, *Caddie* (1976), had previously worked at Film Australia on a series of accomplished documentaries. *Caddie*, featuring a superb performance by Helen Morse, was set in the Depression and told the true story of a former barmaid who, as a single parent, had had to struggle hard to bring up her two children. Crombie's subtle direction was likened to that of John Ford, a comparison given further credence by Crombie's second feature – *The Irishman* (1978) – about the impact of industrial progress on a small town in the Twenties and the resulting break-up of a family. A third film, *Cathy's Child* (1979), about a Maltese woman's attempts to reclaim the baby kidnapped by her husband underlined the director's concern with domestic themes.

Jim Sharman (b. 1945) is a theatre director whose innovative stage productions of *Hair*, *Jesus Christ Superstar* and *The Rocky Horror Picture Show* gained him an international reputation. In Australia he is also known for his excellent productions of plays by Patrick White – indeed his most satisfying film was scripted by White, *The Night the Prowler* (1978). Sharman's most famous feature however, is the cult hit *The Rocky Horror Picture Show* (1975). Horror/fantasy also made the name of **George Miller** (b. 1945). A former doctor, he shot to fame as the director of futuristic thrillers *Mad Max* (1979) and *Mad Max 2* (1982).

A number of young directors preferred to focus on more serious, contemporary themes: Michael Thornhill's *The F.J. Holden* (1977) and John Duigan's *Mouth to Mouth* (1978) and *Winter of Our Dreams* (1981) concerned suburban alienation among the young; while Steven Wallace's powerful *Stir!* (1980) was based on the events leading up to a prison riot. Probably the most original and important of the newer directors is **Paul Cox** (b. 1940), won international acclaim with *Lonely Hearts* (1982), *Man of Flowers* (1983) and *My First Wife* (1984) – intimate, personal and idiosyncratic studies in alienation spiced with daring flashes of sophisticated, dark humour.

Right: Sam Neill as a wealthy young man, and Judy Davis capture each other's fancy in a tender moment from Gillian Armstrong's My Brilliant Career.

Top left: in Newsfront, *recreated newsreel footage is intercut with original documentary. Top right: death in the Dardanelles in* Gallipoli. *Above left: the eerie* Picnic at Hanging Rock *won world-wide acclaim for director Peter Weir and cameraman Russell Boyd. The film is about schoolgirls and their teacher who inexplicably disappear during an outing. Above right: George Miller's* Mad Max *films have become horror/sci-fi classics. In* Mad Max 2, *the desert is the arena for a war between those who have petrol and those who don't. Above: a repressed, wealthy, middle-aged man (Norman Kaye) pays an unemployed girl (Alyson Best) to undress, in* Man of Flowers.

Canada

Long a cultural dependent of the USA, Canada had no significant feature production before the Sixties. The National Film Board was the basis of Canadian film culture and helped to spark off the *cinéma-vérité* movement in Canada that led to such films as *Pour la Suite du Monde* (1964, *The Moontrap*) by Michel Brault and Pierre Perrault and *Warrendale* (1967) by Allan King. The real launching for Canadian cinema came when the new Canadian Film Development Corporation began to finance feature films in 1968. First to win praise was the Quebec cinema and especially the films of Gilles Groulx, Claude Jutra, Gilles Carle, Denys Arcand and Jean-Pierre Lefebvre. These French-language film-makers had the advantage of not having to compete directly with the American cinema; to gain equal attention, the English-language film-makers had to become distinctively 'Canadian'.

Allan King developed an intimate documentary technique, having his biggest success with *A Married Couple* (1969). Robin Spry, after gaining acclaim for *Prologue* in 1969, created an acidic investigative style in such films as *One Man* (1977), about pollution, and *Drying Up the Streets* (1978), about drugs. Other film-makers utilized avant-garde techniques, the most influential being Michael Snow with *Wavelength* (1967), *Back and Forth* (1969), and *La Région Centrale* (1971, The Central Region). David Cronenberg combined science fiction with anti-sexuality in *Stereo* (1969) and *Crimes of the Future* (1970), and then created a series of bizarre, personalized horror films: *The Parasite Murders* (1975, released in Britain as *Shivers*), *Rabid* (1977), *The Brood* (1979), *Scanners* (1981) and *Videodrome* (1983). His disturbing vision of the world has few parallels in the Canadian cinema.

The first English-language director to please both audiences and critics was Donald Shebib with *Goin' Down the Road* (1970), which had a nice, relaxed Canadian quality of its own. Unfortunately, none of his later films has had as much impact, though *Between Friends* (1973) was widely shown. The greatest international success was Ted Kotcheff's 1974 screen version of Mordecai Richler's novel *The Apprenticeship of Duddy Kravitz*, a wryly comic tale of ambition in Montreal that became a box-office hit after winning the Grand Prize at Berlin. Kotcheff, who returned to Canada to make this film after a career in England, did not repeat this success in Canada but moved on to Hollywood.

Many of the most successful Canadian directors, including Norman Jewison, Arthur Hiller, Sidney Furie and Daryl Duke, are not thought of as Canadian, though some returned from Hollywood when the international production era of the late Seventies provided an opportunity. The same was true of a Canadian-born star, Donald Sutherland, who came back for such 'Canadian' co-productions as *The Disappearance* and *Les Liens de Sang/Blood Relatives* (both 1977). Even stars produced by the Canadian cinema itself (Geneviève Bujold, for example) eventually felt the necessity of moving on to Hollywood. The native Canadian industry seemed virtually swamped in the late Seventies by the trend to international film production though in the early Eighties Canada made a small corner in low-budget horror films. However, its biggest hit was the teenage comedy, *Porky's* (1982).

Since the Mid-Forties the French-speaking film-makers of Quebec had striven to create a cinema that would reflect their own culture, thereby loosening Hollywood's stranglehold on the home industry. Between 1944 and 1953, 15 commercially-orientated features were made, starring popular stage and radio performers. For a few years there were dreams of studios, stars, box-office hits and a Hollywood in Montreal. But success was a long time coming and, although a first generation of film-makers learned their skills on these productions, the films made little impact. For every hit, like *Tit-Coq* (1953), there were several failures, such as *Un Homme et Son Péché* (1948, A Man and His Sin), *Le Rossignol et les Cloches* (1951, Nightingale and the Bells) and *La Petite Aurore l'Enfant Martyre* (1952, Little Aurore the Child Martyr). The majority of these films, encouraged (even financially supported) by the all-powerful Quebec Catholic Church of the time, were naive illustrations of what a certain traditional element wished to see as the intrinsic values of French Canadians: devotion to the Church, intense family life, a spirit of sacrifice, respect for authority and, naturally, *joie de vivre*.

The generation of film-makers that appeared at the end of the Fifties, and which would build from nothing the entire Quebec cinema in the following decade, had no deep ties with the archaic Quebec glorified by the post-war features. The new men – some from the artistic bohemia of Montreal, others from the intelligentsia – all began as documentarists and their

experience in this field gave them a passionate feel for their surroundings; the early films they made for the NFB – including *Les Raquetteurs* (1958, Snow-trekkers), *Golden Gloves* (1961) and *La Lutte* (1961, *The Fight*) – indicated the tenor of the whole of Quebec cinema for the next twenty years.

The major split from the past came with the release of three trail-blazing films: Claude Jutra's *A Tout Prendre* (1963, *Take It All*); Michel Brault and Pierre Perrault's collaboration, *Pour la Suite du Monde* (1964, *The Moontrap*); and Gilles Groulx's *Le Chat dans le Sac* (1964, *The Cat in the Bag*). Each of these movies bears defining characteristics of the Quebec screen. There is the charm and unselfconsciousness of Jutra's improvisatory techniques; Brault and Perrault's feel for a meaningful image; the poetic way Groulx handles political themes. These film-makers have remained at the forefront of their national cinema. **Claude Jutra** (b. 1930) had his major success as a director in 1971 with *Mon Oncle Antoine* (*My Uncle Antoine*). It is the portrait of both a provincial adolescent in the Forties and the small mining town where he lives and where exploitation is ingrained in even the most banal day-to-day activities. Abandoning the experimentation of *A Tout Prendre*, Jutra creates in *Mon Oncle Antoine* a perfectly fluent narrative that strongly conveys emotion and atmosphere.

Michel Brault (b.1928), the director of over thirty documentary shorts and an exceptionally talented cinematographer on dozens of other films (including *Mon Oncle Antoine*), has also been attracted to features. His *Entre la Mer et l'Eau Douce* (1967, Between the Sea and Fresh Water) met with only partial critical success, doubtless as a result of the sheer audacity of the project. This film, beautifully photographed and acted mostly by professionals (with Geneviève Bujold as a waitress), starts from a very simple dramatic situation, relies on a linear narrative (a boy from the coast comes down to Montreal to find work), and unpretentiously synthesizes – in a work of fiction – the various techniques Brault had learned in improvisational work.

Brault's effectively balanced use of 'live' methods was repeated with *Les Ordres* (1974, *The Orders*), in which he attempts to fictionalize the political upheavals in Quebec in

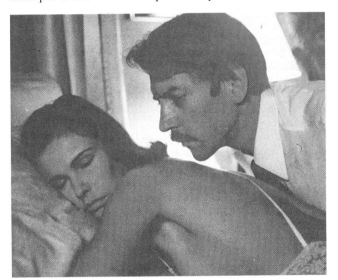

Left: Claude Gauthier and Geneviève Bujold in Michel Brault's Entre la Mer et l'Eau Douce. *Far left: pauperized Indians in Arthur Lamothe's epic documentary* Mistashipu. *Above right: hired gunman Jay Mallory (Donald Sutherland) is concerned with* The Disappearance *of his estranged wife (Francine Racette) and follows her trail from Canada to England. Above left:* The Apprenticeship of Duddy Kravitz *was a great crowd pleaser. Duddy (Richard Dreyfuss) involves his Gentile girlfriend Yvette (Micheline Lanctôt) in negotiating a land deal when the owners will not sell to a Jew. Above far left: two brothers fight a mental duel to the death as they struggle for control of each other's brain in David Cronenberg's* Scanners.

the autumn of 1970. If the film's political analysis is at times confused, its characters are lifelike and its balance between fact (the Trudeau government's passing of the War Emergency Act, the arbitrary imprisonment of hundreds of people, the immediate suppression of local organizations) and fiction is admirably sustained.

Pierre Perrault (b. 1927), radio broadcaster, poet, dramatist and essayist, is, above all, a man of words, and throughout this movies he has forced the camera to 'listen'. The originality of Perrault's approach to film-making owes a lot to the fact that it is the recorded word – though often staged – that becomes the very fabric of such films as *Le Règne du Jour* (1966, The Reign of Day), *Les Voitures d'Eau* (1969, River Schooners) and *Un Pays Sans Bons Sens* (1971, Wake Up, Mes Bons Amis!!!). Well supported by first-class cameramen. Perrault goes in search of the Quebec temperament, past and present, French-speaking or Amerindian. His feature-length films are not documentaries as such, but rather essays – sometimes irritatingly nationalistic but never less than stimulating.

Of all the film-makers of this Quebec first generation, **Gilles Groulx** (b. 1931) was the one who made the greatest impression and who most influenced his peers – and indeed anyone who discovered *Le Chat dans le Sac* in 1964. This is the film which – through its themes (the nationality problem, political responsibility, 'appropriation' of Quebec's landscape), script and the way it sums up Quebec cinema of the Sixties – will always be the essential reference point for any analysis of the revitalized Quebec film industry. It is the story of a young couple (the French-Canadian Claude and the English-Canadian Jew Barbara) who are heading for a break-up. Through their crisis Groulx describes what he called at the time the 'vagueness' of French Canadians. Ultimately the film is just a long dialogue between Claude and Barbara, and more so between Claude and himself, questioning the socio-political reality of his environment and disturbed by his powerlessness to alter it.

Groulx's other films, however accomplished, have not attained the fine balance and lyrical quality of *Le Chat dans le Sac. Où Etes-Vous Donc?* (1969, Where Are You Then?) is a pretty collage and a poetic call to revolution, something which, for all their undeniable merits, *Entre Tu et Vous* (1969, Between Thou and You) and the unreleased *24 Heures ou Plus* (1973–7, 24 Hours or More) never managed to achieve.

From this same generation of young pioneers the names of **Gilles Carle** and **Arthur Lamothe** stand out from diametrically opposed reasons. Carle (b. 1929) has opted to make ostensibly commercial films (though some critics regard them as personal 'quality' films too). *Les Mâles* (1970, The Males), *La Vraie Nature de Bernadette* (1972, The True Nature of Bernadette) and *La Tête de Normande St-Onge* (1975, Normande) – all shown at Cannes and given fairly wide European distribution, and all fulfilling commercial demands with well-heeled social decor, a certain brash sexuality and good acting – are the best known of his persuasive, picturesque films. In 1981 he had a hit with *Les Plouffe* (The Plouffe Family), the amended version of a television mini-series. But his more recent period piece, *Maria Chapdelaine* (1983), was disappointing. His reputation was better served by an entertaining NFB documentary feature, *Jouer Sa Vie* (1982, The Great Chess Movie).

Lamothe (b. 1928) is the epitome of concerned cinema, modest in his means though bold in his deliberate choice of subject-matter. He is basically a documentarist, whose two experiments in fictional films have proved indecisive. After some fine shorts, Lamothe made his name with a feature-length work about the conditions of construction workers around Montreal; *Le Mépris n'Aura Qu'un Temps* (1970, Scorn Won't Last Forever) comes across as a bitter plea on behalf of the exploited, and, filming it, Lamothe discovered his own mood and style, which he has continued to develop. Since 1974 his accusatory films have concentrated, in a simple and disturbing way, on the plight of the Indians of the north coast of St Laurent, a people exiled in their own lands. *Mistashipu* (1974, *La Grande Rivière* – the Great River) and *Ntesi Nana Shepen* (1976, *On Dirait que C'Etait Notre Terre* – You Could Say That It Was Our Land), the two main series of Lamothe's extensive Amerindian cycle, constitute the most balanced approach, both cinematically and ideologically, that any film-maker has ever offered on the facts about Indians living on American soil.

Of the new Quebec film-makers to emerge in the late Sixties and early Seventies, the most important are **Jean-Pierre Lefebvre, Jacques Leduc** and **Denys Arcand** (all b. 1941). Lefebvre, who directed 16 features between 1965 and 1980, is the Quebec film-maker most readily spoken of as an *auteur*. And author he is, working against storms and tides to formulate an *oeuvre* in which every film constitutes a chapter. His movies are by turns rigorous and random, searching and superficial, ordered and slapdash. Although films like *La Chambre Blanche* (1969, House of Light) and *Q-bec-My-Love* (1970) are, with their philosophical discussions, at times pretentious, his work is always strong on narrative and is genuinely emotive, especially *Les Dernières Fiançailles* (1973, The Last Betrothals) and *Avoir Seize Ans* (1979, To Be Sixteen) His charming *Le Jour "S . . ."* (1984, "S as in . . ." A Sentimental Tale) was well received at Cannes.

Below: Esther Auger in Jacques Leduc's first feature film, the powerful On Est Loin du Soleil, *a landmark in the burgeoning Quebec cinema of the early Seventies.*

Leduc, a friend and colleague of Lefebvre, could initially have been seen as one of his disciples, but there is a flavour in his films that hints at something else. His first, *On Est Loin du Soleil* (1971, The Sun Is Far Away) is one of the most original movies of the young Quebec cinema. A portrait of a kind of saint, this film gains from a 'mosaic' structure whose elements – dramatic, thematic, even spiritual – reach a conclusion only once they have run their course. A film entirely restrained, *On Est Loin du Soleil* is a disturbing reflection of the soul of a silent people.

Leduc continued this exploration with a second feature – *Tendresse Ordinaire* (1973, Ordinary Tenderness) – as he did with a long collective documentary in eight parts, *Chronique de la Vie Quotidienne* (1977, Chronicle of Daily Life).

The work of Denys Arcand is of a completely different nature. The author of a famous full-length documentary on textile work, *On Est au Coton* (1971, We Work in Cotton), in the Seventies he made three distinctly original features: *La Maudite Galette* (1972, That Damned Money), *Réjeanne Padovani* (1973), and *Gina* (1974). Complemented by intelligent and vigorous direction and always benefiting from careful control of actors, Arcand's films are genuine social documentaries. As portraits of drop-outs, they say more about Quebec society than countless documentaries. In the Eighties he turned commercial with the soap operatic *Le Crime d'Ovide Plouffe* (1983, The Crime of Ovide Plouffe), a follow-up to Carle's TV series and play. Once again it was made as both six-hour mini-series and two-hour amended film. Arcand made the cinema version while Carle directed the TV-only sections.

For some time now it has been fashionable to say that Quebec's cinema has had its day. The economic crisis gripping the whole of Canada in the early Eighties has gripped the film industry as well. Quebec films produce more unemployment than box-office turnover. The fight still goes on today for a national cinema that can break free from isolation and from Canada's indigenous cultural contradictions; a cinema that must impose itself on audiences more used to the American movies that flood the market.

Artificially maintained (by federal and provincial government), its output underdistributed and often harshly judged, the Quebec film industry is, economically, a fragile structure which new video technology now threatens to destroy. That catastrophe has to be averted at all costs, for, despite its hesitancy, its complacency and its inconsistencies, Quebec cinema remains the most original and stimulating in North America today.

The Third World

During the Sixties the Third World, so-called because it comprised the areas outside the eastern and western power blocs, began to make an unprecedented impact on the western capitalist world. Liberation struggles in Africa, Asia and Latin America had reached a decisive stage across three continents, asserting the ideal of self-determination and the ideology of anti-imperialism. The Cuban Revolution, the Algerian War of Independence, Africa and Vietnam – they were all examplary situations, expressing the global scale of revolutionary consciousness within the oppressed Third World regions.

Third World cinema of the Sixties derived its impetus from these political developments. Its attitude towards cinema necessarily opposed the colonial film practices of the western countries, and was militantly political. Third World film-makers rejected the dominant values of escapist entertainment on the Hollywood model, and redefined the role of cinema as an integral part of the revolutionary process, a 'weapon' to be used against the dominant images of western cinema.

The antipathy towards the dominant Euro-American cinema was legitimate. The major film companies had mono-polized film distribution and exhibition throughout the colonized regions, thereby preventing the emergence of any indigenous cinema industry that could effectively compete. Audiences in Third World countries were bombarded with third-rate films which invariably depicted non-European peoples in pernicious stereotypes. These negative associations, along with the films' idealized images of capitalist society, had a pervasive effect on the consciousness of the audience. Militantly political film-makers recognized the need to counteract these colonial pictures, and to construct alternative themes and images that would express a true identity and dignity. But different parts of the world had had different colonial experiences. Thus in Latin America the main target was American films; in North Africa it was the French and Egyptian film monopolies; and in black Africa the need was to destroy the Tarzan-type jungle mythology and the representation of Africans as 'savages'.

Of course nationalization was correctly seen by the newly formed Third World governments as the crucial factor in developing a national cinema, and therefore in evolving a new self-identity. But any moves in that direction were often met by opposition. When the Algerian government nationalized its film industry in 1964, for example, the major American companies, which controlled 40 per cent of the market, boycotted the country. Similar experiences occurred in other countries, as in Upper Volta in 1972.

Third World films vary widely, ranging from straightfor-ward agit-prop newsreel and didactic documentaries to fictional narratives and films employing complex symbolism. These differences in approach are to a large extent determined by the particular social, political, cultural and historical conditions in which individual film-makers work. But there are also stylistic differences based primarily on the film-maker's own aesthetic preoccupations.

Latin America   Since the arrival of the first projectors and films at the turn of the century, cinema in Latin America has been dominated from abroad. Screens soon filled with images from the United States, while the continent's own producers generally opted for competiton by imitation. *Tango* musicals and *cangaçeiro* Westerns used elements of national cultures, but vulgarized them by adaptation to imposed genres. Some outstanding directors, like the Argentinian **Leopoldo Torre Nilsson** (1924–1978) or the Brazilian **Humberto Mauro** (b. 1897) attempted to treat themes genuinely deriving from the surrounding societies, but in general such explorations were few. Although Mauro was unable to gain a large audience for his films (though these vivid social documents influenced later Brazilian film-makers), Torre Nilsson managed to win international respect. The son of the director Leopoldo Torres Ríos, Torre Nilsson made his first feature, *Días de Odio (Days of Hatred)* in 1954. He achieved worldwide acclaim with *La Casa del Ángel* (1957, House of the Ángel) – the story of a girl unable to break away from the man who has 'raped' her. This was the first of several films Torre Nilsson made in collabor-ation with his wife, the novelist Beatriz Guido. Their subsequent movies combined a highly dramatic visual style and a macabre sense of humour with a tendency towards social criticism – with *La Mano en la Trampa* (1961, The Hand in the Trap) and *Piel de Verano* (1961, Summer Skin) being

Below: an idealist (Alfredo Alcon) joins some rebels to overthrow the government in Los Siete Locos. *Below right: an orphan (Marilina Ross) is comforted by her friend (Luisina Brando) in* Piedre Libre. *Right: barren images of Brazil in Pereira dos Santos'* Barren Lives. *Far right: bandits fearful of their pursuers* in Black God, White Devil. *Below far right: the women of the village discover from the fortune-teller that they are barren in* Blood of the Condor. *Below right:* Antonio-das-Mortes *(1969, Antonio of the Dead) – a revolutionary ballad with Western-style violence.*

particularly fine achievements. In the Sixties, Torre Nilsson became involved in a number of unsuccessful international co-productions and several expensive historical epics, made with government support. However, a series of literary adaptations made the following decade – including *Los Siete Locos* (1972, *The Seven Madmen*), from Robert Arlt's story, and *Piedra Libre* (1976, *Free for All*), from a Beatriz Guido novella – revived his reputation shortly before his death.

In the Fifties and Sixties a different kind of cinema arose. An integral part of the nationalist and revolutionary political tide that was sweeping the continent, this new cinema intended to express a truly Latin American vision of the world, affirming the continent's own cultural heritage and providing an ideological tool that would contribute directly to the struggle for social and political liberation. Its subjects were to be the continent's dispossessed majorities, while its language would only take that which was useful to it from established cinematic traditions, while looking within the continent's own cultural traditions for new resources. The relationship with the audience – intended to be these same dispossessed majorities – would be didactic and interactive, breaking down the passive receptivity encouraged by 'industrial' cinema.

The film-makers of Brazil were among the first to feel the need for a progressive cinema, which they termed *Cinema Novo*. A major impetus for early *Cinema Novo* was Italian neo-realism which pointed the way towards a critical realist method based in few technical resources. Although the movement was to flower fully in the early and mid-Sixties, the groundwork was laid by films such as Alex Viany's *Agulha no Palheiro* (1953, *Needle in a Haystack*) and Nélson

Pereira dos Santos' documentaries on the lives of ordinary people in Rio de Janeiro – *Río, 40 Graus* (1955, Rio, 40 Degrees) and *Río, Zona Norte* (1956, Rio, North Zone).

By the early Sixties *Cinema Novo* was drawing on a wide range of resources in its search for a renovated aesthetic appropriate to the real Brazil of starvation, violence and the gross concentration of wealth in the hands of the few. Styles ranged from the critical realism of Nélson Pereira dos Santos' *Vidas Sêcas* (1963, *Barren Lives*) to the 'baroque poetry' of Gláuber Rocha's films, notably *Terra em Transe* (1967, *Earth in Revolt*). Popular history and myth were the major grounding for the movement. Films such as Rocha's *Barravento* (1962), *Deus e o Diabo na Terra do Sol* (1963, *Black God, White Devil*) and *Antonio-das-Mortes* (1969, Antonio of the Dead) were based on the imagery and ritual of popular culture, proposing these as the essential source for a renewed and authentic Brazilian culture, but simultaneously defining them as insufficient to confront the realities of mid-twentieth-century exploitation and hunger. Carlos Diegues' *Ganga Zumba* (1964), about a seventeenth-century slave revolt, explored the past for its explanations of the present, and Ruy Guerra's *Os Fuzis* (1964, *The Guns*) portrayed the violent yearning for a better life that this culture expressed.

In the later Sixties, *Cinema Novo's* themes moved away from the *sertão* (the harsh north-east) and the *favela* (shanty-town) to examine the culture of the urban middle-class. This reflected a desire not to fall into the trap of romantic primitivism, and to investigate the failures of Brazilian politics after the 1964 military coup. Films such as Paulo Cesar Saraceni's *O Desafío* (1965, The Challenge), Gustavo Dahl's *Os Bravos Guerreiros* (1967, The Brave Warriors) and Carlos

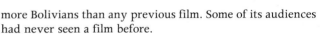

Diegues' *Os Herdeiros* (1969, The Inheritors) examined this latter theme.

However, by the late Sixties, particularly after the intensification of government repression in 1968, *Cinema Novo* declared itself at an end. Film-makers such as Gláuber Rocha and Ruy Guerra went into exile, while others found their films facing violent military censorship as well as the prejudices of commercial distributors.

Brazil's *Cinema Novo* had a sporadic influence on film-making in other Latin American countries. In Bolivia during the mid-Sixties a sustained attempt began to relate cinema to one of the continent's oldest cultures – that of the Quechua and Aymara Indian peoples. In a sequence of six films – including *Yawar Mallku* (1969, *Blood of the Condor*) and *El Coraje del Pueblo* (1972, *Courage of the People*) – the director **Jorge Sanjinés** (b. 1936) and the Ukamau Group production company made fewer and fewer concessions to orthodox structure as they attempted to build a film language from the patterns of Quechua/Aymara culture.

Sanjinés spent ten years making shorts and documentaries before founding the Bolivian National Film Institute and becoming its director. He was dismissed from his post, however, after completion of his first feature film *Ukamau* (1966), also about the sufferings of the Indians, because the government thought it 'too negative'. His second feature film, *Blood of the Condor* was inspired by a newspaper report of a sterilization programme carried out by a team of American doctors on Indian women in a Bolivian mountain region without their knowledge or consent. It was banned until a press campaign and massive street demonstrations forced a change of policy. In its first year of release, it was seen by

more Bolivians than any previous film. Some of its audiences had never seen a film before.

Sanjinés and his colleagues went out to remote country villages where they set up specially prepared presentations. A narrator would tell the story in the age-old village tradition but with the modern aid of photographs. The audience were encouraged to ask questions and to discuss the implications of the events. Then they were shown the film.

Rapport betwen film-makers and film audiences is vital to Sanjinés' working method. Within the general flowering of revolutionary cinema in Latin America, he has pioneered a new way of creating and using film by involving whole communities in its preparation, financing, production and presentation. *Blood of the Condor*, which features the population of the Kaata rural area, was partially financed by students, teachers, technicians, workers and peasants. In his following film, *Courage of the People*, a whole mining community, survivors of a massacre by the Bolivian army in 1967, re-enacted their own story.

In the late Sixties and early Seventies, the Chilean new cinema movement declared itself with the appearance of four films made in 1969; Raúl Ruiz's portrait of urban petty bourgeoise, *Tres Tristes Tigres* (1969, Three Sad Tigers); Miguel Littin's *El Chacal de Nahueltoro* (1970, *The Jackal of Nahueltoro*), about the capture, trial and execution of a notorious murderer; Aldo Francia's *Valparaiso, Mi Amor* (1970, Valparaiso, My Love), about the family of a poor worker who is imprisoned for stealing meat; and Charles Elsesser's *Los Testigos* (1971, The Witnesses), about a murder in a poor part of the capital. Between 1970 and 1973 such film-making flourished under the Allende government.

During the military coup of September 1973, documentarists such as Patricio Guzmán – whose *La Batalla de Chile* (1975–9, *The Battle of Chile*) had to be edited in exile – immersed themselves in current events in order to capture history as it was made. By way of film it was then returned to the ordinary people who had made it for their reflection, discussion and deeper understanding. Directors such as Miguel Littin mobilized the resources of the feature film for a similar end. In his *La Tierra Prometida* (1973, The Promised Land), also edited in exile, past events are reconstructed by using the language and myths of popular memory so as to redeem them from 'official' interpretation and restore them to the people of whose living history they are a part.

Fernado Solanas' *La Hora de los Hornos* (1968, *Hour of the Furnaces*) is the best-known product of new cinema in Argentina. Clandestinely shot during the dictatorship of General Ongania, the film is a series of 'film-essays' exploring aspects of Argentine history and society, including Peronism, the political movement founded by Juan Perón. Strongly influenced by the Algerian writer Frantz Fanon, the film calls for revolutionary violence as being both the only viable political option for liberation and a cathartic cultural necessity.

In all the above countries, right-wing military governments had suffocated the new cinema by the mid-Seventies, killing and imprisoning its practitioners, or driving them into exile. Only in Cuba, where it grew up after rather than before a social and political revolution, has it continued intact.

In 1959, the new revolutionary government led by Fidel Castro set up the Cuban Institute of Cinematographic Art and Industry (ICAIC), only three months after overthrowing the Batista regime. The swiftness of this action shows the importance that was given to cinema in the rebuilding of Cuban society. ICAIC produced several feature films as well as documentaries and weekly newsreels throughout the Sixties. The political and international outlook of progressive Cuban cinema is particularly evident in the documentaries of Santiago Alvarez and in Julio García Espinosa's *Tercer Mundo, Tercera Guerra Mundial* (1970, Third World, Third World War), a documentary shot in North Vietnam and aimed specifically at a politically militant audience.

Politicized film-makers of the Third World were particularly concerned with the role of cinema in relation to the audience; they wanted to counteract the consumer-oriented model of the passive spectator established in Euro-American cinema. Octavio Getino and Fernando Solanas' widely acclaimed, monumental film-essay, *Hours of the Furnaces*, presents a Marxist historical analysis of neo-colonialism and oppression in Argentina in the form of 'chapters' and 'notes' – captioned divisons in the film – designed to form the basis for political discussions with the audience.

Adopting a progressive political perspective entailed raising questions about history, as in *Hour of the Furnaces*. In a different vein, Humberto Solás' *Lucía* (1968) powerfully dramatized three historical moments in the Cuban struggle for liberation, and highlighted the participation of Cuban women in each period. But very few films set out, as *Hour of the Furnaces* did, to activate a critical engagement with the historical process. Most political films were of an agit-prop kind, more concerned with agitation and propaganda than with analysis.

The late Sixties saw a cinema of great promise: notable films of the period were Tomás Gutiérrez Alea's *Muerte de un Burocrata* (1966, *Death of a Bureaucrat*) and *Memorias del Subdesar-*

ollo (1968, *Memories of Underdevelopment*), Pastor Vega's *De la Guerra Americana* (1970, On the American War) and Octavio Gómez's *La Primera Carga al Machete* (1969, *The First Charge of the Machetes*).

Subsequently this impetus seemed lost as official attitudes became less liberal. Among the few important films of later years was Pastor Vega's *Retrato de Teresa* (1979, *Portrait of Teresa*), which considered the difficulties of women fulfilling their potential in a society that, though communist, was still dominated by Latin machismo.

Africa   The effect of colonialism on the continent of Africa was to produce four or five sharp demarcations that deeply affected how the African world perceived and expressed political and cultural activity. The sub-regions included Egypt and the Middle East; North Africa, including Algeria, Morocco and Tunisia; the black French-speaking area; the black English-speaking countries; and the white-dominated

South. These historically-produced divisions help to explain why Africa, unlike Latin America, had been unable to create a forceful cinema by the Sixties. As for black Africa in particular, only the French-speaking countries, with their ready access to France's film-making legacy, had produced any directors of note.

Egyptian films had been widely shown throughout the Arab world since the Thirties. These were mainly escapist comedies and cheap entertainment dramas. The revolution of 1952 led eventually to significant changes. In 1957, Nasser's government established the National Organization for the Cinema and, two years later, set up a film school. The Sixties saw the emergence of 'quality' films such as Youssef Chahine's *An-Nasr Salah Ad-Din* (1963, *Saladin*), which was Egypt's first epic film, and Hussein Kamal's *Al Mostahil* (1965, The Impossible) and *Al Boustagui* (1968, The Postman), while Shadi Abdelsalam's mysterious tale of mummy-robbers in the

early years of this century, *El Mumia* (1970, *The Night of Counting the Years*), broke away completely from earlier conventions.

Another factor which contributed to the reorientation of Arab cinema was the Algerian Revolution. As in the Latin American experience, progressive cinema in Algeria was defined as an integral part of the Algerian cultural renaissance. The Provisional Government of the Algerian Republic set up a film committee in 1961 which became the Cinema Service. It made four films, including Chanderli and Lakhdar Hamina's *Djazaïrouna* (1961), a history of Algeria. Between 1962 and 1971, Algerian 'Cinema Moudjahid' (Arabic for 'freedom fighter') was almost exclusively concerned with anti-colonial war films. There was also an emphasis on big-budget co-productions during this period. For example, Casbah Films, a private production company founded in 1961 by Yacef Saadi, a liberation leader and principal organizer of the battle of Algiers, partly financed major films by European directors, such as Gillo Pontecorvo's *La Battaglia di Algeri* (1966, *Battle of Algiers*).

But Algerian film-makers did not limit their scope to the Algerian experience alone. Like the Cubans, they maintained close relations with other Third World struggles: for instance, Ahmed Rachedi's documentary compilation *L'Aube des Damnés* (1965, The Dawn of the Damned) presented a sharp critique of the European powers' multiple intervention in the African continent and the Third World generally. The concentration on war films during this period was officially encouraged, but young film-makers and audiences alike began to criticize the trend, attacking the films for not dealing with such crucial questions as the status of women in Algerian society, or the abuse of power. But it was not until the agrarian revolution of 1971, which forced a rethinking of political and cultural organization, that a new Algerian cinema emerged. Its vitality was underlined in 1975, when Mohammed Lakhdar Hamina's *Ahdat Sanawouach El-Djamr* (*Chronicle of the Years of Embers*) won the top prize at the Cannes film festival.

During the Seventies and Eighties, **Tunisia** began to produce several notable films, including the Grand Prize winner of the 1980 Carthage Film Festival, *Aziza*, Abdellatif Ben Ammar's fine study of a young girl. Ben Ammar's earlier films, *Une Si Simple Histoire* (1970, A Very Simple Story) and *Sejnane* (1974) were also worthwhile, as was Ridha Bahi's attack on speculative tourist development, *Soleil des Hyènes* (1977, Hyena's Sun) and Naceur Ktari's slick *Assoufara* (1976, The Ambassadors). Morocco, like Tunisia, did not really develop a film industry but still turned out some valuable films, including Ahmed El Maanouni's *Alyam Alyam* (1978, Oh the Days) and Ben Barka Souhel's *Mille et une Mains* (1974, Thousand and One Hands).

During the Sixties, black African cinema consisted of only a handful of film-makers from French-speaking countries such as **Senegal**, **Niger**, **Guinea** and **Chad** – whose films were made in French. Only Ousmane Sembene achieved international recognition, with *Mandabi* (1968, *The Money Order*), his third film, but the first in which he used his own language, Wolof. This use of an indigenous African language in a major film represented a radical shift from conventional practice; it amounted to a way of saying that the film was made by an African for Africans. A forceful African cinema would emerge in the Seventies given impetus by the international respect accorded Sembene's *Emitaï* (1972) and *Ceddo* (1976, Outsiders). Notable among the newer directors were the Senegalese Mahama Johnson Traoré whose films include *Diegue-bi* (1970, The Woman) and *N'Diangane* (1975) and the documentary film-makers Safi Faye and Moussa Bathily.

In the early Eighties several important features were made including *Cry Freedom* (1981) made by Nigeria's Ola Balogun, *Djelli* (1981), by the Ivory Coast's Fadika Krama Lancine, *The Chapel* (1981) from the Congo's Jan-Michel Tchissoukou, *Finye* (1983, The Wind) by Mali's Souleymane Cissi, and *Wend Kuuni* (1983, Gift of God) by the Upper Volta's Gaston Kabore.

The Philippines During the Seventies, the Philippines, the second biggest film-producing country in the world (251 features in 1971), stepped into the limelight of world cinema after long being neglected, despite its prizes gained at Asian festivals. By a quirky chance, the first director from the Philippines to attract attention in Europe was the naive, self-taught Kidlat Tahimik, whose *Mababangong Bangungot* (1977,

The Perfumed Nightmare) appeared like a work of primitive art at that year's Berlin Film Festival and won the Critics' Prize. However, the first director from the Philippines who seemed able to achieve international stature was Lino Brocka. His *Insiang* was shown at Cannes in 1978, to be followed by *Jaguar* in 1980. In 1981, his earlier film *Maynila, sa Mga Kuko ng Liwanag* (1975, *Manila: In the Claws of Darkness*) became the first Filipino film to get commercial distribution in Britain. However, his *Kapit sa Patalim* (1984, Hanging on a Knife), a hard-hitting study of a labour strike, was banned at home, though shown at Cannes; he also underwent a spell of political imprisonment.

In the early Eighties, the Filipino industry was severely hit by economic and political upheavals. Largely thanks to a reduction in the number of imported American films, the industry appeared to recover in 1984, given fresh impetus by the success of Edgardo Reyes' *Bangkang Papel sa Dagat ng Apoy* (1984, Paper Boat in a Sea of Fire) and Mike de Leon's *Sister Stella L.* (1984), both of which confront contemporary social issues.

Iran By 1980, the brilliant cinema that had developed in Iran by the Seventies was virtually dead, with most of its major directors living outside the country and film production practically at a standstill, compared with an output of over a hundred films a year in the late Sixties. This was a real loss, in quality as well as quantity, since the Iranian cinema had produced four directors of international stature during the Seventies. The first to be noticed was Daryush Mehrjui, whose *Gav* (1968, *The Cow*) won the International Critics' Prize at the 1971 Venice Film Festival. The attention paid to *The Cow* soon changed the face of Iranian cinema; by 1973, when Mehrjui helped to found the New Film Group, the Iranian cinema was a creative force of originality and strength. Mehrjui himself had commercial as well as critical success with *Postchi* (1972, The Postman); but he ran into enormous censorship problems from the medical establishment over *Dayereh Mina* (1975, The Cycle).

Bahram Beyzai attracted attention at the first Teheran International Film Festival in 1972 with *Ragbar* (Downpour) and then made a terrific impression with the mysterious *Gharibeh-va-meh* (1974, The Stranger and the Fog). His *Tcherikeh Tara* (1980, The Ballad of Tara) was the last major film to come out of the new Iranian cinema of the Seventies, shot partially before and finished after the revolution. The third major director was Bahman Farmanara, whose *Shazdeh Ehtejab* (Prince Ehtejab) won the Grand Prize at the 1974 Teheran Festival and whose ambitious *Saiehaieh Bolan de Bad* (*Tall Shadows of the Wind*) came out in 1979.

Farmanara and Beyzai both had strong elements of mysticism in their work; the fourth major Iranian director appeared, at least on the surface, to be a pessimistic realist. Sohrab Shahid Saless, one of the most important directors to appear during the Seventies, began his career with the bleak but beautiful *Yek Ettefaghe Sadeh* (1973, A Simple Event), about a poor child, and *Tabiate Bijan* (1974, Still Life), about an old couple. He then went to Germany to make a study in alienation. *In der Fremde* (1975, Far From Home), and became a film-maker in exile, creating a unique, quiet style of desperation that expressed Seventies *angst* in the way that Ingmar Bergman's films had depicted Fifties anguish. Saless has continued to work in Germany and to make outstanding films, including the startling *Ordnung* (1980, All in Order), a reflection on the meaning of madness.

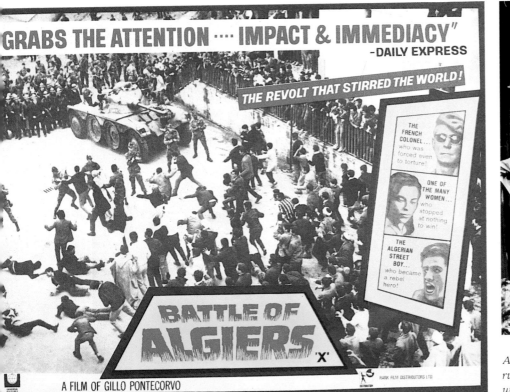

Above: The Money Order *shows the ruination of a poor man with two wives who is sent a money order from Paris.*

Top: Battle of Algiers, *using Algerians to recreate their own history, was a political event in itself. Above: a gentle farmer discovers his beloved cow has died, takes on the identity of his lost love object and becomes* . . . The Cow.

CHAPTER 19
American Cinema Today

The upheavals and crises of the late Sixties and Seventies – the horrors of the Vietnam War, the humiliating political scandal of Watergate – left their mark on the traditional Hollywood genres. Audiences had come to accept and expect a greater degree of realism in terms of plot, character and setting; yet they also yearned to escape into the apparent innocence (and stylishness) of bygone eras. These contradictory desires were amply reflected in the musicals, comedies, thrillers, Westerns, sci-fi and horror films of the period.

Musical Developments

By the end of the Fifties, the producer Arthur Freed's unit at MGM, which had been a conveyor belt of classic musical dream-worlds, was breaking up fast. Stanley Donen and Gene Kelly had left, and were soon involved in mainly non-musical projects, for which there was more demand in a Hollywood with a growing sense of social awareness. In 1960, Vincente Minnelli made his last MGM musical, *Bells Are Ringing*, which also represented the final demise of Freed's group.

While these signs may not have meant the death of the genre, they certainly provided evidence of a shift in sensibility, an adjustment to a more complex world. Paeans in praise of show business, for example, were being rendered somewhat anachronistic by such scorching visions of the world of entertainment as the depictions of Hollywood itself in *Sunset Boulevard* (1950), *The Bad and the Beautiful* (1952) and *The Big Knife* (1955). With Hollywood's broadening outlook, it was becoming harder to make a musical suffused with a sense of fantasy, of the dreamer triumphant over recalcitrant circumstances, and to render it convincing.

Even so, quite a few musicals of the 'hip' Sixties were made by old survivors from MGM, notably Vincente Minnelli, Charles Walters, George Sidney and Gene Kelly. Out of these, Walters, with *Jumbo* (1962) and *The Unsinkable Molly Brown* (1964), and Kelly, with *Hello, Dolly!* (1969), remained the most traditional, with nonetheless pleasing results. Sidney met the challenge of youthful material with a typical brash energy in *Bye Bye Birdie* (1963) and *Viva Las Vegas* (1964), although his less 'swinging' *Half a Sixpence* (1967) was ultimately more inventive. It was Minnelli, though, who showed a real ability to adapt – the formal innovations of *On a Clear Day You Can See Forever* (1970) still seem fresh today.

If these directors were representative of a specialized approach to the genre, the Sixties' and Seventies' musical is really notable for its lack of emphasis on the need for specifically musical talent, in both directors and performers. This was owing partly to a drying-up of reserve musical talent from Broadway, which Hollywood had always relied upon, and partly to a new stress in the genre on such elements as characterization and narrative. Directors and stars were often strongly associated with more apparently realistic genres.

With regard to directors, the results were on the whole surprisingly satisfying. William Wyler, known mainly for prestigious dramas, showed great skill with *Funny Girl* (1968). To prove how easily two already adaptable directors picked up a feel for music, Francis Ford Coppola's *Finian's Rainbow* (1967) was particularly stylish, and Norman Jewison's *Fiddler on the Roof* (1971) was imaginatively conceived for the screen. In 1977, Martin Scorsese, that Italian-American poet of New York street life, made the marvellous *New York, New York*. Perhaps the most noteworthy in this strain of cross-over directors was Robert Wise. Identified more with astringent thrillers, he left his mark upon the Sixties' musical with two film versions of stage hits; *West Side Story* (1961), which won 11 Oscars, and *The Sound of Music* (1965), one of the most popular and successful films ever made. But on the debit side must be set Carol Reed's *Oliver!* (1968), admittedly a big hit, and, still worse, of Richard Fleischer in the hamfisted *Dr Dolittle* (1967).

The pattern is the same for performers. In the theatre or on screen, directors and producers have become accustomed to casting dramatic stars in musicals. When the actor Jack Klugman complained to the lyric-writer Stephen Sondheim of his own poor vocal abilities for the Broadway show *Gypsy*, Sondheim simply replied: 'I don't want a musical star. I want a person I can believe in.'

Of course, there are stars of the two decades who have been connected specifically with film musicals. Julie Andrews' very English charm was crucial to the success of *Mary Poppins* (1964) and *The Sound of Music*. Petula Clark was delightful and underrated in *Finian's Rainbow* and *Goodbye Mr Chips* (1969). Liza Minnelli and Barbra Streisand are both outstanding talents. Nevertheless, Sondheim's 'believable' person is manifest on the screen in such offhand, casual musical performances as those of Rex Harrison in *My Fair Lady* (1964) or Clint Eastwood in *Paint Your Wagon* (1969). It is the approachability of this kind of star's musical manner (especially the sung-spoken style of the numbers, whether or not dubbed) that constitutes their attraction. The effect of the non-musical star depends upon the image brought over from roles in more realistic types of film. The musical has thus harnessed the iconographic significance of such stars as

Left: Francis Coppola, one of the major forces of contemporary American cinema, in a cameo role as the head of a TV film crew in his film Apocalypse Now.

Natalie Wood in *West Side Story* and *Gypsy* (1962), Christopher Plummer in *The Sound of Music*, Richard Harris and Vanessa Redgrave in *Camelot* (1967), Peter O'Toole in *Goodbye Mr Chips*, Lee Marvin and Clint Eastwood in *Paint Your Wagon*, Cybill Shepherd and Burt Reynolds in *At Long Last Love*, and James Caan in *Funny Lady* (both 1975).

Such stars and directors indicated a new emphasis upon the purely dramatic elements of the genre, a need to place the number in a more 'believable' world. Another manifestation of this spirit lay in the genre's growing self-consciousness and a broader social outlook. There was a tendency to deal more with everyday life and real problems, coming to the fore in the depiction of gang warfare and racial tension in *West Side Story*, office life in *How to Succeed in Business Without Really Trying* (1967), thinly-disguised prostitution in *Sweet Charity* (1969), the repression of the Jews in *Fiddler on the Roof*, the rise of Nazism in *Cabaret* (1972) and the harsh treatment of South African blacks in *Lost in the Stars* (1974). As if to clinch the point, the easy resolution, the genre's traditional concluding assertion of 'togetherness', was often eschewed in favour of such distinctly sombre endings as those of *Camelot*, *Goodbye Mr Chips*, *Sweet Charity*, *Paint Your Wagon*, *On a Clear Day You Can See Forever*, *Funny Lady* and *New York, New York*.

Similarly, there was a mocking, self-conscious tone. It is instantly recognizable in the acidic films of Bob Fosse – *Sweet Charity*, *Cabaret* and *All That Jazz* (1979) – where the numbers are explorations of various film-musical stylistic modes. It can be seen, too, in a whole variety of movies that play on the conventions of the genre: the iconography of the pop world and the media is examined in *A Hard Day's Night* (1964), *Phantom of the Paradise* (1974) and *Tommy* (1975); homage is paid to the tradition of the musical in *Let's Make Love* (1960), *At Long Last Love*, *Bugsy Malone* (1976) and *New York, New York*. There is even the camp nostalgia of *Grease* (1978), *Can't Stop the Music* and *Xanadu* (both 1980).

More than ever during the period musicals were based upon Broadway hit shows. Musicals also generally became super-productions, of the type represented by *West Side Story*, *The Sound of Music* and *Funny Girl*. The reason was simple: the rivalry of television. The cinema's tactic was to present audio-visual spectacles unlike anything possible on the small screen, and often to recruit proven successes from the Broadway stage. It did not always work, of course; and when it failed, the financial repercussions could be as crippling as the slow paralysis caused by television. For instance, *Sweet Charity* made no profit for Universal, despite its fresh approach to previously successful material.

What is often complained of, regarding Broadway adaptations, is that the original is treated with too much reverence. But by the late Fifties, Hollywood was dealing with the type of musical drama originally pioneered by Rogers and Hammerstein, which was too integrated to allow the free adaptations once made of original stage works. Further, while these films do follow the stage shows quite closely, the results need not be as slavish and uncinematic as they were in, for example, *Man of La Mancha* (1972) and *Mame* (1973). The long list of more memorable films includes *West Side Story*, *The Music Man* (1962), *My Fair Lady*, *The Sound of Music*, *Camelot*, *Finian's Rainbow*, *Sweet Charity*, *On a Clear Day You Can See Forever* and *Cabaret*.

Of original screen musicals, outstanding by any standards was the Gallic charm of Jacques Demy's romantic evocations of French provincial life in *Les Parapluies de Cherbourg* (1964,

The Umbrellas of Cherbourg) and *Les Demoiselles de Rochefort* (1967, *The Young Girls of Rochefort*). Scorsese's *New York, New York* was an original film musical that explored the form with all the daring and inventiveness once shown by such Betty Comden and Adolph Green scripts as those for *Singin' in the Rain* (1952) and *The Band Wagon* (1953). It centred on the off-beat romance and failed marriage of a jazz saxophonist and a dance-band vocalist. Then there were such pleasant diversions as Marilyn Monroe's penultimate movie *Le's Make Love*, *Robin and the Seven Hoods* (1964), *Thoroughly Modern Millie* (1967) and *Goodbye Mr Chips*. Yet, on the whole, the two decades have not matched the standard of the stream of screen originals once associated, in particular, with MGM.

One of the major developments in the genre during the period was its attempt to come to terms with youth and with post-Beatles popular music. In this the musical has generally taken a patronizing attitude to the energy and subversion of both youth themes and rock music.

Rock musicals themselves usually developed over-simplified youth themes, accompanied by middle-of-the-road music more appropriate to middle-aged audiences. *Godspell* and *Jesus Christ Superstar* (both 1973), for example, merely restated conventional religious values. *Hair* had initiated the Broadway youth-musical vogue in 1968; even then, its nude dancing could only ever have offended a truly Victorian sensibility. When the screen version finally appeared, a safe 11 years later in 1979, it was nothing but a pleasant reminder of an era long since gone, the hippie heyday. Only two screen originals, *Phantom of the Paradise*, a version of the Phantom-of-the-Opera story, and *Tommy*, based on The Who's very successful LP about a deaf, dumb and blind pinball player, came near to creating the anarchy, energy and imagination missing each week from *Top of the Pops* on British television.

Then, in 1977, came *Saturday Night Fever*. All at once, the dance musical was reinvented. The disco craze spread across Europe and the United States; and this film was followed by *Black Joy* (1977), *Thank God It's Friday* (1978), *The Music Machine* (1979), *Can't Stop the Music*, *Xanadu* and *Fame* (1980). All of them pushed the new dance style as the foremost element of the genre – no-one even sings in *Saturday Night Fever*. It was only in *Thank God It's Friday* and *Fame*, though, that the dancing reflected the true energy and invention of the actual disco floor. The exhilarating bursts of movement in these films made the mannered shuffling of *Saturday Night Fever* and the skate-bound plodding of *Xanadu* seem flat-footed.

The classic musical had never fully acknowledged the black origins of such elements as tap-dancing. At least the disco musical made a stab at identifying the cultural context of its subject. The excellent *Black Joy*, concerning immigrant life in London's Brixton, and *Thank God It's Friday*, an evening in the life of a Hollywood disco club, linked the music with black artists, while the sheer skill and subversive eroticism of the solo dancing in *Fame* were inextricable from its black exponent, Gene Anthony Ray. The considerable gay influence upon disco was only limply noticed in the awful *Can't Stop the Music*, in which a pop group, the Village People,

Above: top to bottom: Fanny Brice (Barbra Streisand) has trouble on roller skates in Funny Girl; *Shirley Maclaine (centre) dances Bob Fosse's* choreography *in* Sweet Charity; *John Travolta as Danny Zuko sings 'Greased Lightning' with his gang in* Grease.

were 'normalized' by the presence of the central heterosexual couple.

Both *Saturday Night Fever* and *Xanadu* did identify disco as levelling out social inequalities. *Saturday Night Fever* splendidly utilized the dance floor as a place for stamping out problems, permitting control at least of this environment through skills that anyone could develop. *Xanadu* gave a sense of cultural harmony in its closing vision of disco as a meeting ground free from bias and prejudice.

Disco was seen by the film industry as a convenient and safe way of representing youth music and culture, and it accounted for the bulk of musicals in the late Seventies and early Eighties. But the British *Breaking Glass* (1980) explored, though only tentatively, the area of rock music's 'New Wave'. By the mid-Eighties, dance had moved to the gym with the fashion for aerobics and body-popping, as in *Flashdance* (1983) and then to the street with break-dancing. But *Breakin'* (GB title: *Breakdance*) and *Breakin' 2 Electric Boogaloo* (both 1984) once again obscured the predominantly black and male origins of this form of ethnic display in favour of a utopian vision of togetherness – black, white and Hispanic, male and female – in all-American harmony.

In terms of directors, only Bob Fosse really specialized in the genre. Of the rest, both John Badham, who made *Saturday Night Fever*, and Alan Parker, of *Fame*, showed great potential, with a good feel for music, though a limited ability to provide convincing narrative contexts. All of Martin Scorsese's films were alive with music and movement; *New York, New York* explored the language of the film musical with all the cunning insight of Fosse but without the ego-flexing of the semi-autobiographical *All That Jazz*. *New York, New York* deserves recognition as one of the most entertaining and challenging musicals to appear since Freed's unit at MGM shuddered to a halt back in 1960.

The Rock Movie

During the Sixties, a new genre grew up that was directly geared to the rapidly expanding youth market in the USA and Europe – the rock film. This embraced documentaries on individual artists, or of major concerts, fictionalized vehicles for top groups, movies set in the heady, seamy world of rock and pop and, more loosely, films that depended for much of their drama on the excitement generated by the use of rock music on their soundtracks.

The Seventies should have been a golden era for rock movies. All the portents were favourable. At the start of the decade, *Easy Rider* (1969) and *Woodstock* (1970) had made fortunes both for their backers and for the record companies which had leased the soundtrack rights. Technical improvements in sound recording ensured that live concerts could be taped and reproduced with near-perfect clarity in the cinema (though admittedly few theatres were equipped to take advantage of this). Besides, the Sixties pop-music boom had enriched a large number of rock stars, many of whom looked to the film industry either to invest their new wealth or to expend it.

The teenagers who had purchased pop records in the Sixties in such unprecedented quantities were now reaching their early twenties – the age range that was the most statistically significant in the composition of cinema audiences. This applied equally well to the film-makers themselves; for the first time, films would actually be made by directors who had been part of the rock'n'roll generation.

It was a moment of great promise, then; but such promise would be realized only fitfully. The incontestable achievements were that practically every major rock act did become the subject of a rock movie (Fleetwood Mac and the Beach Boys being exceptions), and that the films that were made spanned a range of territory that adequately reflected the variety of the music itself.

Dennis Hopper's *Easy Rider* was the most commercial film up to that time to have pitted the ideals and aspirations of the counter-culture against the cynicism and violence endemic in American society. The alternative society, drugs and all, was good box-office. Thus cinema audiences suddenly had to stomach a couple of effete student-protest movies, *Getting Straight* and *The Strawberry Statement*, as well as *Joe* (all 1970), a portrait of a foul-mouthed redneck. The depiction in *Joe* of the drug-crazed young was patently absurd, but it was almost redeemed by a performance of massive authority from Peter Boyle in the title role.

Boyle later teamed up with Jane Fonda and Donald Sutherland in the appealing comedy *Steelyard Blues* (1973). The film, with a musical score from Paul Butterfield, Nick Gravenites and the late Mike Bloomfield, examined a group of contemporary misfits sympathetically and plausibly, but by then traces of the alternative society were fast disappearing.

There were other films that clearly took their cue from *Easy Rider*: *Two-Lane Blacktop* (1971), with James Taylor and Dennis Wilson, and *Electra Glide in Blue* (1973), for example, as well as *Cisco Pike* (1971), an excellent thriller about drug-dealing which starred Gene Hackman and, making his debut in a leading role, Kris Kristofferson. The post-*Easy Rider* boom produced few films of lasting merit; and in the aftermath of the collapse of Sixties idealism, the film that most accurately anticipated the mood of the young during the Seventies, and cast its long shadow over the events of the decade, was Stanley Kubrick's futuristic study of teenage violence, *A Clockwork Orange* (1971).

There was one crucial respect in which *Easy Rider* was a pioneer movie – the soundtrack consisted almost entirely of previously released material. This had never been accomplished before in mainstream commercial films; film-makers had adjudged the copyright difficulties to be insuperable, and usually played safe by commissioning an original score, often distinguished for its very lack of originality. *Easy Rider* changed the position completely, although it paid the penalty for its ground-breaking. Contractual problems indeed proved labyrinthine, with the result that the film reached Great Britain several months in advance of its accompanying soundtrack album. Nevertheless, recording and publishing companies subsequently realized that, by over-zealously defending their copyright songs, they were simply denying themselves a potentially lucrative source of extra income. In the long run, the *Easy Rider* breakthrough was decisive, and such directors as George Lucas, in *American Graffiti*, and Martin Scorsese, in *Mean Streets* (both 1973), were able to use more or less the soundtrack material of their choice.

The other major seminal film of the period was *Shaft* (1971). A surprise success itself, it spawned an entire movie sub-genre of superspade thrillers, with original scores fashioned after Isaac Hayes' brilliant prototype. None was very memorable, and only Curtis Mayfield's music for *Superfly* (1972) attained individual distinction.

Much less influential, though much more creditable, was Perry Henzell's *The Harder They Come* (1972), the first Jamaican feature film. Jimmy Cliff offered himself as star and his own experiences, hustling for work in the island's unsavoury music business, as dramatic inspiration. Such authenticity was appropriately garnished with some of Jamaica's finest reggae music.

The rock movie in the Seventies was re-routed by *American Graffiti*, a film concerned with teenage traumas in small-town Northern California in 1962; the period was re-created exactly, though much of the music used came from the Fifties. The strength of the characterization was no less important than the authenticity of the settings, so that the film succeeded as more than mere nostalgia.

Once the hippie dream had dissolved, there had been a resurgence of interest in the uncomplicated sounds of early rock'n'roll. Such films as D.A. Pennebaker's *Keep On Rockin'* (1972) and Sid Levin and Robert Abel's *Let the Good Times Roll* (1973) attested to this shift in popular taste. In the wake of *American Graffiti*, such tastes were not simply gratified, they were satiated. There was an *American Graffiti*-type film for blacks in *Cooley High* (1975), there was one for Jews in *Eskimo Limon* (1978, *Lemon Popsicle*) and arguably there was one for the mentally retarded in *National Lampoon's Animal House* (1978). There was also an official follow-up, *More*

American Graffiti (1979), directed by Bill Norton, who had made *Cisco Pike*.

American Graffiti had included the fondly remembered line, 'Rock'n'roll's been going downhill ever since Buddy Holly died'. The inevitable biopic, *The Buddy Holly Story* (1978), with Gary Busey in the title-roll, succeeded, despite a thorough disregard for factual accuracy, because it achieved a kind of emotional veracity, and because Busey turned in a winning performance.

The British equivalent of *American Graffiti* was *That'll Be the Day* (1973), directed by Claude Whatham from a lively original script by Ray Connolly. This was another evocative film, featuring two sharp central performances by David Essex and Ringo Starr. The Fifties music, however, was used less discriminatingly than it had been in *American Graffiti*. *That'll Be the Day* had a sequel, *Stardust* (1974); but this time the result was a shallow variant of the Beatles' story.

Sixties nostalgia movies on the whole foundered, perhaps because they seemed to be impatient with history, and did not take enough care to reconstruct the Sixties era. The two most notable artefacts of Sixties pop culture were both filmed in

Far left: Donald Sutherland and Peter Boyle in Steelyard Blues. *Above left: Woodstock, Michael Wadleigh's documentary of the epic rock festival held at Bethnal, New York, in August 1969, condensed 'three days of peace, music . . . and love' into three hours. Above: drive-in waitresses in Lucas'* American Graffiti. *Left: Jimmy, melancholy mod hero of Franc Roddam's* Quadrophenia, *prepares to drive himself and the scooter belonging to his former hero over the edge of a cliff.*

Above: Julien Temple's film celebrated Sex Pistols' manager Malcolm McLaren's manipulations of the music business. Top: John Travolta as Tony in Saturday Night Fever.

Above: Prince cranks up the volume in Purple Rain. *Top: Bette Midler as a junkie rock superstar, akin to Janis Joplin, in Mark Rydell's* The Rose.

the Seventies; they were the Beatles' album *Sgt. Pepper's Lonely Hearts Club Band*, in a catastrophic 1978 version, and the musical *Hair*, limply directed by the respected Miloš Forman in 1979. *Quadrophenia* (1979) boasted a cocky central performance from Phil Daniels as a mod, but little else; its period flavour ranged from the superficial to the non-existent. Wildly overrated, it should have been criticized for its lack of genuine understanding of adolescent frustration. The condition has been captured most convincingly in a film that slipped out almost unnoticed several years earlier, Barney Platts-Mills' minor masterpiece *Bronco Bullfrog* (1970).

Some films about the Sixties can be exempted from the general condemnation. In particular, there were two powerful films about the legacy of the Vietnam War, *Coming Home* (1978) and *Who'll Stop the Rain?* (1978, released in Britain as *Dog Soldiers*), both of which used rock music to establish a sense of period. However, the most beguiling, most affectionate re-creation of the Sixties was *I Wanna Hold Your Hand* (1978), which earnestly recaptured the New York atmosphere of the Beatles' first American visit in February 1964.

When looking backwards first became acceptable, in the mid-Seventies, nostalgia probably seemed the decent way

out. After all, rock itself had entered a kind of electric jackboot phase. There were principally two films – both bizarre, baroque extravaganzas – that tried to grasp the nettle of this new mood – *Phantom of the Paradise* and *Tommy*. *Phantom of the Paradise* was a grotesque, saturnine fantasy that amply conformed to the first law of rock: nothing succeeds like excess. *Tommy* was vulgar, garish, highly inventive and very loud; in The Who's rock opera, Ken Russell had found the ideal outlet for his imagination.

The debacle of *Sgt. Pepper's Lonely Hearts Club Band* had badly dented the form-book of Robert Stigwood, whose previous productions, *Saturday Night Fever* and *Grease* both of which starred John Travolta, were the two most commercially successful rock movies of the second half of the Seventies. Trying to explain the appeal of *Grease*, another film about the Fifties, is not altogether easy; certainly its less-than-breathtaking climax – a new hairdo and leather outfit for Olivia Newton-John – does not seem to account for it. *Saturday Night Fever* was at least a genuinely contemporary movie, and it caught the prevailing disco winds perfectly. Its soundtrack double-album became easily the largest-selling record of all time.

Businessmen were not slow to grasp the fact that films and records could achieve a spectacularly commercial symbiosis. Suddenly there were as many films to accompany sound-tracks as vice versa. The most renowned of these, by dint of the excellent Steely Dan title-song on the one hand and the fecklessness of the film itself on the other, was *FM* (1978). When the entertainment industry did manage to create another product where the film and soundtrack vied with each other in commercial potency, it was *Urban Cowboy* (1980), another Travolta vehicle.

By the close of the decade, there was a renewed interest in contemporary themes, partly because of *Saturday Night Fever*, and partly because of the emergence of the British punk or 'New Wave' rock movement. The films concentrating on the new music tended to be made both by the industry, as in the case of Joe Massot's *Dance Craze* (1981), and in spite of the industry – for instance, Don Letts' *Original Punk Rock Movie* (1977). The socio-political invective that accompanied punk found its most eloquent cinematic expression in the Jack Hazan–David Mingay film *Rude Boy* (1980), with the Clash; Derek Jarman found a style to match the new mood of civil disharmony with *Jubilee* (1978), starring Adam Ant and Toyah Willcox.

Of the films that studied the rock business itself, the most effective were the British *Breaking Glass* (1980), again with Phil Daniels, and the American *The Rose* (1979), in which the considerable shortcomings of the film itself were easily outweighed by Bette Midler's performance as the quasi-Janis Joplin figure who overdoses on the life-style that rock stars are expected to conform to. The Sex Pistols' own story was pieced together by Malcolm McLaren, in typically tenden-tious fashion, as *The Great Rock'n'Roll Swindle* (1980).

The Eighties boom in rock videos, aimed primarily at television audiences, resulted in fewer cinema features based around a band or star, though movies continued to use rock music as soundtrack selling-points. Typical of these were the tasteless *Party Party* (1983) which featured top British acts and *Fast Times at Ridgemont High* (1983), which featured top American ones. *Staying Alive* (1983) attempted to repeat the success of *Saturday Night Fever* and failed dismally, though *Flashdance* and *Breakin'* showed that audiences would still flock to see the latest American dance craze. More interest-ingly from the technical, if not the musical or aesthetic points of view, were the cartoon feature *American Pop* (1981) and *Pink Floyd – The Wall* (1982), which also used animation to interesting effect. However in 1984 Prince showed that the rock star's studied charisma could still carry a feature with *Purple Rain*, and Rob Reiner provided a welcome breath of fresh air with *This Is Spinal Tap!*, a deadpan spoof of the rock documentary in general and 'progressive' rock in particular, laden with in-jokes.

The Rock Documentary

Woodstock stands at the head of the rock documentary films produced during the Seventies. Directed by Michael Wad-leigh, the film was a celebration both of the music and of the mythology that the occasion enshrined; but if the gathering at Woodstock represented the zenith of the hippie life-style, it was all too quickly followed by its nadir, the violent Rolling Stones concert at Altamont, brilliantly captured by Albert and David Maysles and Charlotte Zwerin as *Gimme Shelter* (1970).

The other influential film from the start of the Seventies was the Beatles' *Let It Be* (1970). The intention here had been to show them working and recording together as a group. As it happened, togetherness was the characteristic least in evidence, and so the film showed the band actually in the throes of dissolution. Nevertheless, the Beatles had been pioneers in myriad respects, and this was to be no exception. After *Let It Be*, rock's top acts readily agreed to become the subjects of documentary films. In doing so, they were recognizing not only the appeal of the form developed by the Beatles, but also the fact that the old Hollywood notion, of simply building a musical drama around a star name, had happily passed away.

The last person to realize this was Elvis Presley; but he finally did agree to throw away those wretched scripts and be filmed simply as Elvis in two interesting documentary movies, though neither *Elvis – That's the Way It Is* (1970) nor *Elvis on Tour* (1972) could claim to have lifted the veil on the Elvis persona.

Such documentaries appeared regularly throughout the Seventies. Most have titles that speak for themselves: *Pink Floyd à Pompéi* (1972, *Pink Floyd Live at Pompeii*); *Yessongs* (1973); *Genesis – a Band in Concert*; and *The Grateful Dead* (both 1977). *The Kids Are Alright* (1979) went several steps further by providing a retrospective of all aspects of The Who's 15-year career. A fascinating and carefully compiled film, it ended up as a moving tribute to the band's drummer, Keith Moon, who had died while it was being completed.

Of the special-occasion concerts that were filmed, two of the best were *Concert for Bangla Desh* (1972) and *The Last Waltz* (1978). It is just coincidence that both of these featured Bob Dylan, although his charisma undoubtedly contributed greatly to both. Unfortunately, his own four-hour film *Renaldo and Clara* (1978) was insufferably pretentious and unspeakably boring. *The Last Waltz*, directed by Martin Scorsese, contains many excellent performances besides Dylan's and that of The Band, whose farewell concert this was. Other celebrities present included Eric Clapton, Van Morrison, Joni Mitchell and Neil Young, and, like Dylan, they all subsequently featured in their own films.

Documentaries were constructed around Clapton and Morrison individually in *Eric Clapton and his Rolling Hotel* and *Van Morrison in Ireland* (both 1980). Mitchell and Young both made their own films: Joni Mitchell's *Shadows and Light* (1980) was made for television rather than the cinema; Neil Young, under the alias Bernard Shakey, directed two films himself – *Journey Through the Past* (1973) and *Rust Never Sleeps* (1979).

In the Eighties rock manifestly lost much of its former power to provide a focus for social dissent; the rock documentary feature thus became increasingly redundant, being little more than an extended promotion clip for the artist or band in question. Cinema features gave up any attempt to keep up with the fluctuations in fashion in the pop music industry, preferring to appeal to the nostalgic impulse in older rock fans, like the flop cartoon 'history' *American Pop* (1981). *Urgh! A Music War* (1981) offered those who had been asleep during the late Seventies a belated introduction to British and American 'New Wave' performers, while the ageing Rolling Stones were shown going through the motions in Hal Ashby's record of their 1981 US tour, *Let's Spend the Night Together* (1982). Films that attempted to rekindle some sense of youth solidarity in the face of Establishment indifference included *No Nukes* (1981), which, with the exception of Bruce Springsteen, unfortunately presented a number of played-out American stars and, in Britain, Julien

Temple's film of Amnesty International's 1981 fund-raising concert *The Secret Policeman's Other Ball* (1982). This was an enjoyable mix of satirical sketches and rock acts that unconsciously recalled a time when picking up a guitar was a valid subversive act. However in 1984 Jonathan Demme showed that a rock band (Talking Heads) could still prove interesting and stimulating enough to carry a feature-length film with *Stop Making Sense*.

Comic Diversions

As the Seventies began, the continuity of Hollywood comedy appeared to have been ruptured, with virtually all the top-line comedians and most of the leading directors associated with the genre for many years now vanished from the screen. The triumphant survivor among directors was Billy Wilder. But even his output became sporadic, and after the commercial failure of the delightful Italian-set romantic comedy *Avanti!* (1972), he ran for cover with a raucously lively but fairly conservative remake of the old Broadway warhorse *The Front Page* (1974).

The intermittently brilliant ex-cartoonist Frank Tashlin, who died in 1972, had directed the last starring vehicle of Danny Kaye, *The Man From the Diner's Club* (1963). Tashlin concluded his career with *The Private Navy of Sergeant O'Farrell* (1968), one of the brighter spots in the generally disappointing later work of another veteran comic, Bob Hope, who made his most recent appearance in *Cancel My Reservation* (1972).

Jerry Lewis remained active as both performer and director throughout the Sixties, but the quality of his work showed evident signs of decline as the decade wore on. After an uninspired war comedy *Ja Ja Mein General! But Which Way to the Front?* (1970), he retreated into silence, apparently beset by personal difficulties, not to re-emerge until *Hardly Working* (1980), about an unemployed circus clown who pretends to be a variety of characters; the film scored a cult critical success in France but has been less enthusiastically received elsewhere.

The one comic performer who remained a surefire box-office proposition during the Seventies was Peter Sellers in the guise of the bumbling Inspector Clouseau, centrepiece of a string of spin-offs from *The Pink Panther* (1963). These films, including *The Return of the Pink Panther* (1975) and *The Pink Panther Strikes Again* (1976), were elegantly directed by Blake Edwards, who also notched up a success of a different sort with the sex comedy *'10'* (1979), featuring his wife Julie Andrews, later to bare her bosom in his Hollywood satire *S.O.B.* (1981).

Sex comedy, if of a generally rather cautious and compromised kind, proved one of the staples of Hollywood humour in the Seventies. Typical were *The Owl and the Pussycat* (1970), with George Segal exercising his rumpled charm as a timid bookshop assistant caught up with Barbra Streisand's eccentric call-girl, and *A Touch of Class* (1973), with Segal again, this time as an untimid insurance man, partnered by Glenda Jackson as the businesswoman with whom he indulges in an extra-marital affair. Segal starred, too, in *Blume in Love* (1973), an engaging film in which director Paul Mazursky consolidated the instinct he had shown in *Bob & Carol & Ted & Alice* (1969) for sympathetic and inventively funny examinations of modern sexual customs, a talent he was subsequently to develop in *An Unmarried Woman* (1978).

It was the enormous popularity of *The Graduate* (1967), the story of a young man's first encounters with sex and love, that really gave impetus to 'permissive' comedy, while the scale of its success also turned director Mike Nichols into a prestigiously hot property. His blockbuster anti-war satire *Catch-22* (1970), adapted from Joseph Heller's cult novel of the early Sixties, was followed by *Carnal Knowledge* (1971), which, scripted by cartoonist Jules Feiffer, traces the amorous rakes' progress of two erstwhile college boys. Perhaps Nichols' best-achieved film, however, was his least ambitious, *The Fortune* (1975), a knockabout farce set in the Twenties, with Jack Nicholson and Warren Beatty as a pair of incompetent would-be killers.

Nichols initially made a gilded reputation partnering Elaine May, first in nightclubs, then on Broadway, in a series of fashionable satirical sketches. Elaine May was herself to venture into the cinema, as actress and later as director, notably of *A New Leaf* (1971), an acidly amusing little fable about an unprepossessing heiress (May) whom a penniless upper-class loafer (Walter Matthau) seeks to marry for her money.

In the theatre, Nichols directed two plays by the writer who, since the early Sixties, has dominated mainstream

Below: Blake Edwards with Peter Sellers as Inspector Clouseau making The Return of the Pink Panther *(1975). Bottom: Glenda Jackson and George Segal in* A Touch of Class.

humour on Broadway, and increasingly in Hollywood, too – Neil Simon (though, perhaps strangely, Nichols has never directed Simon's work for the cinema). Simon's name rapidly became a byword for profitability, and virtually all his plays have been converted into movies. Simon himself scripted the adaptations of *Barefoot in the Park* (1967), *The Odd Couple* (1968), *The Prisoner of Second Avenue* (1974) *The Sunshine Boys* (1975) and *California Suite* (1978), among others. He also branched out into original screenplays, for conventional situation comedies such as *The Out-of-Towners* (1970), and for two ingenious spoofs of detective fiction, *Murder by Death* (1976) and *The Cheap Detective* (1978). Simon's work can sometimes seem hollow and predictable (as in *Plaza Suite*, 1971) but he retains an uncanny instinct for giving the public what it wants.

Simon's pre-Broadway apprenticeship was served as television writer and gagman, notably for the Sid Caesar programme *Your Show of Shows*, on which his fellow employees included no fewer than three other men who were to become key figures in the cinema – Carl Reiner, Mel Brooks and Woody Allen.

Carl Reiner (b. 1922) first made his name as a comic actor in the Caesar show. He then created the hit series *The Dick Van Dyke Show*, and after writing a couple of nondescript movies (*The Thrill of It All*, 1963; *The Art of Love*, 1965) assumed the mantle of film director. His first feature, *Enter Laughing* (1967), derived from his semi-autobiographical novel, was a somewhat forcedly comic account of a young man's attempts to break into show business, while *The Comic* (1969), his second film, was a falteringly off-beat vehicle for Dick Van Dyke as an unlikeable silent-screen comedian. But in the late Seventies, Reiner was reponsible for two extremely popular comedies showcasing contrasted personalities. *Oh, God!* (1977) is a whimsical joke in which veteran funny-man George Burns essays the role of the Almighty, whilst *The Jerk* (1979) casts Steve Martin in a picaresque farce about an ex-foundling trying without conspicuous success to make good in life. Reiner's best film, though, remains *Where's Poppa?* (1970), a distinctive black comedy featuring Ruth Gordon as a senile Jewish momma and George Segal as her harassed son.

Undoubtedly the outstanding comic talent of the modern American cinema belongs to **Woody Allen** (b. 1935). An ex-

Below: Robert Redford in Barefoot in the Park. *Bottom: love finds would-be singer Annie (Diane Keaton) and comedian Alvy Singer (Woody Allen) in* Annie Hall.

Below: The Odd Couple – *Jack Lemmon and Walter Matthau. Bottom Isaac (Woody Allen) has a moment of happiness with teenage girlfriend Tracy (Mariel Hemingway) in* Manhattan.

Above: Mel Brooks as Moses in The History of the World – Part One. *Top: Cleavon Little as Black Bart in* Blazing Saddles.

cabaret performer and playwright (including *Play It Again, Sam,* filmed in 1972), Allen began his directorial career in the cinema – having earlier written and appeared in *What's New, Pussycat?* (1965) – with modestly budgeted, almost revue-like movies, centring around himself, such as *Take the Money and Run* (1969) and *Bananas* (1971). Then, with Diane Keaton as his dippy co-star, he moved on to the elaborately formulated comedy of *Sleeper* (1973) and *Love and Death* (1975), and thence to the considerable ambition of such overtly thoughtful, personal, but still dazzlingly witty works as the multi-Oscar winning *Annie Hall* (1977), *Manhattan* (1979) and the Fellini-influenced *Stardust Memories* (1980), perhaps his darkest and most disturbing comedy. Central to each is the hero's failure to establish an enduring, happy relationship with a woman, largely owing to his obsessive insecurity.

Allen's admiration for the films of Ingmar Bergman permeated his sole attempt at a 'serious' film, *Interiors* (1978). Despite being nominated for an Academy Award, the movie reflected the worst rather than the best elements of Bergman's work, being self-conscious and pretentious. A Bergman film, *Sommarnattens Leende* (1955, *Smiles of a Summer Night*), also inspired Allen's *A Midsummer Night's Sex Comedy* (1982), which initiated his acting partnership with the increasingly versatile Mia Farrow.

This film's shift towards a more hopeful resolution to the problems of life and love was also discernible in *Zelig* (1983), *Broadway Danny Rose* (1984) and *The Purple Rose of Cairo* (1985). In these films Allen avoided the painful personal confessions of earlier films. The hero of *Broadway Danny Rose*, in particular, triumphs over dangers and comes to the aid of his girlfriend because he knows who he is and knows what is right – a degree of self-confidence and resilience woefully lacking in Allen's protagonists since his bewildered but resourceful time-traveller in *Sleeper* (1973).

Mel Brooks (b. 1927) was formerly a comedy artist in nightclubs and television and the creator of several TV series, including *Get Smart*. In 1967 he burst on to the movie scene as the writer-director of the hilariously tasteless *The Producers*, which starred Zero Mostel and Gene Wilder as a pair of Broadway entrepreneurs who attempt to swindle their investors (rich, lonely old ladies) by putting on a sure-fire flop, 'Springtime for Hitler'. Though panned at the time by over-sensitive US critics, the film has since become a cult favourite. Brooks then attempted a straight literary adaptation, *The Twelve Chairs* (1970), from a Russian comic novel, before returning to the rich vein of parody that he had discovered in *The Producers* with *Blazing Saddles* (1974), in which a timid black sheriff (Cleavon Little) and a neurotic, alcholic former gunfighter (Gene Wilder) save the town of Rock Ridge. In addition to poking fun at the Western, the film satirized modern, white liberal racist attitudes and Hollywood's unscrupulous stereotyping of black performers.

The world-wide success of *Blazing Saddles* was repeated by Brooks' next film, *Young Frankenstein* (1974), his most stylish and sustained work, an affectionate send-up of Hollywood horror movies of the Thirties strikingly photographed in black and white by Gerald Hirschfeld. War films, musicals, suspense films and the world of high finance were debunked in *Silent Movie* (1976), and Hitchcock thrillers in *High Anxiety* (1977). Although both had highly inventive sequences and gags, they were patchy and somewhat indulgent. An air of desperate self-congratulation has subsequently marred Brooks' major Eighties' ventures, *History of the World – Part One* (1981), and *To Be or Not to Be* (1983), a remake of Lubitsch's 1942 comedy drama, in which Brooks and his wife Anne Bancroft took the roles formerly played by Jack Benny and Carole Lombard.

The star of various Brooks movies has been Gene Wilder, a comic actor with a considerable flair for the absurder aspects of neurotic vulnerability, who has occasionally functioned as writer-director of vehicles for himself. *The Adventure of Sherlock Holmes' Smarter Brother* (1975) has some appealing semi-surrealist touches: *The World's Greatest Lover* (1977) is a mainly misfiring farce about Hollywood in the Twenties, the background also of Brooks' *Silent Movie* (1976); and *The Woman in Red* (1984) is a plodding, though commercially successful, sex comedy.

The Crime Film

As law and order became a top domestic issue in the USA, the cop was the new superstar on cinema and television screens. Between 1968 and 1977, movies with police heroes figured prominently among the American top 20 moneymakers of almost every year, as listed by New York's showbiz weekly, *Variety*: *The Detective* in 1968; *Bullitt* (1968) in 1969; *The French Connection* and *Klute*, both in 1971; *Dirty Harry* (1971) and *The New Centurions* in 1972; *Walking Tall* in 1973; *Magnum Force* and *Serpico* (both 1973) in 1974; *Freebie and the*

Bean (1974) in 1975; and *The Enforcer* (1976) in 1977. Cop movies received the industry's acclaim when the Oscars for Best Film of the Year went to *In the Heat of the Night* in 1967, and to *The French Connection* in 1971. In addition to these outstanding box-office hits, studios turned out many more movies with police heroes which did not attain the same critical or cash response. Flashing blue lights and screaming sirens also invaded television screens as shows such as *Ironside, Columbo, Kojak, Policewoman* and *Starsky and Hutch* achieved top ratings.

From 1930 to 1967, only three films with police heroes were listed as top moneymakers: *Bullets or Ballots* in 1936; *Detective Story* in 1951; and *Dragnet* in 1954. Each of these does represent a larger cycle of movies with cop heroes, but none achieved the same popularity or significance as the post-1967 cycle.

The new phase of cop movies was spearheaded by Norman Jewison's *In the Heat of the Night* (1967). This portrayed the conflict between the black, highly trained and professionally skilled northern detective Virgil Tibbs (Sidney Poitier) and Bill Gillespie (Rod Steiger, who won the Best Actor Oscar), the prejudiced, vigilante-style police chief of Sparta, Mississippi. True to the film's liberal message, Gillespie is taught to appreciate the superior power of the college degree over the third degree as Tibbs finds the correct solution to a murder case. Arthur Penn's *The Chase* (1966) had already anticipated similar themes in its depiction of honest Sheriff Calder (Marlon Brando) fighting against Southern bigotry, brutality and corruption. Despite some (mixed) critical acclaim, Penn's film was not a popular success and was only indirectly influential.

In 1968 the flood of cop-movies really began in earnest, including the first two police films directed by Don Siegel, *Madigan* and *Coogan's Bluff*, the second of which marked Clint Eastwood's debut as a cop. In addition, also in 1968, sympathetic lawmen were featured prominently in Jack Smight's *No Way to Treat a Lady* (played by George Segal) and Richard Fleischer's *The Boston Strangler* (played by Henry Fonda).

Gordon Douglas' *The Detective* was notable for being the only *urban* film of the cycle to take a consistently liberal stance on the law-and-order debate. Frank Sinatra plays Joe Leland, a dedicated, skilled and honest cop, loyal to 'The Department' (his father was also a policeman) as an abstract symbol and tradition. Leland is generally humane in his methods, but his extraction of a confession to murder from an innocent suspect by psychological pressure eventually brings about his downfall. The general import is that brutality and illegal methods are not just wrong but also counter-productive. Two aspects of *The Detective* were to be echoed in later examples of the cop cycle. One was the theme of the dedicated, remorselessly honest, lone-wolf, street-level cop pitted against his bureaucratic superiors, who are more concerned with protecting their own promotion prospects by playing it safe than they are with law-enforcement. *The Detective* also foreshadows the rest of the cycle in its relentlessly brutal depiction of urban violence, seediness and decay.

Don Siegel's *Madigan* and Peter Yates' *Bullitt* together mark a transition from liberalism to presidential candidate Richard M. Nixon's hard law-and-order line. Both depict the tension between the pressure on policemen to clear up crime and the requirement that this is subject to 'due process of law'. Steven McQueen as Bullitt is an ambiguous charcter. He wastes cars,

Above: Clint Eastwood puts the boot in as an Arizona cop on a mission to New York in Coogan's Bluff.

buildings and people with abandon yet he does not seem to relish the job. Violence is an unfortunate necessity. The tough, no-nonsense methods of Richard Widmark as Dan Madigan, a street-wise cop, help him get his man but Madigan dies in the process. The final picture is of the city as a jungle, where toughness is the only viable response even if it ultimately solves nothing.

The city-as-jungle theme is most explicit in Siegel's *Coogan's Bluff*, showing the moral and physical confusion and decay of New York City through the eyes of an Arizona deputy sheriff (Clint Eastwood) who, complete with ten-gallon hat and cowboy boots, is tracking down a lost prisoner. Eastwood brings his cowboy persona to the role of Coogan, and the film clinches the connection between the traditional Western hero and the new police image (as does *McCloud*, the television series derived from it). The cop's displacement of the cowboy as folk-hero is best emphasized by the example of John Wayne; after turning down the part of Dirty Harry, he jumped on the paddy-wagon in *McQ* (1974) and *Brannigan* (1975).

The 'order before law' theme of *Madigan* and *Coogan's Bluff* was central in *Dirty Harry*, the next Eastwood-Siegel cop collaboration, a huge hit although condemned by liberals for its approval of police vigilantism. Eastwood's Harry Callahan justifies his disregard for civil rights by seeing crime from the point of view of the victim. In *Magnum Force*, the second Dirty Harry hit, Harry's targets are cops who organize a secret death squad to 'execute' a number of known and vicious gangsters whom the law cannot touch. Why Harry should oppose behaviour not unlike his own previous actions is never satisfactorily explained.

William Friedkin's *The French Connection* presents a message as bleak as – if more ambiguous than – *Dirty Harry's*. Gene Hackman plays 'Popeye' Doyle – based on real-life cop Eddie Egan, who appears in the film in a small part – as a brutal, boorish, boisterous bully but one who usually gets results. He is a dedicated cop; but the pressures of the job have made him so cynical that his relentless pursuit of the heroin traffickers appears socially meaningless, an obsessive chase for its own sake.

Following these hugely successful movies, a glut of derivatives flooded the screen. Jim Brown played a Poitier-like black sheriff in Ralph Nelson's *Tick ... Tick ... Tick* (1970). Poitier himself returned as Virgil Tibbs in Gordon Douglas' *They Call Me Mister Tibbs!* (1970) and Don Medford's *The Organization* (1971). Gene Hackman returned as 'Popeye' Doyle in John Frankenheimer's *French Connection II* (1975), while his real-life prototype, Eddie Egan, was the inspiration for Howard W. Koch's *Badge 373* (1973). Philip D'Antoni, producer of *The French Connection*, directed Hackman's erstwhile partner from that film, Roy Scheider, in *The Seven-Ups* (1973). Real-life Tennessee Sheriff Buford Pusser's exploits were narrated in Phil Karlson's *Walking Tall*, a low-budget, violence-filled sleeper that became a gigantic smash-hit and was followed by *Part 2 Walking Tall* (1975) and *Final Chapter – Walking Tall* (1977). Walter Matthau was a cop in *The Laughing Policeman* (1973) – which, despite its title and star, was a non-humorous, procedural account of the hunt for a mass-murderer – and in *The Taking of Pelham 123* (1974). Novelist Ed McBain's 87th Precinct heroes appeared in *Fuzz* (1972). Real-life prototypes of Starksy and Hutch, the New York cops Dave Greenberg and Bob Hantz, were portrayed in *The Super Cops* (1974); and a similar deadly duo were lampooned by James Caan and Alan Arkin in *Freebie and the Bean*.

Elliott Gould also sent up the police force in Peter Hyams' *Busting* (1974), with a performance reminiscent of *M*A*S*H* (1970). George Peppard and Burt Reynolds played doomed cops in *Newman's Law* (1974) and *Hustle* (1975) respectively. Charles Bronson was a deadly, avenging cop in Michael Winner's *The Stone Killer* (1973), a dry run for his tremendous success as Mr Joe Average turned urban vigilante in the same director's *Death Wish* (1974). *Death Wish* was the most successful of a cycle of private vigilante movies that also included *Gordon's War* (1973), *Framed* (1975), *Fighting Mad* (1976), *The Exterminator* (1980) – and, at a more serious artistic level, *Taxi Driver* (1976).

Whether reactionary, like *Walking Tall*, or liberal, like the Virgil Tibbs series, all these films eulogized their police heroes. But this love affair with the cops was only one side of Hollywood's treatment. In other genres, the police appeared less favourably. The counter-culture movies of the late Sixties, such as *Easy Rider* or *The Strawberry Statement*, showed the cops as kill-joy pigs, an image echoed in the later contemporary-cowboy, driver and trucker movies, such as *J. W. Coop*, *Vanishing Point* (both 1971) and *Convoy* (1978).

A handful of films with cop heroes did not use the conventional crime-story framework. Sidney Lumet's *Serpico*

Above: Frank Sinatra takes a tumble as detective Tony Rome. *Top: Clint Eastwood in the nostalgic private-eye thriller* City Heat, *which teamed him with Burt Reynolds.*

(1973) told of the hero's hounding by colleagues and bosses as he tries to expose corruption within the force. He was based on the real-life cop whose revelations stimulated the Knapp Commission, reporting in 1972 on the wholesale corruption of the New York City Police Department. Al Pacino gave the central role a convincing quality of stubborn idealism.

Electra Glide in Blue was a probing exploration of the psychological roots of police machismo. Robert Blake played John Wintergreen, a short motorcycle cop who boasts of being the same height as Alan Ladd. Shown lovingly donning his boots and gun, Wintergreen dreams of becoming a stetsoned detective, like his idol Harve Pool (Mitchell Ryan). Temporarily assigned to assist the star investigator on a murder case, Wintergreen discovers his hero's impotence as both detective and lover. Back on motorcycle patrol, Wintergreen is gratuitously killed by hippies – an inversion of *Easy Rider's* ending.

The films based on Joseph Wambaugh's novels are in a class of their own. Wambaugh was a 34-year-old Los Angeles

Below left: a dissatisfied cop (Burt Reynolds) falls in love with a call-girl (Catherine Deneuve) in Aldrich's Hustle. *Far left: in Winner's* Death Wish, *prototype of the long-running vigilante cycle, Bronson plays a businessman who avenges his wife's murder by killing any muggers he can find in the streets. Left: Jack Nicholson and Faye Dunaway in Polanski's* Chinatown. *Below: Raymond Chandler's Forties private-eye Philip Marlowe (Elliott Gould) is transplanted to Seventies Los Angeles in Altman's* The Long Goodbye.

police sergeant when he published the 1971 hit novel *The New Centurions*, which was filmed by Richard Fleischer in 1972 starring George C. Scott and Stacy Keach. Wambaugh's subsequent novels have also been filmed: *The Blue Knight* (1973, a television mini-series in the USA); *The Choirboys* (1977); *The Onion Field* (1979); and *The Black Marble* (1980). His work has also inspired two television series, *The Blue Knight* and *Police Story*. These movies are not law-and-order homilies. The cop's struggle is to save his soul and preserve some minimum integrity and decency in an irredeemably savage and amoral world. The films show the routine phases of police work: rounding up prostitutes, spying on gays, rescuing would-be suicides or battered babies, acting as instant marriage-guidance counsellor to battling spouses, as well as shooting it out with liquor-store robbers. What Wambaugh's policeman must ultimately come to terms with is the futility of his efforts as the caretaker – 'centurion' – of a civilization that relentlessly breeds misery and degradation. So he has a tragic vision, a deep pessimism which precludes any hope of social change. The Wambaugh stories do share with the law-and-order cop movies the conflict between the real police work of the street cops and the bureaucratic bungling of their bosses. Wambaugh is a Hollywood maver-

ick who was so incensed by Robert Aldrich's treatment of *The Choirboys* that he took out an injunction against the use of his name in publicizing the movie. Dissatisfied with the handling of his earlier work, Wambaugh himself arranged the independent production of *The Onion Field*, undoubtedly his masterpiece as both book and film, and of *The Black Marble*, accepting only script credits. Despite glowing critical receptions, both of these excellent movies have not received the international acclaim that they deserve.

The late Seventies witnessed the decline but not demise of the cop cycle. Clint Eastwood's *The Gauntlet* (1977) continues the old theme of honest policeman versus corrupt hierarchy, but debunks his earlier lone-cop, machismo mystique. Eastwood plays a policeman proud of being selected for a mission to bring back an important witness, a prostitute (Sondra Locke); but he has been chosen because his corrupt superiors regard him as the most incompetent cop on the force, and they want the witness killed before she can testify. The hero and heroine survive only because the erstwhile loner is repeatedly saved by the advice of the wisecracking girl he is meant to protect. However, Eastwood returned to playing cops in *Sudden Impact* (1983), *Tightrope* and *City Heat* (both 1984).

Although the characteristic law-enforcement hero of the

late Sixties and Seventies was the cop, the more traditional Hollywood staples of the private eye and the gentleman sleuth were not neglected. There were numerous attempts to recapture the tone and atmosphere of the classic private-eye movies of the Forties. The two Raymond Chandler novels which had not yet been filmed at last reached the screen. Paul Bogart's *Marlowe* (1969) was based on Chandler's *The Little Sister* and had James Garner giving a very creditable performance in the title role. In *The Long Goodbye* (1973), Robert Altman brought Marlowe (played by Elliott Gould) up to date, placing him in contemporary Los Angeles. The film deviated pretty sharply from the original novel but it succeeded in capturing Chandler's bleak vision of the great nowhere city. The two most successful of the Forties Marlowe films, *Murder, My Sweet* (1944) and *The Big Sleep* (1946), were remade as Dick Richards' *Farewell, My Lovely* (1975) and Michael Winner's *The Big Sleep* (1978), both starring the excellent Robert Mitchum.

Lew Archer, novelist Ross Macdonald's hero, was brought to the screen with a change of name by Jack Smight in 1966 with Paul Newman as *Harper*. Fast-moving and well-characterized, *Harper* was deservedly one of the most popular private-eye movies of the period. However, it was nearly matched by Gordon Douglas' *Tony Rome* (1967), with Frank Sinatra seemingly made for the Bogart-like role of a Miami-based private eye. *Lady in Cement* (1968) was a respectably workmanlike sequel from the Douglas-Sinatra team.

Gordon Parks' *Shaft* marked a departure for the private-eye movie in featuring a black detective hero. Richard Roundtree's portrayal of Shaft owed more to James Bond than to Philip Marlowe, with the emphasis being on the hero's prowess at sex and violence. Hugely successful, the film spawned two sequels, *Shaft's Big Score!* (1972) and *Shaft in Africa* (1973). Rather more in line with the traditions of the private-eye genre was Bill Cosby's black detective in *Hickey and Boggs* (1972), about a salt-and-pepper pair of down-and-out gumshoes, directed by Robert Culp, who also played Cosby's white partner.

In the Seventies, three films marked the culmination of the private-eye genre to date. Alan J. Pakula's adult thriller *Klute* starred Donald Sutherland in the role of a Tuscarora, Pennsylvania policeman who is hired by a wealthy acquaintance to leave the force and find a missing friend. The only clue is an obscene letter to a New York call-girl, Bree Daniels (Jane Fonda in an Oscar-winning performance). The tense, increasingly paranoiac atmosphere and acute characterization make for compulsive viewing, although the film finally reveals a soft centre as romance blossoms between Klute and the call-girl.

Roman Polanski's *Chinatown* (1974) successfully evoked both the physical and the moral landscape of the Forties' *film noir*. Jack Nicholson was most effective as the private eye uncovering a tangled morass of political and private evil. John Huston, who as director had pioneered the genre with *The Maltese Falcon* (1941), played the personification of corruption through absolute power, and Faye Dunaway was a mysterious *femme fatale*.

Arthur Penn's *Night Moves* (1975) had Gene Hackman as a relentless pursuer of truth, hampered by domestic problems. Derived from an excellent script by Alan Sharp, *Night Moves*, with its bafflingly enigmatic plot, delivered the *coup de grâce* to the central thematic underpinning of the private-eye genre, that integrity and intuition for the moral worth of other people can succeed in resolving problems. Here the moral sensibilities and dedication of the hero lead to disaster for all the characters.

The Seventies also produced some excellent pastiches of the private-eye genre, possibly a sign of the dissolution of the moral assumptions of the straightforward variety. The delightful British *Gumshoe*, directed by Stephen Frears in 1971, starred Albert Finney as a small-time comedian who identifies with Bogart, getting involved in some Chandleresque action in Lancashire and London. In David Giler's *The Black Bird* (1975), George Segal played the son of Sam Spade, hero of *The Maltese Falcon*. Robert Benton's *The Late Show* (1977) had Art Carney as a private eye of pensionable vintage, complete with a hearing-aid which he has to remove before shooting, getting embroiled in a contemporary world of marijuana, murder and mayhem. Most satisfying of all was Richard Dreyfuss' portrayal of a 'clapped-out Marxist gumshoe' (as another character calls him) in Jeremy Paul Kagan's *The Big Fix* (1978). A former college radical of the Sixties turned unsuccessful private eye, he pursues a complex web of political corruption, dragging in tow his Jewish momma and two small kids – his ex-wife dumps them on him as she follows the lastest psychiatric fads.

Robert Moore's *Murder by Death*, with a script by Neil Simon, was a hilarious send-up of the whole detective genre, with an all-star cast playing the best-known screen sleuths, in the traditional setting of a country-house weekend. The partnership of Neil Simon and Robert Moore attempted to repeat the success of this by lampooning the gumshoe genre in *The Cheap Detective*, starring Peter Falk. Like the previously mentioned hits, these films showed that the detective genre was very much alive, although largely in the form of pastiche or nostalgic tribute.

New Ways in the Old West

The Seventies can be regarded as the period in which the Western was dragged kicking and screaming into the twentieth century. The genre's characteristic tone of affirmation or elegy, expressing a nineteenth-century confidence about the future, was transformed into a new tone of cynicism and despair, born of a distinctly modern feeling of helplessness and unease. When the USA bicentenary came along in 1976, the Western – the form which, above all, celebrates the triumphant emergence and civilization of America – could not rise to the occasion. The most typical response came from Robert Altman, with *Buffalo Bill and the Indians . . . or Sitting Bull's History Lesson*, and Arthur Penn, who directed *The Missouri Breaks*. The former shows one of the country's national heroes (played by Paul Newman) as a slow-witted and self-deluding clown; the latter presents as its embodiment of law and order a fat, transvestite sadist (an extraordinary creation by Marlon Brando), who specializes in killing from a distance.

It is perhaps not surprising that the Western should go into a phase of irony and self-criticism. John Ford, the doyen of Western directors and the one who had celebrated the pioneering spirit on film in its purest form, had died in 1973. Other great veteran directors of the genre were to die within the following few years – Howard Hawks in 1977, Raoul Walsh in 1980. After *El Dorado* (1967), Hawks did manage one more variation on his classic *Rio Bravo* (1959), this time called *Rio Lobo* (1970). Significantly, it is one of his darkest films, evoking a world where chivalry between hero and antagonist no longer exists and which seems to be discovering pleasure and sophistication in sadism.

In addition, it seemed that the harrowing vision Sam Peckinpah had presented in *The Wild Bunch* (1969), a film whose nightmarish violence was to reverberate influentially through other directors' Westerns, had exhausted his sensibilities. His major contribution was the distinguished *Pat Garrett and Billy the Kid* (1973), a study of cynical pragmatism and of adjustment to encroaching civilization.

The death or conversion of the gunfighter so that civilization might prosper is a common theme in Sixties Westerns, expressed most poignantly in Ford's *The Man Who Shot Liberty Valance* (1962). There were numerous Westerns at this time about men whose prowess with a gun has helped to tame the country but who, at the point of transition, have to be rejected for their special skill has become both unnecessary and threatening to the new society. It is a theme that recurs in later Westerns, such as Don Siegel's *The Shootist* (1976) and William Wiard's *Tom Horn* (1979), although the inflection tends to be different. The Sixties had accepted this change as painful, but inevitable and necessary. Seventies films seem more bitter. Tom Horn (Steve McQueen in his penultimate film) for example, is framed, tried and condemned for murder by a society that has no further use for him and fears him.

During the Seventies the Western suffered the fate of all genres – it became self-conscious. The previous decade had been preoccupied with reflections on the West – on the gap between fact and legend – and the Western hero who was becoming older and more tired. But it then became absorbed with itself as a form – how a Western is constituted, what its main elements are and mean, and how they have been relayed to mass audiences. This self-consciousness appeared in several forms. There was the broad comic parody of Mel Brooks' *Blazing Saddles*, an irreverent spoof on basic Western situations; while Michael Crichton, the writer and director of *Westworld* (1973), blended cowboy and science fiction in an ingenious tale about programmed robots in a mock frontier town who start killing holidaymakers. In particular, the new films alluded to screen history, referring not to the myth of the West but to the mythology of the Western film. Thus, *The Shootist*, which stars John Wayne as an ex-gunfighter dying of cancer, opens with a montage of scenes from earlier Wayne films, blurring the distinction between the specific character he is playing and the general screen persona he had built up over his career. Both Clint Eastwood's *High Plains Drifter* (1973) and *The Missouri Breaks* play on the audience's recognition of the classic Western hero of George Stevens' *Shane* (1953). Shane was a kind of saviour, an inspirer of men; Eastwood's satanic protagonist in *High Plains Drifter* is an embodiment of what men fear in themselves.

The Seventies' Western tended to be short of conventional heroes. With the exception of Eastwood, there was no actor really identifiable as a natural Western star. Indeed, one of the major themes was the decline of heroism, the absence of charisma. This was true even of Westerns that had the names of central characters in their titles, such as Robert Altman's *McCabe and Mrs Miller* (1971) and Richard Lester's *Butch and Sundance – The Early Days* (1979). In both films the heroes

Left: in the climax of Westworld *a cowboy robut runs amok. Top left: Western old-timers Robert Mitchum, Arthur Hunnicut and John Wayne on the side of law and order in Hawks'* El Dorado. *Above: Paul Newman and Robert Redford down to their last wisecrack in George Roy Hill's multi-Oscar winning, nostalgic* Butch Cassidy and the Sundance Kid *(1969).*

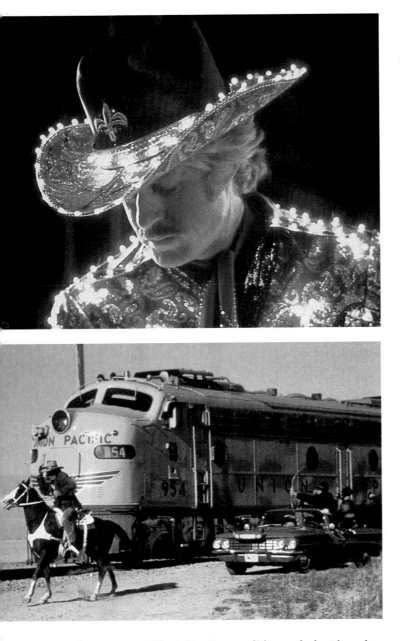

many Seventies Westerns were interested in the years immediately following the American Civil War and the difficulties men found adjusting to postwar society. In *The Outlaw Josey Wales* (1976), Clint Eastwood directed himself as a man whose quest for revenge (after the murder of his family during the war) becomes ultimately less important than his need for peace and emotional security. On the other hand, two remarkable films about the Jesse James and Cole Younger gangs, Philip Kaufman's *The Great Northfield Minnesota Raid* (1972) and Walter Hill's *The Long Riders* (1980), remain abrasive and disillusioned, presenting characters whose war experience makes it hard for them to put down roots, to conform to a new era of materialism.

A number of Seventies Westerns offered interesting variations on modern social themes. Reflecting a contemporary moral malaise, they often drew little distinction between heroes and villains. John Huston's *The Life and Times of Judge Roy Bean* (1972) makes a hero of the hanging judge. In Robert Benton's *Bad Company* (1971) the outlaws are presented as comically endearing even at their most bestial, and the development of the innocent young hero is an inexorable progress towards crime. In the two Westerns he has made for the director Sydney Pollack, *Jeremiah Johnson* (1972) and *The Electric Horseman* (1979), Robert Redford has used the form to proclaim his particular ecological interests, both films employing the majesty of the landscape and the later one, set in the modern day, showing how a resourceful Westerner can outsmart and humiliate big business. William Fraker's *Monte Walsh* (1970) is concerned with the issue of unemployment in the old West, and what happens to cowboys when their skills are superseded by technology.

The Wild West Show, one of only two outlets for the Seventies Western hero, is handled with affectionate respect in Clint Eastwood's *Bronco Billy* (1980); but it is treated savagely in *Buffalo Bill and the Indians ... or Sitting Bull's History Lesson*, which is concerned not with the West as history or legend but as theatre. The film's iconoclastic proposition is that the West does not represent the heart of American adventurism but the origins of American showbiz.

The other outlet is the rodeo, the modern cinema's arena for the activities of those who still have 'Westering' in their blood. The films with this background – including Cliff Robertson's *J. W. Coop* (1971), Stuart Millar's *When the Legends Die* and Sam Peckinpah's *Junior Bonner* (both 1972) – play alternately witty and moving games with the concept of the cowboy in modern civilization.

The conventional Western movie was, then, thoroughly revised in the Seventies. Indeed, *Little Big Man* turned the genre inside out for, as the title suggests, the film is all about paradoxes and contraries, a marvellous inversion of all the old legends.

It was inevitable that the tragedies of recent American history should feed a retrospective doubt into the legends of its pioneering past. Latterday Westerns invariably ask: how did America get to this present from that past? Such a question informs their presentation of history, and issues of 'goodies and baddies' take second place to themes such as the growth of racism and capitalism, or the origins of legitimized violence in the American psyche.

Country-and-Westerns

Country-and-western music grew up with the movies, but the success of Robert Altman's film *Nashville* (1975) made people aware of how strong the country connection had become.

Above: Bronco Billy *(Clint Eastwood) has to deal with modern technology when he briefly becomes a train robber.* Top: *Robert Redford as* The Electric Horseman.

have increasing difficulty in making their presence felt to people busying themselves with the growth of community. And both stage superb gunfights, which are striking precisely because so little notice is taken of them; the townsfolk are too preoccupied to pay much attention to such outmoded confrontations.

The more sceptical and ironical attitude to heroism was probably a response to the infection of cynicism derived from the political traumas of the decade. The influence of the Watergate scandal could be felt in a Western such as *Posse* (1975), with Kirk Douglas directing and starring in a sharp little tale about a ruthlessly opportunistic marshal with political ambitions and a mastery of the publicity machine, who is eventually abandoned by supporters ever more unscrupulous than he is. Vietnam's ghostly and disturbing shadow hung over a number of films. Ralph Nelson's *Soldier Blue* and Arthur Penn's *Little Big Man* (both 1970) both re-create the massacre of Indian villages by the US Cavalry as an analogue to the My Lai massacre.

Indeed, the Vietnam experience might explain why so

Country songs were heard on the soundtracks of films as different as *Bonnie and Clyde* (1967), *Five Easy Pieces* (1970), *The Last Picture Show* (1971) and *Deliverance* (1972); country songs were turned into such successful movies as *Ode to Billy Joe* (1976), *Convoy* and *Harper Valley PTA* (1978); and movie stars with country orientation and country music in their films moved to the top of the popularity polls, most notably Burt Reynolds and Clint Eastwood. By 1980, country music was the most popular form of music in the USA after rock and had become part of the movie mainstream. In 1981, the Best Actress Academy Award went to Sissy Spacek for her impersonation of country singer Loretta Lynn in the box-office hit *Coal Miner's Daughter* (1980).

Country-music films had, however, been around since the beginning of sound, made by small studios. Then a song ('Do not Forsake Me') sung by a country singer, Tex Ritter, won the Academy Award as the Best Film Song of the year in *High Noon* (1952). The success of the film, and of the song, helped to restore the popularity of theme-songs in movies; and country music slowly began to move away from the B-picture studios towards the big time. It took a while, and the main breakthrough did not come until the Seventies, when with the prevalent Seventies demythologizing of the Western, a new character stepped up to fill the cowboy's vacant boots – the country-and-western hero. Hard-drinking, hard-driving, with a song in his heart and a fiercely independent moral code not far removed from that of the old-style Western hero – the trucker and 'honkytonk angel' began to create new myths from America's vast, wide open spaces.

These films drew on a neglected source of acting talent – the stars of the capital of country music, Nashville. The singers Johnny Cash, Kris Kristofferson, Willie Nelson and Dolly Parton thus became sought-after by Hollywood producers. The archetypal country-and-western movie was Sam Peckinpah's *Convoy* (1976), the film version of a hit song. It cast Kristofferson as the leader of a bunch of tough truckers who defy the petty forces of 'law and order'.

Country-music related films provided very profitable vehicles for top stars Burt Reynolds and Clint Eastwood, many of whose films had country-and-western soundtracks. Reynolds starred in John G. Avildsen's *W.W. and the Dixie Dancekings* (1975), about a con-man who turns a no-talent group into Grande Ole Opry stars, which also featured country singers Don Williams and Jerry Reed. Eastwood starred in *Every Which Way But Loose* (1978) as a fighting trucker whose best friend is an orang-utan and whose best girl is a country singer. Its success gave rise to a sequel, *Any Which Way You Can* (1980). The comparatively effete John Travolta donned a check shirt and stetson for *Urban Cowboy* (1980), a *Saturday Night Fever* for country-rock fans.

Some of the best country films had little in the way of star value but a good deal of hard-edged plot. Particularly notable were Daryl Duke's *Payday* (1973), with Rip Torn portraying an ageing country star still trying to make the big time and Gus Trikonis' *Nashville Girl* (1976), made for Roger Corman and starring Monica Gayle as a teenage girl trying to break into the Nashville music world, even at the price of her own self-respect.

In the Eighties, the public's enthusiasm for country-and-westerns began to fade – even Clint Eastwood's charisma could not make *Honkytonk Man* (1982) a success. The music, however, continued to feature regularly on soundtracks whenever a genuine, down-home, 'American' flavour was required by the story and setting.

Top to bottom: country star Barbara Jean (Ronee Blakely) about to break down on stage in Altman's Nashville; *the unknown Loretta Lynn (Sissy Spacek) is introduced to the fans by real-life singer Ernest Tubb in Michael Apted's* Coal Miner's Daughter; *Clint Eastwood as an ailing country singer in* Honky Tonk Man.

Sci-fi, Fantasy and Horror

A major feature of Seventies' cinema was the extraordinary popularity and creativity of its science-fiction and horror films. During the decade, these previously minor genres gained a new vigour and a firm standing at the box-office. *Jaws* (1975) and then *Star Wars* (1977) became the biggest commercial successes the industry had known, according to *Variety*'s 1979 listing.

The major screen manifestation of science fiction in the Sixties had been such impressive television shows as *Dr Who* (1963 onwards), *The Outer Limits* (1963–5) and *Star Trek* (1966–9), to which *Star Trek – The Motion Picture* (1979) was a late follow-up. In the cinema, the genre was not as prolific, although this decade saw the rise of the big-budget treatment of science fiction which was one of the characteristics of the Seventies strain. *The Time Machine* (1960), *Robinson Crusoe on Mars* (1964) and *Fantastic Voyage* (1966) all boasted impressive visuals, although the real precursor of the Seventies' high-technology sheen was Stanley Kubrick's *2001: A Space Odyssey* (1968).

The superproduction aesthetic really arrived with George Lucas' *Star Wars* and *The Empire Strikes Back* (1980, produced by Lucas but directed by Irvin Kershner) and Steven Spielberg's *Close Encounters of the Third Kind* (1977) – ravishing audio-visual experiences which demonstrate the spectacle, power and excitement of high technology.

Star Wars itself spawned a series of derivatives, which sometimes even included cute pet robots. The most obvious is *Battlestar Galactica* (1978), based upon the pilot episode of the television series about the survivors of a doomed planet in search of a new home; but this totally lacks the imagination of its model. *L'Umanoide* (1979, *The Humanoid*), a 'spaghetti' science-fiction film, also flatters by imitation but fails to impress. The only real contender is the underrated Disney production *The Black Hole* (1979). This is almost a remake of *20,000 Leagues Under the Sea* (1954) set in space, with Maximilian Schell playing the mad scientist intent on pushing his knowledge to the very limits.

Star Wars and *Close Encounters of the Third Kind* express a naive faith in space, almost as a new and exciting West to be opened up and explored, which is not necessarily shared by all science-fiction productions. *Alien* (1979) has similar production values, with stunning photography by Derek Vanlint and genuinely other-worldly designs by H.R. Giger, but it fascinatingly tries to combine the cool, abstract manner of Kubrick with the Fifties monster movie – having much the same story as *It! The Terror From Beyond Space* (1958). *Alien* is a menacing, brooding film, with fear and paranoia rife as a virtually indestructible life-form stalks the corridors of a spaceship eating its way through the crew one by one. The heroine (Sigourney Weaver) stands up to this image of male sexual aggression, just as she withstands an attack from a male member of the crew, and comes through as the only survivor in a genre where men usually reign supreme.

Male fantasies are also the subject of two more superproductions, *Superman, The Movie* (1978) and *Flash Gordon* (1980). Both filter the original comic-strip images, and also those drawn from earlier films, through a knowing Seventies sensibility to achieve a finely balanced ironic distance from the material. *Superman, The Movie* is particularly successful because of its range of feelings, from the outrageously comic to a spectacular love scene in the skies over New York City. *Flash Gordon* celebrates the artifice of the original Buster Crabbe series, and along the way exposes the fallacy that only women, and never men, are supposed to be ornamental in films.

Loosely connected to the social-catastrophe element of science fiction (the havoc wrought by falling meteors, marauding monsters, dangerous chemical contamination or atomic blasts), and growing to fill the vacuum left by the passing of the spectacular epic, the disaster movie claimed its share of the box-office in the Seventies. The disaster movie imagines the breakdown of social order and then dusts off old movie stars for their iconographic significance as heroic saviour figures.

At the conclusion of these films, all the marital and romantic problems that have been set out are resolved and old values are restored. The disaster movie may well have been an older generation's way of rejecting life as it developed in the allegedly 'cynical' Seventies and finding solace in the male screen heroism of Richard Harris in *Juggernaut*, Charlton Heston in *Airport 1975* and *Earthquake* (all three 1974), George C. Scott in *The Hindenburg* and Lorne Greene in *Tidal Wave* (both 1975), Rock Hudson in *Avalanche* (1978) and Sean Connery in *Meteor* (1979). But the genre cannot be too easily dismissed. *The Poseidon Adventure* (1972) depicts a world of order so dizzily inverted that the whole film takes place within a liner turned upside down. *The Towering Inferno* (1974), deservedly the most popular film of this type, holds together its various centres of interest with great skill and manages to make the consuming flames profoundly disturbing as they destroy an enormous new skyscraper.

For the variety of themes it tackles and the directorial talent it has attracted, the horror film is certainly one of the most interesting areas of Seventies cinema. As the critic Robin Wood has pointed out:

'It is a commonplace that the (ostensibly) celebratory family film disappeared from the American cinema in the Fifties. What happened was that its implicit content became displaced into the horror film. What is enacted symbolically in *Meet Me in St Louis* (1944) is "realized" in *Night of the Living Dead* (1968).'

In Vincente Minnelli's 1944 film, the child Tootie symbolically destroys her family through attacking a group of snowmen; in George Romero's later film, a daughter kills and then tries to eat her mother. One more late-Sixties film to suggest that the horror derives from within the family was Roman Polanski's *Rosemary's Baby* (1968), in which Rosemary (Mia Farrow) actually gives birth to the Antichrist.

With this trend proceeding into the Seventies, there developed some deeply disturbing visions of values in transition, of growing doubts about the sanctity of the nuclear family and its role in society. Children themselves, traditionally symbols of innocence, and young people are seen as monstrous progeny in *Dead of Night* (1972), *The Exorcist* (1973) and *Exorcist II: The Heretic* (1977), *It's Alive* (1974) and *It Lives Again* (1978), *The Omen* (1976) and *Damien – Omen II* (1978), *Carrie* (1976), *Martin* (1977), *The Fury* (1978) and *The Brood* (1979). The family itself is the collective monster in such films as *Frightmare* (1974) and *The Hills Have Eyes* (1977); and the home becomes the deadliest of traps in *Burnt Offerings* (1976) and *Full Circle* (1977).

The new film-student generation of film-makers seems to have been particularly attracted to fantasy forms. The result has been innovation and exploration, but also a notable amount of homage to the cinematic past. Understandably, Hitchcock is the key influence, both in his identification mechanisms and in the various suspense techniques. The

Above: Christopher Reeve on the wing (thanks to British special effects artists) in Superman, the Movie. *Top: one of the many strange creatures of* Star Wars.

Above: Dennis Weaver overtakes a Juggernaut to his cost in Spielberg's Duel. *Top: Sissy Spacek as the vengeful, telekinetic heroine of De Palma's* Carrie.

most stylistically self-conscious and successful of the new directors are Brian De Palma, Steven Spielberg and John Carpenter.

Brian De Palma (b. 1940) began directing films while studying at Columbia University, and made his first feature, *The Wedding Party* (1967), while a post-graduate at Sarah Lawrence College. His career began to gather impetus when he formed a partnership with producer Charles Hirsch. Their first collaboration, *Greetings* (1968), which followed three young men through a late-Sixties, urban obstacle course of draft dodging, computer dating, pornography and political conspiracy, was an unexpected commercial success. His next films, *Dionysus in '69* and *Hi, Mom!* (both 1970), revealed a film-maker much influenced by the directors of the French *nouvelle vague* and, like them, acutely aware of the way film-making techniques manipulate an audience's responses.

De Palma's subsequent work tended to exploit his earlier insights by applying them to the most 'manipulative' genre of all, that of the horror and suspense film. Fittingly the

dominant influence on his work changed from Jean-Luc Godard to Alfred Hitchcock.

Sisters (1972), the story of murders committed by the survivor of a pair of Siamese twins, contained echoes of Hitchcock's *Rear Window* (1954) and *Psycho* (1960), though the film's black humour has an added modern viciousness. Following a lurid, comic-strip parody of the rock world, *Phantom of the Paradise*, De Palma scored his first major international hit with the horror movie *Carrie*, about a repressed schoolgirl (brilliantly played by Sissy Spacek), who uses her telekinetic powers to wreak vengeance on her bullying schoolmates. *Dressed to Kill* (1980), a controversial *hommage* to *Psycho*, concerning a trans-sexual murderer (Michael Caine) who wears female clothes and slaughters women with a cut-throat razor, also proved popular with the public. However the film's tricksiness and apparent misogyny provoked many critics to lament the deterioration of one of American cinema's most promising talents.

De Palma redeemed himself critically with *Blow Out* (1981), an intriguing updating of Antonioni's *Blow-Up* (1966), characterized by his customary panache and technical mastery. However a bloodthirsty gangster film, *Scarface* (1983), once more laid the director open to charges of cynicism and gratuitous violence.

Steven Spielberg (b. 1947), the supreme popular entertainer of modern cinema, was a movie addict from early childhood and completed two amateur films while still in his teens. After a cinema course at California State College he made *Amblin'* (1969), a prize-winning short that led – at the age of 22 – to his being hired by Universal to direct television movies. In 1971 he directed the tele-feature *Duel*, which was released theatrically in Britain and Europe, thereby establishing his critical reputation.

A mixture of 'road' movie, supernatural tale and paranoid fantasy scripted by sci-fi author Richard Matheson, *Duel* coolly visualizes the travails of an American salesman (Dennis Weaver) whose car is pursued with increasingly murderous intent by a huge truck, the driver of which the audience never sees. Spielberg's direction showed him in absolute control of his material.

With *The Sugarland Express* (1974), his first movie for the cinema, Spielberg moved closer to the picaresque 'road' format then dominating the American cinema. The story derived from an actual incident in Texas, in which – with ultimately disastrous results – a young woman broke her husband out of jail in the hope of forestalling the adoption of their baby. The picture begins on a note of near-farce, and the casting of Goldie Hawn helps to lull the audience into expecting a screwball comedy. Gradually, however, the mood changes as the runaway couple and their lawman hostage push on across country, becoming figures of Bonnie and Clyde-type notoriety.

After working for producers Richard D. Zanuck and David Brown on *The Sugarland Express*, Spielberg continued the association for his next feature. On the face of it, *Jaws* was a routine project, but the film made commercial history; within a few weeks of its US release it had become the biggest grosser of any movie up until that time.

Based on Peter Benchley's best-selling novel, this story of a shark wreaking havoc at an American seaside resort cleverly blended Fifties sci-fi, such as *The Beast From the Ocean Floor* (1954), with the Seventies disaster film, while the climax neatly updated *Moby Dick*. Additional factors in its success were a pulsating score by John Williams and a cleverly mounted publicity campaign (subsequently much imitated and parodied): 'Just when you thought it was safe to go back into the water . . .'

The runaway success of *Jaws* conferred upon Spielberg pre-eminent status in the industry. His next movie, *Close Encounters of the Third Kind*, was his own conception from the very beginning – a grandiose ($21 million), flawed but fascinating attempt to transmute a mystery story about UFOs into a mystic vision of universal brotherhood. It, too, was a gigantic commercial success.

Spielberg then attempted an elaborate and largely unfunny crazy comedy about a rumoured Japanese invasion of California in the wake of Pearl Harbor, *1941* (1979). It was a costly failure, but Spielberg immediately bounced back with yet another blockbuster, *Raiders of the Lost Ark* (1981). This brilliantly revamped Thirties and Forties adventure serials with hair-raising chases and escapes a-plenty, and gave rise to a follow up, *Indiana Jones and the Temple of Doom* (1983).

However Spielberg's supreme commercial triumph of this period was his sci-fi fantasy 'for children of all ages', *E.T. the Extra-Terrestrial* (1982). By January 1983 this story of a little boy's relationship with a disarming visitor from another world had overtaken *Star Wars* (1977) as the most successful film ever made. In 1984 there were few signs that Spielberg's golden touch had deserted him with *Gremlins* (co-produced by him but directed by Joe Dante), another sci-fi fantasy rooted in everyday reality, though the film failed to match *E.T.*'s gentle but acutely observed comedy.

John Carpenter (b. 1948) won the 1970 Oscar for best live-action short with *The Resurrection of Bronco Billy*, made while a student at the University of Southern California. He was thus able to raise the finance to extend his first feature, *Dark Star* (1974), from 16 mm to 35 mm. A cult favourite, the film cleverly dismantled and debunked the machinery and pretensions of films like Stanley Kubrick's *2001: A Space Odyssey*.

Two horror thrillers made Carpenter one of the most popular and influential directors of the Seventies – *Assault on Precinct 13* (1976) and *Halloween* (1978). The first remains Carpenter's best film, brilliantly redeploying the styles and conventions of Westerns such as *Rio Bravo* (1959) and *The Alamo* (1960) in a remorselessly modern setting, as a group of assorted characters, holed up in an abandoned police station in downtown Los Angeles, battle for their lives against hordes of urban terrorists. Even more successful commercially was *Halloween* (which made a star of Jamie Lee Curtis), about an apparently indestructible psychopath with a particularly twisted sense of humour wreaking havoc in suburbia. This regrettably spawned an innumerable series of far less skilful films in which youngsters (mostly female) were terrorized and slaughtered by male perverts.

Carpenter's work has since stayed closer to his B-movie roots – the monsters in *The Fog* (1980) and *The Thing* (1982) being reassuringly supernatural rather than disturbingly human. Unfortunately, though films like these and *Escape to New York* (1981) – set in a gangland of the future – are entertaining enough, they lack the crucial punch and wit of his mid-Seventies successes.

Carpenter is one of several newer directors whose movies have been made at a fraction of the cost of the average Seventies Hollywood product. His films still look quite polished, though, compared to the small-budget productions of such directors as David Cronenberg, Larry Cohen and George Romero. The least interesting of these three directors is Canadian David Cronenberg, whose *The Parasite Murders* (1975, released in Britain as *Shivers*), *Rabid* (1977) and *The Brood* reveal beneath their squalid nastiness an immature attitude towards sexuality and a misogynistic tendency as pronounced as Brian De Palma's.

Larry Cohen and George Romero, on the other hand, make horror films which suggest progressive political attitudes. Cohen's *It's Alive* and *It Lives Again* manipulate images of the home with a creepy accuracy as they relate the stories of mutant babies on the rampage. *Demon* (1976) has been criticized as muddled on the level of sexual politics because of its treatment of the dual-sexed villain; but it ingeniously combines detective movie, science fiction and horror to attack the repressiveness of organized religion.

Romero's brand of political horror is demonstrated by such films as *The Crazies* (1973), about a small rural community fighting back in reaction to being accidentally contaminated with a germ-warfare bug, and *Dawn of the Dead* (1979, released in Britain as *Zombies*), a grim parody of consumerism involving a small group trapped within a huge hypermarket

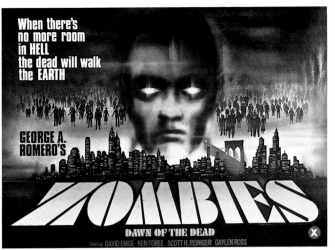

Below: Roy (Richard Drey-fuss) is welcomed aboard the spaceship in Close Encounters of the Third Kind. *Bottom: Harrison Ford in* Raiders of the Lost Ark, *which looked back to the action films of bygone days.*

Above: the murderer exhibits a gruesome sense of humour by dressing up as the ghost of one of his victims as he prepares to claim another in Carpenter's Halloween. *Top: the monstrous Shark attacks in Spielberg's* Jaws. *Top right: Romero's* Zombies *was a terrifying view of modern conformist consumer society. Above right: Henry (John Nance) is decapitated in Lynch's* Eraserhead. *Right: Frederick Treves (Anthony Hopkins) reveals the hideously malformed Merrick to fellow doctors in* The Elephant Man. *Below right: loveable alien meets cute earthling in* E.T. the Extra-Terrestrial.

by hordes of flesh-eating zombies. The black sense of humour running through these films surfaces most distinctly in *Martin*, a vampire film that merely *refers* to the genre conventions as it concentrates upon the theme of sexual repression. Its use of a depressing contemporary suburban location to create atmosphere and its poetic conciseness in exploring Martin's pathological disturbance make it one of the finest films of the Seventies in any genre.

Similar claims can be made for *Eraserhead* (1977), the debut feature of David Lynch (b. 1946), a hissing, clanking, surreal nightmare of a film about a strange man, his fantasies and his howling mutant child. Lynch next scored an international hit with a true-life story, *The Elephant Man* (1980), starring John Hurt as the hideously malformed John Merrick and Anthony Hopkins as the sympathetic surgeon Frederick Treves. These successes prompted Lynch to move into the dangerous waters of the big-budget film with *Dune* (1984).

In Seventies sci-fi, the director was by no means the only effective creator of such films as *Battlestar Galactica*, *Star Wars*, *Close Encounters of the Third Kind*, *Star Trek* and *Alien*. With new techniques in minature photography, computer-linked cameras and automatic systems of mattes, special-effects teams led by such talented people as John Dykstra, Douglas Trumbull and Carlo Rambaldi provided the highly believable physical embodiment of the writers' visions. These manufactured dreams are heady indeed, and their formidable nature seems very much to be the implicit subject of *Star Wars*, *The Empire Strikes Back* and the last forty-five minutes of *Close Encounters of the Third Kind*. The former pair reduce the rich philosophical possibilites of science fiction to a galactic pinball game; and *Close Encounters of the Third Kind*, despite throwing up ideas on the urban nightmare, is ultimately dependent upon its thunderous conclusion, where the dumbstruck extras stand in for the audience's quasi-mystical experience in watching the film.

Two directors especially linked with science fiction in the Seventies were George Lucas and Michael Crichton. Lucas (b. 1945), despite his later epics, will perhaps be most kindly remembered for his feature *THX 1138* (1970). Its abstract images of white chambers and shaved heads, in a futuristic world that denies love or personal identity, reveal a really inventive use of cinema and the genre. Crichton (b. 1942) originally a medical doctor and a novelist, has singlemindedly pursued the theme of dehumanization by technology. He wrote the novels upon which are based the excellent *The Andromeda Strain* (1971) and *The Terminal Man* (1974), and he scripted and directed both *Westworld* and *Coma* (1978). *Westworld* remains his masterpiece, a highly inventive vision of an eerie adult Disney World.

Outside the USA and Canada, fantasy was well represented, although on a smaller scale. From Italy, for example, Dario Argento came out with *Suspiria* (1977), a stylish horror film about demonism in a music college which plays on genre conventions and suspense mechanisms in a fascinating way. Roman Polanski's French movie *Le Locataire* (1976, *The Tenant*) is a horrific tale of loneliness and the bizarre illusions that can lurk beneath deadpan urban existence. Australian director Peter Weir's *The Cars That Ate Paris* (1974) is a consumer fantasy about a community that survives by crashing strangers' cars and then cannibalizing the wreckage. The Russian Andrei Tarkovksy's coolly abstract and metaphysical *Solaris* (1972) portrays an alien planet's ability to manifest visitors' unconscious desires. There is an electric atmosphere generated by some images, but as the critic David

Thomson has commented: 'An episode of *Star Trek* explored this theme with more wit and inegenuity, less sentimentality and a third the length.'

It was an error for Tarkovsky to have attempted to follow *2001*, a cinematic cul-de-sac, especially with a less dramatic use of decor and technology. Kubrick's film may have given fantasy a new respectability; but the way ahead paradoxically proved to be in the backward glance, sometimes with great self-consciousness, at the styles and iconography of an earlier Hollywood – yesterday's dreams and nightmares reassessed in the light of troubled Seventies and Eighties.

Vietnam and Hollywood

The war in Vietnam created in the United States a national trauma unparalleled since the Civil War, and its after-effects may prove to be every bit as enduring in the American consciousness. It was a war fought not only with guns and napalm in South-east Asia, but with placards and truncheons on campuses and streets in large cities throughout the western world. It became the largest, most crucial issue of a generation – virtually taking over such related matters as black protest and the youth-drug subculture – but Hollywood was afraid to deal directly with it, even on a simple level.

Hollywood has traditionally done its best to avoid contemporary politics and especially political controversy, largely for commercial reasons. There is always the danger that a shift in public opinion, or interest, between the time of a film's production and its release date may render a film with a 'timely' subject unmarketable and few producers are ever willing to take such a risk. The profound divisions created by the Vietnam War in American life were too wide to be commercially exploitable – at least while America remained actively involved. Any treatment of the issue was bound to exclude or alienate too large a section of the potential audience.

This happened with *The Green Berets* (1968), co-directed by and starring John Wayne – the only large-scale, simple-minded war film about Vietnam financed by a major Hollywood company. If any major lesson can be extracted from *The Green Berets*, it is that the mythical, heroic archetypes of American soldiers promulgated by Wayne and others during World War II and Korea were no longer as viable or believable for late Sixties audiences.

At the same time, the subject of Vietnam, while seldom confronted directly elsewhere and most often relegated to the background, represented an important undercurrent in many films made during the period. It soon became an inseparable part of the conflicts and considerations that were being dealt with in most youth films. The cultural and generational conflicts of *The Graduate*, *Easy Rider* and *Alice's Restaurant* (1969), the campus revolts of *Getting Straight* and *The Strawberry Statement*, the heightened visions of utopia in *Woodstock* and of apocalypse in *Zabriskie Point* (1970), had reference to, and association with, the war. Even an artist as seemingly apolitical as Ingmar Bergman could scarcely avoid making a comment on the war in a film such as *Persona* (1966), when he showed Elisabeth Vogler (Liv Ullmann) watching the self-immolation of a Buddhist monk in South Vietnam on television, and recoiling in agony – in effect, invaded by the deepest suffering in the modern world.

The fact that American viewers could watch the Vietnam War every day on television tended to blunt its impact – a telling aspect of a movie about private domestic violence such as *Petulia* (1968), where the war is perpetually visible on

Above far left: Elliott Gould as Trapper John, Donald Sutherland as Hawkeye in M*A*S*H.

Above left: The Deer Hunter's *metaphor for war. Above: Kurtz' army in* Apocalypse Now.

Above: Jon Voight as a disabled war veteran and Jane Fonda as the nurse who falls in love with him in Coming Home.

Above: Harvey Keitel as the pimp of a child prostitute, Robert De Niro as her self-appointed protector in Taxi Driver.

diverse television screens, yet remains rigorously unmentioned and undiscussed by the characters. The notion of an *uncontainable* horror eventually produced absurdist, black-humour treatments of modern warfare that conveniently concerned themselves with earlier wars, such as World War II in *Catch-22* and Korea in *M*A*S*H* (1970).

Still another way of approaching the subject obliquely was through the historical allegory provided by the Western. Within these terms, the meditative, slow-motion look at the massive slaughters in *The Wild Bunch* and the tortured examination of the mutual barbarism of Apaches and whites in *Ulzana's Raid* (1972) could both address themselves to the war's wider issues and emotional conflicts.

In all these instances, a certain ambiguity in the film-makers' approaches allowed them to address hawks and doves alike. But it was not until the late Seventies that the subject of Vietnam was finally tackled head-on — after a fashion — by the film industry.

Perhaps by the Nineties a sufficient time gap will have elapsed to allow film-makers to approach the subject of Vietnam in a more detached, balanced and analytical manner. In the meantime, *The Deer Hunter* (1978) and *Apocalypse Now* (1979) both fall into an unavoidable trap. They offer mythical and metaphysical meanings about the war which seem inevitably tailored to the short-term psychic needs of an American or American-influenced audience — namely, the desire to locate the horror of the war within a *containable* image of externalized evil rather than to look at it as the consequence and function of internal ideological processes. As the American journalist Deirdre English succinctly puts it, each film 'takes a fabricated act of Vietnamese terror' – the ultra-sadistic Russian roulette game of *The Deer Hunter*, the hacking off of inoculated childrens' arms in *Apocalypse Now* – 'and elevates it to become the central metaphor of the war'.

In fact, the evasions about Vietnam in the two films work within very different contexts, though the end results may be similar in some ways. For one thing, *The Deer Hunter* operates within a mythic system in which 'the war' is merely an episode, though a crucial one, in a larger structure encompassing the lives of several men – a sort of trial by fire which destroys or seriously marks all of them, but which is given little or no independent significance. In other words, the mere fact that the war functions dramatically as something external to the characters played by Robert De Niro and Christopher Walken – something that happens *to* them rather than because of them, or with their complicity – ensures that the Vietnamese Communist torturers absorb the metaphysical weight of impersonal evil that they are structured to embody.

Despite the childlike naivety of the film-makers and the characters alike, many liberal American critics defended the film on the basis that it was myopic to assume that the Vietnamese Communists did not commit atrocities along with the Americans. At the same time, this naivety allowed the film to function dramatically in old-fashioned terms, with some of the mythic resonance of a John Ford Western – succeeding precisely where *The Green Berets* had failed, because the dramatic needs (which included a feeling for small-town, communal ties) appeared to structure this view of the war rather than the other way round.

In the case of *Apocalypse Now*, the ideological cast seems at once more conscious and more deceptive. Designed and assembled more as an environmental entertainment complex – a 'trip' in every sense of the word – than as a unified drama, the film manages to incorporate a surprising number of mythical and metaphorical ideas to support several positions regarding the war, some of them quite opposed to one another. It can be said without exaggeration that hawks, doves and those in between can all find their beliefs confirmed in the film. This indeed seems reflected in the haphazard manner in which the film was constructed, with John Milius' fanciful right-wing adaptation of Joseph Conrad's anti-colonialist novel *Heart of Darkness* complicated, in turn, by Francis Ford Coppola's preoccupations with megalomania and Michael Herr's cynical narration, some of it virtually adapted from his memorable book *Dispatches*, which mixed personal combat reporting with a sort of lyrical, liberal-humanist rock poetry.

In 1973 the war ended, the soldiers came home and in 1974 Nixon resigned from office in disgrace. More than one commentator had suggested that the Watergate scandal provided Americans with a scapegoat for the traumas occasioned by the American involvement in Vietnam. The sense of national shame was somewhat alleviated in 1976 by the bicentennial celebrations. But though the war was over, the national traumas it had occasioned continued to surface, treated with varying degrees of honesty and directness, in American movies.

Hollywood's New Generation

The Seventies ushered in a new generation of American film-makers – including Martin Scorsese, Steven Spielberg, Francis Ford Coppola and Peter Bogdanovich – who became known as the 'movie brats' because of their comparative youth and because most had learned about film in film school or university rather than by working their way up in the studio system of old Hollywood. Some of these directors were to make, quite early in their careers, films of huge, even unprecedented, commercial success – Coppola's *The Godfather* (1972), Spielberg's *Jaws* and Scorsese's *Taxi Driver*. But what united them more particularly was their indebtedness to the cinema's past, both in terms of using well-established genre material and of alluding directly or indirectly to old movies.

Francis Ford Coppola (b. 1939) began his film-making career in typical 'movie brat' style. After obtaining a degree in theatre arts he studied at the UCLA film school and obtained a job with the producer-director Roger Corman, who part-financed Coppola's first feature, *Dementia 13* (1963). Coppola then worked as a screenwriter for the Seven Arts Company before resuming his directorial career with a wacky, Dick Lester-style comedy, *You're a Big Boy Now* (1966), the unsuccessful musical *Finian's Rainbow*, starring Fred Astaire, and an offbeat drama about loneliness and insecurity, *The Rain People* (1969).

Eager to obtain greater artistic control over his work, Coppola set up a studio, American Zoetrope, in San Francisco with director George Lucas (for whom Coppola produced *American Graffiti* in 1973). The idea of independently producing low-budget features by young directors, exploiting technological developments and escaping not only the unions (more powerful in Los Angeles) but also what Coppola called 'the management breed . . . packages and deals' seemed fine. But Coppola's hustling streak backfired and Warner Brothers, whom he had persuaded to back Zoetrope, so disliked its first feature, Lucas' *THX 1138*, that they instantly withdrew their support. As a result, Zoetrope collapsed.

An Academy Award for co-scripting *Patton* (1970) rescued Coppola's career; despite his patchy record as a director Paramount then hired him to direct *The Godfather*, which won a Best Picture Oscar. *The Conversation*, a superb, low-key thriller about an alienated surveillance expert (Gene Hackman) who becomes involved in a murder plot and the multi-Oscar-winning *The Godfather Part II* (both 1974) briefly established Coppola as the supreme creative force in Hollywood.

He purchased, a theatre, a radio station and San Francisco's *City* magazine. He also bought new production premises and a large share in a distribution company. Most important of all, he resurrected *Apocalypse Now*, a project started by John Milius in 1969. Coppola has stated that his intention was to create 'a film experience that would give its audience a sense of the horror, the madness, the sensuousness and the moral dilemma of the Vietnam War'. The film succeeds most powerfully in the area of sensuousness. For better or for worse, *Apocalypse Now* displays the foul beauty of war, its epic chaos.

Since *Apocalypse Now*, Coppola has become involved in all kinds of activities, ranging from the distribution of Godard's *Sauve Qui Peut (la Vie)* (1980, *Slow Motion*) to the roadshow presentation of Abel Gance's *Napoleon* (1927); the financing of Wim Wenders' *Hammett* (1982) and the temporary rebirth of Zoetrope with the purchase of Hollywood General Studios. However, the crushing failure of his costly romance, *One From the Heart* (1981), came perilously close to putting Coppola out of business. With the lukewarm response accorded *The Outsiders* and *Rumble Fish* (both 1983),

Coppola's plans and pretensions were beginning to seem, like the would-be mogul himself, somewhat anachronistic. His $48 million opus, *The Cotton Club* (1984), seemed unlikely to recover more than a fraction of its cost in the domestic market. Yet its ambitious attempt to combine the musical and the gangster film at least deserved respect.

Martin Scorsese (b. 1942) grew up in New York's Little Italy and the atmosphere of the Lower East Side, and the concerns of its Catholic community – caught between the Mafia and the church – were reflected in his first successful feature, *Mean Streets* (1973). For all its personal concerns and social insights, *Mean Streets* was very much a genre film, drawing on a Hollywood tradition that dates back to movies such as *Angels With Dirty Faces* (1938).

Similarly, Scorsese's next film, *Alice Doesn't Live Here Any More* (1974) – the story of a widow's search for happiness on a trip across America, during which she vacillates between the dream of a career and 'true love' – was clearly related to the sentimental melodramas of Douglas Sirk or Capra, yet interpreted their conventions afresh for a modern audience.

New York City became not only the setting but a major character in *Taxi Driver*, which won the Golden Palm at Cannes and secured Scorsese's reputation as one of the most talented directors of the new American cinema. Given the film's violent modernity and the contemporary relevance of its story of a newly-returned Vietnam veteran's disgust at squalid city corruption, it was surprising to find Scorsese turning to the musical biopics of the Forties and Fifties for inspiration for his musical drama *New York, New York*. This juxtaposed nostalgia for the time when jazz was king with disturbing emotional realism – in particular applied to the central relationship between a musician (Robert De Niro) and a singer (Liza Minnelli).

The Last Waltz, a semi-documentary about The Band, was also a genre film – the concert movie with interviews. In this film the rock music that Scorsese had used so sensitively in his other films, not only to underscore period but to comment on his characters' emotional states and point to ways that popular culture shapes personaltiy, took centre stage. Scorsese's own feeling for the music and respect for the musicians involved in its making lifted *The Last Waltz* above most other rock films. Like *New York, New York*, the film both celebrated and lamented the passing of a musical and cultural era.

In the Eighties, when most of his American contemporaries seemed only concerned with crowd-pleasing sentimentality and escapism, Scorsese began to mix and merge genres to particularly unsettling and stimulating effect. His *Raging Bull*

Above: surveillance expert Harry Caul (Gene Hackman) believes he has been bugged in The Conversation. *Top: Michael Corleone (Al Pacino) seeks the advice of* The Godfather *(Marlon Brando).*

Above: Liza Minnelli and Robert De Niro in New York, New York. *Top: Scorsese's vivid story of small time gangsters,* Mean Streets, *was set in New York's Little Italy but shot in LA.*

(1980) blended the boxing biopic, family melodrama and *film noir* with such sophistication that it could not be said to belong to any genre. The film showed a deepening of Scorsese's favourite concerns, which revolve around his (usually Catholic) sexually insecure male characters' struggles towards status and power. Proving his masculinity by soaking up tremendous punishment in the ring, boxer Jake La Motta (De Niro) counterpunches his way to the championship, but finds it impossible to maintain a loving relationship with a woman, either hopelessly idealizing her or exploding into psychotic jealousy.

A similar complexity and sophistication was evident in Scorsese's masterful satire *The King of Comedy* (1982), in which an unscrupulous, would-be comedian, Rupert Pupkin (De Niro), eventually achieves his desired television celebrity by kidnapping an established star, Jerry Langford (Jerry Lewis). As in *Taxi Driver*, violence is shown to be the only route the 'little man' who seeks to make an impression in Western urban society can take. Scorsese's mature understanding of the viciousness and nastiness, as much as the excitement, glamour and poetry, of modern America makes him one of the USA's most stimulating film-makers. He has been particularly fortunate in having at his disposal a leading man (Robert De Niro) of remarkable versatility.

The first four films of **Peter Bogdanovich** (b. 1939) – *Targets* (1967), *The Last Picture Show* (1971), *What's Up, Doc?* (1972) and *Paper Moon* (1973) – were the work of a man who knew and loved the history of the cinema, and who relished the opportunity of paying tribute to such as Boris Karloff and cheap horror, Forties' black-and-white, screwball comedy, John Ford, Will Rogers and Thirties' child-stars. But the real authority of Bogdanovich's debut was that his celebrations of those earlier styles were always used to enhance his portraits of people and their problems.

With *Targets*, he showed himself so full of wit and invention that he could turn to his own advantage a Roger Corman horror-quickie by making it part of a very original thriller about the film's ageing star, Boris Karloff.

The Last Picture Show is Bogdanovich's best film. Taken from a Larry McMurtry novel, it creates a rural Texan community with the assurance and affection of Jean Renoir's Thirties' French landscapes. With nostalgia for awakening teenage sexuality, it tells the story of several young people who feel trapped in their home-town and are saddened by the closure of the local picture-house.

Another elaborate extension of his skill was the screwball comedy *What's Up, Doc?* about a madcap girl (Barbra Streisand) trying to seduce a musicologist (Ryan O'Neal).

Bogdanovich's career then began to falter, and his films – *Daisy Miller* (1974), *At Long Last Love* (1975) and *Nickolodeon* (1976) – seem smug and slapdash.

After a three-year absence, however, he revived his reputation with a skilled film version of Paul Theroux's *Saint Jack* (1979), about the expatriate American owner of a luxury brothel in Singapore. But the romantic New York comedy *They All Laughed* (1981) achieved only a video release in Britain. *Mask* (1985), however, was a convincing portrait of the relationship between a deformed teenager and his unconventional mother.

The film-maker who has played the genre game to most consistently rewarding effect must, however, be **John Milius** (b. 1944). Milius first won notice by writing two notable studies in old-time individualism, Sydney Pollack's *Jeremiah Johnson* and John Huston's *The Life and Times of Judge Roy Bean*. When Milius, besides writing, also took over the director's chair, the result was the quirkily brilliant *Dillinger* (1973), an account of the Depression-era bankrobber's career couched in terms of a latter-day folk-tale.

Its successor was *The Wind and the Lion* (1975). More ambitious but equally exciting, this film – dramatizing a curious incident of 1904 involving American gunboat diplomacy in Morocco – confirmed Milius' delight in tales of derring-do and in the odd byways of history, as well as his confident skill in staging action sequences. The casting of John Huston in a cameo role set an appropriate seal on the movie's lineage. When Milius moved from modernizing genre material to more openly personal concerns in the semiautobiographical surfing story *Big Wednesday* (1978), the result was appreciably less appealing.

In the Eighties Milius achieved commercial success with the 'sword and sorcery' epic, *Conan the Barbarian* (1981), starring former Olympic weightlifter Arnold Schwarzenegger, and the alarmist, jingoistic *Red Dawn* (1984), in which a group of American students defend their homeland against sadistic Russian and Cuban invaders.

The other most notable promotion to direction from among the ranks of screenwriters was that of **Paul Schrader** (b. 1946), a former critic who wrote several scripts, including Scorsese's *Taxi Driver*, before making his directorial debut with *Blue Collar* (1978). This conspicuously well-crafted movie is on the surface a sharp thriller about trade-union corruption, and below the surface a gripping essay on alienation. Schrader's next film, *Hardcore* (1979), though often intriguing in its response to the Los Angeles underworld, is curiously lacking in narrative plausibility. But *American Gigolo* (1980) is a major achievement: again adopting the frame-work of a suspense story, the film combines a seductively fluid technique with a disquieting foray into the metaphysical realms of guilt and regeneration. His *Cat People* (1982) is a remake of the 1942 Jacques Tourneur/Val Lewton minor classic, and a starring vehicle for Nastassja Kinski.

Another screenwriter who has contributed significantly to modern American cinema – though he has not turned to direction – is **Robert Towne** (b.1935). After rising to modest prominence in the Sixties, he consolidated his position with two very different films. On the one hand, *Chinatown* is a consummate re-creation of an earlier model; on the other, *The Last Detail* (1973) is very much of its own time, and in fact its expletive-strewn dialogue represented something of a breakthrough in the permissible limits of naturalistic speech on the screen. This mordant tragi-comedy about two hard-bitten naval petty officers escorting a naive young sailor to military prison turned the 'road' format to pointedly distinctive use. It clinched the directorial reputation of former film editor **Hal Ashby** (b.1930), who had earlier directed two off-beat comedies, *The Landlord* (1970) and *Harold and Maude* (1971).

Ashby went on to make *Shampoo* (1975), an attractive satirical comedy, changed pace with *Bound for Glory* (1976), a large-scale biopic about folksinger Woody Guthrie, and subsequently returned to the mood of *Shampoo* with an impressively witty and inventive political satire, *Being There* (1979), in which Peter Sellers gave a memorable comedy performance as a near-imbecile who becomes a Presidential adviser – and eventually candidate.

John G. Avildsen (b. 1936) was another director who came to prominence in the Seventies, with *Joe* (1970), which starred Peter Boyle as a gun-slinging anti-hippie. In *Save the Tiger* (1973) a put-upon garment manufacturer (Jack Lemmon) tries

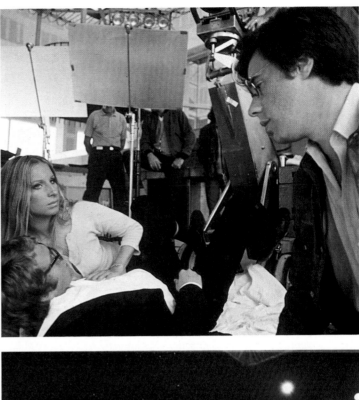

Above: Nastassja Kinski as the haunted heroine of Schrader's Cat People, *a remake of Tourneur's 1942 classic horror film. Top: Robert De Niro as Rupert Pupkin about to realize his ambition to become* King of Comedy.

Above: a k.o. for Sylvester Stallone in the title role of Rocky. *Top: director Peter Bogdanovich (right) rehearses a scene from the comedy* What's Up, Doc? *with the film's stars Ryan O'Neal and Barbra Streisand.*

to save his business by arson. Avildsen's big hit was the consciously old-fashioned boxing melodrama *Rocky* (1976), in which the underdog triumphed – and Avildsen won an Oscar. The film made a star of actor-writer Sylvester Stallone, who promptly turned director for the 1979 and 1982 sequels and other films.

Few of the directors of television movies who graduated to the cinema in the Seventies stamped much of a personality on their big-screen work. A partial exception is **Gilbert Cates** (b. 1934), who showed himself a fluent director in two rather literary movies, *I Never Sang for My Father* (1970) and *Summer Wishes, Winter Dreams* (1973). But his *The Last Married Couple in America* (1980) was a tiresome sex comedy.

Roger Corman, a key influence in encouraging new film-makers in the Sixties, did not on the whole produce a comparable range of talents from his intensive – and immensely profitable – engagement with New World Pictures in the Seventies. However, at least two directors to have come out of New World merit critical attention. Paul Bartel made in *Death Race 2000* (1975) a dynamic and witty comedy about a death-dealing transcontinental road race, that contrived to satirize the popular demand for violence at the same time as satisfying it. His follow-up, *Cannonball* (1976), was virtually a remake.

Crazy Mama (1975), directed by **Jonathan Demme** (b. 1944), made for New World, was an energetic but uneven

Above: country star Tom Frank (Keith Carradine) and one of his several conquests, Linnea (Lily Tomlin), in Nashville.

Above: Robin Williams as the spinach-loving Sailor Man, Shelley Duvall as his beloved Olive Oyl in Popeye.

variation on the period gangster film. But his subsequent work elsewhere qualified him as a director of real skill and versatility. *Citizens Band* (1977) was a spirited updating of Thirties-style populist comedy, whilst *Last Embrace* (1979) was a Hitchcock-like thriller of unflagging style and assurance. Demme's *Melvin and Howard* (1980) might plausibly be seen as a quintessential work of the new American cinema. Putting the 'road' movie formula to unpredictable and very likeable effect, it even manages – since the Howard of the title is the legendary Howard Hughes – to invoke a reference to Hollywood's vanished past as well as pointing encouragingly into the future. But *Swing Shift* (1984) was not a worthy counterpart to the documentary *Rosie the Riveter* (dir. Connie Fields, 1980), which searchingly examined the role of women working in World War II and after.

An independent director from an older generation who nonetheless exerted a strong influence on new American cinema in the Seventies was **Robert Altman** (b. 1925). The financial triumph of M*A*S*H in 1970 made Altman a bankable director in Hollywood at the age of 45. Though he has never had a comparable hit, Altman's work in the Seventies exerted a strong influence on the best young American film-makers.

Having served as a bomber pilot in World War II, Altman made industrial films for the Calvin Company, a job that led to his directing and producing *The Delinquents* and *The James Dean Story* (both 1957). He subsequently directed for television, returning to the cinema with a science-fiction epic, *Countdown* (1967), for Warners. Following a tepid love story, *That Cold Day in the Park* (1969), Altman seized on Ring Lardner Jr's much-rejected script of *M*A*S*H*, which blended farce and anti-establishment satire in its portrayal of life in the Mobile Army Surgical Hospital during the Korean War. Apart from making international stars of its leading actors – Donald Sutherland, Eliott Gould, Sally Kellerman – *M*A*S*H* exhibited Altman's distinctive use of naturalistic, overlapping dialogue for the first time, and an editing technique that audaciously mixed realism with parody. The film's

essential glibness was overlooked by contemporary critics delighted to discover a new, major American film-maker.

Altman followed *M*A*S*H* with a self-indulgent satire, *Brewster McCloud* (1970) and a beguiling story of the Old West, *McCabe and Mrs Miller*. This story of a little man (Warren Beatty) who builds a community with the help of a clever madame (Julie Christie) only to lose it to more powerful interests, is Altman's sharpest visualization of the corruption of the American Dream – a dominant theme in his work. After an attempt at a soft-focus, European-style 'art' film, *Images* (1972), Altman made three movies that focused on American society: *The Long Goodbye*, a clever update of the Chandler novel; *Thieves Like Us* (1974), a grim study of small-time gangsters in the South, set during the Depression; and *California Split* (1974), a smug, satirical comedy about two gamblers (Eliott Gould and George Segal) on the make.

Altman reaffirmed his reputation as a leading American director with the documentary-style *Nashville* (1975), which brilliantly created a microcosm of American life and attitudes from the excesses of Nashville's country music festival, The Grand Ole Opry. It was succeeded by a spirited Western satire, *Buffalo Bill and the Indians . . . or Sitting Bull's History Lesson* and the pretentious, quasi-feminist *Three Women* (1977). *A Wedding* (1978), *A Perfect Couple*, *Quintet* (both 1979), *Health* and *Popeye* (both 1980) quickly followed – none of them fully achieved works, though each contained at least some excellent scenes. Only *Popeye* proved financially successful. For several years in the Seventies, Altman had run his own company, Lion's Gate. This had enabled him to make his own films comparatively cheaply with first-class facilities, to employ a regular 'stock company' of favourite actors and actresses and to support young film-makers such as Alan Rudolph (*Welcome to LA*, 1976) and Robert Benton (*The Late Show*, 1977). The demise of Lion's Gate meant that Altman had reached yet another turning point in his always controversial career by the early Eighties, dependent on his priceless ability to inspire confidence in normally conservative backers. Ever unpredictable, he turned to the theatre, and then promptly made film versions of three plays he had staged, *Come Back to the 5 & Dime Jimmy Dean, Jimmy Dean* (1982), *Streamers* (1983) and *Secret Honor* (1984).

A Question of Colour

Throughout its history, the American cinema has played an important role in popularizing racial stereotypes of black people. Images of blacks have gone through a number of significant changes which, historically, reflect the shifting values and beliefs held in society concerning blacks, as well as the changing status and the emergence of black people within contemporary America.

During the silent-film era, blacks (often played by whites in blackface) were depicted in terms of the American Southern plantation tradition, usually as comic slave types and family retainers. It was during this period that the traditional stereotypes of the Uncle Tom, the Mammy figure and the comic-relief black type were firmly established in the cinematic mythology. By the late Thirties, Hollywood tended to stress relatively gentler images of blacks as subservient types. The Romantic Old South genre continued strongly, reaching a pinnacle in *Gone With the Wind* (1939), for which Hattie McDaniel won an Academy Award (the first black person to do so) as Best Supporting Actress for her performance as the bossy but faithful 'Mammy' to Scarlett O'Hara.

The post-World War II period saw the emergence of a new liberal attitude in Hollywood. The emphasis shifted towards relatively positive images, as more films started to depict black-white relations within a humanistic framework. Clarence Brown's 1949 film version of William Faulkner's novel *Intruder in the Dust* introduced to the screen the figure of the proud and noble black. The liberal attitude was informed by a sense of social equality, and articulated a strong commitment to racial tolerance. One of the recurrent patterns in the Fifties' liberal films is the black-white confrontation motif, in which the black hero is pitted against an intolerant white. This first appears in *No Way Out* (1950), where the central conflict between the Sidney Poitier character and the recalcitrant bigot (Richard Widmark) is eventually resolved with the black emerging as the moral victor. The acceptable black in liberal films eschewed violence – which was the domain of the racially intolerant figures, black and white. A number of films, however, developed the racial-tolerance theme along the lines of mutually hostile black-white confrontation, gradually evolving into mutual respect: in Stanley Kramer's *The Defiant Ones* (1958), the Poitier and Tony Curtis characters are escaped convicts who are shackled together, and therefore forced to work through their opposing attitudes at very close range.

The Fifties' liberal image of a blacks revolved almost entirely around Sidney Poitier; and none of the films placed a woman in the principal role of archetypal noble black. Indeed, they dealt with highly personalized forms of interracial male relationships. Many blacks voiced antipathy towards the 'noble black' image; it was argued that the stereotype effectively pre-empted any idea of black individualism and self-determination.

By the mid-Sixties, the black civil-rights movement was making a tremendous impact on all levels of American society. The general trend was clearly shifting towards militancy and separatism. Blacks re-examined their position in society and began to develop new self-images, in which blackness was an emphatically positive sign of opposition. These social and

Above: black and white bound together – Sidney Poitier and Tony Curtis in The Defiant Ones.

political developments had a broad effect on the Sixties' images of blacks in films: what emerged was the black *as an individual* struggling against society at large, or against his own conscience. The personal qualities of the central black figure provided the focal point in the drama. During this period, blacks also began to appear in a wider variety of story situations and genres, and the characterizations were more fully developed. The incorporation of blacks into otherwise white movies conveyed an image of a plural society, where race relations were part of the complex of human relations. This was dramatized in a number of films concerning a band of men, which included a black, whose common objective – such as robbing a bank – was constantly threatened by personality differences.

Thus the Sixties was a period of maturity, not only in terms of the kinds of racial themes explored in films, but also in terms of the way in which *human* qualities became an integral part in black characterizations. It was now possible for films to construct black characters that possessed some dramatically significant human weakness, without its being interpreted as necessarily pejorative. Norman Jewison's *In the Heat of the Night*, one of the last Hollywood liberal films, explored this theme of the flawed black hero with resounding effect. Low-budget 'art' films such as John Cassavetes' *Shadows* (1960), Shirley Clarke's *The Cool World* (1963), Larry Peerce's *One Potato, Two Potato* and Michael Roemer's *Nothing But a Man* (both 1964) were particularly realistic and sensitive in their approach to racial subjects. But they also tended to express a somewhat cynical view of the black world, and of interracial relations, that placed them outside mainstream conventions. Occasionally this outlook was taken to extremes, as in Robert Downey's satirical *Putney Swope* (1969), set in an advertising agency taken over by blacks.

The latter half of the Sixties saw the re-emergence of political themes in Hollywood, with a number of films concentrating on some aspect of the new militancy. Jules Dassin's *Up Tight!* (1968) dramatized the schisms that arose between separatist militancy and integrationist non-violence in the aftermath of Martin Luther King's assassination. Herbert J. Biberman's *Slaves* (1969) depicted corrupt plantation life and slave rebellion. In *The Lost Man* (1969), Sidney Poitier played a black militant. Generally, Poitier continued to represent the black middle-class image of acceptability. His films were especially popular with white audiences, and he remained Hollywood's top black star well into the Sixties. But he ceased to have the monopoly over the black image, as in the previous decade.

The proliferation of new themes and images in the Sixties opened the way for other black actors and actresses; and this led to other kinds of black types being depicted. One of the more popular was the black male macho figure, then best represented by ex-professional football star Jim Brown. It was to become, in the Seventies, the principal black male stereotype, and highly controversial. Black women also came to the fore in the Sixties, with such actresses as Ruby Dee, Diana Sands, Abbey Lincoln and Diahann Carroll appearing in numerous films, racial and non-racial, playing relatively 'untyped', intelligent roles. But very few films looked at black male-female relationships, *Nothing But a Man* and *For Love of Ivy* (1968) being notable exceptions.

The Seventies witnessed the sudden boom in black exploitation, or 'blaxploitation', films. Their subject-matter, characters and milieu were such that they would appeal primarily to blacks who, for the first time, became a major audience. The films were highly commercial and concentrated mainly on black super-hero types – super-hip, super-slick, super-cool characters capable of super-heroics! They invariably contained a fair amount of sex and violence, and blacks were shown always coming out on top.

Black director Ossie Davis' *Cotton Comes to Harlem* (1970) relied almost entirely on the iconography of the ghetto – its subcultural styles in dress, speech, patterns of behaviour and attitudes – for its effect. The ethnic morality embodied by the two black detective heroes – expressed, for example, by their antipathy towards slick hustlers (white or black) trying to exploit the community – is a theme that reappears in subsequent films.

The new tone of black-slanted films was wonderfully conveyed in black director Gordon Parks' *Shaft*, one of the most successful of the cycle. The film in fact worked within the conventional private-eye detective genre; but it succeeded nevertheless in firmly establishing in the mythology the sophisticated black super-hero. Black director Melvin Van Peebles' extraordinary *Sweet Sweetback's Baadasssss Song* (1971) lacked the sheen of the more mainstream films. But the scenes of the fugitive hero's bizarre sexual adventures, and the overall image of the black man triumphing over the corrupt white establishment, made the film attractive to both black and white audiences. It was a phenomenal success, and established the stereotype of the black super-stud. Gordon Parks Jr's *Superfly* elevated into the mythology the street-hustler cocaine-dealer, a figure that became one of the most popular, and most controversial, black hero-types during the blaxploitation period.

Only a minority of black-oriented films concerned actual black people of stature – notably the Billie Holiday biopic *Lady Sings the Blues* (1972) and Gordon Parks' *Leadbelly* (1976) – or looked at some aspect of black history. Sidney Poitier's first film as director, *Buck and the Preacher* (1972), popularized a neglected part of American history: the period following the Civil War when freed slaves moved west to found homesteads, but were tracked down and forced to return to the South.

The majority of Seventies' blaxploitation films were set in the urban milieu: they glorified the ghetto as a kind of noble jungle, and romanticized the underworld of pimps and pushers. The street-hustler thus became the archetypal anti-establishment, individualistic hero of the period. This image of the black world excited moral indignation in many black-rights organizations and professional bodies. In 1972, the National Association for the Advancement of Colored People (NAACP) and the Congress for Racial Equality (CORE) formed a coalition to attack what they felt had become an intolerable situation. The controversy continued through the Seventies blaxploitation period. A number of black-owned production companies were set up to meet the demands for a more responsible approach to black films. But most of the writers, producers and directors of black-slanted movies in any case were white; and the essential white-owned capitalist structure of the trend remained intact.

A constant theme in the anti-blaxploitation lobby was that the films were psychologically and socially harmful to young blacks, who made up a large proportion of the audience. Certain films were singled out as representing meaningful and positive images of black life. Among these were Gordon Parks' first feature *The Learning Tree* (1969), based on his autobiographical novel about growing up in Kansas during the Thirties; Martin Ritt's *Sounder* (1972), another Thirties' story about a young boy's experiences in the South; Ossie Davis' *Black Girl* (1972); and John Korty's *The Autobiography of Miss Jane Pittman* (1974), an ambitious television film in which Cicely Tyson brilliantly portrayed a 110-year-old black woman who recounts her life from slavery to the civil-rights years. These films reinstated a sense of humanity in the image of blacks – which many believed had been lost in the post-civil-rights Seventies.

The boom in black exploitation films petered out in the late Seventies. At the same time, an independent black film-makers' movement was gaining momentum, examining ethnic themes with creative intelligence and sensitivity.

In the Eighties, Poitier became the most successful black director in Hollywood history, as he had been its most acclaimed actor. He specialized in comedies aimed at black audiences but *Stir Crazy* (1980) crossed over so successfully that it brought in more than $58m in domestic rentals alone. Its star, Richard Pryor, had briefly taken over Poitier's pre-eminence, adding a scathing sense of humour, but was soon challenged by the blander young comedian, Eddie Murphy, in *48 HRS.* (1982), *Trading Places* (1983) and *Beverly Hills Cop* (1984). By the beginning of 1985, *Beverly Hills Cop* had virtually equalled *Stir Crazy* in box-office take, to join it in the all-time top thirty.

Right, top to bottom: Sidney Poitier, for several years virtually the only black star in Hollywood, as detective Virgil Tibbs, who overcomes the racial prejudices of a Southern cop in In the Heat of the Night; *soul star Diana Ross in her first screen role as the heroin-addicted jazz singer Billy Holiday in* Lady Sings the Blues; *Ivy League company executive (Dan Ackroyd) and a streetwise petty criminal (Eddie Murphy) eventually join forces to thwart the machinations of the Big Rich in* Trading Places. *Far right, top to bottom: Starting out as a still photographer, Gordon Parks Sr was one of the first black directors to achieve Hollywood success; Paul Winfield, Kevin Hooks and the dog* Sounder; *Eddie Murphy as the* Beverly Hills Cop, *which consolidated his position as the Eighties' leading black star.*

438

Native Americans

They were called 'redskins', 'savages' and 'hostiles'. They were played by extras wearing feathers and body makeup, or by wooden actors like Chief Yowlachie, the equivalent of store-front Indian figures who were prepared to make a mockery of their own race in white movies. These hostiles had no other apparent life or purpose except to provide a terrible, cruel threat to star actors who sought the frontier, gold and their own happy ending. It was the savages' duty to hurl furious attacks against circles of wagons, lines of cavalry and any pioneer homestead. They wanted to burn, kill, pillage and rape: they were classic barbarians, and as such they served to camouflage much of the brutality of their supposedly civilized opponents.

For the generation that grew up with talking pictures, Hollywood promoted a casual but crushing racial stereotype. It ignored or distorted the history in which whites had invaded Indian territory, exploited the natives, massacred them, put them in camps and stripped them of identity. The American movie – at least until around 1950 – was a steady reinforcement of this legend, and a subtle complement to the fearful mastery whites felt over blacks. Every Indian picture was a commentary on racism in America, and their prejudice was as strident as that of the Nazi *Triumph des Willens* (1934, *Triumph of the Will*).

But there was a changed mood in the early Fifties. Red Indians had fought in World War II, and the demand for civil rights was beginning to emerge in the South. It was not until the late Sixties that books restored the facts of 'Native American' history and culture, and made white America acknowledge the genocide it had committed. No film-maker since then has dared to repeat the stereotypes of racial hostility or subservience. Moreover, several films have had Indians as heroes or tragic victims. But the phrase 'Native American' is still touched with irony. There are still no Native American stars, producers or directors. There is not a Native American cinema, and no sense of ownership or authorship for the natives.

Most Americans admit that the history was a disaster, but how can it be reversed? Should the hideous past not be left decently alone? These questions are heavy with condescension and self-protection, and they suggest how long racist thought prevails. In hindsight, it is even possible to question the alleged tolerance of those famous 'breakthrough' films of the Fifties.

Devil's Doorway (1950) is humane and innovative in its respect for the dilemma of the Indian who has fought on the Union side in the Civil War – presented in the pained handsomeness of Robert Taylor. But in the same year the same director, Anthony Mann, made *Winchester '73*, in which the Indian attack – led by a young Rock Hudson as Young Bull – is so ominous a prospect that Lola Manners (Shelley Winters) is told to keep a last bullet for herself. Nothing betrayed Indians more than the casting of Hollywood stars to play Indian roles, and even though storylines expressed the wrongs done to them, kindness was still a form of superiority. Jeff Chandler played Cochise in *Broken Arrow* (1950), and Rock Hudson brought his great chest to the role of *Taza, Son of Cochise* (1954). It was even possible for an Indian woman to be attractive to a white man, so long as a white actress played the part: Debra Paget in *Broken Arrow*, Elizabeth Threatt in *The Big Sky* (1952), Jean Peters in *Apache*, Marisa Pravan in *Drum Beat* (both 1954), Donna Reed in *The Far Horizons* (1955) and Audrey Hepburn in *The Unforgiven* (1960).

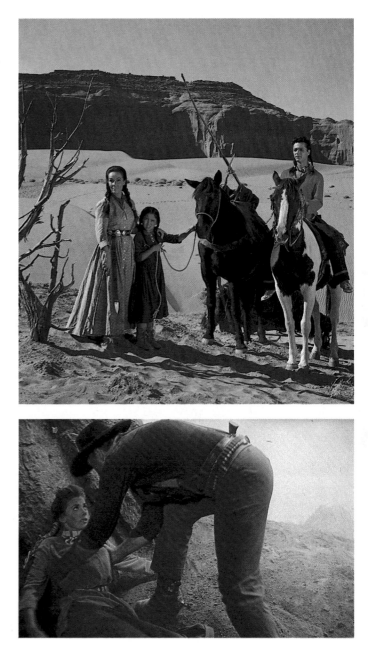

Above: Debbie (Natalie Wood) is rescued against her will from the Comanches by Ethan (John Wayne) in The Searchers. *Top: Indian women robbed of their homes in* Cheyenne Autumn.

Of those films, Robert Aldrich's *Apache* was the most searching study of Indian character and white manipulation. The ending was sentimentalized, and Burt Lancaster's savage was aimed at the box-office; but the picture had unequivocal scorn for white society. Anthony Mann's *The Last Frontier* (1955) still required the casting of Victor Mature as the half-breed scout Jed Cooper, and it settled for the virtues of stockade civilization. But it also recognized the exhilaration of space and liberty for the Indian. Most complex of all in its racial attitudes was Samuel Fuller's *Run of the Arrow* (1957), about a rogue Irish Confederate who marries into the Sioux: Rod Steiger played O'Meara and his bride, Yellow Moccasin, was Sarita Montiel, the Spanish wife of Anthony Mann.

No-one contributed more to the old image of the Indian than John Ford. *The Searchers* (1956) is a very telling metaphor for the stalwarts of racial supremacy having to yield

Above: Ulzana (Joaquin Martinez) leads a war party of Apaches to their death in Ulzana's Raid. *Top: the US cavalry are routed by Indians in* Little Big Man.

McMurphy (Jack Nicholson) finds an ally (Will Sampson) in the asylum in One Flew Over the Cuckoo's Nest. *Top: the bitter reality of America's Indian wars.*

to the new realities of America at the dawn of the civil rights movement. Its story concerns a white girl (Natalie Wood) kidnapped by Indians. The searchers after her are a bastion of white authority (John Wayne) and a mixed-blood companion (Jeffrey Hunter). *The Seachers* is far too tidy in its conclusion, but it shows the old Hollywood racked with uneasiness over race, mixed marriages and the change of an integrated community. Some years later, Ford offered *Cheyenne Autumn* (1964) as a grand, pictorial apology for a century of wrongs. It is far inferior to *The Searchers* and to Nicholas Ray's bold, accurate and disenchanted *Ombre Bianche* (1959, *The Savage Innocents*), about the least-remembered Native American tribe, the Eskimos.

Since then, there have been films made in the shadow of Vietnam, pictures that expose the buffoonery of old heroes like Custer and Buffalo Bill, and which are awash with spilled

blood: *Tell Them Willie Boy Is Here* (1969), *Soldier Blue*, *Little Big Man*, *Ulzana's Raid* (1972). *Billy Jack* (1971) was remarkable for its modern setting, and for the way Tom Laughlin made it so far outside the Hollywood system that his entrepreneurial courage became a symbolic equivalent to Native American independence.

More recently, the Native American in movies has been verging on the mythology of the supernatural. Chief Bromden (Will Sampson) in *One Flew Over the Cuckoo's Nest* (1975) is the spirit of silent knowledge in the American madhouse, the man who brings a merciful death to the tortured white hero and who finally disappears into the forest. And it should not be forgotten that the Overlook Hotel in *The Shining* (1980) has been built on an old Indian burial ground. Perhaps the Indian is the new Frankenstein monster, a man so abused that he will haunt the guilty dreams of white Americans.

CHAPTER 20
The Way Ahead

This history concludes at a moment when the future of the cinema is more uncertain and unpredictable than it has ever been. The century of the cinema has seen more changes – political, social, economic, technological – than at any time in the recorded history of the world; and in the Eighties the cinema itself is undergoing its most radical economic and technological revolutions. The single reassuring certainty is that the world at large still yearns to be told stories by means of moving images, whatever may be the changes in the means through which those images are presented.

After almost seventy years, Hollywood still exerts an unchallenged global domination – economic and therefore cultural. Still able to depend upon the world's richest domestic audience, the American cinema operates on altogether different economic scales from every other country. The average cost of European productions is generally a fraction of that of American films. Hollywood producers may spend tens of millions on one film, knowing that a major commercial success (such as 1984's *Ghostbusters* and *Gremlins*) may bring back hundreds of millions. This kind of success has its price, however: Hollywood in the Eighties has discovered the rewards of addressing the most infantile elements in audience taste. The box-office winners of the period have been child-like stories with an elementary development of narrative and character, compensated by a surfeit of frenetic activity, naive sexuality, gross comedy, physical sensation and special effects. The Hollywood formulas have proved to command a fairly universal market. By the mid-Eighties it was necessary to look outside the Hollywood production industry to find genuine experiment and innovation in the art.

Film-making was by this period depending upon a new and very different economic organization. With the epidemic spread of the video-recorder, cinema audiences in the most affected areas of the world slumped dramatically. In Britain, with the highest per capita number of video machines, cinema admissions dropped by almost one third between 1983 and 1984. Britain was, then, perhaps the most acute demonstration that the domestic box office now made a barely significant contribution to the costs – ever escalating – of film production. Indigenous film production could now only be economically viable given the expectation of box-office success in the USA (1982's *Chariots of Fire* and 1983's *Gandhi*) or a major production contribution from television.

The relation of cinema and television inevitably became crucial to any consideration of the future of the cinema. Since

the early Seventies, the production of quality films in Germany and Italy had depended upon finance from television; and it was with the opening of the fourth television channel and increased investment by the television authorities in film production that Britain, too, saw an apparent revival of the art. In this new situation, with a fair continuity of production of modestly-budgeted films, a whole group of directors (drawn mostly from the theatre and television), which included Bill Forsyth, Richard Eyre, Michael Radford and Neil Jordan, was able to demonstrate the country's resources of promising talent, only waiting to be exercised.

The growing participation of television in film production necessitated some aesthetic revaluation. Particularly in Britain, there had always been an assumption that there were basic (if never clearly specified) distinctions between 'films' and 'television films'. The new, television-subsidized films made in Britain (as had already happened in Germany and Italy) began to break down such illusions of clear-cut distinction, and confusions of media and forms. More often than not there *were* huge differences in the economic and technical resources available to the directors: but the best of the new-generation directors demonstrated that the more significant resources of ambition and imagination were not counted in cash. As Gavin Millar, a director who worked across the spectrum of television and cinema movies, wrote in *Sight and Sound* (Winter 1984–5): ''When Stephen Frears accepts a tenth of the budget and a quarter of the time to do a TV movie, does he apologetically only offer a quarter of his talent? Is *The Hit* necessarily a finer thing than *Sunset Across the Bay*?'' At least one of the British cinema's most outstanding talents, the director Mike Leigh, has only once worked outside television patronage.

By the mid-Eighties it was clear that as a medium television, far from restricting the ambitions of film makers, could actually open up new aesthetic possibilities. Seizing the advantages of extended treatment suggested by the series and serial formula, for instance, Ingmar Bergman's *Fanny och Alexander* (1982, *Fanny and Alexander*), Rainer Werner Fassbinder's *Berlin-Alexanderplatz* (1980) and Edgar Reitz's *Heimat* (1984, Homeland) were able to break out of the set and rigid formats of the theatrical film, and freely and effectively develop narratives at lengths of five, ten and over fifteen hours respectively. These masterly works were a reminder that many literary masterpieces would never have existed if the novel had been limited by rule to, say, two hundred pages.

Outside America and the massive industries of India and the Far East, then, films came increasingly to be financed by television, and viewed on the video screen, whose limitations

Left: little E.T. *the most popular star of 1982–3, 'alone', 'afraid' and 'three million miles from home'.*

of size and quality would be progressively and inevitably reduced. Paradoxically, in a period generally reckoned as marking the slow but ultimate expiration of the cinema, the public across the world saw far more films than ever before. In any one week the British public had available to them, on the regular television channels alone, as many films as the average person would have seen in a year of cinema-going in the theatrical cinema's most booming eras.

The British cinema in the Eighties still suffered under the handicap of being practically the only film industry in Europe, Western as well as Eastern, without any substantial degree of governmental support or any genuine official recognition of the importance of films as a means of national cultural and political expression. (The extent to which American cultural domination has been achieved and maintained through movies is self-evident.) The benefits of official patronage were demonstrated in small degree in the successes of the British Film Institute's Production Fund, which permitted the development of such talents as Bill Douglas, Bill Forsyth and Terence Davies. Elsewhere in the world it was possible to point to country after country – Australia, Sweden and the rest of Scandinavia, Cuba, India and the countries of Socialist Europe – where impressive resurgences of the art, commanding wide international attention, had from time to time resulted directly from state intervention.

State intervention could, of course, be a mixed blessing, as the history of totalitarian socialism had proved. By the mid-Eighties, the Czech cinema, for instance, had still not re-emerged from the suppression in 1968 of the rich flowering of the art that took place in the 'Prague Spring'. The Polish cinema too had seen the dramatic revival of the Solidarity era cut short by martial law, though by 1984, with Krzysztof Zanussi's *Rok Spokojnego Slonca* (*The Year of the Quiet Sun*) and Juliusz Machulski's creditably offensive satire, *Seksmisja*, (Sex Mission) there were signs of speedy revival. The once-great Soviet cinema on the contrary showed no sign of revitalization, with its brightest talent Andrei Tarkovsky in exile, Sergei Paradzhanov still unproductive after years in imprisonment and disgrace and able directors like Andrei Mikhalkov-Konchalovsky and Otar Yoseliani seizing chances to work abroad respectively in America, with *Maria's Lovers*, and France, with *Favoris de la Lune* (Favourites of the Moon).

Among the other socialist countries, while the cinemas of Bulgaria and East Germany intermittently produced international successes, Yugoslavia pursued capricious paths and Albania remained undiscovered, Hungary stood out for the consistent quality and innovation of its work and its constant and enthusiastic development of new talents. The most distinctive quality of Hungarian cinema in the Eighties though was the readiness to face and analyse recent history with a fearlessness uncharacteristic of socialist art, at least since the Soviet Revolution.

Throughout its ninety years, the cinema's history has characteristically been formed by successive and mostly unpredicted upsurges of the art, like the sudden appearances of volcanic springs. From time to time international attention has been focused on new talents and new initiatives in Japan, in India, in Australia, in France, in Scandinavia, in Soviet Russia, in Latin America. Part of the fascination of film history is the impossibility of predicting where the next eruption will be . . . In France, perhaps, where a new generation of *auteurs* has emerged in the train of the pioneers of the *nouvelle vague*? In Germany, which lost a lot of motive force following the death of Fassbinder, but has gained its international con-

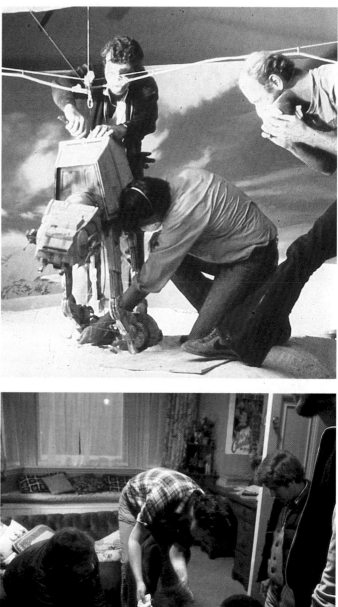

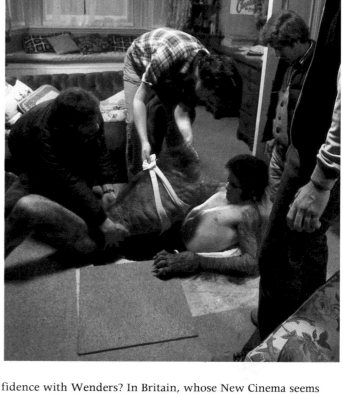

fidence with Wenders? In Britain, whose New Cinema seems stuck in nostalgia and decent craftsmanship, while failing to find a sense of unity and purpose? In China, with the biggest audience in the world and almost virgin film-making resources? In embattled Latin America? In India, with its heterogenous cultures and turbulent political life? In the Far East, where individualists battle for a platform in flourishing popular cinemas? In Australasia, always apparently on the verge of something wonderful? Where will the future of the cinema lie; and what are to be its tasks as this troubled century rushes into its final decade and the obscure future?

Opposite page: special effects have been an important ingredient in the success of movies in the Seventies and Eighties. For the metamorphosis in 1981's An American Werewolf in London (below) the wolf body was attached to the upper part of David Naughton's torso; the rest of his body was hidden under the floor. The four-legged Imperial Walkers in 1980's The Empire Strikes Back (above) were animated using the common 'stop motion' technique in which movements are shot frame by frame.

Left: Terence Stamp and Laura del Sol in The Hit. Above left: Ben Kingsley as Gandhi. Top left: Fanny and Alexander underlined the new artistic possibilities of TV-financed production. Above: The Ploughman's Lunch was one of several British films made in co-operation with Channel 4 TV.   Top: a moment of fear from Favourites of the Moon.

Film Index

Index of Names